Chairman Xi Remakes the PLA

Chairman Xi Remakes the PLA

ASSESSING CHINESE MILITARY REFORMS

Edited by Phillip C. Saunders, Arthur S. Ding, Andrew Scobell,
Andrew N.D. Yang, and Joel Wuthnow

National Defense University Press
Washington, D.C.
2019

Opinions, conclusions, and recommendations expressed or implied within are solely those of the contributors and do not necessarily represent the views of the Defense Department or any other agency of the Federal Government. Cleared for public release; distribution unlimited.

Portions of this book may be quoted or reprinted without permission, provided that a standard source credit line is included. NDU Press would appreciate a courtesy copy of reprints or reviews.

Published in the United States by National Defense University Press
260 Fifth Avenue (Building 64)
Suite 2500
Fort Lesley J. McNair
Washington, DC 20319

Library of Congress Cataloging-in-Publication Data
A catalog record of this publication may be found at the Library of Congress.

Book design by Jamie Harvey, U.S. Government Printing Office

This volume is dedicated to the memory of Dr. Richard H. Yang, founder and former Chairman of the Chinese Council of Advanced Policy Studies (CAPS).

Dr. Yang was a scholar with strong conviction and strategic vision who believed the world should pay close attention to the People's Republic of China's military modernization and efforts to rebuild China into a great power. He acted on this conviction by encouraging academics and experts to apply scientific methodology to study the modernization of the People's Liberation Army (PLA) and its impact on the regional security environment. Beginning in 1987, Richard organized the international conference on PLA affairs on an annual basis and used the conference proceedings as the basis for books that have stimulated debates and become important sources of knowledge. Many young scholars and experts have benefited from the international efforts that grew out of Richard's inspiration and hard work.

This volume and the continuing international PLA conference series are efforts to build on the foundation that Richard created.

CONTENTS

Part III: Overhauling Services

Part IV: Centralizing Authority

Part V: Integrating with Society

ACKNOWLEDGMENTS

Other than the introduction and conclusion, all the chapters in this book were originally presented as part of the PLA conference series co-sponsored by Taiwan's Council of Advanced Policy Studies (CAPS), National Defense University (NDU), and the RAND Corporation. The editors thank the authors for their patience and hard work in revising and updating their papers for publication.

The editors gratefully acknowledge the presenters, discussants, and participants at the CAPS-RAND-NDU 2016 PLA Conference in Arlington, Virginia, at the RAND Washington Office: Ken Allen, Dennis Blasko, Ed Burke, Arthur Chan, Michael Chase, Richard Chen, Tai Ming Cheung, Roger Cliff, Cortez Cooper, Jeff Engstrom, David Finkelstein, Scott Harold, Tim Heath, Lonnie Henley, Alexander Huang, Jeffrey Lewis, Nan Li, Lin Ying-yu, LeighAnn Luce, Ma Chengkun, Oriana Mastro, Frank Miller, Erin Richter, Mark Stokes, and Dennis Wilder. They also thank Megan Bishop at RAND, Yi-su Yang and Polly Shen from CAPS, and Don Mosser at NDU for logistical and administrative support. MAJ Jason Halub and Patrick Shaw of the Joint Staff played an important role in obtaining permission for NDU to co-sponsor the conference.

The editors gratefully acknowledge the presenters, discussants, and participants at the CAPS-CSS-NDU-RAND 2017 PLA Conference in Taipei, Taiwan, at the Far Eastern Plaza Hotel: Ken Allen, John Chen, Richard Chen, Chia-Shen Chen, Cortez Cooper, Mark Cozad, Arthur Ding, Andrew Erickson, Kim Fassler, Dan Gearin, Scott Harold, Alexander C. Huang, Yen-Chi Hsu, Taeho Kim, Brian Lafferty, Ying-Yu Lin, Wei-The Li, Chengkun Ma, Ian Burns McCaslin, Joel McFadden, Joe McReynolds, Frank Miller, Brendan Mulvaney, Nathan Beauchamp Mustafaga, Weichong Ong, Jagannath Panda, Angela Poh, Phillip Saunders, Andrew Scobell, Ming-Shih Shen, Hsiang-Huang Shu, Michael Swaine, Stanley Weeks, Joel Wuthnow, Shinji Yamaguchi, Andrew N.D. Yang, Meng-Zhang Yang, Stanley Yang, Tiehlin Yen, and Tsung-Chu Yu. They also thank Betsy Kammer and Megan Bishop at RAND, Yi-su Yang and Polly Shen from CAPS, and Catherine Reese and Lucianna Perez-Pikelny at NDU for logistical and administrative support.

In addition to the conference participants, others provided assistance in the preparation of the book manuscript. The editors thank NDU contract researchers Alex Jeffers and Ian Burns McCaslin for their hard work in reformatting chapters, tracking down details of missing notes and ensuring consistent formatting, and helping with the translation of terms to and from Chinese in the text and the notes. MAJ Ryan Neely provided assistance in resolving copyediting queries on several chapters. The editors thank William Eliason and Ms. Joey Seich at NDU Press and Cameron Morse and Daniel Chykirda at the OSD Security Review office for their assistance in clearing the chapters for publication. NDU Press executive editor Jeffrey Smotherman copyedited the book and oversaw the production process.

Phillip C. Saunders and Joel Wuthnow thank Dennis J. Blasko, David M. Finkelstein, Frank G. Hoffman, Frank Miller, Andrew Scobell, and David Stilwell for comments and suggestions on the introduction and conclusion. They also thank Ian Burns McCaslin for translation and research assistance for chapter 9, and Ken Allen for providing several useful sources. John Costello and Joe McReynolds thank Joel Wuthnow,

Alex Crowther, and Frank Miller for their peer reviews of chapter 13, and Jim Chen, MAJ Ryan Neely, and Maj. Adam Greer for proofreading the chapter.

Thanks to the following experts for their help in proofreading the final manuscript: Susan Carroll, John Chen, Adam Greer, Nicolas Gruenwald, MAJ Jason Halub, Corey Howell, Rob Miltersen, Paul Nantulya, MAJ Ryan Neeley, Lt. Col. Martin C. Poon, Edward Haofeng Tang, Jennifer Thurman, Lt. Col. Terry Vance, and Emily Walz.

And final thanks to Susan Carroll, who indexed the book.

CHAIRMAN XI REMAKES THE PLA

Joel Wuthnow and Phillip C. Saunders

Integral to Xi Jinping's vision of restoring China to greatness—what he defines as the "great rejuvenation of the Chinese nation" [*zhonghua minzu weida fuxing*, 中华民族伟大复兴]—is building a more modern, capable, and disciplined military. China's economic development, territorial integrity, and even the survival of the Chinese Communist Party (CCP) itself cannot be guaranteed without an army that can fight and prevail in modern warfare. Articulating the need for a stronger military, Xi and his colleagues have reflected on periods of Chinese weakness, such as the era of imperial decline in the late 19th century and the Japanese occupation in the 1930s and 1940s. In Xi's words, a "nation's backwardness in military affairs has a profound influence on a nation's security. I often peruse the annals of modern Chinese history and feel heartbroken at the tragic scenes of us being beaten because of our ineptitude."[1] Such humiliations, in his view, should never be repeated.

Xi's ambition to reshape and modernize the People's Liberation Army (PLA) has been apparent from his early days as CCP general secretary and Central Military Commission (CMC) chairman. At the third plenum of the 18th Party Congress, held in October 2013, Xi and other Party elites declared their intention to overhaul the military's command structure, update its training and logistics systems, adjust the size and composition of the services, unveil new rules and regulations governing military personnel, and strengthen civil-military cooperation in technological development and other areas.[2] In early 2014, Xi assumed leadership of a leading group on military reform, symbolizing his central role in the process. At the group's first meeting, Xi declared that "national defense and military reform are an important part and an important symbol of China's overall reform," noting that the overriding goal was to produce a military that can "fight and win battles."[3]

Following an interval of study and assessment, Xi announced a series of major organizational changes in late 2015 and early 2016.[4] Some of the key reforms included a reorganization of the bureaucratic structure under the CMC, creation of a system of five joint theater commands (TCs), and establishment of two new quasi-services that will support joint operations: the Strategic Support Force (SSF) and Joint Logistics Support Force (JLSF). This initial tranche of reforms was followed by a series of additional changes, such as the execution of a 300,000-person force reduction, elimination of a number of group armies and conversion of army (and some air force) divisions to brigades, and an overhaul of the PLA's professional military education system (more specifics on the reforms are provided later).

These changes help support the longer term vision for military transformation articulated by Xi at the 19th Party Congress in October 2017:

- by 2020, the PLA should basically achieve mechanization and make strides in applying information technology and developing strategic capabilities
- by 2035, national defense modernization should be basically completed
- by mid-century, the people's armed forces (including the PLA, People's Armed Police, and militia) should become "world-class forces" [*shijie yiliu jun*, 世界一流军].[5]

The Xi-era reforms represent the latest stage in a decades-long process of organizational realignment and modernization. According to Chinese sources, the PLA underwent 10 major restructurings between 1949 and 2013, most of which attempted to reduce end strength, professionalize the officer and noncommissioned officer corps, and adapt military force structure to meet new operational challenges.[6] Many of the focus areas of the current (11th) round of reforms, such as strengthening the PLA's ability to conduct joint operations and rebalancing the military's composition from the ground forces to the naval, air, and missile forces, were conceived in the 1980s and 1990s.[7] This agenda followed changes to Chinese military strategy to focus less on preparing for a general war with the Soviet Union or the United States—which had driven China's defense planning during the Cold War—and more on a smaller scale conflict around China's borders.[8] Key events signaling the need for reform included the 1990–1991 Gulf War, which showcased the U.S. military's advantages in doctrine and technology, and the 1995–1996 Taiwan Strait crisis, which exposed the PLA's inability to deter Taiwan independence forces or counter U.S. intervention on Taipei's behalf.[9]

However, fundamental reforms eluded Xi's two predecessors, Jiang Zemin and Hu Jintao. The PLA's service composition remained heavily skewed toward the ground force, for instance, and the outmoded command structure was not geared toward rapid crisis response or joint operations. The problem likely resulted from a combination of Jiang and Hu's weak political influence over the military, bureaucratic inertia, and opposition from corrupt senior officers who profited, quite literally, from a continuation of the status quo. What is unique about Xi's reforms is not the agenda itself, but his ability to overcome bureaucratic resistance.[10] He has done this through his own personal charisma as well as savvy political tactics, such as leveraging anti-corruption investigations over opponents and handpicking loyalists for key positions. The result has been a more extensive organizational transformation than what Jiang and Hu were able to achieve, and perhaps the most important set of reforms in the PLA's 90-year history.

The implications of the Xi-era reforms for China's neighbors and potential adversaries are significant. A better trained, organized, and equipped PLA will be in a stronger position to accomplish its three primary functions: winning modern wars, especially what the U.S. Department of Defense terms *short-duration, high-intensity regional conflicts*; deterring both larger and smaller competitors; and protecting Chinese interests within and beyond Asia.[11] Rival territorial claimants, such as Vietnam, the Philippines, Japan, and India, will face a more confident and capable adversary in the South and East China seas and across the Sino-Indian border. Taiwan will have to contend with a PLA that can more credibly plan and execute joint operations, such as amphibious landings, blockades, and joint firepower strikes.[12] U.S. forces operating throughout the Indo-Pacific region will need to anticipate a PLA that can respond more quickly to regional crises and conduct counter-intervention operations more effectively.

Foreign analysts have only begun to explore the contents, drivers, and possible implications of Xi's campaign to restructure the PLA.[13] Many issues remain shrouded in uncertainty and warrant further examination. These include:

- what impacts the reforms are having on PLA operations, training, and logistics
- the prospects for the ground forces as the reforms' nominal biggest loser, as well as the other services
- challenges the PLA is facing in cultivating operational commanders
- the structure, roles, and missions of the SSF and JLSF
- how the downsizing is being carried out, and what impact it might have on social stability
- the implications of reform for Party control over, and Xi's influence within, the PLA
- whether and how the reforms will improve coordination between the PLA and the civilian science and technology sector
- what the implications might be for the defense acquisition process.

This volume explores these and other dimensions of China's military reforms as they were planned and implemented between 2013 and 2018. The chapters are based on papers presented at the 2016 and 2017 PLA conferences co-organized by the U.S. National Defense University, RAND, and Taiwan's Council of Advanced Policy Studies, updated to account for more recent developments.[14] The goal is to assess the motivations of Xi and his associates, chronicle key successes and outstanding problems, and consider what the net effect of the reforms will be as the PLA strives to become a "world-class" military by mid-century, if not much sooner. This introduction provides an overview of the major elements and goals of the reforms and summarizes the 17 substantive chapters. A brief conclusion at the end of the book assesses the progress of the reforms to date and sketches the way ahead.

Major Elements

On New Year's Day 2016, the CMC issued a blueprint for reform that explained how the PLA would develop into a "modern military with Chinese characteristics that can win information-age wars" by 2020.[15] The initial phase of the reforms involved "above the neck" [*bozi yishang*, 脖子以上] changes to the PLA's three major organizational pillars—the services, CMC, and theaters—and was introduced by Xi in a series of announcements in the winter of 2015–2016. The new PLA structure is depicted in figure 1. First, on December 31, 2015, Xi announced three service-related changes:

- The Second Artillery Force, responsible for the country's land-based nuclear and conventional missiles, was renamed the Rocket Force and upgraded to full-service [*junzhong*, 军种] status, equal to the army, navy, and air force.[16] As David Logan argues in this volume, this was mainly a symbolic change, though some anticipated that it could imply greater resources and expanded missions for the Rocket Force.

- The Strategic Support Force was created with the status of an independent branch [*budui*, 部队], though with a bureaucratic grade equivalent to a service.[17] This new organization consolidated a variety of functions related to the information domain, including space and cyber operations, electronic warfare, and even some psychological warfare capabilities.[18] (Another new force, the Joint Logistics Support Force, was established in September 2016 to provide strategic and operational logistics support to the new joint theater commands.)[19]

Figure 1. New PLA Structure

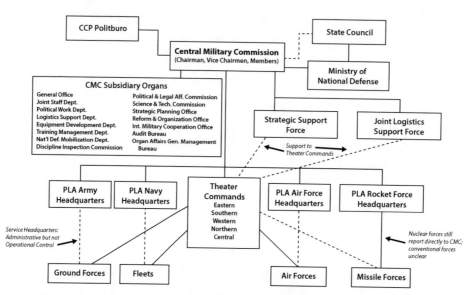

- Headquarters for the PLA ground forces, which had previously been commanded and administered by the general departments, were established at the national and theater levels. This reduced the army's importance by placing it on the same bureaucratic level as the navy, air force, and Rocket Force.

Second, on January 11, 2016, Xi announced that the four general departments—the General Staff Department (GSD), General Political Department, General Logistics Department (GLD), and General Armament Department (GAD)—had been disbanded.[20] Built on the Soviet model, these departments had developed into sprawling, semi-independent fiefdoms with limited external oversight. This autonomy meant that corruption had festered during the Jiang and Hu eras, especially in areas such as the promotions and logistics systems.[21] The general departments were replaced by 15 smaller functional CMC departments, commissions, and offices that would report directly to the CMC (via the CMC General Office, which was ranked first among these organizations).[22] These are depicted in figure 2, and described in detail in the appendix to this chapter.

Figure 2. New CMC Organization

The CMC reshuffle impacted the former general departments in different ways. Most affected was the GSD, whose diverse portfolio was distributed among new and existing organizations. Core operations and intelligence analysis functions were transferred to a smaller CMC Joint Staff Department (JSD), while signals intelligence and electronic warfare went to the SSF and army aviation was sent to the new army headquarters. The GSD's training, strategic planning, and mobilization departments were all removed from the successor JSD and placed under direct CMC control, indicting both their significance and the need for more top-level oversight over these functions. The other general departments were less affected, though as discussed later, several changes were made to the former GPD to encourage greater Party control and discipline in the PLA. In addition, the GAD's Science and Technology Commission was placed under direct CMC oversight, signaling Xi's intent to improve management of military innovation.

Third, the previous system of seven military regions was replaced by five joint theater commands. The military regions were largely administrative constructs that had no operational control over air, naval, and missile forces in peacetime. By contrast, theater commanders would be able to draw on conventional forces within their respective areas of responsibility to plan and execute operations (theater-based nuclear forces remained under the tight control of the CMC). Each of the theaters has a specific set of missions that it is primarily responsible for: the Eastern Theater is responsible for Taiwan and the East China Sea, the Southern Theater handles the South China Sea and land borders with Southeast Asian states, the Western Theater covers the land borders with India and Central Asian states (as well as the restive regions of Xinjiang and Tibet), the Northern Theater would deal with a Korea contingency, and the Central Theater focuses on the defense of Beijing and can provide support to other theaters as needed. A map of the new theater boundaries appears in figure 3.

In planning and executing these major organizational changes, the PLA clearly drew inspiration from the U.S. military. Assigning service chiefs a force building function and investing operational authority in joint theater commands paralleled similar changes made in the U.S. system after World War II and solidified in the 1986 Goldwater-Nichols Act. The similarities, however, should not be overstated. For instance, the PLA's new regional command structure was geographically confined to China and its immediate environs, unlike the globe-spanning U.S. combatant command system. The PLA also retained a number of Leninist features that have no

Figure 3. TC Boundaries

All locations are approximate.
Boundary representation is not necessarily authoritative.

parallel in the U.S. or other militaries in democratic countries, such as political commissars and Party committees. Indeed the reforms, as discussed below, strengthened those features in important ways.

Following a CMC work conference on military reform in December 2016, the PLA embarked on a second phase of reforms. Several notable changes were carried out in 2017 and 2018 that affected the PLA's size, composition, and personnel. First was a reduction of the PLA by 300,000 personnel, a goal that Xi had announced at a military parade in September 2015.[23] The focus was on reducing the ground forces, which had constituted nearly 70 percent of PLA personnel on the eve of reform. Following the reduction, Chinese sources claim that the army's share declined to less than 50 percent.[24] If true, this would represent a major step toward the longstanding goal of rebalancing the force toward the other services. The reduction also targeted noncombat personnel, such as headquarters staff, allowing more resources to be devoted to combat troops and equipment that would give the PLA a "stronger battle capability."[25] Overall, more than 30 percent of commissioned officers were reportedly cut.[26] Some personnel transitioned to jobs in local governments, state-owned enterprises, or the private sector, while others became PLA civilians.[27] The reduction was declared "basically complete" in March 2018 (though interviewees note that the downsizing might not be fully complete until 2020).[28]

Second were a series of below-the-neck [*bozi yixia*, 脖子以下] force structure changes. In April 2017, Xi announced that 84 "corps-level units" had been established or adjusted, forming what he called an "indestructible combat force."[29] Few details were provided, though the announcement signaled that the reforms were beginning to address organizational problems at lowers levels of the PLA.[30] Some of the changes included:

■ The army continued its transformation from a group army-division-regiment structure to a standardized group army-brigade-battalion structure, which had begun in the early 2000s. The lineup of group armies was cut from 18 to 13, 15 former army divisions were converted into two brigades apiece, and combat brigades were transformed into combined arms brigades. Revisions were also made at the level of combined arms battalions, which the ground forces had earlier announced as the "basic combat unit" [*jiben zuozhan danwei*, 基本作战单位] capable of independent maneuver.[31] There has also been an increase in the number of more rapidly deployable army units, such as army aviation and special operations forces.[32]

- The navy has expanded its marine corps, which stood at around 12,000 personnel prior to the reforms. With the conversion of one army motorized infantry brigade and up to three coastal defense units to marine brigades, the marine corps may have tripled in strength to roughly 36,000 personnel distributed among the North, East, and South Sea fleets.[33]

- The air force continued its attempts to move from a division-regiment structure to a base-brigade structure for fighters and ground attack aircraft units under the theater command air forces. (Bombers, as well as transport and specialized aircraft, remain organized in divisions.)[34]

- In December 2017, the People's Armed Police, previously under the dual command of the State Council and CMC, was placed solely under CMC leadership. Its internal organization was also significantly revised; changes included losing its responsibilities for protecting China's gold, forestry, and hydropower resources and gaining oversight of the coast guard, which previously reported to the State Oceanic Administration.[35]

Third were changes designed to improve the competence and quality of PLA personnel. Bonuses and other incentives were adopted to increase the share of college graduates among active-duty officers, while the reserve officer program was altered to accept only college graduates.[36] To retain qualified officers, the PLA reportedly offered a modest pay increase drawn from defense budgets that continued to grow by more than 8 percent a year.[37] The professional military educational system was restructured, with 77 institutes reduced to 43 (many were merged into the National Defense University (NDU) and National University of Defense Technology).[38] Curricular changes were adopted to focus on practical skills in areas such as computer science, information technology, and aerospace studies.[39] NDU created a new training course in joint operations for mid-level officers and inaugurated a specialized joint operations track for its senior commanders' course.[40] Reforms to the grade and rank system were also initiated, though the results of this effort had not been announced as of mid-2018.[41]

Another step in the reforms came at the 19th Party Congress, when Xi announced an overhaul of the CMC membership. The congress provided Xi an opportunity to hand pick leaders that he could trust to implement the remainder of his agenda and remove those either too old, unreliable, or corrupt to serve, all of whom had been selected by his predecessors. (Two former CMC members, Fang Fenghui and Zhang Yang, were targeted by anti-corruption investigators; Zhang later committed suicide.)[42] As detailed in the chapter in this volume by Joel McFadden, Kim Fassler, and Justin Godby, the new CMC was also reduced in size from 11 to 7 members, which notably did not include the service chiefs or heads of the successor organizations to the GLD or GAD. This suggested Xi's desire to rein in those organizations. Added was the secretary of the Discipline Inspection Commission, which is responsible for anti-corruption investigations in the PLA. Figure 4 lists the old and new CMC members.

Table. Old and New CMCs			
18th Central Committee CMC (2012–2017)		**19th Central Committee CMC (2017–2022)**	
Xi Jinping	Chairman	Xi Jinping	Chairman
Fan Changlong	Vice Chairman	Xu Qiliang	Vice Chairman
Xu Qiliang	Vice Chairman	Zhang Youxia	Vice Chairman
Chang Wanquan	Defense Minister	Wei Fenghe	Defense Minister
Fang Fenghui	GSD Director	Li Zuocheng	Joint Staff Department Director
Zhang Yang	GPD Director	Miao Hua	Political Work Department Director
Zhao Keshi	GLD Director	Zhang Shengmin	Discipline Inspection Commission Secretary
Zhang Youxia	GAD Director		
Wu Shengli	Navy Commander		
Ma Xiaotian	Air Force Commander		
Wei Fenghe	Second Artillery Commander		

Key: GAD: General Armament Department; GLD: General Logistics Department; GPD: General Political Department; GSD: General Staff Department.

What the Reforms Sought to Achieve

While broadly focused on building a military that can, in Xi's words, "fight and win battles," reformers also pursued three more specific objectives. First was strengthening the PLA's ability to plan and conduct joint operations. This was not a new goal: by the late 1990s, Chinese military strategists understood that success on the modern battlefield would require the PLA to better integrate the activities and capabilities of units from the different services and do so with the support of advanced command, control, communications, computers, intelligence, surveillance, and reconnaissance systems and logistics systems. Part of this judgment resulted from observations of the changing character of war, especially lessons derived from U.S. operations during the Gulf War and in the Balkans, while part resulted from the specific requirements of preparing for conflict with Taiwan (including denying U.S. forces the ability to intervene on Taiwan's behalf, as they had done during the 1995–1996 crisis).[43] As Mark Cozad explains in his chapter, PLA doctrine and training exercises increasingly focused on joint operations in the 1990s and 2000s.

Previous reforms had failed to address several persistent weaknesses. The most significant challenge was an organizational culture that prioritized the interests of the ground forces over the other services. As noted, the army represented a large majority of all PLA personnel, while ground forces officers occupied most key command and staff billets. This was out of sync with the growing importance of developing capabilities and expertise in the maritime, air, and space domains. A related problem was the lack of a joint command structure. In peacetime, air and naval forces were under the operational control of their respective service headquarters, while the military regions took charge of army units. Prosecuting a joint campaign would have required temporary "war zones" [战区] to be established, a process that, while useful to signal strategic intent and non-kinetic escalation, would have slowed the PLA's ability to respond to an emerging crisis and denied it the element of surprise in a campaign against Taiwan. Yet another shortcoming was the failure of the military's training and education systems to produce qualified joint commanders.[44]

The impetus for further reform was not only a result of these limitations but also changes in China's security environment. In his chapter in this volume, David Finkelstein notes that Chinese security assessments became increasingly dire under Xi, with a particular emphasis on challenges posed by the United States (especially the Barack Obama administration's pivot to Asia, which many in China interpreted as strategic encirclement), Japan and other regional territorial rivals, and separatist forces on Taiwan. Xi and his colleagues also closely followed the global revolution in military affairs, in which other major powers were making strides in new technologies. All this meant that the PLA would have to be prepared to win what Chinese military strategy termed *informationized local wars* [*xinxihua jubu zhanzheng*, 信息化局部战争], the cornerstone of which is an ability to conduct joint operations.[45]

Reforms undertaken between 2015 and 2018 advanced this agenda in several ways. In brief, these included:

- rebalancing service composition to put more weight on naval, air, and missile forces
- creating the SSF and JLSF, which provided critical operational support to joint commanders
- removing the service chiefs from operational chain of command, while granting theater commanders operational oversight over all conventional forces within their respective regions
- establishing an independent training department under the CMC to formulate and enforce joint training standards
- revising professional military educational curricula to put more emphasis on joint operations
- increasing specialized forces, such as amphibious and helicopter units, that would be essential to a joint campaign.

These adjustments coincided with personnel changes that placed more navy and air force officers in key positions, including as commanders of two of the five theaters.[46]

Second was a desire to revitalize Party control and discipline within the PLA. The PLA has always been a "Party-army," which must follow the

CCP's instructions and defend its interests. Nevertheless, Xi and his colleagues worried that Party control may have been atrophying to dangerous levels. One problem was the possibility that some in the military could prioritize the interests of the people, or the nation as a whole, over the Party. This was an issue during the 1989 Tiananmen crackdown, in which some local PLA units refused to obey the Party's orders to use force against the student protesters.[47] Along these lines, Xi revived concerns that some—usually unnamed—officers were lobbying for the PLA to be transformed from the armed wing of the CCP into a "national army" [*jundui guojia-hua*, 军队国家化], which if true could represent a serious threat to Party survival.[48] Moreover, the example of the 1991 Soviet military coup (which Chinese analyses suggested was partially the result of the Soviet Communist Party's loosening grip over the military) is never far out of mind.[49]

Another problem is PLA officers placing their own personal interests ahead of the Party's. Xi recognized that corruption in the officer corps—a problem that had been festering on a large scale since the 1980s—could blemish the Party's image among the public, impede readiness and morale, and limit the willingness of senior officers to tolerate major reforms. Combating this challenge was thus a major theme of his leadership. At a 2014 speech in Gutian, site of the 1929 Party Congress that established the principle of Party control over the PLA, Xi commented on problems in cadres' "ideology, politics, and work style," castigating the "lax" supervision of PLA personnel and pointing to Guo Boxiong and Xu Caihou, CMC vice chairmen under Hu who were targeted in Xi's anti-corruption campaigns, as cautionary examples.[50] He instead urged the PLA to develop officers both loyal to the Party and capable of "leading soldiers to fight and win battles."[51]

Central to restoring Party control was elevating Xi's own status and authority within the PLA. This is critical to arresting the trend of too much power being delegated to corrupt military elites and helped ensure that his vision for military transformation was being implemented. (It was also part of Xi's broader consolidation of power within the Party-state as a whole.) Thus, Xi emphasized what the 1982 PRC Constitution termed the "CMC Chairman

Responsibility System" [*zhongyang junwei zerenzhi*, 中央军委责任制], which stated that ultimate authority over military affairs rested with that individual (who usually serves concurrently as Party general-secretary). Other steps he took to assert control over the PLA included attending military events at a greater rate than Hu, personally leading reform efforts, weighing in on senior officer promotions, and publishing military treatises that became "required reading" for soldiers.[52]

Xi also oversaw a series of structural and personnel changes designed to combat graft and ensure political orthodoxy among the officer corps. One part was adjusting the PLA's supervisory mechanisms. Prior to the reforms, supervision was centralized in the general departments, which, as noted, were notoriously corrupt. Xi changed this situation by disbanding the general departments, elevating the Discipline Inspection Commission to independent status, and placing its secretary on the CMC—and likewise placing the audit bureau and military court system under direct CMC oversight. The Political Work Department continued to oversee personnel files, political indoctrination, and the political commissar and Party committee systems. This meant that the PLA now had several independent, but mutually reinforcing channels to monitor and fight ideological laxity and corruption. This adjustment was complemented by continuing anti-corruption investigations and a rotation of senior officers intended, in part, to break up patronage networks.[53]

Third was the need for improvements in the area of "civil-military integration" (CMI) [*junmin ronghe*, 军民融合]. The term refers primarily to the process whereby the military could leverage breakthroughs in the civilian science and technology sector, though it also encompasses other types of cooperation between the military and civilian realms. Examples include expanding reliance on civilian contractors in the military supply chain, which is cheaper and more efficient than relying on traditional suppliers, and the incorporation of military specifications into the design of civilian transport ships, which could be appropriated during wartime (especially during an amphibious invasion of Taiwan). As Brian Lafferty discusses in this volume, strengthening CMI has been part of the PLA's reform agenda since the 1990s, but its implementation was hindered by ineffectual top-level management, bureaucratic stovepiping, and other obstacles.

Xi attempted to make progress in the CMI arena through various changes. One was upgrading the PLA's Science and Technology Commission, previously housed within the GAD, to direct CMC supervision. This commission is responsible for the military's coordination with outside civilian experts in critical technological areas. Another was reforms to the military research system. For instance, several technical institutes were merged into the PLA's Academy of Military Science, helping to more closely integrate technical advances with innovations in China's military doctrine.[54] To improve management and supervision of the process, the government created a new Central Commission for Integrated Military and Civilian Development in January 2017, with Xi as chairman.[55] In sum, these motives—operational, political, and technological—were not new, but taken together shaped an agenda that Xi and his fellow reformers acted on to create a "world-class" force by mid-century.

Outline of the Book

The following chapters explore the reforms from a variety of angles and are divided into five thematic sections. Part I analyzes the strategic and bureaucratic context in which the reforms are occurring. In chapter 2, David Finkelstein considers how domestic politics, operational requirements, and changing external security assessments provided the impetus for reform and shaped its contents. He also asks who (other than Xi) played a critical role in the process. Chapter 3, by Andrew Scobell and Nathan Beauchamp-Mustafaga, discusses how the reforms are occurring alongside the creation of a more "global" PLA that is being tasked with protecting China's overseas interests. On the bureaucratic front, chapter 4 by John Chen explains why the ground forces—which had the most to lose from restructuring—reluctantly opted to endorse the changes. In chapter 5, Ian Burns McCaslin and Andrew Erickson examine the impact of reform on the navy's modernization plans and document the emerging rivalries as the services position themselves to be *the* critical part of the joint force.

Part II considers several features of the PLA's attempts to forge a stronger joint operations capability. Chapter 6, written by Mark Cozad, traces the PLA's progress in the areas of joint training, doctrine, and personnel education since the 1990s, showing why previous reforms failed and how more recent changes aim to rectify the situation. In chapter 7, Edmund Burke and Arthur Chan explain the role of the new joint theater commands and identify several challenges to the effectiveness of the new system, including resistance by the services (which have continued to lead some types of operations).[56] Chapter 8, by LeighAnn Luce and Erin Richter, examines the trajectory and key features of the PLA's logistics reforms, one component of which is creating a "precision" system that provides "comprehensive, timely, and accurate logistics support to PLA joint operations." In chapter 9, Joel Wuthnow and Phillip C. Saunders assess the challenges facing the PLA in cultivating highly qualified joint commanders, and how Xi and his colleagues are seeking improvements in this arena.

Part III digs deeper into how the reforms are affecting the PLA's services. Chapter 10, by Daniel Gearin, places the recent downsizing in the context of previous force reductions and assesses the implications for the ground forces. In chapter 11, Dennis J. Blasko discusses the army's new structure, recent training and deployments, and changes to its logistics, doctrine, and educational systems, concluding that despite new equipment, the army's modernization process has been slower and perhaps less effective than the more technical services. Even as it remains the largest single service, Blakso concludes that the army is the "biggest loser" in the current reforms. Chapter 12, by David Logan, addresses the status of the Rocket Force, which he asserts is "arguably the biggest winner in the reforms" because it retained control over nuclear forces, increased its status, and strengthened its ability to compete for resources. In chapter 13, John Costello and Joe McReynolds provide a comprehensive overview of the SSF, detailing this new force's background, structure, and missions. The authors also raise important questions about whether the rise of the SSF was more about organizational innovation or the desire by top leaders to centralize control over China's strategic resources.

Part IV assesses the implications of the reforms for defense acquisition and the relationship between the PLA and civilian sector writ large. Tai Ming Cheung, in chapter 14, shows how the reforms complement the defense industry's transformation "from a follower to an original innovation leader" and outlines continuing weaknesses in that sector. In chapter 15, Brian Lafferty explores the CMI dimensions of the reforms. He concludes that despite important structural changes, the historical "track record suggests that even positive returns will involve a longer and more difficult process than the Party currently acknowledges." Chapter 16, by Ma Chengkun and John Chen, explores the impact of the downsizing on military-locality relations and documents the range of policies and tactics the government has used to try to compensate the reforms' losers and mitigate discontent among demobilized soldiers.

Part V turns to the political elite dimensions of the reforms, focusing on Xi's role and status as CMC chairman. Chapter 17, by Phillip C. Saunders and Joel Wuthnow, examines the political and ideological challenges Xi sought to rectify through the reforms as well as his political strategy for bringing the process to a successful outcome. Chapter 18, by Joel McFadden, Kim Fassler, and Justin Godby, looks at the new CMC lineup that was announced at the 19th Party Congress in October 2017. They conclude that "there is little doubt that Xi and his generals emerged in a stronger position to steer the PLA toward fulfilling its part in the 'great rejuvenation' of the Chinese nation."

Taken together, the chapters suggest that the PLA has been able to make major strides, within a short period of time, toward completing the unfinished business of organizational transformation left over from the Jiang and Hu eras. This is both a testament to Xi's ability to push structural changes through a bureaucracy that has historically resisted them and an indication that the PLA is on track to field a more professional and capable joint force by 2020. However, the chapters also reveal persistent weaknesses, such as encouraging operational flexibility in a system that prizes top-down political control; cultivating proficient joint commanders in the absence of real combat experience (China has not fought a war since 1979); reducing interservice rivalry and the influence of the ground forces, which remains by far the largest service and continues to hold most senior command billets; and forging stronger connections between the PLA and civilian technological innovators. Resolving these deeper problems will require that Xi and his successor—whenever one is named—remain focused on the agenda even after 2020 and be prepared to counter resistance if and when it resurfaces.

Notes

[1] Li Xuanliang and Wang Jingguo, "Focus the Building of Elite Forces on Winning in War" [聚焦打赢砺雄师], Xinhua, September 21, 2017, available at <www.xinhuanet.com/politics/2017-09/21/c_1121704641.htm>.

[2] "CCP Central Committee Decision on Deepening of Reforms for Major Issues" [中共中央关于全面深化改革若干重大问题的决定], Xinhua, November 15, 2013, available at <http://news.xinhuanet.com/politics/2013-11/15/c_118164235.htm>.

[3] "Xi Leads China's Military Reform, Stresses Strong Army," Xinhua, March 15, 2014, available at <http://english.cntv.cn/20140315/102892.shtml>

[4] For a summary, see Joel Wuthnow and Phillip C. Saunders, *Chinese Military Reforms in the Age of Xi Jinping: Drivers, Challenges, and Implications*, China Strategic Perspectives 10 (Washington, DC: NDU Press, 2017), 6–22.

[5] "Full Text of Xi Jinping's Report at the 19th CPC National Congress," Xinhua, November 3, 2017, available at <www.xinhuanet.com/english/special/2017-11/03/c_136725942.htm>.

[6] "Previous PLA Reorganizations Since the Founding of the Republic" [建国以来解放军历次体制编制调整改革], *Caixin Online* [财新网], November 27, 2015, available at <http://china.caixin.com/2015-11-27/100878949.html>.

[7] For a discussion of People's Liberation Army (PLA) reforms during the Jiang era, see Kenneth W. Allen et al., *Institutional Reforms of the Chinese People's Liberation Army: Overview and Challenges* (Alexandria, VA: CNA Corporation, 2002).

[8] See, for example, Taylor Fravel, "Shifts in Warfare and Party Unity: Explaining China's Changes in Military Strategy," *International Security* 42, no. 3 (Winter

2017/2018), 37–83; and David M. Finkelstein, "China's National Military Strategy," in *Right Sizing the People's Liberation Army: Exploring the Contours of China's Military*, ed. Andrew Scobell and Roy Kamphausen (Carlisle Barracks, PA: Strategic Studies Institute, 2007), 99–145.

[9] Dean Cheng, "Chinese Lessons from the Gulf Wars," in *Chinese Lessons from Other Peoples' Wars*, ed. Andrew Scobell, David Lai, and Roy Kamphausen (Carlisle Barracks, PA: Strategic Studies Institute, 2011), 153–200.

[10] See Arthur S. Ding, "The PLA and Taiwan Policy under Xi Jinping: One Joint Actor Without Its Own Agenda," *Issues & Studies* 53, no. 2 (June 2017), 1–24; and the chapter by Saunders and Wuthnow in this volume.

[11] *Annual Report to Congress: Military and Security Developments Involving the People's Republic of China, 2016* (Washington, DC: Office of the Secretary of Defense, 2016), i; "China's Military Strategy (Full Text)," Xinhua, May 27, 2015, available at <http://english.gov.cn/archive/white_paper/2015/05/27/content_281475115610833.htm>.

[12] Phillip C. Saunders and Joel Wuthnow, "What Do China's Military Reforms Mean for Taiwan?" *NBR Commentary*, May 19, 2016, available at <http://nbr.org/research/activity.aspx?id=692>.

[13] See, for example, Wuthnow and Saunders, *Chinese Military Reforms in the Age of Xi Jinping*; David M. Finkelstein, *Initial Thoughts on the Reorganization and Reform of the PLA* (Arlington, VA: CNA, 2016); David M. Finkelstein, *Get Ready for the Second Phase of Chinese Military Reform* (Arlington, VA: CNA, 2017); and the special section on Chinese military reform in *Joint Force Quarterly* 83 (4th Quarter, 2016).

[14] The Taiwan Ministry of National Defense Center for Strategic Studies was also a co-sponsor of the 2017 conference.

[15] "China Releases Guidelines on Military Reform," Xinhua, January 1, 2016, available at <www.xinhuanet.com/english/2016-01/01/c_134970353.htm>.

[16] "Xi Inaugurates PLA Rocket Force as Military Reform Deepens," Xinhua, January 1, 2016, available at <www.xinhuanet.com/english/2016-01/01/c_134970564.htm>. Previously, the Second Artillery was a branch of the ground forces.

[17] Like the service headquarters, the Strategic Support Force headquarters is a theater command commander [正战区级] grade organization.

[18] See chapter by John Costello and Joe McReynolds in this volume.

[19] "China Establishes Joint Logistic Support Force," *China Military Online*, September 13, 2016, available at <http://eng.mod.gov.cn/TopNews/2016-09/13/

content_4730336.htm>. See also chapter by LeighAnn Luce and Erin Richter in this volume.

²⁰ "China Reshuffles Military Headquarters," Xinhua, January 11, 2016, available at <www.xinhuanet.com/english/2016-01/11/c_134998692.htm>.

²¹ As Tai Ming Cheung notes in this volume, the PLA has been less transparent about corruption in the weapons research and development system since those programs are mostly classified.

²² For a discussion, see Joel Wuthnow, "The CMC General Office: Recentralizing Power in the PLA," *China Brief* 17, no. 7 (May 2017), available at <https://jamestown.org/program/cmc-general-office-recentralizing-power-pla/>.

²³ "China to Cut Troops by 300,000: Xi," Xinhua, September 3, 2015, available at <www.xinhuanet.com/english/2015-09/03/c_134583730.htm>.

²⁴ However, it is unclear if this figure accounts for army officers serving in "joint" positions within the Central Military Commission departments and theaters. See "Facts and Figures on China's Military Reform," Xinhua, December 19, 2017, available at <www.xinhuanet.com/english/2017-12/19/c_136837189.htm>.

²⁵ "PLA Non-Battle Personnel Downsized as Part of Military Reform: Report," *Global Times* (Beijing), March 5, 2018, available at <http://eng.chinamil.com.cn/view/2018-03/05/content_7959328.htm>.

²⁶ "Facts and Figures on China's Military Reform."

²⁷ Authors' interviews with PLA officers, 2017–2018.

²⁸ "Premier Li: China Has Reduced Army Size by 300,000," *ChinaMil.com*, March 5, 2018, available at <http://eng.chinamil.com.cn/view/2018-03/05/content_7959842.htm>; authors' interviews, 2017–2018.

²⁹ "China Reshuffles 84 Corps-Level Military Units," Xinhua, April 18, 2017, available at <www.xinhuanet.com/english/2017-04/18/c_136218258.htm>.

³⁰ Chinese media did reveal that the newly realigned group armies were included in the 84 corps. See "PLA Reveals New Designation for First Time," *China Daily* (Beijing), April 25, 2017, available at <www.chinadaily.com.cn/china/2017-04/25/content_29076824.htm>. A Hong Kong newspaper published a purported list of the 84 units, which included major commands in all the services and Strategic Support Force. See "What Are the 84 Corps-Grade Units?" [84个军级单位是什么?], *Ming Pao* [明报], April 20, 2017, available at <www.mingpaocanada.com/tor/htm/News/20170420/tcab1_r.htm>.

³¹ For an overview, see Dennis J. Blasko, "What Is Known and Unknown about Changes to the PLA's Ground Combat Units," *China Brief* 17, no. 7 (May

2017), available at <https://jamestown.org/program/known-unknown-changes-plas-ground-combat-units/>.

[32] See the chapter by Blasko in this volume, as well as Dennis J. Blasko, "Recent Developments in the Chinese Army's Helicopter Force," *China Brief* 17, no. 8 (June 2017), available at <https://jamestown.org/program/recent-developments-chinese-armys-helicopter-force/>.

[33] Thanks to Dennis Blasko for these observations.

[34] Lawrence Trevethan, *"Brigadization" of the PLA Air Force* (Maxwell Air Force Base, AL: China Aerospace Studies Institute, 2018).

[35] Kristin Huang, "China Brings People's Armed Police under Control of Top Military Chiefs," *South China Morning Post* (Hong Kong), December 27, 2017, available at <www.scmp.com/news/china/diplomacy-defence/article/2125880/china-brings-peoples-armed-police-under-control-top>; Lyle Morris, "China Welcomes Its Newest Armed Force: The Coast Guard," *War on the Rocks*, April 4, 2018, available at <https://warontherocks.com/2018/04/china-welcomes-its-newest-armed-force-the-coast-guard/>. In addition, changes were made to the People's Armed Police (PAP) internal security [*neiwei*, 内卫] forces, with 14 mobile divisions disbanded and replaced by a mix of mobile *zongdui* and *zhidui* distributed among provincial PAP commands. Thanks to Dennis J. Blasko for this observation.

[36] "College Students Account for Large Majority of New Military Recruits," *ChinaMil.com*, September 10, 2017, available at <http://eng.chinamil.com.cn/view/2017-09/10/content_7750599.htm>; "China Changes Student Enrollment Policies for Army," Xinhua, May 26, 2017, available at <www.xinhuanet.com/english/2017-05/26/c_136317920.htm>.

[37] Minnie Chan, "China Raises Pay, Pensions for Trimmed Down Military, Announces Plans for Veterans' Ministry," *South China Morning Post* (Hong Kong), March 13, 2017, available at <www.scmp.com/news/china/diplomacy-defence/article/2137008/china-raises-pay-pensions-trimmed-down-military>.

[38] "Xi Calls for World-Class Military Research, Educational Institutions," Xinhua, July 7, 2017, available at <www.xinhuanet.com/english/2017-07/19/c_136456748.htm>.

[39] "PLA Schools to Expand Recruitment, Help China Win Information War," *Global Times* (Beijing), June 12, 2017, available at <http://en.people.cn/n3/2017/0612/c90000-9227234.html>.

[40] Luo Jimnu, "Building a World-Class Joint Operations University" [建设世界一流综合性联合指挥大学], *Enlightenment Daily* [光明日报], October 19,

2017, available at <http://epaper.gmw.cn/gmrb/html/2017-10/19/nw.D110000g-mrb_20171019_1-13.htm>; Huang Panyue, "PLA Aims to Cultivate Commanding Talents for Joint Operations," *ChinaMil.com*, September 7, 2017, available at <http://english.chinamil.com.cn/view/2017-09/07/content_7747234.htm>.

41 Kenneth W. Allen, "China Announces Reform of Military Ranks," *China Brief* 17, no. 2 (January 2017), available at <https://jamestown.org/program/china-announces-reform-military-ranks/>.

42 "PLA Backs Investigation of Senior Military Official," Xinhua, January 10, 2018, available at <www.xinhuanet.com/english/2018-01/10/c_136885601.htm>.

43 Joel Wuthnow, "A Brave New World for Chinese Joint Operations," *Journal of Strategic Studies* 40, nos. 1–2 (February 2017), 169–195.

44 See the chapter by Wuthnow and Saunders in this volume.

45 M. Taylor Fravel, "China's New Military Strategy: 'Winning Informationized Local Wars,'" *China Brief* 15, no. 13 (July 2015), available at <https://jamestown.org/program/chinas-new-military-strategy-winning-informationized-local-wars/>.

46 Those were Vice Admiral Yuan Yubai, who was named Southern Theater commander, and General Yi Xiaoguang, who was named Central Theater commander.

47 See Andrew J. Nathan and Perry Link, eds., *The Tiananmen Papers* (New York: PublicAffairs, 2001).

48 For a discussion, see Andrew Scobell, "China's Evolving Civil-Military Relations: Creeping Guojiahua," *Armed Forces & Society* 31, no. 2 (January 2005), 227–244; a forthcoming volume by Chen Yali (Princeton University Press); and chapter by Saunders and Wuthnow in this volume.

49 William Wan, "In China, Soviet Union's Failure Drives Decisions on Reform," *Washington Post*, March 23, 2013, available at <www.washingtonpost.com/world/asia_pacific/in-china-soviet-unions-failure-drives-decisions-on-reform/2013/03/23/9c090012-92ef-11e2-ba5b-550c7abf6384_story.html?noredirect=on&utm_term=.b9e61cff20ac>.

50 James C. Mulvenon, "Hotel Gutian: We Haven't Had That Spirit Here Since 1929," *China Leadership Monitor*, no. 46 (Winter 2015), available at <www.hoover.org/sites/default/files/research/docs/clm46jm.pdf>

51 "Xi Stresses CPC's Absolute Leadership Over Army," Xinhua, November 2, 2014, available at <www.chinadaily.com.cn/china/2014-11/02/content_18843109.htm>.

52 See chapter by Saunders and Wuthnow in this volume.

53 Ibid.

54 Authors' interviews with PLA Academy of Military Science personnel, 2017.

[55] "Xi to Head Central Commission for Integrated Military, Civilian Development," Xinhua, January 22, 2017, available at <www.xinhuanet.com/english/2017-01/22/c_136004750.htm>.

[56] For instance, the PLA Navy headquarters continues to lead anti-piracy task forces (authors' interviews, 2017), while David C. Logan's chapter in this volume clarifies that the Rocket Force retained control over land-based nuclear weapons.

APPENDIX

Central Military Commission Reforms

This appendix analyzes the organizational logic behind the People's Liberation Army (PLA) shift from a system centered on a small Central Military Commission (CMC) staff and the four general departments to a much larger post-reform CMC staff that incorporates many of the functions of the former general departments. It also describes the functions of the 15 new CMC departments, commissions, and offices that were announced on January 11, 2016.[1]

From the General Departments to an Expanded CMC

The pre-reform CMC had 11 members, including a civilian chairman, 2 military vice chairmen, minister of defense, heads of the four general departments, and commanders of the navy, air force, and Second Artillery. The four general departments—the General Staff Department (GSD), General Political Department (GPD), General Logistics Department (GLD), and (from 1998) General Armament Department (GAD)—were led by army officers and collectively served as the ground force headquarters, among other functions. The CMC members supervised the general departments, services, and seven military regions and were supported by a relatively small staff of about 1,000 people in the CMC General Office.[2] In this setup, the heads of the general departments and services represented their organizations in CMC debates and were responsible for implementing CMC decisions within their organizations. The CMC chairman (who served concurrently as the Chinese Community Party general-secretary and state president) nominally had the final word on decisions, though during the Jiang Zemin and Hu Jintao eras, considerable decisionmaking authority and autonomy were delegated to the uniformed vice chairmen.

The post-reform CMC has only seven members, with the GLD, GAD, and service commanders losing their seats, and the director of the CMC Discipline Inspection Commission gaining a seat on the CMC proper (see table 1). (See the chapter by McFadden, Fassler, and Godby in this volume for an analysis of the post-reform CMC leadership.)

Table 1. Pre- and Post-Reform Central Military Commission (CMC) Membership			
Position	Pre-Reform CMC Status	Post-Reform Position	Post-Reform CMC Status
CMC Chairman	CMC Chairman	CMC Chairman	CMC Chairman
CMC Vice Chairman	CMC Vice Chairman	CMC Vice Chairman	CMC Vice Chairman
CMC Vice Chairman	CMC Vice Chairman	CMC Vice Chairman	CMC Vice Chairman
Minister of Defense	CMC Member	Minister of Defense	CMC Member
GSD Director	CMC Member	CMC Joint Staff Department Director	CMC Member
GPD Director	CMC Member	CMC Political Work Department Director	CMC Member
GLD Director	CMC Member	CMC Logistics Department Director	—
GAD Director	CMC Member	CMC Equipment Development Department Director	—
Navy Commander	CMC Member	Navy Commander	—
Air Force Commander	CMC Member	Air Force Commander	—
Second Artillery Commander	CMC Member	Rocket Force Commander	—
Discipline Inspection Commission Director	—	CMC Discipline Inspection Commission Secretary	CMC Member

Key: GAD: General Armament Department; GLD: General Logistics Department; GPD: General Political Department; GSD: General Staff Department.

The four general departments were abolished, and the post-reform CMC staff grew into a much larger organization that now includes 15 departments, commissions, and offices. The parts of the general departments that focused on managing the ground forces moved into the new army headquarters, while those involved in executing space, cyber, signals intelligence, electronic warfare, and psychological warfare operations mostly moved to the Strategic Support Force. The remaining parts of the general departments were either converted into successor CMC departments (the CMC Joint Staff Department, CMC Political Work Department, CMC Logistics Support Department, and CMC Equipment Development Department) or elevated to the status of independent CMC departments, commissions, or offices (see table 2).

Table 2. CMC Departments, Commissions, and Offices			
Name	Predecessor	Initial Director	Current Director
General Office [办公厅]	General Office	GEN Qin Shengxiang [秦生祥]	MG Zhong Shaojun [钟绍军]
Joint Staff Department [联合参谋部]	General Staff Department (GSD)	GEN Fang Fenghui [房峰辉]	GEN Li Zuocheng [李作成]
Political Work Department [政治工作部]	General Political Department (GPD)	GEN Zhang Yang [张阳]	ADM Miao Hua [苗华]
Logistics Support Department [后勤保障部]	General Logistics Department (GLD)	GEN Zhao Keshi [赵克石]	GEN Song Puxuan [宋普选]
Equipment Development Department [装备发展部]	General Armaments Department (GAD)	GEN Zhang Youxia [张又侠]	LTG Li Shangfu [李尚福]
Training and Administration Department [训练管理部]	GSD Military Training Department	LTG Zheng He [郑和]	LTG Li Huohui [黎火辉]
National Defense Mobilization Department [国防动员部]	GSD Mobilization Department	MG Sheng Bin [盛斌]	LTG Sheng Bin [盛斌]
Discipline Inspection Commission [纪律检查委员会]	GPD Discipline Inspection Commission	GEN Du Jincai [杜金才]	GEN Zhang Shengmin [张升民]
Political and Legal Affairs Commission [政法委员会]	GPD Military Procuratorate	LTG Li Xiaofeng [李晓峰]	LTG Song Dan [宋丹]
Science and Technology Commission [科学技术委员会]	GAD Science and Technology Commission	LTG Liu Guozhi [刘国治]	LTG Liu Guozhi [刘国治]
Strategic Planning Office [战略规划办公室]	GSD Strategic Planning Department	MG Wang Huiqing [王辉青]	MG Wang Huiqing [王辉青]

Table 2. CMC Departments, Commissions, and Offices

Name	Predecessor	Initial Director	Current Director
Reform and Organization Office [改革和编制办公室]	GSD Military Affairs Department	MG Wang Chengzhi [王成志]	MG Zhang Yu [张宇]
Office of International Military Cooperation [国际军事合作办公室]	MND/CMC Foreign Affairs Office	RADM Guan Youfei [关友飞]	MG Hu Changming [胡昌明]
Audit Bureau [审计署]	GLD Audit Bureau	MG Guo Chunfu [郭春富]	MG Guo Chunfu [郭春富]
Organ Affairs General Management Bureau [机关事务管理总部]	GSD Management Support Department	MG Liu Zhiming [刘志明]	MG Liu Zhiming [刘志明]

Key: GAD: General Armament Department; GLD: General Logistics Department; GPD: General Political Department; GSD: General Staff Department.

This shift from a PLA centered on the general department system to one managed by the CMC and CMC staff reflects the three broad drivers of PLA reforms described in the introduction:

- strengthening the PLA's ability to plan and conduct joint operations in order to fight and win informationized wars
- revitalizing party control and discipline within the PLA
- improving "civil-military integration" so that the PLA can tap civilian resources and leverage breakthroughs in the civilian science and technology sector.

Strengthening the PLA's Ability to Plan and Conduct Joint Operations

One way the reorganization strengthened the PLA's ability to conduct joint operations is by reducing CMC responsibilities to allow greater focus on jointness and managing operations. Freed from the need to serve as army headquarters and operate technical intelligence collection and space operations, the expanded CMC staff can concentrate on building a joint force and supervising joint operations. The removal of service commanders from CMC membership weakens the services relative to the CMC, although ground force dominance and the service-centric organizational culture within the PLA remain obstacles to building a joint force. Key functions such as joint training (including military education), national defense mobilization, and strategic planning were elevated from second-level departments within the GSD to the status of independent departments and offices within the CMC staff, allowing the CMC chairman and vice chairmen direct oversight over these functions and improving their ability to push forward a joint agenda without obstruction from a GSD or Joint Staff Department director concerned about ground force equities. Some new CMC organs, such as the reform and organization office, were created to help implement leadership priorities.

Revitalizing Party Control and Discipline within the PLA

Bringing the general departments and most of their functions inside the CMC strengthens the ability of the CMC chairman and vice chairmen to monitor those personnel and activities. The CMC General Office is the key CMC staff organization responsible for ensuring compliance with CMC directives and gathering information on what the larger CMC bureaucracy is doing. That office's critical role is reinforced by the fact that Zhong Shaojun, a longtime civilian aide [秘书] to Xi Jinping, was installed as a key General Office official to serve as Xi's trusted eyes and ears within the military.[3] Zhong followed Xi to Beijing, was appointed deputy director with a military rank of senior colonel, and was subsequently promoted to major general before being named as General Office director in 2018.[4] The reorganization also seeks to strengthen the effectiveness of monitoring and control mechanisms by giving the Discipline Inspection Commission, Political and Legal Affairs Commission, and Audit Bureau independent status and the ability to report directly to CMC leaders without interference from their superiors.

Elevation of the CMC Discipline Inspection Commission director to CMC member status increases the authority of that organization within the PLA (and likely the effectiveness of its subsidiary discipline inspection commissions throughout major parts of the PLA). According to interviews, the discipline inspection system now functions as a parallel chain of information that reaches directly up to Xi and provides an independent assessment of the performance of commanders, political commissars, and party committees.[5]

This arrangement should reduce opportunities for commanders and political commissars to engage in corrupt practices and provide an independent source of information for Xi to use when making promotion decisions.

Improving Civil-Military Integration

The reorganization also strengthens parts of the PLA that collaborate with civilian counterparts in the state and party apparatus. The Science and Technology Commission, previously under the GAD, is now an independent CMC organ.[6] The commission will promote civil-military cooperation in defense research and development and strengthen high-level guidance for the research, development, test, and evaluation (RDT&E) system. The National Defense Mobilization Department, which manages the military districts and garrisons that interface with the party and civilian government organs that run China's provinces and cities, is now an independent department that reports directly to top CMC leaders. The CMC's Office of International Military Cooperation helps ensure that military diplomacy is coordinated with China's broader foreign policy objectives.

Assessing Effectiveness of CMC Reforms

While the shift from the general department system to an expanded CMC staff system has a clear organizational logic that corresponds to the goals that PLA reforms are intended to advance, this does not necessarily mean that the organizational reforms will achieve their intended results. The reforms should increase effectiveness and improve monitoring by creating a clearer division of responsibilities and improving the flow of information from the agents (CMC staff organs) to the principal (CMC chairman and vice chairmen). Our assessment is that the PLA has adopted a CMC organizational structure that can support development of a more effective joint force, but that result is by no means guaranteed.

Challenges include the fact that the expanded CMC staff is a larger, more complex organization to run than its smaller predecessor, which delegated more responsibilities to the general departments. As in other aspects of current

Chinese government reforms, this reflects an impulse to centralize power and Xi's reluctance to delegate responsibilities to others. The "CMC Chairman Responsibility System" calls for Xi to make all the important military decisions. Given that the scarcest resource in government is high-level attention, how much time can Xi actually devote to these responsibilities?[7] Does he trust the CMC vice chairmen enough to delegate some decisions to them?

This challenge is aggravated by the fact that the PLA's organizational culture does not encourage independent decisionmaking and taking responsibility, which suggests that greater centralization may slow down decisionmaking. According to one PLA source, many of the senior officers Xi has appointed are relatively inexperienced and reluctant to make decisions. Instead, they pass the buck to their superiors.[8] Xi's promulgation of his own thought on military matters—now required study within the PLA—may also make senior officers more reluctant to challenge suboptimal decisions from the top. The result may be slower decisionmaking and difficulty in correcting mistakes.

Finally, most key CMC and CMC staff positions are held by army officers, and all of them are staffed by officers whose careers have been spent in a military dominated by the ground forces and with rigid promotion and assignment systems. Will their decisions reflect their personal experiences in a PLA with limited jointness or the leadership's goal of building a military capable of conducting integrated joint operations? Can the PLA move from a service-centric mentality to a joint mentality? Even if the structure of the reorganized CMC supports efforts to build an effective joint military force, the individuals in key leadership positions may frustrate that objective. Building a joint force with capable joint commanders and staff officers may ultimately require generational change.

Overview of CMC Departments, Commissions, and Offices

The rest of this appendix describes the composition of the post-reform CMC and functions of the new CMC departments, commissions, and offices that were announced on January 11, 2016. These departments, commissions, and offices are presented in the protocol order provided by authoritative People's Republic of China media accounts.[9]

CMC Departments [*bu*, 部/*ting*, 厅]
General Office [*bangongting*, 办公厅]

The CMC retained a General Office whose key responsibilities include managing information flows between CMC members and subsidiary departments, providing advice, and conducting policy research.[10] Under Xi, a key mission of the General Office has been implementing the CMC Chairman Responsibility System, which refers to the principle that all important decisions ultimately rest with Xi.[11] Authoritative Chinese sources list the General Office ahead of all other CMC departments, including those led by former general department directors (that is, Joint Staff, Political Work, Logistics Support, and Equipment Development), underscoring its importance in ensuring that CMC orders are being implemented across the PLA. The office's director from 2012 through 2017 was Lieutenant General Qin Shengxiang, who previously served as director of the General Political Department Organization Department.[12] In late 2017, Qin departed to serve as the PLA Navy's political commissar but a successor was not immediately announced. Major General Zhong Shaojun, one of Xi's longtime civilian aides, was promoted from his position as deputy director to CMC General Office director in 2018.[13]

Joint Staff Department [*lianhe canmou bu*, 联合参谋部]

The Joint Staff Department is responsible for command and control (C2), "combat command support" [*zuozhan zhihui baozhang*, 作战指挥保障], campaign planning, formulating military strategy, organizing joint training, performing combat capability assessments, and working to ensure combat readiness [*zhanbei jianshe*, 战备建设].[14] Thus, the department performs many of the functions of the former General Staff Department Operations Department [*zongcan zuozhan bu*, 总参作战部].[15] The Joint Staff Department also likely absorbed some of the GSD's role in intelligence collection and analysis (former 2PLA) and, as documented in the chapter in this volume by Costello and McReynolds, plays a role in cyber and electronic warfare management through its Network-Electronic Bureau (former 4PLA). Other former GSD functions were transferred to the Strategic Support Force and service headquarters. The organization plays a significant role in the evolving joint C2 structure by serving as the institutional link between the CMC and five joint theater commands, though the nature of that role remains unclear.[16] Its initial director was former Chief of the General Staff General Fang Fenghui. In August 2017, Fang, who had become embroiled in an anti-corruption investigation, was replaced by former PLA ground force commander Li Zuocheng. Li serves concurrently as a CMC member.

Political Work Department [*zhengzhi gongzuo bu*, 政治工作部]

The Political Work Department performs the duties of the previous GPD, including overseeing political education, "human resources management," and party organizations within the military, in addition to managing the PLA's internal and external propaganda arms. Some have speculated that the Political Work Department might have assumed the former GSD Military Affairs Department's role in enlisted personnel management.[17] This department is instrumental in strengthening the party's "absolute leadership" over the military, which has been a consistent theme of the reforms.[18] However, unlike the former GPD, the Political Work Department does not oversee party discipline inspection or the military prosecutorial system; those functions migrated to independent Discipline Inspection and Political and Legal Affairs commissions under the CMC. It was initially led by former GPD Director General Zhang Yang. Zhang, who like Fang Fenghui was caught up in an anti-corruption investigation, was replaced in September 2017 by Admiral Miao Hua, former PLA Navy political commissar. Miao serves concurrently as a CMC member.

Logistics Support Department [*houqin baozhang bu*, 后勤保障部]

The Logistics Support Department is responsible for overseeing logistics support, setting standards, performing inspections, and carrying out other duties previously entrusted to the General Logistics Department.[19] As Luce and Richter note in their chapter in this volume, the Logistics Support Department also plays a role in "facilities management, contracting, budget management and funds disbursement, international military engagement, and overall administration of PLA hospitals and medical programs." A key focus of the department is managing the logistics system, though combat support appears to be carried out by the Joint Logistics Support Force and its subordinate units.[20] Its first director was former GLD Director General Zhao Keshi, who retired in October 2017, and was replaced by former Northern Theater commander General Song Puxuan.

Equipment Development Department [*zhuangbei fazhan bu*, 装备发展部]

Like its predecessor, the General Armaments Department, the Equipment Development Department performs RDT&E functions and oversees procurement management and information systems building [*xinxi xitong jianshe*, 信息系统建设]. However, the GAD's Science and Technology Commission did not migrate to this department and was instead placed directly under the CMC (see below). In addition, the GAD's role in overseeing equipment development for the ground forces was sent to the new army headquarters. According to the Ministry of National Defense (MND), the PLA aims for a division of labor in RDT&E between the new CMC department, services, and theaters, but how this will work in practice is unclear.[21] The initial director was former GAD Director General Zhang Youxia. Following Zhang's elevation to CMC vice chairman in October 2017, the department was directed by Lieutenant General Li Shangfu, a previous deputy commander of the Strategic Support Force.

Training and Administration Department [*xunlian guanli bu*, 训练管理部]

The Training and Administration Department is responsible for overseeing training and professional military education, and likely coordinates with the Joint Staff Department, theater commands, and services to develop joint training requirements and assess training programs. It replaced the former GSD Military Training Department [*zongcan junxun bu*, 总参军训部], which had been stood up in 2011.[22] Establishing a training department under direct CMC supervision underscores the importance of strengthening "realistic" joint training across the PLA.[23] The first director was Lieutenant General Zheng He, who went on to serve as president of the PLA Academy of Military Sciences and later the PLA National Defense University. He was replaced by Lieutenant General Li Huohui, who was previously commander of the 31st Group Army, one of the PLA's elite units.

National Defense Mobilization Department [*guofang dongyuan bu*, 国防动员部]
The National Defense Mobilization Department oversees the reserve forces and the provincial military districts [*sheng junqu*, 省军区] and below, other than the Tibet and Xinjiang Military Districts and the Beijing Garrison (which were placed under the army headquarters in part due to their higher bureaucratic grade).[24] This department succeeds the former GSD Mobilization Department [*canmou dongyuan bu*, 总参动员部]. Elevating mobilization to a separate CMC department highlights the importance of civil-military integration, given the office's oversight over reserve force and mobilization planning.[25] The first director was Lieutenant General Sheng Bin, who was previously deputy commander of the Shenyang Military Region.

CMC Commissions [*weiyuanhui*, 委员会]
Discipline Inspection Commission [*jilu jiancha weiyuanhui*, 纪律检查委员会]
The CMC Discipline Inspection Commission is responsible for enforcing party discipline within the PLA, including conducting investigations of suspected corrupt personnel. Its mission parallels that of the civilian Central Discipline Inspection Commission, which has played a prominent role in China's anti-corruption campaign since late 2012. Although Chinese sources describe this as a new organization,[26] the CMC has had a discipline inspection commission since November 1980.[27] However, the work of that commission was reportedly carried out by the GPD. Its inaugural secretary was General Du Jincai, a previous GPD deputy director. In

March 2017, Du was replaced by General Zhang Shengmin, who had been political commissar of the CMC Logistics Support Department. Zhang was appointed a CMC member at the 19th Party Congress.

Political and Legal Affairs Commission [*zhengfa weiyuanhui*, 政法委员会]

This organization establishes regulations and legal norms to improve the administration of the PLA—what the Chinese armed forces call "regularization" [*zhengguihua*, 正规化].[28] It also helps to "prevent, investigate, and deal with" criminal activities in the military.[29] Centralizing the military's legal system reduces the potential for interference with the enforcement of laws and regulations at lower levels. Previously, the military court system and Military Procuratorate (which conducted police investigations) were under the GPD. The organization parallels the civilian Central Political and Legal Affairs Commission, formerly under Zhou Yongkang, which supervises the legal and police systems. The first secretary of the CMC Politics and Law Commission was Lieutenant General Li Xiaofeng, who previously served as the PLA's chief procurator. In March 2017, he was replaced by Lieutenant General Song Dan, previously the commission's deputy secretary.

Science and Technology Commission [*kexue jishu weiyuanhui*, 科学技术委员会]

As part of the CMC reshuffling, the PLA's Science and Technology Commission was transferred from the GAD to direct CMC oversight.[30] It continues to be responsible for advising PLA leadership on weapons development and serving as a nexus for collaboration between the armed forces and defense industry.[31] Moving the commission to the CMC highlights the importance of civil-military integration to the PLA, a theme of the larger reforms. The commission's director remained Lieutenant General Liu Guozhi, who was appointed to his position in 2014.[32]

CMC Offices [*bangongshi*, 办公室/*shu*, 署/*zongju*, 总局]

Strategic Planning Office [*zhanlüe guihua bangongshi*, 战略规划办公室]

The Strategic Planning Office is responsible for centralizing authority over "military strategic planning."[33] It replaced the GSD Strategic Planning Department, which was established in 2011 and carried out functions such as long-term strategic analysis, resource allocation analysis, and organizational reform analysis.[34] The new department continues to perform some of these roles, including managing military budgets and project evaluation and accountability systems.[35] Organizational reform issues, however, appear more likely to be addressed within the CMC Reform and Organization Office (see below). Major General Wang Huiqing remained as the office's director after its transfer from the GSD.

Reform and Organization Office [*gaige he bianzhi bangongshi*, 改革和编制办公室]
The Reform and Organization Office is responsible for coordinating military reforms and managing the PLA's organizational structure.[36] The organization likely coordinates closely with the CMC's military reform leading small group [*zhongyang junwei zhenhua guofang he jundui gaige liangdao xiaozu*, 中央军委深化国防和军队改革领导小组], which was established in 2014 to provide guidance for the entire reform process under Xi's leadership.[37] It appears to replace some functions of the former GSD Military Affairs Department [*zongcan junwu bu*, 总参军务部] and may also have acquired some responsibilities from the former GSD Strategic Planning Department related to organizational reform.[38] The office's first director was Major General Wang Chengzhi, who formerly led the GPD's Direct Work Department [*zong zheng zhishu gongzuo bu*, 总政直属工作部]. In 2017, he was replaced by Major General Zhang Yu, who previously served as the office's deputy director.

Office of International Military Cooperation [*guoji junshi hezuo bangongshi*, 国际军事合作办公室]
The CMC Office of International Military Cooperation is responsible for managing foreign military exchanges and cooperation and supervising foreign affairs work throughout the PLA.[39] It replaced the previous MND Foreign Affairs Office [*guofang bu waishi bangongshi*, 国防部外事办公

室], which had doubled as the CMC General Office Foreign Affairs Office (FAO). However, the MND Information Affairs Bureau [*guofang bu xinwen shiwu ju*, 国防部新闻事务局], part of the former FAO that conducts news briefings, remained within the MND. Clarifying the office's status within the CMC underscores the importance of military diplomacy, which has been an emphasis of Xi.[40] The first director of the office was Rear Admiral Guan Youfei, who previously headed the MND Foreign Affairs Office.[41] In May 2017, Guan was replaced by Major General Hu Changming, who had previously served as the office's deputy director.

Audit Bureau [*shenji shu*, 审计署]

The Audit Bureau is responsible for inspecting PLA finances and supervising the military's audit system.[42] This office was previously located within the GLD but moved to the CMC in November 2014.[43] Like the Discipline Inspection Commission, the Audit Bureau sends inspection teams to units throughout the PLA to ensure compliance with rules and root out corruption.[44] Major General Guo Chunfu was appointed to lead the office in December 2015.[45]

Organ Affairs General Management Bureau [*jiguan shiwu guanli zongbu*, 机关事务管理总部]

This is a new organization responsible for providing administrative support to CMC departments and subsidiary organs.[46] The office was apparently the result of a merger between the former GSD Management Support Department [*canmou guanli baozhang bu*, 总参管理保障部], which served a logistics function (for example, facilities management), and similar offices from the other general departments.[47] The new bureau appears to continue to play a role in provisioning supplies as well as in managing military wages.[48] One role of the office is "cutting support units and personnel," which suggests that it has played a role in implementing the PLA's planned 300,000-person force reduction.[49] The bureau's first director was Major General Liu Zhiming, former head of the Shenyang Military Region Joint Logistics Department.

Notes

[1] "China Reshuffles Military Headquarters," Xinhua, January 11, 2016, available at <http://news.xinhuanet.com/english/2016-01/11/c_134998692.htm>; "MND Holds Press Conference on CMC Organ Reshuffle," *China Military Online*, January 12, 2016, available at <http://english.chinamil.com.cn/news-channels/china-military-news/2016-01/12/content_6854444.htm>. This appendix is adapted from Joel Wuthnow and Phillip C. Saunders, *Chinese Military Reforms in the Age of Xi Jinping: Drivers, Challenges, and Implications*, China Strategic Perspectives 10 (Washington, DC: NDU Press, 2017), 61–65.

[2] Tai Ming Cheung, "The Riddle in the Middle: China's Central Military Commission in the Twenty-First Century," in *PLA Influence on China's National Security Policymaking*, ed. Phillip C. Saunders and Andrew Scobell (Stanford: Stanford University Press, 2015), 90–92.

[3] Edward Wong, "The 'Gatekeeper' in Xi Jinping's Inner Circle," *New York Times*, September 30, 2015, available at <https://sinosphere.blogs.nytimes.com/2015/09/30/the-gatekeeper-in-xi-jinpings-inner-circle/>.

[4] "Zhong Shaojun Takes Up the Post of CMC General Office Director" [钟绍军出任军委办公厅主任], Sina News [新浪网], September 18, 2018, available at <http://news.sina.com.cn/o/2018-09-18-doc-ifxeuwwr5766185.shtml>.

[5] Authors' interviews, December 2017.

[6] For details on the pre-reform General Armament Department, see Kevin Pollpeter and Amy Chang, "General Armament Department," in *The PLA as Organization v2.0*, ed. Kevin Pollpeter and Kenneth W. Allen (Vienna, VA: DGI, Inc., 2015), 228–231.

[7] This rule is also known as the Saunders Theorem.

[8] Authors' interviews, December 2017.

[9] "China Reshuffles Military Headquarters"; "MND Holds Press Conference on CMC Organ Reshuffle."

[10] Cheung, "The Riddle in the Middle," 90–92.

[11] Tian Yixiang, "Faithfully Implement the Duties and Responsibilities of the CMC General Office" [忠实履行军委办公厅职责使命], *PLA Daily* [解放军报], April 28, 2016, available at <https://web.archive.org/web/20170523011041/http://www.mod.gov.cn/topnews/2016-04/28/content_4651306.htm>.

[12] "Which Generals Will Be on the CMC after the Reform?" [哪些将军这次会后调进中央军委?], *China Youth Online* [中国青年网], January 12, 2016, available at <http://military.china.com/important/11132797/20160112/21122496.html>. For biographical details on Lieutenant General Qin, see "CMC General Office Director

Qin Shengxiang Promoted to Lieutenant General" [中央军委办公厅主任秦生祥晋升中将], *Caixin Wang* [财新王], July 21, 2015, available at <http://china.caixin.com/2015-07-21/100830965.html>.

[13] "Zhong Shaojun Takes Up the Post of CMC General Office Director."

[14] "MND Holds Press Conference on CMC Organ Reshuffle."

[15] The Operations Department was sometimes known as the 1st Department [总参一部], a second-level (corps leader grade) department within General Services Department. See Mark A. Stokes and Ian Easton, "The Chinese People's Liberation Army General Staff Department: Evolving Organizations and Missions," in *The PLA as Organization v2.0*, 142–145.

[16] Alice Miller, "The Central Military Commission," in *The PLA as Organization v2.0*, 97.

[17] Kenneth W. Allen, Dennis J. Blasko, and John F. Corbett, Jr., "The PLA's New Organizational Structure: What Is Known, Unknown, Or Speculation (Part 1)," *China Brief* 16, no. 3 (February 4, 2016), available at <www.jamestown.org/single/?tx_ttnews%5Btt_news%5D=45069&no_cache=1#.VxfOffnR_RY>.

[18] "MND Holds Press Conference on CMC Organ Reshuffle."

[19] Ibid.

[20] See chapter in this volume by Luce and Richter.

[21] "MND Holds Press Conference on CMC Organ Reshuffle."

[22] Stokes and Easton, "The Chinese People's Liberation Army General Staff Department," 154–157.

[23] See "Reform Efforts Should Be Focused on the 'Strategic Hubs'" [改革要向"战略枢纽"聚焦用力], *PLA Daily* [解放军报], April 22, 2014, available at <http://theory.people.com.cn/n/2014/0422/c40531-24927666.html>.

[24] Allen, Blasko, and Corbett, "The PLA's New Organizational Structure."

[25] This theme was highlighted in a Chinese report about the initial activities of the department. See "Demystifying the Newly Established CMC National Defense Mobilization Department" [揭秘新成立的中央军委国防动员部], *China Youth Daily* [中国青年报], January 29, 2016, available at <http://zqb.cyol.com/html/2016-01/29/nw.D110000zgqnb_20160129_1-06.htm>.

[26] "MND Holds Press Conference on CMC Organ Reshuffle."

[27] Roy Kamphausen, "The General Political Department," in *The PLA as Organization v2.0*, 173.

[28] For a discussion, see Thomas A. Bickford, "Regularization and the Chinese People's Liberation Army," *Asian Survey* 40, no. 3 (May–June 2000), 456–474.

29 Strengthening the "socialist rule of law" [社会主义法制] is a theme of the broader national reforms, highlighted in particular at the 4ᵗʰ Plenum of the 18ᵗʰ Central Committee held in October 2014. See "Highlights of Communique of 4ᵗʰ Plenary Session of CPC Central Committee," Xinhua, October 23, 2014, available at <http://news.xinhuanet.com/english/china/2014-10/23/c_133737957.htm>.

30 Kevin Pollpeter and Amy Chang, "General Armament Department," in *The PLA as Organization v2.0*, 223–224.

31 "MND Holds Press Conference on CMC Organ Reshuffle."

32 "Which Generals Will Be on the CMC After the Reform?"

33 "MND Holds Press Conference on CMC Organ Reshuffle."

34 Stokes and Easton, "The Chinese People's Liberation Army General Staff Department," 153–154.

35 Li Guang, "Promote the Innovative Development of Military Strategic Planning" [推进军队战略规划工作创新发展], *PLA Daily* [解放军报], April 28, 2016, available at <https://web.archive.org/web/20180110124955/http://www.mod.gov.cn/topnews/2016-04/28/content_4651317.htm>.

36 "MND Holds Press Conference on CMC Organ Reshuffle."

37 See "Xi Leads China's Military Reform, Stresses Strong Army," Xinhua, March 15, 2014, available at <http://news.xinhuanet.com/english/china/2014-03/15/c_133188618.htm>.

38 The GSD Military Affairs Department was also responsible for welfare and benefits and served as the personnel center for enlisted servicemen. It is unclear if the new CMC office will assume these duties. See Stokes and Easton, 159–160.

39 "MND Holds Press Conference on CMC Organ Reshuffle."

40 "Xi Jinping: Further Innovate a New Situation in Military Diplomacy" [习近平: 进一步开创军事外交新局面], Xinhua, January 29, 2015, available at <http://news.xinhuanet.com/politics/2015-01/29/c_1114183775.htm>.

41 "Which Generals Will Be on the CMC After the Reform?"

42 This organization has also been translated as "Audit Office." However, "Audit Bureau" may be a better translation of *shu* [署] and distinguish it from *bangongshi* [办公室] ("office").

43 "China Military Reaches Key Decision to Strengthen Auditing," Xinhua, November 4, 2014, available at <http://eng.mod.gov.cn/TopNews/2014-11/06/content_4550175.htm>.

44 "MND Holds Press Conference on CMC Organ Reshuffle."

[45] "Guo Chunfu Becomes Director of PLA Audit Office, in a New Role Twice In a Year" [郭春富任解放军审计署审计长 年内两度履新], *Caixin Online* [财新网], December 30, 2015, available at <http://china.caixin.com/2015-12-30/100894397.html>.

[46] *Jiguan* [机关] may also be translated as "office" or "organization."

[47] Allen, Blasko, and Corbett, "The PLA's New Organizational Structure."

[48] Li Tongzhu, "Focus On Building a New-Type Service Support System" [着力构建新型服务保障体系], *PLA Daily* [解放军报], January 25, 2016, available at <https://web.archive.org/web/20170802163930/http://www.mod.gov.cn:80/topnews/2016-01-25/content_4638461.htm>.

[49] "MND Holds Press Conference on CMC Organ Reshuffle."

PART I

DRIVERS AND STRATEGIC CONTEXT

CHAPTER 1

BREAKING THE PARADIGM

Drivers Behind the PLA's Current Period of Reform

David M. Finkelstein

Closely embrace the building of a military that listens to the

Party's commands, which can fight and win, with a superior work style.

—Third Plenum "Decision," November 2013

I n late 2015, Xi Jinping launched the Chinese People's Liberation Army (PLA) into a period of much anticipated reform that will continue for many years. In 2016 alone, the PLA made significant changes to a legacy organizational structure that had its roots in the 1950s, when Soviet advisors helped to shape the People's Republic of China (PRC) defense establishment. Swept away were the four general departments—traditional bastions of authority over operations and training, Party work and personnel affairs, logistics, and equipment development.[2] In their stead emerged an expanded and more powerful Central Military Commission (CMC) that includes a newly formed Joint Staff Department, among other subordinate departments and organs.[3]

Also disestablished were the PLA's seven geographic military regions: ground force–dominated entities that harkened back to the immediate "post-liberation" period after 1949, when they were created to consolidate Communist rule after a long civil war and to defend the borders and coast of the newly established PRC against potential external attack.[4] These have been replaced by five joint theater commands that will focus on planning and conducting operations outward along various "strategic directions."[5]

These organizational changes have been accompanied by major adjustments in roles, authorities, and responsibilities. With the disestablishment of the four general departments, the CMC now has direct control over the five joint theater commands and services, the latter now serving as force providers responsible for training, equipping, and modernizing their respective organizations.[6] Moreover, peacetime and wartime command and control relationships have been streamlined and authorities clarified, at least in theory.[7] This is just the beginning of Beijing's ambitious military reform agenda.[8] On December 2–3, 2016, President Xi convened and chaired the CMC Work Conference on Armed Forces Scale, Structure, and Force Composition Reform. This conclave launched the second tranche of major organizational reforms focused mostly on force reductions, a rebalancing among the services, a reorganization of major ground force units, and institutional reforms such as a reorganization of the expansive system of military academies.[9]

Beyond changes to the PLA's line-and-block chart, the heart and soul of this enterprise will be myriad institutional and systemic changes that were announced as part of the military reform agenda in the Central Committee's "Decision" at the Third Plenum of the 18th Party Congress in November 2013, that were discussed at the November 2015 CMC Work Conference on Military Structural Reform, and that were included in the authoritative *Central Military Commission Opinion on Deepening Reform of National Defense and the Armed Forces*, which was issued on January 1, 2016.[10] These institutional, systemic, and procedural reforms—some 46 identified in the Third Plenum Decision—cover major areas such as:

- national military strategy
- command and control relationships
- the balance of forces among the services
- service structure and size
- force deployments within China
- the ratio of combat to noncombat organizations

- the balance between officers, noncommissioned officers, and enlisted personnel
- the officer personnel management system (promotions and assignments)
- professional military education
- budget and finance
- oversight and compliance.

Although the PLA's timetable for enacting change in all of these areas is unknown, the year 2020 has been set as the target date for completion.[11]

Needless to say, this is a bold undertaking. In some areas, such as organizational changes, the decisions to date have already gone far beyond previous periods of reform, and more developments are expected. For example, as initial versions of this chapter were being drafted, the PLA announced the establishment of the Joint Logistics Support Force under the CMC.[12] As for institutional reforms, that enterprise has just begun, but it will be marching over well-trampled fields. The PLA will seek to push through change in systemic problem areas that have long bedeviled China's armed forces. Overall, the range of issues on the reform agenda suggests the PLA is seeking to make significant adjustments to organizational, institutional, and operational attributes that have defined it for decades. They are looking to break out of old paradigms.

What is driving this current period of military reform? To what ends? Why now? This chapter argues that this period of reenergized military reform is being impelled by three drivers that are all interacting at a moment in time: domestic political factors, operational factors, and assessments of China's national security situation. When this process is complete, Beijing hopes to have a military that is more tightly tied to the Chinese Communist Party (CCP) and more operationally capable of winning joint, high-tech wars fought primarily in the maritime and aerospace domains.

The remainder of this chapter looks at each of these three drivers of reform in greater depth. The analysis is based almost exclusively on PLA and other Chinese materials that have been placed in the public domain, mostly in the Chinese media. Indeed, PLA leadership and a wide range of officers have not been shy about discussing what they intend to achieve and why they need to achieve it through speeches, journal articles, and PLA media. While the details may be slow in coming (if at all in some cases), the general contours of what is transpiring are in the public domain.

The Political Dimensions of Military Reform

Four key and interrelated political drivers are behind this reform enterprise. First and foremost is a need to tighten the CCP-PLA linkage in an era of perceived internal and external challenges to the Chinese Party-state. Second is pulling the PLA into the larger national reform agenda that Xi and the CCP have set for the PRC. Third is strengthening Xi's personal power. Fourth is the need to preemptively roll over any potential resistance within the PLA to the military reform enterprise. Each is examined in turn.

Reaffirming Party Control of the PLA

Since this period of reform was announced at the Third Plenum in 2013, a significant dimension of the accompanying internal propaganda campaign directed at the PLA has focused on reinforcing fundamental political principles: that the PLA is a Party-army and the armed wing of the CCP. In short, the PLA needs to remain a force that "listens to the commands of the Party." "Adhere to the correct political direction" was the first of the six "Basic Principles" for the reform outlined in the authoritative CMC "Opinion" issued on January 1, 2016:

> Adhere to the correct political direction. It is necessary to consolidate and perfect the basic principles and system of the Party's absolute leadership over the military, maintain the nature and purposes of the people's military, carry forward our military's glorious traditions and excellent work style, comprehensively implement the Central Military Commission chairmanship responsibility system, and ensure that the supreme leadership

right and command right of the military are concentrated in the [Communist Party of China] Central Committee and in the Central Military Commission.[13]

It is easy to dismiss these reaffirmations of Party control of the PLA as standard CCP rhetoric [*tifa*, 提法], for there is nothing new at all in these exhortations. However, the amount of hand-wringing over this issue is worth noting. At a time when the CCP is facing a challenging domestic agenda, Party leadership appears determined that there be no slippage whatsoever in CCP-PLA connectivity.[14] A strong CCP-PLA connection is considered especially critical at this point in time under "the new situation" [*xin xingshi*, 新形势] when the Party perceives that it is facing mounting internal and external security challenges, some of which are viewed as interconnected—an assessment that is captured in the CCP's shorthand phrase "the two big situations" [*liangge da ju*, 两个大局].

There continue to be concerns that "anti-Party forces" from within and without China pose a real threat to the CCP-led regime. Xi Jinping has spoken of the need to "achieve political security as our fundamental task."[15] There is no dearth of public commentary about perceived threats to the political system. One authoritative example comes from the publicly released 2015 defense white paper that transmitted China's national military strategy. The document declared that "China faces a formidable task to maintain political security" and that "anti-China forces have never given up their attempt to instigate a 'color revolution' in this country."[16] Besides persistent concerns about color revolutions, the example of the fall of the Communist Party of the Soviet Union stands as a stark reminder of what can happen when a Party-army loses its political direction. Party leaders no doubt also keep in the backs of their minds the momentary confusion in the ranks of the PLA at one point in 1989 when some units refused to obey orders to enforce martial law. In the face of these political threats and challenges, a PLA *not* loyal to the CCP could pose an existential threat to the regime, and so requires constant vigilance.

Second, and directly related to the above, over the past few years senior CCP and PLA leaders have felt a need to vociferously attack the notion of the "nationalization" or "de-politicization" of the PLA. In 2011, for example, the former director of the General Political Department, General Li Jinai, wrote a widely disseminated editorial in *PLA Daily* that lambasted the idea of depoliticizing the PLA as an attempt by "domestic and foreign hostile forces" to overthrow the CCP, a common theme.[17] (In August 2016, an uncorroborated news report alleged General Li was arrested in retirement as part of the anticorruption campaign in the PLA.[18]) In August 2013, in a long article on military reform in *Seeking Truth* [*Qiushi*, 求是], the CCP's flagship journal, then–CMC Vice Chairman General Fan Changlong warned that the PLA must "resolutely refute and reject the erroneous political viewpoints of 'disassociating the military from the Party, depoliticizing the armed forces' and 'putting the armed forces under the state.'"[19] And, of course, Xi's speech at the All Army Political Work Conference held in Gutian in November 2014, 1 year after the Third Plenum and 1 year before the CMC Opinion on military reform, was a top-down exercise in "re-redding" the PLA.[20] Addressing concerns about "erroneous views" on depoliticizing the PLA in conjunction with the current period of reform is likely a combination of a periodic need to exorcise this ultimate demon that CCP and PLA officials have conjured up in their worst nightmares, a need to counter the arguments of some Western scholars who argue from time to time that the PLA cannot become a professional force until it is a national force, and possibly a response to a real discourse on this issue that may have been taking place in some quarters of the PLA, but into which outside observers have little visibility.[21]

Third, there are intriguing hints, though based on thin gruel, that over the years the absolute power and authority of the CMC (and hence, the Central Committee) over the PLA had somehow been diluted and that the reorganization would correct this. One article in *PLA Daily* spoke of "overly concentrated power" in the four general departments resulting in them taking on some of the prerogatives of the CMC, and that the four general departments "in reality form[ed] an independent level of leadership" serving as "a substitute for several functions of the CMC"—not an acceptable situation.[22] As for the military regions, the same author used a historical-literary allusion from the Western Zhou Dynasty (11th BCE) to assert that as a result of the new organizational changes to the PLA, the "large military regions will also no longer have feudal powers over their domains."[23]

Pulling the PLA "Inside the Tent"

Another political dimension of the current military reform enterprise is bringing the military establishment inside the CCP's "tent" and chipping away at what one might refer to as the PLA's tradition of *bureaucratic exceptionalism*. What is meant by this term? To be clear, it is *not* meant to imply that the PLA is a rogue or independent actor within the Chinese Party-state system or to question its institutional loyalty to the CCP. It *does* mean that the PLA has been left mostly to its own devices to manage itself, regulate itself, and set its own institutional priorities with little or no oversight or accountability from outside the PLA. This extreme institutional autonomy has resulted in two significant problems for the PLA: rampant corruption throughout the officer corps (including at its highest levels) and a lack of political will to take on the deeply vested bureaucratic, institutional, and personal interests that have stood in the way of implementing reforms necessary to enhance the PLA's capabilities as a warfighting organization.

The anticorruption campaign sweeping through the PLA and the mind-boggling number of senior officers who have been arrested speaks volumes to Xi Jinping's determination that the PLA not elude the larger ongoing anticorruption campaign within the greater CCP. Through this campaign he is underscoring that the PLA, and especially its top leaders, is subject to the same type of Party discipline as civilian CCP members. A *PLA Daily* commentator article in October 2016 strongly suggested the anticorruption campaign in the PLA is far from over and will continue for some time to come.[24]

As for the need to move forward on much needed military reforms, the PLA has been given its marching orders directly from the CCP to make tough decisions and show progress despite the number of "rice bowls" that will be upended. Military reform and modernization have been made a part of Xi's and the CCP's larger national reform agenda—military reform is not just the PLA's business at this point.

The importance of military modernization to the larger CCP agenda has been clear since the 18th Party Congress in 2012 and was reaffirmed at the Third Plenum in 2013. We recall that the 18th Party Congress work report called for "accelerating" defense reform and made its accomplishment "a strategic task of China's modernization drive," directing the PLA to "make major progress."[25] The Central Committee's "Decision on Major Issues Concerning Comprehensively Deepening Reforms" coming out of the Third Plenum placed military reform in the context of a larger national reform agenda that included the economic system, government functions, the fiscal and tax systems, urban-rural issues, the "socialist democratic political system," the legal system, accountability of officials, social services, and environmental issues.

Announcing the key components of the current military reform effort at a Central Committee plenum, and not at an expanded meeting of the CMC as in the past, has been described by some PLA officers as unprecedented. Moreover, as one PLA analyst has written, this was the "first time China's national defense and military reforms have been integrated into overall national reforms and been considered an important part of executing a national strategy."[26] Finally, as students of Chinese affairs are well aware, an important component of the CCP's "China Dream" [*zhongguo meng*, 中国梦] is the "Strong Army Dream" [*qiangjun meng*, 强军梦]. Having been handed its own "Goldwater-Nichols moment" by the Party, the PLA must now produce results no matter how dislocating or painful it may be for various stakeholders.

Strengthening Xi's Power

Finally, another result of the political muscle movements associated with this current PLA reform and modernization enterprise has been strengthening Xi Jinping's control over the PLA, and hence his control over the Party itself. Xi is chairman of the "CMC Leading Small Group for Deepening National Defense and Military Reform" [*zhongyang junwei shenhua guofang he jundui gaige lingdao xiaozu*, 中央军委深化国防和军队改革领导小组], an organ that was established after the Third Plenum to oversee the development and implementation of military reform and modernization plans. The implication is that Xi is personally involved in this process to make sure it happens. In the past, the four general departments were responsible for carrying out the stated military reform objectives of the CMC. This usually resulted in foot-dragging or less than bold initiatives. This time, overseeing and enforcing change has been taken over by the CMC chairman himself (Xi), who has taken the four general departments out of the process, disbanding them and absorbing many of their former functions and responsibilities into the CMC. Second, the PLA and Party literature explaining the new organizational and command and control arrangements are awash with explanations of the need to strengthen the "chairman responsibility system" [*junwei zhuxi fuze zhi*, 军委主席负责制]—that is, placing more authority in the hands of the CMC chairman, namely Xi. As one article put it, the new arrangements "will be more advantageous to strengthening the concentrated unified leadership of the CMC, and better implementing the chairman responsibility system . . . to safeguard the firm grasp of the highest leadership and command authority over the nation's armed forces of Chairman Xi and the CMC."[27] Third, the anticorruption campaign and the netting of such high-level generals as former CMC Vice Chairmen General Xu Caihou and General Guo Boxiong make clear to everyone in uniform how powerful Xi is. Indeed, Xi is getting tough with the PLA just as Mao Zedong and Deng Xiaoping did. The symbolism of Xi convening the November 2014 All Army Political Work Conference in Gutian, the site of one of Mao's early triumphs over the Red Army (1929), could not have been lost on those who attended (and the rest of the officer corps not in attendance, thanks to a barrage of articles in *PLA Daily*). Xi's alleged criticisms of the PLA are reminiscent of Deng, especially Deng's famous 1975 speech, "The Task of Consolidating Our Army," in which he famously criticized the PLA for "bloating, laxity, conceit, extravagance, and inertia."[28] Finally, because of the reorganization, Xi is the first CMC chairman to take on the title commander-in-chief of the Joint Operations Command Center.[29]

At this point, there should be no question in the PLA (or the CCP) about who is in charge of the armed forces. Nothing says "I'm in charge" like arresting active-duty and retired generals, chairing the group overseeing the reform enterprise, having your expositions on national defense and army-building published and studied, taking on new titles, and disestablishing organizations that have provided the bases for personal power and institutional authority for decades. To oppose or stand in the way of military reform is to oppose the will of the Central Committee and Xi Jinping. Such a large degree of political power behind the military reforms is considered a necessary prerequisite for a successful reform program simply because of the challenges of bureaucratic inertia and resistance to change based on vested interests. The PLA has been attempting many of these reforms for decades, but unsuccessfully due at times to resistance from within the armed forces. CMC Vice Chairman General Xu Qiliang, an important political voice of the reform, has hammered home the need to get with the program as directed by the CCP. Typical of his exhortations: "It is necessary to break through the restrictions of traditional thoughts, break through the obstruction of vested interests, and muster up the courage of blazing a trail when facing a mountain."[30] And a steep mountain it is that the PLA is trying to climb, for the guts of this enterprise is aimed at enhancing the PLA's capability to conduct a type of warfare it has never fought before.

Operational Imperatives

The most significant driver of this reform enterprise is the need to improve the operational capabilities of the PLA as a joint warfighting force—one that can prevail in information-intensive joint operations in the maritime-aerospace domains, and other high-tech battle spaces. In addition to strengthening the CCP-PLA linkage, the PLA must come out the other end of this period of reform more capable of prosecuting joint warfare, an objective it has been pursuing for over two decades. In addition to prevailing in a joint, high-tech fight, the PLA is being told to better position itself to deal with an expanding list of nontraditional security threats faced by Beijing and to be able to secure Chinese national interests, many of which are increasingly abroad. All of these missions require enhanced operational capabilities.

The demand signal from the CCP for such a military is captured in the opening paragraph of the section on defense and military affairs in the work report of the 18th Party Congress:

> Building a strong national defense and powerful armed forces that are commensurate with China's international standing and meet the needs of its security and development interests is a strategic task of China's modernization drive. China is faced with interwoven problems affecting its survival and development security as well as traditional and nontraditional security threats. To address these problems and threats, we must make major progress in modernizing national defense and the armed forces.[31]

At bottom, the PLA is being told that it must become a force that can "fight and win." It is Xi himself who is demanding that the PLA enhance its actual operational capabilities and focus its energies on warfighting.

Xi is quoted ad infinitum in articles in the PLA media and professional military journals emphasizing that all facets of the military reform program must be focused on the Party's "strong army objective" [*qiangjun mubiao*, 强军目标] and that the most important criterion for moving forward with a reform initiative is whether it will unleash combat power and meet the "warfighting standard" [*zhandouli biaozhun*, 战斗力标准]. The following passage from *The Selected Important Expositions of Xi Jinping on National Defense and Army Building* (cited by a PLA author) makes the point indelibly clear:

> The military must develop the ability to fight and win wars. We must strengthen the ability of officers and men to fight wars, to

lead troops in battle, and train soldiers in a warfighting way of thinking. We must firmly establish warfighting capability as the fundamental and sole standard. We must build according to the requirements of warfighting; grasp preparations; and ensure that the army will respond to the call, fight, and win.[32]

Xi reportedly underscored this point at the first meeting of the CMC's Leading Small Group on Military Reform (March 15, 2014) when he stated that:

it is necessary to firmly grasp the focal point of being able to fight and win. Persistently take preparations for military struggle [PMS] as the lead, persistently adhere to the orientation of problem solving, focus reforms on settling crucial and difficult issues in preparations for military struggle and overcoming the weak links in combat power building.[33]

There are two phrases in the statement that merit comment. The first phrase of note is "preparations for military struggle" [*junshi douzheng zhunbei*, 军事斗争准备], which some also translate as "military combat preparations." This PLA term speaks to the need to be able to equip, train, and especially employ a military force to engage in a specific *type* of conflict. It is a capabilities-based perspective.[34] To a large extent, many if not all of the facets of this current period of military reform are centered on the need to be able to fight a specific type of conflict. What type of conflict is the PLA being told to prepare for? The answer was provided by Beijing in the publicly released 2015 defense white paper. The paper told readers that China's current military strategy ("Military Strategic Guideline of Active Defense Under the New Situation"[35]) requires the PLA to prepare to fight "informationized local wars, highlighting maritime military struggle and maritime PMS."[36]

There is no dearth of PLA writing or analyses to help us understand what type of conflict the Chinese armed forces are being told to prepare for. Briefly, first and foremost, it means a joint fight that integrates all of PLA services and key capabilities. It means a high-tech and information-dominant conflict.

It is anticipated by the PLA that operations will primarily be fought in the maritime-aerospace domains, with actions also taking place in cyberspace, outer space, and across the electromagnetic spectrum. The ability to fight and win this type of fight is what the PLA reform enterprise must accomplish.

The second phrase of note in Xi's statement is *overcoming the weak links in combat power building*. This is important to highlight because the PLA currently assesses that it is not yet where it needs to be when it comes to fighting and winning the kind of joint conflict it currently identifies as the "focal point" for its "preparations for military struggle."

Those who are steeped in Chinese military literature and who regularly read the comments and articles of commanders, political commissars, and Chinese military analysts appreciate that there is no greater critic of the PLA than the PLA itself. PLA expert Dennis Blasko has written and commented extensively on this point.[37] The PLA (and Xi Jinping) have multiple self-critical phrases that capture the PLA's various self-assessed shortcomings. One of the most common is the "two incompatibles" [*liangge buxiang shiying*, 两个不相适应], which assesses that the PLA's level of modernization is not yet at the point of being able to win information-based local wars, nor can the PLA fulfill all of its new "historic missions in the new phase of the new century."[38] Another common phrase is "the two big gaps" [*liangge chaju hen da*, 两个差距很大], which states that there is still a large gap between the capabilities of the PLA and the overall demands of national security and between the PLA's state of modernization compared with the world's most advanced militaries.[39]

What seem to be the problems? Where are the "weak links" Xi Jinping spoke of that must be addressed during this urgent period of military reform? Even a cursory answer to these questions is far beyond the scope of this chapter. However, to oversimplify, they reside in two big bins: technologies (weapons and systems) and institutions (organization, people, and processes).

On the technologies side, the PLA is not satisfied that it has the weapons and systems it needs to sustain and prevail in modern warfare. For example, there are still problems with China's defense industrial system, with indigenous innovation, and in manufacturing key components of some weapons systems or platforms. Aircraft engines are one persistent example where there is still difficulty in the defense industrial sector. The current reforms aim to address the perennial problems in China's defense industrial sector *again* (as they have been attempting to do for almost three decades). The emphasis in the current period of reform on enhanced "civil-military integration" [*junmin ronghe,* 军民融合] as part of the solution is not a new concept; it goes back decades (see the respective chapters by Cheung and Lafferty in this volume).

Moreover, the PLA speaks of itself as unevenly modernized across a force of some 2 million personnel (after the 300,000-troop cut that Xi Jinping announced in September 2015 has been implemented). The PLA still describes itself as only partly mechanized and partly "informationized"—not only in equipment but also in operational mindsets. The PLA views itself as a force operating in two military epochs simultaneously: the previous age of mechanization and the current information era, with some forces only partially residing in either. In the year 2013, when this period of reform was launched, the PLA was not where it planned to be in making these transitions, even in achieving full mechanization, as called for in its own 30-year military modernization plan known as the "three step development strategy" [*san buzou fazhan zhanlüe,* 三步走发展战略], promulgated in 1997.[40]

These problems notwithstanding, there has been great progress on the weapons and systems fronts over the years that the current reform enterprise aims to build on and accelerate. China's defense industries have demonstrated that they can indigenously produce (or reverse engineer and reproduce) impressive weapons, systems, components, and technologies that today give the PLA more reach, more punch, and more situational awareness than at any time in the past. The Chinese have demonstrated the *capacity* to field systems credible enough to elicit concerns and reactions from among the foreign defense establishments in China's neighborhood and beyond, to include the United States. The U.S. Department of Defense's annual reports to Congress on Chinese military power, and other types of publications, are replete with examples of impressive systems being fielded by the PLA (and the high rate by which they are being produced): various types of missiles, surface vessels, submarines, aircraft, tanks, long-range artillery, satellites and antisatellite systems, radars, cyber capabilities, and a nuclear force that is being modernized. The list goes on.[41] And there are certainly pockets of excellence in defense innovation, so positive strides are being made in some sectors in China.

The more vexing issues for the PLA seem to reside on the institutional front. There appear to be deep-seated concerns, and a full appreciation, that the *capacity* to produce first-rate weapons and systems does not automatically translate into operational *capability*. The latter is the result of real operational know-how (experience), coupled with the necessary command and control assets, and organizational structures that allow commanders to employ, integrate, and manage forces on the modern battlefield. In short, the PLA is concerned about the practical but increasingly complex matters associated with *operational art*, to borrow a term from the U.S. military. The PLA is painfully aware that it has not been tested in battle for many years, and there are questions in its own mind about how it might fare in real-world operations. As a commentator article in *PLA Daily* put it, "it should be noted that our military forces have not fought any major battle for over 30 years, and have not undergone the tempering of actual operations under informationized conditions."[42] Some of the comments attributed to Xi Jinping about the capabilities of the PLA's operational commanders are both blunt and surprising. For example, PLA press articles often refer to Xi pointing out that many PLA commanders suffer from the "five cannots" [*wuge buhui*, 五个不会]. These commanders cannot:

- analyze a situation
- understand higher echelon intent
- make a decision on a course of action

- deploy forces
- handle unexpected situations.[43]

Beyond technological shortfalls and the lack of recent real-world operational experience, the literature surrounding this current period of reform strongly suggests that the CCP and PLA leadership believe the real inhibitors to generating operational capability and combat power are systemic. There is an acute acknowledgment that the PLA's legacy organizational structures, processes and procedures, and even its institutional culture and the level of operational acumen of its personnel (especially commanders) are such that they are inhibiting the generation of combat power. This is borne out by a careful read of the military section of the Central Committee's Decision from the Third Plenum. Almost all of the areas identified as needing reform or change are organizational, institutional, procedural, or administrative in nature. The CMC's authoritative Opinion on Reform (2016) speaks of the necessity of "resolving systematic obstacles, structural contradictions, and policy problems that constrain national defense and military development."[44] Writing in *People's Daily* over a year before the Opinion was published, CMC Vice Chairman Xu Qiliang used almost the same language, calling for the pressing need to "break through the restrictions" to accruing combat power and operational capability caused by "institutional obstacles," "structural contradictions," and "policy-related problems."[45]

The persistence of institutional and systemic problems inhibiting warfighting capability must be a source of great frustration, for the PLA has been working at resolving a host of these issues for decades. This is not the first time in recent memory that the PLA has attempted to surge its reform efforts. Students of Chinese military affairs will recall the late 1990s and early 2000s, when the PLA introduced myriad systemic changes to doctrine, organization, personnel management, training, logistics, professional military education, and "civil-military integration" in the realm of defense industries.[46] Among some analysts of the PLA, this author included, 1999 was referred to as "the year of regulations" in recognition of the amount of systemic change the

PLA was attempting to undergo by enacting new administrative regulations and guidelines as well as new operational doctrine. All of these areas (and others) are being looked at again during this current reform period. One can only surmise that the fixes of the past did not solve the problems they were intended to mitigate, were not actually put into place or enforced, or did not keep up with the rapidly changing nature of global military affairs. One must also surmise that the political will to enable bold but necessary changes was not present until recently (see the chapter by Wuthnow and Saunders in this volume for an overview of the changes being discussed).

In terms of "bold but necessary changes," the recent disestablishment of the former seven "military regions" [*junqu*, 军区] and creation of the five "theater commands" [*zhanqu*, 战区] stands out as a prime example of what the PLA is attempting to achieve by way of improving its ability to conduct joint operations.

After working assiduously since the early-1990s to develop the capacity to conduct joint operations, a major stumbling block was apparently command and control arrangements. The wholesale disestablishment in February 2016 of the legacy military region system makes clear that the PLA assessed it was unable to effectively superimpose the requirements of joint warfighting onto the military region system, *especially* with respect to command and control arrangements. This is not surprising. The military regions were conceived in the late 1940s based on internal geographic and political considerations: internal political defense of the new CCP regime and the defense of the new Party-state's borders and coastlines from attack or invasion. Moreover, throughout their existence, the military regions were ground force–centric entities, with other services and forces stationed in the military regions commanded or managed by their respective service headquarters, elements within the four general departments, or the military region headquarters. No arrangement could be less conducive to joint warfare.

The five newly created joint theater commands are conceptually different from the old military regions in various significant ways. (See the chapter by Burke and Chan in this volume.) The most important difference is that they are joint entities focused on projecting military power externally against designated contingencies—"strategic directions" [*zhanlüe fang-xiang*, 战略方向], in the parlance of the PLA. Along with new command and control relationships and authorities, the PLA hopes that this organizational change will do the following:

- Simplify command and control relationships by having the theater commands report directly to the CMC.
- Establish unity of command by giving the five joint theater commanders operational control over all forces assigned to their theaters.
- Achieve unity of effort by assigning specific strategic directions—that is, contingencies—to each theater command for planning and warfighting purposes.
- Focus warfighters on warfighting by making theater commanders responsible for war planning and joint training and relegating the services to the role of force providers.
- Quickly transition from peacetime training to wartime operations by creating standing joint theater staffs versus the previous ad hoc command and control arrangements.

This is but one example that underscores the operational factors behind the current reform period.

Before leaving this section of the chapter, it is important to state that the preceding discussion of the PLA's self-assessment of its own operational or institutional shortcomings, and those pointed out, should not be misconstrued for an argument that the Chinese armed forces are not an increasingly capable, increasingly advanced, and potentially formidable force.

National Security Assessments: The Third Driver of Reform

The third major driver of this period of reform is a set of assessments that the CCP and PLA have made about China's current security challenges, as well as concerns about the accelerating nature of the global revolution in military affairs. Both are justifying and adding a sense of urgency to the military reform enterprise.

The increasingly "stern," "complex," and "uncertain" security environment the Chinese state and CCP itself are said to be facing is being touted by Xi Jinping and senior PLA leadership as another critical reason why the military must "accelerate" reform and modernization while the "strategic window of opportunity" remains open. Then–CMC Vice Chairman General Fan Changlong urged PLA personnel to think of the current reform period as "a race against time," further stating, the "complexity and sternness of our country's security situation require that substantial development be made in national defense and army building."[47] A 2014 article in *PLA Daily* declared, "to successfully accomplish our mission in the relay race of history, our Party cadres in the military, no matter at what positions, should have a stronger sense of trouble and crisis and a stronger sense of mission, and dare to take on duties and commitments in work."[48]

The CCP still officially adheres to the ideologically important judgment that "peace and development" [*heping yu fazhan*, 和平与发展] remains the "keynote of the times" [*shidai zhuti*, 时代主题]. This judgment was made by Deng Xiaoping back in 1985 and revalidated in 1999 during an extended public and internal debate triggered by the errant North Atlantic Treaty Organization bombing of the PRC embassy in Belgrade. At its most basic level, this judgment holds that a world war that could involve China is not imminent and that China has the opportunity to develop in a fundamentally peaceful environment. That said, this larger judgment provides a good deal of analytic space for challenges to China's national security interests. These include the possibility of local wars, regional conflicts, nontraditional security threats, and other breeches of the peace that could involve China or directly and adversely affect Beijing's key national interests. Changes in assessments in this space can result in adjustments to foreign policy, military policy, and domestic security policies. Consequently, it is important to stay abreast of how the Chinese security community assesses its proximate security situation at any given time.[49]

Since the military reform enterprise was launched at the Third Plenum, various assessments of China's security situation placed in the public domain strongly suggest that Beijing sees challenges to Chinese national security on the rise both externally and internally (the "two big situations," in CCP speak). This is discernable in publicly released PRC government documents such as the defense white papers of 2012 and 2015. These concerns are especially driven home in much starker language in PLA-authored articles in military and Party journals as well as in editorials and commentaries in the PLA's media complex—venues meant for internal consumption.

Beyond the need to fight a joint, high-tech, information-intensive war off China's littorals, what other threats and challenges are being discussed? What are some of the other perceived challenges to Chinese national security that are currently being transmitted down through the PLA and are associated with the need for military reform and modernization? Below is a brief sampling, not comprehensive by any means.[50]

The Rising Challenges of "Hegemonism, Power Politics, and Neo-Interventionism"

Both the April 2013 and May 2015 editions of the PRC defense white paper called out concerns about "hegemonism, power politics, and neo-interventionism." In 2013 then–CMC Vice Chairman Fan Changlong wrote that "Hegemonism, power politics, neo-interventionism are *on the rise.*"[51] In 2014, the dean of the Nanjing Army Command Academy parroted this assessment in an article in *China Military Science*, stating that "Hegemonism, great power politics, and 'new interventionism' have all risen to some extent."[52]

External Pressures Aimed at Preventing China's Rise

There is also an assessment often found in the PLA and Party literature that "outside powers" are working to undermine China's ascension to great power status and retard China's rise. A February 2014 commentator article in *PLA Daily* declared that "some Western countries are not willing to see socialist China's development and strengthening, and try by all means to carry out strategic containment and encirclement against China."[53] This assessment was made in the context of urging the PLA to study Xi Jinping's

newly published *Expositions* on national defense and army building in 2014.
A *PLA Daily* editorial on August 1, 2014, commemorating the founding
of the PLA stated that "external hostile forces do not want to see China
growing strong, and try by various means to contain and restrict China's
development."[54] A variation on this argument is that as China continues to
grow and gather strength, there will be pushback from outside powers—
especially the United States. In May 2014, Major General Gao Guanghui
(at the time commander of the 16th Group Army) made these arguments:

> As the country's comprehensive national strength has rapidly
> increased, so too the structure of its national interests produced
> great influence. The friction between containment and anti-con-
> tainment continues to play out. This is especially true of the [U.S.]
> Asia-Pacific "Rebalance" strategy, which strengthens containment
> of China and brings about great change to the political, economic,
> and strategic situation in the Asia-Pacific region.[55]

In an eye-catching passage from the 2013 edition of *Science of Military
Strategy* (published by the PLA Academy of Military Science), the authors
provided this admittedly low-probability but high-impact scenario when
it comes to thinking about the possible conflicts China could find itself in:

> At this crucial stage in our country's peaceful development, our
> country cannot rule out the possibility of hegemonic countries
> inciting war *with the goal of delaying or interrupting our country's
> rise*. The factors leading to war may be a crisis getting out of con-
> trol and gradually escalating, or a premeditated plot that arises
> suddenly. The probability of this kind of conflict breaking out is
> low, but its degree of danger is high.[56] (Emphasis added).

The "Three Main Dangers"

According to some Chinese public domain articles, Xi Jinping himself has
articulated the need for the Party and PLA to remain vigilant in defending

against the "three main dangers." In a long 2015 interview with *Huanqiu Wang*, Admiral Sun Jianguo, a deputy chief of the General Staff whose PLA portfolio included military intelligence and foreign affairs, asserted that "President Xi has made a general survey of today's changing world and has clearly presented strategic determinations such as 'three major trends,' 'three unprecedented situations,' and 'three main dangers.'" In the interview, Admiral Sun states, "looking at the matter from the point of view of the threats facing national security, the main dangers are the nation being invaded, being subverted, and being split; the danger of the overall state of reform, development, and stability being damaged; and the danger of an interruption in the development of socialism with Chinese characteristics."[57] This formulation has appeared in other PLA-authored articles. For example, in a May 2014 article in *China Military Science*, Major General Wang Pei and Major General Zhang Zhihui, both of the Nanjing Army Command Academy, wrote the following under the heading "The Security Situation Has Grown Severely Complicated, Presenting New Demands for the Military's Warfighting Capabilities":

> We face a severely complex national security situation. We must ensure that the country is not invaded, subverted, or split up; ensure that the general situation of reform and development is not broken; and ensure that the process of building socialism with Chinese characteristics is not interrupted.[58]

In yet another variation on this theme, the deputy political commissar of the PLA National Defense University argued in a January 2014 article that the PLA must enhance its ability to fight and win informationized local wars "so as to guarantee that our nation will not be turned into a target of aggression, subversion, and division."[59]

The near verbatim verbiage of these and other statements strongly suggests that this language is contained in official internal study materials associated with the military reform enterprise, perhaps in Xi's *Expositions* (published in February 2014) on national defense or some other speeches not in the public domain. One notes the three dangers cover the physical security of China, China's development, and political security—issues in line with Xi's concept of "holistic security" [*quanmian anquan guan*, 全面安全观] as articulated in his April 2014 speech at the first meeting of the National Security Commission.[60]

Political Subversion and Threats to Sovereignty

Related to the three main dangers are concerns about political subversion—specifically, the undermining of CCP rule. This is not a new worry, but it has been a prominent theme associated with the internal propaganda campaign associated with the current military reform program. As mentioned, China's military strategy, as transmitted in the 2015 defense white paper, called out "anti-China forces" that are alleged to be "attempting to instigate a 'color revolution'" in China.[61] In his aforementioned interview with *Huanqiu Wang*, Admiral Sun Jianguo likened the "occupy" movement in Hong Kong to a color revolution and then went on to explain the concern in more detail:

> Instigating "color revolutions" is a customary trick of certain Western nations to fly the flag of "democratization" and subvert the regimes of other nations. With China's constant development, their aim to infiltrate and harm China has become all the clearer, their activities are all the more rampant, and they are stepping up the implementation of an online "cultural Cold War" and "political genetic engineering." Struggles in the area of ideology are acute and complex—iron-forged souls vs. the souls of termites, solid roots vs. the roots of destruction. The contest is growing more intense and is becoming a major danger facing China's political security and regime security.[62]

Related to the concern about the subversion of China's political and ideological unity are concerns about "separatist forces" determined to undermine China's geographic unity. PLA articles continue to emphasize challenges posed by separatist cliques and forces operating within and out-side of China to separate Taiwan, Tibet, and Xinjiang from the mainland. The challenges in Xinjiang in particular are associated with the incantation of the "three evil forces" [*san gu shili*, 三股势力]: terrorism, separatism and extremism. As stated by Major General Wang Pei:

> the "three evil forces" are interlinked within and outside of Chinese territory. They have intensified separatist movements, repeatedly produced incidents, and posed serious threats to the political security and social stability of the country. This demonstrates that China's security problems are becoming more integrated, complex, variable, and unprecedentedly strong.[63]

Beyond the various forms of threats and challenges to China's geographic, political, and "developmental" security, the evolving "global revolution in military affairs" is touted as another reason why the PLA must make significant progress in modernization and reform. Specifically, the Chinese argue that the global revolution in military affairs continues to forge ahead, China must keep up, China is not necessarily keeping up in all domains, and various other nations are making progress that, in some cases, is troubling. From a 2014 *PLA Daily* commentator article:

> The accelerating development of the world's new revolution in military affairs also poses a stern challenge to our national defense and armed forces building. With the rapid development of new and high technologies with information technology as the core, military technologies and the pattern of war are also undergoing revolutionary changes. The major countries in the world are all stepping up their military transformations in an attempt to seize the commanding heights in the future military competition. At present, there remains a substantial gap between the modernization level of our military and the world's advanced military level.[64]

Then–CMC Vice Chairman Fan Changlong used much the same language in his own 2013 *Qiushi* article, writing that the "world's new revolution in military affairs is still accelerating. All major countries are stepping up military transformation. *This poses a stern challenge to our military.*"[65] Fan's then-colleague, CMC Vice Chairman Xu Qiliang, has also beat this drum, stating that "deepening national defense and military reform is an urgent need in adapting to the accelerating development of the world's new revolution in military affairs and the profound evolution of the warfighting patterns and operational forms."[66] In particular, the United States, Russia, and Japan are commonly cited in PLA articles as nations whose progress in military modernization bears China's attention, for they are often touted as being on the leading edge of the global revolution in military affairs. For instance, one PLA author argues in *China Military Science* that:

> Currently the new worldwide revolution in military affairs has developed quickly. Competition [among] countries in the speed of advancement and development of quality is increasingly fierce. The American military relies on the continuous development of science and technology, draws support from enriched combat practices, and continues the revolution in military affairs. It openly emphasizes "we must ensure that the U.S. military is a few steps ahead of any potential opponent." Russia has announced that it must speed up the process of its military "stepping into the 21st-century electronic world," so that [it] can return to a place as one of the world's most influential powers. . . . Japan is accelerating the pace of its military reforms and attempting to build an offensive force that can operate regionally and globally. India is committed to promoting "a military capable of exerting influence both regionally and globally." Faced with these severe challenges and pressing situations, we must view matters soberly.[67]

What usually follows these narratives of progress among the world's top militaries is the "sober" assessment of China's lack of progress and the invoking of the various self-critical phrases mentioned earlier, such as the "two incompatibles" or laments about the lack of progress in reaching "full mechanization" and "informationization" as called for in the PLA's "three step strategy" for modernization of the force. "The foundations of army building are weak. We are still engaged in the complex development stage of mechanization, semi-mechanization, and informationization," wrote Major General Gao Guanghui.[68] Moreover, a *PLA Daily* commentator article stated:

> The major countries in the world are all stepping up their military transformations in an attempt to seize the commanding heights in the future military competition. At present, there remains a substantial gap between the modernization level of our military and the world's advanced military level; the modernization level of our military is still not in keeping with the requirement of winning local wars under informationized conditions.[69]

For his part, Fan Changlong argues that the PLA is getting closer to its modernization objectives, but is not there yet:

> We are now so close to the strong army dream like never before, and are more confident in and more capable of fulfilling the goal [of] strengthening the military. However, we should be soberly aware that, at present, our military is situated at the stage of having not yet accomplished mechanization and also accelerating the development of informationization, there remains a substantial gap between our military's modernization level and the world's advanced military level, and our current condition remains out of keeping with the requirement of national security.[70]

And so it goes. As one reads through PLA and Party materials, it is clear that the sense of urgency in moving forward with the military reform enterprise is being driven by assessments that China's threat environment is becoming more acute, that the state of PLA modernization is inadequate, that the global revolution in military affairs is accelerating, but that there is still a window of opportunity for China to make substantial progress if the PLA can just push through some bold reforms. How much of this threat assessment does the Party and PLA truly believe, and to what extent are these fears and concerns being hyped to justify some tough decisions? The answer is probably a mix of both. What really matters is that this is what the PLA is telling itself, this is what the officers and troops are imbibing, this is the narrative being carried in important Party media outlets—and one strongly suspects also being expounded on in internal Party-PLA documents.

Who Are the Architects of Reform?

To this point, this chapter has focused on the reasons for the reform enterprise. An equally important question is *who* is behind these reforms. Who devised these changes? As far as any single individual or specific group of officers goes, the answer to this question is unclear, at least to this author. Nevertheless, some brief speculation is in order.

Certainly, Xi Jinping's fingerprints are indelibly stamped on this military reform enterprise, and it will undoubtedly be part of his legacy. Like other aspects of the Chinese Party-state, Xi is attempting to move the PLA into the post-Dengist era. His *Expositions* on national defense and "army building" serve as a political primer to justify the reforms, and his chairmanship of the CMC Leading Small Group for Deepening National Defense and Military Reform places him in the center of all major decisions on military reform. Overall, it would not be unreasonable to posit that Xi is the most engaged CMC chairman since Deng Xiaoping, and there should be no question that Xi's role in this reform process has been vital. Specifically, Xi has served as the enabling and catalyzing agent who has provided the political muscle necessary to force the PLA to overcome its own bureaucratic inertia and force it to move forward with significant organizational and institutional reform. Nevertheless, Xi is not the architect of these reforms, deft Marxist theoretician though he may be.

The reforms we have seen to date, and those yet to be announced, could only have come from the military professionals within the PLA itself. However, one is hard-pressed to point to any single general officer or group of officers publicly identified as being highly influential in the current reform effort as in the past. In the 1980s, for example, General Li Jijun was closely associated with the creation of the group armies [*jituan jun*, 集团军] and combined arms doctrine for the ground forces. Also in the 1980s, General/ Admiral Liu Huaqing was associated with the modernization of the PLA Navy. In the late 1990s, General Chen Bingde was sometimes associated with the new iteration of operational doctrine that was issued circa 1999 (specifically, the "new generation operations regulations" [*xin yidai zuozhan tiaoling*, 新一代作战条令]). Today, the PLA professionals who devised the current reform program remain largely anonymous.

Without question, this current reform enterprise is the result of a protracted institutional effort across the PLA. It is undoubtedly based on many years of study, experimentation, and planning. Lessons learned from the practices of militaries abroad were clearly studied by the cohort of military analysts and scholars who comprise the PLA's foreign military studies community. We should assume the PLA military intelligence community supported that effort. PLA journal articles strongly suggest that military reforms and operational practices of the armed forces of Russia and the United States in particular were carefully followed and studied. More than likely, PLA delegations traveling abroad and PLA officers studying at foreign institutions of professional military education would have had ideas to offer. So too would officers participating in combined exercises with other nations' militaries be in a position to understand best practices from abroad.

More than anything else, perhaps, the results of nearly two decades of joint exercises and experimentation were probably critical in formulating fixes to the PLA's more intractable operational problems, especially those associated with joint command and control arrangements. The exercises involve not only forces in the field but also observers and analysts from Beijing and other centers of operations research throughout the PLA.

One can imagine organizations such as the Academy of Military Science, National Defense University, PLA Navy Research Institute, various service-level command academies across China, and other organizations that comprise the PLA's large military research complex all working on the key problems, both through their focused research efforts and as observers in field settings.

Staff officers in the former four general departments must have played a role in thinking through the operational and administrative challenges of the reorganization effort, likewise for officers in headquarters of the former military regions. One does wonder with hindsight whether the establishment of the PLA's Strategic Planning Department [*zhanlüe guihua bu*, 战略规划部] in November 2011 was a harbinger of serious preparation for the reorganization of late 2015 and the accompanying reforms.

Moreover, professionals from across the PLA were invited to write papers and do their own research, a sort of "mass line" [*qunzhong luxian*, 群众路线] approach to gathering good ideas for change and practical fixes to vexing problems. Some officers associated with the reforms have asserted that the PLA has indeed taken a bottom-up as well as top-down approach to seeking solutions to its problems. This becomes quite apparent when reading the titles of articles in the table of contents in *China Military Science* over time, especially between 2013 (post–Third Plenum) and continuing over the following 3 years, especially under the journal's section heading of "National Defense and Armed Forces Building." Many of these articles identify shortcomings in various practices and offer solutions. And, of course, as is the proclivity of the PLA, one imagines interminable conferences, meetings, symposia, workshops, and seminars at which ideas were floated, rejected, adjusted, refined, and then sent up the chain of command as recommendations.

Undoubtedly, the CMC Leading Small Group for Deepening National Defense and Military Reform, as well as the new CMC Reform and Organization Office [*junwei gaige he bianzhi bangongshi*, 军委改革和编制办公室], have played a critical role in gathering data, taking in recommendations, and sending decision papers up to Xi and the top leadership of the Leading Small Group—whose full membership remains unpublicized, although General Fan Changlong and General Xu Qilaing were both reported to be vice chairmen.

This is the best we can do using public domain data: speculate about how this process may have taken place, without knowing who the creative military professionals are who devised the blueprints of the most ambitious reform and reorganization enterprise in the history of the PLA. Hopefully, that institutional history will be written one day and available.

Conclusion

This chapter has focused on the drivers behind the current military reform enterprise—the reasons why the PLA is being told this is necessary and why modernization must be accelerated. Three major drivers have been identified: political factors, operational factors, and national security assessments. There are undoubtedly other ways that the catalysts for the current reform effort could have been parsed, presented, or analyzed. These three were chosen because they represent how the PLA is explaining the need for significant systemic change to itself.

For many outside observers, certainly for countries in the Asia-Pacific region and for the United States, the operational imperatives for Chinese military reform will undoubtedly be the most important. A PLA that is better organized, equipped, and trained to conduct joint operations along various strategic directions—especially in the maritime-aerospace domains beyond the Chinese littoral—will have a wide range of strategic and operational implications. And truly, reorganizing and reforming to become a military that "can fight and win" is at the heart of this endeavor.

Yet the Chinese would surely say that the political drivers are equally important. The survival and protection of the CCP as the ruling political Party of China is Beijing's number one national security priority: "political security," to borrow a phrase from the PLA and Party literature. One is struck by the degree to which Party and PLA leaders see the CCP itself as the real target of internal and external threats. Consequently, a PLA that is tightly tied to the CCP and that will defend the regime from political threats both from within China and from abroad is deemed absolutely essential. This is likely why the paramilitary People's Armed Police was brought under the sole control of the Central Military Commission in January 2018, whereas previously it was under the dual command of the CMC and State Council.

The sober assessments of China's national security situation (even as the Chinese judge that they are still in "a period of strategic opportunity") are clearly being used to justify why military reform must be accelerated and why extraordinary measures are necessary. So too with the judgment that the global revolution in military affairs is moving quickly and that the PLA cannot miss this opportunity. Indeed, one gets the sense that they believe that if they do not fix their biggest problems now, they will only find themselves further behind than they believe they are now compared to other modern militaries.

The need to maintain the momentum in military modernization and reform was reiterated as a political task by the CCP in the work report of the 19th Party Congress in October 2017. The year 2020 was set as the time by which the PLA must achieve full "mechanization" and significant progress toward "informationization." The report deemed the year 2035 as the point at which the PLA will "basically realize modernization of national defense and military." By mid-century, the CCP aim is to have "a world-class military" [*shijie yiliu jun*, 世界一流军]. These are ambitious objectives.[71]

What the PLA actually initiated with the issuing of the *Central Military Commission Opinion on Deepening Reform of National Defense and the Armed Forces* on January 1, 2016, is a generational undertaking. Being joint is not merely changing the line and block charts; it is a capability born of a deep set of professional and operational experiences, a product of the professional military education system, adjustments based on training experiments and real-world operations, and sustained by institutional incentives that reward joint service.

How this will unfold for the PLA will depend on many factors, not least of which is the quality, training, and capabilities of personnel in the force, especially its commanders. From a professional and institutional perspective, some of the more interesting reforms coming down the road will be those that address the PLA's perpetual problems with attracting, training, managing, and retaining the personnel it needs to fight the high-tech wars it is convinced it must be able to fight (see the chapter by Wuthnow and Saunders in this volume). As Jiang Zemin is alleged to have once stated about the PLA, "Everything will be empty talk without qualified personnel and knowledge." Yet for all of its problems, the PLA continues to demonstrate that it is a "learning organization." For those of us who study this fascinating military organization, the next few years will hold our attention.

Notes

[1] The formal name of the "Decision" of the Third Plenum of the 18th Central Committee is "Decision of the Central Committee of the Communist Party of China on Some Major Issues Concerning Comprehensively Deepening Reforms," November 12, 2013, available at <www.china.org.cn/china/third_plenary_session/201401/16/content_31212602.htm>.

[2] The four general departments were the General Staff Department [*zong canmo bu*, 总参谋部], General Political Department [*zong zhengzhi bu*, 总政治部], General Logistics Department [*zong houqin bu*, 总后勤部], and General Equipment Department [*zong zhuangbei bu*, 总装备部].

[3] The Central Military Committee (CMC) is a Chinese Communist Party (CCP) organization, an organ of the Central Committee. Its formal name is Military Commission of the Central Committee of the Chinese Communist Party [*zhongguo gongchandang zhongyang junshi weiyuanhui*, 中国共产党中央军事委员会]. It is usually chaired by the General Secretary of the CCP.

[4] The number of military regions and their borders have changed over the years (in 1985, there were 11). Until their recent disestablishment, they were the most important and powerful sub-national organizations in the People's Liberation Army (PLA) structure.

[5] In the PLA doctrinal lexicon the term "strategic direction" [*zhanlüe fangxiang*, 战略方向] is used to identify either a general direction from the mainland

from which China perceives a military threat that requires preparations or a specific contingency. For example, since at least 1993, the PLA has identified Taiwan as its "main strategic direction" [*zhuyao zhanlüe fangxiang*, 主要战略方向]. For more on strategic directions, see David M. Finkelstein, "China's National Military Strategy: An Overview of the Military Strategic Guidelines," in *Right-Sizing the People's Liberation Army: Exploring the Contours of China's Military*, ed. Roy Kamphausen and Andrew Scobell (Carlisle Barracks, PA: Strategic Studies Institute, 2007), 69–140.

⁶ The PLA's four services are the PLA Army, PLA Navy, PLA Air Force, and PLA Rocket Force.

⁷ Other key organizational changes included the elevation of the former Second Artillery (hitherto a branch of the ground forces) to an independent service [*junzhong*, 军种], the establishment of a separate headquarters for the ground forces (the PLA Army), the creation of the Strategic Support Force, and a Joint Logistics Support Force. Other new organizations may be announced as time rolls on.

⁸ For analyses of the first tranche of changes that took place in the first half of 2016, see David M. Finkelstein, *Initial Thoughts on the Reorganization and Reform of the PLA* (Arlington, VA: CNA, 2016); and Dennis J. Blasko, "Integrating the Services and Harnessing the Military Area Commands," *Journal of Strategic Studies* 39, nos. 5–6 (August 3, 2016), 685–708.

⁹ See David M. Finkelstein, *Get Ready for the Second Phase of Chinese Military Reform* (Arlington, VA: CNA, 2017).

¹⁰ For reportage on the November 2015 conference, see Cao Zhi, Li Xuanliang, and Wang Shibin [曹智, 李宣良, 王士彬], "At CMC Reform Work Meeting, Xi Jinping Stresses: Comprehensively Implement Reform and Military Strengthening Strategy, Resolutely Take the Path to a Strong Military with Chinese Characteristics" [在中央军委改革工作会议上强调习近平: 全面实施改革强军战略 坚定不移 走中国特色强军之路], Xinhua, November 26, 2015, available at <http://cpc.people. com.cn/n/2015/1127/c64094-27861889.html>. The CMC "Opinion" was published by Xinhua on January 1, 2016, under the title "Central Military Commission's 'Opinions on Deepening Reforms of National Defense and Armed Forces'" [中 央军委"关于深化国防和军队改革的意见"系统阐述为什么改、改什么、怎么改], available at <www.xinhuanet.com/mil/2016-01/01/c_128588726.htm>.

¹¹ Wang Jingguo, Sun Yanxin, and Huang Yifang [王经国, 孙彦新, 黄益方], "Defense Ministry Spokesman Gives Detailed Explanation on Relevant Issues of Deepening National Defense and Army Reforms" [国防部新闻发言人详解深化

国防和军队改革有关问题], Xinhua, January 1, 2016, available at <http://news. xinhuanet.com/politics/2016-01/01/c_1117646764.htm>.

[12] "Make Vigorous Efforts to Build a Strong Modern Logistics Support Force" [努力建设一支强大的现代化联勤保障部队], *PLA Daily* [解放军报], September 14, 2016, available at <www.81.cn/jfjbmap/content/2016-09/14/content_156621.htm>.

[13] "Central Military Commission's 'Opinions on Deepening Reforms of National Defense and Armed Forces.'"

[14] The CCP's challenging domestic agenda is laid out in the same Decision from the Third Plenum (2013) that also included the requirement for military reform.

[15] "A Holistic View of National Security," speech by Xi Jinping to the first meeting of the National Security Commission, April 15, 2014, in *Xi Jinping: The Governance of China* (Beijing: Foreign Language Press, 2014), 220.

[16] See *China's Military Strategy* (Beijing: People's Republic of China Ministry of National Defense, May 26, 2015), available at <http://eng.mod.gov.cn/Defense-News/2015-05/26/content_4586748.htm>.

[17] "No Nationalization of Military in China: Senior PLA Officer," Embassy of the People's Republic of China in the United States of America, June 20, 2011, available at <www.china-embassy.org/eng/gdxw/t832372.htm>.

[18] Minnie Chan and Choi Chi-yuk, "Two More of China's Former Top Commanders Taken Away for Corruption Investigation: Military Sources," *South China Morning Post* (Hong Kong), August 5, 2016, available at <www.scmp.com/news/china/policies-politics/article/1999535/two-more-chinas-former-top-commanders-taken-away>.

[19] Fan Changlong [范长龙], "Strive to Build the People's Army That Obeys the Party's Orders, Is Able to Fight Victorious Battles, Keeps a Good Style—Study and Implement Chairman Xi's Important Thinking on the Party's Strong Army Goal Under the New Situation" [为建设一支听党指挥能打胜仗作风优良的人民军队而奋斗：学习贯彻习主席关于党在新形势下的强军目标重要思想], *Qiushi* [求是], no. 15 (August 2013).

[20] For an overview of the Gutian Conference of 2014, see James C. Mulvenon, "Hotel Gutian: We Haven't Had That Spirit Here Since 1929," *China Leadership Monitor*, no. 46 (Winter 2015), available at <www.hoover.org/research/hotel-guti-an-we-havent-had-spirit-here-1929>.

[21] See Peter Mattis, "Is China Scared of a Coup?" *The Diplomat*, July 4, 2012, available at <https://thediplomat.com/2012/07/is-china-scare-of-a-coup/>; and Liz Carter, "Whom Should the Chinese Army Serve—the Party or

the State?" *The Atlantic*, October 25, 2012, available at <www.theatlantic.com/international/archive/2012/10/whom-should-the-chinese-army-serve-the-party-or-the-state/264104/>.

[22] Wu Ming [吴铭], "Remolding Our Military's Leadership and Command Structure Is a Necessary Choice for a Strong and Revitalized Military" [重塑我军领导指挥体制是强军兴军的必然选择], *PLA Daily* [解放军报], November 30, 2015, available at <www.81.cn/jfjbmap/content/2015-11/30/content_130735.htm>.

[23] On the military regions, Wu Ming stated that the "large military regions will also no longer have feudal powers over their domain" [大军区也不再是权力很大的"一方诸侯"]. The term *yifang zhuhou*, 一方诸侯 is said to originate from the Western Zhou, and is a reference to the king's siblings and other relatives, the nobles, and other key personages. These individuals had high autonomy over their lands, including military rights, not unlike a small nation, but they also had to report to the king and pay taxes and support military expenses on a regular basis. Today, the term is used to describe someone with great influence or power over a certain area. The author is indebted to James Bellacqua of CNA and Alice Miller of the Hoover Institution for their help in understanding this obscure reference.

[24] "Continuously Enhance Consciousness and Firmness to Thoroughly Purge the Pernicious Influence of Guo Boxiong and Xu Caihou" [不断增强全面彻底肃清郭伯雄徐才厚流毒影响的自觉性和坚定性], *PLA Daily* [解放军报], October 16, 2016, available at <www.81.cn/jfjbmap/content/2016-10/11/content_158578.htm>.

[25] "Hu Jintao's Report at 17th Party Congress," October 15, 2007, available at <www.china.org.cn/english/congress/229611.htm>; "Full Text of Hu Jintao's Report at 18th Party Congress," Embassy of the People's Republic of China in the United States of America, November 27, 2012, available at <www.china-embassy.org/eng/zt/18th_CPC_National_Congress_Eng/t992917.htm>.

[26] Conference paper by a PLA author, 2014. See also Xiong Zhengyan, "Admiral Sun Jianguo: China Is in Danger of Being Invaded; Using Struggle to Seek a Win-Win for China and the United States" [孙建国上将: 中国有被侵略危险 用斗争谋中美共赢], *Huanqiu Wang*, March 2, 2015, available at <http://mil.huanqiu.com/observation/2015-03/5793682.html>. In this interview, Admiral Sun stated, "For the first time, national defense and armed forces reform has been incorporated into the national reform layout, upgrading it to the will of the Party and national action."

[27] Wu, "Remolding Our Military's Leadership and Command Structure Is a Necessary Choice for a Strong and Revitalized Military"; James C. Mulvenon,

"The Yuan Stops Here: Xi Jinping and the 'Chairman Responsibility System,'" *China Leadership Monitor*, vol. 47 (Summer 2015), available at <www.hoover.org/publications/china-leadership-monitor>.

[28] Deng Xiaoping, "The Task of Consolidating Our Army," speech at an enlarged meeting of the Military Commission of the Central Committee of the Communist Party of China, July 14, 1975, in *Selected Works of Deng Xiaoping, 1975–1982* (Beijing: Foreign Language Press, 1984), 27.

[29] "China's Xi Jinping Takes Commander in Chief Military Title," BBC News, April 21, 2016, available at <www.bbc.com/news/world-asia-china-36101140>.

[30] Xu Qiliang [许其亮], "Firmly Push Forward Reform of National Defense and the Armed Forces" [许其亮: 坚定不移推进国防和军队改革], *People's Daily* [人民日报], November 21, 2013, available at <http://cpc.people.com.cn/n/2013/1121/c64094-23610085.html>.

[31] "Full Text of Hu Jintao's Report at 18th Party Congress."

[32] This citation from p. 92 of *The Selected Important Expositions of Xi Jinping on National Defense and Army Building* comes from an article written by Major General Hu Yang, at the time Jilin Military District Political Commissar. See "Key Issues on Implementing Standards for Warfighting Capability in Peacetime," *China Military Science* [中国军事科学], May 2014. *The Selected Important Expositions of Xi Jinping on National Defense and Army Building* is not in the public domain. According to *PLA Daily* (February 21, 2014), it was published in February 2014, but its distribution was restricted to PLA officers at and above the regimental level. See "'The Selected Important Expositions of Xi Jinping on National Defense and Army Building' Issued by the Army General Political Department, Calling for Members of the Armed Forces to Conscientiously Organize Their Studies" ["习近平关于国防和军队建设重要论述选编"印发全军总政治部下发通知要求全军和武警部队认真组织学习], available at <www.mod.gov.cn/auth/2014-02/21/content_4491893.htm>.

[33] "Xi Jinping Presides Over the First Meeting of the CMC Deepening Defense and Armed Forces Reform Leading Small Group, Emphasizes Applying the Military Strengthening Objective to Direct Reforms, Push Forward Reforms Around Military Strengthening Objective, Provide Strong Institutional Support for Building and Consolidating National Defense and a Powerful Armed Forces" [习近平主持召开中央军委深化国防和军队改革领导小组第一次全体会议强调 坚持以强军目标引领改革围绕强军目标推进改革为建设巩固国防和强大军队提供有力制度支撑], Xinhua, March 15, 2014, available at <http://news.sina.com.cn/c/2014-03-15/150629715381.shtml>.

[34] As opposed to a contingency-based perspective that speaks to planning for specific campaigns against a specific enemy. For a detailed explanation of this term, see Finkelstein, "China's National Military Strategy."

[35] Liu Hang [刘航], ed.,"The Military Strategic Guideline of Active Defense Under the New Situation" [新形势下积极防御军事战略方针], *PLA Daily* [解放军报], August 12, 2015, available at <www.81.cn/jmywyl/2015-08/12/content_6625850_4.htm>.

[36] *China's Military Strategy.*

[37] See, for example, Dennis J. Blasko, "The 'Two Incompatibles' and PLA Self-Assessments of Military Capability," *China Brief* 13, no. 10 (May 9, 2013), available at <https://jamestown.org/program/the-two-incompatibles-and-pla-self-assessments-of-military-capability/>.

[38] The PLA's "new historic missions" refer to the expanding set of traditional and nontraditional security missions the PLA must address as China's role as a global economic and political power grows. For more on the missions, see Daniel M. Hartnett, "The 'New Historic Missions': Reflections on Hu Jintao's Military Legacy," in *Assessing the People's Liberation Army in the Hu Jintao Era*, ed. Roy Kamphausen, David Lai, and Travis Tanner (Carlisle Barracks, PA: Strategic Studies Institute, 2014).

[39] See Dennis J. Blasko, "The New PLA Joint Headquarters and Internal Assessments of PLA Capabilities," *China Brief* 16, no. 10 (June 21, 2016), available at <https://jamestown.org/program/the-new-pla-joint-headquarters-and-internal-assessments-of-pla-capabilities/>.

[40] According to the People's Republic of China (PRC) Web site "National Defense Policy": "China pursues a three-step development strategy in modernizing its national defense and armed forces, in accordance with the state's overall plan to realize modernization. The first step is to lay a solid foundation by 2010, the second is to make major progress around 2020, and the third is to basically reach the strategic goal of building 'informationized' armed forces and being capable of winning 'informationized' wars by the mid-21st century." Available at <www.china.org.cn/english/features/book/194485.htm>. See also "Defense Policy," People's Republic of China Ministry of National Defense, available at <www.eng.mod.gov.cn/Database/defensePolicy/index.htm>.

[41] For the most recent report, see *Annual Report to Congress: Military and Security Developments Involving the People's Republic of China 2017* (Washington, DC: Office of the Secretary of Defense, 2017), available at <www.defense.gov/Portals/1/Documents/pubs/2017_China_Military_Power_Report.PDF>.

[42] Xi Jinping, "Start the New March in the Course of Military Strengthening and Development; Deeply Study and Implement Chairman Xi's Important Expositions on National Defense and Armed Forces Building" [深入学习贯彻习主席关于国防和军队建设的重要论述], *PLA Daily* [解放军报], February 17, 2014, available at <http://cpc.people.com.cn/n/2014/0217/c83083-24376791.html>.

[43] Many thanks to colleague Dennis J. Blasko and Alan Burns for multiple references for this phrase.

[44] "Central Military Commission's 'Opinions on Deepening Reforms of National Defense and Armed Forces.'"

[45] Xu, "Firmly Push Forward Reform of National Defense and the Armed Forces."

[46] For an overview of key systemic reforms during these years, see David M. Finkelstein et al., *Institutional Reforms of the Chinese People's Liberation Army: Overview and Challenges* (Alexandria, VA: CNA, 2002). See also David M. Finkelstein and James C. Mulvenon, eds., *China's Revolution in Doctrinal Affairs: Emerging Trends in the Operational Art of the Chinese People's Liberation Army* (Washington, DC: Beaver Press, December 2005).

[47] Fan, "Strive to Build the People's Army."

[48] Xi, "Start the New March."

[49] For the significance of the determination that "peace and development" remains the "keynote of the times," see David M. Finkelstein, *China Reconsiders Its National Security: The "Great Peace and Development Debate" of 1999* (Alexandria, VA: CNA, December 2000).

[50] Not all of these perceived challenges may be new ones. Even if not new, they are being articulated as part of the ideological campaign supporting the military reform effort.

[51] Fan, "Strive to Build the People's Army." Emphasis added.

[52] Wang Pei and Zhang Zhihui, "Adhere to the Sole and Fundamental Standard of Warfighting Capability—A Thorough Study of Xi Jinping's Important Expositions on the Standard of Warfighting Capability," *China Military Science* [中国军事科学], May 2014, 22–31.

[53] Xi, "Start the New March."

[54] "Faithfully Perform the Missions and Tasks Assigned by the Party and the People—Warmly Celebrate the 87th Anniversary of the Founding of the PLA" [忠实履行党和人民赋予的使命任务 ——热烈庆祝中国人民解放军建军87周年], *PLA Daily* [解放军报], August 1, 2014, available at <www.81.cn/jfjbmap/content/2014-08/01/content_83384.htm>.

55 Gao Guanghui [高光辉], "Consideration on Adhering to the Standard of Warfighting Capability in the New Situation" [新型式下坚持战斗力标准的思考], *China Military Science* [中国军事科学], May 2014, 32–41.

56 *The Science of Military Strategy* (Beijing: Military Science Publishing House, 2013), 99. Emphasis added.

57 Xiong, "Admiral Sun Jianguo."

58 Wang and Zhang, "Adhere." Also see the editorial "Faithfully Perform the Missions and Tasks Assigned by the Party and the People," which used nearly identical language, stating that military reform is necessary to ensure that China "will not fall into a target of aggression, subversion, division; the overall interests of reform, development, and stability will not be harmed; [and] the development process of socialism with Chinese characteristics will not be interrupted."

59 Major General Wu Jieming, "Adhere to the Party's Mass Line, Strive to Achieve the Goal of Military Strengthening," *Qiushi* [求是], January 16, 2014.

60 "Xi Jinping Chairs First Meeting of CPC Central Committee's National Security Commission" [习近平主持召开中央国家安全委员会第一次会议] Xinhua, April 15, 2014.

61 *China's Military Strategy*.

62 Xiong, "Admiral Sun Jianguo." These comments help to explain the mindset behind recent PRC laws governing foreign nongovernmental organizations operating in China.

63 Wang and Zhang, "Adhere." For more on China's terrorism concerns, see Murray Scot Tanner and James Bellacqua, *China's Response to Terrorism* (Arlington, VA: CNA, 2016).

64 Xi, "Start the New March."

65 Fan, "Strive to Build the People's Army." Emphasis added.

66 Xu, "Firmly Push Forward Reform of National Defense and the Armed Forces."

67 Gao, "Consideration on Adhering to the Standard of Warfighting Capability in the New Situation." Emphasis added.

68 Ibid.

69 Xi, "Start the New March."

70 Fan, "Strive to Build the People's Army."

71 Xi Jinping, "Secure a Decisive Victory in Building a Moderately Prosperous Society in All Respects and Strive for the Great Success of Socialism with Chinese Characteristics for a New Era," 19th National Congress of the Communist Party of China, October 18, 2017, available at <www.xinhuanet.com/english/special/2017-11/03/c_136725942.htm>.

CHAPTER 2

CHOOSING THE "LEAST BAD OPTION"

Organizational Interests and Change in the PLA Ground Forces

John Chen

The People's Liberation Army (PLA) is currently undergoing a series of organizational reforms unprecedented in its 90-year history. Beginning in September 2015, Chinese Communist Party (CCP) General Secretary and Central Military Commission (CMC) Chairman Xi Jinping announced a force reduction of 300,000 PLA personnel, kicking off a rapid-fire sequence of organizational and structural reforms. The PLA has undergone significant revisions to multiple levels of its command structure, constituent branches and services, and force structure that broadly conform to a dictum that the CMC will handle general management, newly formed theater commands (TCs) will focus on operations, and the services will handle force building [*junwei guanzong, zhanqu zhuzhan, junzhong zhujian*, 军委管总, 战区主战, 军种主建].[1] These are major changes, and their complete impact may not be fully understood and appreciated for some time to come.

Changes in China's external security challenges, altered perceptions of the character of warfare, and new political directives all likely played critical roles in driving these latest adaptations in the PLA ground forces. These drivers, however, appear better suited for explaining the gradual, spasmodic pace of PLA Army reform that has taken place over the past 25 years rather than the sweeping changes enacted over the past 2 ½ years. If these three main drivers offer only partial explanations, what explains the dramatic and unprecedented changes in the ground forces announced in the latest organizational reforms?

This chapter argues that the army's organizational and bureaucratic interests are a valuable lens for interpreting the 2015 reforms and that these same considerations may have contributed to the recent disruptive changes aimed at fielding a PLA ground force that serves as a true ground component of a joint force. To the extent that organizational interests prove to be important steering factors of the future army, they may push the PLA ground forces toward a more offensive-oriented role for a PLA ground force that has previously been tasked to defend and deter.

This chapter proceeds in four parts. The first section summarizes several possible drivers for change within the PLA ground forces since the collapse of the Soviet Union, briefly outlining a variety of motivations and the expected "new type of army" [*xinxing lujun*, 新型陆军] that would result from each. The second section examines past and present changes in the army, arguing that while each driver has some explanatory value, the existing explanations for adaptation are incomplete. The third section identifies organizational incentives and behavior as a valuable lens for explaining the drawn-out nature of army reforms. The final section describes the implications of army organizational behavior as a possible explanation for the latest tranche of PLA reforms.

Drivers for Changes

Many of the existing explanations for the 2015 reforms fall into three broad categories: changes in China's external security environment, changes in Chinese views on the character of warfare, and response to new political imperatives. While these categories of drivers are typically offered in explanation of change in the PLA writ large, they are equally applicable to changes in the ground forces.[2]

Changes in External Security Outlook

Changes in China's external security outlook could have motivated significant changes to the PLA ground forces. A broader reorientation of security threats along China's land borders, or a change in enemy war plans along those borders, could have led to major changes in the ground forces. Any change in threat perception from China's surrounding waters would also have had an impact on the ground forces. If changes in China's overall external security outlook are the main determinant for changes in the PLA Army, new doctrinal thinking, force structures, and training patterns should emerge following any new assessment of China's land security situation. Conversely, relative continuity in China's security situation should trigger no major changes in the ground forces.

The most consequential change in China's external security outlook in the last three decades was the disappearance of the Soviet Union as a major land threat. Shortly after the December 1991 dissolution of the Soviet Union, top Chinese leaders assessed that a major land invasion of the Chinese homeland from the north no longer posed an existential threat. This relative confidence in the security of China's land borders is reflected in the 1993 *Military Strategic Guideline for the New Period* [*xinshiqi junshi zhanlüe fangzhen*, 新时期军事战略方针], which called for the PLA to shift its attention away from defending the Chinese mainland from large scale invasion to preparing to fight local wars under high-technology conditions along China's periphery.[3] The 1993 guideline held that the most likely sites of local wars were on China's land borders, along with near seas and associated airspaces.[4]

The dissolution of a major land threat on China's northern border has been accompanied by an intensified emphasis on offshore threats. Military scholars argued that future wars would increasingly threaten targets along China's coastline and involve maritime and air operations,[5] and the 2004 defense white paper called for increased prioritization of naval, air, and missile forces in accordance with this new threat perception.[6] The most recent defense white paper, published in 2015, reiterated the need to shift emphasis away from land and toward the sea, arguing that China "must break the traditional thinking that land outweighs sea" [*bixu tupo zhonglu qinghai de chuantong siwei*, 必须突破重陆轻海的传统思维].[7] This language was a prominent part of the development of the latest iteration of China's military strategy.[8] The overall intent was clear: the PLA as a whole would focus less of its resources and attention on land threats.

These altered views on China's external security outlook had a clear impact on reshaping the PLA ground forces. The dramatic decrease of the land threat to China led to a reduction in the PLA Army's end strength, while the increasing priority placed on sea threats nudged the army toward becoming the ground component of a joint force. The introduction of the 1993 military strategic guideline was followed by a force reduction of 500,000 personnel in 1997 that reduced the ground forces by some 19 percent, while only trimming the navy by 11.6 percent and the air force by 11 percent;[9] further reductions in 2005 and 2015 also disproportionately impacted the ground forces.[10] The losses in end strength have been accompanied by increasing emphasis on maritime threats and joint training in the years following the 1993 military strategic guideline, with the army increasing the size of its amphibious forces after the 1997 troop reduction by transforming the first army division to an amphibious mechanized infantry division in 2000 and adding other amphibious units to the order of battle in the former Nanjing and Guangzhou military regions (MRs).[11] The army began discussing and implementing its interpretation of "integrated joint operations" [*yitihua lianhe zuozhan*, 一体化联合作战], which inevitably broached an increasing maritime orientation when it was established as the main form of operations beginning in 2004.[12]

Changing Views on the Character of Warfare

A second explanation for changes in the PLA ground forces could be that broader changes in views on new technology and the character of warfare drove military reforms within the PLA and its ground forces. The rise of new warfighting technologies and their implications for force structure and employment may be driving adaptations in the ground forces, and new technology may drive new tactics and ways of conducting warfare. Increased emphasis on technological developments, changes in force structure, and rapid integration of new technologies into the force following new assessments of the character and conduct of warfare would indicate that the PLA ground forces are adapting to changes in the way warfare is carried out. Relative continuity within the ground forces during perceived periods of fundamental change in the character of war, especially in doctrinal thinking, would suggest that any army changes are responding to a different determinant.

PLA strategy documents have envisioned at least three notable shifts in the character of warfare over the past 25 years, namely "local war under high-technology conditions" [*gaojishu tiaojian xia de jubu zhanzheng*, 高技术条件下的局部战争], "local war under informationized conditions" [*xinxihua tiaojian xia de jubu zhanzheng*, 信息化条件下的局部战争], and "informationized local war" [*xinxihua jubu zhanzheng*, 信息化局部战争]. Two of these fundamental changes in how the PLA views the character of warfare were strongly influenced by recent conflicts: local war under high-technology conditions was informed by the 1991 Persian Gulf War, and local war under informationized conditions was informed by the 1999 Kosovo War and the 2003 Iraq War.[13] Scholars have argued that the third, informationized local war, was not influenced by any particular past conflict.[14]

The lessons derived by PLA academicians from these conflicts place a premium on mobility, range, command of information, and increased operability in multiple domains, including land, sea, air, space, and the electromagnetic spectrum. High-technology warfare is "focused on superior weapons technology; battlefield integration between air, land, and sea; high-speed, all-weather operations; new modes of long-range warfare, especially missile, electronic, and air warfare; and a premium on [command, control, communications, and intelligence] dominance."[15] War under informationized conditions is characterized as an intermediate step toward informationized war, using "information systems and a defined degree of informationized weapons to carry out war."[16] Informationized warfare "relies upon networked information systems and informationized weapons, fighting on air, land, sea, space, and in the electromagnetic spectrum."[17]

These lessons have not been lost on the PLA ground forces, which have translated them into ground forces more capable of meeting the requirements of high-technology and informationized warfare, especially by emphasizing increased mobility and more multifunctional [*duoneng hua*, 多能化] units. Army transformation theorists argued that future PLA ground forces would need diverse capabilities to enable army units to fight under different conditions of informationization.[18] Accordingly, PLA ground forces began to stress mobility and more organic cross-domain capabilities like aviation and electronic countermeasures units. Army training has placed special emphasis on transregional mobility and operations in complex electromagnetic environments since at least 2008.[19] The ground forces have been adding aviation units and building them in size and capability since the first formation of an army aviation brigade in 2009.[20] These changes in force structure and training strongly suggest that the PLA ground forces have been gradually adapting to a shift in the character of warfare that has called for better mobility and multifunctionality.

Response to New Political Directives

The PLA's role as a Leninist military organization subject to CCP command means that military reforms could alternatively be the direct result of military obedience to new political directives emanating from the Party. Political directives that could have spurred doctrinal and organizational change in the ground forces could include anything from the articulation of new missions for the ground forces to exhortations to embrace joint warfare. Timely changes in PLA ground forces in direct response to CCP orders would suggest that obedience to Party directive is the main driver of reform in the ground forces. On the other hand, delays in implementation or repeated CCP orders would suggest that changes in the ground forces are not necessarily responses to Party commands.

Hu Jintao's 2004 articulation of a set of New Historic Missions [*xin de lishi shiming*, 新的历史使命] for the PLA is one obvious example of a new political directive shaping PLA ground forces. Hu's speech called for the PLA to protect CCP rule, guarantee strategic opportunity for national development, provide strategic support for defending national interests, and protect world peace and security,[21] and thereupon laid the groundwork for increasing prioritization of military operations other than war (MOOTW). The MOOTW concept made its first appearance in the 2008 defense white paper, signifying its elevation in status to that of a critical military task.[22]

The PLA ground forces have made adaptations in accordance with these New Historic Missions, with many of the changes falling in line with the new political directive. Doctrinally, the PLA ground forces began to embrace their newly articulated MOOTW role in a series of research works detailing the army's role in a variety of MOOTW operations, including counterterrorism, protection of social stability, peacekeeping, and disaster relief.[23] Force structure concepts like "modularity" [*mokuai hua*, 模块化] were originally intended to create more independent, deployable army units capable of quickly adapting to a wide variety of missions in combat,[24] but quickly proved applicable for units training for different types of MOOTW operations and yielded obvious utility for units rotating into and out of peacekeeping operations abroad.[25] At home, PLA ground force units routinely practiced rapid-reaction maneuvers to the point where the official distinction between designated "rapid-reaction units" and "regular units" has been mostly dissolved.[26] Abroad, army soldiers make up the majority of China's peacekeeping forces,[27] and some have gained combat experience during their time overseas.[28]

Taken separately, these three drivers for army reform would have resulted in three distinct types of ground forces, each with different projected opponents, force compositions, geographic orientation, and types of operations. The characteristics of these different types of ground forces are summarized briefly in table 1.

Table 1. Drivers of PLA Army Changes and Resultant Types of PLA Ground Forces			
	Changes in External Threat Environment	Changes in Nature of Warfare	New Political Directives
Change	Land threat perception greatly reduced; maritime threat perception increases	Shifting from large land conflict to long-range, noncontact warfare	Focus on New Historic Missions and military operations other than war
Role	Ground component of joint force	Defend and deter; survive and thrive in noncontact warfare	Guarantee Party rule; secure China's overseas interests
Required Force Size and Structure	Reduced size, increased amphibious capabilities	Multifunctional, mobile	Modularity, mobile
Training	Joint training with other services; amphibious training	Cross-domain training; joint training with other services	Rapid deployment, experience overseas

In reality, however, all three of these drivers have stimulated adaptations in the PLA ground forces in the past and continue to manifest themselves in the 2015 reforms. The PLA ground forces appear to have responded to changes in China's external threat environment, changes in views on the character of warfare, and new political directives by implementing many of the changes in table 1 to varying degrees over the past 25 years. Many of these changes are still under way as a direct result of the 2015 reforms: the army continues its seaward orientation,[29] revisions to force structure have stressed multifunctionality in army units by creating combined arms brigades [hecheng lü, 合成旅] from divisions,[30] and the army continues to play a large (and increased) role in peacekeeping operations overseas.[31]

Yet an explanation that attributes the 2015 changes in the army solely to some combination of the three drivers identified here would be incomplete. None of the specific factors described were especially pressing or unique to the period immediately preceding the 2015 reforms. The explanatory gaps associated with each of these drivers are covered in more detail in the following section.

Gaps in Explaining the 2015 Reforms

Despite the fundamental nature of the existing explanations for reform, none of these three main drivers is sufficient explanation for the 2015 reforms. Many of the critical indicators of change in the PLA ground forces were present long before the 2015 reforms came about. Changes in doctrinal thinking, force structure adjustments, and new training regimens all suggest that the three main drivers for changes in the ground forces have been motivating a number of different adjustments in the army for some time.

Changes in Threat Environment?

Changes in China's external threat environment are unlikely to have been the primary determinants of the 2015 changes to the PLA ground forces. Current analysis indicates that the 2015 reforms were designed to enhance the PLA's ability to conduct joint operations,[32] which would strongly suggest that PLA leaders envisioned a change in China's external security environment or in the character of warfare dramatic enough to warrant a major reorganization of the PLA ground forces—and yet no such tectonic shifts are obvious in the period immediately preceding the 2015 reforms. In fact, many of the factors driving the 2015 reforms have been unvarying components of army transformation for years.

The 2015 force reductions that might be correlated to a shifting threat assessment are not unique to the latest tranche of reforms. While these latest troop reductions undoubtedly help reorient the army away from land and toward the sea, they are better understood as part of a long-running effort dating back to the 1990s to create a much smaller [*xiaoxing hua*, 小型化] army. The 1999 *Science of Military Strategy* noted that combat forces were trending toward smaller and lighter formations, and the 2001 *Science of Military Strategy* called for the PLA to reduce the size of the armed forces as much as possible without compromising victory.[33] By early 2008, army researchers had called for overall force reductions and specifically cited army reductions as a key component of ground force transformation.[34] Force reductions to implement this new type of ground force have taken place intermittently since the 1993 military strategic guideline, with reductions announced in 1997, 2005, and 2015.[35]

Although the latest reforms purport to push the army toward a maritime orientation, they have not yet added amphibious capabilities to the army commensurate with a substantial reorientation toward a maritime threat. Some army capabilities, like special operations, aviation, and electronic warfare units, are useful for offshore maritime operations, but PLA and army leaders have been calling for more of these units since at least 2011, as noted in the 2013 Academy of Military Science (AMS) edition of the *Science of Military Strategy*, which called for reductions in "traditional" army units in favor of expansions in special operations, electronic countermeasures, network attack and defense, tactical guided-missile, and army aviation units.[36] These types of units have been growing in size and number since at least 2009.[37] If anything, rumors about the conversion of army units in Northern China to navy-controlled marine brigades seem to suggest that other services with more relevant maritime capabilities will benefit at the expense of the army.[38]

Most importantly, the highest-level strategic articulations of army missions have remained consistent since the early 2000s, coalescing around regional threats including Taiwan, Korean Peninsula, and various forms of territorial disputes along China's borders. These missions are expressed in the 2004 and 2015 defense white papers, which represent close approximations of revised military strategic guidelines, but are also reflected in more granular PLA texts from the years dating back to at least 2004 and preceding years.[39] For instance, army academic research confirms the service's previously anticipated roles in addressing regional threats: a 2011 AMS volume identified several regional threats that China was likely to face, including potential land conflict hotspots like the Korean Peninsula to the east, Afghanistan and Central Asia to the west, and Kashmir to the south. Tibetan independence and Xinjiang independence were also specifically identified as security challenges within Chinese land borders.[40] For their part, army researchers regularly stressed "anti-Taiwan separatist" operational training[41] and emphasized preparations for potential border conflict with India.[42] The 2015 white paper repeats almost all of these regional land security threats, with an added emphasis on threats to the security of Chinese overseas energy resources, overseas personnel and assets, and strategic sea lines of communication.[43] In short, past doctrinal thinking on the army's main missions roughly matched the thinking immediately prior to the 2015 reforms, albeit with an additional emphasis on maritime threats in recent years.

Changes in the external security outlook certainly affected army modernization, but the nature and scope of those changes may have been insufficient to force large-scale, organizationally disruptive reforms. The reduction of the Soviet military threat permitted change but did not compel the PLA to adapt quickly to confront a major new threat. The rise of the threat of Taiwan independence in the mid-1990s created the need for army capabilities to deter Taiwan via the threat of punishment, a relatively modest goal. Building the capability to successfully invade Taiwan in the face of U.S. military intervention was a much more ambitious goal, but one that lacked urgency given the acceptability of the status quo, so long as Taiwan did not move toward de jure independence.

Changes in the Character of Warfare?

A fundamental shift in views regarding the character of warfare is similarly unlikely to have been the primary driver of the 2015 reforms. Many of the indicators of such a shift predate Xi Jinping's rule and have been in play for many years before the 2015 reforms, suggesting that other factors combined to push the 2015 reforms through. Although evidence suggests that PLA theorists believe informationized warfare [*xinxihua zhanzheng*, 信息化战争] to be a departure from warfare under informationized conditions [*xinxihua tiaojian xia zhanzheng*, 信息化条件下战争], the changes in the army instituted by the latest reforms have been undergoing trial and experimentation for a decade or more, suggesting that a new conception of the character of warfare among army leaders may not be a primary reason for the 2015 reforms.

The PLA ground forces have been pushing toward the multifunctionality [*duonenghua,* 多能化] associated with changes in the character of warfare since long before 2015, suggesting that it was not a substantial change in the way Chinese leaders perceived warfare that directly precipitated the 2015 reforms. The effort to build a "multifunctional" army has been justified by a perception that the PLA's ground forces must adapt to a variety of different missions since the early 1990s. For instance, the 1999 *Science of Military Strategy* argued that "local wars" were by nature "diverse situations," and called for the PLA to better prepare for missions on land, at sea, and in air.[44] A 2011 AMS work called for the development of multifunctional forces to fulfill the needs of a "mission-oriented" combat structure.[45] This attitude had filtered down to operational army units by mid-2013, when a deputy commander of the former Shenyang MR emphasized the importance of being able to complete a wide variety of missions.[46] These same views were expressed in various authoritative PLA writings leading up to the 2015 reforms[47] and have been implemented in the restructuring of group armies to accommodate combined arms brigades.[48] This implementation, however, is the culmination of years of efforts that predate the 2015 reforms, suggesting that it was not a fundamental change in PLA views of the character of warfare that drove the increased multifunctionality in the latest reforms.

An emphasis on increased mobility emblematic of a shift in the character of warfare has likewise been a consistent feature of army training for more than a decade before the 2015 reforms. Doctrinally, the army has stressed increased mobility and flexibility since before 2000: the 2000 defense white paper noted that the army was moving toward smaller, modularized, and multifunctional forces as the army "reoriented from theater defense to trans-theater mobility."[49] The army began to implement some of these concepts by adding aviation units in 2009, while exercises beginning in 2006 emphasized transregional mobility and operations in complex electromagnetic environments.[50] The 2015 reforms may have accelerated implementation of these concepts, but the reforms are implementing changes suggested in response to a shift in PLA views of warfare that was elucidated many years before.

Army views on the character of warfare have evolved in the past 25 years, but there is no evidence that a major change in the Army's view of warfare occurred immediately prior to the 2015 reforms to prompt major organizational changes. Many of the changes implemented in the reforms were experimented with and agreed on long before they were actually executed, suggesting that other factors were at play in determining the timing of the reforms.

New Political Directives?

Some analysts argue that a new political directive from Xi Jinping may have driven the 2015 reforms, but the issuance of a new political directive alone is unlikely to have prompted such swift and sweeping change in the ground forces. Past political directives have not always been fully heeded or executed in a timely fashion. While a new political dictum was issued in March 2013 calling for the military to obey CCP command, fight and win wars, and develop an excellent work style (that is, not be corrupt) [*ting dang zhihui, neng da sheng zhang, zuofeng youliang*, 听党指挥, 能大胜仗, 作风优良],[51] this broad formulation did not imply a specific organizational structure or translate directly into distinctive guidance for PLA reforms. The outlines of the military reforms were unveiled in the third plenum decision document approved by the CCP Central Committee in November 2013,[52] but it took an additional 2 years of work within the PLA to flesh out the details, some of which are still being refined as the reforms are implemented. The new military strategic guideline that eventually resulted (which was announced in the 2015 white paper on China's military strategy) was a minor adjustment rather than a major change. (See the chapter by Wuthnow and Saunders in this volume for discussion of Xi's role in the reforms).

While the 2015 reforms were undoubtedly accompanied by a new political urgency, the actual military content of the latest political directive appears to be based on longstanding past appeals by PLA reformers, including the emphasis on improving the PLA's ability to plan and execute joint operations.[53] (See the chapter by Finkelstein in this volume.) Immediately after the reforms were announced at the end of 2015, newly anointed commander of the army Li Zuocheng called for the service to dispense with the "Big Army Mentality" [*da lujun siwei*, 大陆军思维], avoid the belief that "land warfare is outdated and the army is useless" [*luzhan guoshi, lujun wuyong*, 陆战过时，陆军无用], and construct a "new type of army,"[54] ostensibly marking a new political directive to the army endorsed by Xi Jinping himself.[55] These expressions, however, are not new. A 2009 AMS volume on army command in joint operations listed "countering the influence of the Big Army" [*kefu da lujun de yingxiang*, 克服大陆军的影响] as the first among many steps to establish better coordination among the services,[56] and a 2011 volume noted that the PLA should abandon Big Army tradition in order to better embrace integrated joint operations.[57]

Even if the most recent political directive had significant new content, the PLA's track record of executing political orders in a timely manner is mixed. Hu Jintao's New Historic Missions were announced in 2004, but the PLA ground forces did not appear to fully embrace the study of MOOTW operations until an extensive series of instructional materials were published in 2008.[58] The details of Xi Jinping's new type of army are likely being interpreted in a similarly delayed approach: the flurry of recently published articles by army officers "studying" Xi's new type of army suggests that the ground forces are still translating this latest political directive in ways that may yield additional changes further in the future.[59] Hu Jintao reportedly contemplated organizational reforms to establish joint command structures in 2008–2009, but was unable to push the reforms through against opposition by the ground forces.

These examples indicate a distinctive new political directive was not the primary driver of recent army reforms. Hu's inability to carry out reforms may have been thanks to a lack of political capital or the resistance of corrupt senior army officers, such as CMC vice chairmen Guo Boxiong or Xu Caihou. The familiar content of the latest political instructions to the PLA suggests that that Xi Jinping's personal involvement in the reforms and use of a multifaceted political strategy to see them through likely affected the timing and implementation of the reforms, but the content of the reforms was largely derived from ideas about joint operations that had been advocated by PLA reformers for years.

The main body of available PLA literature suggests that army theorists arrived at a clear answer for their service's modernization by the end of the first decade of the 21st century at the latest: the future army was to be a smaller, modular, multifunctional force shaped to conduct informationized joint operations with a primary focus on threats emanating from the sea. Many of these concepts were well-worn and not unique to the immediate period leading up to the 2015 reforms. Even the new political directive to abandon the Big Army Mentality was based on previously articulated exhortations.

The existing explanations for the 2015 reforms fail to account for the timing and implementation of the most recent changes to the army. What explains the time lag between development of army reform concepts and the actual implementation after the 2015 reforms, and what could explain the timing of the actual implementation of these concepts within the army at scale once the 2015 reforms began?

Army Changes from an Organizational Perspective

The inadequacies of several existing explanations for the timing and implementation of the 2015 reforms leave at least one major question unanswered. If many of the changes that comprise the 2015 reforms are not substantively new ideas, what explains the long lag time between the genesis of these ideas and their actual implementation in 2015, and what may have caused the changes to actually happen? Though direct evidence of organizational motivation to reform is hard to find, examining the changes from the organizational perspective of the army yields several compelling insights and possible explanations for the long delay and the timing of the 2015 reforms.

The rough typology of PLA ground force organizational interests that follows is based on past studies of organizational behavior that chart the typical organizational interests of a bureaucracy, as well as evidence of army concern about these broad categories of organizational interests. It is neither exhaustive nor necessarily fully borne out by direct evidence that may be difficult to obtain; instead, the sections below provide a useful framework for evaluating army changes from an organizational perspective.

Uniqueness and Identity

Like any other military organization, the PLA ground forces appear to place a premium on a unique service identity driven by unique service capabilities and a monopoly of expertise. Early scholars of bureaucracies identified monopoly of expertise as a formidable and indispensable source of bureaucratic power.[60] Monopoly of expertise and a bureaucracy's "technical superiority over any other form of organization" ensure that a bureaucracy is the only unit capable of executing a task and virtually forces society to rely on that organization to execute policy.[61]

PLA Army scholars view the service's unique capability to seize and hold territory as the defining hallmark of its identity, even as the advent of integrated joint operations carves out even greater roles for the other services. Army theoreticians have argued that even though naval, air, and missile capabilities have replaced many of the army's traditional strengths, the army continues to have a special role even in the context of joint warfare, namely to seize, hold, and control strategically important territories.[62]

Autonomy

The army's unique capabilities and identity are inextricably linked to autonomy, which is a critical organizational interest for the service. This emphasis on autonomy is particularly pronounced when related to control of the budget, as the expenditure of funds determines the essence and priority of an organization's activities. Organizations frequently seek total operational control over the personnel and resources required to carry out a mission.[63] Autonomy is valued by bureaucracies "at least as much as resources" and signals that the agency "has a supportive constituency base and a coherent set of tasks that can provide the basis for a strong and widely shared sense of mission."[64]

One proxy for the army's relative autonomy is its relationship with the other PLA services, which is theoretically moving away from single-service thinking and toward more interservice cooperation as a result of increased emphasis on joint warfare. Army researchers openly acknowledge that the service's relative freedom to act on its own singular objectives is fast waning as the rest of the PLA adopts joint warfare as the primary mode of operations and the other services gain in prominence.[65] On top of that, PLA theorists have noted that army commanders must increasingly understand and consider the requirements, strengths, weaknesses, and specialties of other services, especially in the era of joint operations.[66] This rhetoric suggests a steadily decreasing amount of autonomy for army commanders and units, especially when engaged in joint operations or exercises.

Budget

A third army organizational interest is budget. An organization's budget may be the most important of the metrics of bureaucratic power, as money enables a bureaucracy to hire personnel, buy equipment, gain prestige, and otherwise increase an organization's capabilities and strengthen its ability to get what it wants.[67] Scholars have compared bureaucracies to firms, articulating a vision of bureaucracies as budget maximizers (instead of profit maximizers). The problems of making changes and managing a bureaucracy are at least partially alleviated by an increase in the total budget, and organizations will frequently maximize their budget relative to the production output expected of them by the sponsor of the organization's budget.[68] In brief, money is important to the extent that it enables production and eases management, and organizations (and their leaders) will pursue higher budgets as rational actors.

Available army writings almost never explicitly reveal budget-maximizing behavior, but the importance of the army's budgetary disposition is not lost on PLA researchers. Past researchers have called for increased overall defense expenditures to enable more investment on army weapons,[69] while more recent articles have argued that overall army expenditure is excessive in comparison to the spending of other services.[70] These contrasting viewpoints illustrate that service budgets have long been a point of debate within the PLA, in spite of an overall lack of budgetary transparency.

Presence in Command Billets

A final organizational interest is the number of influential positions held by army personnel. Scholars have argued that in order for a bureaucracy to provide governance, its officials must "occupy the most important positions in policy making, and further, they must be in sufficient numbers to be able to make their decisions effective."[71] Quantity of positions held has a quality all its own, in that sheer preponderance of positions held may itself increase bureaucratic power.[72] Staffers, ad hoc players, and lower level officials are also critical, wielding substantial influence over action channels and agenda-setting.[73]

PLA Army theorists understand the importance of having qualified personnel occupying key billets in a given command structure. Army researchers have recognized the importance of developing relevant army talent to occupy billets that might require army expertise,[74] and past analysis has identified the lack of qualified army technical personnel in key billets as a major bottleneck for the advancement of transformation.[75] One prominent researcher proposed the establishment of an army command organ, among other specifically army-controlled organizations like military academies, research units, and logistics support units, to remedy this problem as far back as 2009.[76]

Becoming a Joint Force Component: Choosing the "Least Bad Option"

While organizational and bureaucratic interests (some would say pathologies) may have held up the reforms until 2015, these same interests could also have enabled the reforms by helping the army to evaluate its future force choices. Interpreting the army's menu of options for its future force through the lens of the service's organizational interests yields an interesting perspective: of the three variants of a new type of army, becoming the ground component of a joint force may have been the least objectionable option for the army as an organization. The contours of these three different models for a future ground forces are summarized briefly in table 2 and described in more detail in the sections that follow.

Table 2. Future PLA Ground Force Roles			
	"Defend and Deter"	Constabulary Force	Ground Component of Joint Force
Missions	Deterrence	Military operations other than war	Taiwan
Unique Capabilities	Defend homeland	Defend Chinese Communist Party at home	Seize and hold territory
Relationship with PLA Partners	Reliant on naval, rocket, and air forces for protection and strike	Reliant on naval and air forces for overseas transportation	Reliant on naval and air forces for transportation and support; naval, rocket, and air forces for strike
Budgetary Implications	Limited budget; investment in equipment for defensive and deterrence operations	Smallest budget; limited investment for personnel and minimum necessary equipment	Comparatively reduced budget; investment in heavy power-projection
Command Implications	Stay at home; limited role in command of high-end combat operations	Stay loyal; little to no role in command of high-end combat operations	Reduced but continued role in command of complex combat operations

Defend and Deter

The PLA ground force is currently shaped as a force designed to defend and deter, largely thanks to China's longstanding strategic posture and periodic modifications in the way PLA leaders perceived the character of warfare. The PLA and its ground forces place a heavy emphasis on deterrence and defense of China; offense is typically referenced in the context of "active defense," in which China would task its armed forces to attack only when threatened.[77] Force modernization resulting from changes in perceptions about warfare under high-technology conditions to informationized conditions laid the groundwork for a force that is increasingly mechanized and informationized, with growing but limited-range power projection capabilities in its special operations and aviation components.[78] Taken together, these components represent the army's status quo, forming the basis for an army shaped primarily to defend the Chinese homeland and deter any violations of Chinese territory.

A ground force shaped for defense and deterrence confers specific bureaucratic advantages, capitalizing on the army's unique capability among the PLA's services to hold territory in defense of China's landmass. While the navy and air force each have ground force components, and the Rocket Force is based on land, the army alone has sufficient numbers and heavy weapons to assure China's territorial integrity on land.

At the same time, however, an army shaped for defense and deterrence is saddled with distinct bureaucratic disadvantages. While the army could benefit from interior lines for transportation and logistical support, it would be heavily reliant upon the PLA's naval and air forces and Rocket Force for protection and strike, even while operating inside friendly territory. PLA academics acknowledge this reliance, commenting that army operations are "near impossible without reliable air cover"[79] and that the army should make maximum use of long-range firepower strikes from the other services to achieve its goals.[80]

This reliance generates some significant potential budgetary and command limitations for the PLA Army. Comparatively greater portions of the defense budget would go to the navy, Rocket Force, and air force to buy high-end equipment needed for their operations. Meanwhile, with limited power projection capabilities and missions, army commanders would gradually be given commands limited to homeland defense and would only participate in high-end joint combat operations to the extent that they are needed to coordinate with other services tasked with protecting the ground forces.

The PLA ground forces have already run up against many of these limitations. The army does not command strategic air defense assets, which belong to the air force, and the long-range strike weapons used to keep China's enemies far afield are under the command of the Rocket Force and air and naval forces, which are perceived to be naturally better suited to use long-range firepower.[81] These trends have contributed to an army with limited power projection capabilities designed primarily to secure Chinese territorial integrity.

A Constabulary Force

Hu Jintao's New Historic Missions offered the army a glimpse at a future bureaucratic disposition far worse than the one army leaders were accustomed to during the runup to the 2015 reforms. A PLA ground force that fully embraced Hu's New Historic Missions would have focused more of its time and resources on MOOTW missions like antiterrorism, peacekeeping, and internal security, at the expense of training and equipping for complex combat operations against peer adversaries. The result would have been an army that more closely resembled an enhanced constabulary force with limited expeditionary capabilities instead of one designed to defeat the militaries of peer competitors.

While the call to participate in MOOTW missions under the aegis of Hu's New Historic Missions offered bureaucratic opportunities for the army, the unique and most politically important of these was not one that the PLA ground forces especially savored. Party leaders have continued to champion the army as the final line of defense for ensuring continued CCP rule,[82] but internal security was a mission that army leaders did not especially want. Some officers have candidly expressed their distaste for this particular duty.[83] Indeed, the existence of the People's Armed Police helps distance the PLA from this internal security mission.[84]

A constabulary army could have expected a greatly reduced share of the budget and significantly lessened command responsibility for the types of complex combat operations that armies typically embrace. Its unique role as the defender of the CCP would not have required extensive modernization that could justify budgetary largesse, and modernization funds would likely be funneled to selected units tasked with overseas peacekeeping, antiterrorism, and other MOOTW operations, eschewing the advanced capabilities needed to fight peer adversaries in favor of lighter rapid reaction forces. The increased emphasis on MOOTW would divert training time and resources away from more intensive combat operations, which would ultimately diminish the number of army officers holding prestigious command billets charged with executing complex combat operations against peer adversaries offshore from China.

It is no surprise that the PLA ground forces have not fully embraced the constabulary model that MOOTW missions would have foisted upon the service. Some evidence suggests that army theorists increasingly conceive of MOOTW operations within the context of larger, more complex operations rather than a set of separate, dedicated missions.[85] This is preliminary evidence that army theorists appear inclined to include MOOTW missions as lesser included tasks, even though MOOTW operations remain enshrined as one of the "three basic ways to use military power" cited in the 2013 *Science of Military Strategy*[86] and offer unique opportunities for the army to gain experience in combat support skills.[87] Given the significant bureaucratic disadvantages, army leaders are unlikely to endorse or adopt anything resembling the constabulary model if they can help it.

Ground Component of a Joint Force

Given the options described here, becoming the ground component of a joint force appears to be the best option from the perspective of the army's bureaucratic interests. While a full embrace of joint warfare would reduce the service's budget allocation, control over command billets, and leave the army reliant on other services for transportation and support, it nonetheless presents the strongest case for continued force modernization, making it the best option for the ground forces from the standpoint of organizational and bureaucratic interests.

Fully transforming into the ground component of a joint force would result in a bureaucratic retreat on multiple fronts, damaging the army's organizational interests and priming the way for significantly reduced influence. The army would lose some of its monopoly of expertise as other services begin to absorb or compete for army roles, such as amphibious operations. Accordingly, the army's share of budgetary appropriation relative to other PLA services would fall as the navy, air force, and Rocket Force funnel money toward costlier systems and training needed for complex joint operations. Army dominance of command billets would end as officers from other services increased their proficiency in joint operations and begin to rise through the ranks, demanding greater control commensurate with the rising importance of the other services.

Many of these bureaucratic retreats have already come to fruition during the recent reforms, though the army lost at least some of these bureaucratic battles more than a decade ago. Recent changes have captured the most attention. For instance, key chief of staff and theater commander billets in the newly formed theater commands are increasingly being filled by officers from other PLA services.[88] If true, rumors that an army brigade would be converted to a marine corps unit would have dealt a further blow to the army's weakening monopoly of expertise on amphibious operations.[89] Still, it is clear that the army likely lost some important bureaucratic clashes years before—the prioritization of informationization over mechanization and the announcement that the navy, air force, and Second Artillery would have modernization priority in the 2004 defense white paper hinted at major bureaucratic defeats for the army.[90]

In context, however, becoming the ground component of a joint force entails comparably fewer bureaucratic concessions than the other two options. Should the army ultimately be tasked with a future invasion of Taiwan, for instance, it would reap the budgetary benefits of continued modernization directed at defeating a technologically advanced Taiwan military and the U.S. military might that the PLA expects to confront in such a scenario. The aggregate number of officers occupying command billets responsible for joint operations would fall, but the army would still retain a legitimate claim to a substantial number of critical command positions given its continued role in a joint PLA. An army that is an equal participant in joint operations could ameliorate its reliance on other PLA services for protection and transportation by contributing niche capabilities to joint operations with other PLA services.

Given the comparatively lesser bureaucratic losses to the army, it is not entirely surprising that the undeniably painful transition toward a joint force is fully under way. This transition, evinced by numerous blows to the army's bureaucratic standing, will likely continue to be shaped by not only the army's organizational interests but also broader strategic and political directives described in previous sections of this chapter. In the end, however, organizational interests may have helped push army leaders and experts toward making the best of a worsening bureaucratic environment.

Explaining Incremental Change: Organizational Backsliding with Chinese Characteristics, or Risk Aversion?

If the transition to a ground component of a joint force was ultimately in the army's best organizational interest, what explains the lag time between the introduction of reform concepts in the 2000s and actual implementation in 2015?

The first and most simple explanation for the delay is that the army simply saw no strategic imperative for dramatic changes to its fighting force after the 1993 military strategic guideline, which marked a new era in how the PLA and the ground forces should have perceived land security challenges—a shift toward fighting local wars under high-technology and later under informationized conditions called for a smaller, more versatile, and mobile ground force. According to this explanation, the army's changes, or lack thereof, were a response to the new strategic directives laid down by the 1993 guideline, and subsequent modifications were appropriate responses to comparatively minor adjustments in China's national military strategy. The army continues to implement the directives handed down to them by higher authorities and does so with sufficient speed and effectiveness.[91] The consistency in the army's perceptions of land security challenges is a function of the enduring nature of China's remaining land security challenges, which is an especially plausible explanation given that China has mostly settled its territorial disputes, save for a select few outstanding trouble spots.[92]

But the evidence suggests that this "strategic" explanation is incomplete. If the PLA and its ground forces were as responsive to higher level strategic directives as the CCP and the military would have observers believe, one might expect quicker and more pronounced changes in doctrine or force structure than those described in the previous sections of this chapter. One prominent example of this explanatory gap is the apparent multiple attempts to adopt the smaller ground force structure that is consistently upheld and reiterated seemingly ad infinitum as a key pillar of army modernization. Since the introduction of the 1993 guidelines, the PLA has undergone several troop reductions: 500,000 personnel in 1997, 200,000 more in 2005, and an additional 300,000 announced in 2015.[93] The latest reductions were reportedly completed in March 2018,[94] nearly a full 25 years after the strategic need for a smaller ground force was first articulated in 1993 and 20 years since the first personnel reduction under the "military strategic guideline in the new period" was undertaken. Are these reductions deliberate and precise responses to changes in China's land security threats and views on the character of warfare, or have they been conducted in a delayed and piecemeal fashion because the PLA (and especially its ground forces) was unwilling or unable to reduce the size of the force? How much of the delay can be attributed to the consensus-driven nature of the PLA's organizational culture, and how much is due to opposition or resistance? Given the relative consistency in China's views on land security threats since 1993, the timing of the iterative, piecemeal force reductions cannot be readily explained by adjustments in perceptions of land security threats.

A second explanation involves PLA (and especially ground force) resistance to implementing its conclusion that smaller, modular, and multifunctional forces were necessary because these changes went against parochial organizational interests within the ground forces. Seasoned PLA experts point out that the PLA does not always respond rapidly to decisions it does not like. There is ample scholarship supporting the idea that the PLA and its ground forces may be less than fully willing to follow through on CCP directives,[95] and history is replete with concrete instances of serious friction between the Party and army. One recent example is the November 2015 announcement of a 3-year phase out of PLA commercial businesses, which came nearly two decades after the famous 1997 divestiture of PLA businesses ordered by Jiang Zemin, which was apparently not as effective or complete as civilian leaders had hoped.[96] Through this lens, one might attribute the slow and small-scale changes in army priorities to organizational backsliding and unwillingness to break "iron rice bowls" within the service. The army's professional role as land warfare experts gives the service excellent bona fides upon which to execute this particular form of doctrinal disobedience, as with any other service. The long series of experimental exercises in the former Jinan MR may have been an expression of this resistance, serving as an excuse to put off implementation of needed reforms rather than a genuine effort to change the army.[97] Was the army's laggard pace of change actually a result of a deliberate campaign of military slow walking?

A third possible explanation for the army's relative failure to adapt to a new type of force centers on a potential organizational inability to do so, or at least do so in a radical way. Military organizations, like their nonmilitary counterparts, are typically deeply resistant to change, except under conditions of competition or doctrinal innovation from a foreign opponent.[98] A review of scholarly literature on organizational behavior suggests that organizations rarely adopt radical change, preferring instead to engage in incremental innovation characterized by the adoption of policy options that bear a strong resemblance to choices adopted in the past.[99] On its face, the main body of PLA and army literature regarding land security threats appears to conform to these patterns of behavior—views on regional challenges and the future shape of the force have remained nearly identical, while changes to emphasize amphibious operations use many of the same intellectual language and constructs employed before the latest revision to China's military strategic guideline.[100] This suggests that the ground forces may have previously been organizationally unable to innovate, hindered by a particular brand of organizational pathology that emphasizes hierarchy and consensus-driven processes.[101]

Evidence to assess the relative weight of these explanations is difficult to come by, but some details from the PLA reforms give hints that all three of these explanations may be valid to varying degrees. Some of the latest reforms appear to be directed at remedying selected residual outcomes that could have resulted from the above three explanations, especially any deliberate slow-rolling or inability to foster doctrinal innovation. For instance, the reduction of army influence at the highest levels of administrative and operational command, exemplified by the reassignment of several former General Staff Department functions to competing organizations[102] and the formation of joint operations command centers [*lianhe zuozhan zhihui zhongxin*, 联合作战指挥中心] at the new theater commands,[103] would likely reduce any army-led efforts to obstruct or hinder the development of a "joint" PLA. The heavier presence of air force and navy officers at the theater commands is likely to force their army counterparts to interact more with other doctrinal schools of thought.[104] The bevy of first-time military delegates to the latest Party congress may also hint at a broader displacement of army personnel who were professionally disinclined toward change.[105]

While it remains difficult to determine precisely which of the above explanations best describes the army's pace and scope of change, the relative validities of these explanations nonetheless have much larger implications for the army, the PLA writ large, and the state of Party-military relations in China.

If the army failed to adjust in the past based on limited adjustments in strategy or views on the character of warfare, the latest changes in the ground forces suggest that a dramatic reorientation in the army's future force is coming to fruition. Many of the changes that army theorists have discussed at length over the past 20-odd years are finally being realized, shortly after the issuance of a new military strategic guideline strongly emphasizing maritime threats. Reforms from the "neck down" [*bozi yixia gaige,* 脖子以下改革] have resulted in significant reductions and changes to army units, including the elimination of five group army headquarters and the redistribution and reassignment of many of their subordinate units, personnel, and equipment. The remaining group armies command combined arms brigades instead of divisions, and have been redesignated, reduced in size, and completely reorganized.[106] If the army is responsive to the latest military strategic guideline, it will continue to work toward developing smaller, modularized, and multifunctional forces, primarily for use in joint maritime operations.

If the ground forces were backsliding, some elements of the reforms may be better interpreted as deliberately disruptive measures. The process of "discarding Big Army Mentality" may have motivated the removal of individual leaders and precipitated the abolition of certain institutions and departments, and any further perceived Big Army Mentality may result in further disruption within the PLA ground forces. A concerted move against the army would bode ill for the Party-army relationship, and analysts should expect to see much more stringent efforts at political control of the army in particular. Ground force personnel associated with corruption may be drummed out of the force en masse, and the remaining forces and their commanders will likely experience a sharp uptick in political work emphasizing political and personal loyalty to Xi Jinping. For career army personnel, it will likely pay to be "Red."

If the ground forces are simply risk averse and organizationally incapable of articulating a radically different view of land security challenges, the process of discarding Big Army Mentality is likely to be gentler and more gradual, although just as jarring in the end. Party and military leaders may increase the army officers' exposure to other components of the PLA, namely the air force, navy, and Rocket Force, in an attempt to diversify army doctrinal and operational thinking. Older officers will be ushered out of their posts in order to be replaced by a new generation that is more inclined to value joint operations with other services. One obvious price of becoming more accepting of change in the army, however, is that the service's bureaucratic status and influence are likely to continue to decrease as a result of any "radical" changes in views on land security challenges.

These three paths are not necessarily mutually exclusive, and some of the recently announced changes from the reforms could be indicators of all three explanations of army theoretical and actual change. One major issue going forward is that absent better data, much of the evidence gleaned from the reforms can be interpreted as supporting evidence for multiple theories explaining the army's views on land security challenges. For instance, army leadership reductions and reassignments resulting from the group army reorganization could be part of the service's response to a new strategy, serve as a punishment to some backsliding officers, or remove organizational and bureaucratic obstacles to needed change. On balance, such a leadership change probably achieves all three of those objectives, which makes it difficult to determine which explanation is most valid.

As it stands, the key findings of this chapter suggest that while changes in China's external security challenges, altered perceptions of the character of warfare, and new political directives all likely played critical roles in driving these latest adaptations in the PLA ground forces, these explanations for reform neglect the army's organizational interests as a potential driver and enabler of reform. While an organizational explanation may still be unable to account for exactly what happened to push the 2015 reforms to fruition, the existing body of literature on bureaucratic behavior in general and on the ground forces suggests that army organizational interests almost certainly influenced the scale and timing of reforms.

To the extent that army organizational interests prove to be important determinants of the future service, they may push the PLA ground forces toward a more offensive-oriented role for a PLA ground force that has previously been tasked to defend and deter. This is not to say that the PLA or the highest CCP leadership will opt to use the ground forces in an offensive manner, but rather to imply that a more joint PLA ground force would have a greater organizational preference for offensive actions within the context of the PLA's broader posture of active defense. This may be especially true in a Taiwan scenario in which the ground forces may be called upon to invade the island.

Ultimately, the ongoing transformation of the army into the ground component of a joint force is still not good for the service's bureaucratic standing. An altered strategic paradigm will likely precipitate a continued decline in army bureaucratic power and influence. Organizational opposition or simple organizational pathology is likely to trigger similar outcomes, albeit with varying degrees of disruption. Given these possible explanations and outcomes, the other PLA services and branches will likely continue to gain at the expense of the ground forces as the PLA continues to implement the next slate of reforms. Nonetheless, the army's embrace of joint warfare will likely continue to be its "least bad" organizational choice, especially in light of its other options.

The author is indebted to Dennis J. Blasko, Morgan Clemens, and Phillip C. Saunders for their generous help in reviewing previous versions of this chapter. Any errors are the author's alone.

Notes

[1] Zhang Jiaoying [张骄瀛], ed., "CMC Opinions on Deepening National Defense and Military Reforms" [中央军委关于深化国防和军队改革的意见], Xinhua [新华社], January 1, 2016, available at <www.xinhuanet.com/mil/2016-01/01/c_128588503.htm>.

[2] For a similar but distinct categorization of the factors that spur changes in military strategy, see M. Taylor Fravel, "Shifts in Warfare and Party Unity: Explaining China's Changes in Military Strategy," *International Security* 42, no. 3 (Winter 2017/2018), 40–44.

³ For an extensive description of the formulation, content, and significance of the 1993 military strategic guideline, see David M. Finkelstein, "China's National Military Strategy: An Overview of the 'Military Strategic Guidelines,'" in *Right Sizing the People's Liberation Army: Exploring the Contours of China's Military*, ed. Andrew Scobell and Roy Kamphausen (Carlisle Barracks, PA: Strategic Studies Institute, 2007), 69–140.

⁴ Wang Xiangfu [王祥富] et al., eds., *Study Guide on Jiang Zemin National Defense and Military Construction Thought* [江泽民国防和军队建设思想学习读本] (Beijing: Chinese Communist Party History Press [中共党史出版社], 2002), 75.

⁵ Shan Xiufa [单秀法], ed., *Research on Jiang Zemin National Defense and Military Construction Thought* [江泽民国防和军队建设思想研究] (Beijing: Academy of Military Science Press [军事科学出版社], 2004), cited in Finkelstein, "China's National Military Strategy," 106.

⁶ *China's National Defense in 2004* [2004 年中国的国防] (Beijing: State Council Information Office of the People's Republic of China, December 2004), available at <www.mod.gov.cn/affair/2011-01/06/content_4249947.htm>.

⁷ *China's Military Strategy* [中国的军事战略] (Beijing: State Council Information Office of the People's Republic of China, May 2015), available at <www.mod.gov.cn/auth/2015-05/26/content_4586723.htm>.

⁸ Language calling for the military to rid itself of the "big army" [大陆军] mentality appeared in several papers published by *China Military Science* in a two-part 2014 study of Xi Jinping's thoughts on the military. For examples of this language, see Gao Guanghui [高光辉], "Considerations on Adhering to the Standard of Warfighting Capability in the New Situation" [新形势下坚持战斗力标准的思考], *China Military Science* [中国军事科学], vol. 3 (2014), 34; and Wang Pei and Zhang Zhihui [王培, 张志辉], "Adhere to the Sole and Fundamental Standard of Warfighting Capability—A Thorough Study of Xi Jinping's Important Expositions on the Standard of Warfighting Capability" [坚持战斗力这个唯一的根本的标准—深入学习领会习近平关于战斗力标准的重要论述], *China Military Science* [中国军事科学], vol. 3 (2014), 29.

⁹ *China's National Defense in 1998* [1998 年中国的国防] (Beijing: State Council Information Office of the People's Republic of China, September 1998), available at <http://60.people.com.cn/GB/166974/9988169.html>.

¹⁰ Li Tao [李涛], "Ten Historical Troop Reductions of the People's Liberation Army" [人民解放军历史上的10次大裁军], *PLA Daily* [解放军报], November 18, 2015, available at <www.81.cn/20151126jg/2015-11/18/content_6885147.htm>.

[11] See Dennis J. Blasko, *The Chinese Army Today,* 2nd ed. (New York: Routledge, 2012), 96; and Dennis J. Blasko, "PLA Amphibious Capabilities: Structured for Deterrence," *China Brief* 10, no. 17 (August 19, 2010), available at <https://jamestown.org/program/pla-amphibious-capabilities-structured-for-deterrence/>.

[12] Fravel, "Shifts in Warfare and Party Unity," 79.

[13] Ibid., 80.

[14] Ibid., 81.

[15] Chang Qiaozhang and Cui Shuxia [常巧章, 崔叔霞], "High-Technology Warfare" [高技术战争], in *China Military Encyclopedia* [中国军事百科全书], *Military Science I* [军事学术1], ed. Song Shilun and Xiao Ke [宋时轮, 萧克] (Beijing: Academy of Military Science Press [军事科学出版社], 1997), 126–127.

[16] All-Military Military Terminology Management Committee [全军军事术语管理委员会], *People's Liberation Army Military Terminology* [中国人民解放军军语] (Beijing: Academy of Military Science Press, 2011), 48.

[17] Ibid.

[18] Zhan Yu [战玉], ed., *Research on Army Transformation under Informationized Conditions* [信息化条件下陆军转型研究] (Beijing: Academy of Military Science Press, 2009), 270–271.

[19] For a detailed analysis of the People's Liberation Army (PLA) ground forces' transregional exercises involving other services, see Dennis J. Blasko, "Clarity of Intentions: People's Liberation Army Transregional Exercises to Defend China's Borders," in *Learning by Doing: The PLA Trains at Home and Abroad*, ed. Roy Kamphausen, David Lai, and Travis Tanner (Carlisle Barracks, PA: Strategic Studies Institute, 2012), 171–212; and his chapter in this volume. See also Kevin McCauley, *PLA System of System Operations: Enabling Joint Operations* (Washington, DC: The Jamestown Foundation, 2017), 67.

[20] Dennis J. Blasko, "Recent Developments in the Chinese Army's Helicopter Force," *China Brief* 17, no. 8 (June 9, 2017), available at <https://jamestown.org/program/recent-developments-chinese-armys-helicopter-force/>.

[21] Hu Jintao, "Recognize Historical Missions of Our Military in the New Period of the New Century" [认清新世纪新阶段我军历史使命], speech to session of the Central Military Commission, Beijing, December 24, 2004, available at <http://gfjy.jxnews.com.cn/system/2010/04/16/011353408.shtml>.

[22] Morgan Clemens, "PLA Thinking on Military Operations other Than War," in *China's Evolving Military Strategy*, ed. Joe McReynolds (Washington, DC: The Jamestown Foundation, 2016), 338.

²³ In 2008, the Academy of Military Science published a series of books for military distribution only through the Nanjing Army Command College [南京陆军指挥学院] on military operations other than war. The series included volumes on the army's role in counterterrorism, protection of social stability, peacekeeping operations, and disaster relief, among others. See Zhang Jian [张健], ed., *Military Operations other Than War Research Series* [非战争军事行动系列研究] (Beijing: Academy of Military Science Press, 2008).

²⁴ See Zhan Yu [战玉], "Strategic Considerations on Army Transformation" [对陆军转型的战略思考], *China Military Science* [中国军事科学], vol. 2 (2008), 97; and Zhan, *Research on Army Transformation*, 271–272.

²⁵ For a discussion of how PLA academicians conceived of peacekeeping rotations, see Li Chunyuan [李春元], ed., *Army Peacekeeping Operations Research* [陆军维和行动研究] (Beijing: Academy of Military Science Press, 2008), 100–106.

²⁶ Blasko, *The Chinese Army Today*, 84.

²⁷ Yin Shijie [尹世杰], ed., "Army Begins Organizing Peacekeeping Unit Awaiting Orders" [陆军启动组建6类19支维和待命部队], Xinhua Online [新华网], November 18, 2017, available at <www.xinhuanet.com/2017-11/18/c_1121976423.htm>.

²⁸ Zhuang Pinghui, "Two Chinese UN Peacekeepers Killed, Two Seriously Injured in Attack in South Sudan," *South China Morning Post* (Hong Kong), July 12, 2016, available at <www.scmp.com/news/china/diplomacy-defence/article/1988348/two-chinese-un-peacekeepers-killed-two-seriously>.

²⁹ *China's Military Strategy.*

³⁰ Dennis J. Blasko, "PLA Army Group Army Reorganization: An Initial Analysis," October 2017, available at <www.ashtreeanalytics.com/wp-content/uploads/2017/10/PLA-Army-Group-Army-Reorganization-An-Initial-Analysis.pdf>.

³¹ Sarah Zhang, "China Completes Registration of 8,000-Strong UN Peacekeeping Force, Defense Ministry Says," *South China Morning Post* (Hong Kong), September 29, 2017, available at <www.scmp.com/news/china/diplomacy-defence/article/2113436/china-completes-registration-8000-strong-un>.

³² Phillip C. Saunders and Joel Wuthnow, *China's Goldwater-Nichols? Assessing PLA Organizational Reform*, INSS Strategic Forum 294 (Washington, DC: NDU Press, April 2016), 1–9.

³³ Researchers at PLA's National Defense University began work on the 1999 version of the *Science of Military Strategy* in 1992, and Academy of Military Science researchers from the Strategy Research Department began work on the 2001 edition of the *Science of Military Strategy* in 1996. For information on the drafting

processes for both of these volumes, see Wang Wenrong [王文荣], ed., *Science of Military Strategy* [战略学] (Beijing: National Defense University Press [国防大学出版社], 1999), 1; and Peng Guangqian and Yao Youzhi [彭光谦, 姚有志], eds., *Science of Military Strategy* [战略学] (Beijing: Academy of Military Science Press, 2001), 509–510. For relevant text on force reduction, see Wang, *Science of Military Strategy*, 273–274, 383; and Peng and Yao, *Science of Military Strategy*, 203.

[34] Zhan, "Strategic Considerations on Army Transformation," 97–98. Similar calls for army force reductions were echoed in a 2009 book edited by the same author. For one example of many, see Zhan, *Research on Army Transformation under Informationized Conditions*, 31–33.

[35] Li, "Ten Historical Troop Reductions of the People's Liberation Army."

[36] Shou Xiaosong [寿晓松], ed., *Science of Military Strategy* [战略学] (Beijing: Academy of Military Science Press, 2013), 201.

[37] Blasko, "Recent Developments in the Chinese Army's Helicopter Force."

[38] For rumors of a transfer of a 26th Group Army brigade to the PLA Navy Marine Corps, see "Two Generals Strike a Pose: Chinese Marine Corps About to Expand?" [这两位少将亮相, 中国海军陆战队要扩编成军?], May 29, 2017, available at <www.guancha.cn/military-affairs/2017_05_29_410685.shtml>.

[39] For a seminal treatment of the importance of the military strategic guideline in understanding China's national military strategy, see Finkelstein, "China's National Military Strategy," 69–140. For a discussion of the uncertainty surrounding the existence of the military strategic guideline as a single document, see Timothy R. Heath, "An Overview of China's National Military Strategy," in *China's Evolving Military Strategy*, 4–6. See also China's *National Defense in 2004* and *China's Military Strategy*.

[40] Wang Fa'an [王法安], ed., *Strong Military Strategy Amidst China's Peaceful Development* [中国和平发展中的强军战略] (Beijing: Academy of Military Science Press, 2011), 58, 78.

[41] For an example, see Zhan, *Research on Army Transformation under Informationized Conditions*, 291.

[42] PLA academics have written extensively about India's military strategy and the threat India poses to China. For a candid 2005 assessment of the Indian border threat, see Geng Weidong and Zhou Zhenfeng [耿卫东, 周振锋], eds., *Joint Border Operations at the Group Army Level* [集团军级边境联合作战] (Beijing, Academy of Military Science Press, 2005), 1–18.

[43] *China's Military Strategy.*

44 Wang, *Science of Military Strategy*, 282–283.

45 Wang, *Strong Military Strategy Amidst China's Peaceful Development*, 177.

46 Wang Xixin [王西欣], "Understanding of and Consideration on Improving Warfighting Capabilities of the PLA Infantry Forces" [对提高陆军部队实战能力的认识与思考], *China Military Science* [中国军事科学], vol. 4 (2013), 103–107.

47 See Xiao Tianliang [肖天亮], ed., *Science of Military Strategy* [战略学] (Beijing: National Defense University Press [国防大学出版社], 2015), 330, 332; Shi Zhongwu [石忠武], "Considerations on Promoting the Transformation of the PLA Army" [推进陆军转型建设的几点思考], *China Military Science* [中国军事科学], vol. 6 (2016), 106–107; Wang Jishan [王吉山], "A Study of Real Combat Training of the PLA Army" [陆军实战化训练研究], *China Military Science* [中国军事科学], vol. 5 (2015), 127–128; Zhang Dongjiang, Xu Zhen, and Lü Tao [张东江, 许震, 吕涛], "Guidance of Xi Jinping's Important Thought on 'Building a Human Community of Shared Destiny' for China's Military Strategy" [习近平"构建人类命运共同体"重要思想对中国军事战略的指导意义], *China Military Science* [中国军事科学], vol. 2 (2017), 9.

48 Blasko, "PLA Army Group Army Reorganization."

49 *China's National Defense in 2000* [2000年中国的国防] (Beijing: State Council Information Office of the People's Republic of China, October 16, 2000), available at <*www.scio.gov.cn/zfbps/ndhf/2000/Document/307949/307949.htm*>.

50 Blasko, "Clarity of Intentions," 171–212. See also McCauley, 67.

51 Xi Jinping, "Build a People's Military That Obeys Party Command, Can Fight and Win Wars, and Has an Excellent Work Style" [建设一支听党指挥, 能打胜仗, 作风优良的人民军队], *News of the Chinese Communist Party* [中国共产党新闻网], March 11, 2013, available at <http://cpc.people.com.cn/xuexi/n/2015/0720/c397563-27332090.html>.

52 "CPC Central Committee Decision on Deepening of Reforms for Major Issues" [中共中央关于全面深化改革若干重大问题的决定], Xinhua, November 15, 2013, available at <http://news.xinhuanet.com/politics/2013-11/15/c_118164235.htm>.

53 See Xi Jinping, "Speech at a Ceremony Marking the 90th Anniversary of the Founding of the People's Liberation Army," *Qiushi Journal* 9, no. 4 (October–December 2017), available at <http://english.qstheory.cn/2017-11/28/c_1122006806.htm>.

54 Shao Beizhen and Ren Lihong [邵贝真, 任丽虹], eds., "Army Commander Li Zuocheng: Build a Strong Modernized New Type of Army" [陆军司令员李作成: 建设强大的现代化新型陆军], *People's Daily* [人民日报], January 31, 2016, available at <http://sn.people.com.cn/n2/2016/0131/c358036-27662181.html>.

[55] Jiang Pingping and Cheng Hongyi [姜萍萍, 程宏毅], eds., "Work Hard to Build a Strong, Modernized New Type of Army—Deep Study Implementation of Chairman Xi's Important Thoughts Regarding Army Building" [努力建设一支强大的现代化新型陆军—深入学习贯彻习近平主席关于陆军建设重要论述], *Qiushi* [求是], February 26, 2016, available at <http://theory.people.com.cn/n1/2016/0216/c40531-28128055.html>.

[56] Li Chunyuan and Li Zhangrui [李春元, 李章瑞], eds., *Army Command in Joint Operations* [联合作战中的陆军指挥] (Beijing: Academy of Military Science Press, 2009), 20.

[57] Wang, ed., 75.

[58] See Zhang, ed.

[59] For instance, see Guo Tong [郭统], "Adhere to Guiding Army Transformation by Xi Jinping's Thought on Military Strategy" [坚持以习近平军事战略思想指导陆军转型建设], *China Military Science* [中国军事科学], vol. 3 (2017), 32–39; and Chen Genhua and Fu Minghua [沈根华, 付明华], "Consolidate the Political Guarantee for Army Transformation—A Strategic Consideration of Strengthening Army's Ideological and Political Construction" [强化陆军转型建设的政治保证—加强陆军思想政治建设的战略思考], *China Military Science* [中国军事科学], vol. 3 (2017), 40–48.

[60] See Max Weber, "Essay on Bureaucracy," in *Bureaucratic Power in National Policy Making*, 4th ed., ed. Francis E. Rourke (Boston: Little, Brown and Company, 1986), 69; and David Beetham, *Bureaucracy* (Minneapolis: University of Minnesota Press, 1987), 60, 75.

[61] Weber, 67–73.

[62] See Zhan, ed., 144; and Li and Li, eds., 27.

[63] Morton H. Halperin and Priscilla A. Clapp, *Bureaucratic Politics and Foreign Policy*, 2nd ed. (Washington, DC: Brookings Institution Press, 2006), 51.

[64] James Q. Wilson, *Bureaucracy: What Government Agencies Do and Why They Do It* (New York: Basic Books, 1989), 195.

[65] Li and Li, eds., 21.

[66] Ibid., 25–29.

[67] William A. Niskanen, *Bureaucracy and Public Economics* (Brookfield, VT: Edward Elgar, 1994), 38.

[68] Ibid., 36–42.

[69] Yan Jia and Shi Jianfeng [严佳, 施剑峰], "An Analysis of the Weaponry Funds Distributed to the Army in the Future" [我军陆军武器装备经费投入预期], *Military Economics Research* [军事经济研究], vol. 9 (2002), 35–36.

[70] An Wenchao, Hao Lu, and Jiang Nan [安文超, 郝路, 姜楠], "Problems and Solutions in National Defense Budget Allocation Efficiency" [国防预算配置效率的困境与出路], *Military Economics Research* [军事经济研究], vol. 11 (2011), 18–20.

[71] B. Guy Peters, *The Politics of Bureaucracy: An Introduction to Comparative Public Administration* (New York: Routledge, 2010), 204.

[72] Ibid., 205.

[73] Graham Allison and Philip Zelikow, *Essence of Decision: Explaining the Cuban Missile Crisis*, 2nd ed. (New York: Addison-Wesley, 1999), 296.

[74] Zhan, ed., 276.

[75] Ibid., 221.

[76] Ibid., 247–248.

[77] Dennis J. Blasko, "China's Evolving Approach to Strategic Deterrence," in *China's Evolving Military Strategy*, 315–334.

[78] Blasko, "PLA Army Group Army Reorganization."

[79] Li and Li, eds., 27.

[80] Zhan, ed., 144.

[81] Ibid., 142.

[82] Murray Scot Tanner, "How China Manages Internal Security Challenges and Its Impact on PLA Missions," in *Beyond the Strait: PLA Missions Other Than Taiwan*, ed. Roy Kamphausen, David Lai, and Andrew Scobell (Carlisle Barracks, PA: Strategic Studies Institute, 2009), 40.

[83] General Xu Qinxian, commander of the 38th Group Army, refused to lead his forces into Tiananmen Square to clear out student protestors in 1989. Other officials have registered their disapproval: former Defense Minister General Chi Haotian asserted that the actions at Tiananmen Square "would not happen again." See Verna Yu, "No Regrets for Defiant Tiananmen General," *South China Morning Post* (Hong Kong), February 25, 2011, available at <www.scmp.com/article/738185/no-regrets-defiant-tiananmen-general>; and Dennis J. Blasko and John F. Corbett, Jr., "No More Tiananmens: The People's Armed Police and Stability in China, 1997," *China Strategic Review* 3, no. 1 (1998), 88–89.

[84] Roy Kamphausen, "China's Land Forces: New Priorities and Capabilities," in *Strategic Asia 2012–2013: China's Military Challenge*, ed. Ashley J. Tellis and Travis Tanner (Seattle: National Bureau of Asian Research, 2012), 32.

[85] In the past, PLA Army writings have allocated dedicated and extensive coverage to a range of stand-alone military operations other than war (MOOTW)

missions; one recent volume, however, makes reference to counterterrorism and social stability operations in the context of joint border campaign operations, not as part of a broader MOOTW construct. See Zhang, ed., for an example of the former; and Cao Zhengrong, Sun Longhai, and Yang Ying [曹正荣, 孙龙海, 杨颖], eds., *Informationized Army Operations* [信息化陆军作战] (Beijing: National Defense University Press [国防大学出版社], 2014), 246–247, for an example of the latter.

[86] Shou, ed., 6. See also Blasko, "China's Evolving Approach," 317–318.

[87] Zhang Tao, ed., "Monthly Press Conference of the Ministry of National Defense on September 28," Ministry of National Defense, September 28, 2017, available at <http://eng.mod.gov.cn/focus/2017-09/28/content_4793398.htm>.

[88] Joel Wuthnow and Phillip C. Saunders, *Chinese Military Reform in the Age of Xi Jinping: Drivers, Challenges, and Implications*, China Strategic Perspectives 10 (Washington, DC: NDU Press, 2017), 18–19; and Chi-yuk Choi, "Admiral Named to Head PLA's New Southern Theater Command," *South China Morning Post* (Hong Kong), January 19, 2017, available at <www.scmp.com/news/china/policies-politics/article/2063649/admiral-named-head-plas-southern-theatre-command>.

[89] "Two Generals Strike a Pose."

[90] The 2002 defense white paper claimed that the PLA would pursue both mechanization and informationization, but the 2004 white paper announced that the PLA would transition from mechanization to informationization, cementing a shift in priorities that would ultimately benefit other services over the army. See *China's National Defense in 2002* [中国的军事战略] (Beijing: State Council Information Office of the People's Republic of China, December 2002), available at *<eng.mod.gov.cn/Database/WhitePapers/2002.htm>*; and *China's National Defense in 2004*.

[91] This is almost certainly the narrative that the Chinese Communist Party wants both the PLA and the outside world to believe. Defense white papers produced for public consumption constantly reiterate that the army will "continue to" carry out modernization according to strategic directives from on high. Any alternative narratives would seriously undermine the governing principle of Party-army relations, namely that the "Party Controls the Gun" (党指挥枪). See note 34 for an example of the careful and differential use of English and Chinese to convey separate messages to Chinese and foreign audiences.

[92] M. Taylor Fravel, *Strong Borders, Secure Nation* (Princeton: Princeton University Press, 2008), 300–319.

[93] Li.

94 "Defense Ministry's Regular Press Conference on March 29," *China Military Online*, March 30, 2018, available at <http://english.chinamil.com.cn/view/2018-03/30/content_7987841.htm>.

95 Volumes have been written on the topic of tensions in China's civil-military relationship. Among other works, see Harlan W. Jencks, *From Muskets to Missiles: Politics and Professionalism in the Chinese Army* (Boulder, CO: Westview Press, 1982); Michael Kiselycynyk and Phillip C. Saunders, *Civil-Military Relations in China: Assessing the PLA's Role in Elite Politics*, China Strategic Perspectives 2 (Washington, DC: NDU Press, 2010); James C. Mulvenon, "China: Conditional Compliance" in *Coercion and Governance: The Declining Political Role of the Military in Asia*, ed. Muthiah Alagappa (Stanford: Stanford University Press, 2001).

96 For an analysis of the November 2015 announcement, see James C. Mulvenon, "PLA Divestiture 2.0: We Mean It This Time," *China Leadership Monitor*, no. 50 (2016). For a study of the 1998 divestiture, see James C. Mulvenon, *Soldiers of Fortune: The Rise and Fall of the Chinese Military-Business Complex 1978–1998* (Armonk, NY: M.E. Sharpe, 2001), which follows up on the problem that apparently never ends.

97 Blasko, "Clarity of Intentions," 171–212.

98 Much of the literature on organizational behavior can be found in the eponymously named classic on organizations by March and Simon. See James G. March and Herbert A. Simon, *Organizations* (New York: John Wiley and Sons, 1958). For discussions of change within militaries based upon these academic studies of organizational behavior, see Kimberly Marten-Zisk, *Engaging the Enemy: Organization Theory and Soviet Military Innovation, 1955–1991* (Princeton: Princeton University Press, 1993); and Barry Posen, *The Sources of Military Doctrine: France, Britain, and Germany between the World Wars* (Ithaca, NY: Cornell University Press, 1984).

99 The main threads of this argument are laid out in a study of American government organizations in Charles E. Lindblom, "The Science of 'Muddling Through,'" *Public Administration Review* 19, no. 2 (Spring 1959), 79–88. The framework was extended to an analysis of 1970s Soviet policymaking in Valerie Bunce and John M. Echols III, "Power and Policy in Communist Systems: The Problem of 'Incrementalism,'" *The Journal of Politics* 40, no. 4 (August 1978), 911–932.

100 Multiple army theoreticians, for example, have repeatedly urged caution about the scale and the shape of ground force drawdowns throughout the entire period of study covered in this chapter.

101 One fitting and obvious example of the PLA's emphasis on consensus comes from examining the authorship of PLA books. The most authoritative works within

the ecosystem of PLA academic literature are typically recognized as ones authored by large committee(s) or attributed to entire organizations. Nearly all major PLA academic works are edited or vetted by a research or supervisory committee.

[102] For a detailed examination of which sub-departments and functions were redistributed to which organizations, see Wuthnow and Saunders, 10–13.

[103] Chen Jian [陈剑], ed., "Beginning a New Trend Amidst Fluttering Red Flags—Post-Establishment Observations of the Theater Commands" [开局新风起 猎猎战旗红—东南西北中五战区成立伊始见闻], Xinhua [新华社], February 3, 2016, available at <www.xinhuanet.com/politics/2016-02/02/c_1117973365.htm>.

[104] Wuthnow and Saunders, 18–19.

[105] Cheng Li, "Forecasting China's Largest-Ever Turnover of Military Elite at the 19th Party Congress," Brookings, September 18, 2017, available at <www.brookings.edu/opinions/forecasting-chinas-largest-ever-turnover-of-military-elite-at-the-19th-party-congress/>.

[106] For a detailed analysis of these "neck-down" reforms to the PLA ground forces, see Dennis J. Blasko, "PLA Army Group Army Reorganization."

CHAPTER 3

THE IMPACT OF XI-ERA REFORMS ON THE CHINESE NAVY

By Ian Burns McCaslin and Andrew S. Erickson

This chapter examines how China has come to declare itself a maritime country and how the reforms of the People's Liberation Army (PLA) under Xi Jinping affect the navy's ability to protect and advance China's maritime interests and its own organizational interests. It examines the context within which China's maritime evolution is occurring, explores three vectors of naval modernization, and considers the difference that PLA reforms might make for each. Xi, general-secretary of the Chinese Communist Party, chairman of the Central Military Commission (CMC), and commander in chief of the armed forces, has stated that his "China Dream" includes a "strong military dream" and has tasked the PLA to be able to fight and win informationized wars. In pursuit of this goal, Xi has implemented ambitious reforms intended to force collaboration between the services and improve their ability to conduct joint operations. The PLA Navy (PLAN) stands to benefit from a reduction in traditional ground force dominance, but the reforms may also shift the trajectory of naval modernization efforts in directions less supportive of an independent navy.

This chapter is organized in five sections. The first frames China's maritime development by examining its strategic drivers. The second outlines the navy's three vectors of modernization: hardware and "software" developments aimed at creating a blue-water navy capable of power projection; creation of a maritime component that can work effectively with other services as part of a joint PLA; and further development of an "interagency" maritime force wherein the navy works with the coast guard, maritime militia, and other parts of the Chinese government to advance China's maritime sovereignty claims. Sections two, three, and four lay out each of these vectors and examine the impact of the reforms on it. The last section offers broad findings concerning the reform of China's sea forces and related implications, with particular focus on the tensions among the three modernization vectors.

Strategic Drivers of China's Maritime Development

"Reform and Opening Up," "Going Out," and "New Historic Missions"

Since Deng Xiaoping ushered in the policy of "Reform and Opening Up" in late 1978, the People's Republic of China (PRC) has become increasingly integrated into the global economy. China took full advantage of opportunities provided by globalization, with foreign companies investing in China to tap cheap labor and Chinese state and private companies gradually developing the expertise and technology to produce for export markets. Rapid economic growth increased Chinese demand for imported components, oil and natural gas, and food and tied the employment of millions of Chinese workers to exports. China's integration with the global economy received a further boost when Hu Jintao urged Chinese companies to "go out" into the world by investing abroad to acquire natural resources and technology and to compete for foreign construction contracts.[1]

The growing importance of sea-borne trade and increased PRC investment and citizen presence overseas, some in unstable places, prompted Beijing to take measures to secure its new interests. In 2004, Hu Jintao gave the PLA "New Historic Missions," including defending China's expanding international interests.[2] Under this aegis, the PLA Navy has conducted counterpiracy patrols in the Gulf of Aden since December 2008 and participated in evacuations of PRC citizens during unrest in Libya and Yemen. Social media and press coverage have produced growing calls for the Chinese government to better protect PRC citizens abroad.[3] China's overseas presence has continued to deepen with Xi Jinping's Belt and Road Initiative, an ambitious plan to fund infrastructure construction to increase China's connectivity with Eurasia and the rest of the world. The initiative now even includes an additional maritime component, a proposed "Polar Silk Road" through the Arctic Ocean.[4]

Navy Primed to Take Advantage of China's New Orientation

Of all the services, the navy was best positioned to exploit the increasing importance of the outside world. The navy has long worked to articulate the importance of Chinese maritime interests and to advocate for a more capable navy to protect these interests.[5] PLAN leaders like Vice Admiral Chen Ming-shan have argued since the early 1990s that the navy is "a direct defender of its [China's] economy, especially its maritime economy and foreign trade."[6] Chinese analysts have insisted that the navy needs capabilities "to protect [China's] long and increasingly vital maritime energy supply lines."[7] PLAN publications such as *Modern Navy*[8] have emphasized topics such as "maritime resources" more frequently than mainstream civilian publications and general defense publications.[9] The Chinese maritime lobby has grown to include officials in maritime provinces, state-owned and private firms reliant on overseas trade, companies that build equipment and technology used to seize and build on claimed areas, and military and civilian organizations charged with seizing, building, and administering claimed areas.[10]

The navy not only leveraged the growing importance of the sea for China's economy but also stressed the growing importance of China's maritime and sovereignty claims. China's three highest profile sovereignty disputes (Taiwan, South China Sea, and East China Sea) all involve islands or other physical features surrounded by vast bodies of water. The navy and marines have occupied physical features in the Paracels and the Spratlys for decades. As maritime and sovereignty disputes in the South China Sea and East China Sea intensified after 2012, the navy took center stage in defending China's interests. Efforts by the Chinese naval and maritime lobby to emphasize the growing importance of Chinese maritime interests helped attract resources for naval modernization and culminated in the 18th Party Congress work report in November 2012 that set the task of "building China into a sea power nation."[11]

Calls for greater efforts to protect Chinese maritime interests were supported by rapid economic growth following China's reform and opening up that enabled the PLA to receive double-digit budget increases for decades. Higher budgets benefited all PLA services, but the navy received an increasing share of the defense budget beginning in 2004, allowing it to create and expand a fleet of modern warships and aircraft. Improved underwater, surface, and aerial platforms have allowed the navy to operate farther from the PRC more frequently and for longer periods of time. Given exposure from port calls, international military exercises, and its increasing presence in the South China Sea, East China Sea, and Indian Ocean, the navy has in many ways become the face of the PLA to the world.

Chinese Naval Modernization

China's naval modernization can be analyzed in terms of three vectors of modernization. The first involves hardware and "software" developments aimed at creating a blue-water navy capable of power projection. The second is creation of a potent maritime component that can work effectively with other services to achieve operational synergies as part of a joint PLA capable of fighting and winning wars against advanced militaries. The third is further development of an "interagency" maritime force where the navy works with the coast guard, maritime militia (which the U.S. Department of Defense refers to as the People's Armed Force's Maritime Militia), and other parts of the Chinese government to advance China's maritime sovereignty claims. Each vector is driven by certain factors, is supported by certain actors, emphasizes different missions, and is optimized for use in different areas. As resources are finite, any increase in resources for one particular vector potentially reduces those available for the others, thereby affecting the composition of the navy and its capacity to perform other missions.[12] The table illustrates key aspects of each vector.

Table. Three Modernization Vectors for the PLA Navy			
	Blue-Water Navy	Joint Operations Force for the Maritime Domain	"Interagency" Maritime Force
Type/Mode of Operation	Combined-arms naval operations	Joint operations	Sovereignty claim advancement operations
Maritime Challenges	SLOC protection, far-seas defense, power projection, military diplomacy	War vs. high-tech adversary, Taiwan, ECS, long-range piece of joint campaign	Maritime territorial disputes, regional naval clashes
Missions	ASuW, ASW, strike, amphibious operations, nuclear deterrence	ASuW, ASW, strike, transportation, amphibious operations, nuclear deterrence	Presence, deterrence, C2, escalation control
Partners	Navy branches	Other services	CCG, PAFMM, MoFA, SOEs
What Do Partners Provide?	Nothing	ASBMs, long-range strike, manpower for land ops., air control, air defense, airlift, cyberspace capabilities, counter-space	White hulls, fishing vessels, deniability, messaging, numbers (swarming), asymmetric approach

Key: SLOC: sea lines of communication; ASuW: anti-surface warfare; ASW: anti-submarine warfare; ECS: East China Sea; ASBM: anti-ship ballistic missile; C2: command and control; CCG: China coast guard; PAFMM: People's Armed Forces Maritime Militia; MoFA: Ministry of Foreign Affairs; SOE: state-owned enterprise.

First Vector: Blue-Water Navy

Possession of a blue-water navy has been the "blue dream" of every great power since technology made such fleets possible.[13] A blue-water fleet is commonly seen as the epitome of naval development, with the ability to operate far from the homeland and perform combined arms naval operations. In the Chinese context, such a fleet would allow the navy to operate independently to address the maritime challenges of protecting sea lines of communication, far-seas defense, power projection, and military diplomacy in distant seas. It would also require the navy to perform the missions of antisurface warfare, anti-submarine warfare, strike, amphibious operations, and nuclear deterrence.

The navy has been working for decades to create its own blue-water fleet. This involves two main elements: hardware modernization (military equipment) and software modernization (education, training, doctrine, and so forth). This vector of modernization supports PLAN interests by providing a rationale for moving beyond its original role as a support force for the army toward an independent operational capability.

Building the Fleet

The navy had been undergoing modernization for decades prior to Xi's reforms. Early Soviet (1950–1960), later American (1980s), and post–Cold War Russian (1991–present) assistance for Chinese naval modernization have been largely supplanted by efforts to replace foreign equipment and tech-nology with indigenously developed or improved Chinese versions. Soviet support created an initial foundation for the navy, both in terms of hardware and personnel training.[14] However, the withdrawal of Soviet advisors in 1960 and the Western technology blockade forced China to rely on indigenous efforts to reverse-engineer foreign technology and to make incremental improvements on Soviet designs. Rapprochement with the United States eventually allowed China access to some Western arms and military tech-nology, but this window largely closed after the Tiananmen massacre in 1989, when the United States and Europe imposed bans on arms sales to China.

Improved relations with the Soviet Union in the late 1980s and its eventual breakup gave the Chinese military and defense industry access to advanced weapons such as the *Kilo*-class submarine, Su-27 fighter (assembled in China, then reverse-engineered and produced as the J-11), *Sovremmeny*-class destroyers (and their advanced antiship cruise mis-siles), and S-300 surface-to-air missile systems. The combination of broad improvements in China's technology base, direct access to advanced Russian weapons, assistance from weapons scientists from the former Soviet Union, and industrial espionage helped the Chinese defense industry assimilate advanced technologies into more advanced weapons systems.

Rapid economic growth spurred on by Deng's reform and opening up initiative provided both technology and resources that allowed the PLA to import greater numbers of more advanced equipment and weapons and procure the increasingly advanced weapons produced by the Chinese defense industry. The PLA's limited ability to respond to the deployment of two U.S. carriers during the 1995–1996 Taiwan Strait crisis and the accidental bombing of the Chinese embassy in Belgrade in 1999 during the Kosovo War persuaded Chinese leadership to increase funding for military modernization. Preparing for a potential invasion or blockade of Taiwan in the face of U.S. intervention became the chief scenario for PLA planning and force modernization, with the maritime aspects of the Taiwan scenario supporting PLAN efforts to procure a range of advanced weapons systems.

China's naval modernization includes the development and deployment of advanced surface ships, submarines, aircraft and aircraft carriers, and amphibious vessels that will improve the PLAN ability to conduct a range of missions. China's shipyards are now launching new ships at a brisk pace, but have also shifted to focus on "quality over quantity."[15] The old surface fleet, based on largely antiquated 1950s Soviet technology with some indigenous improvements, is being replaced with new advanced vessels, such as the Type 054/054A frigate, Type 052C/D destroyer, and cruiser-sized Type 055 destroyer. These vessels feature advanced weapons and modern design features such as vertical launch systems capable of launching different types of antiship, antiaircraft, and land-attack missiles, phased-array radars, and improved air and cruise missile defenses.[16] The navy had no corvettes prior to 2014, but had 37 Type 056/056A ships as of November 2017.[17]

The notoriously noisy PLAN submarines have been gradually reducing their noise footprint.[18] The submarine force consists primarily of diesel-powered attack submarines, most of which are capable of launching advanced antiship cruise missiles. The navy has also added 10 nuclear submarines to the force since 2002, including 6 longer range nuclear-powered attack submarines, and 4 nuclear-powered ballistic missile submarines (SSBNs). The submarine force may grow to between 69 and 78 submarines by 2020.[19]

China's first aircraft carrier, the *Liaoning* (Type 001), began sea trials in August 2011 and was declared combat ready in November 2016. The *Liaoning* carries J-15 fighters that launch off its ski jump–style flight deck. The navy is currently developing two more advanced aircraft carriers, with the Type 001A carrier beginning sea trials in May 2018.[20] The planned inclusion of an integrated propulsion system on the Type 002 aircraft carrier, which would support an electromagnetic aircraft launch system, could allow more rapid aircraft launches.[21] Xinhua hailed the launch of China's first carrier as a symbolic step forward: "building a strong navy that is commensurate with China's rising status is a necessary step and an inevitable choice for the country to safeguard its increasingly globalized national interests."[22]

Due to their value and vulnerability to attack, aircraft carriers typically operate as part of a carrier group with multiple vessels protecting and supporting them.[23] The navy has made clear its intent to establish carrier groups by rushing production of the Type 055 destroyer. The Type 055 destroyers will join the growing array of vessels and weapon systems that will provide Chinese carriers protection against air and cruise missile attack and allow them to operate more safely outside the range of land-based aircraft. The navy has also been producing a new type of large replenishment ship, the Type 901, which is similar in size to those used by the U.S. Navy.[24] The production of such support vessels is particularly important given the continuing poor ratio of support vessels to frontline ships of the navy, especially when compared with the U.S. Navy.[25]

The navy has also been deploying new ships to improve its limited amphibious capabilities. These include semi-submersible amphibious landing vessels, the Type 726A air-cushioned landing craft, and the Type 071 landing platform dock. The new ships, coupled with the PLA Navy Marine Corps expansion to add additional marine brigades, should significantly improve PLAN amphibious warfare capabilities.[26]

Creating a "New Type" of Sailor for the New Navy: Recruiting, Educating, and Training

Naval modernization also requires talented personnel capable of executing independent and joint operations far from the country's shores. The service and its branches have reformed their efforts to recruit higher caliber personnel to fill their ranks, especially with graduates from civilian universities.[27] From 1999 onward, the navy planned to recruit 600 officers from civilian higher education institutions each year.[28] Naval aviation began recruiting its own personnel in 1988, an important step toward achieving independence from the PLA Air Force (PLAAF), which enabled it to educate and train individuals for aeronautical operations in the maritime domain from the beginning of their careers.[29]

The navy has also reformed the education and training of recruits. Since 1987, the navy has utilized the training ship *Zheng He*, a "classroom at sea," to help train its cadets.[30] This ship has been an "especially prolific traveler," even embarking on the first circumnavigation of the world by a Chinese navy training ship in mid-2012.[31] This has allowed the navy to give thousands of cadets hands-on experience in a variety of maritime environments around the world.[32] The navy has also recently added a "tall ship," the *Polang*, as well as the advanced naval training ships, *Qi Jiguang* and *Yupeng*. These ships and the push for naval personnel to undergo "tempering" on a vessel allowed the navy to provide onboard experience for 92 percent of the 3,000 "new soldiers" trained by the South Sea Fleet from 2011 to 2012.[33] To give its aviators at-sea experience, the navy launched the air training ship *Shichang* in 1996.[34] The PLAN aviation training base at Huangdicun has added land-based facilities and equipment, such as ski jumps on runways, to allow pilots to practice carrier takeoffs and landings more safely, and added catapult launch systems to support training for the Type 002 carrier.[35]

Similarly, the navy created Vessel Training Centers in the 1980s for each of its fleets to provide more detailed and vessel-specific training, facilitating the introduction of new classes of ships. The centers can assemble military personnel, industry representatives, and other experts to help create an "Outline for Military Training and Evaluation" specific to each class of vessel to accelerate training for the first crews.[36] This was seen with the *Bengbu*, the first *Jiangdao*-class (Type 056) corvette to be introduced to the East Sea Fleet.[37]

An increased operational tempo contributes to training of the force. *China Daily* stated that "each year every combat vessel and submarine will spend nearly eight months at sea, carrying out patrols, drills, and training. Every day, dozens of aircraft, more than 100 ships and submarines, and thousands of navy personnel are in operation."[38] Since December 2008, PLAN activity has included continuous deployment of an escort task force in the Gulf of Aden to conduct escort and counterpiracy operations. This high operations tempo is paralleled by more port calls and increased participation in international military exercises. The navy only conducted 11 port calls from 2003 to 2008, but conducted 40 in 2015 alone. The navy has also led the way in international military exercises. From 2003 to 2016, the navy conducted almost half of all international military exercises that involved the PLA, more than any other service. The navy has also begun to participate in multilateral exercises such as the U.S. Rim of the Pacific exercise series.[39]

A growing number of these exercises, especially those with Russia, include combat or combat-support elements. The navy "completed its first overseas joint beach landing drill" as part of the Joint Sea–2015 exercise in Russia.[40] Sino-Russian naval exercises are being held in new locations, such as in the Baltic Sea, Mediterranean Sea, and Sea of Okhotsk, expanding the operational horizons of the navy. Some Sino-Russian naval exercises have expanded to include combined arms operations with the participation of multiple branches.[41] Spurred on by their increasing experience and confidence, some navy officers have even begun using run-ins with foreign forces as training opportunities, and they have been recognized and rewarded for their actions.[42]

All these exercises and training have begun to pay off as the traditionally strict control by senior officers is starting to relax, giving operational commanders more flexibility. Submarine units have been applauded in recent military media reports for undertaking significant operations without additional senior officers onboard, whose presence often reduced the captain of a submarine to a "duty officer."[43] Naval aviation began introducing greater "pilot autonomy" back in 2013, marking a shift from "nanny-style" control of pilots by superior officers.[44]

Years after the army first established special operations forces (SOF) units in the 1980s, the navy finally established its own SOF regiment in the South Sea Fleet.[45] This regiment has been able to gain operational experience from the navy's antipiracy patrols, which have included a SOF contingent with every flotilla.[46] PLA SOF operators have also benefited from the establishment of the Special Operations Academy in Guangzhou and have sought to gain experience from foreign units by participating in international SOF competitions.[47] The navy's SOF regiment is augmented by smaller units established in at least two marine corps brigades.[48]

The PLA marines corps functions as the naval infantry branch of the navy but has recently established a separate headquarters and is expanding its number of operational brigades as part of PLA reforms. The marines were relatively late in joining the rest of the PLA in exercising abroad but performed their first overseas exercise in Thailand in 2010.[49] The marines also appear to now have their own helicopters, which had previously been provided by naval aviation.[50] The Marine Corps College now boasts more than 20 professional programs, an educated faculty, and simulation training systems.[51] Faculty are being encouraged to participate in exercises to rectify their lack of combat and operational experience.[52]

Other branches such as naval aviation are making similar efforts to improve education and training to produce officers and seaman capable of operating modern weapons. To leverage carriers, the Naval Aviation Academy and Naval Aeronautical Engineering Institute have been combined to form the Naval Aviation University/Naval Aeronautical University, which will train China's carrier-based fighter pilots.[53] The new university has recruited 450 pilot cadets, which will eventually translate into a significant boost in naval aviation personnel to support the deployment of more carriers.[54] Naval aviation has also changed the way it trains pilots to emphasize extended daytime and nighttime operations and increasing flights over water and at low altitudes.[55] To improve the quality and realism of training, naval aviation held its first actual combat confrontation exercise between different aircraft models in 2011.[56]

Impact of Reforms on the Blue-Water Navy Vector of Modernization

The reforms have three main effects on the blue-water navy vector of modernization: altering the role of the services, assigning operational control to the theater commands, and improving PLA education, training, and personnel systems. First, the services are now responsible for force-building rather than operations. This should reduce the operational role of navy headquarters. However, the navy appears to be utilizing several methods to keep a not-insignificant role in operations. PLAN headquarters appears to have retained operational responsibility for counterpiracy deployments to the Gulf of Aden. The headquarters role in force-building and setting naval training requirements allows the navy to use training exercises to maintain an operational role, since virtually anything can be promoted as having "training" value. The navy refers to this as moving from "separation of training and operations" [*xunzhan fenli*, 训战分离] to "embedding training in operations" [*yizhan zaixun*, 以战载训].[57] The navy headquarters also appears to be using tri-fleet exercises, which do not fall under the responsibility of any particular theater command, as another way to hold onto some operational responsibilities.[58] An unintended consequence of attempting to relegate service headquarters to training and force-building is that it frees time and resources for the headquarters to advocate for the interests of its individual service.[59] Such lobbying is more important as the Chinese economy slows, which has already led to slowdowns in military budget growth. For the navy, this could lead to clashes with the other services and with the new theater commands, which have their own distinct interests. Some platforms, like land-based aircraft, are highly relevant for the Eastern Theater Command in planning for the invasion of Taiwan, while blue-water systems such as aircraft carriers are less relevant. It remains unclear how such discrepancies in interests will be resolved.

The second major impact, placing the theater commands in charge of operations, reduces the navy's autonomy in conducting operations. It also complicates operations to protect China's maritime sovereignty claims by adding another bureaucratic actor into the mix, especially if a non-navy officer is in charge of the theater. However, the navy has used theater command geographic constraints to lead some operations. The Indian Ocean, for example, falls outside of the geographic jurisdiction of the theater commands, giving the navy headquarters a strong case for continued leadership in counterpiracy operations, even if these have joint elements.[60] Port calls and exercises with foreign militaries also fall outside the geographic responsibilities of the theater commands, giving navy headquarters another opportunity. However, while navy headquarters can task its components to meet certain requirements through training, the theater commands nominally control naval forces within their jurisdiction and may have different priorities. This situation is complicated by the fact that the service chiefs are no longer on the CMC but are now theater-leader grade, putting them on equal footing with the heads of the theater commands.[61] Neither side has the authority to force the other to follow orders. It is unclear whether one of the CMC vice chairmen, or perhaps even Xi himself, will arbitrate such disputes.

While the Joint Staff Department Overseas Operations Office coordinates army peacekeeping operations, the navy appears to control its far-seas operations.[62] This might be partly due to the unique nature of navies and the history of "independent command at sea" that they cherish.[63] Despite the increasing number of military diplomacy activities and exercises involving naval forces, the theater commands do not appear to have been able to curtail these activities to increase focus on joint training and theater-specific missions.[64]

The third major impact of the reforms on this vector of modernization involves personnel issues. Some of the most important aspects of the reforms and anticorruption campaign have to do with career paths and the health of the military force as a whole. As of April 2018, PLA personnel have received two pay increases since Xi announced the 300,000-troop cut in September 2015.[65] How any military deals with its veterans is of immense importance for recruiting and for the morale of existing active-duty personnel. The PLA has historically been parsimonious toward honoring commitments to its veterans.[66] To address these shortcomings, Xi announced that the government would "set up an agency that will manage veterans and protect their legal rights and interests,"[67] and a new Ministry of Veterans Affairs was established to care for the PLA's 57 million retired personnel.[68] Ensuring fair treatment of veterans will help "make a career in the military one that is revered and respected by all."[69] As subsequent large-scale veterans protests have demonstrated, this is still one area where the armed forces and civilian government are struggling.[70]

The anticorruption crackdown within the PLA may also make a military career more attractive and respected. While the campaign has often selectively removed individuals who were seen as potentially disloyal to the Party or to Xi himself, many of those individuals were nonetheless spectacularly corrupt.[71] The anticorruption campaign has helped officers who resented the negative effects corruption has had on the PLA, those unable to afford the bribes necessary to advance within a corrupt system, and junior officers who can advance more quickly to fulfill positions vacated by corrupt officers.[72] This should allow professional military criteria to become more important for career advancement, especially for the officer corps.

Second Vector: Naval Component of a Joint Force

The PLA is a "latecomer" to joint operations.[73] Its first and only real joint operation was the attack and conquest of the Yijiangshan Islands in 1955.[74] An effective joint force, in the Chinese context, can respond to the maritime challenges of war against a high-tech adversary, an attempted conquest of Taiwan or the Senkakus, and the long-range aspect of joint campaigns in the near seas. Officers have acknowledged that the PLA must become more joint, which is seen as a fundamental part of modern warfare.[75] For this to happen, the concept of winning as a joint force must replace the old concept of a "single service victory" [*danyi junzhong zhisheng,* 单一军种制胜].[76] The push for jointness has undercut the army's traditional dominance of the PLA to the benefit of the other services. While the navy looks to be a big winner under the reforms, interservice rivalry and competition for resources and missions remain powerful obstacles to jointness and may have some negative impact on navy interests. Moreover, jointness implies that naval operations will be conducted via joint command and control structures, potentially undercutting the navy's efforts to develop more autonomy and the ability to conduct its own combined arms operations in the far seas.

Joint Education and Training

The PLA's conceptualization of jointness involves achieving victory by fusing the "operational strengths" of the separate services together to achieve collectively what no service could accomplish alone.[77] Jointness received a much-needed boost following the ground force–dominated PLA's inability to respond effectively to the U.S. Navy's sending two aircraft carrier battle groups toward Taiwan in March 1996. The role of airpower in the Kosovo War and sea power in the Falklands War impressed upon the PLA the strategic importance of other services.[78] However, despite frequent mention of jointness in articles and internal publications, the reality of jointness still lags far behind the rhetoric.

The PLA has tried to rectify the imbalance among the services by adding the commanders of other services to the CMC (2004–2017) and by increasing students and faculty from services other than the army at PLA National Defense University and the Academy of Military Science. The presence of these officers was intended to facilitate joint thinking by ensuring that non-army perspectives are included in the classroom and in important debates.

PLA texts acknowledge that China's armed forces still have a long way to go to achieve true jointness.[79] Even with increased focus on educating joint commanders and theater command staff, joint experience remains a widely acknowledged weakness of the PLA as a whole.[80] Officers complain that the lack of joint command experience could reduce its joint commanders to mere "armchair strategists" [*zhishang tanbing*, 纸上谈兵].[81] The 2015 book *Theater Joint Operations Command* [*zhanqu lianhe zuozhan zhihui*, 战区联合作战指挥] suggested that the PLA should engage more in exchanges and exercises with foreign militaries to compensate for this lack of experience.[82] However, despite increasing PLA participation in international military exercises, only a few of these (a mere 7 percent from 2003–2016) involve two or more PLA services.[83] The navy has been most active in international exercises, but these are usually combined arms exercises with multiple navy branches rather than joint exercises with multiple PLA services.

Joint training between the various services continues to be limited, but some progress is being made.[84] The navy (including surface vessels, marines, and naval aviation) and air force participated together in a Sino-Russian international exercise, Joint Sea–2015 (II), for the first time in 2015.[85] However, in the words of one expert, "true joint interoperability remains largely a work in progress for the PLA."[86] The navy and air force are doing some joint training, most notably in name-brand exercises, such as Sharp Sword–2015.[87] In some of the highest profile joint exercises between naval aviation and air force, including Golden Helmet–2015, the two were actually competing against one another as opposing forces rather than working together.[88]

Training between the navy and army is also limited, though this appears to be changing as well. One example involves army aviation and naval aviation providing air support for marines during amphibious training exercises.[89] Another involves joint amphibious exercises with army amphibious and ground force units, which would provide the bulk of the troops for large-scale amphibious landings, such as an invasion of Taiwan.[90]

In reviewing PLA joint exercises, press reports highlight "cases in which PLA commanders were not well-versed in the wide range of capabilities at their disposal, failed to coordinate and share information among the units under their command, and demonstrated their weak command and organization skills."[91] The lack of qualified joint commanders and staff officers continues to plague China's armed forces.[92] Without significant progress, the PLA's lack of jointness will result in "deconflicted operations," where the services operate in proximity to, but not with, each other.[93]

Reduced Army Dominance

Recognition of the increasing value of the maritime domain and the push for jointness have benefited navy modernization efforts. One of the earliest indicators of a shift in attention and resources away from the army was the 2003 force reduction, when it took a disproportionate share of the cuts.[94] (Blasko's chapter in this volume argues that the army is the biggest loser in the current PLA personnel reductions, as the PLA places more emphasis on the other services.)

Decreasing army dominance can also be seen in the PLA's changing strategic outlook. When the 2002 defense white paper stated that the "primary missions" of each service were to be performed "independently or jointly," it simultaneously encouraged the services not only to work together jointly, but also to be able to operate on their own.[95] Non-army services received a further boost with the 2004 defense white paper, which explicitly stated the PLA would "enhance the development of its operational strength with priority given to the navy, air force, and Second Artillery Force."[96] Acknowledgment of the important role non-army services would play in an invasion of Taiwan also gave the navy a new toehold in operational planning.

While the navy's focus has gradually shifted outward from coastal to offshore defense, establishment of an "active defense" strategy for the PLA saw the military leadership formally inaugurate a shift in focus from China and its immediately periphery, which favored the army, toward "open seas protection," which favors the navy.[97] These changes were illustrated in the 2013 edition of the *Science of Military Strategy* that argued, "the main threat of war has already shifted from traditional inland direction to the ocean direction." In addition, the "strong enemy," a common PLA euphemism for the United States, "will rely on its comprehensive distant combat superiority from the ocean direction." Under such circumstances, it will be "increasingly difficult to protect the homeland from the homeland and the near seas from near seas, it might even become untenable." Therefore, defensive operations should be pushed farther away from Chinese territory.[98] Efforts to "push forward the strategic frontier" to gain additional strategic space boosted the navy because the geography of the region means that additional strategic space is maritime space. As maritime concerns—such as Taiwan, the South China Sea, and sea-borne trade—have grown over the years, the navy appears to have been increasingly successful at capitalizing on them to bolster itself as a service.

The push for jointness has opened new opportunities for the navy to make itself relevant for additional missions. The service has moved beyond its initial coastal defense and sealift missions into missions ranging from interdiction to amphibious operations to nuclear deterrence.

Increased Competition for Maritime Missions

The increased priority of maritime missions not only favors the navy, but has also encouraged other services to encroach on PLAN turf by highlighting the relevance of their own current and future capabilities to the maritime domain. The navy has responded by further developing its own ability to perform "diversified tasks" to reduce the need for help from the other services.[99] These trends highlight the tension between the navy's desire to be able to conduct independent operations (especially in blue water far from China's coast) and the potential for other services to contribute useful capabilities in a joint operational context.

As growth in PLA budgets has slowed, the air force, army, and even Rocket Force are attempting to carve out new maritime responsibilities (and associated budget claims). The air force has made the clearest effort to ensure that it is not left out of the new emphasis on the maritime domain. In the past few years, it has taken significant steps to emphasize operations over water, the traditional domain of the navy and naval aviation.[100] This has been marked by a number of firsts, including flights over the Western Pacific through new air corridors,[101] PLAAF H-6K bombers practicing attacks on Guam,[102] and deploying some of the air force's most advanced aircraft, such as the Su-35, to the South China Sea. The air force has also expanded the role of its vessel troops to support maritime combat operations.[103] A professor from the Air Force Command Academy stated that South China Sea deployments showed PLAAF "resolution to implement missions in the new era and firmly maintain national sovereignty and security and maritime interests."[104]

The air force has overhauled training for its pilots to emphasize operations over water, including those farther from shore.[105] These included the creation of new textbooks, including *A Practical Handbook on Maritime Live-Fire Training with Trainer Aircraft* and *Safety Checklist for Maritime Live-Fire Training.*[106] Classroom work has been augmented by "regular high seas training" that began in 2015.[107] The air force has held seminars attended by senior officers to review its progress in overwater training.[108] These efforts put the air force in direct competition with the navy for maritime missions and resources.

The air force has followed the PLAN lead in using the need to protect China's economic interests as an argument to support its strategic relevance. Then–PLAAF Commander Ma Xiaotian gave a speech in 2014 emphasizing the importance of airpower for the maritime domain. According to Ma, "[W]inning the initiative in the air is important in effectively responding to all kinds of security threats at sea. . . . [We must] fully recognize the new circumstances in the defense of maritime rights; [it] gives the air force new meaning to accelerate the transition from territorial air defense toward attack and defense. . . . [We must] transform the 'center of gravity' of sea operations toward the employment of airpower."[109]

The air force is acquiring two types of aircraft that will expand its maritime capabilities. The first is the Y-20 long-range transport, which can carry paratroopers and their equipment to the remote physical features controlled by China in the South China Sea.[110] Paratroopers have conducted simulated airdrops over "unfamiliar island targets" in exercises.[111] The second is the acquisition of additional and updated tankers, such as the IL-78/

MIDAS, to augment its small and aging fleet of tankers.[112] Expansion of the PLAAF tanker fleet, including the rumored development of a tanker variant of the Y-20, would increase the range of PLAAF fighters, surveillance aircraft, and bombers, improving their ability to operate far over the ocean from land bases in China.[113]

By contrast, the army has found it harder to carve out a maritime role. Although Taiwan has been the main driver of PLA modernization for decades, the army only had one amphibious tank brigade in 1997.[114] The army's amphibious force has grown since then, but these units only spend 3 to 4 months a year on amphibious operations, with the rest of their time spent on nonamphibious training.[115] In 2010, only one army ship group was exclusively focused on amphibious support.[116] However, it has been trying to make itself more relevant for maritime missions. Army amphibious units have traditionally focused on the conquest of Taiwan, where the need for large numbers of ground troops would guarantee it a prominent role. PLAN marines have primary responsibility for amphibious operations involving smaller physical features, such as the land features that dot the South China Sea. However, the army has recently suggested that it could too have a role in capturing and holding smaller islands.[117]

Even the Rocket Force, the "hermit" of the PLA, is pushing into the maritime domain. Its control of the PLA's land-based antiship ballistic missiles (ASBM) represents another attempt by a land-based service to "use the land to control the sea" [*yi luzhihai*, 以陆制海].[118] Literature from the Second Artillery Force (now the Rocket Force) has been overwhelmingly positive on the development and future utility of ASBMs, while PLAN analysts have been more pessimistic about the weapon's value.[119] The DF-21D ASBM, dubbed the "carrier-killer," is an obvious attempt to credibly hold U.S. carriers at risk. It is joined by the Rocket Force's DF-26, which also has an ASBM variant and has the range to target U.S. facilities on Guam.[120]

The Rocket Force can also use its arsenal of conventional ballistic missiles to hit maritime-relevant land targets, such as ports. The 2006 edition of *The Science of Campaigns* discussed how conventional cruise missiles can be used to "implement sea blockades" and "capture localized campaign sea superiority."[121] Other tactics, such as a "missile fire blockade" [*daodan huoli fengsuo*, 导弹火力封锁], can disrupt facilities important for naval forces, such as ports and relevant airfields.[122] While these efforts could be done jointly in coordination with the navy and air force, the Rocket Force could also conduct such campaigns independently, inserting itself into operations for "sea blockades" and "sea dominance."[123]

This competition for roles and missions goes both ways. The navy now has submarines that can compete with Rocket Force conventional and nuclear assets. The navy has four SSBNs armed with nuclear intercontinental ballistic missiles and attack submarines that can carry land-attack cruise missiles.[124] Such assets allow the navy to duplicate some Rocket Force capabilities, potentially with greater survivability than land-based Rocket Force assets. The navy also has numerous surface vessels and aircraft armed with antiship cruise missiles, which give it a strong tool to beat back Rocket Force efforts to intrude too far onto navy turf.[125] These systems, and the Rocket Force's desire to maintain primacy in nuclear deterrence and long-range conventional strike missions, are likely to limit the Rocket Force's ability to carve out too much space in the maritime domain.[126] Despite the clear interest of other services in competing for maritime missions and associated resources, spending too much time on these missions may compromise their combat effectiveness in their primary missions.[127]

The final advantage the navy has over the other services in the maritime domain is presence. It is the only service that can operate assets on or over the high seas for long periods of time. It also has advantages in its ability to use overseas bases and commercial port facilities to provide logistics support for its peacetime operations. PLAN ability to launch and recover helicopters and planes from frigates and carriers allows it to maintain an air presence much longer than the air-refuelable land-based aircraft that the air force operates.[128] The navy can loiter under the waves, on the waves, and in the sky—something no other service can do.

Impact of Reforms on Joint Force Vector of Modernization

The reduction of army dominance presents new opportunities for the navy to promote its own interests, advocate for increased focus on Chinese maritime interests, and argue for new military capabilities to protect those interests. However, the intent to eliminate the operational role of the service headquarters and to conduct operations via joint command and control structures also implies a reduction in PLAN autonomy and increased competition for maritime roles and missions from other services.

The shifting of operational responsibilities away from the military regions and service headquarters to joint theater commands is perhaps the most significant operational change instituted by the reforms. The establishment of new joint command structures ends the PLA's reliance on army-dominated military regions and ad hoc wartime joint command structures. This shift, combined with placing some non-army officers in charge of theater commands (Navy Vice Admiral Yuan Yubai in the Southern Theater Command and PLAAF General Yi Xiaoguang in the Central Theater Command) and presence of non-army staff in all the theater commands, constitutes an important step toward a more joint force.

The role of theater commands in leading military operations within their geographic purview presents both a challenge and opportunity for the navy. If the head of a theater command is a naval officer, as in the Southern Theater Command, then the navy can theoretically run non-navy operations there and decide how to integrate relevant capabilities of other services into naval operations.[129] Even if another service is in charge of a theater command, each of the theater commands with a fleet (Northern, Eastern, and Southern) has a navy officer as a deputy commander in change of theater command naval forces. Much will depend on how much centralized control the theater commander exerts over the theater ground, naval, and air components and how much authority the commander is willing to delegate to his component commanders. The fact that army officers have little experience in commanding naval operations, and the fact that the navy can perform many of its near-seas missions using its own assets to conduct combined arms operations, suggests that navy component commanders are likely to retain a great deal of autonomy in most circumstances. Most PLA operations in the South China Sea, for example, are kept below the threshold where another country would respond with force. However, PLA planning for a Taiwan contingency, which would involve both coastal operations to support an amphibious landing and blue-water operations to delay U.S. intervention, would require the Eastern Theater Commander (currently an army officer) to make difficult choices about priorities.

Third Vector: "Interagency" Operations

China has a long history of drawing on military and militia vessels, as well as civilian ships and fishing boats, to compensate for its limited naval capabilities. However, in recent decades, the PLA has increasingly cooperated with other parts of the Chinese government and civilian actors to respond to maritime and territorial sovereignty disputes and possible regional naval clashes in the East China Sea and South China Sea. The heightened importance of the maritime domain and maritime sovereignty disputes, as well as the proven utility of other components of China's armed forces such as the coast guard and maritime militia in pressing Beijing's claims, have helped drive this vector of modernization. However, the other two vectors of modernization have also allowed the navy to build capabilities that strengthen its ability to conduct "interagency" operations.

These operations involve the navy working with the maritime militia and coast guard, as well as utilizing a network of bases and outposts throughout the South China Sea.[130] Civilian agencies are involved in some aspects: the Ministry of Foreign Affairs and state-run media, for instance, play an important role in shaping and propagating the narrative of the day.

Navy Leading from Behind

China's approach to the South China Sea involves seeking to use a range of military, paramilitary, legal, and administrative tactics to expand Chinese control of disputed features and waters, while minimizing the chances of military conflict breaking out. The PRC has adopted three lines of "defense" in this effort, with the maritime militia as the first, maritime law enforcement agencies as the second, and the PLA (especially the navy) as the third.[131] While the navy is deliberately kept away from the frontline to minimize escalation risks, it played a significant role in crafting the strategy and continues to directly and indirectly support the other actors.[132]

China's maritime militia has always been an integral component of China's maritime forces, and in recent years, its importance and interactions with the navy have increased significantly.[133] The maritime militia has benefited from a generous building program that has seen its branches acquire new, large steel-hulled vessels.[134] Trends seen in the PLA at large, such as a shift toward greater professionalism and phasing out less advanced units, are also evident in the maritime militia.[135] Leading personnel in the maritime militia are being militarized, professionalized, and incentivized; the organization can now call on elite units for more specialized and challenging tasks. Some maritime militia branches have become so well trained and are so useful that they have even been referred to as a "veritable 'light cavalry.'"[136] Some maritime militia detachments have developed specialized combat support and technical skills to better aid the navy in operations.[137] While the maritime militia organization has a limited ability to engage in high-end warfare, it is optimized for sovereignty advancement operations that stay below the threshold of military conflict.[138]

The navy also has been closely tied to the coast guard since the latter was formed by merging several different maritime law enforcement agencies. Its role in protecting disputed Chinese maritime and sovereignty claims and projecting Chinese domestic law into disputed waters have led many to call it "China's second navy."[139] The PLA influenced its creation, and the navy plays a significant role in planning, coordinating, and conducting coast guard operations.[140] Like the maritime militia, coast guard vessels have been significantly upgraded in recent years. Some are actually former PLAN vessels with some weapons systems removed.[141] Some larger coast guard vessels even have 76mm main guns, among other armaments.[142]

The maritime militia and coast guard have carried out several successful interagency operations against foreign countries in cooperation with the navy. Two examples are the *Impeccable* incident in March 2009 and HYSY-981 oil rig incident in May–July 2014.

Impeccable *Incident, March 8–9, 2009.* The *Impeccable* incident involved the USNS *Impeccable*, an ocean surveillance ship that was shadowed and harassed by Chinese vessels that maneuvered in ways that threatened its safety. The Chinese ships and aircraft involved included a PLAN frigate, Fisheries Law Enforcement patrol vessel, State Oceanic Administration patrol vessel, two trawlers (one of which was from the Sanya maritime militia), and at least one Y-12 aircraft.[143] The Chinese action involved multiple military and civilian government organizations and maritime militia vessels, necessitating a certain level of coordination. Chinese vessels came dangerously close to the *Impeccable*, dropped objects directly in its path, tried to snag its acoustics equipment, and even obstructed it after it announced it was trying to leave the area.[144] At one point a Chinese Y-12 buzzed the *Impeccable* 11 times.[145] The Chinese operation was reportedly led by then-head of the Fisheries Law Enforcement's South China Sea Bureau, Wu Zheng.[146] Given the variety of Chinese assets and their close proximity to each other and to the *Impeccable*, a high degree of communication and control was necessary to coordinate actions and avoid collisions.

HYSY-981 Oil Rig Incident, May 2–July 15, 2014. The HYSY-981 oil rig incident is China's largest and most sophisticated "Three-Sea-Force" operation to date.[147] Throughout the operation, China maintained between 110 and 115 vessels around the oil rig in an approximately 10 nautical mile cordon. These included four navy vessels, 35 to 40 coast guard ships, 30 transport and tugs, and more than 40 maritime militia vessels.[148] While the cordon radiated about 10 nautical miles out from the rig, the Chinese side utilized maritime militia and "fishing vessels" to harass, and in some cases attack and sink, Vietnamese fishing vessels operating miles beyond the cordon.[149] During the incident, China was able to maintain around twice as many vessels as Vietnam did in the area.[150] Operating a cordon of so many vessels from so many different organizations over such a long period, while sending out skirmishing parties to attack Vietnamese vessels miles from the cordon, required careful coordination across multiple military and civilian organizations. This included cooperation with the China National Offshore Oil Corporation, a state-owned enterprise that owned and operated the HYSY-981 drilling platform.

The maritime militia was given mobilization orders for the operation by the Guangzhou Military Region. In the case of the participating Sansha City maritime militia, a sea command post was set up and a command and coordination group was sent to the coast guard's "forward command post at sea."[151]

China appears to plan to conduct more operations like these in the future. While the navy is the main military service involved in maritime sovereignty defense operations, at least one training event featured limited involvement by other services. A 2014 joint escort defense and joint oil rig defense exercise in the Gulf of Tonkin involved a maritime police unit under the navy's South Sea Fleet, personnel and vessels from fisheries, maritime police, and maritime militia, as well as aircraft from naval aviation and the air force. Just as in the HYSY-981 oil rig incident, a maritime command post was set up to help coordinate the effort. The exercise took the "defensive" actions utilized in the HYSY-981 oil rig a step further when fighter aircraft and surface vessels armed with missiles "destroyed" enemy vessels during the escort part of the mission. To defend the rig, the Chinese forces practiced blocking the passage of a "suspicious fishing boat" and shooting the water to prevent frogmen from getting close to the rig. The exercise ended with the arrest of "militants" and a journalist on the boat.[152] Although this example involved limited participation of the air force, the navy continues to regularly perform such drills without the participation of another service.

Artificial "Islands," More Than Just the "Big Three." While China's "Big Three" artificial islands in the South China Sea (Fiery Cross, Mischief, and Subi Reefs) have dominated the coverage of China's artificial island–building activities in the region, they are part of a larger network of Chinese bases and outposts scattered across the South China Sea.[153] While PLAAF aircraft might be able to operate from runways on the artificial islands, the navy regularly operates from both larger and smaller land features in cooperation with the coast guard, maritime militia, and other Chinese government organizations.

The 2013 edition of the *Science of Military Strategy* argued that China relies on islands and reefs to help create a "large-area maritime defense system" [*da quyu haishang fangwei tixi*, 大区域海上防卫体系] for power projection.[154] In addition to the large artificial islands that have harbors and airstrips, the smaller, but still vital, islands and reefs have facilities called "coastal defense militia outposts" [*haifang minbing shaosuo*, 海防民兵哨所], which are staffed by maritime militia and People's Armed Forces Department personnel, to monitor the maritime domain.[155] This type of force can help maintain a constant forward presence and play peacetime (and potentially wartime) operations roles that would be much more visible and sensitive if performed by military units.

Reform Impact on the Interagency Vector of Modernization

The PLA reforms have facilitated some aspects of interagency maritime operations but have also created new organizational roles and responsibilities that may complicate existing understandings and procedures. The reforms placed the coast guard under the authority of the People's Armed Police, which was itself subordinated to report solely to the CMC.[156] This gives the CMC the ability to issue orders to both the PLA and coast guard, facilitating interagency planning and operations. Certain elite and specialized branches of the maritime militia have also drawn much closer to the navy and coast guard in terms of funding, equipment, training, personnel, and coordination in recent years.[157] Such closer relations should help reduce the coordination burden in interagency maritime operations.

That said, the PRC appears to lack a permanent mechanism to coordinate operations of the maritime militia and coast guard with services other than the navy. Previous coordination mechanisms appear to have been run through PLAN headquarters and the three fleets, with no or limited involvement of the military regions. The establishment of new joint theater commands will require adjustments in these command and coordination mechanisms, which may be challenging since the theater commands have no natural channels to coordinate with national-level ministries and state-owned enterprises. The challenge is further increased because some maritime militia units are designed primarily for use in peacetime sovereignty advancement operations, while others are designed to provide support during combat operations. Given the high number of maritime militia branches and specialized units within those branches and the local nature of these branches, the lack of a mechanism to coordinate with non-PLAN services will limit the ability of these forces to contribute to joint operations with other services. For the time being, the navy will likely have to coordinate directly with the maritime militias and coast guard and then coordinate joint operations with the other services on behalf of China's maritime forces.

Conclusion

Like any large organization, the PLA is made up of different bureaucratic actors, each with its own interests. As with any military, there is disagreement among the services, and even between different branches of the same service, as to how the force should develop. The three vectors of modernization employed in this chapter are a useful device for highlighting these divergent interests and thinking about how they may affect decisions about PLA modernization in general, and navy modernization in particular.

We argue that there will be continued tension between the PLAN desire to create a blue-water navy optimized for independent operations in the far seas and the desire of the CMC and theater commands for a naval component that is optimized for joint operations and executing theater contingency plans. Theater commanders are likely to advocate for naval forces that suit the specific missions and geography of their region and use their operational control to focus the naval components in their theaters on those particular priorities. This tension will likely manifest itself in arguments over how PLAN headquarters and the theater commands want naval units to spend their time and potentially even what platforms are assigned to what theaters. However, because the interagency navy vector of modernization involves support for a high national priority (defending and advancing China's maritime sovereignty claims) and does not involve expensive weapons development requirements, this mission set is not likely to be a major focus of tensions between the headquarters and theater commands.

There will also be tension among the services over what level of joint-ness they are comfortable with, since true jointness will require each service to give up some of its autonomy and limit its ability to maximize its orga-nizational interests. The pursuit of joint synergies will inevitably involve creating new dependencies on other services to provide critical capabilities for joint operations. The logic of a blue-water navy whose different branches provide all the capabilities needed for far seas operations has inherent contradictions with the interdependence and cross-service coordination that are the essence of jointness. There may even be resentment between the navy and interagency maritime forces because resources going to the coast guard and maritime militia will not provide much support for the PLAN's own "blue dream." The navy's efforts to seeks an even greater role in the training, education, personnel, and operations of the coast guard and maritime militia may also remove the gossamer-thin façade that these forces are mainly concerned with maritime safety and fishing.

In the short-term, it is hard to tell how the various bureaucratic actors in the navy, PLA as a whole, interagency maritime force, and civilian gov-ernment will respond to the impacts of the reforms. The navy has made progress in all three vectors of modernization in recent years, as is evident in its improving capability to execute independent operations far from China's coastline, in the PLA's improving capability to execute joint operations, and in the interagency maritime force's capabilities to outclass the paramilitary or military forces of any other South China Sea claimant and to continue advancing China's maritime claims.

The longer term impact is even harder to predict. For the navy, the biggest factor will be how well it can sell itself as a service capable of contributing to the various missions each modernization vector is designed to serve. If the navy cannot convince Chinese and PLA leaders of the importance of a blue-water fleet, its efforts to develop blue-water capabilities will be hampered. If the navy does not play nice in pursuing jointness while holding off efforts of the other services to play greater roles in the maritime domain, it may find its roles and missions reduced along with its share of the budget. The navy could even lose out on resources if the interagency maritime force is too successful, with more resources going to the paramilitary and militia forces that are the frontline and public-facing elements of the maritime sovereignty defense strategy. On the whole, the reforms have provided new resources and new opportunities for the navy, but there are challenges on the horizon. How the navy meets them will decide its future as a service.

Notes

[1] Nargiza Salidjanova, *Going Out: An Overview of China's Outward Foreign Direct Investment* (Washington, DC: U.S.-China Security and Economic Review Commission, March 30, 2011).

[2] Daniel M. Hartnett, *The PLA's Domestic and Foreign Activities and Orientation* (Washington, DC: U.S.-China Economic and Security Review Commission, March 4, 2009), available at <www.uscc.gov/sites/default/files/3.4.09Hartnett.pdf>.

[3] Jonas Parello-Plesner and Mathieu Duchatel, *China's Strong Arm: Protecting Citizens and Assets Abroad* (New York: Routledge, 2015), 37–41.

[4] See "China Focus: China Publishes Arctic Policy, Eyeing Vision of 'Polar Silk Road,'" Xinhua Online, January 26, 2018, available at <www.xinhuanet.com/english/2018-01/26/c_136927327.htm>.

[5] See Christopher D. Yung, "The PLA Navy Lobby and Its Influence over China's Maritime Sovereignty Policies," in *PLA Influence on China's National Security Policymaking*, ed. Phillip C. Saunders and Andrew Scobell (Stanford: Stanford University Press, 2015), 286–292.

[6] Gordon Jacobs, "Chinese Naval Developments Post–Gulf War," *Jane's Intelligence Review* 5, no. 2 (February 1993), 82.

7 See Gabriel B. Collins, Andrew S. Erickson, and Lyle J. Goldstein, "Chinese Naval Analysts Consider the Energy Question," in *China's Energy Strategy: The Impact on Beijing's Maritime Policies*, ed. Gabriel B. Collins et al. (Annapolis, MD: China Maritime Studies Institute and the Naval Institute Press, 2008), 299.

8 While some experts translate *xiandai haijun* [现代海军] as *Modern Navy* or *Contemporary Navy*, the authors use the official English translation of *Navy Today*.

9 M. Taylor Fravel and Alexander Liebman, "Beyond the Moat: The PLAN's Evolving Interests and Potential Influence," in *The Chinese Navy: Expanding Capabilities, Evolving Roles*, ed. Phillip C. Saunders et al. (Washington, DC: NDU Press, 2011), 55–56.

10 For more on some of the civilian supporters and potential members of the maritime lobby, see Ian Burns McCaslin, *Role of the PLA in China's Foreign Policy and Behavior Abroad* (Singapore: National University of Singapore, 2016), 138–145.

11 See Wu Xiaoyan, *China's "Sea Power Nation" Strategy* (Stockholm: Institute for Security and Development Policy, 2014).

12 The extent to which this is a problem in practice depends on how fungible particular assets are across the three vectors of modernization.

13 For more on the attempts of non-Chinese powers in the modern era to build such fleets, see Andrew S. Erickson, Lyle J. Goldstein, and Carnes Lord, eds., *China Goes to Sea: Maritime Transformation in Comparative Historical Perspective* (Annapolis, MD: Naval Institute Press, 2009), 121–233.

14 From July 1949 to July 1960, the "Chinese Navy alone employed 3,390 Soviet advisers and experts." Soviet advisers and experts were critical because many Chinese officers knew little about the forces they were charged with commanding or the equipment they were supposed to use. See Zhihua Shen and Danhui Li, *After Leaning to One Side: China and Its Allies in the Cold War* (Stanford: Stanford University Press, 2011), 118–121.

15 A 2013 estimate by the U.S. Office of Naval Intelligence indicated that the PLA Navy could have between 313 and 342 warships (including submarines) by 2020. See Craig Murray, Andrew Berglund, and Kimberly Hsu, *China's Naval Modernization and Implications for the United States* (Washington, DC: U.S.-China Economic and Security Review Commission, August 26, 2013), 6–7. For more on the quality-over-quantity shift in navy vessels, see *The People's Liberation Army Navy: A Modern Navy with Chinese Characteristics* (Washington, DC: Office of Naval Intelligence, August 2009), 16–20.

[16] Gabe Collins and Andrew Erickson, "The Type 054/054A Frigate Series: China's Most Produced and Deployed Large Modern Surface Combatant," *China SignPost*, August 2, 2015, available at <www.chinasignpost.com/2015/08/02/the-type- 054054a-frigate-series-chinas-most-produced-and-deployed-large-modern-surface- combatant/>.

[17] Ronald O'Rourke, *China Naval Modernization: Implications for U.S. Navy Capabilities—Background and Issues for Congress*, RL33153 (Washington, DC: Congressional Research Service, May 21, 2018), 3.

[18] *The People's Liberation Army Navy*, 22–23.

[19] *Annual Report to Congress: Military and Security Developments Involving the People's Republic of China 2017* (Washington, DC: Office of the Secretary of Defense, May 15, 2017), 24.

[20] For a comparison of the China's first and second aircraft carrier, see "What Do We Know (So Far) about China's Second Aircraft Carrier?" *China Power*, available at <https://chinapower.csis.org/china-aircraft-carrier-type-001a/>.

[21] Minnie Chan, "Breakthrough to Power Most Advanced Jet Launch System on China's Second Home-Grown Aircraft Carrier," *South China Morning Post* (Hong Kong), November 1, 2017, available at <www.scmp.com/news/china/diplomacy-defence/article/2117947/breakthrough-power-most-advanced-jet-launch-system?utm_source=t.co&utm_medium=referral>.

[22] Chris Buckley, "China Launches First Aircraft Carrier on Maiden Sea Trial," Reuters, August 9, 2011, available at <www.reuters.com/article/us-china-military-carrier/china-launches-first-aircraft-carrier-on-maiden-sea-trial-idUSTRE77900D20110810>.

[23] A senior Chinese official stated in the mid-2000s that until recently carriers had "not been the best use of national resources" because the country lacked the platforms necessary for an "escort fleet." See Andrew S. Erickson and Andrew R. Wilson, "China's Aircraft Carrier Dilemma," in *China's Future Nuclear Submarine Force*, ed. Andrew S. Erickson et al. (Annapolis, MD: Naval Institute Press, 2007), 230.

[24] Andrew S. Erickson and Christopher P. Carlson, "Sustained Support: The PLAN Evolves Its Expeditionary Logistics Strategy," *Jane's Navy International*, March 9, 2016.

[25] The U.S. Navy enjoys a ratio of 1:5 of replenishment ships to frontline ships, while, as of December 2016, the PLA Navy only had a ratio of 1:15. See "PLAN First Type 901 Replenishment Oiler Started Sea Trails of Shenzhen, China," *Navy Recognition*, December 23, 2016, available at <www.navyrecognition.com/

index.php/news/defence-news/2016/december-2016-navy-naval-forces-defense-industry-technology-maritime-security-global-news/4720-plan-first-type-901-replenishment-oiler-started-sea-trials-off-shenzhen-china.html>.

26 "868 Semi-Submersible Vessel Enters Service in the South Sea Fleet Can Carry European Bison Which Will Impact Island Attack" [868号半潜船入役南海舰队可载欧洲野牛冲击岛礁], *ifeng.com* [凤凰网], July 13, 2015, available at <http://news.ifeng.com/a/20150713/44156468_0.shtml#p=1>; Henri Kenhmann, "China Launches Mass Production of the New LCAC Type 726A" [La Chine lance la production en série de son nouveau LCAC Type 726A], *East Pendulum*, February 5, 2017, available at <www.eastpendulum.com/la-chine-lance-la-production-en-serie-de-son-nouveau-lcac-type-726a>; Andrew Tate, "China Launches Fifth LPD for PLAN," *Jane's 360*, June 16, 2017, available at <www.janes.com/article/71491/china-launches-fifth-lpd-for-plan>.

27 This effort was aided by earlier PLA-wide reforms that sought to encourage civilians to work for the PLA. See Thomas J. Bickford, "Trends in Education and Training, 1924–2007: From Whampoa to Nanjing Polytechnic," in *The "People" in the PLA: Recruitment, Training, and Education in China's Military*, ed. Roy Kamphausen, Andrew Scobell, and Travis Tanner (Carlisle Barracks, PA: Strategic Studies Institute, 2008), 36–37.

28 Roy D. Kamphausen, "ROTC with Chinese Characteristics: Training the PLA in Civilian Universities," *China Brief* 7, no. 6 (April 13, 2007), available at <https://jamestown.org/program/rotc-with-chinese-characteristics-training-the-pla-in-civilian-universities-3/>. In an effort to further diversify those it recruits, the marines even began partnering with wushu schools, such as the Tagou Wushu School in Henan, to hold recruitment events at wushu competitions. See Li Faxin, *The PLA Marines* (Beijing: China Intercontinental Press, 2013), 78–80.

29 Kenneth W. Allen, *PLA Air Force, Naval Aviation, and Army Aviation Aviator Recruitment, Education, and Training* (Washington, DC: Jamestown Foundation, 2015), 38.

30 This move was in part done to address the complaint that cadets' education focused too much on theory and not enough on gaining practical skills and experience. See Kenneth W. Allen and Morgan Clemens, *The Recruitment, Education, and Training of PLA Navy Personnel* (Newport, RI: China Maritime Studies Institute, August 2014), 7.

31 Kenneth W. Allen, Phillip C. Saunders, and John Chen, *Chinese Military Diplomacy, 2003–2016*, China Strategic Perspectives 11 (Washington, DC: NDU Press, July 2017), 35; Zhang Xiaomin, "Naval Training Ship Going Round the

Globe," *China Daily* (Beijing), April 17, 2012, available at <http://usa.chinadaily.com.cn/china/2012-04/17/content_15063312.htm>.

[32] Between April 1987 and August 1993, the *Zheng He* trained more than 6,000 navy cadets. See Srikanth Kondapalli, *China's Naval Power* (New Delhi: Knowledge World, January 2001), 146.

[33] Allen and Clemens, *The Recruitment, Education, and Training of PLA Navy Personnel*, 32.

[34] "82 *Shichang* National Defense Mobilization Ship" [82 世昌号国防动员船], *haijun360.com* [海军360], available at <www.haijun360.com/news/QTFZCZ/2011/716/11716153820777C426CG301J1KC379.html>.

[35] Vinayak Bhat, "Satellite Images Reveal China's State-of-Art Naval Air Base," *The Print*, October 17, 2017, available at <https://theprint.in/2017/10/17/satellite-images-reveal-china-naval-airbase/>.

[36] Dale C. Rielage, "Chinese Navy Trains and Takes Risks," U.S. Naval Institute *Proceedings* 142, no. 5 (May 2016), available at <www.usni.org/magazines/proceedings/2016-05/chinese-navy-trains-and-takes-risks>.

[37] Yan Jiangzhou, Fu Qiang, and Ren Wei [闫江洲, 付强, 任伟], "'First Ship' Brilliantly Draws Sword" ["首舰" 精彩亮剑], *People's Navy* [人民海军], June 9, 2014, 4.

[38] Zhao Lei, "Navy Training Exercises Deemed Success," *China Daily* (Beijing), April 24, 2017, available at <www.chinadaily.com.cn/china/2017-04/24/content_29050321.htm>.

[39] Allen, Saunders, and Chen, *Chinese Military Diplomacy*, 23. Notably, however, the United States disinvited the PLA Navy from Rim of the Pacific exercise 2018.

[40] Yang Jie, "Navy Completes Joint Beach Drill," *China Daily* (Beijing), August 26, 2015, available at <www.chinadaily.com.cn/kindle/2015-08/26/content_21711187.htm>.

[41] Allen, Saunders, and Chen, *Chinese Military Diplomacy*, 24–26.

[42] See Zhao Lei, "PLA Submarines Defy Death in the Depths," *China Daily* (Beijing), December 18, 2014, available at <www.chinadaily.com.cn/china/2014-12/18/content_19111841.htm>.

[43] Rielage, "Chinese Navy Trains and Takes Risks."

[44] Kenneth W. Allen and Lyle J. Morris, *PLA Naval Aviation Training and Operations: Missions, Organizational Structure and Training (2013–2015)* (Maxwell Air Force Base, AL: China Aerospace Studies Institute, 2017), 7.

[45] Fan Jianghuai, Cao Haihua, and Shao Longfei [范江怀, 曹海华, 邵龙飞],

"These Self-Styled Special Forces—South Sea Fleet Units' Special Mission, Training, and Knowledge" [这些自讨苦吃的特种兵——南海舰队某特种团训练见闻], *China Military Online* [中国军网], January 23, 2013, available at <www.81.cn/tzjy/2013-01/23/content_5500379.htm>.

    46 Dennis J. Blasko, "PLA Special Operations Forces: Organizations, Missions, and Training," *China Brief* 15, no. 9 (May 1, 2015), 8. For the activities of naval special operations forces detachments on the antipiracy missions, see Li, *The PLA Marines*, 66–76.

    47 See Jeffrey Lin and P.W. Singer, "Chinese Special Forces Take 1st, 2nd, and 4th at 'Olympics' for Elite Warriors," *Popular Science*, May 19, 2014, available at <www.popsci.com/blog-network/eastern-arsenal/chinese-special-forces-take-1st-2nd-and-4th-place-%E2%80%9Colympics%E2%80%9D-elite>; "Chinese Airborne Troops Win Glory in International Special Forces Competition," *China Military Online*, July 10, 2015, available at <http://english.chinamil.com.cn/news-channels/china-military-news/2015-07/10/content_6581621.htm>.

    48 Dennis J. Blasko, "SOF a Priority in China," *The Cipher Brief*, March 15, 2017, available at <https://www.thecipherbrief.com/sof-a-priority-in-china>.

    49 *China's National Defense in 2010* (Beijing: Information Office of the State Council, 2010), available at <http://english.gov.cn/archive/white_paper/2014/09/09/content_281474986284525.htm>; Takeshi Yuzawa, "ASEAN in the Era of Japan-China Tensions: Diplomatic Opportunities or Strategic Dilemmas?" in *International Security in the Asia-Pacific*, ed. Alan Chong (New York: Palgrave Macmillan, 2018), 161. The marines were involved in joint exercises with foreign militaries prior to 2010, such as Peace Mission 2005 with Russia. See Li, *The PLA Marines*, 176–177.

    50 Li, *The PLA Marines*, 122. In at least one Chinese-language book that was part of a series that had the "strong support and guidance" of the Ministry of National Defense, the helicopters used by the marines were referred to as being part of a "海军陆战队直升机分队." See Li Faxin [李发新], *The PLA Marines* [中国人民解放军海军陆战队] (Beijing: China Intercontinental Press [五洲传播出版社], 2013), 107.

    51 "Chinese People's Liberation Army Marine Corps College Brief Introduction" [中国人民解放军海军陆战学院简介], *KaoYan.com* [考研帮], April 22, 2014, available at <http://yz.kaoyan.com/hjbzzhxy/jianjie/>.

    52 See Li Tang, Zhou Yuan, and Liu Chuan [李唐, 周园, 刘川], "Military Teachers, to Teach Warfighting First Must Train on the Frontline" [军校教员, 教打仗先到一线练打仗], *PLA Daily* [解放军报], April 26, 2015, available at <www.81.cn/jmywyl/2015-04/26/content_6460539.htm>.

[53] Both names have been used by official state media outlets. The new university will be located in Yantai, Shandong, with a campus and training base in Qingdao, as well as training bases in Huludao, Liaoning, in Changzhi, Shanxi, and in Qinhuangdao, Hebei. See Wang Lei, "China's Only University to Train Carrier-Based Fighter Pilots Makes Debut," *CGTN.com*, May 29, 2017, available at <https://news.cgtn.com/news/3d517a4e3241444e/share_p.html>.

[54] Deng Xiaoci, "PLA Navy to Streamline Pilot Training as More Aircraft Carriers Expected," *Global Times* (Beijing), January 7, 2018, available at <www.globaltimes.cn/content/1083697.shtml>.

[55] Zhang Dabin and Gao Yi [张大宾, 高毅], "Night Training Bids Goodbye to Calm Winds and Waves—To Aim for Accurate Real Combat Night Training Environment, a South Sea Fleet Aviation Bombing Regiment Concentrates on Refining Night Combat Capability" [夜训告别 "风平浪带"—瞄准实战构设夜训环境, 潜心锤炼夜战本领. 南海舰队航空兵某轰炸机团], *People's Navy* [人民海军], May 18, 2015, 3; Allen and Morris, *PLA Naval Aviation Training and Operations*, 8.

[56] Allen and Morris, *PLA Naval Aviation Training and Operations*, 16. This training is important; the international militaries that naval aviation is most likely to come into conflict with—namely those of the United States, Japan, Taiwan, and South Korea—do not fly the same aircraft as it does.

[57] Dai Zongfeng, Wan Minwu, and Wu Dengfeng [代宗锋, 宛敏武, 吴登峰], "A Report on How PLA's First AIP Submarine Unit Improves Its Ability to Win Battle" [全军首支AIP潜艇部队提升打胜仗能力纪实], Xinhua [新华], June 25, 2018.

[58] Authors' discussions with Chinese naval officers in 2017. The navy performed its first tri-fleet exercise in 2010. See Christian Le Miere, *Maritime Diplomacy in the 21ˢᵗ Century: Drivers and Challenges* (New York: Routledge, 2014), 135.

[59] Even in the U.S. military, years after the Goldwater-Nichols Department of Defense Reorganization Act of 1986, the Services still engaged in "Service parochialism" to the point where "it is the single most important factor in force planning." See William A. Owens, "Making the Joint Journey," *Joint Force Quarterly* 34 (Spring 2003), 76.

[60] During a far-sea training exercise, a flotilla from the navy's South Sea Fleet performed "over 20 training items including joint area air defense, joint maritime rights protection, sea and air combined assaults, close counterattacks and in-depth land strike and so on." Despite being described as joint actions, they only involved naval forces. See Huang Panyue, ed., "PLA Fleet Returns to Homeport from Far-Sea Training," *China Military Online*, February 26, 2018, available at <http://eng.chinamil.com.cn/view/2018-02/26/content_7952635.htm>.

61 The PLA service commanders were Central Military Commission (CMC) members from 2004 to 2017.

62 For more on the CMC's level of control and involvement in overseas naval actions via the Joint Staff Department Overseas Operations Office, see Huang Jiafu [黄家福], "Take Command of and Provide Support for Overseas Military Actions" [海外军事行动的指挥与保障], *Naval and Merchant Ships* [舰船知识] (September 2017), 75–76.

63 Carl H. Builder, *The Masks of War: American Military Styles in Strategy and Analysis* (Baltimore: Johns Hopkins University Press, 1989), 18.

64 Allen, Saunders, and Chen, *Chinese Military Diplomacy*, 18.

65 Minnie Chan, "China Raises Pay, Pensions for Trimmed Down Military, Announces Plans for Veterans' Ministry," *South China Morning Post* (Hong Kong), March 13, 2018, available at <www.scmp.com/news/china/diplomacy-defence/article/2137008/china-raises-pay-pensions-trimmed-down-military>.

66 Neil J. Diamant, *Embattled Glory: Veterans, Military Families, and the Politics of Patriotism in China, 1949–2007* (Lanham, MD: Rowman & Littlefield Publishers, Inc., 2010), 6–7.

67 Luisetta Mudie, trans. and ed., "Chinese Military Veterans Skeptical over President's Promise to 'Protect Their Rights,'" *Radio Free Asia*, October 23, 2017, available <www.rfa.org/english/news/china/veterans-10232017114254.html>.

68 Chan, "China Raises Pay."

69 Mudie, "Chinese Military Veterans Skeptical." This claim has been undercut by continuing mistreatment and abuse of veterans by officials and police. See Yang Fan and Luisette Mudie, trans. and ed., "Chinese Military Veterans Detained, Beaten in Beijing after Pension Petition," *Radio Free Asia*, December 5, 2017, available at <www.rfa.org/english/news/china/chinese-military-veterans-detained-beaten-in-beijing-after-pension-petition-12052017110040.html>.

70 Wong Siu-san et al., trans. and ed., "Chinese Military Veterans Converge on Zhenjiang as Protests Swell," *Radio Free Asia*, June 22, 2018, available at <www.rfa.org/english/news/china/chinese-military-veterans-converge-on-zhenjiang-06222018111306.html>.

71 "Former Top China Military Officer Hoarded Cash, Jade in Basement: Phoenix," Reuters, November 20, 2014, available at <www.reuters.com/article/us-china-politics-corruption/former-top-china-military-officer-hoarded-cash-jade-in-basement-phoenix-idUSKCN0J412Q20141120>.

72 See Peng Wang, "Military Corruption in China: The Role of *Guanxi* in the

Buying and Selling of Military Positions," *China Quarterly*, no. 228 (December 2016), 970–991.

⁷³ Joel Wuthnow, "A Brave New World for Chinese Joint Operations," *Journal of Strategic Studies* 40, nos. 1–2 (2017), 174.

⁷⁴ Jeffrey Engstrom and Michael Chase, "Enhancing China's Status as a Great Power," *The Cipher Brief*, August 1, 2017, available at <www.thecipherbrief.com/enhancing-chinas-status-great-power-1091>; also see Kevin McCauley, "PLA Yijiangshan Joint Amphibious Operation: Past Is Prologue," *China Brief* 16, no. 4 (September 13, 2016), 12–16.

⁷⁵ Li Dianren [李殿仁] et al., "Foreword" [前言], *Study on the Development of Joint Commanding Officers* [联合作战指挥人才培养] (Beijing: National Defense University Press [国防大学出版社], 2008), 1.

⁷⁶ Liu Wei [刘伟], ed., "Theater Joint Operations Command" [战区联合作战指挥], (Beijing: National Defense University Press [国防大学出版社], 2016), 293.

⁷⁷ Mark R. Cozad, *PLA Joint Training and Implications for Future Expeditionary Capabilities* (Santa Monica, CA: RAND, January 2016), 2, available at <www.rand.org/pubs/testimonies/CT451.html>.

⁷⁸ June Teufel Dreyer, "People's Liberation Army Lessons from Foreign Conflicts: The Air War in Kosovo," in *Chinese Lessons from Other People's Wars*, ed. Andrew Scobell, David Lai, and Roy Kamphausen (Carlisle Barracks, PA: Strategic Studies Institute, November 2011), 33–73; Christopher D. Yung, "Sinica Rules the Waves? The People's Liberation Army Navy's Power Projection and Anti-Access/Area Denial Lessons from the Falklands/Malvinas Conflict," in *Chinese Lessons from Other People's Wars*, 75–114.

⁷⁹ Li et al., *Study on the Development of Joint Commanding Officers*, 2.

⁸⁰ Dennis J. Blasko, "The PLA Joint Headquarters and Internal Assessments of PLA Capabilities," *China Brief* 16, no.10 (June 21, 2016), 8–9.

⁸¹ Liu, "Theater Joint Operations Command," 311.

⁸² Ibid., 312.

⁸³ Allen, Saunders, and Chen, *Chinese Military Diplomacy*, 32–33.

⁸⁴ One expert stated that the PLA Air Force's "most glaring" training weakness is the limited training that it conducts with other services. See Lee Fuell, "Broad Trends in Chinese Air Force and Missile Modernization," Testimony Before the U.S.-China Security and Economic Review Commission, January 30, 2014, 9. More "robust" operations between the air force and navy only began "recently." See Mark R. Cozad and Nathan Beauchamp-Mustafaga, *The People's Liberation*

Army Air Force Operations over Water: Maintaining Relevance in China's Changing Security Environment (Santa Monica, CA: RAND, 2017), 49.

85 Zhang Zhongkai and Wu Dengfeng [张钟凯, 吴登峰], "Military Experts Explain the Sino-Russian 'Joint Sea-2015 (II)' Exercise Highlights" [军事专家详解中俄 "海上联合—2015(II)" 演习亮点], Xinhua Online [新华网], August 24, 2015, available at <http://news.xinhuanet.com/world/2015-08/24/c_1116357242.htm>; Yang Jie, "Navy Completes Joint Beach Drill," *China Daily* (Beijing), August 26, 2015, available at <www.chinadaily.com.cn/kindle/2015-08/26/content_21711187.htm>.

86 Fuell, "Broad Trends in Chinese Air Force and Missile Modernization," 10.

87 Qiu Yue and Yan Jiaqi [邱越, 闫嘉琪], "Expert: Joint Navy and Air Force Exercise to Control the Contest of Air Supremacy Helps to Exert the Navy's Strike Capability" [专家: 海空军联演助力制空权争夺发挥海军打击能力], *People's Daily Online* [人民网], November 4, 2015, available at <http://military.people.com.cn/n/2015/1104/c1011-27774164.html>.

88 See Liu Wenping and Zhao Haitao, "Flying Against a 'Golden Helmet,'" *China Armed Forces* 32, no. 2 (2015), 82–83. In exercises involving naval aviation and the air force, the two are mostly used as training opponents rather than operating on the same side as they would in a real conflict. See Zhang Heng [张恒], "Confrontation Between Different Models 'Back-to-Back' in Progress: Naval Aviation and Air Force Joint Training Deepening" [异型机对抗 "背靠背" 进行], *PLA Daily* [解放军报], September 21, 2015, available at <http://kj.81.cn/content/2015-09/21/content_6690270.htm>.

89 Jeffrey Lin and P.W. Singer, "China's Marine Corps Is Getting Bigger and Stronger," *Popular Science*, March 29, 2017, available at <www.popsci.com/chinas-marine-corps-expansion-reorganization>. It is unclear how the marines having their own aviation assets will impact the level and frequency of joint training with army aviation units.

90 Ian Easton, *The Chinese Invasion Threat: Taiwan's Defense and American Strategy in Asia* (Arlington, VA: Project 2049 Institute, 2017), 173–175.

91 Cozad, *PLA Joint Training*, 11.

92 Zhao Lei, "PLA Restructuring Changes Focus at Military Schools," *China Daily* (Beijing), April 28, 2016, available at <www.chinadaily.com.cn/china/2016-04/28/content_24911350.htm>.

93 Fuell, "Broad Trends in Chinese Air Force and Missile Modernization," 10–11.

94 "China to Cut Troops by 300,000: Xi," Xinhua, September 3, 2015, available at <www.xinhuanet.com/english/2015-09/03/c_134583730.htm>.

[95] *China's National Defense in 2002* (Beijing: Information Office of the State Council, December 2002), available at <www.china.org.cn/e-white/20021209/index.htm>.

[96] *China's National Defense in 2004* (Beijing: Information Office of the State Council, December 2004), available at <http://en.people.cn/whitepaper/defense2004/defense2004.html>.

[97] "White Paper Outlines China's 'Active Defense' Strategy," Xinhua, May 26, 2015, available at <http://en.people.cn/n/2015/0526/c90786-8898060.html>.

[98] Shou Xiaosong [寿晓松], ed., *Science of Military Strategy* [战略学] (Beijing: Military Science Press [军事科学出版社], December 2013), 106.

[99] Li Youtao [黎友陶], "Diversified Activities Will Help to Calmly Chase Navy Blue Dream" [行动多样化: 逐梦深蓝更加从容], *Navy Today* [当代海军], no. 273 (June 2016), 18–19.

[100] Cozad and Beauchamp-Mustafaga, *The People's Liberation Army Air Force Operations over Water*.

[101] "PLA Air Force Conducts First Training in West Pacific," *China Military Online*, March 30, 2015, available at <http://english.chinamil.com.cn/news-channels/2015-03/30/content_6420538.htm>.

[102] Tara Copp, "China Has Practiced Bombing Runs Targeting Guam, U.S. Says," *Defense News*, October 31, 2017, available at <www.defensenews.com/flashpoints/2017/10/31/china-has-practiced-bombing-runs-against-guam-us-says/>.

[103] These include armed combat vessels for wartime maritime search and rescue missions. See Li Jiayao, ed., "Vessel Troops of the PLA Air Force," *China Military Online*, January 19, 2018, available at <http://english.pladaily.com.cn/view/2018-01/19/content_7914789.htm>.

[104] Huang Panyue, ed., "Su-35, J-20 Fighter Jets Help Maintain China's Airspace Safety," *China Military Online*, February 12, 2018, available at <http://english.pladaily.com.cn/view/2018-02/12/content_7942685.htm>.

[105] According to air force spokesperson Senior Colonel Shen Jinke, "in the two years since the Chinese air force launched distant sea training, interference from various obstacles had been dealt with, engaged in reconnaissance and early warning, maritime patrolling, maritime assault, and mid-air refueling training, which improved distant sea mobility and tested distant sea combat capability." See Zhang Yuqing and Zhang Mimi [张玉清, 张汩汩], "China's Air Force Strengthens Distant Sea Training to Improve Strategic Capability" [中国空军加强远海训练提升战略能力], Xinhua Online [新华网], December 15, 2016, available at <http://news.xinhuanet.com/2016-12/15/c_1120123755.htm>.

106 Li Kaiqiang and Zhang Hongwei [李开强, 张宏伟], "Air Force Organized First Live Fire Training at Sea for Flight School" [空军首次组织飞行院校海上实弹打靶], *PLA Daily* [解放军报], May 20, 2015, available at <www.mod.gov.cn/academy/2015-05/20/content_4585772.htm>.

107 Liangyu, ed., "Chinese Air Force Patrol South China Sea," Xinhua Online, November 23, 2017, available at <http://news.xinhuanet.com/english/2017-11/23/c_136774671.htm>. The Air Force Aviation University performed its first live-fire training at sea in 2015. See Li Kaiqiang and Zhang Hongwei [李开强, 张宏伟], "Air Force Organized First Live Fire Training at Sea for Flight School" [空军首次组织飞行院校海上实弹打靶], *PLA Daily* [解放军报], May 20, 2015, available at <www.mod.gov.cn/academy/2015-05/20/content_4585772.htm>.

108 Cozad and Beauchamp-Mustafaga, *The People's Liberation Army Air Force Operations over Water*, 19.

109 Ma Xiaotian [马晓天], "Strive to Improve the Ability of the Air Force to Fight and Win" [努力提高空军部队能打仗打胜仗能力], *PLA Daily* [解放军报], April 2, 2014, available at <www.81.cn/2014-content_18620/2014-04/02/content_6153511.htm>.

110 Jeffrey Lin and P.W. Singer, "The World's Largest Military Plane in Production Is China's Y-20," *Popular Science*, June 20, 2016, available at <www.popsci.com/worlds-largest-military-plane-in-production-is-chinas-y-20>.

111 Yi Wenbo and Jiang Long [尹闻博, 蒋龙], "Achieving Airdrop Capability Through All-Domain Direct Reach Operations: Air Force Airborne's Air Transport Brigade Carries Out Simulated Airdrop Over Unfamiliar Island Targets" [全域直达练就能降: 空降兵某航运旅对陌生海岛目标实施模拟空降训练小记] *Air Force Daily* [空军报], June 7, 2017, 1.

112 Jeffrey Lin and P.W. Singer, "Finally, a Modern Chinese Aerial Tanker," *Popular Science*, April 2, 2014, available at <www.popsci.com/blog-network/eastern-arsenal/finally-modern-chinese-aerial-tanker>.

113 "'Chubby Girl's' Sister to Boost China's Military Capability," *Asia Times* (Hong Kong), December 14, 2017, available at <www.atimes.com/article/chubby-girls-sister-boost-chinas-military-capability/>.

114 For more on the conquest of Taiwan being the prime driver of the PLA for decades, see Easton, *The Chinese Invasion Threat*, 16–19; and Dennis J. Blasko, "PLA Amphibious Capabilities: Structured for Deterrence," *China Brief* 10, no. 17 (August 19, 2010), 5.

[115] Blasko, "PLA Amphibious Capabilities," 6.

[116] Ibid., 7.

[117] Cao Zhengrong, Sun Longhai, and Yang Ying, eds., *Informationized Army Operations* [信息化陆军作战] (Beijing: National Defense University Press [国防大学出版社], 2014), 12–14.

[118] Andrew S. Erickson, *Chinese Anti-Ship Ballistic Missile Development: Drivers, Trajectories, and Strategic Implications* (Washington, DC: Jamestown Foundation, May 2013), 6–7.

[119] Andrew S. Erickson and David D. Yang, "Using the Land to Control the Sea: Chinese Analysts Consider the Antiship Ballistic Missile," *Naval War College Review* 62, no. 4 (Autumn 2009), 73.

[120] Chen Heying, "New Missiles for Defensive Purposes Only," *Global Times* (Beijing), September 4, 2015, available at <www.globaltimes.cn/content/940518.shtml>.

[121] *The Science of Campaigns* [战役学] (Beijing: National Defense University [国防大学出版社], 2006), 629–630. *The Science of Second Artillery Campaigns* similarly indicated the Second Artillery force, now the Rocket Force, would work with the navy to "execute focused naval blockades" and "achieve command of the seas." *The Science of Second Artillery Campaigns* [第二炮兵战役学] (Beijing: PLA Press [中国人民解放军出版社], 2004), 140, 317–318.

[122] *The Science of Campaigns* [战役学] (Beijing: National Defense University [国防大学出版社], 2006), 634–635.

[123] Erickson and Yang, "Using the Land to Control the Sea," 60; *The Science of Campaigns*, 623, 629.

[124] For more on China's nuclear-armed submarines, see Eric Heginbotham et al., *China's Evolving Nuclear Deterrent: Major Drivers and Issues for the United States* (Santa Monica, CA: RAND, 2017), 107–110.

[125] For analysis on navy antiship cruise missiles, see Dennis M. Gormley, Andrew S. Erickson, and Jingdong Yuan, *A Low-Visibility Force Multiplier: Assessing China's Cruise Missile Ambitions* (Washington, DC: NDU Press, 2014), 15–23.

[126] Anthony H. Cordesman, *The PLA Rocket Force: Evolving Beyond the Second Artillery Corps and Nuclear Dimension* (Washington, DC: Center for Strategic and International Studies, 2016), 5–6.

[127] This happened to the Imperial Japanese Navy aviation force when it took the lead aviation role in a land war in China. See Mark R. Peattie, *Sunburst: The Rise of Japanese Naval Air Power, 1909–1941* (Annapolis, MD: Naval Institute Press, 2001), 126.

[128] The air force has historically had limited mid-air refueling capabilities. See

Eric Heginbotham et al., *The U.S.-China Military Scorecard: Forces, Geography, and the Evolving Balance of Power* (Santa Monica, CA: RAND, 2015), 33.

[129] In early 2017, Vice Admiral Yuan Yubai was appointed to lead the Southern Theater Command. See Nan Li, "The Southern Theater Command and China's Maritime Strategy," *China Brief* 17, no. 8 (June 9, 2017), 8. This appointment was important not only for what it signaled about the military's view and orientation toward this region but also because he was the "first . . . non-army officer ever to command a military region or theater command." See Dennis J. Blasko, "A 'First' for the People's Liberation Army: A Navy Admiral Becomes a Joint, Regional, Commander," *China Brief* 17, no. 5 (March 31, 2017), 7.

[130] The more formal name for the maritime militia was proposed in Conor M. Kennedy and Andrew S. Erickson, "China's Third Sea Force, The People's Armed Forces Maritime Militia: Tethered to the PLA," *China Maritime Report*, no. 1 (March 2017), 1.

[131] Wang Xiaobin, "Sansha City Promotes Military-Police-Community Joint Defense Mechanism to Construct a Three-Line Maritime Protection Structure" [三沙市推动军警民联防机制 构建三线海上维权格局], China News Service [中国新闻网], November 20, 2014, available at <www.chinanews.com/gn/2014/11-21/6803776.shtml>.

[132] For more on the involvement and influence by the PLA, and specifically the navy, see McCaslin, *Role of the PLA in China's Foreign Policy and Behavior Abroad*, 114–121, 132.

[133] For more on the PLA's control of the maritime militia, see Kennedy and Erickson, "China's Third Sea Force," 2–10. Some maritime militia units, such as Tanmen's, have been involved with Chinese naval activity in the South China Sea for decades. See "Spratlys Reef Construction Project" [南沙礁盘建设工程], *360doc.com* [个人图书馆], June 10, 2014, available at <www.360doc.com/content/14/0610/11/15447134_385347297.shtml>.

[134] Yi Xiucheng [易修呈], "Tanmen Militia: Riding Dark Blue Waves of a New Journey" [潭门民兵: 踏浪深蓝新征程], China National Defense Daily [中国国防报], December 24, 2015, available at <http://news.mod.gov.cn/militia/2015-12/24/content_4634045.htm>.

[135] In the PLA writ large, there has been a long-term reduction in overall numbers of maritime militia units, with some less advanced units (in equipment and capabilities) being phased out, even as units of unprecedented sophistication are introduced. See "On the Construction of the Militia Since the Reform and Opening-Up" [在创新发展中前行——改革开放以来民兵建设综述], Ministry

of National Defense [国防部网站], December 15, 2011, available at <www.gov.cn/gzdt/2011-12/15/content_2020745.htm>.

[136] Gao Chen [高辰], ed., "South China Sea Sanya Militia Handles Incursions by Foreign Fishing Boats (from) Mischief Reef" [南海三沙民兵处置侵入领海外籍渔船 部署美济礁], China News Service [中国新闻网], January 1, 2016, available at <www.chinanews.com/mil/2016/01-27/7735164.shtml>.

[137] Wu Weiman [吴维满], "China's New Type of Service Militia Detachments Stage Battlefield to Adapt to Combat Requirements" [中国新型军兵种民兵分队上演兵场 适应作战需要], *PLA Daily* [解放军报], December 27, 2010, available at <http://mil.sohu.com/20101227/n278525284.shtml>. These navy militia detachments include ones specialized in oil-replenishment security and mobile ship repair.

[138] Official Chinese media have referred to there being three lines of defense to protect China's disputed maritime and sovereignty claims. They state that the maritime militia is the first line, with maritime law enforcement being the second, and navy being the third. See Wang Xiaobin [王晓斌], "Sansha Promotes Military, Police, and Militia Joint Defense Mechanism, Constructs a Three Line Maritime Rights Protection Structure" [三沙市推动军警民联防机制 构建三线海上维权格局], China News Service [中国新闻网], November 20, 2014, available at <www.chinanews.com/gn/2014/11-21/6803776.shtml>. Even though such a defensive line system reduces the frontline role of the navy, interviews conducted by Christopher D. Yung indicate that the PLA "supports the idea that civilian law enforcement vessels should be on the 'frontline' while the military is 'in the rear.'" See Christopher D. Yung, "The PLA Navy Lobby and Its Influence over China's Maritime Sovereignty Policies," in *PLA Influence on China's National Security Policymaking*, 292.

[139] The coast guard is composed of four previously separate maritime law enforcement agencies: China Marine Surveillance (CMS), China Fisheries Law Enforcement, Border Defense Coast Guard, and Maritime Anti-Smuggling Police. The CMS fleet is by far the most militant and outward-looking element of the coast guard, so much so that authoritative Chinese publications openly refer to the CMS fleet as the country's "second navy." See Ryan D. Martinson, "China's Second Navy," U.S. Naval Institute *Proceedings* 141, no. 4 (April 2015), available at <www.usni.org/magazines/proceedings/2015-04-0/chinas-second-navy>.

[140] Yung, "The PLA Navy Lobby," 292.

[141] Franz-Stefan Gady, "Is China's Coast Guard about to Field a Modified PLA Warship?" *The Diplomat*, June 3, 2016, available at <http://thediplomat.com/2016/06/is-chinas-coast-guard-about-to-field-a-modified-pla- warship/>.

142   Andrew S. Erickson, "Numbers Matter: China's Three 'Navies' Each Have the World's Most Ships," *The National Interest*, February 26, 2018, available at <http://nationalinterest.org/feature/numbers-matter-chinas-three-navies-each-have-the-worlds-most-24653>.

143   Andrew S. Erickson and Conor M. Kennedy, *China's Daring Vanguard: Introducing Sanya City's Maritime Militia* (Washington, DC: Center for International Maritime Security, 2015), available at <http://cimsec.org/chinas-daring-vanguard-introducing-sanya-citys-maritime-militia/19753>.

144   "Pentagon Says Chinese Vessels Harassed U.S. Ship," CNN, March 9, 2009, available at <www.cnn.com/2009/POLITICS/03/09/us.navy.china/index.html>.

145   "Raw Data: Pentagon Statement on Chinese Incident with U.S. Navy," Fox News, March 9, 2009, available at <www.foxnews.com/politics/2009/03/09/raw-data-pentagon-statement-chinese-incident navy.html>.

146   Ryan D. Martinson, "From Words to Actions: The Creation of the China Coast Guard," paper prepared for China as a "Maritime Power" conference, CNA, Arlington, VA, July 28–29, 2015, 20.

147   "Three-Sea Force" is a reference to the three maritime forces being employed by China: navy, maritime law enforcement agencies, and maritime militia.

148   Erickson, "Numbers Matter."

149   One report, as well as video evidence, indicate that *Qiongdongfang* 11209 from Dongfang City intentionally rammed and sank a Vietnamese fishing vessel 7 miles outside of the cordon. See "The Latest on the Situation in the South China Sea: Vietnamese Media Says a Chinese Fishing Boat Crashed into and Sank a Vietnamese Fishing Boat Near (the) Haiyang (Shiyou) 981 (Oil Rig)" [南海局势最新消息: 越媒称中国渔船在海洋981附近撞沉越南渔船], *Guancha* [观察], May 27, 2014, available at <www.guancha.cn/Neighbors/2015_03_25_313539.shtml>. At least 10 vessels and 200 militia members from the Tanmen maritime militia were involved in the Chinese operation. See "Qionghai Wang Shumao: National Model Worker, the New Era of 'Dinghai Shenzhen'" [琼海王书茂: 全国劳动模范, 新时期的"定海神针"], *Qionghai Shichuang* [琼海视窗], May 8, 2015, available at <www.qionghais.com/html/2015/jiaoyu/18391.html>. Sanya City's maritime militia supplied 29 trawlers for the Chinese operation. See Erickson and Kennedy, "China's Daring Vanguard."

150   "Japanese Media: Vietnamese Tried to Obstruct China's Completion of Oil Drilling Preparations in the Paracels of the South China Sea" [日媒: 克服越南船只阻挠 中国在南海西沙群岛海域完成钻探石油准备], *Guancha* [观察], May 12, 2014, available at <www.guancha.cn/Neighbors/2014_05_12_228824.shtml>.

;7

[151] Conor M. Kennedy and Andrew S. Erickson, *Riding a New Wave of Professionalization and Militarization: Sansha City's Maritime Militia* (Washington, DC: Center for International Maritime Security, 2016), available at <http://cimsec.org/riding-new-wave-professionalization-militarization-sansha-citys-maritime-militia/27689>.

[152] Zhang Yigen and He Peng [张毅根, 何鹏], "Protection of Drilling Platforms: Military Police and Civilians Surround and Annihilate in South China Sea Drill" [保护钻井平台: 军警民南海演练围歼], *China National Defense Daily—Military Affairs Special Edition* [中国国防报—军事特刊], August 23, 2014, available at <www.81.cn/jmywyl/2014-08/23/content_6107899.htm>.

[153] "Updated: China's Big Three Near Completion," Asia Maritime Transparency Initiative, June 29, 2017, available at <https://amti.csis.org/chinas-big-three-near-completion/>.

[154] Shou, *Science of Military Strategy*, 214.

[155] Gao "South China Sea Sanya Militia Handles Incursions."

[156] Liu Zhen, "China's Military Police Given Control of Coast Guard as Beijing Boosts Maritime Security," *South China Morning Post* (Hong Kong), March 21, 2018, available at <www.scmp.com/news/china/diplomacy-defence/article/2138257/chinas-military-police-given-control-coastguard-beijing>.

[157] Liu Weihua, Xu Qiang, and Zhang Ning [刘卫华, 徐强, 张宁], "Service Building, How Do Militia Specialized Detachments Correspond?" [军种主建, 民兵专业分队如何对接?] *China National Defense Daily* [中国国防报], January 27, 2016, available at <www.81.cn/mb/2016-01/27/content_7071697.htm>.

CHAPTER 4

THE FLAG LAGS BUT FOLLOWS

The PLA and China's Great Leap Outward

By Andrew Scobell and Nathan Beauchamp-Mustafaga

D oes trade follow the flag, or does the flag follow trade? In China's "reform and opening" policy, the sequence appears to be first trade, then investment in resources and infrastructure—now codified under the so-called One Belt, One Road (OBOR) or Belt and Road Initiative (BRI)—followed by efforts to protect the physical manifestations of extended engagement with the outside world. While "trade follows the flag" may have been "a reasonable maxim for 19th-century imperialism," it does not appear to be a viable course of action for a 21th-century great power in a globalized world economy.[1]

Since the late 1970s, the People's Republic of China (PRC) has been engaged in a sustained economic outreach to the world beyond its borders, initially focused mostly on its immediate neighborhood, but eventually extending far beyond the Asia-Pacific region. In contrast to the most ambitious economic development policy initiative of the first three decades of the PRC, the Great Leap Forward, China's most ambitious economic development policy initiative since then constitutes a Great Leap Outward.[2] While the former effort was autarkic and internally focused, the latter effort is global in scope and projected externally. Moreover, while the earlier effort was a catastrophic failure and abandoned 3 years after its launch, the more recent effort has been a stunning success sustained for four decades and counting.

This chapter first examines possible options available to protect what have been labeled China's overseas interests—a category of national interests that has become much more meaningful because of the successes of Beijing's ongoing Great Leap Outward. Second, it analyzes People's Liberation Army (PLA) thinking about the security dimensions of OBOR and the role of the armed forces.[3] Third, this chapter considers three case studies to explore what securing China's overseas interests involves in concrete terms. Finally, it summarizes the findings and their implications. Before proceeding, we briefly discuss Chinese national interests and summarize the phases of China's Great Leap Outward.

Much attention has focused on China's core interests but far less on China's overseas interests. The former category of national interests has understandably drawn considerable focus because when China designates interests as core, this means they are considered worth fighting and dying for—such as the PRC's sovereignty claims over Taiwan. But Beijing's overseas interests have grown in importance and are now routinely identified as important interests to be protected. For example, they are mentioned in China's defense white papers and elsewhere. Overseas interests include—but are not limited to—PRC citizens living, working, and traveling abroad, as well as PRC property and investments located abroad. President Jiang Zemin announced the "going out" strategy in 2002, and his successor Hu Jintao gave the PLA four "new historic missions" in 2004, including protecting China's expanding interests. The Chinese military's strategic guidelines were revised that same year (the first revision since 1994) to include "threats to overseas interests" as a primary threat for the first time.[4] The volume and strategic significance of this category of national interests have expanded considerably since Xi Jinping officially launched OBOR in two major speeches in 2013.

The PRC's prolonged Great Leap Outward has moved through three discernible phrases. It began as a quest to sell Chinese exports to the developed world, which stimulated demand for commodities and raw materials from the developing world. Gradually, China's initial heavy focus on exports to the developed world broadened to include greater attention to the developing world. This second phase saw China starting to invest and build infrastructure in the countries of the Asia-Pacific, Middle East, Africa, and Latin America in support of trade and investment in these regions. A third phase emerged as Beijing started to recognize that since many parts of the developing world are unstable and vulnerable to a range of threats, it was necessary to figure out how to protect PRC citizens, investments, and Chinese-built infrastructure around the globe.

Options for Protecting China's Overseas Interests

The PRC's expanding overseas interests have prompted a lively discourse about how best to protect them. At least five ways have been identified. China could:

- continue to free ride on the coattails of other countries
- rethink its aversion to alliances
- reassess its policy of not posting military forces in bases abroad
- enhance the nascent power projection capabilities of the PLA
- outsource the protection of its overseas interests to host countries or private contractors.

Free Riding

To date, Beijing's primary means of protecting overseas interests have been to rely on the kindness of acquaintances. Certainly, this is not China's preferred option, but given the severe limitations of the PLA and other instruments of national power in past decades, Beijing has had little alternative but to look to other great powers, especially the United States, for help. Indeed, China has been free riding on the U.S. Navy since the 1980s and more recently on the U.S. Army in places like Afghanistan.[5] The U.S. Navy has been actively patrolling the sea lanes of the world's oceans and in the process protecting not only U.S. commercial vessels but also the flagged vessels of other countries, including China. But China would prefer not to depend on the altruism of the United States; indeed, Beijing is suspicious of U.S. intentions and worries that if bilateral relations sour and conflict looms, then Washington would restrict or block access to PRC commercial vessels. The so-called Malacca Dilemma is about both China's heavy reliance on one narrow shipping channel and Beijing's perceived vulnerability to blockade by the U.S. Navy. Consequently, there is an active and ongoing discourse about possible alternatives to protecting China's citizens and assets, whether on the high seas or land.

Rethinking Alliances

After decades of insisting that China does not "do alliances," in recent years, Chinese scholars and analysts have been debating the pros and cons of having allies. Moreover, although the PRC has strongly criticized the U.S. alliance system in Asia and Chinese elites have generally avoided advocating for China adopting similar formal security arrangements, Beijing has developed closer security cooperation with other countries.[6] Indeed, if an alliance is defined as "a formal or informal relationship of security cooperation between two or more sovereign states," then China may already have allies.[7]

North Korea stands out as a sui generis case of a Chinese "ally." Formally known as the Democratic People's Republic of Korea (DPRK), North Korea is China's only official treaty ally as of 2017. The official alliance was established by the 1961 Treaty of Mutual Friendship signed between Beijing and Pyongyang. However, the security and military-to-military components of the bilateral relationship have long been essentially nonexistent, and more recently political ties have soured.[8] In short, 21st-century military ties between the PRC and DPRK look nothing like a functioning alliance (ironically, China acted like a real ally prior to the penning of the treaty—in the 1950s when Chinese forces fought side by side with the DPRK Korean People's Army during the Korean War). In fact, in 2017 China has a far more robust bilateral security relationship with Pakistan and a more vibrant multilateral security relationship with the member countries of the Shanghai Cooperation Organisation, including Russia (see below).

One of the leading proponents of more formalized security relationships for the PRC is Yan Xuetong of Tsinghua University. Professor Yan has argued that "China should consider having military bases in countries it considers allies," but acknowledges that this may be in the distant future because the "Chinese government [unfortunately] insists on a nonaligned principle. . . . The major obstacle to China abandoning its nonaligned principle is years of propaganda criticizing alliances as part of a Cold War mentality."[9] Discounting the argument that China's lack of alliances is due to a weak military, Yan framed his support for alliances as befitting a great power: "China has become the world's second-largest power, and the nonaligned principle no longer serves its interests." However, Yan does not think that China's OBOR project will lead to a fundamental transformation of partners into official treaty allies: "I don't think China's One Belt, One Road initiative for economic development across Eurasia can fundamentally change the nature of the relations." He believes that China's embracing of alliances would not drive another Cold War but rather improve U.S.-China relations because the "more allies China makes, the more balanced and stable the relationship will be. The more China shies away from alliances, the greater the chance that Washington will contain China, therefore resulting in an unstable relationship." Clearly, some in China are rethinking alliances.

But if China were to select a 21st-century military ally, the most likely candidate would be Pakistan or Russia; both countries have proven records of extended strategic cooperation with China. Chinese leaders are deeply distrustful of outsiders and other states and trust takes time to develop.

Pakistan is one of the few countries that has been able to sustain good relations with China across multiple decades.[10] From Beijing's perspective, Islamabad has shown itself to be a trusted partner both during the Cold War and after. From Pakistan's perspective, China has proved itself to be an "all-weather" friend. Moreover, neither country has any good alternatives for trustworthy strategic partners in the tumultuous neighborhoods of South and Central Asia. Thus, while Beijing has never fought side by side with Islamabad or directly come to Pakistan's aid in any of its serial conflicts with India, China has provided considerable conventional military assistance, critical support for Islamabad's nuclear program, and the PLA has sustained interactions with Pakistan's armed forces over many decades.

Russia is another logical potential ally for China, but this alliance option comes with heavy baggage for each country. Both Beijing and Moscow are undoubtedly wary of entering another alliance because of the fate of their 20th-century effort. The newly established PRC looked to its socialist elder brother—the Soviet Union—for military support and economic aid. Months after formally establishing a new communist party-state in China, Mao Zedong traveled to Moscow to meet with Joseph Stalin and sign the Treaty of Friendship, Alliance, and Mutual Assistance in February 1950. But a decade later, the alliance fractured because of ideological differences, political tensions, and personality conflicts between two headstrong leaders.[11] These fundamental tensions persist today. Indeed, as one Chinese analyst opined, China and Russia will not cement a 21st-century alliance unless driven to do so by the United States.[12] A scholar at the China Academy of Social Sciences wrote in 2016 that he could find "no evidence supporting the possibility or necessity of a China-Russia military alliance."[13] The expert highlighted the absence of any contributing factors, including lack of a clear direct military threat (from the United States), major differences between Chinese and Russia national interests, and fundamental skepticism that even a formal treaty would guarantee that one country would come to the aid of the other in the event of an attack by a third country.

Moreover, nothing in official PRC rhetoric suggests that Beijing might pursue a military alliance in the near future. President Xi's May 2014 speech to the Conference on Interaction and Confidence Building Measures in Asia made clear that China opposes the U.S. alliance system in Asia.[14]

Referring to U.S. alliances, the Chinese leader stated, "One cannot live in the 21st century with the outdated thinking from the age of Cold War and zero-sum game. . . . [T]o beef up and entrench a military alliance targeted at a third party is not conducive to maintaining common security." Instead, he advocated that security cooperation must be "universal . . . equal . . . [and] inclusive" and that China needs "to innovate [its] security concept, establish a new regional security cooperation architecture, and jointly build a road for security of Asia that is shared by and win-win to all." Reflecting a regional security order that excluded the United States, Xi concluded that "it is for the people of Asia to run the affairs of Asia, solve the problems of Asia, and uphold the security of Asia." Speaking in September 2017, a Foreign Ministry spokesperson clarified China's interest in partnerships over alliances: "We advocate that regional countries should make joint efforts to engage in dialogue instead of confrontation, forge partnerships instead of alliances, and build an Asia-Pacific partnership featuring mutual trust, inclusiveness, and mutually beneficial cooperation."[15] Such strident rhetorical positioning leaves little room for China to enter into a formal alliance.

Yet at least some of China's relationships with other states are starting to resemble alliances, and just because China does not call something an alliance does not mean that it may not be or become one. But for Chinese leaders and analysts, the term *alliance* has negative connotations because it is seen as denoting a security relationship between two states that targets a third state. Indeed, China tends to be both critical and wary of U.S. alliances in the Asia-Pacific because they are perceived to be directed against China.[16]

Overseas Basing

One manifestation of an alliance can be the military bases of one country on the territory of another. In this chapter, we treat overseas bases as an analytically distinct option separate from an alliance (but, of course, they may go together). Beijing's new base in Djibouti is a case in point—despite China's military installation, there is no expanded military cooperation between the two countries. Indeed, Djibouti plays host to the military bases of multiple foreign states, including the United States, France, Italy, and Japan, but none of these countries could be characterized as an ally of Djibouti.

China's approach to overseas bases has undergone the clearest and most dramatic shift in terms of how China thinks about protecting its overseas interests. China has long adhered to its policy of non-interference in the internal affairs of others, which would ostensibly preclude military bases in foreign countries. Yet China's deployment in the Gulf of Aden since 2008 has triggered discussion among the Chinese public and elites of the need for bases to support forward-deployed forces, and in 2017, the Chinese government finally announced it would establish a military base in Djibouti (discussed below).

China's growing economic interests and the increased presence of PRC citizens abroad have largely driven public expectations for the Chinese government to protect these interests and related support for overseas bases to accomplish this mission. According to an in-depth report on Chinese overseas basing requirements, "polling data suggest the Chinese public has a positive attitude toward overseas bases."[17] Indeed, the majority of respondents to polls as early as 2009 supported the construction of an overseas base, and bases were the most popular responses to a separate survey that same year asking how best to improve the PLA Navy (PLAN).[18]

Linked closely with public interest in overseas basing was elite advocacy for the Chinese government to establish such bases. A wide range of Chinese scholars and military commentators began discussing and recommending this course of action, especially after 2008. However, in January 2010, PLAN media commentator Zhang Zhaozhong instead stated that the odds were low that China would build an overseas base.[19] Academics also joined in the debate, with professor Shen Dingli in January 2010 explaining the four responsibilities such a base would accomplish: protecting "people and fortunes overseas . . . [and] trading," as well as preventing "overseas intervention which harms the unity of the country; and the defense against foreign invasion."[20] Discussions have waxed and waned in the years since, but general enthusiasm has persisted.

Chinese military officials have occasionally tactically supported the idea of overseas bases, or at least logistics facilities, to support operations far from Chinese shores. The PLA has studied U.S. operations in World War II and British operations in the early 1980s for the Falkland Islands to understand the requirements of distant sea logistics, suggesting at least an interest in such strategies.[21] After reports suggested China may be interested in establishing a base in the Seychelles in 2011, the Ministry of National Defense stated, "Based on our demand in the escort mission, China will consider stopping over at ports of Seychelles or other countries for supply."[22]

With Djibouti establishing precedent for Chinese overseas bases, this raises the question of whether more will be built, and where they might be. Pakistan is a likely future choice. Civilian strategist Yan Xuetong advocates that China should consider military bases in countries that it considers allies and notes that "China now has only one real ally, Pakistan." Nevertheless, he argued in February 2016 that it is "too early to say where China would build military bases."[23] Pakistan's close security cooperation with China generates intense speculation that it may play host to a Chinese base in the future. It has been suggested in 2014—before serious rumors began about the Djibouti base—that "Pakistan's status as a trusted strategic partner whose interests are closely aligned with China's make the country the most likely location for an overseas Chinese military base."[24] Following the official announcement for Djibouti, the 2016 Department of Defense annual report to Congress suggested that Pakistan may host a future Chinese base.[25] Nevertheless, the exact location of the proposed base is unclear. While Gwadar is mentioned most often, other sites, including Karachi and Jiwani, have been discussed.[26]

Extended Power Projection

Another way to provide greater security for China's overseas interests is to enhance and expand PLA power projection capabilities to be able to respond quickly to specific threats. Of course, this could be done in conjunction with other options, not merely as a standalone option. An important element of expanding power projection would be developing expeditionary capabilities, which would likely emphasize maritime and aviation components.[27]

China's military modernization over the last 20 years has begun to lay the foundation for a blue water navy, but China does not yet have the capability to project power beyond East Asia. The PLAN has deployed its submarines outside Asia with more frequency in recent years and has recently deployed new longer range nuclear submarines, but its submarine force remains insufficient to protect the sea lines of communications along the OBOR route. China's growing fleet of aircraft carriers represents a much more visible "flag" for deployment abroad, but so far Beijing has kept the *Liaoning* in Asia, and it will likely take years if not decades for Beijing to develop carrier strike groups capable of conducting U.S.-style offensive operations around the world. Lastly, reporting suggests the PLAN will expand its marine corps to 100,000 servicemembers (partly by transferring PLA amphibious brigades).[28] This suggests following the U.S. model in order to have the option of deploying a land-based presence to combat terrorism or local instability along the OBOR. Further investment in submarines and more distant deployments of future aircraft carriers may suggest some Chinese interest in actively replacing the U.S. Navy's long-standing role as the ensurer of freedom of navigation, but China does not appear to have made this decision yet.

While China's Navy has led the way in developing power projection capabilities, the PLA Air Force is now beginning to demonstrate its power projection capabilities within the region. China's indigenously produced Y-20 provides a more capable strategic airlift capacity that may enable Beijing to deploy troops—such as its future marine force—quickly in a crisis along OBOR. The September 2016 announcement of the future H-20 next-generation strategic bomber will also extend the air force's reach further from the Chinese homeland, but this would likely have to be paired with an expansion of overseas military basing to support high-intensity operations abroad. One potential solution to this basing requirement would be to make its bomber refuelable, which is reportedly under development.[29] Other future aerial power projection capabilities that may enable Beijing to avoid overseas basing would be to pursue unmanned combat aerial vehicles, such as the *Lijian*.[30] The air force's development of long-range capabilities may alleviate the direct requirement for bases abroad if Chinese aircraft can target hotspots along OBOR with aerial refueling, but the U.S. model clearly shows force projection on a global scale works best with bases abroad.

China has begun to use these more capable military assets in contingencies abroad. The PLA has participated in the United Nations–mandated Gulf of Aden antipiracy mission since 2008, already establishing a limited Chinese presence along the OBOR route years ahead of time. This was followed by noncombat evacuation operations (NEOs) from Libya in 2011 using PLA Air Force cargo planes and Yemen in 2015 using PLAN ships (for details see below).[31] Greater Chinese investment and workers in countries along the OBOR route mean that it is likely the PLA will remain in the business of conducting NEOs.

While China has a growing suite of military hardware that can power project abroad to secure its interests, China's ability to use these platforms has so far been constrained by a lack of dedicated facilities. One study suggested six potential logistics models that China could adopt for its overseas operations: "the pit stop model, lean colonial model, dual use logistics facility, string of pearls model, warehouse model, and model USA."[32] After discounting the lean colonial, warehouse, and U.S. models because they violate China's non-interference policy and too closely mirror often criticized "hegemonic power," the study suggests the dual use logistics facility and string of pearls models. However, "China appears to be planning for a relatively modest set of missions to support its overseas interests," and the study rejects the possibility that China is pursuing the ability to conduct major combat operations abroad via a string of pearls strategy. Such operations would require hospitals; ordnance resupply; petroleum, oil, and lubricant stocks; and likely "bases to provide air cover for naval forces and to defend bases and logistics facilities from attack." These are not evident at any China-related facilities abroad.[33] Looking to the future, the study concludes that "the most efficient means of supporting more robust [PLA] out of area military operations would be a limited network of facilities that distribute functional responsibility geographically" and that such bases would be dual-use and "probably would be characterized by a light footprint with 100 to 500 military personnel conducting supply and logistics functions." Indeed, the Djibouti base is intended to solve many of these challenges and is discussed in the following case study section. Finally, the PLA acknowledges its overseas operations are constrained by many factors, including legal ones.[34]

Outsourcing

Another option is to rely on the host country and/or private contractors to handle security arrangements for China's burgeoning overseas interests. The former is what happened in Pakistan. After the 2007 Red Mosque incident in which PRC citizens were murdered and others were taken hostage, Islamabad, under pressure from Beijing, reportedly established a security force exclusively charged with protecting Chinese citizens in Pakistan.[35] In other countries, PRC state-owned enterprises have relied on their own security guards or hired private security contractors—the Chinese equivalent of Blackwater—composed of retired PLA personnel.[36]

But no matter which one of these options—or combination of options—Beijing decides to pursue to provide security for China's expanding overseas interests, it seems inevitable that the PLA will be expected to play a greater role. The potential set of PLA missions for specific PRC overseas interests is outlined in the table.

Table. Overseas Interests and Potential PLA Missions	
Expanded Chinese Interest	Potential Corresponding PLA Missions
Protection of Chinese citizens living abroad	Noncombatant evacuation operations, humanitarian assistance/disaster relief, counterterrorism, counterinsurgency, training and building partner capacity, special operations ashore, riverine operations, military criminal investigation functions, military diplomacy
Protection of Chinese property/assets	Counterterrorism, counterinsurgency, humanitarian assistance/disaster relief, training and building partner capacity, special operations ashore, military criminal investigation, physical security/force protection, riverine operations, military diplomacy, presence operations
Protection of Chinese shipping against pirates and other nontraditional threats	Counterpiracy, escort shipping, maritime intercept operations; training and building partner capacity; sector patrolling; special operations ashore; visit, board, search, and seizure; replenishment at sea; seaborne logistics; military diplomacy
Protection of sea lines of communication against adversary states	Antisubmarine warfare, antiair warfare, antisurface warfare, carrier operations, escort shipping, maritime intercept operations, air operations off ships, helicopter operations, vertical replenishment, replenishment at sea, seaborne logistics operations, military diplomacy, mine countermeasures

Source: Christopher D. Yung and Ross Rustici, *"Not an Idea We Have to Shun": Chinese Overseas Basing Requirements in the 21st Century*, with Scott Devary and Jenny Lin, China Strategic Perspectives 7 (Washington, DC: NDU Press, 2014), 9.

PLA Thinking about OBOR

OBOR's focus on economics and diplomacy has generated limited attention on the security dimension, and the PLA's voice on this issue has tended to be rather muted. Nevertheless, there is a discernable discourse on the subject.

Discourse

Previous research on PLA views of OBOR have been sporadic and mainly focused on military commentators in high-profile but mainstream publications, which are less authoritative than official PLA ones.[37] Earlier work by these authors found that most PLA discussions of OBOR focused on the benefits accruing to China from economic cooperation, especially against the backdrop of U.S.-China competition for influence in Asia, but did not focus on PLA responsibilities to protect these trade routes or overseas assets. A survey of PLA writings on the topic through 2015 by Andrea Ghiselli argued that while all "support the idea that the PLA should protect Chinese interests along the One Belt and One Road, they disagree about whether the PLA is capable of doing so" and that this debate within the PLA about its role in the initiative outside Asia was likely more representative of PLA opinion rather than pure propaganda work.[38]

Some PLA experts placed greater emphasis on military involvement in the Silk Road Economic Belt or Maritime Silk Road—usually based on their service affiliation, with the navy favoring the Maritime Silk Road and the Army and Air Force favoring the Silk Road Economic Belt. Retired PLA Army analyst Major General Zhu Chenghu cautioned that while overseas bases were necessary, negative global opinion and domestic elections in host nations challenge the feasibility of the idea, and retired PLA Air Force Major General Qiao Liang suggested a solution to this problem through focusing on air force power projection in times of crisis instead of permanent naval deployments. Lyle Goldstein analyzes two articles by PLA authors and finds, "while it still seems quite far-fetched to argue that military strategy is a major impulse for the [Maritime Silk Road], there is a clear strain of threat perception," possibly as opportunistic bandwagoning to justify a larger PLA role in Chinese foreign policy.[39] Most PLA writings cited focus on nontraditional threats and do not envision fighting a conventional adversary, mirroring Western academic consensus about likely PLA operations abroad.[40]

Limited PLA Analysis of OBOR

A broad review of PLA sources suggests the Chinese military has yet to engage in a substantive debate over its roles and missions for OBOR. Indeed, as Goldstein stated, "such writings are rather rare. . . . Chinese military publications have been much more reticent to comment, preferring to stay with safe and relatively straightforward strategic issues, such as the maritime disputes."[41] This is likely the reason most Western analysis of PLA views of the initiative has focused on PLA "talking heads," since they are the only ones providing even superficial analysis from the military. This lack of discussion could be due to a lack of senior-level consensus on the PLA's role, sensitivity to imbuing a military angle to President Xi's premier economic and diplomatic initiative, or because the military deems discussion about operations abroad as classified.[42]

A review of all Chinese military region newspapers, service newspapers, and military academic journals revealed few references to OBOR. OBOR has never been referenced in *China Military Science*, the PLA's most authoritative journal, or in many of the operational and equipment journals that typically feature debates over the future of PLA capabilities and missions. These include *Ordnance Knowledge* [兵器知识], *Winged Missiles* [飞航导弹], and *Missiles and Space Vehicles* [导弹与航天运载技术]. The authors could find only two references to OBOR in the PLA Air Force's *Kongjun Bao*, one in the PLA Navy's *Renmin Haijun*, and none in the PLA Rocket Force's *Huojian Bao*.[43]

There is some evidence that PLA entities studied OBOR in the summer of 2015. That June, PLA Air Force Commander Ma Xiaotian and other senior leaders held a conference with the Academy of Military Science titled the National Aerospace Security and Development Forum.[44] According to *Kongjun Bao*, "the forum was aimed at implementing Chairman Xi's important instruction, serving the national strategy of 'One Belt, One Road,' strengthening the research of the informationized warfare winning mechanism, [and] providing theory support for winning local wars under informationized conditions." While this may seem like empty rhetoric, the forum focused on the PLA Air Force's responsibilities in the maritime domain, which is the most likely area for the service's foreign operations along OBOR. It concluded "that the nation 'will thrive if being oriented to the sea, and will decline if giving up the sea.' . . . The maritime direction has become an important strategic direction concerning the nation's economic lifeline and the expansion of its development interests, and [it] holds a more prominent status in the safeguarding of the national sovereignty, security, and development interests." In explaining the PLA Air Force's role, the forum argued that "aerospace has become closely tied to the seas to an unprecedented extent" and that "no battlefield will be isolated."

PLA Pays Lip Service to OBOR

The PLA does, however, appear to pay lip service to the concept, likely as a way to demonstrate political loyalty to President Xi by supporting his key initiative and perhaps lobby for additional funding and resources. *PLA Daily* references to OBOR jumped dramatically during May 2017, when the first OBOR Forum was held in Beijing. This rhetorical support is common in the PLA's military diplomacy, where OBOR is a common item discussed with foreign interlocutors.

PLA Uses OBOR Opportunity to Reduce Threat Perceptions Abroad

The PLA commonly uses OBOR, and especially the historical Silk Road, as evidence that China's current global outreach and presence is simply a continuation of China's longstanding involvement in global affairs and that this involvement has always been peaceful. On the PLA Navy's 60th anniversary in 2009, Commander Wu Shengli stated: [45]

Figure. *PLA Daily* References to One Belt and One Road Initiative, 2014–2017

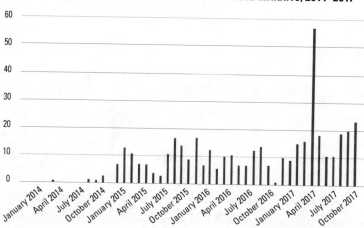

Source: China National Knowledge Infrastructure (data through November 2017).

The maritime silk road starting from China's coastal areas became a friendship bond for spreading China's advanced civilization to the other parts of the world. More than 600 years ago, Zheng He, the famous Chinese navigator of the Ming Dynasty, led the then world's strongest fleets to sail the western seas seven times, reaching as far as the Red Sea and the eastern coast of Africa, and visiting more than 30 countries and regions. They did not sign any unequal treaties, did not claim any territory, and did not bring back even one slave. They wiped out pirates for the countries along their course, broad[ly] disseminated benevolence to friendly nations, brought China's tea, silk, cloth, chinaware, and Oriental civilization to the countries they visited, brought back other people's trust and friendship toward the Chinese nation, and created a world-level example of peaceful and friendly maritime exchanges.

Mini–Case Studies in Protecting China's Overseas Interests

This section examines three examples of PRC efforts to protect overseas interests. These cases have been selected to illustrate the full range of measures Beijing is employing. The first examines the establishment of China's first military base beyond its borders; the second examines the first overseas evacuation of civilians wholly planned and executed by the PLA; and the third examines host-nation efforts to provide enhanced protection for PRC citizens.

Establishing a Base in Djibouti (2017). There have long been rumors about the possibility of China establishing an overseas base, and this speculation has only increased as the PLA has become more involved in United Nations peacekeeping operations (since the 1990s) and anti-piracy operations in the Gulf of Aden (since December 2008). The matter was sensitive in China, and PRC officials routinely denied that Beijing was considering establishing any base overseas. Thus, when questioned in 2011 as to whether the PRC was going to open a base in the Seychelles, a Ministry of Foreign

Affairs spokesman emphatically denied it, stating, "China has never set up military bases in other countries."[46] Moreover, Beijing repeatedly denied that China was going to locate an installation in Djibouti. Even after the Djibouti president publicly announced in May 2016 that the two countries were discussing the prospect, the PRC Ministry of National Defense continued to deny the reports.[47]

Nevertheless, Chinese civilian and military analysts had for years openly discussed the possibility and logic of such an unprecedented move. According to Senior Colonel Dai Xu, the criteria for locating "overseas bases," included not only "the needs of escorting [commercial vessels] and peacekeeping . . . [but] also . . . the long-term protection of [China's] overseas interests."[48] Djibouti was a logical choice for several reasons. First, it is almost certainly the least controversial location. As noted above, other states already have military installations there, and Beijing knew it would be hard for critics inside or outside of China to accuse the PRC of creating a new alliance, or strengthening an existing alliance, and/or threatening third countries. If China had established its first overseas military base in Pakistan, the move would have likely provoked tremendous controversy, especially from India.[49]

Second, the location makes great sense considering PLA recent activities in the Middle East and North Africa and China's growing interests in the region. China officially has described the facility as a "logistics facility," which will provide valuable support for ongoing PLAN anti-piracy operations in the Gulf of Aden and potentially for Chinese forces involved in multiple United Nations peacekeeping operations in the region, including South Sudan and Lebanon. Furthermore, Chinese overseas interests in the area are significant and only likely to grow since the Middle East constitutes the nexus of the overland "belt" and maritime "road" of the PRC OBOR initiative. Not only does China have substantial economic investments in countries of the region, but there are also approximately 500,000 PRC citizens living and working in the Middle East and as many as 1 million citizens on the African continent.[50]

China's base in Djibouti positions it to extend military power and strategic influence over a critical part of OBOR, and the base appears to be designed with room to grow as Chinese interests expand in the coming years. Although rumors of China's troop strength initially went as high as 10,000, it appears China began with stationing several hundred troops there, including some marines.[51] This makes it comparable to most other foreign bases, though the United States has 4,000 troops.[52] The 90-acre base is reportedly capable of supporting a brigade, with a heliport (including a 400-meter runway), ammunition, as well as petroleum, oil, and lubricant storage.[53] The base has already conducted several live-fire exercises since it opened in August 2017, and according to one analysis, it "will be able to accommodate all but the two largest ships in China's fleet."[54]

Evacuating Citizens from Yemen (2015). Beijing is increasingly concerned about the safety of its citizens in hot spots around the world, and for more than two decades the PRC has been engaged in efforts to extract civilians from harm's way. Despite modest capabilities, the Ministry of Foreign Affairs has effectively conducted more than two dozen evacuations from countries around the globe. All but two of these operations have been purely civilian with no discernible involvement of PLA personnel or assets. The first exception was in 2011, when Beijing organized the extraction of approximately 36,000 PRC citizens from the chaos of post–Muammar Qadhafi Libya, mostly using civilian and commercial vessels with some support from one PLA naval vessel in the Mediterranean. Some civilians were flown out on chartered commercial airliners, but several hundred were evacuated on PLA Air Force transports via Sudan.[55]

The second and most noteworthy participation by the PLA in an overseas evacuation operation was the 2015 NEO from Yemen. The operation, while coordinated with the other PRC bureaucratic actors, notably the Ministry of Foreign Affairs, marked the first time that the PLA took the central role in planning and executing an evacuation of Chinese citizens from a crisis zone far from home. In response to Saudi Arabia's decision to attack Houthi rebels in Yemen, China evacuated more than 600 Chinese citizens and nearly 300 foreign citizens over a week from multiple ports in Yemen using three PLAN ships.[56] Some of these people were initially transported to Djibouti before flying home to China, underscoring the strategic location of China's first overseas military base.[57]

The operation clearly showed the benefits of China's military deployments abroad. Most importantly, the evacuation began quickly because the PLAN ships involved were drawn from Gulf of Aden patrols, reaching port to start evacuations in 3 days.[58] By comparison, a naval deployment from the Chinese mainland would likely have taken upward of 2 weeks. Second, the security situation was likely too dangerous for private companies to transport the evacuees, showing the limits of relying primarily on commercial assets as in the Libya NEO.[59] Third, evacuating foreign citizens allowed China, and especially the PLA, to frame Chinese foreign deployments as beneficial to others. The Ministry of Foreign Affairs stated that the NEO was a "special action by the Chinese government to evacuate foreign nationals," which embodied the notions of 'putting the people first.'"[60] This narrative was also touted at home as a reflection of President Xi's "strong army dream."[61]

Outsourcing Security of PRC Citizens in Pakistan (Since 2007). Since the 1990s when Chinese citizens have been more active traveling and living overseas, they have been subject to crimes and acts of violence. Of course, PRC citizens can be victimized by criminals or terrorists in any country, but they are more vulnerable in some countries and regions than others. Chinese nationals have been killed and/or kidnapped in tumultuous and unstable countries in Central Asia, South Asia, the Middle East, and Africa.

While the thousands of Chinese living and working in Pakistan had been occasionally victimized by criminals and extremists, until the mid-2000s, they had not been targeted by militants to the same extent Westerners had. The turning point was the Red Mosque incident in mid-2007 after seven Chinese massage parlor workers were kidnapped by Islamic extremists in Islamabad.[62] The PRC citizens were eventually released unharmed, but the episode culminated in the siege and storming of the Red Mosque complex in July 2007. Pakistani commandos stormed the fortified mosque defended by armed Islamic extremists on July 10, and 20 hours later the complex was secured at the cost of more than 100 fatalities. The battle was the most intense and sustained combat that Pakistan's capital city had ever witnessed.[63]

The June kidnapping of the seven Chinese workers prompted a proactive response by PRC officials starting with PRC ambassador to Pakistan, Luo Zhaohui. Luo reached out to numerous Pakistani political figures, including the sitting prime minister, former officials, and even the leader of the militants holding the Chinese hostages. PRC Minister of Public Security Zhou Yongkang also spoke with his Pakistani counterpart, and PLA leaders communicated with Pakistani military leaders. In addition, President Hu Jintao telephoned Pakistan President Pervez Musharraf on the matter.[64]

Although the Chinese workers were released unharmed, Chinese citizens in Pakistan became targets after the bloody end to the Red Mosque incident, as many Islamic radicals blamed China for the crackdown. In response, PRC leaders demanded that the Pakistan government do much more to protect Chinese citizens. Islamabad established a National Crisis Management Cell to coordinate the protection of PRC citizens working in Pakistan.[65] The cell also formed a joint liaison committee that included PRC diplomats. Furthermore, a 24-hour hotline was created linking China's embassy in Islamabad with Pakistan's interior ministry and provincial authorities across the country. In addition, "thousands" of additional security personnel were added to secure Chinese construction projects, and Chinese workers were transported in armed convoys.

According to one account, by December 2008, Pakistan mobilized nine thousand soldiers and police to guard PRC citizens. Moreover, the PRC reportedly contributed almost $300 million worth of new security equipment for Pakistani police.[66] The increased efforts appear to have improved the security of PRC citizens in-country. Beijing was sufficiently satisfied. The improved security situation allowed Xi to make a visit to Pakistan in April 2015 and to declare that Beijing was committing $46 billion worth of infrastructure investments to develop an ambitious China-Pakistan Economic Corridor.[67]

Conclusions

As China's national interests have expanded further beyond the shores of the PRC, Beijing has gradually embraced the idea that China is responsible for protecting these interests and that the PLA ought to play a key role in safeguarding these interests against both traditional and nontraditional security threats.

The PLA constitutes only one set of tools—albeit an important set—in the larger PRC toolkit available to protect China's interests abroad. But no matter which of the five security options discussed above Beijing adopts to protect its burgeoning overseas interests, the PLA will be expected and will be ordered to play a greater role. While China's armed forces will salute and do their best to obey, the PRC's flag continues to lag in terms of available capabilities and resources especially for out-of-area security requirements.

Of the five discrete alternatives identified in this chapter, free riding and outsourcing seem destined to continue for the foreseeable future. Both are appealing options in the absence of robust enhanced PLA capabilities. Indeed, the PLA's power projection capabilities are likely to grow only incrementally and remain extremely limited, especially for out-of-area deployments and employments in the near to medium term. Meanwhile, barring a dramatic worsening of the strategic environment, China is unlikely to go much beyond "rethinking" alliances. The most likely developments in coming years are the establishment of at least one or two more military bases overseas, with Pakistan being perhaps the most plausible location. With the construction of a logistics facility in Djibouti, China has effectively broken the taboo of building military installations beyond the borders of the PRC.

Although OBOR is officially a new foreign policy initiative under President Xi, the overseas interests at stake for the PLA to protect have slowly been growing in these places since the 1990s. The PLA has already used some of its newer military capabilities in contingencies along the route—mainly evacuating Chinese citizens from warzones, such as Libya in 2011 and Yemen in 2015. As greater numbers of more advanced platforms come online—including aircraft carriers, submarines, strategic airlift and long-distance bombers—an important question is how hard the PLA will be pressed to employ these capabilities far from China's shores.

Notes

[1] "Trade No Longer Follows the Flag, Prime Minister," *Financial Times*, November 13, 2015, available at <www.ft.com/content/cd0d47b8-8a04-11e5-9f8c-a8d619fa707c>.

[2] The phrase *Great Leap Outward* was coined by one of the authors. See Andrew Scobell, "Introduction," in *China's Great Leap Outward: The Hard and Soft Dimensions of a Rising Power*, ed. Andrew Scobell and Marylena Mantas (New York: Academy of Political Science, 2014), 5–6.

[3] For good overviews of One Belt, One Road (OBOR), see Nadege Rolland, *China's Eurasian Century? Political and Strategic Implications of the Belt and Road Initiative* (Seattle: National Bureau of Asian Research, May 2017); and Joel Wuthnow, *Chinese Perspectives on the Belt and Road Initiative: Strategic Rationales, Risks, and Implications*, China Strategic Perspectives 12 (Washington, DC: NDU Press, 2017).

[4] Daniel Hartnett, "The 'New Historic Missions': Reflections on Hu Jintao's Military Legacy," in *Assessing the People's Liberation Army in the Hu Jintao Era*, ed. Roy Kamphausen, David Lai, and Travis Tanner (Carlisle, PA: Strategic Studies Institute, April 2014), 31–80; Daniel Hartnett, *Towards a Globally Focused Chinese Military: The Historic Missions of the Chinese Armed Forces* (Alexandria, VA: CNA, 2008); David M. Finkelstein, "China's National Military Strategy," in *The People's Liberation Army in the Information Age*, ed. James C. Mulvenon and Richard H. Yang (Santa Monica, CA: RAND, 1999), 99–145.

[5] Jonas Parello-Plesner and Mathieu Duchâtel, *China's Strong Arm: Protecting Citizens and Assets Abroad* (London: International Institute for Strategic Studies, 2015), 69.

[6] Chinese government officials, media, and experts castigate U.S. alliances as the cause of much of the tensions in Asia. See, for example, Timothy R. Heath, "China and the U.S. Alliance System," *The Diplomat*, available at <http://thediplomat.com/2014/06/china-and-the-u-s-alliance-system/>; and Adam P. Liff, "China and the U.S. Alliance System," *China Quarterly*, no. 233 (March 2018), 137–165.

[7] Stephen Walt, *The Origins of Alliances* (Cornell, NY: Cornell University Press, 1987), 1, 1n and 12n.

[8] Andrew Scobell and Mark Cozad, "China's North Korea Policy: Rethink or Recharge?" *Parameters* 44, no. 1 (Spring 2014), 51–63.

[9] Huang Yufan, "Yan Xuetong Urges China to Adopt a More Assertive Foreign Policy," *New York Times*, February 9, 2016, available at <www.nytimes.com/2016/02/10/world/asia/china-foreign-policy-yan-xuetong.html>.

[10] On the China-Pakistan relationship, see Andrew Small, *The China-Pakistan Axis: Asia's New Geopolitics* (New York: Oxford University Press, 2015). On China's security relations with the Shanghai Cooperation Organisation, see Andrew Scobell, Ely Ratner, and Michael Beckley, *China's Strategy Toward South and Central Asia: An Empty Fortress* (Santa Monica, CA: RAND, 2014.)

[11] Odd Arne Westad, *Brothers in Arms: The Rise and Fall of the Sino-Soviet Alliance, 1945–1963* (Washington, DC: Woodrow Wilson Center Press, 1998); Chen Jian, *Mao's China and the Cold War* (Chapel Hill: University of North Carolina Press, 2001).

[12] Chen Dingding, "Are China and Russia Moving Toward a Formal Alliance?" *The Diplomat*, May 30, 2014, available at <http://thediplomat.com/2014/05/are-china-and-russia-moving-toward-a-formal-alliance/>.

[13] Zheng Yu, "China and Russia: Alliance or No Alliance?," *China-U.S. Focus*, July 29, 2016, available at <www.chinausfocus.com/foreign-policy/china-and-russia-alliance-or-no-alliance>.

[14] Xi Jinping [习近平], "New Asian Security Concept for New Progress in Security Cooperation" [积极树立亚洲安全观共创安全合作新局面], speech delivered to the Fourth Summit of the Conference on Interaction and Confidence Building Measures in Asia, Shanghai, May 21, 2014, available at <www.fmprc.gov.cn/mfa_eng/zxxx_662805/t1159951.shtml>.

[15] "Foreign Ministry Spokesperson Hua Chunying's Regular Press Conference on September 14, 2017," Chinese Ministry of Foreign Affairs, September 14, 2017, available at <www.fmprc.gov.cn/mfa_eng/xwfw_665399/s2510_665401/2511_665403/t1493166.shtml>. See also the white paper *China's Policies of Asia-Pacific Security Cooperation* (Beijing: State Council Information Office of the People's Republic of China, January 2017), available at <www.fmprc.gov.cn/mfa_eng/zxxx_662805/t1429771.shtml>.

[16] Heath, "China and the U.S. Alliance System."

[17] Christopher D. Yung and Ross Rustici, *"Not an Idea We Have to Shun": Chinese Overseas Basing Requirements in the 21st Century*, China Strategic Perspectives 7, with Scott Devary and Jenny Lin (Washington, DC: NDU Press, 2014), 53.

[18] Ibid.; Gao Youbin [高友斌], "Netizens Call for Overseas Base, Aircraft Carrier Formation to Maintain Distant Sea Rights and Interests" [网民呼吁寻求

海外基地组航母编队维护远洋利益], *Global Times* [环球时报], October 21, 2009, available at <http://mil.huanqiu.com/china/2009-10/608793.html>.

[19] "Zhang Zhaozhong: Probability That China Builds Overseas Base Not Large" [张召忠：中国在海外建军事基地的可能性不大], *QQ.com*, January 19, 2010, available at <http://news.qq.com/a/20100119/002913.htm>.

[20] Yung and Rustici, *"Not an Idea We Have to Shun,"* 8.

[21] Ibid., 10; Christopher D. Yung, "Sinica Rules the Waves? The People's Liberation Army Navy's Power Projection and Anti-Access/Area Denial Lessons from the Falklands/Malvinas Conflict," in *Chinese Lessons from Other People's Wars*, ed. Andrew Scobell, David Lai, and Roy Kamphausen (Carlisle, PA: Strategic Studies Institute, 2011).

[22] Li Zhenyu, "China Denies Overseas Military Base Rumors," *People's Daily Online*, December 14, 2011, available at <http://en.people.cn/90786/7676578.html>.

[23] Yufan, "Yan Xuetong Urges China to Adopt a More Assertive Foreign Policy."

[24] Yung and Rustici, *"Not an Idea We Have to Shun,"* 2.

[25] *Annual Report to Congress: Military and Security Developments Involving the People's Republic of China 2017* (Washington, DC: Office of the Secretary of Defense, 2017), 5.

[26] Rajeswari Pillai Rajagopalan, "A New China Military Base in Pakistan?" *The Diplomat*, February 9, 2018, available at <https://thediplomat.com/2018/02/a-new-china-military-base-in-pakistan/>.

[27] See, for example, Cristina L. Garafola and Timothy R. Heath, *The Chinese Air Force's First Steps Toward Becoming an Expeditionary Air Force* (Santa Monica, CA: RAND, 2017).

[28] Minnie Chan, "As Overseas Ambitions Expand, China Plans 400 Per Cent Increase to Marine Corps Numbers, Sources Say," *South China Morning Post* (Hong Kong), March 13, 2017, available at <www.scmp.com/news/china/diplomacy-defence/article/2078245/overseas-ambitions-expand-china-plans-400pc-increase>.

[29] "Expert: If the Airborne Refuelable-6K Is True, Its Range Will Exceed 10,000 Kilometers" [专家：空中受油型轰-6K若属实 其航程将超1万公里], *People's Daily Online*, August 18, 2017, available at <http://military.people.com.cn/n1/2017/0818/c1011-29479619.html>.

[30] Jeffrey Lin and P.W. Singer, "Meet China's Sharp Sword, a Stealth Drone That Can Likely Carry 2 Tons of Bombs," *Popular Science*, January 18, 2017.

[31] On People's Liberation Army (PLA) involvement in these operations, see Degang Sun, "China's Military Relations with the Middle East," in *The Red Star*

and the Crescent: China and the Middle East, ed. James Reardon-Anderson (New York: Oxford University Press, 2018), 99–100.

[32] Yung and Rustici, *"Not an Idea We Have to Shun,"* 1.

[33] Ibid., 11.

[34] An Puzhong [安普忠], "Accelerating the Legislation of Overseas Non-War Military Operations" [加快海外非战争军事行动立法], *PLA Daily*, March 10, 2015, available at <www.81.cn/2015qglh/2015-03/10/content_6388233.htm>.

[35] Parello-Plesner and Duchâtel, *China's Strong Arm*, 79–81.

[36] Charles Clover, "Chinese Private Security Companies Go Global," *Financial Times*, February 26, 2017, available at <www.ft.com/content/2a1ce1c8-fa7c-11e6-9516-2d969e0d3b65>; and Zi Yang, "China's Private Security Companies: Domestic and International Roles," *China Brief* 16, no. 15 (October 4, 2016), available at <https://jamestown.org/program/chinas-private-security-companies-domes-tic-international-roles/>.

[37] Nathan Beauchamp-Mustafaga, "Dispatch from Beijing: PLA Writings on the New Silk Road," *China Brief* 15, no. 4 (February 20, 2015), available at <https://jamestown.org/program/dispatch-from-beijing-pla-writings-on-the-new-silk-road/>; Nathan Beauchamp-Mustafaga, "Rolling Out the New Silk Road: Railroads Undergird Beijing's Strategy," *China Brief* 15, no. 8 (April 16, 2015), available at <https://jamestown.org/program/rolling-out-the-new-silk-road-railroads-under-gird-beijings-strategy/>; Andrea Ghiselli, "The Belt, the Road and the PLA," *China Brief* 15, no. 20 (October 19, 2015), available at <https://jamestown.org/program/the-belt-the-road-and-the-pla/>. See also, Wuthnow, *Chinese Perspectives on the Belt and Road Initiative*.

[38] PLA commentators are first and foremost propaganda outlets. See Andrew Chubb, "Propaganda, Not Policy: Explaining the PLA's 'Hawkish Faction' (Part One)," *China Brief* 13, no. 15 (July 25, 2013), available at <https://jamestown.org/program/propaganda-not-policy-explaining-the-plas-hawkish-faction-part-one/>.

[39] Lyle Goldstein, "China's 'One Belt One Road' Is a Big Deal. So What Is the Role for Beijing's Military?" *National Interest*, November 20, 2016, available at <http://nationalinterest.org/print/feature/chinas-one-belt-one-road-big-deal-so-what-the-role-beijings-18456>.

[40] Parello-Plesner and Duchâtel, *China's Strong Arm*; and Oriana Skylar Mastro, "China's Military Is about to Go Global," *National Interest*, December 18, 2014, available at <http://nationalinterest.org/feature/chinas-military-about-go-global-11882>.

[41] Goldstein, "China's 'One Belt One Road' Is a Big Deal."

⁴² Almost all People's Republic of China (PRC) official speeches and writings stress the economic cooperation aspect of One Belt, One Road (OBOR) and downplay/deny any strategic ambitions. See Wuthnow, *Chinese Perspectives on the Belt and Road Initiative.*

⁴³ There was one reference to the historical silk road in *Renmin Haijun* from April 2009 and two from *Kongjun Bao* in January 2010 and October 2010. For articles that mention OBOR specifically, see Gong Benhai and Xu Yi [巩本海, 许毅], "Third 'National Aerospace Security and Development Forum' Is Held in Beijing" [第三届 "国家空天安全与发展论坛"在京举行], *Kongjun Bao* [空军报], June 24, 2015, 1; Gao Jie [高杰], "Resolutely Maintain the Core, Speed Up the Strategic Transformation: Theory Study Central Group of the PLA Air Force Party Committee Holds a Concentrated Study Session on 'Promoting the In-Depth Implementation of Safeguarding the Core and Obeying Command, Speeding Up the Process of the Air Force's Strategic Transformation from the New Starting Point of Reform and Military Strengthening'" [坚定维护核心加速战略转型: 空军党委理论学习中心组开展 "推动维护核心, 听从指挥落深落实,在改革强军新起点上加速推进空军战略转型" 专题集中学习综述], *Kongjun Bao* [空军报], June 26, 2017, 1; and Zhao Xin [赵新], "Vigorously Strengthen the 'Four Counters' Work to Build a Defense Line for Covert Struggle" [大力加强"四反"工作筑牢隐蔽斗争防线], *Renmin Haijun* [人民海军], July 3, 2017, 3.

⁴⁴ Gong and Xu, "Third 'National Aerospace Security and Development Forum' Is Held in Beijing," 1.

⁴⁵ Wu Shengli [吴胜利], "Make Concerted Efforts to Jointly Build Harmonious Ocean" [同心协力共建和谐海洋], *Renmin Haijun* [人民海军], April 22, 2009, 1.

⁴⁶ Li Zhenyu, "China Denies Overseas Military Base Rumors," *People's Daily Online*, December 14, 2011, available at <http://en.people.cn/90786/7676578.html>.

⁴⁷ Ben Blanchard, "China Military Declines to Confirm Djibouti Base Plan," Reuters, June 25, 2015, available at <www.reuters.com/article/us-china-defence-djibouti/china-military-declines-to-confirm-djibouti-base-plan-idUSKBN0P51CV20150625>; and Kristina Wong, "China's Military Makes Move into Africa," *The Hill*, November 24, 2015, available at <https://thehill.com/policy/defense/261153-chinas-military-makes-move-into-africa>.

⁴⁸ Retired Rear Admiral Yin Zhuo proposed the idea of a PLA base in Djibouti. See Yung and Rustici, *"Not an Idea We Have to Shun,"* 11.

⁴⁹ Sarah Zheng, "China's Djibouti Military Base: 'Logistics Facility,' or Platform for Geopolitical Ambitions Overseas?" *South China Morning Post* (Hong

Kong), October 1, 2017, available at <www.scmp.com/news/china/diplomacy-defence/article/2113300/chinas-djibouti-military-base-logistics-facility-or>.

[50] For estimates on the number of PRC citizens in the Middle East and Africa, see, respectively, Andrew Scobell and Alireza Nader, *China in the Middle East: The Wary Dragon* (Santa Monica, CA: RAND, 2016), 18; and Howard W. French, *China's Second Continent: How a Million Migrants Are Building a New Empire in Africa* (New York: Random House, 2015).

[51] "China Formally Opens First Overseas Military Base in Djibouti," Reuters, August 1, 2017, available at <www.reuters.com/article/us-china-djibouti/china-formally-opens-first-overseas-military-base-in-djibouti-idUSKBN1AH3E3>.

[52] Of the eight countries with facilities there, most are small, and France and the United States have the largest troop levels, 2,000 and 4,000, respectively. See Erica Downs, Jeffrey Becker, and Patrick deGategno, *China's Military Support Facility in Djibouti: The Economic and Security Dimensions of China's First Overseas Base* (Arlington, VA: CNA, July 2017).

[53] Mike Yeo, "Satellite Imagery Offers Clues to China's Intentions in Djibouti," *Defense News*, November 8, 2017, available at <www.defensenews.com/global/mideast-africa/2017/11/08/satellite-imagery-offers-clues-to-chinas-intentions-in-djibouti/>.

[54] Kinling Lo, "Chinese Troops Head Back into the Djibouti Desert for Live-Fire Drills," *South China Morning Post* (Hong Kong), November 25, 2017, available at <www.scmp.com/news/china/diplomacy-defence/article/2121547/chinese-troops-head-back-djibouti-desert-live-fire>; Downs, Becker, and deGategno, *China's Military Support Facility in Djibouti*.

[55] Gabe Collins and Andrew Erickson, "Implications of China's Military Evacuation of Citizens from Libya," *China Brief* 11, no. 4 (March 11, 2011), available at <https://jamestown.org/program/implications-of-chinas-military-evacuation-of-citizens-from-libya/>.

[56] "Spotlight: China Completes Evacuation from Yemen, Assisting 629 Nationals, 279 Foreigners," Xinhua, April 7, 2015, available at <http://news.xinhuanet.com/english/2015-04/07/c_134130679.htm>.

[57] "Chinese Warship Carrying 83 Evacuees from Yemen Arrives in Djibouti," Xinhua, April 7, 2015, available at <http://news.xinhuanet.com/english/2015-04/07/c_134129830.htm>.

[58] Guo Yuandan and Yu Wen [郭媛丹, 于文], "Chinese Navy Has Temporarily Paused Patrols in the Gulf of Aden: Expert—May Be to Participate in

Yemen Evacuation" [中国海军暂停亚丁湾护航 专家：或赴也门参加撤侨], *Global Times* [环球时报], March 28, 2015, available at <http://world.huanqiu.com/exclusive/2015-03/6033036.html>.

59 Zhang Yunbi, "Navy Wins Praise for Evacuating Foreigners," *China Daily* (Beijing), April 7, 2015, available at <www.chinadaily.com.cn/china/2015-04/07/content_20012083.htm>; and Xie Chuanjiao, "Cool under Fire, Captain Leads by Example," *China Daily*, September 3, 2015, available at <www.chinadaily.com.cn/cndy/2015-09/03/content_21782031.htm>.

60 "Foreign Ministry Spokesperson Hua Chunying's Regular Press Conference on April 3, 2015," Ministry of Foreign Affairs, April 3, 2015, available at <www.fmprc.gov.cn/mfa_eng/xwfw_665399/s2510_665401/2511_665403/t1251976.shtml>.

61 Fan Jianghuai, Zhou Meng, and Zhou Yuan [范江怀, 周猛, 周远], "To Raise the Strong Army Dream, the Rule of Law Is the Cornerstone" [托举强军梦, 法治基石坚如磐], *PLA Daily* (Beijing), October 28, 2016, available at <www.81.cn/2016gtzghy/2016-10/28/content_7331168.htm>.

62 Small, *The China-Pakistan Axis*, 111.

63 Ibid., ix–xvi.

64 Ibid., xii–xiv.

65 Ibid., 111–112.

66 Isaac B. Kardon, *China and Pakistan: Emerging Strains in the Entente Cordiale* (Arlington, VA: Project 2049 Institute, 2011), 14, 16.

67 Nevertheless, PRC security concerns persist, and in February 2016, Pakistan promised to create a "special force" of 10,000 troops to protect Chinese workers and investments. See Shannon Tiezzi, "Pakistan Will Provide 'Special Force' to Defend Chinese Investments," *The Diplomat*, February 5, 2016, available at <https://thediplomat.com/2016/02/pakistan-will-provide-special-force-to-defend-chinese-investments>.

PART II

BUILDING A JOINT FORCE

CHAPTER 5

TOWARD A MORE JOINT, COMBAT-READY PLA?

By Mark R. Cozad

Military reform has been a central element of Xi Jinping's military program since ascending to the top positions in both the Community Party of China and military in 2012. The need to prepare and equip the People's Liberation Army (PLA) to "fight and win informationized wars" has been a central, if not *the* central, theme driving these reform and modernization efforts. Accordingly, joint operations factor heavily into the PLA's assessments of the capabilities it needs to improve its status as a modern, informationized military. During Xi's tenure, the PLA has placed significant focus on all aspects of improving joint operations, including personnel, architecture, organization, training, and concept development. These renewed efforts under Xi are building on several years of similar programs, all of which sought to build on lessons learned derived from observations of recent foreign military developments, particularly those involving U.S. operations. These lessons have magnified the importance of joint operations in modern warfare. From this standpoint, Xi's interest in joint operations has not been so much a new start as a top-level reinforcement of previous efforts and a recognition that future success will rely upon substantive, sustained progress in joint operations capacity.

This chapter addresses the question of how much progress the PLA has made in the joint operations arena during Xi's tenure. To accomplish this, the chapter examines how joint operations have evolved in the PLA since 2000 in order to identify where Xi's policies have diverged from earlier practices and where they have maintained continuity. Similarly, this chapter provides context on how previous reform efforts relevant to joint operations development have fared. While the PLA has outlined new initiatives in recent years designed to improve PLA readiness for actual combat, previous efforts in similar areas have met with limited success over the past two decades. Lastly, this chapter discusses specific criteria for evaluating PLA joint operations progress.

The overall conclusions provided in this chapter do not address two key areas: organization and service-related personnel decisions within that structure. Clearly, these two areas are essential elements in building a military culture that embraces joint operations; however, these structural questions become significantly less important if the basic building blocks of joint operations have not been developed and put into effect. These building blocks include operational concepts; personnel development, training, and education; and field training, experimentation, and exercises. Absent developments in these three core areas, organizational reforms, personnel changes at senior levels, and information architecture achieve few, if any, tangible improvements in capability.

Recent PLA Reforms in Context

The 1990s were a watershed in PLA history. Military and civilian leaders in the People's Republic of China (PRC) closely observed U.S. operations in the Middle East and North Atlantic Treaty Organization operations in southeastern Europe and realized how far their forces had fallen behind these technologically advanced militaries in several key areas. On further study, PLA leaders identified not only major shortfalls in technology and weapons systems, but also in conceptual development, organizational structure, and personnel. Concerned that China's forces were unprepared for modern combat, PRC analysts studied the successes and failures of the Gulf War and Kosovo campaigns, drawing lessons for the PLA about "asymmetrical war" and "local wars under high-tech conditions," focusing particularly on joint operations as a means for efficiently fighting in future wars that relied on information technology, networks, and advanced weapons controlled by different parts of the military.[1] Their research led to a wholesale restructuring of all PLA services that encompassed a new military strategy, new operational concepts, the pursuit of advanced technologies, and accelerated purchases of advanced Russian weapons and platforms.[2] Improved joint operations capability was viewed as an imperative.

In particular, the operational surprises and resulting lessons learned from U.S. operations in the First Gulf War and Kosovo compelled the PLA to confront its weaknesses and step up its modernization efforts. U.S. operations demonstrated that modern forces—particularly air forces—equipped with precision weapons; advanced command, control, communications, computers, intelligence, surveillance, and reconnaissance (C4ISR) capabilities; and aerial refueling offered an unprecedented threat to the survivability of the PRC's most strategically significant infrastructure.[3] Many PLA observers thus argued that joint operations—particularly the effective integration of offensive air and naval operations—would define future conflicts, requiring the PLA to invest in a networked system of systems encompassing precision munitions, automated command and control systems, and intelligence, surveillance, and reconnaissance (ISR).[4]

These same observers also noted that U.S. and allied forces had easily gained and maintained the initiative in each conflict, deploying with impunity around the periphery of the countries under attack and operating with little concern for defending their own assets against attack.[5] In the face of such overwhelming adversary forces, the PLA could no longer rely solely on massive numbers of ground forces. Instead, future conflicts would depend on having significant maneuverability and destructive capacity. In short, many capabilities applicable to future combat resided outside of the

PLA ground forces. The need for developing joint operations concepts and capabilities became understood as the critical link for bringing together the PLA's full range of combat capabilities.

Calls within the PLA for new programs to develop commanders and improve training highlighted the importance of developing the PLA's joint operations capability. Broad efforts within the PLA to improve the overall quality of its personnel focused on a variety of aspects such as recruitment, retention, technical training, and military education. With the growing demand for technically competent people, PLA efforts required a dedicated program to ensure that its new officers and soldiers were suited for modern military operations. The need for commanders versed in modern warfare was particularly important. These commanders were envisioned as the primary ingredient necessary to "master joint operations under modern high-tech conditions."[6] Moreover, they were expected to possess "keen political insight" and a "deep strategic mind" along with mastery of "high-tech operational theories and compatible science and technology."[7] Programs to cultivate talented personnel were subsequently focused on emphasizing the ability to command joint operations.[8] These efforts culminated in efforts throughout the military regions to improve training for commanders and mid-level staffs and develop the competency of technical personnel needed for future joint operations.[9]

The PLA has also treated training reform efforts as a means for improving joint force readiness. Since 2001, the PLA has issued its third *Outline of Military Training and Evaluation* (OMTE). The 2001 version was largely focused on improving the framework for how PLA training was performed and evaluated. It followed an extended period of study and experimentation in the 1990s to ensure that new training methods could be implemented effectively across the PLA and that innovations had been tested extensively. The 2009 OMTE placed particular emphasis on building joint operations capacity. The new guideline treated joint operations as its primary theme.[10] The most recent iteration of the OMTE has likewise placed joint operations as a core element.

These examples demonstrate that the need for joint operations and the infrastructure required to support its development was recognized well in advance of Xi's leadership. The programs to develop commanders and improve training were widely touted within the PLA as important steps toward creating a modern, high-tech—later informationized—military. Likewise, joint operations concept development began in earnest in the early 1990s and gained significant momentum during the 10th and 11th Five Year Plans.

PLA Joint Operations Concepts

In the 1993 revision of the *Military Strategic Guidelines in the New Era* (still in force today with minor adjustments), the PLA's observations coalesced into the core objective of conducting integrated joint operations, a concept that predates Xi and has, since its inception, guided the development of new systems and operational concepts.[11] The PLA textbook *Science of Campaigns* defines *integrated joint operations* as "using integrated methods and information technology, blending an operational system from all services and arms and other types of armed strengths with operational units to form an integrated whole."[12] The PLA's evolving framework for integrated joint operations forms the foundation for its current joint operations concept and is a driving force behind two key concepts—noncontact warfare and target-centric warfare.[13] In order to achieve success in local wars under informationized conditions, the PLA recognizes that it must link military information systems and networks that will enable PRC military planners to fuse "operational strengths" from each of the PLA's services.[14] These integrated joint operations in theory rely on a flexible system that permits and enables adjustments and coordination over the entire depth of the battlespace and within all domains as the situation requires. This flexibility allows for more precise applications of military force based on new information as it becomes available and is assimilated into the PLA's command automation system. As one senior PLA officer argued in the early conceptual development stages, these types of operations are driven by "the guiding ideology of 'comprehensive supremacy, precision strike, and destruction of systems.'"[15]

Integrated joint operations are linked conceptually with the continuing imperatives to improve the PLA's level of "informationization" that enables "system-of-systems operations."[16] Informationization has been a core concept in PLA modernization formally for over a decade.[17] In turn, informationization is the essence of integrated joint operations, which rely on information networks to integrate and systematize operations designed to obtain information superiority.[18] An informationized architecture forms the basis for nearly all facets of integrated joint operations. Integrated joint operations thus are considered "the basic form and necessary requirement for informationized war," particularly in terms of ensuring real-time information support, effective precision weapon employment, and a system capable of rapidly deploying and configuring the necessary forces for a range of environments and contingencies.[19] Informationization will permit the realization of truly integrated joint operations through the development of precision timing for maneuvers, precise position data for fire strikes, and precision support for forces across the battlespace.[20] Accordingly, efforts to develop informationized capabilities serve as a key unifying theme in much of the experimentation that supported development of important new operational concepts, including noncontact and target-centric warfare.

Another central element in the PLA's joint operations development is found in its emphasis on system-of-systems operations—an area that presents commanders and their staffs with significant challenges. This concept is based on linking command automation, ISR, precision strike, and mobility in ways that permit rapidly and efficiently striking vital sites and key nodes in an enemy's systems.[21] Conceptually these "combat systems" optimize operational strengths from across the PLA's services. These systems should be optimized to meet specific operational objects and ensure that critical weapons and capabilities are used as efficiently as possible.[22] *The Campaign Theory Study Guide*, an early PLA textbook that addressed system-of-systems, identified the connection between campaigns and combat systems in the following manner:

Paralyzing the enemy's combat system has become an important means of winning a war. . . . Once there are problems in key links of the system, the entire weapon system and combat system will lose its combat effectiveness, or will even become paralyzed. This illustrates that modern campaigns are the confrontation between combat systems. Advanced weapons and equipment and good strategy and planning both depend upon the integrity and coordination of combat systems. Therefore, in modern campaigns, attacking and paralyzing key nodes in the enemy's combat system while ensuring the integrity and coordination of one's own combat systems has become an important way of winning.[23]

This important PLA teaching text—although an early version—highlighted two imperatives for success in future wars that remain central to PLA thinking on system-of-systems operations and, by extension, integrated joint operations. The first imperative is the need to build and protect one's own combat system, while the second involves simultaneously identifying and attacking an adversary's critical weaknesses. These ideas, developed and tested as part of the PLA's military science research efforts, provide the underpinnings for many of the PLA's most recent joint exercises.

Key Joint Operations Concepts

PLA joint operations capability development efforts have not taken place in a functional vacuum; they have been tailored to correspond to major trends in global military development over the past two-and-a-half decades. The methods of warfare that PLA observers identified during U.S. and allied operations since the 1990s have led to the development of new ideas within the PLA about how future wars will be fought and the capabilities necessary to succeed in this environment. As discussed earlier, these observations focus on information and weapon systems that can be integrated efficiently to target an adversary's war-making capacity. These types of operations placed a premium on air and naval power. Likewise, PLA observers concluded that future conflicts were much less likely to involve ground-heavy, brute-force conflicts of attrition that characterized military operations in previous generations. The strategic importance placed on gaining superiority in the air, at sea, in space, and in information domains presented an imperative to PRC political and military leaders: reorient the PLA to become more joint, agile, and efficient or fail to keep pace with the demands of the global revolution in military affairs.

One of the most significant developments in modern warfare that shaped PLA recognition for the need for a credible joint operations capability was the emergence of "noncontact warfare." According to several senior PLA writers who developed the concept, this new form of warfare constituted a significant departure from earlier models of warfare in several important respects.[24] Until the 1990s, they argued, warfare was based on a model of attrition that sought the destruction of fielded forces; military success was primarily achieved by mass deployments of mechanized forces. U.S. operations in the former Yugoslavia demonstrated that warfare no longer conformed to this model. The objective of military operations had changed from attrition to the destruction of an enemy's war potential, embodied in strategic targets like leadership, energy, industry, communications, and key infrastructure.[25] Long-range precision strikes on these targets, enabled by advanced C4ISR capabilities, would be the cornerstone of modern warfare. The noncontact warfare model required PLA commanders to bring together each service's firepower capabilities in unprecedented ways. It was therefore necessary for PLA commanders to understand the entire range of kinetic and nonkinetic capabilities at their disposal.

The PLA's latest operational concept is target-centric warfare, which has been under development since at least 2011. It appears to be a further refinement of the noncontact warfare model primarily oriented toward the joint integration of PLA Air Force and PLA ground forces. The general concept behind target-centric warfare is that by employing ISR sensors and target analysis, PLA commanders can identify—and subsequently aim to destroy—the most critical targets in an enemy's combat system.[26]

This operational concept seeks to make efficient use of firepower assets, provide timely targeting of the most essential targets on the battlefield, and ensure that combat plans are able to adapt in an agile manner that addresses rapid changes in a dynamic environment. Recent target-centric warfare experimentation has focused on engaging mobile targets and employing opposition forces in order to challenge exercise participants.[27] Though this concept is under development, there has been a limited amount of literature available describing its evolution and key elements. Regardless, its existence provides an overarching context by which to evaluate key areas of progress in the PLA's development of integrated joint operations.

Training and Experimentation

The PLA initiated its program to develop joint operations concepts in 2001 with the *Five Year Plan on Headquarters' Informationization Building, 2001–2005*.[28] This multifaceted effort involved conceptual development that brought together a broad body of military science research, technology development, new training guidelines, and operational experimentation. The plan culminated with two exercises named Sharp Sword 2005, led by units in the Chengdu and Nanjing Military Regions (MRs). PLA leaders tasked units from the Chengdu MR with exploring new modes of integrated joint training, along with air-land integration between the PLA Army and Air Force.[29] They also tasked units from the Nanjing MR with experimenting on firepower strike coordination, integrated training methods, and interservice coordination mechanisms.[30] Although this geographically dispersed exercise highlighted several shortcomings in the PLA's capability to perform integrated joint operations, it marked a significant foundational basis that guided follow-on efforts in the next two Five Year Plans.[31]

PLA joint operations training entered a "standardized development" phase as the 11th Five Year Plan ended in 2010, presumably to experiment and test the joint operations concepts and practices that emerged from the Sharp Sword exercises. In 2009, the PLA claimed a total of 18 large-scale exercises that explored a wide range of joint operations subject matter, including civil-military integration, naval and air force power projection, "systemic operations," joint training methods, and war zone–level command and control.[32] Three key exercises during 2009 and 2010—Firepower 2009, Stride 2009, and Mission Action 2010—demonstrated the PLA's progress in joint operations during the 11th Five Year Plan. More importantly, the underlying themes guiding these exercises and evaluations would serve as the basis for many components of the major exercises seen in the subsequent 12th Five Year Plan.

In August 2009, four PLA divisions subordinate to the Shenyang, Lanzhou, Jinan, and Guangzhou MRs conducted "the first large-scale, intertheater, live-forces, checkout-type exercises since the founding of the Chinese People's Liberation Army," named Stride 2009.[33] Participating units deployed to a PLA combined tactical training base located outside of their respective MRs. Subjects ranged from practical evaluations of training practices and procedures to long-range mobility. PLA training methods were further enhanced through the use of dedicated opposition forces and the newly deployed Army Unit Exercise and Evaluation System.[34] Substantively, exercise participants tested new equipment types, including multiple features of the Beidou navigation and positioning system, electronic warfare systems, and psychological warfare support vehicles, among many others.[35] Stride 2009 also served as a comprehensive test in multiple specialty mobility–related areas, including fuel and material resupply, medical support, war compensation, and political work.[36]

Shortly after Stride 2009 began in October 2009, the PLA General Staff Department's Military Training and Arms Department convened an All-Army Symposium named Firepower 2009, which examined precision strike under informationized conditions. This 3-day event brought together PLA experts and scholars tasked with developing new approaches and models for an advanced warfighting concept capable of integrating "precision reconnaissance, precision command, precision firing, and precision evaluation."[37] In contrast with the evaluation- and test-focused aspects of Stride 2009, Firepower 2009 served almost exclusively as a means for experimentation using demonstrations and working groups composed of military science researchers and operators. The symposium's content clearly reflected PLA thinking on the intersections between joint operations and system-of-systems concepts.

Mission Action 2010 marked the culmination of the 11th Five Year Plan's joint operations training efforts. This exercise involved multiple units from across multiple MRs in a test exercise that focused on transregional maneuver and testing of key operational functions, including joint campaign command, joint firepower strike, comprehensive protection, and precision support.[38] Overall, the exercise stretched for 20 days and included participants from the Beijing, Chengdu, and Lanzhou MRs, along with elements from both the PLA Air Force and PLA Navy. Most notably, Mission Action 2010 marked the first time that operational forces crossed MR boundaries to participate in an operationally oriented joint exercise.

More recently, since the beginning of the 12th Five Year Plan, joint exercises have become even more of a centerpiece in PLA military modernization and experimentation. Primarily, they provide a means by which PRC senior leaders can measure PLA progress toward achieving its most important modernization objectives. In contrast to the heavy emphasis placed on experimentation and concept development in the major joint exercises during the 10th and 11th Five Year Plans, more recent joint exercises have focused on testing and evaluating a wider range of operational missions intended to produce a more flexible, adaptable, and deployable military. At the same time, the integrated joint training methods examined in earlier exercises—along with recognition among senior leaders that training quality needed to be improved overall—have evolved into a broader effort to improve realism and more effectively evaluate unit performance. Although many press reports following these events highlight shortcomings that continue to hinder PLA progress in the field of joint operations, they also portray significant improvements in realism and complexity, as the units involved are placed in much more dynamic scenarios away from their familiar surroundings and with dedicated opposition forces providing more-than-token resistance. Based on these improvements, the capabilities developed during these joint exercises are essential for meeting the PLA's objective of being able to fight local wars under the conditions of informationization. The progression of joint operations exercises spanning the 10th, 11th, and 12th Five Year Plans demonstrates a sustained focus on the key elements of PLA joint operations concepts developed over a decade ago—informationized, system-of-systems-based, high-tempo, multidimensional operations that integrate all PLA combat strengths.[39]

Evaluating Progress Under Xi

The preceding discussion and examples demonstrate that joint operations development was under way within the PLA on many levels prior to Xi's coming to power. In no sense was the effort lacking in resources or high-level interest. In addition, it appeared to make progress in several areas despite some acknowledged setbacks by the commanders leading key pieces of experimentation. Furthermore, a wide range of literature was being made available to PLA professional military education institutions in order to educate future commanders in joint operations theory. In sum, the range of PLA activities dedicated to building joint operations concepts and capabilities increased significantly and methodically attempted to address a wide range of critical questions.

The primary issue related to Xi's impact on joint operations development appears to be greater emphasis and a new organizational structure that ensures responsibility for joint training will be overseen by the theater commands—the PLA organizations responsible for operational planning and warfighting.[40] Although many efforts were in place to develop concepts, improve personnel and education, and reform training, each of these programs had met with mixed success and were heavily focused on theoretical aspects of joint operations. In some cases, personnel and training reforms were rolled out in multiple iterations, each time acknowledging many of the same longstanding shortfalls in key areas. While in many respects these reforms may signal gradual improvements in practice or changes based on the state of the-art, in most cases they appear to be redesigned efforts to address longstanding problems and shortfalls.

Xi's imprint on joint operations has nonetheless been significant. His guidance to prepare for military struggle has begun taking hold at multiple levels as evidenced by a body of new training guidance. Most notably, at the beginning of 2014, the Central Military Commission released the *Opinions on Raising the Level of the Realistic Battle Orientation of Training*, and in 2015, the General Staff Department issued the *Opinions on Strengthening and Improving Campaign and Tactical Training*.[41] While these directives build on earlier efforts to improve and reform training, they appear to be a corrective to the emphasis under Hu Jintao on nonmilitary operations. Similar programs have been designed to educate and train commanders to better equip them because the requirements of joint operations have gained momentum under Xi's leadership. In general, Xi's imprint will most likely be felt in three key areas: education, training, and personnel.

In addition, new training regulations clearly outline responsibilities for joint training. Most notably, joint training has been identified as the key driver for service-specific training requirements. As such, the services still maintain their overall responsibility for building general proficiency based on service capabilities while the theater commands—overseen by the Central Military Commission—are given the authority to ensure that combat-related joint training meets PLA specifications and operational requirements.[42] As explained by the Eastern theater's commander, the new system was designed to have "the theater command taking the lead" to ensure "alignment of training with combat operations" and "shaping of systems of systems."[43] Under this system, the theater command generates joint training plans based on its missions and operational training requirements, delegating key training decisions to the theater commanders responsible for combat operations. This approach is a significant departure from the highly centralized system overseen by the General Staff Department prior to the reorganization.

Personnel

The PLA has embarked on a program to train and cultivate talented personnel for command positions in joint operational roles. Key elements of the program were discussed in Beijing at a July 2016 gathering of some two dozen military education and research institutions, theater commands, and the armed services that sought to identify measures to improve the cadre of qualified commanders.[44] The program highlighted several areas by which the PLA could accomplish these goals, generally in the development of strategic leadership, command capabilities, and management commensurate with the PLA's future requirements.[45] Overall, the effort is dedicated to improving the manner in which commanders are selected and trained. From a training perspective, this process will rely on intensified training for commanders and staffs in eight areas that range from emergency situation training to theater joint command organization.[46]

Another critical component in the effort to improve the quality and preparedness of personnel taking joint command and staff positions has been developing common standards and training requirements. These standards range from educational materials to criteria for evaluating performance and progress of individuals in both educational and field training settings.[47] In particular, these guidelines are designed to provide a long-term, structured framework for ensuring that PLA personnel are groomed at early points in their military career for the positions they will ascend to in the future.

Education

A key element of these personnel reforms involves improved education in joint operations. One of the most challenging problems facing the PLA education system is determining "what kinds of ideas and models" should be used in educating future joint commanders.[48] Based on previous military science research and experimentation efforts, this realization is illuminating in terms of the PLA's view of its own progress in the field of joint operations. In line with the effort to "cultivate talented joint operations commanding personnel" the General Staff Department's Military Training Department (prior to its dissolution) alluded to new programs at the National Defense University (NDU), National University of Defense Technology, and service and branch command colleges to enhance the content and quality of teaching on joint operations topics. Interestingly, the program's development comes shortly following new editions of key joint operations teaching materials used to educate PLA officers.[49] The new NDU Joint Operations College at Shijiazhuang is likely to play a critical role in educating officers for joint positions. It will offer a year-long course for division and "brigadier level" officers and train staff below the rank of colonel who will serve in joint positions.[50]

Training

Progress in training overall has been a notable success for the PLA. Over the past 10 years, exercises have grown in scale, complexity, and number reflecting the priority the PLA has assigned to developing joint operations capability in a number of potential scenarios. These exercises also have attempted to incorporate more realistic scenarios and rigorous evaluation of performance through all exercise stages. Many of the most significant problems highlighted in previous iterations of the OMTE appear to be improving across the board. The primary uncertainty, however, is the extent to which these innovations reflect true improvements or set piece additions that give the appearance of progress. Based on the sources available, it is difficult to make a definitive assessment. Regardless, the joint operations exercise program and quality of the exercises themselves predates Xi. Exercises performed during the 11th Five Year Plan provided an important bridge between the PLA's earlier experimentation and the major exercises that have become routine during the 12th Five Year Plan. Based on this steady progression, it seems that the PLA's progress in this area is real but not attributable to Xi's reforms.

Xi's primary influence is clear in two key areas. The first is in the direction given to the PLA to prepare for military struggle, which came forward shortly after the 2009 OMTE. Based on the PLA's recent discussions about this directive, it seems clear that new rigor is being applied to exercise content, intensity, and evaluation under Xi.

The second area is closely related to recent efforts to cultivate talented personnel and improve education—training joint commanders in realistic conditions. Since the PLA reorganization, each of the major theaters has highlighted efforts to ensure that joint command is a key topic in their specific training programs.[51] In addition, several units have attempted to address perceived shortcomings in joint command, referred to as the "Five Incapables."[52] These examples demonstrate that this critical piece of training reform is at the forefront of PLA joint operations training. As in previous years, the idea of rigorous training has taken hold across the PLA, and units are now attempting to implement these guidelines. The degree to which these new directives are being highlighted in PLA media suggests that there is added impetus behind ensuring that evaluations and commander training are dealt with more substantively than in the past. In April 2016, Xi visited the newly established Central Military Commission Joint Operations Command Center and emphasized the critical importance of developing both operational- and strategic-level command capabilities necessary for modern conflicts.[53] Additional reports, both before and after Xi's visit, highlighted programs and training initiatives across the PLA and within various theater commands designed to implement and test new joint command programs and procedures.[54]

Conclusion

Overall, it is clear that the PLA has made substantial progress in several key areas relating to joint operations capability.[55] Exercises have become considerably larger and more sophisticated. They now involve units from across the PLA, frequently in scenarios that require them to deploy considerable distances from their home bases and familiar training facilities. Attempts to improve realism by adding uncertain situations have also been noted in several PLA media accounts as enhancing the overall quality of joint training. Similarly, joint training increasingly has involved the use of new command automation systems to exercise the use of capabilities from across the PLA's services and branches. Participating commanders and staffs are being challenged like never before. These developments have built on to earlier experimentation and development efforts in clear, steady progression from a long-term effort. The progress is real, but it is not a result of Xi's policies.

Xi's policies likely will have the most significant impact in the areas of personnel and education. "New" programs to cultivate better joint commanders are evidence of previous failures and a desire to change the PLA culture. Much of the declaratory statements about why these programs are important reveal a recognition that earlier reform attempts fell short of their intended mark. In addition, the stated need to improve military education instruction and content suggests a similar dissatisfaction with the materials that are currently available. This second issue is particularly striking due to the amount of time and energy devoted to joint operations concept development since 2001. The degree to which these two areas are considered shortfalls is uncertain, and the extent to which bureaucratic branding is at play should temper future assessments. However, the attention devoted to these two areas over the past 3 years strongly suggests that PLA leaders, including Xi, perceive a major problem. The reorganization of the PLA military education system announced in July 2017 is intended to address these shortfalls.

Similarly, the most recent training reforms also suggest dissatisfaction with the progress and quality of training across the PLA. Two iterations of the OMTE prior to 2010 were touted as solutions to the very problems that Xi's directive to prepare for military struggle was designed to solve. The new OMTE, issued in January 2018, reinforced Xi's core themes and ensured that recent organizational reforms are embodied in these new training guidelines. In general, directing the PLA to prepare for military struggle following nearly two decades of training reform indicates that Xi and other leaders were concerned the PLA's training was not sufficient.

As with any assessment of the PLA that relies on official media, there are significant uncertainties due to the quality and veracity of the information. While these latest reforms suggest problems continue beneath the surface, visible signs of improved training are readily available. The PLA has made progress in joint operations, and its ability to perform many joint functions is better today than it was in 2001 when these programs were initiated. Regardless, the repeated reintroduction of reform initiatives to address longstanding problems strongly suggests that there are significant impediments to progress.

Over the past two-and-a-half decades, the PLA has devoted considerable time and resources to becoming a modern, informationized military. There is no shortage of PLA analysis of the problems and potential solutions required for China's military to develop the capabilities necessary for bringing it up to the standards of the world's most modern military, that of the United States. Despite some degree of progress, the long lineage of problem identification, experimentation, implementation, and reorganization has not achieved several of the PLA's most important objectives, particularly in the area of joint operations. In part, this is due to the backward state of the PLA when it embarked on its current modernization effort in the early 1990s. Major changes evolve over time. However, a major reason why many of these problems persist is due to the PLA's organizational culture, which has favored the army over other services, fostered a lack of initiative and creativity within the officer corps, and discouraged risk-taking. It appears that reforms under Xi are focused on changing these aspects of the PLA's culture in ways previous reforms could not.

Absent a crisis that necessitates rapid change to survive, change in organizational culture often requires considerable time for personnel transitions, bureaucratic acceptance, and acculturation. Xi's reforms attempt to tackle these issues. They provide new professional incentives, bureaucratic authorities, and organizational responsibilities that ultimately will guide how current and future military officers will approach joint operations and command. At this stage in the current reform effort, it is unclear whether these cultural changes will take root and be assimilated successfully. Senior-level interest, although important, is not the sole determinant of success, as evidenced by previous efforts to build a joint culture within China's military. Xi's reforms are an important departure from previous efforts and address several of the PLA's most challenging systemic problems. Assessing the prospects of success at this early point in the reform effort is difficult, largely due to the number of known and unknown variables that might shape the PLA's actions in coming years. However, Xi's reforms offer an important departure from earlier efforts and provide what appears to be a sustainable baseline for cultural change—a critical element in making joint operations reforms viable over the long term.

Notes

[1] Two key studies include Huang Bin [黄斌], *Research into the Kosovo War* [科索沃战争研究] (Beijing: Liberation Army Publishing House, 2000); and Wang Yongming, Liu Xiaoli, and Xiao Yunhua [王永明, 刘小力, 肖允化], *Research into the Iraq War* [伊拉克战争研究] (Beijing: Military Science Press [军事科学出版社], 2003). These two studies, along with numerous other military science journal and military press publications, highlight intense People's Liberation Army (PLA) focus on foreign military developments, particularly those involving the United States. As this chapter discusses, many of these lessons are captured in PLA operational concepts developed to respond to specific operational requirements. For an English language overview, see Andrew Scobell, David Lai, and Roy Kamphausen, eds., *Chinese Lessons from Other Peoples' Wars* (Carlisle Barracks, PA: Strategic Studies Institute, 2010).

[2] For a discussion of the Military Strategic Guidelines and the central role they play in delineating planning and modernization requirements, see David Finkelstein, "China's National Military Strategy: An Overview of the 'Military Strategic Guidelines,'" in *Right-Sizing the People's Liberation Army: Exploring the Contours of China's Military*, ed. Roy Kamphausen and Andrew Scobell (Carlisle Barracks, PA: Strategic Studies Institute, May 2007), 82–87. See also James C. Mulvenon and Andrew N.D. Yang, eds., "A Poverty of Riches: New Challenges and Opportunities in PLA Research," CF-189-NSRD, RAND Conference Proceedings, 2004.

3 Peng Guangqian and Yao Youzhi [彭光谦, 姚有志], eds., *The Science of Military Strategy* [战略学] (Beijing: Military Science Press [军事科学出版社], 2005), 321–322; and Ge Dongsheng [葛东升], ed., *On National Security Strategy* [国家安全战略论] (Beijing: Military Science Press [军事科学出版社], 2006), 234.

4 Wang Houqing and Zhang Xingye [王厚卿,张兴业], eds., *Science of Campaigns* [战役学] (Beijing: National Defense University Press [国防大学出版社], 2001), 418–422; Ge, *On National Security Strategy*, 231–235.

5 Huang, *Research into the Kosovo War*, 140–144; and Wang, Liu, and Xiao, *Research into the Iraq War*, 199. In addition, see Ge, *On National Security Strategy*, 234; and Zhang Yuliang [张玉良], ed., *The Science of Campaigns* [战役学] (Beijing: National Defense University Press [国防大学出版社], 2006), 97.

6 Zhong Shengqin, "Establish New Train of Thought for Training Commanders," *PLA Daily* [解放军报], February 9, 1999, 6.

7 Ibid.

8 Li Dianren [李殿仁], "Fundamental Principle of Strengthening the Building of Military Academies—Understanding on the Study of Central Military Commission Chairman Jiang Zemin's Important Expositions on Military Academy Education" [加强军队院校建设的根本指针], *PLA Daily* [解放军报], May 18, 2000, 6.

9 "Fostering High-Caliber Personnel and Promoting Leaps-and-Bounds Development of Chinese Armed Forces—Excerpts from Forum on Implementing Strategic Talent Project and Speeding Up Personnel Training" [大力培养高素质人才 推进我军跨越式发展—全军实施人才战略工程加速人才培养座谈会经验摘登], *PLA Daily* [解放军报], June 6, 2003, 2.

10 Liu Fengan and Wu Tianmin [刘逢安, 武天敏], "New-Generation 'Outline of Military Training and Evaluation' Promulgated" [新一代"军事训练与考核大纲"颁发], *PLA Daily* [解放军报], July 25, 2008, 1.

11 Zhang, *The Science of Campaigns*, 63.

12 Ibid., 80.

13 Shou Xiaosong [寿晓松], ed., *The Science of Military Strategy* [战略学] (Beijing: Military Science Press [军事科学出版社], 2013), 125.

14 Ibid.

15 Zhan Yu [战玉], "A Study of the Theory of Integrated Joint Operations" [一体化联合作战理论探要], *China Military Science* [中国军事科学], no. 6 (2007), 11–21.

16 Shou, *The Science of Military Strategy*, 125.

17 Ge, *On National Security Strategy*, 62, 280; Hao Yuqing and Cai Renzhao, eds., *Science of Armed Forces Building* (Beijing: National Defense University Press

[国防大学出版社], 2007), 280–282; and Zhang, *The Science of Campaigns*, 85. For an English language analysis, see Dean Cheng, *Cyber Dragon: Inside China's Information Warfare and Cyber Operations* (Santa Barbara, CA: Praeger, 2017).

    18 Song Youfa and Hong Yaobin [宋有法, 洪耀斌], eds., *Integrated Joint Operations Command Headquarters Work* [一体化联合作战指挥总部工作] (Beijing: Military Science Press [军事科学出版社], 2005), 1.

    19 Zhang, *The Science of Campaigns*, 80; and Shou, *The Science of Military Strategy*, 127.

    20 Shou, *The Science of Military Strategy*, 127.

    21 Ibid., 126. For English language analysis, see Kevin McCauley, *PLA System of System Operations: Enabling Joint Operations* (Washington, DC: The Jamestown Foundation, 2017); and Jeffrey Engstrom, *Systems Confrontation and System Destruction Warfare: How the Chinese People's Liberation Army Seeks to Wage Modern Warfare* (Santa Monica, CA: RAND, 2018), available at <www.rand.org/pubs/research_reports/RR1708.html>.

    22 Ibid.

    23 Xue Xinglin [薛兴林], ed., *Campaign Theory Study Guide* [战役理论学习指南] (Beijing: National Defense University Press [国防大学出版社], 2001), 66. Emphasis added.

    24 See Liu Yuejun [刘粤军], ed., *Non-Contact Warfare* [非接触战争] (Beijing: Military Science Press [军事科学出版社], 2004); Pan Youmu [潘友木], *The Study of Non-Contact Warfare* [非接触战争研究] (Beijing: National Defense University Press [国防大学出版社], 2003); and Shao Guopei [邵国培], ed., *Information Operations in Non-Contact Wars* [非接触战争的信息作战] (Beijing: Liberation Army Publishing House, 2004).

    25 Liu, *Non-Contact Warfare*, 8–9; and Pan, *The Study of Non-Contact Warfare*, 50.

    26 Liu Shenyang [刘沈扬], "The Theory and Practice of Target-Centric Warfare" [目标中心战的理论与实践], *China Military Science* [中国军事科学], no. 5 (2013), 83–92.

    27 Ding Yahan and Li Dezhong [丁雅涵, 李德忠], "In This Battle, Aiming at the 'Vulnerable Spot' When Firing—Close-Up View of the Military Region's 'Queshan Decisive Victory-2013A' Exercises with Troops, Part III" [这一丈, 瞄准"七寸"打 — 近观军区"确山决胜—2013A"实兵演习之三], *Vanguard News* [前卫报], December 8, 2013, 2; and Chang Xin [常欣], "Use Military Innovation Theory to Guide Substantial Leap in Combat Power" [以军事创新理论牵引战斗力实质跃升], *Vanguard News* [前卫报], March 31, 2013, 4.

28 "Push Forward Revolution in Military Affairs with Chinese Character-istics, Build Informationized Command Organs—Excerpts of Advanced Typical Experiences from the All-Army Conference on Headquarters Building," *PLA Daily* [解放军报], September 28, 2004, 3.

29 Zhuang Lijun [庄利军] et al., "A Rapidly Expanding Transformation in the Training Domain" [训练领域一场方兴未艾的变革], *PLA Daily* [解放军报], February 6, 2006; Cheng Sixun, "Exploration and Practice of Integrated Training of Military Region Units: Part One," *Battle Flag News* [战旗报], February 9, 2006; and Cheng Sixun, "Exploration and Practice of Integrated Training of Military Region Units: Part Two," *Battle Flag News* [战旗报], February 10, 2006.

30 Zhuang, "A Rapidly Expanding Transformation in the Training Domain"; Zhang Wenping and Yan Wenbo, "Advance Phase of Second Artillery's Integrated Training Starts—Establishing Steering Group on Integrated Training, Organizing Trial Comprehensive Integration and Integrated Training, Conducting Theoretical Study on Integrated Combat and Training, and Exploring Characteristics and Laws of Integrated Training," *Rocket Forces News* [火箭兵报], July 13, 2004, 1; and Lu Feng and Ni Menzhi, "Mobile and Camouflaged Launches Using New Equipment Under Complex Weather and Terrain Conditions," *People's Front* [人民前线], July 28, 2004.

31 "An Expedition That Spans History," *Battle Flag News* [战旗报], March 9, 2006; and Wang Jianmin, "Footprints of the Forerunner," *Battle Flag News* [战旗报], February 16, 2006.

32 "Overview of PLA Military Training in 2009," *PLA Daily* [解放军报], December 30, 2009.

33 Li Yun, Liu Fengan, and Wu Tianmin [黎云, 刘逢安, 武天敏], "Stride 2009: A Major Exercise Sticking Close to Actual War" ["跨越—2009": 一场贴近实战的大练兵], *PLA Daily* [解放军报], August 11, 2009, 1.

34 Ibid.

35 Ibid.

36 Ibid.

37 "All-Army Artillery and Air Defense Forces' Symposium on Precision Attack Exercises Under Informationized Conditions Concludes" [探索信息化条件下作战训练的新理念新模式新手段 全军炮兵防空兵精确打击演练研讨结束], *PLA Daily* [解放军报], October 15, 2009.

38 Cai Pengcheng and LiYun [蔡鹏程, 黎云],"Mission Action 2010 Trans–Military Region Mobile Exercise Concluded" ["使命行动—2010" 跨区机动演习结束], *PLA Daily* [解放军报], November 4, 2010.

[39] Shou, *The Science of Military Strategy*, 93–98.

[40] Dai Feng and Cheng Yongliang [代烽, 程永亮], "Joint Training Makes Progress along the Course Charted by the Rules—An Account of Efforts Made by the Eastern Theater Command to Propel Rules-Based Joint Training" [联合训练, 在法治轨道运行—东部战区依据法规推动联合训练纪事], *PLA Daily* [解放军报], January 2, 2018.

[41] Xu Tongxuan [徐同宣], "Where Does Training Go from Here? Viewing Realistic Battle Training During Informationized Transformation from the Perspective of Air Force Defense Penetration and Assault Competitive Assessments" [训练向哪里去:从空军突防突击竞赛性考核看信息化转型时期实战化训练], *Kongjun Bao* [空军报], July 16, 2015, 3.

[42] Dai and Cheng, "Joint Training Makes Progress Along the Course Charted by the Rules."

[43] Ibid.

[44] Wu Xu and Liu Yiwei [吴旭, 刘一伟], "Eight Measures to Intensify the Cultivation for Joint Operational Command Personnel" [八项举措加紧培养联合作战指挥人才], *PLA Daily* [解放军报], July 24, 2016.

[45] He Sheng [贺胜], "Create a Combined Operational Mode" [打造联合作战工作模式], *PLA Daily* [解放军报], May 17, 2016. Also see the chapter by Wuthnow and Saunders in this volume.

[46] Wu and Liu, "New-Generation 'Outline of Military Training and Evaluation' Promulgated."

[47] Liang Pengfei and Li Yuming [梁蓬飞, 李玉明], "Our Armed Forces Completely Launch the Professional Joint Operations Talented Commanding Personnel Cultivation Model" [我军全面推开联合作战指挥人才专业化培养模式], *PLA Daily* [解放军报], December 20, 2014.

[48] Ibid.

[49] Two recent examples include Tan Yadong [谭亚东], ed., *Joint Operations Course Materials* [联合作战教程] (Beijing: Academy of Military Science Press [军事科学出版社], 2013); and Li Yousheng and Wang Yonghua [李友生, 王永华], eds., *Lectures on the Science of Joint Campaigns* [联合战役教程] (Beijing: Military Science Press, 2012).

[50] Author interviews with PLA officers, December 2017.

[51] Dai Feng and Cheng Yongliang [代烽, 程永亮], "Eastern Theater Focuses on Main Battle Roles as It Accelerates the Development of New-Type Combat Command Talent" [东部战区聚焦主战职能加速推进新型作战指挥人才培养],

PLA Daily [解放军报], September 1, 2016; Huang Honggui and Meng Bin [黄宏贵, 孟斌], "Toward Joint, Necessary to Form Links and Also Link in Spiritual" [走向联合, 既要形联更要神联], *PLA Daily* [解放军报], April 22, 2016; and Wang Jun and Shi Liu [王军, 石榴], "Push Forward 'Eight Changes' with Focus on Combat Functions" [聚焦主战推进 "八个转变"] *PLA Daily* [解放军报], March 23, 2016.

⁵² Hou Guorong and Wang Guangli [侯国荣, 王广利], "Strengthening Leadership Teams in Order to Strengthen Armed Forces; Training Commanders Before Troops" [强军先强班子练兵先练指挥], *PLA Daily* [解放军报], March 27, 2016; Wang Tianlin, Ding Rongzhen, and Tian Liang [王天林, 丁荣帧, 田亮], "Understanding Causes of Loss, Admitting Failure, and Trying to Win the Loser's Game" [败得明白输得服气更要 败中求胜赢得精彩], *Huojianbing Bao* [火箭兵报], December 26, 2015; and An Weiping [安卫平], "Thoughts on the Practice of Solving the Problem of the 'Five Incapables'" [破解 '五个不会' 问题的实践思考], *Qianjin Bao* [前进报], April 30, 2015, 4.

⁵³ Hua Xia, ed., "Xi Stresses Joint Battle Command for Military Reform," Xinhua, April 20, 2016, available at <www.xinhuanet.com/english/2016-04/20/c_135297662.htm>.

⁵⁴ Wu and Liu, "New-Generation 'Outline of Military Training and Evaluation' Promulgated." For a more detailed discussion of these programs and initiatives, see Wuthnow and Saunders, "A Modern Major General."

⁵⁵ Joel Wuthnow, "A Brave New World for Chinese Joint Operations," *Journal of Strategic Studies* 40, no. 1–2 (January 2, 2017), 169–195.

CHAPTER 6

COMING TO A (NEW) THEATER NEAR YOU

Command, Control, and Forces

By Edmund J. Burke and Arthur Chan

In late 2015, China enacted a series of sweeping military reforms that ostensibly laid the groundwork for a more viable joint force.[1] These reforms—long anticipated by Western observers due to the gap between the command structure of the People's Liberation Army (PLA) and its force development goals—give the military an opportunity to align its organizations and processes with these objectives. Consolidating the former seven military regions (MRs) into five new theater commands (TCs) (see figures 1 and 2); abolishing the four general departments; forming the Strategic Support Force to consolidate space, cyber, and electronic warfare responsibilities; and creating a separate army command are all massive steps meant to address many chronic shortcomings that constrained the development of the joint force and generation of combat power.

Among many details that are not yet clear and will no doubt require years for Western observers (and the PLA) to sort out, perhaps the most important is its success or failure in implementing a new approach to commanding and controlling theater forces. As PLA expert Roger Cliff points out, there are significant cultural, doctrinal, and technical impediments ahead before the PLA arrives at even an interim joint capability at the theater level.[2]

Figure 1. MR System Boundaries

All locations are approximate.
Boundary representation is not necessarily authoritative.

Source: *Annual Report to Congress: Military and Security Developments Involving the People's Republic of China* (Washington, DC: Department of Defense, 2016), 2.

Figure 2. Approximate TC Boundaries

All locations are approximate.
Boundary representation is not necessarily authoritative.

Source: *Annual Report to Congress: Military and Security Developments Involving the People's Republic of China* (Washington, DC: Department of Defense, 2016), 2.

Despite more than a decade of experimentation and sometimes citing a generation gap, critiques in official press continue to highlight the inexperience and lack of commitment to "informationization" [*xinxi hua*, 信息化] on the part of PLA officers and leaders.[3] Nonetheless, the decision to finally set aside the MR structure in favor of a joint TC construct has removed perhaps the biggest obstacle in executing integrated joint operations [*yitihua lianhe zuozhan*, 一体化联合作战], which is how the PLA seeks to operate jointly under informationized conditions.

This chapter examines in depth one aspect of these new reforms: the shift from military regions to theater commands. In so doing, it consults a broad range of Chinese and English sources, including authoritative news media, publications by Chinese military institutions, and commentary by PLA experts. The first section examines the logic behind this shift, particularly what Chinese leaders hope to achieve from such a transition. The second section looks at the missions and responsibilities of each of the five new TCs. It further presents a draft order of battle, sketching out what ground, naval, air, and other assets have been assigned to the new theater commands. The third section looks at the prospects of success for these reforms.

The Logic Behind the Shift to Theater Commands

When trying to quantify the importance of the reforms—and the dissolution of the MR system, in particular—it is necessary to revisit a long arc of study and publications on military theory and the nature of modern warfare by the PLA and its political leaders. This section reviews the background of PLA efforts to improve its ability to conduct integrated joint operations. It further examines how these efforts are connected with the shift from MRs to TCs and what Chinese leaders hope to achieve.

Over the past 20 years, PLA thought leaders have written extensively on the criticality of information technology for military innovation, prompted by the U.S.-led coalition's success in the First Gulf War and in particular by its perceived ability to effectively command and control joint forces in dynamic maneuver warfare. Their exploration of the topic highlighted the important role of integrating advanced information technology with joint forces. This led to the incorporation of a number of related concepts in the Chinese military lexicon, including information warfare [*xinxi zhanzheng,* 信息战争], digital forces [*dianzi budui,* 电子部队], and information operations [*xinxi zuozhan,* 信息作战]. The PLA eventually settled on Information System–based System of Systems Operations [*jiyu xinxi xitong tixi zuozhan,* 基于信息系统体系作战] as their approach to conflict.[4]

Many of these themes are illustrated in a 2010 interview with a prominent PLA theorist at the Chinese National Defense University of Science and Technology. Citing the U.S. military's experience not only in the Gulf War but also in Operation *Iraqi Freedom* as well as *Joint Vision 2020* materials, the article laid out China's information system–based system of systems operations as "basically identical or similar" to the Western concept of network-centric warfare.[5] A background section prefacing the article laid out what can be interpreted as an official PLA endorsement of its new approach: "System operations based on the information system have become a basic pattern of joint operations under informationized conditions, and information capability has become the primary capability in joint operations." Moreover, after describing the critical importance of new command information systems and weapons platforms to the PLA, the senior Chinese strategist quoted in the article cited joint air strike operations during Operation *Desert Storm* as evidence that it was "absolutely impossible to use traditional command means and methods to successfully direct a complicated informationized joint operation, and it is necessary to rely on an integrated command information system."[6] The PLA's command system itself, then, was a major impediment to achieving longstanding force development and capability goals.

Both the command structure changes and the path to joint operations writ large have been arduous and nonlinear. As PLA analyst Kevin Pollpeter notes, Chinese leaders in the late 1990s began to aim for the creation of an informationized force, and one of the ways to achieve this was through jointness. In 1999, the PLA issued a *gangyao* [纲要], or outline, that formally instituted joint operations into PLA warfighting. Pollpeter notes that in 2009, "the General Staff Department (GSD) provided training objectives that for the first time fully committed the services to joint operations."[7] Yet during this period, the PLA made less progress toward achieving jointness than hoped. This was due to a combination of factors, including a focus on coordination rather than true jointness, the lack of permanent joint structures, and a mindset of single service domination. Individual services during this period were able to develop robust vertical command and control systems but failed to take the initiative to do the same across services.[8]

Chinese leaders have also attempted to change the PLA's mindset regarding joint operations. As Defense Intelligence Agency analysts Wanda Ayuso and Lonnie Henley detail, from 2008 onward, these efforts centered on three areas: "developing the expertise of academic faculty in the military educational institutions; getting PLA commanders and staff to think in terms of joint training rather than combined arms training; and developing information systems and material solutions to facilitate joint command."[9] The PLA also gained knowledge from its interactions with other countries in bilateral and multilateral exercises.[10] In spite of these efforts, however, the PLA continued to have difficulty applying joint operational concepts to actual situations and in changing its way of thinking about military conflict.

The shift from an MR to TC system may be viewed in this context as the continuation of these previous efforts to achieve jointness for the PLA. China watchers and analysts for decades have pointed out the limitations of China's MR system, with its built-in impediments to deploying maneuver forces across or in the air over invisible lines at MR boundaries and the PLA's reliance on this structure to provision logistics and other combat service support in both peacetime and wartime.[11] Even veteran PLA officers recognized that the MR system was not a functional command and control system for modern warfare. PLA campaign literature makes clear that an ad hoc joint command and control system would be employed in wartime. This ad hoc entity would have been led by an army general attached to the GSD, but potentially by an MR officer in smaller army-dominated contingencies such as a small border crisis with a Southeast Asian neighbor. Maneuver and strike forces would be led by GSD officers for large joint operations, but potentially could be led by army leader to MR leader grade officers drawn from participating military regions.

Over the past decade, as joint training and joint operations increasingly became focal points for the PLA, the MR construct became a greater impediment for operational forces in terms of exercising command and control and in training realism. If the joint command element would be formed from and by the Central Military Commission (CMC) and staffed with GSD officers in wartime, how realistic could the operational/maneuver force training have been in the absence of a real command element exercising with them? If MR staff officers were not responsible for joint training, how could they simulate this command element in a realistic manner? How could anyone gain useful joint command experience in this structure? The following section explains how the TC system helps to rectify these issues.

Chinese Explanations of the TC System

Chinese researchers framed the need for restructuring as a strategic requirement—even as the framework of the radical reforms was being debated and shaped. In September 2015, Senior Colonel Wang Xiaohui of the Strategy Research and Teaching Department at China's National Defense University highlighted what he saw as the most pressing strategic preparations [*zhanlüe zhunbei*, 战略准备] the PLA needed to make. While not necessarily authoritative, Wang concisely detailed the shortfalls that would soon be addressed with the broad military reforms later that year.[12] First, Wang contended that China could not exercise unified command over the joint force without first establishing what he termed an integrated joint operation command system [*yitihua lianhe zuozhan zhihui tizhi*, 一体化联合作战指挥体制] to command and control all PLA forces, to which the theater system would be subordinate. He specifically cited the U.S. military experience with combatant commands, highlighting that its most prominent features are a simple hierarchy and command smoothness and that the campaign and tactical command levels from theater to division were reduced from five to three. The envisioned Chinese command entity would be responsible for training theater forces in peacetime and operational command in wartime. The supporting theater departments—manpower and personnel, intelligence, operations, training, and support—would then be formed under the theater command.

Second, Wang noted the weakness of combining military administration with operational command, pointing to the U.S. experience separating the two. Wang went on at length regarding the challenges the PLA faced under its current system:

> For example, the command organs are oversized and overstaffed, with unreasonable internal structure. Functions of various departments in a command organ are overlapped to a serious extent. Most departments are responsible for peacetime training, management, and support. As a result, over a long period, there were two major shortcomings in our military's leadership and command system: First, the function of commanding forces to fight battles was weak. Second, the strategic management capability of directing the whole military's building and development was weak. Such a state of affairs is far from meeting the required "flat-shaped" joint operation command system in informationized warfare, and also directly restricts and affects the conducting of scientific leadership and management of national defense and armed forces building.

Third, Wang emphatically highlighted the often-cited imbalance of forces due to the historic primacy of the PLA Army and the need to rationalize the mix of combat to noncombat forces:

> Furthermore, the most prominent issue related to the quantity and scale of the Chinese military forces is the inappropriate proportion of forces in the army, the navy, the air force, and the Second

233

Artillery, the inappropriate proportion of combat units to non-combat units, the inappropriate proportion of combat personnel to noncombat personnel, and consequently the inappropriate proportion of officers to enlisted personnel. . . . In particular, it is necessary to energetically reinforce the building of the navy and the air force, improve the proportion of various services, establish a scientific and reasonable ratio of combat personnel to noncombat personnel, and thus enhance the combat power of the Chinese armed forces.

The strategic drivers that Wang laid out no doubt reflect the arguments that won the day in terms of the reforms. Official statements and commentary by experts within and outside of the PLA cite four primary reasons for the shift from MRs to TCs:

- streamlining responsibilities
- strengthening jointness
- increasing readiness
- making China's military policy vis-à-vis external actors more coherent.

This section discusses each of these factors.

Streamlined Responsibilities

First, under the old system, the MRs fulfilled a wide range of functions, which included force-building, management, command, and peacetime administration.[13] This made the MR a type of composite organization that ended up dealing more with routine administration in peacetime than actual preparations for wartime operations. As noted, during wartime the affected MRs would have been replaced by a command drawn from staff in Beijing, not exclusively officers from the particular MR.[14] This was the case in 1979, when the GSD set up a separate ad hoc organ responsible for the overall prosecution of the Sino-Vietnamese War. The MRs adjoining Vietnam continued to conduct operations separately and provide support for their specific strategic direction.[15] In the context of the Cold War, this was considered an optimal setup, as China's political and military leaders judged that if a war were to break out, it would likely be an all-out war. Thus, it was better to leave the responsibility for preparing operations to the GSD, which would create temporary theater command organs as needed.[16] The shift brought about by the reforms is an attempt to move away from this arrangement by stripping the new TCs of many of their non-warfighting functions, moving these responsibilities to other leadership organs, and making the TCs solely responsible for joint training and operations. Mobilization, for example, now falls to the CMC's National Defense Mobilization Department, 1 of its 15 new functional departments.

At the same time, the reforms clarify the lines of authority flowing from various PLA leadership organs. The new system allows the CMC to more effectively and directly exercise overall authority over the country's armed forces. Meanwhile, the TCs are responsible for operations, and the services are responsible for force-building.[17] Under this arrangement, the TCs are able to concentrate on performing a more narrowly defined, clearer set of roles, theoretically allowing them to do so more effectively and with better results than under the responsibilities assigned to the military regions.

Strengthened Jointness

Second, the TCs' focus on joint operations and training, in turn, supports another longstanding force development goal: increasing jointness among the armed forces. As mentioned, Chinese military experts strongly believe that informationized warfare and system of systems warfare will predominate in modern conflicts and that only a truly joint force is suited for this.[18] However, there was a noticeable lack of jointness under the old MR system. In particular, regional naval and air forces commanders were dual-hatted as deputy MR commanders, but under their dual chain of command they also reported to their service chiefs in Beijing in peacetime. This duality impeded a true sense of jointness at the MR echelon. In a February 2016 interview, Southern TC Commander Wang Jiaocheng explained the rationale for separating administrative management and command of regional forces from preparing for joint combat:

> In the traditional military region structure, the functions of combat command and construction management were combined, construction and use were integrated, and because of that the combat command function was weakened, and the joint operations structure was not complete enough. Faced with the new challenges of the revolution in military affairs, the shortcomings of joint command and joint operations were worsened further. The lack of smoothness in the joint operations command structure also constrained the building of joint training and joint support structures. That contradiction became the most significant structural impediment to our armed forces' ability to fight [win] battles.[19]

While the precise command and control relationship between conventional missile forces at the brigade echelon and the theaters in which they are based is unclear, like other conventional forces they will be available to support any of the five theaters through theater joint operations command centers if needed. Nuclear forces, on the other hand, are different. One *Global Times* article notes that "According to tradition, nuclear weapons are instruments of the utmost importance to the nation. In all countries, they are controlled by the highest authority and cannot be assigned to the theater commands."[20] Logically, though, if theater commanders and their staffs have responsibility for planning for their strategic direction, then conventional missile forces will almost certainly be part of planning considerations not only in the theaters in which they are based but also in supporting other theaters.[21] Beijing fielded these operational forces based on perceived wartime needs, and those needs have not changed under the reforms. These forces would be under the command and control of those theater commanders in wartime, but able to support other theaters as well. Assigning the theater commander responsibility for an operational direction and large-scale training of the joint force for that contingency are strong arguments for wartime command and control of conventional forces for strike missions in that theater.

Increased Readiness

Third, a primary aim of the introduction of TCs is to increase the readiness of the PLA. Indeed, Xi Jinping has been emphatic about the PLA concentrating on combat readiness.[22] Modern PLA military texts stress that limited, localized wars are far likelier than the all-out wars (and the concomitant long warning times that accompany these conflicts) anticipated during the Cold War period. For instance, of the four likeliest future wars that China will have to fight that are listed in the 2013 *Science of Military Strategy*, three are essentially localized wars. One is a relatively large-scale, high-intensity conflict with Taiwan. Another is a medium- to small-scale, mid- to low-intensity war against bordering countries. The last is a small-scale, low-intensity war to counter terrorist activities, maintain stability, and maintain sovereignty.[23] Rather than create temporary joint headquarters, Chinese planners argue that it makes more sense to have TCs already established for each strategic direction so that China will have planned and be prepared for its most likely contingencies. Such a system is envisioned to "allow for the rapid shift from a peacetime to wartime stance ... [and] greatly improve the nation's ability to respond to crises and protect national security."[24]

The new command mechanisms to promote both jointness and readiness include new standing joint command entities known as Joint Operations Command Centers, which exist at two levels. At the national level, there is the CMC Joint Operations Command Center, of which Xi is commander in chief. Each TC also has its own Joint Operations Command Center.[25] How these centers will work in practice, or who will serve in specific leadership positions beyond the identified theater commanders and deputies, is not currently known. For example, will theater joint commanders still exercise command and control through operations groups, or will those entities now be subsumed at the theater level? What seems certain is that, in the short term, these command positions will continue to be dominated by army officers as the PLA works through the process of promoting more officers from other services into staff and leadership positions at the theater level.

Greater Coherency Externally

Fourth, a further consequence of establishing theaters with operational control of forces within their assigned geographic regions is to provide greater coherency to China's military policy vis-à-vis external actors. As the example of the Sino-Vietnamese War demonstrates, the old system had more than one MR for each strategic direction. In the event of a conflict, the ad hoc "front" approach meant that coordination had to take place across MR boundaries, thereby complicating planning, mobilization, and communications at precisely the wrong time. As Yang Yujun, spokesman for the Ministry of National Defense, stated, the "TC will serve as the sole supreme joint operational command organ for its strategic direction."[26] How the new TC system attempts to accomplish this goal is discussed in the following section.

Finally, it may also be worth noting the role that outside sources of inspiration have played. Several commentary pieces have compared China's theater commands to Russia's joint strategic commands (military districts) and U.S. unified combatant commands.[27] The shift to TCs, in that sense, suggests a desire to demonstrate that the PLA aspires to be a peer of the Russian and U.S. militaries in terms of how it plans and prepares for conflict. The ultimate goal of this, as China's civilian and military leadership has stressed repeatedly, is to make the PLA capable of fighting and winning wars.[28]

Theater Command Responsibilities

Each of the new TCs has its own defined set of roles and is responsible for a particular strategic direction. In general, each TC has under its command ground and air forces, and some capacity to either call for fires or have some command authority over conventional missile units based in the TC (see table). The three coastal TCs (Northern, Eastern, and Southern) also have an assigned naval fleet, while the Central TC most likely includes some lower echelon naval elements not subordinate to one of China's three fleets. Of course, various support and nuclear missile units are based in each theater, but their chain of command is not under question: The consensus among analysts is that they remain directly under the command of the CMC and would support any of the theaters or directions at CMC discretion.

Table. Order of Battle for Theater Commands

Theater Command	Group Armies	Fleet	Air Assets	Rocket Force Base (Brigades)/Unit
Eastern	71st, 72nd, 73rd	East Sea Fleet	10th Bomber Division; 40th, 41st, and 42nd fighter brigades; 26th Special Mission Division; 83rd Attack Brigade; Fuzhou Base; Shanghai Base	61 Base (807, 811, 815, 817, 819, 820 brigades), 96180 Unit
Southern	74th, 75th	South Sea Fleet	4th, 5th, 6th, 25th, 26th, 27th, 52nd, 54th, 96th, 98th, and 99th fighter brigades; 8th Bomber Division; 13th Transport Division; 20th Special Mission Division; Kunming Base; Nanning Base	61 Base (818 brigade), 96166 Unit; 62 Base (802, 808, 821, 825 brigades), 96212 Unit; 63 Base (803, 805, 814, 824, 826 brigades)
Western	76th, 77th	N/A	16th Fighter Brigade; 36th Bomber Division; 4th Transport Division; Lanzhou Base; Urumqi Base; Xi'an Flying Academy	64 Base (809, 812, 823 brigades)
Northern	78th, 79th, 80th	North Sea Fleet	15th, 31st, 32nd attack brigades; 34th, 35th, 36th, 61st, and 63rd fighter brigades; 16th Special Mission Division; Dalian Base; Jinan Base; Harbin Flying Academy	65 Base (810, 816, 822 brigades)
Central	81st, 82nd, 83rd	N/A	19th, 55th, 56th, 70th, 71st, and 72nd fighter brigades; 43rd and 44th fighter/attack brigades; Datong Base; Wuhan Base; Shijiazhuang Flying Academy	65 Base (806 Brigade); 66 Base (801, 804, 813, 827 brigades)

Sources: For ground and naval assets, *The Military Balance 2018* (London: International Institute for Strategic Studies, 2018); for air assets, *The Military Balance 2018*, and Lawrence Trevethan, *"Brigadization" of the PLA Air Force* (Montgomery, AL: China Aerospace Studies Institute, 2018); for Rocket Force brigades and bases, *Directory of PRC Military Personalities* (Washington, DC: Defense Intelligence Agency, 2018), and various Chinese and English media reports.

Another important facet of the military reforms is the establishment of separate service headquarters for PLA Army units within each of the five theaters, thereby creating an equivalency between all services in the new theater construct. These perform the same function as TC air forces and TC navy forces—operational and administrative oversight of operational units, in this case group armies. More than that, the TC service headquarters will likely play an important role in ensuring that units meet training requirements, in line with the new division of labor within the PLA—with the CMC exercising overall control, the theater commands responsible for operations, and the services responsible for force-building. These would include both service-specific and joint requirements. As one commentator noted, Xi Jinping in his report at the 19th Party Congress stressed the need to build a modern operational system with Chinese characteristics. For the services to "implement and carry out the spirit of the commander's speech, they must not only do a good job of building their own weapons/armaments and operations systems, [but] they must also improve their consciousness of the overall situation, their joint thinking, and do a good job of resolving the problem of integrating theater services command into the theater joint operational command system."[29]

Eastern Theater Command

Headquartered in Nanjing, the Eastern TC area of jurisdiction is exactly identical to that of the former Nanjing MR. It has responsibility for Shanghai, Jiangsu, Zhejiang, Anhui, Fujian, and Jiangxi and initially had command of all of the Nanjing MR's group armies—the 12th, 1st, and 31st.[30] In late April 2017, the PLA ground force underwent another reform that saw the number of group armies reduced from 18 to 13 in addition to being renumbered from 71 through 83.[31] The 12th, 1st, and 31st Group Armies were redesignated as the 71st, 72nd, and 73rd Group Armies, respectively.[32] For the maritime dimension, the Eastern TC has responsibility for the East China Sea and Taiwan. The East Sea Fleet has been assigned to the Eastern TC, with the fleet commander simultaneously serving as deputy theater commander and commander of the Eastern TC naval forces, which were initally referred to as the East Sea Fleet and then referred to as the Eastern TC Navy as of February 2018.[33]

Because the Eastern TC includes the same provinces as the former Nanjing MR, it should theoretically also have retained its air assets. According to the 2018 edition of the *Military Balance*, the Eastern TC's air assets currently include the 10th Bomber Division, 14th and 32nd Fighter Divisions, 26th Special Mission Division, 28th Attack Division, Fuzhou Base, and Shanghai Base.[34] (All PLA Air Force fighter divisions and attack divisions have now been converted into brigades. The table shows the new brigade designations for each TC.). Finally, the Rocket Force's 52 Base, now known as the 61 Base and headquartered at Huangshan in Anhui, is based in the Eastern TC as well.[35] While command and control of PLA Rocket Force nuclear units will remain held at the CMC level, 61 Base's subordinate conventional missile units will no doubt feature prominently in Eastern TC planning. Much of China's conventional missile firepower is also based within the Eastern TC, as it was fielded there to support Taiwan contingency operations. As mentioned previously, these highly maneuverable assets would be allocated to any TC at CMC direction.[36]

Southern Theater Command

The Southern TC is headquartered in Guangzhou and was created by combining parts of the Guangzhou and Chengdu MRs. From the former, it received the provinces of Hunan, Guangdong (and by extension, the Hong Kong and Macau Special Administrative Regions), Guangxi, and Hainan, as well as the 41st and 42nd Group Armies. From the latter, it received the provinces of Yunnan and Guizhou and the 14th Group Army.[37] Following the changes to the group armies in April 2017, the 14th Group Army was eliminated, while the 41st and 42nd were renumbered as the 74th and 75th, respectively.[38]

The South Sea Fleet has additionally been assigned to the Southern TC, serving as its naval force component.[39] According to Liang Fang, professor at China's National Defense University, the Southern TC has responsibility for the South China Sea.[40] Perhaps mirroring the importance of the South China Sea in its planning, in early 2017 the Southern TC became the first to be led by a PLA Navy officer when Admiral Yuan Yubai was named commander, replacing PLA Army General Wang Jiaocheng.[41] While this may be a primary planning task for the theater, operational units of the former Guangzhou MR also had responsibility for Taiwan contingencies and participated in high-profile exercises on the Taiwan Strait. The Southern TC may have at least partially inherited this responsibility. It may no longer lead planning and preparation for conflict with Taiwan, but it will still have to support the Eastern TC. Southern theater commanders will therefore have to ensure that it schedules and accomplishes rigorous joint training for a variety of contingencies, some of which it may not command. Moreover, the theater has added border regions with Laos and Myanmar. While the combat tasks and campaigns are the same, planning for border conflicts in terms of intelligence preparation, terrain analyses, and logistics is presumably more complex when planning for multiple opponents.

In terms of air assets, the 2018 *Military Balance* notes the Southern TC as having the 2nd, 9th, and 18th Fighter Divisions; 8th Bomber Division; 13th Transport Division; 20th Special Mission Division; Kunming Base; and Nanning Base.[42]

Western Theater Command

In terms of geographic extent, the Western TC is the largest of the five new theaters. It is headquartered in Chengdu and has responsibility for most of the provinces under the Chengdu and Lanzhou MRs. From the former, it received Sichuan, Tibet, Chongqing, and the 13th Group Army. From the latter, it received Gansu, Ningxia, Qinghai, and Xinjiang, as well as the 21st and 47th Group Armies.[43] Later on, the 47th Group Army was eliminated, while the 21st and 13th Group Armies were respectively renumbered as the 76th and 77th Group Armies.[44] Initial reporting from *Global Person* argues that this TC is in an especially strategically sensitive position because it borders multiple countries in Central Asia and India.[45] This range of border issues suggests that counterterrorism will also be prominent in mission planning.

While it lacks subordinate naval forces, from a planning perspective, the Western TC staff is responsible for a potential conflict with India, which could certainly include a maritime dimension requiring PLA Navy involvement. As a result, naval forces likely would be operationally controlled by the Western TC command but overseen by a naval command element deployed to the area to command an operations group in a large-scale conflict with India. It is unclear if the units subordinate to the Central TC are assigned some responsibility for an India contingency, as some Central TC ground units no doubt are. With the planning contingencies relative to India ranging from a quick border crisis to a full-scale conflict between two nuclear powers, the theater planners will have to coordinate closely with navy counterparts based in multiple theaters, as well as working through service lines of authority to complete their diverse tasks.

For air assets, the 2018 *Military Balance* notes that the Western TC has the 4th Transport Division, 6th and 33rd Fighter Divisions, 36th Bomber Division, Lanzhou Base, Urumqi Base, and Xi'an Flying Academy.[46]

Northern Theater Command

The Northern TC is headquartered in Shenyang and has jurisdiction over all three provinces formerly under the Shenyang MR opposite the Korean Peninsula—Jilin, Heilongjiang, and Liaoning. It is further responsible for Inner Mongolia, formerly under the Beijing MR.[47] It has under its command all three group armies from the former Shenyang MR—the 16th, 39th, and 40th—as well as the 26th Group Army from the former Jinan MR.[48] The Northern TC further has jurisdiction over Shandong, which was also formerly under the Jinan MR. Following the most recent reform to the PLA Ground Force, the 40th Group Army was eliminated, while the 16th, 39th, and 26th Group Armies, respectively, became the 78th, 79th, and 80th Group Armies.[49]

In terms of other component services under this command, there was some initial speculation that the North Sea Fleet would be placed under the Central TC,[50] but this was clarified in March 2016 when Rear Admiral Yuan Yubai, then-commander of the North Sea Fleet, was appointed to the additional positions of deputy commander of the Northern TC and commander of the Northern TC naval forces.[51] Inclusion in the Northern TC makes more sense from a planning perspective, as this theater is responsible for conflict on the Korean Peninsula, which could require heavy navy participation in both the air and maritime domains.

According to the 2018 *Military Balance*, the Northern TC has the 5th and 11th Attack Divisions, 12th and 21st Fighter Divisions, 16th Special Mission Division, Dalian Base, and Jinan Base.[52]

Central Theater Command

Chinese military experts describe the Central TC as being an innovation of China's system: Its unique position allows it to respond to crises on its own while also being able to provide support to other theater commands. It subsumed the former Jinan MR, which also served this role for the CMC.[53] As a result, the Central TC provides the capital region with its own dedicated military force, allowing it to respond to crises without having to rely on troop transfers from other parts of the country. Defense of the capital is a primary role; perhaps reflecting that defense of China's leadership against enemy air attack is a top consideration, the Central TC is now commanded by PLA Air Force General Yi Xiaoguang.[54] It is headquartered in Beijing and was created on the foundations of the Beijing and Jinan MRs. From the former, units based in Hebei, Shanxi, Beijing, and Tianjin were presumably reassigned, as well as the 27th, 38th, and 65th Group Armies. From the latter, it received Henan-based units and the 20th and 54th Group Armies.[55] It further has jurisdiction over Shaanxi, formerly under the Lanzhou MR, and Hubei, formerly under the Guangzhou MR.[56] This setup makes the Central TC the most diverse of the new commands in terms of its origins as well as the largest in terms of the number of group armies assigned to it. It also added the distinction of being the first TC to have a group army relocate: the 27th Group Army reportedly moved its headquarters from Hebei to Shanxi

Province by early January 2016 according to PLA press reporting.[57] The relocation likely accommodated the establishment of the TC army command at Shijiazhuang,[58] which was formerly the site of the 27th Group Army headquarters. Like their counterparts in the other TCs, the group armies in the Central TC also underwent changes in late April 2017. Both the 20th and 27th Group Armies were eliminated, while the 65th, 38th, and 54th Group Armies, respectively, became the 81st, 82nd, and 83rd Group Armies.[59]

According to Xinhua, the component services of the Central TC include not only Ground Force but also navy, air force, and missile units.[60] The Hong Kong–based *Ming Pao* newspaper noted that there are no military ports within the Central TC, but there are a number of technical stations and training bases for naval aviation. These include the "naval aviation training base located at Qinhuangdao; its associated Shanhaiguan airfield; the naval aviation academy at Changzhi, Shanxi; and at Jiyuan, Henan, the fighter aircraft branch of the naval aviation academy."[61] In early August 2016, it was reported that a Ground Force air defense brigade from the Central TC had conducted exercises with naval aviation units around the Bohai area.[62] In light of this, it appears that naval forces based in the Central TC will not include surface vessels but encompass the other service branches of the navy based in this geographic area. Until further information is available, however, the exact nature of the naval component of the Central TC remains a matter of speculation.

The 2018 *Military Balance* notes that the Central TC has the following air assets: the 7th and 19th Fighter Divisions, 15th Fighter/Attack Division, 24th Fighter Division, Datong Base, Wuhan Base, and Shijiazhuang Flying Academy.[63]

Prospects for Success

Whether or not these reforms to the PLA succeed will depend greatly on the ability of Chinese leaders to overcome a number of continuing challenges in the medium to long term. This section identifies several remaining challenges for the new TC system, including training of command personnel, command and control, and potential service resistance in a still-army-dominated military.

Phillip Saunders and Joel Wuthnow of the U.S. National Defense University have dubbed the reforms as "Goldwater-Nichols with Chinese characteristics,"[64] which seems an apt description that promises the same opportunities and pitfalls for the PLA. Much of the promise for increased jointness will not be realized for years—well past 2020, and probably more realistically by about 2030.

In the near term, success will depend on the details of the practical, day-to-day relationship between the services and theaters in training units for new joint operational capabilities. To be most effective, theater-level training departments will need to have a mechanism to provide input into (or at least a way to express their requirements to) services responsible for force development. Similarly, theater commanders need to have staffs and mechanisms in place to express their capability requirements both up a command chain to the CMC level and to the military services, which are peer organizations at the same grade. This is not to suggest that the PLA lacks the personnel to staff these organizations because it clearly does not. However, these kinds of relationships are not the norm in the PLA and represent a substantial cultural change in that new relationships among theater and service staffs may be workable in theory but are untested, which will lead to uncertainty and confusion.

In addition, TCs will likely also be advising on and overseeing professional military education initiatives for senior officers steeped in their old systems, as well as for more junior officers presumably less invested in old processes. All of this precedes the complexities of joint training, which requires not only designing new training approaches but also becoming more familiar with existing service training plans in order to integrate them across service lines among like and similar operational elements in ways the PLA has never done.

The changing dynamics of the command and control relationship between theater commanders and theater-based operational forces will also take some time to sort out. These dynamics are different from those that officers have experienced throughout their careers. The forces allocated to each theater presumably meet some kind of basic planning factor for that theater based on their historic missions and strategic directions under the MR system, but the theater no longer has to be concerned with the administration of subordinate forces. The separation of administrative responsibilities from operational command and warfighting responsibilities may be sensible and best for operations, but this division of labor will not be a matter of habit or standard procedure for commanders for some time.

The continued dominance of ground commanders at the TC level is also problematic. A jaundiced view of the reforms from a non–PLA Army viewpoint would be that the names of the organizations have changed, but the uniforms are predominantly still green at the TC level. As mentioned, the five new army headquarters give the army, navy, and air force counterpart commands at the operational echelon, presumably commanded by officers of the same rank. The theater Joint Operations Command Centers' staff is ostensibly the venue through which jointness among these services will manifest itself for the time being. The elevation of navy Admiral Yuan Yubai to Southern TC commander in January 2017 and the assignment of air force General Yi Xiaoguang as Central TC commander in August 2017 also signal the CMC's intent to break this ground dominance, especially where it makes more operational sense to do so.[65]

Conclusion

The decision to do away with the old military regions and replace them with theater commands is a major step in a decades-long effort to create an informationized joint force. By doing so, Chinese military leaders aim to streamline responsibilities, strengthen jointness among the services, increase PLA readiness, foster a more coherent external military policy, and, ultimately, create a force that is capable of fighting and winning wars. The attainment of such a goal may not be so simple as replacing one organizational system with another, however. Chinese leaders have undertaken multiple initiatives since 1999, when joint operations were officially instituted in PLA warfighting, to achieve this goal. These have ranged from developing new command and control technologies to altering the curricula at PLA academic institutions to exercises with foreign partners. Yet progress to date has been slow. Multiple fundamental challenges remain, particularly those related to prevailing mindsets within the PLA. Chinese leaders will have to address these as well in order for their reforms to be truly effective.

This round of Chinese military reforms is continuing, as the renumbering of group armies and Rocket Force bases attests. Areas for further research begin with the most basic, foundational information: orders of battle for each TC and service are now uncertain, as are unit designators. Evidence of the evolving command relationships between TC commanders and service chiefs, both in Beijing and at the TC level, also bears watching; it will probably become available via Chinese official and non-official media outlets. The Chinese version of joint forces could well differ from Western concepts, so researchers will be best served by gaining insights and evidence not only indirectly but also through engagement with Chinese military officials.

As a point of reference, U.S. military efforts to achieve greater jointness theoretically began immediately after World War II with the passage of the National Security Act of 1947, which eliminated independent Cabinet-level departments for each of the Services in favor of a single unified Department of Defense. The subsequent Defense Reorganization Act of 1958 strengthened the control and authority of the Secretary of Defense over the Services in part by authorizing that each department be organized under its own secretary who then reported to the Secretary of Defense; it also established "unified or specified combatant commands" responsible to the President and Secretary of Defense.[66] Almost 30 years later came the Goldwater-Nichols Department of Defense Reorganization Act of 1986 which, among other measures, "redesigned personnel incentives in order to prioritize 'jointness' among the Services—a characteristic that the U.S. Department of Defense demonstrably lacked prior to the reforms."[67] Even by 2013, as former Chairman of the Joint Chiefs of Staff Martin Dempsey noted as he advocated for globally integrated operations, "efforts to create a fully joint force [were] not yet complete."[68] In

2016, former Secretary of Defense Ash Carter stressed what he saw as the need for updates to Goldwater-Nichols that would, among other measures, redefine "joint duty assignment" to include operational functions beyond "just" planning and command and control.[69]

Goldwater-Nichols with Chinese characteristics sounds like a much lower bar than what the U.S. military has achieved over the years, but it certainly hinges on achieving substantial progress on planning and command and control if the PLA is to make headway on truly joint capabilities. Chinese leadership has taken decisive steps toward the future with its organizational reforms; it is now up to PLA officers at the theater level and throughout the services to execute these reforms. It will be a long time before we know the outcome.

Notes

[1] For an excellent overview of the reforms, see Michael S. Chase and Jeffrey Engstrom, "China's Military Reforms: An Optimistic Take," *Joint Force Quarterly* 83 (4th Quarter 2016), 49–52.

[2] Roger Cliff, "Chinese Military Reforms: A Pessimistic Take," *Joint Force Quarterly* 83 (4th Quarter 2016), 53–56.

[3] Dennis J. Blasko, "The New PLA Joint Headquarters and Internal Assessments of PLA Capabilities," *China Brief* 16, no. 10 (June 21, 2016), available at <www.jamestown.org/single/?tx_ttnews%5Btt_news%5D=45511&no_cache=1#.V83n65MrIb0>. See also Michael S. Chase et al., *China's Incomplete Military Transformation: Assessing the Weaknesses of the People's Liberation Army* (Santa Monica, CA: RAND, 2015), available at <www.rand.org/content/dam/rand/pubs/research_reports/RR800/RR893/RAND_RR893.pdf>.

[4] For an excellent discussion of how the People's Liberation Army (PLA) will approach conflict in the future, see Jeffrey Engstrom, *Systems Confrontation and System Destruction Warfare: How the Chinese People's Liberation Army Seeks to Wage Modern Warfare* (Santa Monica, CA: RAND, 2018), available at <www.rand.org/pubs/research_reports/RR1708.html>.

[5] Wang Wowen [王握文], "Information Capability: Primary Capability of Joint Operations—Interview with Kuang Xinghua, Professor and Doctoral Adviser at the National Defense University of Science and Technology" [信息能力: 联合作战的第

一能力——访国防科学技术大学教授、博士生导师匡兴华], *PLA Daily* [解放军报], May 27, 2010, available at <www.mod.gov.cn/gflt/2010-05/27/content_4160027_2.htm>.

⁶ Ibid.

⁷ Kevin Pollpeter, "Toward an Integrative C4ISR System: Informationization and Joint Operations in the People's Liberation Army," in *The PLA at Home and Abroad: Assessing the Operational Capabilities of China's Military*, ed. Roy Kamphausen, David Lai, and Andrew Scobell (Carlisle Barracks, PA: Strategic Studies Institute, 2010), 194–195.

⁸ Ibid., 193–237.

⁹ Wanda Ayuso and Lonnie Henley, "Aspiring to Jointness: PLA Training, Exercises, and Doctrine, 2008–2012," in *Assessing the People's Liberation Army in the Hu Jintao Era*, ed. Roy Kamphausen, David Lai, and Travis Tanner (Carlisle Barracks, PA: Strategic Studies Institute, 2014), 171–207.

¹⁰ See Kenneth W. Allen, Phillip C. Saunders, and John Chen, *Chinese Military Diplomacy, 2003–2016: Trends and Implications*, China Strategic Perspectives 11 (Washington, DC: NDU Press, July 2017), available at <http://ndupress.ndu.edu/Media/News/Article/1249864/chinese-military-diplomacy-20032016-trends-and-implications/>.

¹¹ For a more in-depth discussion, see Dean Cheng, "The PLA's Wartime Structure" in *The PLA as Organization v2.0*, ed. Kevin Pollpeter and Kenneth W. Allen (Vienna, VA: DGI, 2015), 453–476.

¹² Wang Xiaohui [王晓辉], "What Strategic Preparations Should the Chinese Armed Forces Make?" [中国军队要做哪些战略准备], *Southern Weekend* [南方周末], September 11, 2015.

¹³ Ma Ho-leung [马浩亮], "Beijing Watch: Five Major Differences Between Theater Commands and Military Districts" [北京观察: 战区与军区五大不同], *Ta Kung Pao* [大公报], February 2, 2016, available at <http://news.takungpao.com/mainland/focus/2016-02/3276428.html>.

¹⁴ Han Xudong [韩旭东], "The Difference Between Military Regions and Theater Commands" [军区与战区的不同], *Global People* [环球人物], vol. 11 (April 2014), available at <http://paper.people.com.cn/hqrw/html/2014-04/26/content_1422529.htm>.

¹⁵ Ibid.

¹⁶ Han Xudong [韩旭东], "Decrypting the Military Reforms: 'Military Regions' Become 'Theater Commands,' Getting War Preparations Right" [军改解码: "军区"改"战区", 为战争做好准备], *Southern Weekend* [南方周末], April 27, 2016, available at <www.infzm.com/content/116612>.

17   Yang Yujun [杨宇军], "Transcript for MND Special Press Conference" [国防部专题新闻发布会文字实录], People's Republic of China Ministry of National Defense [中华人民共和国国防部], February 1, 2016, available at <www.mod.gov.cn/info/2016-02/01/content_4642553.htm>.

18   Han, "Decrypting the Military Reforms."

19   Feng Chunmei and Ni Guanghui [冯春梅, 倪光辉], "Interview of Southern Theater Commander Wang Jiaocheng: 'Creating a Joint Operations Command Structure Which Is Comprehensively Up-to-the-Mark'" [锻造全面过硬的联合作战指挥机构], Renmin Ribao [人民日报], February 28, 2016, 6.

20   Guo Yuandan [郭媛丹], "Decrypting the Military Reforms: North Sea Fleet Assigned to Northern Theater Command, Missile Force Directly Under CMC" [军改解读: 北海舰队属北部战区 火箭军直属军委], *Global Times* [环球时报], February 5, 2016, available at <http://mil.huanqiu.com/observation/2016-02/8510312.html>.

21   *Strategic direction* [*zhanlüe fangxiang*, 战略方向] is a military term used by the PLA. It is the "operational direction that has a major impact on the overall war situation. It points toward strategic targets, possesses a certain depth and breadth, and encompasses a multidimensional space that includes both the ground and its associated air space, maritime space, and outer space." There is a single primary strategic direction and multiple secondary strategic directions. For more information, see Lu Mingshan [陆明山], "Strategic Direction" [战略方向], *Chinese Military Encyclopedia: Military Learning II* [军事百科全书: 军事学术II] (Beijing: Academy of Military Science Press [军事科学出版社], July 1997), 715.

22   "Focus Vigorously and Solidly on the Work of Military Training for Combat Readiness—Second Commentary on Studying and Implementing the Important Speech Given by Chairman Xi Jinping on His Inspection Tour of the Ground Force Headquarters of the PLA Southern Theater Command" [抓紧抓实练兵备战工作—二谈学习贯彻习主席视察南部战区陆军机关时的重要讲话], *PLA Daily* [解放军报], April 24, 2017.

23   Shou Xiaosong [寿晓松], ed., *Science of Military Strategy* [战略学] (Beijing: Academy of Military Science Press [军事科学出版社], December 2013), 99.

24   Han, "Decryping the Military Reforms."

25   Wang Shibin, An Puzhong, and Liang Pengfei [王士彬, 安普忠, 梁蓬飞], "Xi Jinping Inspects CMC Joint Operations Command Center" [习近平视察军委联合作战指挥中心], People's Republic of China Ministry of National Defense [中华人民共和国国防部], April 20, 2016, available at <www.mod.gov.cn/leaders/2016-04/20/content_4650183.htm>.

[26] Yang, "Transcript for MND Special Press Conference."

[27] Jiang Congxiao [蒋骢骁], "Topic: What Theater Commands and Military Districts Do the U.S. and Russia Have?" [谈资: 美俄都有哪些战区和军区], Xinhua, February 2, 2016, available at <http://news.xinhuanet.com/world/2016-02/02/c_128695079.htm>; and Han, "Decrypting the Military Reforms."

[28] Li Xuanliang [李宣良], "PLA Theater Command Establishment Ceremony Held in Beijing" [中国人民解放军战区成立大会在北京举行], Xinhua, February 1, 2016, available at <http://news.xinhuanet.com/politics/2016-02/01/c_1117960554.htm>.

[29] Guo Ping [郭平], "Focusing on Advancing the Integration of Theater Services Command into Theater Joint Command" [着力推进战区军种指挥融入战区联指], *Rocket Force News* [火箭兵报], November 14, 2017.

[30] Xiao Ying and Zheng Xinyi [肖莹, 郑心仪], "New Layout for the Five Theater Commands" [五大战区心布局], *Global Person* [环球人物], February 1, 2016, available at <http://paper.people.com.cn/hqrw/html/2016-03/06/content_1668987.htm>; and "A Month Since the Five Theater Commands Have Been Established, Where Are the 18 Group Armies?" [五大戰區成立1個月 18個集團軍隸屬哪], *Wen Wei Po* [文匯報], February 28, 2016, available at <http://news.wenweipo.com/2016/02/28/IN1602280050.htm>.

[31] "Former 18 Group Armies Used as Basis in Adjustment and Establishment of 13 Group Armies" [以原18个集团军为基础，调整组建13个集团军], People's Republic of China Ministry of National Defense [中华人民共和国国防部], April 27, 2017, available at <www.mod.gov.cn/info/2017-04/27/content_4779505.htm>.

[32] Dennis J. Blasko, "What Is Known and Unknown about Changes to the PLA's Ground Combat Units," *China Brief* 17, no. 7 (May 11, 2017), available at <https://jamestown.org/program/known-unknown-changes-plas-ground-combat-units/>.

[33] "The Arrangement of the Five Theater Commands: Under Which Theater Command's Protection Does Your Hometown Fall?" [五大战区划设: 你的家乡在哪个战区的保护之下?], *Global Times* [环球时报], February 11, 2016, available at <http://mil.huanqiu.com/observation/2016-02/8526693.html>.

[34] "Chapter Six: Asia," *The Military Balance* 118, no. 1 (February 2018), 257, available at <www.tandfonline.com/doi/abs/10.1080/04597222.2018.1416982>.

[35] Kenneth W. Allen and Maryanne Kivlehan-Wise, "Implementing PLA Second Artillery Doctrinal Reform," in *China's Revolution in Doctrinal Affairs: Emerging Trends in the Operational Art of the Chinese People's Liberation Army*, ed. James C. Mulvenon and David Finkelstein (Arlington, VA: CNA, 2005), 176. The new 60 series designations for Rocket Force bases are found in the *2017 Report to*

Congress of the U.S.-China Economic and Security Review Commission (Washington, DC: Government Publishing Office, 2017), 219–220.

36   Dennis J. Blasko, *The Chinese Army Today: Tradition and Transformation for the 21st Century*, 2nd ed. (New York: Routledge, 2012), 108–109.

37   Xiao and Zheng, "New Layout for the Five Theater Commands"; and "A Month Since the Five Theater Commands Have Been Established, Where Are the 18 Group Armies?"

38   Blasko, "What Is Known and Unknown about Changes to the PLA's Ground Combat Units."

39   Shen Fan [沈凡], "59-Year-Old Du Benyin Reassigned as Southern Theater Command Naval Forces Deputy Political Commissar" [59岁杜本印改任南部战区海军副政委], *Caixin* [财新], March 5, 2016, available at <http://china.caixin.com/2016-03-05/100916536.html>.

40   Guo Yuandan, Ren Zhong, and Lan Yage [郭媛丹, 任重, 蓝雅歌], "Focused on the Potential Strategic Threats of Surrounding Areas, the Reason for Establishing the Five Theater Commands Is Very Clear" [针对周边潜在战略威胁 五代战区成立的目标很清晰], *Global Times* [环球时报], February 2, 2016, available at <http://world.huanqiu.com/exclusive/2016-02/8488105.html>.

41   Choi Chi-yuk, "Admiral Named to Head PLA's New Southern Theatre Command," *South China Morning Post* (Hong Kong), January 19, 2017, available at <www.scmp.com/news/china/policies-politics/article/2063649/admiral-named-head-plas-southern-theatre-command>.

42   "Chapter Six: Asia," 258.

43   "A Month Since the Five Theater Commands Have Been Established, Where Are the 18 Group Armies?"

44   Blasko, "What Is Known and Unknown about Changes to the PLA's Ground Combat Units."

45   Xiao and Zheng, "New Layout for the Five Theater Commands."

46   "Chapter Six: Asia," 257.

47   Xiao and Zheng, "New Layout for the Five Theater Commands."

48   "A Month Since the Five Theater Commands Have Been Established, Where Are the 18 Group Armies?"

49   Blasko, "What Is Known and Unknown about Changes to the PLA's Ground Combat Units."

50   Minnie Chan and Liu Zhen, "China's North Sea Fleet Put Under Central Command to Help Safeguard the Capital: Sources," *South China Morning Post* (Hong

Kong), February 2, 2016, available at <www.scmp.com/news/china/diplomacy-defence/article/1908768/chinas-north-sea-fleet-put-under-central-command-jinan>.

[51] Jiang Ziwen [蒋子文], "North Sea Fleet Commander Yuan Yubai Becomes Deputy Commander of Northern Theater Command and TC Naval Forces Commander" [北海舰队司令员袁誉柏任北部战区副司令员兼战区海军司令员], *The Paper* [澎湃], March 20, 2016, available at <www.thepaper.cn/newsDetail_forward_1446278>.

[52] "Chapter Six: Asia," 256.

[53] Han, "Decrypting the Military Reforms."

[54] Teddy Ng, "China's Air Force Gets a Lift with Pilot's Promotion to Top Military Job," *South China Morning Post* (Hong Kong), February 14, 2018, available at <www.scmp.com/news/china/diplomacy-defence/article/2133405/chinas-air-force-gets-lift-pilots-promotion-top>.

[55] Xiao and Zheng, "New Layout for the Five Theater Commands"; and "A Month Since the Five Theater Commands Have Been Established, Where Are the 18 Group Armies?"

[56] "Central Theater Command Areas of Jurisdiction Revealed: Area of Jurisdiction Includes 7 Provinces/Municipalities, Including Shaanxi and Hubei" [中部战区辖区曝光 辖区包括陕西湖北等7个省市], *Global Times* [环球时报], March 27, 2016, available at <http://mil.huanqiu.com/china/2016-03/8777452.html>.

[57] Guo Kai, "27th Group Army Becomes First Army in PLA to Relocate HQ," *China Daily* (Beijing), February 25, 2016, available at <www.chinadaily.com.cn/china/2016-02/25/content_23643856.htm>.

[58] "Military Theater Commands' Army HQs Identified: Source," *Global Times* (Beijing), February 4, 2016, available at <www.globaltimes.cn/content/967289.shtml>.

[59] Blasko, "What Is Known and Unknown about Changes to the PLA's Ground Combat Units."

[60] Li Wenji [李文姬], "Five Theater Commands, Four Have Already Clearly Established Naval Forces" [五大战区 4个明确已经建立海军], Xinhua, April 4, 2016, available at <http://news.xinhuanet.com/mil/2016-04/04/c_128861501.htm>.

[61] "Although It Has No Military Ports, Official Media Confirms Central Theater Command Has Naval Forces" [雖無軍港 官媒證中部戰區有海軍], *Ming Pao* [明報], April 2, 2016, available at <http://news.mingpao.com/pns/dailynews/web_tc/article/20160403/s00013/1459619554477>.

[62] Zhou Fei [邹菲], "A Certain Ground Force Air Defense Brigade and Naval Units from the Central Theater Command Jointly Create a Realistic Training Environment" [中部战区陆军某防空旅与海军部队共同构建逼真联训环境],

People's Daily [人民日报], August 1, 2016, available at <http://military.people.com.cn/n1/2016/0801/c1011-28600205.html>.

[63] "Chapter Six: Asia," 256.

[64] Phillip C. Saunders and Joel Wuthnow, *China's Goldwater-Nichols? Assessing PLA Organizational Reforms*, Strategic Forum No. 294 (Washington, DC: NDU Press, April 2016), 3.

[65] Choi, "Admiral Named to Head PLA's New Southern Theatre Command."

[66] *Department of Defense Reorganization Act of 1958*, Pub. L. 85-599, 85th Cong., 2nd sess., August 6, 1958.

[67] Kathleen J. McInnis, *Goldwater-Nichols at 30: Defense Reform and Issues for Congress*, R44474 (Washington, DC: Congressional Research Service, June 2, 2016), available at <www.fas.org/sgp/crs/natsec/R44474.pdf>.

[68] Martin E. Dempsey, "The Future of Joint Operations: Real Cooperation for Real Threats," *Foreign Affairs*, June 20, 2013, available at <www.foreignaffairs.com/articles/united-states/2013-06-20/future-joint-operations>.

[69] Lisa Ferdinando, "Carter Proposes Updates to Goldwater-Nichols Act," *DOD News*, April 5, 2016, available at <www.defense.gov/News/Article/Article/713930/carter-proposes-updates-to-goldwater-nichols-act>.

CHAPTER 7

HANDLING LOGISTICS IN A REFORMED PLA

The Long March Toward Joint Logistics

By LeighAnn Luce and Erin Richter

This chapter introduces People's Liberation Army (PLA) logistics modernization as an outgrowth of demands to ready the PLA for joint operations and high-tech warfare while satisfying domestic economic and political objectives for civil-military fusion. To forecast future reforms and their impact, we examine the three interrelated logistics requirements that Chinese sources have identified as requisite for the implementation of a joint logistics system: centralized command, advanced information systems, and civil-military fusion [*junmin ronghe*, 军民融合], also known as civil-military integration. We highlight constraints on PLA logistics transformation, including ingrained corruption and weak oversight mechanisms for the military and political elite, which will continue to degrade logistics efficiency and overall combat readiness.

The research underlying this chapter relies on a range of Chinese language sources. Published speeches, interviews, and editorials provided Chinese Community Party (CCP) and PLA leadership judgments regarding future requirements for military logistics. Official Chinese news media provided official statements relating to organizational reform. Finally, civilian and military academic and industry publications provided additional insights into the strategy and logic behind reform objectives, specific examples and assessments of operational capabilities, and suggestions for future developments. This chapter also benefits from and builds on prior expert assessments by Susan Puska and Dennis Blasko, as well as James Mulvenon's research on corruption within the PLA.[1]

The PLA's long-term goal of logistics reform is a precision logistics system that enables comprehensive, timely, and accurate logistics support to PLA joint operations. Implementing a joint logistics system is the primary means of achieving this goal. The PLA defines *joint logistics* as a system that "unifies the organization of the services to implement basic logistics work; avoids duplicate staffing, organizations, and facilities; and rationally distributes workforce, material, and financial resources to support joint operations and joint activities."[2] Alternatively and more colloquially, the system provides logistics support at the right time, at the right place, in the required amount.[3] This reform does not mean to eliminate specialized logistics support from the services, but rather seeks to consolidate general logistic support and achieve efficiencies wherever possible. According to PLA authors, an ideal joint logistics support system:

- provides precision logistics support for high-tempo, dynamic joint combat operations
- achieves strategic unity of effort by implementing an integrated joint logistics command system that is itself fully integrated with a strategic joint operations command system
- leverages the full potential of China's comprehensive national power through civil-military fusion to maximize combat power, ensure peacetime efficiencies, and maintain a constant state of combat readiness.[4]

Inspired by the U.S. *Joint Vision 2020*, the PLA has directed logistics modernization and civil-military fusion initiatives over the last two decades toward the development of a joint logistics system.[5] While many procedural, organizational, infrastructure, and equipment changes have been implemented, some changes necessary to unify and centralize logistics command remain incomplete. Consolidating and centralizing logistics command require more than just organizational reforms; it also requires the integration of logistics information systems to provide logisticians with timely and accurate information on the location, movement, status, and identity of units, personnel, equipment, material, and supplies.[6] For the PLA, this requirement also extends to civilian resources and demands standardized catalogs of available resources and associated attributes, regulations for military procurement, joint equipment development, and knowledge transfer. All of these objectives are enabled through integrated information systems.[7]

At the Third Plenum of the 18th Party Congress in November 2013, the CCP formally announced a series of significant military reforms intended to ensure that the PLA can fight and win high-tech modern wars. These reforms, to be implemented by 2020, alter the PLA's logistics command, infrastructure, and civil support systems to better support and sustain combat operations. In March 2016, the PLA renamed the General Logistics Department (GLD) as the Central Military Commission (CMC) Logistics Support Department (LSD), but delayed the execution of additional reform measures pending the September 13, 2016, establishment of the Joint Logistics Support Force (JLSF) [*junwei lianhe houqin baozhang budui*, 军委联合后勤保障部队].[8] The reason for this delay is unclear, but the broader restructuring of the PLA headquarters and military regions (MRs) to CMC and joint theater commands (TCs) may have been a necessary precursor.

With the establishment of the JLSF, PLA leaders separated logistics management responsibilities (resource management and regulatory activities) from combat service support (sustainment activities). Logistics management is now to be carried out by the CMC LSD, and combat service support is to be carried out by the JLSF. This move parallels wider PLA reform efforts to separate warfighting from force management. This change reduces the responsibilities of LSD offices, purportedly enabling the LSD to concentrate on resource management, training, infrastructure construction, and procedural oversight. (This reduction in responsibilities may explain why the current director of the CMC LSD, Song Puxuan, no longer has an ex officio seat on the Central Military Commission.) A more focused LSD will theoretically result in a greater standardization of logistics management and support procedures across the force, more efficient use of financial and materiel resources, streamlining of bureaucratic processes, and an overall decrease in corrupt practices by logistics professionals. Meanwhile, the JLSF is free to focus on planning and executing integrated joint logistics support for strategic and campaign operations.

These structural reforms create opportunities for greater centralization of command and control that allow the PLA to more effectively capitalize on two decades of information technology (IT), transportation, and facility improvements; maturing combat service support doctrine and training; and civil-military fusion that collectively improve PLA capabilities to manage and execute precision logistics support.

A New Logistics System for a New PLA

The CCP and PLA vision for future combat capabilities requires a modernized, centralized, efficient logistics system, but in many ways, the PLA military logistics support system has persisted as a relic from the Chinese civil war. Logistics organizations resisted numerous previous efforts to reform the system to more effectively support joint logistics. This section first reviews early attempts at and thinking on joint logistic reform. It then examines advances in three areas that appear necessary to meet national defense and economic logistics expectations: unification and centralization of command, IT integration (or *informationization*), and civil-military fusion. It then examines corruption within PLA logistics organizations as an obstacle to logistics reform.

Early Attempts at Reform

Joint logistics was first raised by Zhou Enlai in a 1952 report to the Joint Military Affairs Commission. Over the next four decades, the PLA unsuccessfully experimented with various methods of implementing joint logistics. PLA analysts attribute these failures to external events that made structural reform of the PLA's logistics system impossible. These include the Cultural Revolution, the death of Lin Biao in 1971, and PLA force reductions in the 1980s.[9]

In the 1990s, Jiang Zemin, as CMC chairman, directed the PLA to research and draft a series of military reforms. Drivers for the reforms included PLA logistics failures in the 1979 Sino-Vietnam war, observations of U.S. military operations in the Balkans and Persian Gulf, the PLA's inferior military capabilities revealed in the 1995–1996 Taiwan Strait crisis, and a general lack of combat readiness. In December 1998, the CMC enacted a series of military reforms intended to transform the PLA into a modern and professional joint operations force. These were subsequently outlined in the January 24, 1999, PLA Joint Combat Program. Nested in the program was a 10-year PLA logistics support system reform plan that emphasized implementation of a joint logistics system, socialization of support functions, modernization of logistics equipment, and improvements to logistics training and resource management.[10]

As a result of these reforms, the PLA logistics system now appears to be capable of effectively supporting large-scale military campaigns along internal lines of communication and has a nascent capability to sustain external force projection operations.[11] However, in 2014, the PLA identified several areas that required additional emphasis in order to advance PLA joint warfighting capabilities. These included unifying logistic units from all services under one command center and establishing mutual support relationships among and between joint and service units. The PLA needed additional improvements to logistics information systems in order to obtain the data necessary to command joint operations. The PLA also needed to diversify force projection capabilities to support operations both at home and abroad. This diversification required enhancing intermodal transport capabilities and developing new air and maritime transport platforms that leveraged the potential of the civilian sector. Most importantly, the PLA needed to reduce corruption within the logistics system to guarantee that the limited resources of the military are used to meet the actual needs of armed forces building and combat readiness.[12]

Unified and Centralized Logistics Command

Centralization of PLA logistics under one unified system has been an objective of PLA leaders since the 1950s. In 1952, the separate supply systems for the army, navy, and air force were unified under the leadership of the General Rear Area Services Department (later named the GLD).[13] On at least five separate occasions between 1965 and 1985, the PLA experimented with more comprehensive implementations of joint logistics command, but these were never fully executed.[14] This was likely due to a lack of joint culture in the broader PLA, but an internal power struggle may also have played a role.[15] The PLA's 1998 joint operations reforms under Jiang Zemin were a necessary precursor to real joint logistics command integration.[16]

By 2002, Joint Logistics Departments (JLDs) were established under each MR. The JLDs unified most transportation, medical, and material support; infrastructure construction; equipment procurement; and financial management functions under one headquarters. This allowed the PLA to eliminate many redundant structures previously maintained by the navy, air force, and Second Artillery Force; these services retained control of their specialized facilities and units.[17] By 2005, eight division-level logistics organizations, 94 rear depots, 47 hospitals, and nearly 2,000 other support organizations were eliminated, and a professional civilian cadre system was instituted to further reduce active-duty military manpower requirements. The cuts enabled the PLA to reduce its size by at least 135,000 troops.[18]

In July 2004, the GLD initiated a joint logistics pilot test in the Jinan MR, combining MR joint logistics and service logistics organization under the newly named Jinan War Zone JLD.[19] The War Zone JLD brought together logistics officers from the MR JLD, and MR army, navy, air force, and Second Artillery commands to jointly plan and direct logistics support for all PLA units operating in the MR. After the conclusion of the pilot in

July 2006, GLD evaluations concluded that a fully integrated joint logistics system improves the speed and efficiency of logistics support by centrally managing logistics command and control at the theater/war zone level, consolidating logistics facilities and organizations, and reducing the amount of combat service support capabilities required to support joint operations by creating joint task-organized logistics support formations.[20]

However, the test identified some barriers that prevented implementation of the integrated joint logistics support system across the PLA. While the new system enabled centrally managed logistics planning and direction at the theater/war zone level, IT deficiencies undermined the JLD's ability to maintain visibility over logistics assets. The JLD was unable to direct the distribution of materials and service in time to support operational demands.[21] Established logistics standards, regulations, policies, and procedures did not adequately support the effective execution of joint logistics operations. A period of comprehensive research and development was necessary to make adjustments that fully integrated the requirements of the navy, air force, and Second Artillery. Also, CMC leaders concluded that PLA-wide structural reforms would be required to effectively centralize logistics command. Presumably, this included the transition from MRs to TCs.

In December 2007, the CMC promulgated "An Outline on Comprehensively Building Modern Logistics," which directed logistics modernization tasks required to fully transition the joint logistics system by 2020.[22] From 2007 onward, the Jinan MR continued to operate an integrated joint logistics system at the MR level. This provided unified direction for service and general logistics support activities in order to identify what command, communications, procedural, and operational changes would be necessary for PLA-wide implementation.[23] The MR would also continue to experiment with organizing joint logistics support for deployed combat formations. This involved task-organizing joint and service logistics units and fostering mutual support relationships between services.[24]

Between 2009 and 2015, with the exception of Jinan, the MRs continued to operate separate logistics systems for shared and service-specific requirements. However, they also experimented with centralized theater logistics command structures to inform planning for future PLA-wide structural reforms. MR exercises emphasized the use of integrated logistics command systems to direct logistics operations, and ad hoc joint logistics commands were integrated into maturing joint operations command structures for increasingly sophisticated campaign-level exercises.[25] PLA informationization, or IT integration, projects used these exercises to refine systems to horizontally and vertically link all logistics activities.

Informationized Logistics

PRC experts on informationization recognize that the ability to aggregate, process, and access large quantities of data, in near real-time, is an absolute requirement to conduct precision logistics. Moreover, examination of PLA logistics information system research suggests that the foundational technological requirements necessary for centralized joint logistics were not met as of 2012. This suggests that there were significant technical barriers to creating a centralized, joint logistics command organization.[26]

Despite the high degree of abstraction that this term has consistently carried in PLA theoretical discussions, at its core, informationization (*xinxihua*, 信息化) emphasizes the integration of information technology and other science and technology developments. As former Deputy Director of the All-Military Informationization Work Office Hou Xigui expounds in the 2002 publication *Military Informationization Construction Research*, the "application of information technology to logistics support promises to achieve more accurate and more intense logistics support. When information, logistics, and transportation are brought together, it fundamentally changes the traditional delivery support mode, achieving more accurate, precise, and intense support."[27] This publication also depicts the logistics support system as one essential IT component together with combined armed forces; each service's operations platforms; communication systems; and intelligence, surveillance, and reconnaissance systems as components of information technology. According to the author, these collectively form an integrated command platform that will provide a breakthrough in the capabilities of the battlefield command and control system.[28]

PLA researchers recognize that the PLA's desired logistics system involves a large number of technical challenges. Two experts on logistics informationization and information aggregation at the PLA Logistics Command University raised a tentative list of technology requirements:[29]

- unified military logistics standards, required to achieve logistics system interconnectivity and interoperability
- military logistics sensing and collection equipment, such as the comprehensive application of radio frequency identification (RFID), GPS, and other Internet of Things sensing and identification technology that allows for real-time, dynamic visualization and control
- construction of a ubiquitous information transmission network, using an All-Military Joint Communication Network, Military Comprehensive Information Network, and other network resources to form a Military Logistics Information Transmission Backbone Network
- a robust information management platform, to enable data storage, efficient processing, rapid retrieval, with intelligent processing to prevent abuse
- development of comprehensive enterprise applications.

This list lays out the technical milestones for the PLA to achieve visualized, precise, intelligent, coordinated logistics support. Over the last decade, the PLA has concentrated on making improvements in several areas, including inventory visibility and management; standardization, which would enhance networking of logistics information; tracking of materiel and equipment throughout the distribution process; and information management.[30] Warehouse and transportation management information systems, RFID and GPS, and camera and aerospace surveillance systems have all been sporadically integrated and networked to military logistics command centers.[31] Standardized logistics funding and material management platforms and a suite of online procurement systems have been launched to integrate logistics managers with commercial suppliers for materiel procurement and distribution.[32] PLA logisticians continue to modify sustainment planning factors that are used to drive logistics information systems based on exercise consumption and the characteristics of newly fielded equipment.[33] In 2013, the PLA created the All-Military Logistics Information Center in Beijing to integrate logistics system standards to provide a framework for the large-scale integration of logistics information systems.[34]

Informationization programs show that the PRC has prioritized a development path that will enable military logistics organizations to coordinate and integrate information sources from outside civilian entities with military information systems. One recent example is the new Forces Medical Cloud, which leverages cloud technology to implement horizontal and vertical integration between information systems between military medical organizations and related Civilian Information Systems, such as between military hospitals and China's center for disease control. According to a 2014 presentation by Han Wei, one of China's leading experts on military medical information systems, this system design leverages cloud computing–based technology, Software as a Service, Infrastructure as a Service, and Platform as a Service to create a managed, scalable foundation to develop big data information-sharing capabilities.[35]

The Forces Medical Cloud project appeared to progress rapidly and created network linkages between civilian and military organizations over a wide geographic area, a requirement for centralized logistics. Specifically, the design specifications show that the information services were available via mobile and fixed-line networks, including three presumably military networks, a military 3G mobile network, local area networks, as well as a medical telework network interface, allowing for information-sharing and coordination. The project progressed from the research and planning phase in January 2013 through intermediate phases to arrive at the application expansion phase in September 2014. Moreover, the project was expected to reach the final summary phase by January 2015. Thus, in 2 years, Han Wei argues that the cloud-based model provided significant improvements to the information platform that would allow cost-efficient, scalable information systems infrastructure.[36]

The Forces Medical Cloud project also highlights systemic weaknesses within the PLA's previous IT development programs, which suffered from a lack of leadership and foresight and resulted in the creation of inefficient, cumbersome IT systems that could not easily evolve or scale. In its early years of development, the Forces Medical Cloud suffered from technical impediments to the integration and centralization of data and was not reasonably operational until 2015. According to Han Wei, developers faced five major situational challenges:

- numerous organizations were involved and were widely distributed
- numerous systems were involved and were not easy to use
- it was difficult to extend and difficult to maintain
- there was insufficient funding and insufficient technology
- the system was fixed, not mobile.

Furthermore, he described the pre–cloud computing development environment as characterized by stovepipe style applications that required intensive investments and that were difficult to manage. Notably, several of the challenges faced by the developers, such as dealing with numerous, cumbersome systems, insufficient funding and technology, as well as stovepiped development models, demonstrate larger systemic failures in leadership and program management. Other logistics information systems likely suffered from similar early development setbacks but have similarly benefited from advances in project development strategy and technology capabilities in recent years.

Civilian Military Fusion

A third focus for PLA joint logistics reform is civil-military fusion, also known as civil-military integration (see the chapter by Lafferty in this volume for more details). Civil-military fusion aims to leverage the full potential of a state's comprehensive national power to maximize combat capabilities, ensure peacetime efficiencies, and guarantee a constant state of combat readiness. Within China, it also emphasizes the fusion of economic development and military modernization to support the country's overall economic and social development. China's goals are not only to leverage national resources in order to support military requirements but also to promote economic growth through advancements in military capabilities.[37] One Chinese National Defense University professor highlights the Beidou system as an example that was developed for national defense, but when commercialized can yield 400–500 billion yuan (63–79 billion USD) in returns by 2020.[38]

As part of logistics reform, civil-military fusion seeks to separate from the PLA those operations where civilian resources can be used as part of a larger strategy to strengthen the national economic system and reduce military operating costs. This involves outsourcing logistical support to the civilian sector wherever operationally feasbile.[39] The target of this reform is to "incorporate the development of military logistical services into the state economic and social development system and embed military production in the civilian sector."[40] Between 2000 and 2007, more than 5,200 administrative, subsistence, medical, and construction services were outsourced to the civilian sector. Subsequently, troops deployed in China for exercises and contingency operations have received some level of civilian support through support-the-front offices or mobilized militia units.[41]

The PLA is also working to leverage the capabilities of the civilian sector to support a variety of logistics operations. Many of China's maturing logistics information systems utilize commercial technologies already widely employed by international civilian and military logistics systems.[42] In addition, Chinese regulations and laws issued between 2003 and 2016 facilitated the PLA's ability to use transportation capacity from the civilian sector and encouraged civil transportation construction projects, both infrastructure and equipment, to take military support requirements into consideration.[43] These projects have improved PLA strategic mobility along internal lines of communication through improved infrastructure and transport equipment, neither of which must be regularly maintained by the military.[44] In addition, the construction of dual-use air and maritime platforms and infrastructure, usually retained in the civil sector, has allowed the PLA to make modest improvements in its ability to support external force projection operations.[45]

China's 2015 defense white paper, *China's Military Strategy*, also emphasizes the importance of civil-military fusion. The document notes that through 2020, the PLA will continue to focus on "developing uniform military and civilian standards for infrastructure, key technological areas, and major industries, exploring methods for training military personnel in civilian educational institutions, developing weaponry and equipment by national defense industries, and outsourcing logistics support to civilian support systems."[46] The paper also calls on the PLA to enhance force projection capabilities and support overseas operations. The PLA will likely rely heavily on mobilized or contracted civilian support resources to do so.

Corruption as an Enduring Constraint

As the PLA's logistic system has developed in the modern era, fiscal corruption and links to the private sector have distracted from its mission. This section addresses increased corruption within logistics as an outgrowth of CCP policies in the 1980s and 1990s, which was compounded as logistics organizations operated in an environment that lacked transparency and independent oversight. After characterizing the environment, it examines the impact of corruption in undermining logistics system reform efforts.

Deng Xiaoping's economic reforms in the 1980s helped cultivate an environment for corruption in the PLA that persisted to the 2010s, as they encouraged the PLA to participate in commercial activities while not incentivizing proper behavior or providing adequate internal or external oversight mechanisms.[47] According to late 1990 estimates, there were over 15,000 PLA-run companies at one point, generating billions of yuan each year.[48] However, the military's activities were shrouded and rarely discussed publicly, although corruption was considered a serious issue.[49] In July 1998, Jiang Zemin declared that the PLA would divest itself from all commercial activity, a pronouncement reiterated in his plans for PLA modernization.[50] As a result, the GLD rapidly shed many of its corporate investments, handing over factories and other commercial businesses to the civilian sector, and dissolved GLD organizations responsible for managing much of the PLA's commercial enterprise and factory system.[51]

However, while many businesses were formally removed from military control, in practice many remained under the control of relatives or close associates of active-duty officers.[52] CMC directives to outsource allowed senior PLA officials to direct contracts for services to these companies, enhancing their profits or to individuals with whom they desired to curry favor. Graft was rampant.[53] According to the *Global Times*, as of May 2016, the PLA remained active in commercial businesses in sectors such as telecommunications, personnel training, logistics, technology, and health care.[54] Furthermore, PLA regulations allowed the compensatory transfer of land use rights (with GLD approval) and for units to form partnerships with local governments and build real estate projects together on PLA-owned land.[55]

This set of semi-legal and outright illegal involvements of PLA officials in commercial ventures hobbled PLA logistics reforms in particular because senior GLD leaders responsible for implementing reforms had a great deal to lose in the process. GLD officials managed most of the PLA's land and facilities, oversaw its construction and procurement contracts, managed its material and much of its equipment, approved budgets, and accounted for and disbursed its funding.[56] The GLD also managed the PLA audit system and was responsible for ensuring the fiscal discipline of senior PLA officials, until the CMC transferred the audit system to its direct control in 2014.[57]

Anti-corruption measures have been in full swing since January 2012 when then-GLD Deputy Director Liu Yuan declared war on the establishment, promising to fight corruption to the end. President Xi Jinping soon championed this fight.[58] According to press reports, at least 17 deputy-corps level or higher logistics officials were charged with corruption as of September 2016, and many others, including former GLD Director Liao Xilong, are rumored to be under investigation.[59] However, these are just the tip of the iceberg of structural, endemic corruption within the PLA and especially within its logistic system. The elevation of the director of the CMC Discipline Inspection Commission to CMC member status in

October 2017 is an indicator of the continuing extent of the corruption problem and of Xi's determination to try to address it.

Examining the efficacy of future PLA logistics reforms will require consideration of the extent to which Xi has successfully curbed corruption. Emphasis on civil-military fusion will compound this challenge, as military and civilian logisticians must operate in the same ecosystem. One problem is that China's civilian logistics industry appears to also function in an opaque environment that makes identifying corruption difficult.[60] FTI Consulting's Asia branch has observed some standard practices within the logistics industry that create risk and waste resources: bribery of staff, unauthorized subcontracting to third parties, collusion between suppliers in the bidding process, and undisclosed conflicts of interest between purchasing or management staff. Overall, the industry appears to lack transparency and legislative control, especially when examining the supply chain beyond first-tier suppliers. Reforms to the PLA logistics system are bound to fail if there is not a similar holistic overhaul of business processes within the civilian sector. That would be a particularly ambitious goal given China's demand for economic growth.

A "Reformed" PLA Logistics System

On February 1, 2016, the PLA announced the permanent transition to a joint operations command system comprised of five theater commands centrally directed by the CMC.[61] By creating a unified command structure at the strategic level, this decision set the conditions under which an integrated joint logistics system could be established across the PLA.[62]

The September 13, 2016, inauguration of the JLSF marked the implementation of the PLA's new logistics system. During its establishment ceremony, Xi Jinping identified the JLSF as the CMC's main force for implementing joint logistics support for strategic and campaign operations.[63] Identification of the JLSF as subordinate to the CMC and not the LSD suggests that, in sync with wider PLA organizational reforms, joint logistics support for PLA operations will be separated from force management.

The LSD appears to be continuing previous GLD responsibilities of PLA-wide strategic logistics planning, material management and procurement, facilities management, contracting, budget management and funds disbursement, international military engagement, and overall administration of PLA hospitals and medical programs.[64] To strengthen PLA logistics support as a whole, the LSD is pursuing improved mechanisms to draw support from China's commercial enterprises to support PLA logistics operations, develop technologies to enhance logistics planning and execution, and improve logistics support equipment.[65] In addition, the LSD appears to be spearheading initiatives to standardize information technology for logistics management across PLA services to improve data integration required to support joint logistics execution.[66]

The JLSF now coordinates the execution of logistics support to theater commands, assuming the responsibilities of previous GLD direct subordinate units and MR JLDs. Its responsibilities include managing the storage and distribution of material, fuel, ordnance, and directing transportation, field medical, and subsistence support to PLA units assigned to theater operations.[67] Despite its designation as CMC subordinate, it is possible that the JLSF remains administratively organized under the LSD, but it is almost certainly operationally subordinate to the CMC Joint Staff Department.

The JLSF is a force led by the army leader grade Wuhan Joint Logistics Support Base (JLSB), which directs five joint logistics support centers (JLSCs), each aligned to a theater command (see figure 1).[68] Each of these centers is a deputy army leader grade organization. Before the reforms, the Wuhan JLSB was responsible for providing strategic material support to the entire PLA. The base had some subordinate units that controlled equipment, weapons, fuel, material, and munitions depots spread throughout central China. In wartime, it was tasked with providing strategic logistics support to war zones/theaters.[69] The base will likely continue in this role, with an altered command structure.

The JLSF as a whole appears to operate separately from but in general support of the theater commands in order to facilitate the movement of

Figure 1. Organization of the Central Military Commission Joint Logistics Support Force

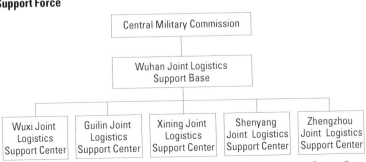

Source: Zhang Tao, ed., "Defense Ministry Holds News Conference on Joint Logistic Support System Reform," *China Military Online*, September 14, 2016, available at <http://english.chinamil.com.cn/view/2016-09/14/content_7258622.htm>.

resources across theater boundaries as required. The JLSCs are subordinate to the Wuhan JLSB but provide direct support to TC operations and general support to all units garrisoned and/or operating within their designated theater command. JLSCs also appear to have some authority in tasking military districts (MDs) and service logistics units within their area to provide support to units operating nearby, regardless of service affiliation.[70]

How JLSCs are tasked to support TC elements is unclear, as there is no evidence of a logistics department or staff directly subordinate to the TC headquarters after reform. Each TC army and air force headquarters does have a subordinate logistics department.[71] It is possible TC subordinate units or service components request support directly from the JLSC without consulting the TC headquarters, indicating the logistics system [xitong, 系统] is distinct from the operational system, but this is unlikely given the PLA's overarching drive toward integrated joint operations. More likely, there is a yet to be identified logistics coordinating entity within the headquarters responsible for prioritizing the logistics requirements of subordinate units based on overall operational needs (see figure 2).

JLSCs are new organizations. Rather than just renaming five MR JLDs and transitioning their staffs to support the new theater commands, the PLA created entirely new commands geographically separate from the

Figure 2. JLSF May Act as a Supporting Command Separate from Theater Commands

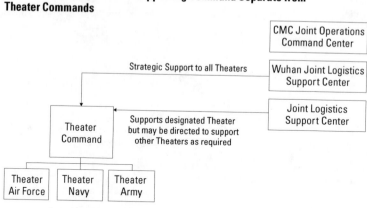

Source: Zhang Tao, ed., "Defense Ministry Holds News Conference on Joint Logistic Support System Reform," China Military Online, September 14, 2016, available at <http://english.chinamil.com.cn/

TC headquarters.[72] The JLSCs were probably redesignated and elevated to deputy army leader grade organizations from five of the PLA's previous 26 division leader grade joint logistics support departments (JLSDs), which were subordinate to MR JLDs (see table).[73]

Table. Probable Association of Former Joint Logistics Subdepartments to New Joint Logistics Support Force		
Previous Designation	New Designation	Supports
Wuhan Rear Base (MUCD 62101)	Wuhan Joint JLSB	Strategic Support to all Theaters
13th JLSD (MUCD 73801)	Wuxi JLSC	Eastern Theater Command
20th JLSD (MUCD 76140)	Guilin JLSC	Southern Theater Command
25th JLSD (MUCD 68060)	Xining JLSC	Western Theater Command
2nd JLSD (MUCD 65133)	Shenyang JLSC	Northern Theater Command
33rd JLSD (MUCD 72495)	Zhengzhou JLSC	Central Theater Command

Key: JLSB: joint logistics support base; JLSC: joint logistics support center; JLSD: joint logistics support department; MUCD: Military Unit Cover Designator.

The reason for the separation of JLSCs from the TC headquarters remains unclear. It is possible that PLA planners, in line with establishing theater commands that can smoothly transition to support wartime operations without significant changes to staff, wanted to establish standing theater rear command posts to manage logistics, equipment, and mobilization support work in war and peace.[74] If this is the case, theater mobilization for contingencies may be improved since a full-time rear command post would standardize command and support relationships among the JLSCs, theater logistics forces, militia, reserve, and civilian supporting organizations. However, at present there is no evidence that JLSCs are responsible for equipment support or mobilization activities outside of material procurement and transportation.

Some formerly disparate units appear to have been consolidated under the JLSCs, most notably the former GLD transportation military representative offices (MROs) and possibly elements of former MD maritime transport units. The following organizations have been listed as subordinate to JLSCs in various press reports, though the distinction between second- and third-level organizations remains unclear:[75]

- Political Work Department
- Medical Service Support Department
- PLA Hospitals
- Military Facilities and Construction Division
- Procurement Division
- Supplies Division
- Military Representatives Division
- Navigational Affairs MRO
- Transportation MRO
- Railway MRO
- Airport MRO
- Subordinate Work Division
- Fuel, Supply, and Ordnance Depots
- Ship Transport Units
- Waterway Technical Support Unit.

Figure 3. JLSD Organization Prior to PLA Reform

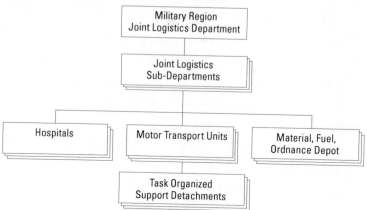

Source: Cheng Yunjie and Xu Jinzhang, "PLA Continues Long March of Logistics Reform," Xinhua, July 28, 2007, available at <http://web.archive.org/web/20081025011030/http://news.xinhuanet.com/english/2007-07/28/content_6441943.htm>.

Prior to reform, each MR JLD had between three and five subordinate division leader grade logistics units responsible for providing general logistics support to all PLA units operating within their assigned area and task organizing detachments to provide direct support to deploying units as required (see figure 3). JLSDs also controlled a number of subordinate regiment leader grade material, ordnance, and fuel depots; subsistence support and transportation units; and hospitals.[76] These units were the core of the PLA's joint logistics support system.

While five former JLSDs have been redesignated as JLSCs, there is currently little information available on the other JLSDs. It is possible that the PLA may separate the remaining JLSD fixed and mobile logistics capabilities into separate but interconnected systems in order to increase readiness to support power projection operations. JLSDs have been experimenting with various methods of task organizing contingency support brigades for two decades and could carve these units out into their own direct support echelon under the JLSC, while other echelons manage fixed sites and general support capabilities. This may allow a consolidation of some fixed storage areas and allow for a reduction of support personnel.[77]

Figure 4. Possible Organization of JLSCs with Separated Fixed and Mobile Groups

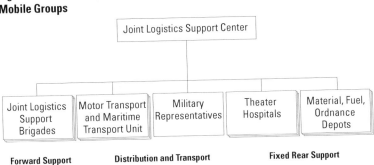

Source: Cheng Yunjie and Xu Jinzhang, "PLA Continues Long March of Logistics Reform," Xinhua, July 28, 2007, available at <http://web.archive.org/web/20081025011030/http://news.xinhuanet.com/english/2007-07/28/content_6441943.htm>.

The JLSCs are likely to maintain separate maritime and motor transport units to support the distribution of materials from rear to forward areas supplemented by military representatives who coordinate civilian transport support to theater operations as required, under both peacetime and wartime conditions (see figure 4).

A flattening of the logistics organizational structure at the theater level may enable an overall reduction in the size of the PLA logistics force while increasing its operational efficiency by designating full-time forward support units that can concentrate on mission-specific combat logistics support tasks, while retaining a robust theater storage and distribution system. By subordinating the military representative system under JLSCs, the PLA may also be able to more effectively leverage growing civil-transport capabilities, creating economies of force. If the supply support system follows a similar model as the transport system, the PLA may be able to more effectively procure materials from local commercial suppliers, reducing theater material storage requirements.

There is little information available to date on planned changes to navy, air force, or Rocket Force logistic organizations. However, some consolidation of these organizations is likely where efficiencies can be found. The newly designated PLA Army will likely inherit some facilities in order to establish its own organic service logistics system separate from the joint system. Media reports suggest that the GLD's Qinghai-Tibet Military Depot has already been transferred to the army.[78]

It remains unclear exactly what the relationship between JLSCs and TC service logistics units will be in the future. PLA officials have indicated that service logistics systems will continue to maintain specialized capabilities and manage material specific to each service, while the JLSF will manage all general support.[79] This is in itself not a break from previous practice; however, it is possible under the "reformed" PLA logistics system that the JLSF will have greater authority to task service logistics units to provide support to other units where and when necessary, procedures required for precision logistics. It appears that JLSCs are much more joint in composition than their JLD predecessors, indicating staffs are more likely to understand service-specific requirements and capabilities and be capable of integrating this information into joint logistics planning and execution.[80]

Conclusion and Questions for Further Research

Through 2020, the PLA will likely complete the reorganization of its logistics command structure, centralizing support for theater operations under a joint logistics headquarters that is more capable of leveraging the civilian sector for support. However, legacy logistics infrastructure, leadership, and culture, especially corruption, continue to exist as barriers to reform. The future sustainability of PLA logistics reform efforts will depend on how effectively the PLA can professionalize logistics operations to ensure reliability within the system and modernize its information technology to effectively integrate information systems among military units, and between military and civilian logistics entities.

The PLA appears to be increasing the centralized management of logistics IT projects, while continuing to outsource support work to the civilian sector. Both efforts appear focused on rectifying problems associated with stovepiped, outdated, and cumbersome systems that impede joint logistics and operational planning and execution. The PLA has now introduced organizations dedicated to IT standardization and integration to achieve PLA-wide interoperability and compatibility. At the same time, the PRC is prioritizing dual-use technology and unified civilian and military technology standards that may allow the PLA to more effectively integrate disparate information systems currently in use and speed the fielding of newer and more technologically advanced platforms. In particular, PRC adoption of new data science methodologies, and development of cloud computing and Internet of Things technologies, have the potential to significantly advance logistics management for the PLA.[81] These technologies are necessary for the PLA to capitalize on structural changes designed to enhance joint operations and overcome previous organizational and informational stovepipes.

One major question that remains unanswered is how the PLA will modernize its logistics system to support overseas operations. The structural reforms under way and efforts to integrate civilian information systems into PLA decision and planning systems all emphasize improvements to logistics support along internal lines of communication and outward along China's immediate periphery. There appears to be little emphasis on developing true strategic force projection capabilities to support PLA overseas operations beyond the production of large Y-20 military transport aircraft. In 2014, PLA leaders identified the development of force protection and sustainment capabilities as goals for PLA logistics modernization, yet to date there has been little discussion about how this will be technically and procedurally achieved, or even what organization will be responsible for these operations since they are beyond the current responsibilities of any theater command.[82]

On July 11, 2017, the PLA officially established China's first overseas military base in Djibouti, ostensibly under the PLA Navy. The base is purportedly intended to enhance support to naval operations in the Gulf of Aden, though other joint missions are likely in the future.[83] It remains unclear how the PLA will permanently sustain operations from this base, though it will most likely involve regular support from Chinese commercial shipping and logistics enterprises to reduce the demand on military lift platforms. Closely watching the development of logistics mechanisms associated with the Djibouti base will be critical to understanding how and how well the PLA will regularly sustain operational forces along external lines of communication. Future academic research on PLA logistics should emphasize civil-military coordination mechanisms to leverage national resources to support PLA operations overseas as well as the development of PLA expeditionary logistics capabilities with particular emphasis on the maturation of reception, staging, onward movement, and integration procedures and supporting technological enablers.

Notes

[1] Susan Puska, "Taming the Hydra: Trends in China's Military Logistics Since 2000," in *The PLA at Home and Abroad: Assessing the Operational Capabilities of China's Military*, ed. Roy Kamphausen, David Lai, and Andrew Scobell (Carlisle, PA: Strategic Studies Institute, 2010), 553–624; Dennis J. Blasko, *People's War Lives On: Chinese Military Logistics in the War Zone* (Santa Monica, CA: RAND, 2004); James C. Mulvenon, "To Get Rich Is Unprofessional: Chinese Military Corruption in the Jiang Era," *China Leadership Monitor*, vol. 6 (Spring 2003); and James C. Mulvenon, "So Crooked They Have to Screw Their Pants On—Part 3: The Guo Boxiong Edition," *China Leadership Monitor*, vol. 48 (Fall 2015).

[2] *China Military Logistics Encyclopedia* [中国军事后勤百科全书] (Beijing: Golden Shield Publishing House [金盾出版社], August 2002), vol. I, 43.

[3] Liu Wei and Yu Xin [刘炜, 于鑫], *Food and Fodder Go First* [粮草先行] (Hunan: Hunan Science and Technology Press [湖南科学技术出版社], 2005); Zhang Zhende [张振德] "'Precision Logistics'—The Focus of Military Logistics Reform" ['精确后勤':军事后勤变革的聚焦点], *PLA Daily* [解放军报], September 23, 2003.

[4] Liu Zhigang [刘志刚], "We Should Focus on Three Types of Changes in Logistics Reform" [后勤改革要着眼三种转变], *PLA Daily* [解放军报], September 9, 2014; Wang Haibo, Gao Zhiwen, and Hua Xiao [汪海波, 高志文,花晓], "The Grand Program for Building Modern Logistics—An Interview of Zhou Songhe, Chief of Staff of the General Logistics Department's Headquarters Department on Issues Concerning the Logistic Work in the New Year" [谋篇布势: 建设现代

后勤展宏图—总后司令部参谋长周松和就新年度后勤工作有关问题答记者问],
PLA Daily [解放军报], February 12, 2014; Liao Xilong [廖锡龙], "Comprehensively
Develop Modern Logistics with Scientific Development Concept as Guide" [以科
学发展观为指导全面建设现代后勤], *Qiushi* [求是], July 16, 2006; Cheng Ying
and Xu Jinzhang [程瑛, 徐金章] "Inside Story of PLA Logistics Reforms" [解放军
后勤变化内情], *Liaowang Dongfang Zhoukan* [瞭望东方周刊], no. 3 (January 19,
2006), 33–34, 36–38; Ma Shuming [马书铭], "Issues on the Theory and Practice
of the PLA's Joint Logistics" [解放军联合后勤理论和实践的问题], *China Military
Science* [中国军事科学], no. 2 (2000), 14–20.

   ⁵ *Joint Vision 2020—America's Military: Preparing for Tomorrow* (Washington, DC: The Joint Staff, June 2000).

   ⁶ Joint Publication 4-01.8, *Joint Tactics, Techniques, and Procedures for Reception, Staging, Onward Movement, and Integration* (Washington, DC: The Joint Staff, June 13, 2000).

   ⁷ Liu and Yu, Food and Fodder Go First; Ma Haoliang [马浩亮], "Civil-Military Fusion" [军民深度融合多管齐下支撑强军路], *Ta Kung Pao* [大公报], November 4, 2015, available at <http://news.sina.com.cn/o/2015-11-04/ doc-ifxk-mrvp5097082.shtml>.

   ⁸ Xu Qiliang [许其亮], "Firmly Push Forward Reform of National Defense and the Armed Forces" [坚定不移推进国防和军队改革], *People's Daily* [人民日报], November 20, 2013; Cao Zhi, Li Xuanliang, and Wang Shibin [曹智, 李宣良, 王士彬], "At CMC Reform Work Meeting, Xi Jinping Stresses: Comprehensively Implement Reform and Military Strengthening Strategy, Resolutely Take Path to Strong Military with Chinese Characteristics" [习近平在中央军委改革工作会议上强调全面实施改革强军战略坚定不移走中国特色强军之路], Xinhua, November 30, 2015; "Inaugural Meeting of Joint Logistics Support Force of Central Military Commission Held in Beijing; Xi Jinping Confers Army Flags to Wuhan Joint Logistics Support Base and Various Joint Logistics Support Centers and Delivers Speech" [中央军委联勤保障部队成立大会在京举行习近平向武汉联勤保障基地和各联勤保障中心授予军旗并致训词], Xinhua, September 13, 2016, available at <http://politics.people.com.cn/n1/2016/0914/c1024-28714073.html>.

   ⁹ Zhang Liansong and Liu Jing [张连松, 刘晶], "From Self-Supporting Arms and Services to Joint Support for the Three Services: The 50-Year History of Our Army's Joint Logistics Reform" [从军兵种自我保障到三军联合保障-我军联勤改革50年的历史跨越], *History of the People's Liberation Army* [人民军队史], April 2004, available at <www.hprc.org.cn/pdf/JLSY200404005.pdf>.

[10] Pei Fang, "Major Operation to Be Performed on Military Logistics System," *Kuang Chiao Ching* [广角镜], no. 318 (March 16, 1999), 50–52. The People's Liberation Army (PLA) defines *socialization of support functions* as replacing military support personnel with civilian professionals and contracting out logistics services to civilian companies. See Shi Wennian and Wang Haibo [石文年, 汪海波], "The History and Theory of the Socialization of Military Logistics" [军人后勤保障社会化的历史及理论研究], *China Military Science* [中国军事科学], no. 2 (2001), 57–61.

[11] *Annual Report to Congress: Military and Security Developments Involving the People's Republic of China 2016* (Washington, DC: Office of the Secretary of Defense, April 26, 2016), available at <www.defense.gov/Portals/1/Documents/pubs/2016%20China%20Military%20Power%20Report.pdf>; Dennis J. Blasko, "Clarity of Intentions: People's Liberation Army Transregional Exercises to Defend China's Borders," in *Learning by Doing: The PLA Trains at Home and Abroad*, ed. Roy Kamphausen, David Lai, and Travis Tanner (Carlisle Barracks, PA: Strategic Studies Institute, 2012), 171–212; Feng Chunmei [冯春梅], "The Shenyang Military Region Explores a New Way of Military-Civilian Integration Strengthening Logistic Support by Complementing Each Other and Seeking Win-Win Results" [沈阳军区探索军民融合新路子—互补共赢强保障], *People's Daily* [人民日报], February 11, 2011.

[12] Gao and Hua, "The Grand Program for Building Modern Logistics"; Liu Zhigang [刘志刚], "We Should Focus on Three Types of Changes in Logistics Reform" [后勤改革要着眼三种转变], *PLA Daily* [解放军报], September 9, 2014.

[13] *China Military Logistics Encyclopedia*, vol. I, 43.

[14] Zhang and Liu, "From Self-Supporting Arms and Services to Joint Support for the Three Services."

[15] Ibid.

[16] Puska, "Taming the Hydra"; Pei, "Major Operation to Be Performed on Military Logistics System."

[17] Liao Xilong [廖锡龙], "Personally Experiencing Jinan Theater's Major Joint Logistics Reform" [亲历济南战区大联勤改革], *PLA Daily* [解放军报], December 16, 2008, available at <http://military.people.com.cn/GB/1076/52984/8527794.html>.

[18] *China's National Defense in 2006* (Beijing: State Council Information Office, 2006), available at <www.china.org.cn/english/China/194332.htm on>; Liao, "Personally Experiencing Jinan Theater's Major Joint Logistics Reform"; Hao Yingquan and Li Xuanlian, "PLA Begins to Implement System of Non-Active Service Staff in 2006," Xinhua, February 15 2006; "Documentary for Military" [军事纪事], CCTV-7, June 22, 2009.

[19] Under the old system, a peacetime military region would become a "war zone" in a war situation, and the war zone commander would gain operational control over air force and navy units within the war zone. Under the new theater command system, the theater commander has operational control of army, navy, air force, and perhaps conventional Rocket Force units in both peacetime and wartime.

[20] Liao, "Personally Experiencing Jinan Theater's Major Joint Logistics Reform."

[21] Wang Fan [王帆], "Benefits Opened Up by Distributed Support" [配送式保障开辟的效益途径], *PLA Daily* [解放军报], January 29, 2009.

[22] Liao, "Personally Experiencing Jinan Theater's Major Joint Logistics Reform."

[23] Dong Zhaoxin and Zhao Jianwei, "From Separate Logistics System to Joint Logistics of Three Services," *PLA Daily*, January 17, 2007; Zhao Jianwei [赵建伟], "Strategic Concept for China's Military Logistics," *Guangming Daily* [光明日报], January 17, 2007.

[24] Zhang Lianwu [张练武], ed., "Theme Word: Integrated Joint Logistics" [主题词:一体化联勤], *Qianwei Bao* [前卫报], April 2, 2008.

[25] Chen Biao and Wang Yijie, "Logistics Command College Cultivates Commanders of Joint Logistics," *PLA Daily*, November 10, 2009; Zhang Shuo [张硕], "Riveting Attention on Winning, Striving for Breakthroughs—General Review of Shenyang Military Region's Efforts for Strengthening Combat Capability Building" [紧盯打赢求突破—军区加强作战能力建设综述], *Qianjin Bao* [前进报], November 11, 2009; Lin Siping, Ning Jianhong, and Tian Yong [林思平, 宁剑宏, 田勇], "Play the Thunderous Music of Joint Support—An Eye-Witness Account of a Joint Campaign Logistics Support Exercise Conducted by a Guangzhou Military Region Emergency Army Service Station" [奏响联合保障最强音—某分部应急兵站联合战役后勤保障演练见闻], *Renmin Qianxian* [人民前线], October 11, 2011; Zhang Fenghai [张风海] et al., "Crossing Hundreds of Miles to Conduct Major Exercise—Overview of 'Mission Action-2013A' Cross-Region Mobility Campaign Exercise" [千里跨越大演兵—'使命行动-2013A'跨区机动战役演习综述], *Renmin Qianxian* [人民前线], September 25, 2013, 2–3; Zhan Qi [战旗] et al., "Three Services Come Together to Cast Sharp Swords—Actual Accounts of Explorations on Joint Operation Training Innovation by 26th Group Army" [三军联挟制利剑—第26集团军探索联合作战训练创新纪实], *Qianwei Bao* [前卫报], November 16, 2014, 3; Lei Jianghai and Zheng Xiaogang [雷江海, 郑孝刚], "Lanzhou MR Carries Out All-Element Training in Campaign Logistics Support" [兰州军区全要素演练战役后勤保障], *PLA Daily* [解放军报], September 21, 2015.

[26] Guo Shijun, Luo Ting, and Qing Taiping [郭石军, 罗挺, 卿太平], "Application of IoT Technology in Integrated Military Logistics Information System" [物联网技术在一体化军事物流信息系统中的应用], *Logistics Technology* [物流技术], no. 2 (2012), 209–212, available at <cf.lcchina.org.cn/docbak/5/6/d/163862_50dbea604056d.pdf>.

[27] "Communications Troops Achieve Three Great Leaps from 'One Half' Radio" [通讯兵从"一部半"电台实现三大跨越], *Guangming Daily* [光明日报], July 11, 2007, available at <http://news.xinhuanet.com/mil/2007-07/11/content_6358114.htm>; Hou Xigui [侯喜贵], "Military Informationization Construction Research" [军队信息化建设研究], *The Basic Characteristics of Military Informationization* [军队信息化的基 本 特性] (Beijing: PLA Press [解放军出版社], 2002), 63.

[28] Hou, "Military Informationization Construction Research."

[29] Guo, Luo, and Qing, "Application of IoT Technology in Integrated Military Logistics Information System."

[30] Puska, "Taming the Hydra."

[31] Liu Zhigang [刘志刚], "We Should Focus on Three Types of Changes in Logistics Reform" [后勤改革要着眼三种转变], *PLA Daily* [解放军报], September 9, 2014; Zhang, "'Precision Logistics'—The Focus of Military Logistics Reform."

[32] Cheng and Xu, "Inside Story of PLA Logistics Reforms"; Cui Rongli and Fan Juwei, "PLA Shapes Up New Concept Model for Integrated Material Procurement and Support," *PLA Daily*, August 17, 2006.

[33] Gao and Hua, "The Grand Program for Building Modern Logistics."

[34] "PLA Logistics Information Center Established," *PLA Daily*, July 8, 2013.

[35] Han Wei, "Forces Medical Cloud 'Research and Development' Integration Design and Concept" [部队卫生云 '研建用管'一体化设计与思考], Presentation at the Next Generation Medical Information Technology Foundation Forum, Beijing, August 2014, 24, available at <www.hit180.com/wp-content/uploads/zhuanti/wuxi/wuxi_012.pdf>.

[36] Ibid.

[37] Jiang Luming [姜鲁鸣], "Military-Civilian Integration: The Shield of Modern National Defense" [军民融合: 现代国防安全之盾], *Loose Leaf Anthology* [活页文选], no. 71 (2015), 34, available at <http://dangjian.com/djw2016sy/djw2016wkztl/wkztl2016xihy/201604/t20160414_3287764.shtml>.

[38] Jiang Luming [姜鲁鸣], "Why to Raise Civil-Military Integration to the Status of National Strategy" [为何把军民融合上升为国家战略], *People's Daily* [人民日报], May 31, 2015.

39 Liao, "Comprehensively Develop Modern Logistics with Scientific Development Concept as Guide"; Yuan Jianda, Xu Jinzhang, and Xu Zhuangzhi, "The Liberation Army Will Basically Put in Place Modern Logistical Services in 2020—Exclusive Interview with Liberation Army General Logistics Department Deputy Director Li Maifu," Xinhua, December 24, 2007.

40 Ibid.

41 "Joint Action 2015D," *Hsiang Kang Shang Pao* [香港商报], August 11, 2015; Liao, "Comprehensively Develop Modern Logistics with Scientific Development Concept as Guide"; Zhang Hongwei and Du Qingguo, "The 'Fusion' Effect Is Everywhere—Eyewitness Account of the Theater's Promotion of Joint Logistics Support Structure Reform," *Qianwei Bao*, August 22, 2010, 3; Huai Qianjian, Nie Jun, and Su Fengshou [怀前进, 桌军, 苏丰收], "Providing Strong and Solid Support for Victory in Battle—An Overview of the Public Relations Work During the Large-Scale Battle Training Exercise across Five Provinces, 'Mission Action-2013A,' Conducted by the Nanjing Military Region" [为能打胜仗提供坚强有力保障—'使命行动 -2013A'跨区机动战役演习群众工作概述], *Renmin Qianxian* [人民前线], October 18, 2013; Wang Wei and Yang Zhen [王伟, 杨振], "Recent Development in the Study of the Thought of People's War Under Informationized Conditions" [信息化条件下人民战争思想研究的新进展], *China Military Science* [中国军事科学], no. 2 (2009).

42 Puska, "Taming the Hydra."

43 "National Defense Transportation Law of the People's Republic of China," Xinhua, September 3, 2016; and Yao Jianing, ed., "China Passes New Law on National Defense Transport," Xinhua, September 3, 2016, available at <http://english.chinamil.com.cn/view/2016-09/03/content_7241207.htm>; "Regulations on National Defense Mobilization of Civil Means of Transportation" [授权发布:《民用运力国防动员条例》(全文)], Xinhua [新华网], October 9, 2003, available at <http://news.sina.com.cn/c/2003-10-09/1654886729s.shtml>.

44 Blasko, "Clarity of Intentions"; "Liao Xilong Urges to Accelerate Military Transportation Mobilization Drive," *PLA Daily*, June 23, 2010; Gao Xiaowen [高效文] et al., "Stars Shine Down on the Vast Flat Lands and the Moon Floods the Great Rivers—Looking Back on the 2010 Military-Wide Joint Combined Operations Drill" [星垂平野阔月—回眸2010年全军联], *Jiefangjun Huabao* [解放军画报], January 6, 2011, 6.

45 Sang Yongliang, Lin Lin, and He Mingxiang [桑永亮, 林琳, 何名享], "Engaging in Emergency Support at Sea" [应急保障在海上进行], *Jiefangjun Huabao* [解放军画报], October 16, 2010, 54–55; Lin Hongmei and Qu Baichun [林红

梅, 屈百春], "Our Country Holds Emergency Logistical Support Exercise at Sea in Jinan Theater to Test Transportation Combat Readiness" [我国交通战备海上应急保障演练在济南战区举行], Xinhua, July 18, 2010; *Annual Report to Congress: Military and Security Developments Involving the People's Republic of China 2016.*

⁴⁶ *China's Military Strategy* (Beijing: State Council Information Office of the People's Republic of China, May 2015), available at <http://eng.mod.gov.cn/Press/2015-05/26/content_4586805.htm>; "China's Military Strategy" [中国的军事战略], Xinhua, May 26, 2015.

⁴⁷ James C. Mulvenon, *Soldiers of Fortune: The Rise and Fall of the Chinese Military-Business Complex, 1978–1998* (Armonk, NY: M.E. Sharp, 2000).

⁴⁸ "PLA Bans Commercial Activities as Anti-Graft Drive Gains Momentum," *Global Times*, May 5, 2016, available at <www.globaltimes.cn/content/981596.shtml>.

⁴⁹ Mulvenon, *Soldiers of Fortune.*

⁵⁰ "Hu Jintao Emphasizes Importance of Closing PLA Businesses," Xinhua, July 28, 1998.

⁵¹ Cao Haili, "The Chinese Army Has Sailed Out of the Business Sea," *Beijing Zhongguo Qingnian* [北京中國青年], February 15, 1999, 4–7; Mulvenon, *Soldiers of Fortune*; "PLA Bans Commercial Activities as Anti-Graft Drive Gains Momentum."

⁵² James C. Mulvenon, "PLA Divestiture 2.0: We Mean It This Time," *China Leadership Monitor*, no. 50 (Summer 2016), available at <www.hoover.org/research/pla-divestiture-20-we-mean-it-time>; State Council Information Office, "China's National Defense in 2002," December 9, 2002, available at <https://fas.org/nuke/guide/china/doctrine/natdef2002.html>.

⁵³ Li Xuanliang [李宣良], "All Units of the Armed Forces to Deal with Commercial Bribery" [中国军队开展治理商业贿赂专项工作], Xinhua [新华网], August 2, 2006, available at <http://jczs.news.sina.com.cn/2006-08-02/1642387932.html>.

⁵⁴ "PLA Bans Commercial Activities as Anti-Graft Drive Gains Momentum."

⁵⁵ Ibid.

⁵⁶ Puska, "Taming the Hydra."

⁵⁷ Yuan Hao and Fan Juwei [袁浩, 范炬炜], "Liao Xilong Speaks at Plenary Session of All-Army Leading Group for the Work of Auditing Economic Responsibility of Leading Cadres; Calls for All-Round, In-Depth Implementation of the Work of Auditing Economic Responsibility of Leading Cadres in the Whole Army" [廖锡龙在全军领导干部经济责任审计工作领导小组全体会议上强调全面推进军队领导干部经济责任审计工作深入开展], *PLA Daily* [解放军报], July 21, 2006, 1; An Puzhong and Zhang Xiaoqi [安普忠, 张晓祺], "According to the Order

Signed by Chairman Xi, the PLA Audit Office Is Turned into an Organ Under the Central Military Commission; Fan Changlong Attends and Addresses the Event for Announcing the Order; Xu Qiliang Reads Out the Order; Zhao Keshi Attends the Event" [近平主席签署命令解放军审计署划归中央军委建制 范长龙出席宣布命令大会并讲话 许其亮宣读命令赵克石一同出席], *PLA Daily* [解放军报], November 7, 2014; Minnie Chan, "Xi Jinping Shifts Control of PLA Audit Office to Military's Top Decision-Making Body," *South China Morning Post* (Hong Kong), November 7, 2014, available at <www.scmp.com/news/china/article/1633802/xi-jinping-shifts-control-pla-audit-office-militarys-top-decision-making>.

⁵⁸ John Garnaut, "Chinese General to Fight Corruption," *Sydney Morning Herald*, January 19, 2012, available at <www.smh.com.au/world/chinese-general-to-fight-corruption-20120118-1q6n2.html>.

⁵⁹ Li Hao [李昊] , "Corruption Is Serious in the Former CPC Central Military Commission Joint Support Force" [中共军委联勤保障部队成立前身腐败严重], *Epoch Times* [大纪元], September 14, 2016, available at <www.epochtimes.com/gb/16/9/13/n8296789.htm>; Minnie Chan and Choi Chi-yuk, "Two More of China's Former Top Commanders Taken Away for Corruption Investigation," *South China Morning Post* (Hong Kong), August 5, 2016, available at <www.scmp.com/news/china/policies-politics/article/1999535/two-more-chinas-former-top-commanders-taken-away>.

⁶⁰ Greg Hallahan, "Collusion, Creative Bribery & Subcontracting," FTI Consulting, October 30, 2014, available at <www.fticonsulting-asia.com/~/media/Files/us-files/insights/articles/collusion-creative-bribery-subcontracting.pdf>.

⁶¹ Jiang Jie, "China Unveils Five New Theater Commands," *Global Times* (Beijing), February 1, 2016, available at <www.globaltimes.cn/content/966860.shtml>.

⁶² Liu and Yu, Food and Fodder Go First.

⁶³ Ibid.

⁶⁴ Wang Ke [王克], "Military Logistics" [军事后勤], in *Chinese Military Encyclopedia* [中国军事百科全书], Song Shilun and Xiao Ke [宋时轮,萧克], eds., vol. IV (Beijing: Military Science Publishing House [军事科学出版社], 1997), 1–8; Guo Jing and Luo Guojin [郭晶, 罗国金], "Fourth Great Wall International Forum on Military Medicine Successfully Held" [第四届长城国际军事医学论坛在京成功举办], Xinhua, April 2, 2017, available at <http://news.xinhuanet.com/mil/2017-04/02/c_129523752.htm>; Huang Panyue, "PLA Releases Self-Heating Meals Research and Development Project to the Public," *China Military Online*, March 28, 2017, available at <www.81.cn/jwywpd/2017-03/28/

content_7542387.htm>; "PLA Starts Test and Trial of 'Dog Tags,'" *China Military Online*, February 21, 2017, available at <http://eng.chinamil.com.cn/view/2017-02/21/content_7496278.htm>; "China, Israel Vow to Enhance Military Logistics Cooperation," *China Military Online*, February 21, 2017, available at <http://eng.chinamil.com.cn/view/2017-02/21/content_7496087.htm>; "PLA Makes Headway in Improving Combat Protective Outfit System," *China Military Online*, February 13, 2017, available at <http://eng.chinamil.com.cn/view/2017-02/13/content_7487395.htm>.

[65] "PLA Takes Extraordinary Measures to Ensure Rations Supply," *China Military Online*, March 28, 2017, available at <http://eng.chinamil.com.cn/view/2017-03/28/content_7542292.htm>; Zhao Jie and Lu Qingguo [赵杰, 陆庆国], "Comprehensive Upgrade of Military Oxygen Support System for Plateau Region" [装备多样化供给标准化管理制度化我军高原制供氧保障全面升级], *PLA Daily* [解放军报], March 14, 2017, available at <www.81.cn/jfjbmap/content/2017-03/14/content_171675.htm>.

[66] "Meeting on Application and Demonstration of All-Military Logistics Operations Processing Platform Held in Beijing" [全军后勤业务处理平台应用示范现场会在火箭军举行], *Rocket Force News* [火箭兵报], November 20, 2016, 1.

[67] Ibid.

[68] "Defense Ministry Holds News Conference on Joint Logistic Support System Reform," *China Military Online*, September 14, 2016, available at <http://english.chinamil.com.cn/view/201609/14/content_7258622.htm>.

[69] Information accessed at <www.cgw.cn> and "The General Logistics Department, an Expert Mission to Wuhan Rear Base for the Intelligence Services," May 13, 2012, available at <www.chinamil.com.cn/site1/xwpdxw/2009-06/09/content_1792344.htm> and <www.wwgc.cc/luntan/viewthread.php?tid=80838&page=4>; "PLA General Logistics Department's Wuhan Rear Base Organizes 100-Odd Principal Military Commanding Officers for Centralized Military Training Conducted in Line With Updated Military Training Outline," *PLA Daily*, June 9, 2009; Fan Juwei, Li Yong, and Kuang Xiaowen, "Rear Base of GLD Provides Massive Support of Disaster Relief Materials," *PLA Daily* [解放军报], June 2, 2008; Xu Xianhong and Luo Xianning [许先洪, 罗贤宁], "GLD Certain Vehicle Depot Takes Measures to Improve Personnel Quality" [总后某汽车仓库多措并举提高人员素质], *PLA Daily* [解放军报], May 13, 2012, available at <http://web.archive.org/web/20130709094828/http://www.chinamil.com.cn/site1/xwpdxw/2009-05/28/content_1778894.htm >; Wei Xiaojun and Weng Huainan [魏小俊, 翁淮南], "General Logistics Department Base Holds

Strategic Support Exercise" [运行快捷协同密切保障精确—总后某基地首次实施战略支援保障演练], *PLA Daily* [解放军报], October 7, 2006, 1.

70 Liu Jianwei [刘建伟] et al., "The Joint Logistic Support Force, Please Receive Five 'Letters From Users'" [联勤保障部队,请收5封"用户来信"], *PLA Daily* [解放军报], May 2, 2017, available at <www.81.cn/jmywyl/2017-05/02/content_7583691.htm>; Gao Jie [高洁], "The Wuxi Joint Logistics Support Center: Strengthen the Service Mindset, Improve the Service Form" [联勤保障中心: 运行满月,新风扑面无锡联勤保障中心强化服务意识改进保障方式], *PLA Daily* [解放军报], October 16, 2016; Liu Jianwei and Liu Lei [刘建伟, 刘磊], "The Shenyang Joint Logistic Support Center: Quicken the Integration of Support Data for the Missions" [沈阳联勤保障中心着眼使命加速保障数据融合], *PLA Daily* [解放军报], October 16, 2016; Zhao Jie and Zheng Xiaogang [赵杰, 郑孝刚], "Xining Joint Logistical Support Center Explores Support Methods for Joint Operations and Joint Training: Integrating 'Provision Officers' into Joint Operations System" [西宁联勤保障中心探索联战联训联保模式:'粮草官'融入联合作战体系], *PLA Daily* [解放军报], February 24, 2017.

71 Qiu Xinli and Zhou Yuan [邱新力, 周远], "When Ordinarily Using Electronic Expense Submissions, What's to Be Done When Met with Emergency Assignments During Network Outages?" [平时采用无货币报销, 断网遇有紧急任务时又该怎么办?], *Junbao Jizhe* [军报记者], May 23, 2017, available at <http://zb.81.cn/content/2017-05/23/content_7614223.htm>; "'Three Capabilities' Qualification Competition Develops Comprehensive Quality" ['三能'达标考核锤炼综合素质], *PLA Daily* [解放军报], February 13, 2017, available at <www.81.cn/jfjbmap/content/2017-02/13/content_169266.htm>; Zhang Cunguo and Li Jianwen [张存国, 李建文], "Military-Civilian Dual-Use Airport Support No Longer Has Each Side Focus Solely on Its Own Tasks," [军地机场保障不再'各扫门前雪'], *PLA Daily* [解放军报], October 27, 2016, 2, available at <www.81.cn/jfjbmap/content/2016-10/27/content_160029.htm>.

72 "Defense Ministry Holds News Conference on Joint Logistic Support System Reform," *China Military Online*, September 14, 2016, available at <http://eng.chinamil.com.cn/view/2016-09/14/content_7258622.htm>; "Army Adjustment and Establishment Completed in Five Theater Commands," *China Military Online*, February 4, 2016, available at <http://english.chinamil.com.cn/news-channels/china-military-news/2016-02/04/content_6890499.htm>.

73 Gao Jie [高洁], "The Wuxi Joint Logistic Support Center: Strengthen the Service Mindset, Improve the Service Form" [联勤保障中心: 运行满月,新风扑面无锡联勤保障中心强化服务意识改进保障方式], *PLA Daily* [解放军报], October 16,

2016; "People's Liberation Army (Including Armed Police) Designation Code and Garrison Situation" [解放军（含武警）番号, 代号及驻防情况], October 25, 2014; "Military and Civilians Work Together to Build a Harmonious Society" [军民同心共建和谐社会], People's Liberation Army 101ˢᵗ Hospital [中国人民解放军第101医院], March 9, 2016, available at <www.wx101.com/Item/976.aspx>; "China Life Guilin Branch Celebrates the 87ᵗʰ Anniversary of the Founding" [国寿桂林分公司举行庆祝建党八十七周年纪念活动], Guangxi Insurance Association Network [广西保险行业协会], August 28, 2008, available at <www.gxbx.com.cn/bencandy. php?fid-122-id-10021-page-1.htm>; "Zhengzhou Military and Police Forces Work Together to Green the Yellow River Beach" [郑州军警部队二日一起来绿化黄河滩], Henan Cultural Industry Network, April 5, 2010, available at <www.henanci. com/Pages/2010/04/05/20100405044918.shtml>.

⁷⁴ Dang Chongmin [党崇民], ed., *Staff Officer Work in Joint Operations* [联合作战参谋工作] (Beijing: PLA Press [解放军出版社], August 2006).

⁷⁵ Lai Yuhong and Wang Xiaowei [赖瑜鸿, 王晓伟], "Army Establishes Rapid Commodity Distribution," *China Military Online* [中国军网], May 3, 2017, available at <www.81.cn/sydbt/2017-05/03/content_7585404.htm>; Gao Aiguo [高爱国] et al., "From 'Health' to 'Medical Service': Far More Than Just Changing the Name of an Organization" [从卫生到卫勤: 远不止改个机构名称这么简单], *China Military Online* [中国军网综合], April 28, 2017, available at <www.81.cn/jmy-wyl/2017-04/28/content_7581050.htm>; Wang Jun [王俊], "Xie Donghui Becomes Director of Wuhan Joint Logistics Support Base Political Work Department" [谢东辉已担任武汉联勤保障基地政治工作部主任], *The Paper* [澎湃], March 22, 2017, available at <www.thepaper.cn/newsDetail_forward_1644897>; Guo Bin and Lin Youwei [郭彬, 林幼卫], "Wuxi Joint Logistics Support Center Forges a Contingent of Elite Maritime Soldiers" [无锡联勤保障中心锻造一支海上尖兵], *Zhongguo Guofang Bao* [中国国防报], March 21, 2017, available at <www.81.cn/gfbmap/con-tent/2017-03/21/content_172344.htm>; Tang Zhichao and Sun Xingwei [汤智超, 孙兴维], "Military Representatives Occupy Apartment of Shanghai-Based Vehicle Battalion" [无锡联勤保障中心探索公寓住房区域保障模式军代表住上汽车营公寓房], *PLA Daily* [解放军报], March 20, 2017, available at <www.81.cn/jfjbmap/content/1/2017-03/20/02/2017032002_pdf.pdf>; Yang Yucheng and Zhou Peng [杨玉成, 周鹏], "Organizing the Strengthening of Military Supply Station Leaders in Fujian and Jiangxi" [组织闽赣两省军供站长加钢淬火], *Zhongguo Guofang Bao* [中国国防报], December 1, 2016, available at <www.81.cn/gfbmap/content/2016-12/01/content_162993.htm>; Lai Yuhong and Huang Yi [赖瑜鸿, 黄翊], "Guilin Joint

Logistics Support Center and Civil Airline Sign Cooperation Agreement on Air Ticketing Service" [桂林联勤保障中心与某航空公司签订合作协议助推惠军服务升级], *PLA Daily* [解放军报], March 7, 2017, available at <www.81.cn/jfjbmap/content/2017-03/07/content_171096.htm>; Gao Jie, Sun Yan, and Liu Jian [高洁, 孙燕, 刘健], "PLA No. 85 Hospital of Wuxi Joint Logistics Support Center Provides Services for Island-Stationed Troops" [解放军无锡联勤保障中心第八五医院团队为海岛官兵服务], China News Service, February 8, 2017, available at <www.chinanews.com/mil/2017/02-08/8143867.shtml>.

76 Yu Zhiming [於志明], "Command of Joint Logistics Subdepartments" [联勤分部指挥], *China Military Logistics Encyclopedia* [中国军事后勤百科全书] (Beijing: Gold Shield Press [金盾出版社], 2002), vol. 1, 252–253; Fu Quanyou and Liang Guanglie [傅全有, 梁光烈], "Joint Logistics Sub-Department" [联勤分部], in *Chinese Encyclopedia: Military Affairs* [中国军事百科全书] (Beijing: Encyclopedia of China Publishing House [中国大百科全书出版社], 2005), 509.

77 Lonnie Henley, "PLA Logistics and Doctrine Reforms, 1999–2009," in *People's Liberation Army after Next*, ed. Susan Puska (Carlisle Barracks, PA: Strategic Studies Institute, 2000); Dennis J. Blasko, *The Chinese Army Today: Tradition and Transformation for the 21st Century*, 2nd ed. (London: Routledge, 2012), 52.

78 "Details of Military Reforms Come to Light: Personnel of CMC's Two New Departments Has Been Decided" [军委细节曝光: 军委两新部门人事已定], *Chaoji Pingguo Wang* [超级苹果网], December 28, 2015; He Yongmin [何勇民], "How Is the Qinghai-Tibet Highway Military Supplies Depot, Which Has Undergone Reforms Five Times, Facing Reorganization" [历经5次调整改革的青藏兵站部如何面对改革], *PLA Daily* [解放军报], December 21, 2015, available at <web.archive.org/web/20170220014703/http://www.81.cn/jwgz/2015-12/21/content_6824329.htm >; Ding Li and Li Wei [丁丽, 李伟], "Military Report" [军事报道], CCTV-7, June 21, 2016, available at <www.youtube.com/watch?v=r2K1r-80mUw>.

79 Zhang Tao, ed., "Defense Ministry Holds News Conference on Joint Logistic Support System Reform," *China Military Online*, September 14, 2016, available at <http://english.chinamil.com.cn/view/2016-09/14/content_7258622.htm>.

80 Zhao Jiaqing [赵佳庆], "Shenyang Joint Logistics Center Organizes Severe Cold Weather Training" [沈阳联勤保障中心组织冬季严寒条件下的训练], *China Network* [中国网], January 26, 2017, available at <www.china.com.cn/military/2017-01/26/content_40184471.htm>.

81 Jiang, "Military-Civilian Integration."

[82] Liu Zhigang [刘志刚], "We Should Focus on Three Types of Changes in Logistics Reform" [后勤改革要着眼三种转变], *PLA Daily* [解放军报], September 9, 2014.

[83] "PLA Djibouti Base Must Be Viewed Objectively," *Global Times* (Beijing), July 13, 2017, available at <www.globaltimes.cn/content/1056127.shtml>; Huang Jingjing and Guo Yuandan, "China's Logistic Hub in Djibouti to Stabilize Region, Protect Interests," *Global Times* (Beijing), March 15, 2016, available at <www.globaltimes.cn/content/973900.shtml>; Zhou Bo, "Station Looks Beyond Anti-Piracy Mission," *China Daily Online*, March 17, 2016, available at <http://usa.chinadaily.com.cn/epaper/2016-03/18/content_23948894.htm>.

CHAPTER 8

A MODERN MAJOR GENERAL

Building Joint Commanders in the PLA

By Joel Wuthnow and Phillip C. Saunders

Among the key ingredients in fielding a modern joint military force is cultivating a cadre of high-caliber commanders and staff officers to plan and lead operations. This has been a perennial challenge for all modern militaries, as the scope and scale of warfare has extended past single battle campaigns of short duration. Since the end of World War II, for instance, the U.S. military has considered and reconsidered ways in which officers can be given the requisite training, experience, and education to work effectively across Service boundaries and within joint organizations such as the combatant commands and Joint Staff. The Goldwater-Nichols Department of Defense Reorganization Act of 1986 mandated joint professional military education and joint assignments as requirements for promotion, yet the creation of a deeply rooted joint culture remains elusive—if achievable at all.[1]

For decades, China's People's Liberation Army (PLA) has also struggled with producing the officers it needs to perform joint operations. Reforms carried out during the 1990s and 2000s attempted to reorient the PLA toward a stronger joint operational capability, but weaknesses in the human resource domain persisted. Key problems included senior and mid-level officers with limited exposure to other services, few opportunities for non–ground force officers to get joint assignments, and training that paid lip service to joint operations via superficial involvement of other services to allow portraying service exercises as "joint." Yet the need for qualified personnel has only increased as the PLA, under Xi Jinping, has been tasked with being able to fight and win "informationized local wars," which are inherently joint.[2] Xi and his fellow reformers in the PLA understand the problem and have adopted several initiatives designed to alleviate it, but the effectiveness of those reforms remains unclear.

This chapter documents how the PLA has tried to cultivate joint commanders before and during the current reform cycle, and comments on obstacles limiting the chances for success. It is divided into five sections. The first discusses the motivation for human capital reforms under Xi. The next reviews reforms instituted during the preceding two administrations. This is followed by a discussion of identified weaknesses as well as solutions considered in PLA sources prior to the Xi era. The fourth assesses reforms undertaken since 2016 to build qualified joint commanders in three areas: professional military education (PME), personnel management, and training. The conclusion assesses possible obstacles to current reforms and states the implications for the PLA.

Impetus for Reform

An overarching operational objective of the current PLA reform cycle is to create the conditions for better planning and execution of joint operations.[3] This focus on joint operations mirrors changes in PLA doctrine over the preceding 30 years that required commanders to integrate the unique combat capabilities of the individual services (army, navy, air force, and Rocket Force), along with combat support units in areas ranging from logistics to space-based surveillance, in order to conduct complex operational missions. The current doctrinal rubric is known as informationized local wars [*xinxihua jubu zhanzheng*, 信息化局部战争], which focuses on executing high-tech, integrated joint operations. Key types of campaigns include amphibious assaults, blockades and counter-blockades, joint firepower strikes, and anti–air raid operations.[4] Conducting these types of operations effectively would be a key to success in larger campaigns against Taiwan and other regional adversaries—and to counter U.S. military intervention in a conflict.

Reforms launched in late 2015 and early 2016 sought to improve China's joint operations capabilities in several ways. Most prominent was the creation of a two-tiered permanent joint command structure, in which the Central Military Commission (CMC), aided by a Joint Staff Department in Beijing, would oversee operations led by five theater commands (replacing the previous seven military regions), each focused on a specific set of regional contingencies. For instance, the Eastern Theater Command (TC) would be responsible for operations against Taiwan, while the Northern TC would lead operations in the Yellow Sea and on the Korean Peninsula. The commanders would have peacetime and wartime control of the ground, naval, air, and conventional missile units within their theaters.[5] A related goal was rebalancing the services in favor of maritime and aerospace forces, which had been greatly outnumbered by the ground forces throughout the PLA's history.[6] Joint "enablers" were consolidated in the creation of the Strategic Support Force (responsible for space, cyber, and electronic warfare) and the Joint Logistics Support Force.

Xi and his fellow reformers understood that structural changes would be of little value without corresponding human capital reforms, especially in the officer corps. The initial reform outline presented at the Third Plenum of the 18th Party Congress in November 2013 discussed the need to build "new-type operational forces" [*xinxing zuozhan liliang*, 新型作战力量], denoting highly qualified personnel with the requisite training and education to succeed in modern combat.[7] CMC Vice Chairman Xu Qiliang noted that achieving this goal would demand changes across the PLA's human resources system, including in the areas of promotions, benefits, and career paths.[8] The formal 5-year reform agenda unveiled on January 1, 2016, further described the need to cultivate "new-type military talent" [*xinxing junshi rencai*, 新型军事人才], requiring improvements in PME, training, and personnel management.[9]

Nevertheless, recruiting and retaining higher quality officers (as well as noncommissioned officers [NCOs]) would only be a first step. Given its operational requirements, the PLA would also need a cadre of officers with the specialized knowledge and skills required to understand, plan, and carry out joint operations. At a tour of the PLA National Defense University (NDU) in March 2016, Xi Jinping stated that the entire PLA must focus on "grooming talented personnel in commanding joint military operations, a complex and large project involving many factors."[10] Xi reiterated this message during a tour of the CMC's new joint operations command center in April 2016, when he called on the PLA to adopt "extraordinary measures" to train joint commanders and achieve a "big breakthrough as quickly as possible."[11] An accompanying *PLA Daily* report argued that without sufficient progress, "joint operations will be only a slogan, and winning battles will be impossible to achieve."[12] These statements indicate that a second phase of the current reforms will move beyond changes to PLA organizational structure and focus on building the softer skills necessary for executing joint operations.[13]

Earlier Reforms

Xi's call for more qualified joint commanders was more an exhortation for the PLA to complete unfinished business than a radical innovation. The PLA's overall focus on planning and conducting joint operations did not originate with Xi, but rather began in earnest in the 1990s.[14] Contributing factors included the observation that success on the modern battlefield required strong coordination between units from different services, as exhibited by the U.S. military during the 1990–1991 Gulf War, and the deterioration of cross-Strait relations, culminating in the 1995–1996 Taiwan Strait crisis, which spurred new thinking on the types of missions the PLA must be prepared to conduct to deter Taiwan independence or invade and occupy the island if necessary.[15] This focus on joint operations led to a number of changes in the PME system, personnel management, and the training arena.

PME Reforms

A series of PME changes were designed to better educate officers in joint operational arts. PLA NDU [*guofang daxue*, 国防大学] was established in 1985 primarily in order to train senior officers (major generals and rear admirals) from all the services, preparing them for command positions.[16] Reflecting changes in PLA doctrine, both Jiang Zemin and Hu Jintao called for that institution to produce commanders capable of leading joint operations.[17] Accordingly, during the 2000s, NDU added content in that subject, such as by offering courses in "joint firepower strikes under complex electromagnetic conditions."[18] This was complemented by the publication of new teaching materials, likely derived at least in part from classified doctrinal sources. For instance, in 2012 and 2013 the PLA Academy of Military Science [*junshi kexue yuan*, 军事科学院]—the PLA's primary center for doctrinal development—released two new teaching volumes designed to give students more exposure to joint operations concepts.[19]

PME reforms also affected lower level service academic institutions and military regions. In June 2007, for instance, the former General Staff Department spearheaded an effort to promote closer collaboration between NDU and the service command academies in the area of joint operations instruction.[20] Although the details of this program are unclear, the goal was likely to introduce joint operational concepts to officers earlier in their careers.[21] A separate program sponsored by the Shenyang Military Region between 2004 and 2009 tried to foster stronger interservice understanding and esprit de corps by giving officers the chance to cross-enroll in PME institutes outside their home service.[22] In addition, the 2010 defense white paper noted that the PLA was "laying stress on the training of officers for joint operations," in part by publishing "basic readers" on the subject and holding lectures across all branches and services.[23]

Personnel System Reforms

Earlier reforms in the personnel system sought to develop human capital on two levels. As a first step, the PLA needed to attract and retain a high-quality, educated officer corps from which joint commanders could be developed. Post-Mao professionalization of the officer corps began during the 1980s, but took new strides in the 1990s with the recruitment of civilian college graduates. National defense scholarships were also established at civilian colleges in order to attract more highly educated and technically proficient personnel, a task complicated by growing opportunities in the civilian economy.[24] Service academies and command colleges increased emphasis on science and technology in their curricula.[25] Pay and benefits also increased as a way to retain top performers. Salaries doubled for some officers between 1999 and 2000, for instance, and perks included subsidized housing, new cars, and study opportunities.[26]

Personnel system changes also tried, in limited ways, to enhance officers' exposure to different services and provide joint opportunities. Several military regions experimented with cross-posting officers to temporary assignments in different services during the 2000s. For instance, in 2006 a North Sea Fleet deputy chief of staff was temporarily posted as a Nanjing Military Region group army deputy commander.[27] During the mid-2000s, 100 officers took part in a Shenyang Military Region program involving short-term duty in a different service.[28] In addition, a handful of senior officers took positions in nominally joint billets, giving them broader (and likely career-enhancing) experiences.[29] Examples include Ma Xiaotian and Wu Shengli's assignments as deputy chief of the general staff prior to assuming command of the air force and navy, respectively, and Ma and Song Puxuan's service as NDU president.[30] Joint assignments for lower level non–ground force officers, however, were few and far between.

Training Reforms

Following an overall pattern of increasing complexity and realism in the training arena, PLA officers gained more experience in joint training during the 2000s and 2010s. Major joint exercises in the early 2000s in the Nanjing and Guangzhou Military Regions focused on Taiwan scenarios, while those in the Jinan Military Region focused on problems in command

and control, logistics, and other areas.[31] Mark Cozad documents the evolution of joint training during the 11th and 12th 5-year plans (2006–2010, 2011–2015), describing a growing number of joint exercises (for instance, 18 were held in 2009 alone); a broadening range of subjects, such as war zone–level command and control, civil-military integration, and air force and naval power projection; and, especially during the latter period, increasingly realistic conditions, including operations in unfamiliar terrain and "dedicated opposition forces providing more-than-token resistance."[32]

The PLA also took steps toward greater standardization and supervision of joint training. Perhaps the most important change was the creation of the General Staff Department Military Training Department in December 2011. Compared to its predecessor organization, the new department was intended to focus on not only ground force training but also training across all the services. It reportedly included a bureau responsible specifically for joint training.[33] As part of its oversight of the PME system, the Military Training Department also sought to "cultivate talented joint operations commanding personnel" by devising new programs on joint operations at NDU, the National University of Defense Technology [*guofang keji daxue*, 国防科技大学], and service and branch academies.[34] In short, the PLA adopted (or at least experimented with) a variety of measures to cultivate joint commanders during the tenures of Xi's two immediate predecessors.

Problems and Proposed Solutions

Despite these initiatives, weaknesses persisted in the development of joint commanders and staff officers. Helping to justify Xi's focus on improvement in this area, a Xinhua report on the newly created Central Theater Command headquarters noted that most staff officers were "proficient" in the operations of their own services, but joint operations were "rather strange to them. So there exists an obvious gap in the capability of taking command of joint operations."[35] A senior PLA interlocutor likewise argued in June 2016 that deficiencies in talent cultivation meant that it would be "many years" before non–ground force officers would be able to exercise command over army operations, while army commanders had much to learn about employing air and naval assets.[36] Some senior PLA officers judged the effort to increase jointness by cross-service assignments to be a failure. While a cross-service assignment increased the officer's familiarity with another service, cross-posted officers served for too short a time (typically 6 to 9 months) and lacked the knowledge to be given substantive command responsibilities.[37]

PLA sources describe several interrelated factors contributing to this situation. First are general weaknesses in leadership and technical skills. Poor command skills are reflected in recent slogans such as the "two insufficient capabilities" [*liangge nengli bugou*, 两个能力不够], referring to the inability of the PLA to fight, and cadres at all levels to command, modern wars; and the "five cannots" [*wuge buhui*, 五个不会], meaning commanders who cannot judge the situation, understand the intentions of higher echelons, make command decisions, deploy forces, and deal with exigent circumstances.[38] Lack of technical proficiency is also a commonly cited problem. A human resources scholar at the Xi'an Political Academy, for instance, bemoaned the fact that while the PLA has acquired "cutting-edge weapons" and equipment, it lacks personnel qualified to use many of those systems.[39]

Second is the lack of "joint" education throughout the PME system. One concern is that officers are not receiving adequate joint operations content in the NDU course for senior commanders, which is a requisite step for high-level command billets.[40] Another problem is that, despite earlier experiments, service academies below the NDU level lack the experienced faculty and curriculum necessary to educate officers in joint operational concepts. One PLA command academy commandant lamented that his institute was lagging behind in its ability to provide joint education because it was still struggling with bringing its students (at the colonel/senior colonel grade) to an acceptable level of proficiency in *combined arms* (that is, intraservice) operations.[41] Yet another issue is that command academies tend to include students only from a single service, and even then are segregated according to branch specialty, reducing the ability of officers to interact with colleagues from different services.[42]

Third are quality assurance and credentialing problems. Generally, the PLA continues to face problems such as "weak and out of date courses," instructors that are "out of touch with modern operational requirements," and academic fraud and corruption.[43] Certification of officers well beyond their actual operational abilities has also been a longstanding problem for the PME system.[44] Exacerbating this situation is the lack of standardized criteria for the selection of joint commanders. One PLA source, for instance, contrasts the PLA with the U.S. and other Western militaries, which have "strict requirements" under which officers must demonstrate proficiency in joint operations (such as through graduation from a joint PME course or by serving in a joint assignment) in order to advance.[45]

Fourth is a continuing paucity of joint operational experience among PLA personnel. One hurdle is that few active-duty PLA officers have any combat experience; those who do, such as current CMC member Li Zuocheng and CMC Vice Chairman Zhang Youxia, served in the 1979 border war with Vietnam and subsequent skirmishes, which did not involve extensive naval or air force operations.[46] A retired PLA flag officer identified the lack of combat experience as a significant deficiency and noted that efforts to gain experience via assignments to United Nations peacekeeping forces and exercises with foreign militaries were of limited effectiveness.[47] Although more intensive and realistic operational and joint training likely compensates somewhat for limited combat experience, PLA sources continue to suggest constraints on training quality. A report on two 2016 exercises held in the Northern Theater Command, for example, found that jointness was achieved only "in form rather than in spirit . . . on the surface, rather than in essence . . . and in might rather than in mind."[48]

Fifth is inadequate career incentives for officers to aspire to joint assignments in the first place. A useful point of comparison is the U.S. military prior to Goldwater-Nichols, in which officers were rewarded for excelling within their respective Services and appointment to joint organizations was seen as detrimental to one's career.[49] That problem was only rectified when joint assignments (and joint PME) became congressionally mandated requirements for promotion. A 2015 NDU volume suggests that a similar problem might be at work in the PLA, noting that most officers are not pursuing joint command or staff positions.[50] In the PLA Navy, for instance, key criteria affecting career prospects included experience at sea, overseas experience, education level, participation in party affairs, and personal connections—but not experience in joint positions.[51] The incentives problem was exacerbated by the lack of opportunities for joint assignments.

Sixth is that the PLA is a relative latecomer in efforts to cultivate qualified joint command personnel. One source notes that the PLA did not begin focusing on joint operations until after the Gulf War, years after the U.S. military began to emphasize joint warfare.[52] Another source similarly notes that both Russia and the United States began the process of training joint commanders in the mid-20th century and argues that both countries assessed that it would take 25 years to develop a cadre of fully qualified joint commanders. Implicit in this critique is the notion that building a joint culture, in which officers look beyond their own service's parochial interests, perspectives, and traditions, can appreciate different service viewpoints, and can work effectively across service lines, is a generational process. If U.S. experience is a guide, the goal of genuine joint consciousness might never be fully attainable. Yet the author concludes that China "does not have 25 years and must adopt extraordinary measures" to catch up.[53]

Given these problems, Chinese analysts have considered various proposals on how to improve human capital for joint operations. One set of recommendations centers on strengthening joint operations instruction across the PME system. Echoing initiatives sponsored in the mid-2000s, one study notes that training for joint commanders cannot be accomplished "all at once," but needs to be pursued at different stages in an officer's career.[54] Pursuing a "multitiered" joint PME system, in which instruction would begin as early as the major level, would also bring China into conformity with the U.S., British, German, and other advanced militaries.[55] Other suggestions include curriculum reforms, increasing study abroad opportunities, better integrating PME institutes with joint exercises, and creating more online courses to facilitate distance learning.[56]

Another proposal concerned changes to the personnel management system. A 2008 internal-circulation volume published by NDU envisioned a "joint specialization" (similar to a U.S. military occupational specialty) in which a select group of junior officers would be designated as future joint commanders and be provided with relevant experience and education at different career point. For instance, between the 15- to 20-year mark in their careers, ground force officers would be assigned to joint positions as staff officers, then receive intermediate-level combined arms education, then take a unit command position within a group army, and then receive more advanced joint staff officer instruction. This would culminate with appointment as a joint commander at the 35- to 40-year mark. Another study argued that promotion criteria for joint commanders needed to be clarified and standardized.[57]

Other suggestions focused on the need for practical experience. The 2013 *Science of Military Strategy* broadly argues for deepening joint training and completing a more effective joint training management system.[58] A 2016 PLA NDU volume noted that "war is the best crucible for forging command talent" but identified several areas in which commanders might attain useful experience short of actual conflict, including joint exercises, use of computer simulations, combined exercises with advanced foreign militaries, and participation in military operations other than war, such as humanitarian assistance and disaster relief, search and rescue, and escort duty. Without such real-world expertise, the authors feared that many PLA joint commanders would be little more than "armchair strategists" [*zhishang tanbing*, 纸上谈兵].[59]

Xi-Era Reforms

PLA human capital reforms after 2015 resulted from three factors: the practical imperative to build the requisite talent to plan and lead joint operations, the foundation provided by previous attempts to adjust the

PLA's human resources systems to achieve that goal, and assessments of why the PLA faced continuing weaknesses in this arena. Even prior to the structural changes announced in late 2015 and early 2016, the need to adopt corresponding human capital changes was likely weighed by Xi and the CMC leading small group on reform, which was established in January 2014 to lead the process and consider policy adjustments. As CMC Vice Chairman Xu Qiliang remarked, the reforms would be a "complex systems engineering project," in which the major elements had to be considered in parallel, even if they were announced sequentially.[60] By late 2017, the PLA had begun to unveil changes to the PME, personnel, and training systems.

PME Reforms

During his March 2016 visit to the PLA NDU, Xi set the tone for revamping the PME system to better educate aspiring joint commanders, calling for new teaching concepts, updated course content, improved teaching models, and a stronger faculty.[61] That guidance led to several changes. First, the NDU senior commanders' course was restructured so that the students, who had previously been grouped together, were divided into joint operational command and leadership management tracks. The first group focused on joint operations, including through case study analysis and briefings on "key issues" facing each of the theater commands. The second group, destined for senior-level staff posts (such as in service headquarters and CMC departments), placed more emphasis on administrative issues.[62] This change was accompanied by an updated syllabus, including six new courses in joint operations. According to one PLA NDU professor, 80 to 90 percent of the course content was new.[63]

Second, PME institutes directly under the CMC expanded their course offerings in joint operations. For instance, PLA NDU created a 10-month course to expose lower level officers to joint operations. Launched in the 2017–2018 academic year, the program was focused on officers at the battalion to deputy regiment leader levels (majors through colonels), and included staff officers working in each of the TC headquarters.[64] According to PLA media, completion of the program would eventually be a precondition for certain theater command billets—a goal that, if implemented, may help to resolve problems of standardized credentialing.[65] This change coincided with the announcement that, as part of a larger realignment of the PME system, the PLA NDU would oversee a new joint operations college, which apparently succeeded the Shijiazhuang Army Command College (though few details on that new organization were immediately available).[66] The National University of Defense Technology likewise unveiled new courses on joint operations intelligence support for TC staff officers.[67]

Third, lower level service PME institutes placed a new emphasis on joint operations. One report noted that the PLA Rocket Force Command College had signed a cooperative agreement with five other service command colleges that would allow cross-training of students, broader research cooperation, and "sharing of talent resources."[68] That college also introduced new rules stating that more than 60 percent of its Ph.D. students would be required to complete dissertations focused on joint operations.[69] A PLA service command college commandant also noted that his institute had increased focus on joint operations, pointing out a system in which student groups would have the opportunity to spend a month at each of the other service command colleges.[70]

Fourth, stronger partnerships were established among PME institutes, theater commands, and the services. Although faculty from the PLA NDU and other institutes previously had opportunities to lecture and observe training in the military regions, PLA media suggested that those relationships had deepened after the reforms. For instance, a report from the Western Theater Command noted that in 2016, professors from 10 different academies had given lectures or conducted seminars on joint operational command, while volumes published by NDU were being used to train headquarters staff.[71] Another report noted that a single lecture by an NDU professor drew more than 1,900 officers from the Southern Theater Command headquarters and service component commands.[72] Moreover, PLA NDU announced that it would invite commanders and staff officers from the theater commands to give lectures to its students in Beijing, bringing insights from the field to the classroom.[73]

Personnel System Reforms

Building on previous reforms, changes were also made within the personnel system to develop stronger joint commanders. One area involved attempts to incentivize high performers. A program in the Eastern Theater Command, for instance, matched performance in joint operations study and training with incentives including promotions, priority in selecting future billets, and other "awards."[74] Likewise, the Southern Theater Command stated that it would grant awards, citations, and promotions to officers who had achieved satisfactory results on tests measuring aptitude in joint operational command skills.[75] The impending shift to a system based on ranks, rather than grades, may also have the effect of incentivizing joint commanders. According to one NDU professor, higher ranks would be reserved for personnel who "directly participate in operations," rather than noncombat positions.[76] If the PLA does replace the senior colonel rank with a flag-level brigadier general rank, some PLA sources have suggested that this rank may be reserved for operational commanders and that senior colonels in support roles might be demoted.[77]

The reforms also expanded opportunities for non–ground force officers to serve in joint positions, especially within the theater commands. Key examples include the appointment of a naval officer (Yuan Yubai) and an air force officer (Yi Xiaoguang) as commanders of the Southern and Central Theater Commands, respectively. Those appointments reflect the recognition that naval and air force experience is valuable, and even preferable, in those theaters with heavy maritime and air defense responsibilities. Changes also occurred at the theater deputy commander level, in which the proportion of non-army officers rose from less than one-third to more than one-half post-reform.[78] Opportunities for naval, air force, Rocket Force, and Strategic Support Force personnel at lower levels are less clear, though reports suggest that joint operations command centers are staffed with personnel from every service.[79]

However, more ambitious changes to the personnel system were still being debated in late 2017. PLA interlocutors have described proposals to create a rotational system in which officers are able (and required) to move among theater command headquarters, operational units, and CMC departments.[80] Some evidence that these proposals were making their way into practice was seen in 2017 with the rotation of 100 Beijing-based officers to western provinces and the reshuffling of group army commanders (though part of the rationale for the latter development was likely breaking up patronage networks).[81] Establishment of a rotational system for officers would represent a significant departure from the current system, in which officers spend most of their careers within a single theater. Although it would provide future joint commanders with a broader range of experience, rotational assignments would likely be an unwelcome change for those officers who benefit from residing in more affluent regions, where their families have access to better housing, education, and health care—and who choose to remain in the PLA because of those circumstances. These practical considerations are a significant obstacle to a more radical transformation of the assignment system.

Broader changes to the personnel system could also result in a more streamlined and competent officer corps. For instance, changes to the promotion system may encourage greater transparency and competition among qualified officers. One early indication was a competition held in the Western Theater Command in late 2017, in which 2 officers were selected from a pool of 14 applicants to fill open brigade commander positions. The candidates were screened through a standard assessment gauging their knowledge and command skills.[82] A separate, but perhaps related, proposal that has been discussed in recent years has been to "civilianize" more of the PLA workforce, especially noncombat positions currently filled by officers. This would build on previous PLA efforts to contract out some nonessential tasks as part of civil-military integration. Discussions with PLA officers indicate that the previous civilian cadre [*wenzhi ganbu*, 文职干部] system is being eliminated and that some military positions will become civilian contract positions as part of efforts to meet force reduction targets. However, some officers are reluctant to move from the active force to civilian positions due to lower pensions and reduced benefits.[83]

Training Reforms

A final set of reforms aimed to improve the quality of PLA joint training. Structurally, the former General Staff Department Military Training Department was replaced with a separate Training and Administration Department under direct CMC supervision.[84] That department exercises its authority by both establishing training standards and conducting inspections of training events across the PLA, including "theater command–level joint training," to ensure that standards are being met.[85] Inspections completed in early 2017, for instance, uncovered violations by 57 units and 99 personnel from all of the services and meted out a variety of punishments.[86] The department has also been involved in setting the content of PME reforms, including reducing the number of doctoral students in military academies and redirecting their focus to "practical" subjects, such as joint operations.[87]

Table. Theater Command Training for Joint Commanders and Staff	
Theater Command (TC)	Example Initiatives/Exercises
Eastern TC	Command post exercise involving more than 100 joint operations commanders.
Southern TC	Training class for joint commanders involving lectures from NDU scholars.
Central TC	Command post exercise focused on handling an "unidentified air object."
Northern TC	Training courses for headquarters staff involving case study analysis, lectures from theater commanders, and external speakers.
Western TC	Embedding headquarters staff in field exercises carried out by frontline units.

Sources: Dai Feng and Cheng Yongliang [代烽, 程永亮], "Upgrading Capabilities, Strengthening Skills in Joint Operations and Joint Training" [能力升级，练强联战联训过硬本领], *PLA Daily* [解放军报], September 1, 2016, available at <http://www.81.cn/jfjbmap/content/2016-09/01/content_155319.htm>; Li Huamin and Jiang Boxi [李华敏, 姜博西], "Speed Up Training for Joint Operations Command Talent" [加快联合指挥人才培训], *PLA Daily* [解放军报], August 15, 2016, available at <www.81.cn/jfjbmap/content/2016-08/15/content_153536.htm>; Yang Danpu and Yang Qinggang [杨丹谱, 杨清刚], "'Joint Forum' Focuses on Real Combat Capabilities" ['联合大讲堂' 聚焦实战长本事], *PLA Daily* [解放军报], April 16, 2016, available at <http://www.81.cn/jfjbmap/content/2016-04/16/content_141747.htm>; Du Shanguo and Shi Liu [杜善国, 石榴], "With This Type of Training, We Will Have Confidence in Future Battles" [这样练下去，将来打起仗来心里就有底了], *China Youth Daily* [中国青年报], April 12, 2017, available at <http://news.xinhuanet.com/mil/2017-04/12/c_129529922.htm>.

Training reforms have also been conducted at the TC level. A key focus has been on providing officers with practical training related to joint operations. Likely intended in part to demonstrate compliance with directives from Xi and the PLA top brass, each of the theater commands have announced relevant on-the-job training programs. Captured in the table, these ranged from command post exercises, to lectures, to participation in unit-level exercises. A Central TC program, for instance, focused on six capabilities junior officers would need to run the theater's joint operations command center, including drafting documents, marking maps, performing calculations, performing data searches, providing support to decisionmakers, and using the data link command system.[88] A December 2017 competition of 100 staff officers in the Central TC tested skills ranging from relaying orders to assessing adversary threats.[89] Based on a similar training program, the Eastern Theater Command required personnel to pass a "joint duty qualification test" that evaluated officers' understanding of the weapons, equipment, and operational principles of different services.[90]

Some changes have also started to appear in joint field training. While a comparison of pre- and post-reform joint exercises is beyond the scope of this chapter, it is worth noting that the shift from military regions to theater commands may be instrumental in spurring more intensive joint training. Speaking during an air-ground exercise, a Southern TC air force officer explained that his service often previously paid only lip service to joint training, given weak authorities of the military regions over non-army units. Under the new system, theater air forces are more responsive to training requirements being set by TC headquarters.[91] Theater joint training has also allowed non-army officers to gain experience in commanding ground forces. For instance, in October 2016, the East Sea Fleet staged an amphibious drill in which the activities of army, naval, and air force units were directed by a maritime joint command center.[92] The latest iteration of the CMC's authoritative training guidance, promulgated in January 2018, also emphasizes joint operations as a focus of training across the PLA.[93]

Conclusion and Implications

The first phase of the reforms announced in late 2015 and early 2016 involved major changes to the organizational structure of the PLA. These included disbanding the four general departments and transferring most of their functions into departments within a revised CMC structure; restructuring the seven military regions into five joint theater commands aligned against specific regional threats; and removing the operational command role of the service headquarters and giving them (including a new PLA Army service headquarters) an "organize, train, and equip" mission. These shifts were followed by an October 2017 restructuring of the membership of the CMC, which eliminated ex officio representation for the service chiefs and the heads of the CMC Joint Logistics Department and Joint Armaments Department.[94] These structural reforms collectively constitute a major shift in where power and responsibilities lie within different parts of the PLA, which is why they were resisted by vested interests (especially the ground forces) for more than a decade. Nevertheless, these "above the neck" reforms did not affect the organization of most PLA operational units and had only a limited impact on average PLA officers, NCOs, and enlisted personnel. For most PLA ground force and air force units, the "below the neck" reforms to move to a group army-brigade-battalion structure were likely more significant.

However, reforms to address the "software" and human capital problems discussed in this chapter have the potential to be much more disruptive for the daily lives of the PLA officer corps. (The reduction of 300,000 personnel—declared to be "basically complete" in March 2018—has also been extremely disruptive for the military.) Building a "modern major general" capable of commanding integrated joint operations will likely involve significant changes to PLA recruitment and retention policies; to the military educational system (at the academy level and throughout the service and joint PME system); to the rank/grade, assignment, and promotion systems; and to the conduct and evaluation of joint exercises. Put another way, these reforms could change who joins the PLA, criteria for promotion and advancement, what a successful career looks like, and what quality of life is available for a successful officer and his or her family. They could also have a negative impact on the careers of current officers, who were recruited, promoted, and assigned using a different set of criteria and incentives.

PLA writings and statements by Xi Jinping and PLA leaders suggest that the PLA is aware of a number of deficiencies in its current recruitment, educational, personnel management, and training practices that inhibit the development of effective joint commanders. Moreover, a wide range of solutions are being discussed, some of which would involve significant reforms to longstanding PLA regulations and practices. Some of the reforms, such as increasing the joint content of PME courses and increasing interactions between the field and schoolhouse, are underway and will be relatively easy to implement. Others, such as reforming the grade/rank, assignment, and promotion systems, will be much more disruptive to the military as a whole and to the career prospects of the current officer corps. The degree of difficulty is likely to be even higher because changes in one area affect many of the other areas.

Making major changes in a military typically requires making major changes in the incentives that ambitious military officers face as they try to win promotion and advance to senior leadership positions. But changing the incentives and promotion criteria also entails changes in who decides which officers will get promoted, and this will undermine existing power and patronage networks within the PLA. For example, increasing the joint content of PME courses is relatively easy, but making these courses more rigorous and having the results of classroom evaluations and performance on tests influence promotion decisions take autonomy away from the local commanders and political commissars who currently determine promotions. These officers (who have succeeded under the old criteria) are likely to argue that proven operational command ability and political reliability should outweigh classroom performance.[95] The current system where officers spend most of their careers within one service and one theater up to corps leader grade means that winning the approval of one's local commanders and political commissars is critical for success. But rotational assignments to a different service or outside the theater will loosen these bonds; the "new guy" will always be at a disadvantage compared to officers who have known and worked for the commander and political commissar for a decade or more. The U.S. military seeks to avoid these problems by having centralized promotion boards within each Service, which reduces (but does not eliminate) the role of patronage in promotions. The PLA could potentially adopt such a system, but it would constitute a major change from current practice, which is adapted to Chinese culture, Chinese Communist Party rule, and the PLA's own organizational culture and values.

Some of the proposals being discussed suggest focusing resources and attention on a subset of junior officers who the PLA believes have the potential to be effective joint commanders. (This is already being put into practice in a limited way by the NDU distinction between "command" and "staff" tracks, although this appears to be based on career fields.) One challenge is identifying officers with high potential early enough in their careers to steer them into the right mix of joint, educational, and operational assignments to develop well-rounded commanders. The idea of a "joint specialization" is envisioned as one vehicle for achieving this goal. However, a separate career track also has the potential to be a career ghetto if the senior leaders deciding on promotions (currently local commanders and political commissars within the officer's service) value a different set of criteria (for example, excellence in command rather than a well-rounded set of skills). Moreover, if the promotion system discriminates against effective service commanders who are *not* selected for joint specialization early in their careers, it is likely to be regarded as unfair. Some militaries have adopted joint staff or general staff systems that constitute a separate career track, but these usually involve strategy, planning, or staff functions rather than operational command of troops.[96] The PLA, like any military, will resent and resist a promotion system that does not reward and promote its most operationally proficient commanders, even if that proficiency is demonstrated primarily in single-service operations.

This suggests that the success of reforms to the recruitment, education, assignment, and promotion systems is interdependent with PLA efforts to give operational units more stringent joint training requirements and more opportunities to practice and meet those requirements in joint exercises. This would create the possibility of a virtuous cycle where company and battalion commanders understand how their units fit into joint operations (and the benefits of jointness for their ability to carry out their assigned missions) and bring that knowledge into PME courses and staff assignments in a theater service headquarters or command post. That education and experience, in turn, would make them more effective in exercising further responsibility at the brigade level and then prepare them for higher level joint positions at the theater or CMC level. However, this sort of virtuous cycle involves generational change to be fully effective. The PLA leadership faces difficult choices in deciding what changes are needed to get from here to there and how to keep faith with existing officers and NCOs while building the military of the future.

PLA leaders have concluded that cultivating "new-type military talent" is necessary to build "new-type operational forces" capable of fighting and winning the informationized wars of the future. This chapter describes some of the changes to current PLA recruitment, educational, personnel management, and training practices that will likely be necessary. Some aspects of these changes are likely to be observable as the PLA decides what to do and promulgates new regulations to implement reforms in these areas. However, it will be harder to understand precisely how these changes affect the career incentives of PLA officers and to assess their cumulative impact. Military-to-military exchanges offer a limited but valuable window on the issues the PLA is grappling with, but U.S. interlocutors should be careful not to offer the PLA answers to the problems it faces. At the same time, U.S. policymakers should expect the PLA to engage other advanced militaries, including U.S. allies, in its efforts to survey and evaluate the range of potential solutions.[97]

Building a "modern major general" capable of effectively commanding integrated joint operations is a challenging task that may take the PLA decades to achieve. The PLA assesses that its current efforts fall short of the mark and is contemplating significant changes to its recruitment, education, assignment, and promotion systems and training practices. The extent to which the PLA is willing and able to change how it does business to develop more effective joint commanders—and its ability to "fix the plane while flying it"—will be a major determinant in how successful it is in realizing the potential combat capability created by PLA investments in modernizing its weapons systems and developing joint doctrine.

The authors are grateful to Ian Burns McCaslin for invaluable research assistance.

Notes

[1] On problems of joint culture, see David T. Fatua, "The Paradox of Joint Culture," *Joint Force Quarterly* 26 (Autumn 2000), 81–86. Nevertheless, creating a common joint culture remains an aspiration. For instance, the U.S. *Joint Officer Handbook* encourages officers to "foster a joint culture that is not mutually exclusive of any one Service culture, but instead advocates all Service cultures and leverages the best aspect of each." *Joint Officer Handbook* (Washington, DC: The Joint Staff, August 2012), 70.

[2] For a discussion, see M. Taylor Fravel, "China's New Military Strategy: 'Winning Informationized Local Wars,'" *China Brief* 15, no. 13 (July 2, 2015), available at <https://jamestown.org/program/chinas-new-military-strategy-winning-informationized-local-wars/>.

[3] Joel Wuthnow and Phillip C. Saunders, *Chinese Military Reforms in the Age of Xi Jinping: Drivers, Challenges, and Implications*, China Strategic Perspectives 10 (Washington, DC: NDU Press, 2017), 23–32, available at <inss.ndu.edu/Portals/68/Documents/stratperspective/china/ChinaPerspectives-10.pdf>.

[4] Joel Wuthnow, "A Brave New World for Chinese Joint Operations," *Journal of Strategic Studies* 40, nos. 1–2 (2017), 174–179. These campaigns are described at length in Dang Chongmin and Zhang Yu [党崇民, 张羽], *Science of Joint Campaigns* [联合作战学] (Beijing: People's Liberation Army Press [中国人民解放军出版社], 2009); Zhang Yuliang [张玉良], *Science of Campaigns* [战役学] (Beijing: National Defense University Press [国防大学出版社], 2006), 273–326. For an earlier discussion, see Jianxiang Bi, "Joint Operations: Developing a New Paradigm," in *China's*

Revolution in Doctrinal Affairs, ed. James C. Mulvenon and David M. Finkelstein (Arlington, VA: CNA, 2002), 29–78.

5 In practice, this control would be exercised through service component commands and operational command posts in each theater. The precise mechanisms that theater commanders use to exercise operational control over conventional rocket force units in their theaters remain unclear. See Wuthnow and Saunders, *Chinese Military Reforms in the Age of Xi Jinping*, 24–28.

6 Prior to the reforms, the People's Liberation Army (PLA) ground forces held around 69 percent of all PLA end strength, while the navy, air force, and Rocket Force account for around 10 percent, 17 percent, and 4 percent, respectively. Wuthnow and Saunders, *Chinese Military Reforms in the Age of Xi Jinping*, 29. As of writing, it was unclear whether the size of the navy and air force will increase in absolute terms or merely in relation to the ground forces.

7 "Decision of the Central Committee of the Communist Party of China on Some Major Issues Concerning Comprehensively Deepening the Reform," Xinhua, November 12, 2013, available at <www.china.org.cn/china/third_plenary_session/2014-01/16/content_31212602.htm>.

8 Xu Qiliang [许其亮], "Firmly Push Forward Reform of National Defense and Armed Forces" [坚定不移推进国防和军队改革], *People's Daily* [人民日报], November 21, 2013, 6.

9 "CMC Opinions on Deepening National Defense and Military Reforms" [中央军委关于深化国防和军队改革的意见], Xinhua [新华], January 1, 2016, available at <http://news.xinhuanet.com/mil/2016-01/01/c_1117646695.htm>.

10 Li Xuanling and Wang Yitao [李宣良, 王逸涛], "Xi Jinping: To Achieve the China Dream and the Strong Army Dream, Supply Human Talent and Knowledge Support" [习近平: 为实现中国梦强军梦提供人才和智力支持], Xinhua [新华], March 23, 2016, available at <http://news.xinhuanet.com/politics/2016-03/23/c_1118422270.htm>.

11 Wang Wenyue [王文跃], "'The Most Difficult Battle Preparations' Cannot Be Slowed" ["最艰巨的战争准备"慢不得], *PLA Daily* [解放军报], May 6, 2016, available at <www.81.cn/jfjbmap/content/2016-05/06/content_143686.htm>.

12 Ibid.

13 For an overview of the PLA reform agenda through 2020, see Wuthnow and Saunders, *Chinese Military Reforms in the Age of Xi Jinping*, 49–52.

14 The PLA traces its experience with joint operations to the 1955 battle of Yijiangshan, in which air force, ground, and naval units coordinated to land on and

occupy Nationalist-held islands off the Chinese coast. However, preparations for joint operations were limited during most of the Cold War due to a preoccupation with preparing for People's War, centering on ground force operations.

[15] Wuthnow, "A Brave New World for Chinese Joint Operations." For a discussion of Chinese lessons from the Gulf War, see Dean Cheng, "Chinese Lessons from the Gulf War," in *Chinese Lessons from Other Peoples' Wars*, ed. Andrew Scobell, David Lai, and Roy Kamphausen (Carlisle, PA: Strategic Studies Institute, 2011), 161–162.

[16] Its first president, Zhang Zhen, actively investigated how foreign militaries pursued "joint professional military education" (PME), for instance asking detailed questions during visits to the U.S. National Defense University (NDU). See Paul H.B. Godwin, "The Cradle of Generals: Strategists, Commanders, and the PLA–National Defense University," in *The "People" in the PLA: Recruitment, Training, and Education in China's Military*, ed. Roy Kamphausen, Andrew Scobell, and Travis Tanner (Carlisle Barracks, PA: Strategic Studies Institute, 2008), 322.

[17] Jia Yong [贾永] et al., "Record of Jiang Zemin's Concern for the PLA National Defense University Training New-Type Military Talent" [江泽民关心国防大学培养新型军事人才纪实], Xinhua [新华], December 4, 2002, available at <www.people.com.cn/GB/shizheng/16/20021204/881361.html>; "Record of Hu Jintao's Attendance at the PLA National Defense University's 80th Anniversary Celebration" [胡锦涛主席出席国防大学80周年校庆活动纪实], Xinhua [新华], December 7, 2007, available at <http://news.ifeng.com/mainland/200712/1207_17_324697.shtml>.

[18] Nan Li, "Educating 'New-Type Military Talent': The PLA's Command Colleges," in *The "People" in the PLA*, 300–301.

[19] These volumes were Tan Yadong [谭亚东], ed., *Joint Operations Course Materials* (Beijing: Academy of Military Sciences Press [军事科学院出版社], 2013); and Li Yousheng and Wang Youhua [李友生, 王永华], *Lectures on the Science of Joint Campaigns* (Beijing: Military Science Press [军事科学出版社], 2012). See the chapter by Cozad in this volume. Of note, the PLA NDU also tried to foster greater critical thinking among its students through greater use of seminar discussions, case studies, and wargaming. How much these techniques were used in the study of joint operations, however, is unclear. See Li, "Educating 'New-Type Military Talent,'" 301.

[20] Godwin, "The Cradle of Generals," 332.

[21] Typically, PLA officers only began study of joint operations upon attendance at the PLA NDU's senior command course for major generals and rear admirals.

[22] Between 2004 and 2009, 200 officers in the Shenyang Military Region participated in cross-college training, while 100 officers served in a different service.

See Kevin McCauley, *PLA System of System Operations: Enabling Joint Operations* (Washington, DC: The Jamestown Foundation, 2017), 42.

[23] "China's National Defense in 2010," Information Office of the State Council, March 31, 2011, available at <www.china.org.cn/government/whitepaper/node_7114675.htm>.

[24] Thomas J. Bickford, "Searching for a Twenty-First-Century Officer Corps," in *Civil-Military Relations in Today's China: Swimming in a New Sea*, ed. David M. Finkelstein and Kristen A. Gunness (New York: Routledge, 2007), 176–177. See also Kristen A. Gunness, "Educating the Officer Corps: The Chinese People's Liberation Army and Its Interactions with Civilian Academic Institutions," in *Civil-Military Relations in Today's China*, 187–201.

[25] Author's visit to Army Command College and Air Force Command College, 2005.

[26] Bickford, "Searching for a Twenty-First-Century Officer Corps," 180.

[27] Elizabeth Hague, "PLA Career Progressions and Policies," in *The "People" in the PLA*, 274.

[28] McCauley, *PLA System of Systems Operations*, 42.

[29] However, it is worth noting that the PLA did not have a formal joint assignment system, such as exists in the U.S. military.

[30] Kenneth W. Allen, "Assessing the PLA Air Force's Ten Pillars," *China Brief* 11, no. 3 (February 11, 2011), 5–9, available at <https://jamestown.org/program/assessing-the-pla-air-forces-ten-pillars/>.

[31] McCauley, *PLA System of Systems Operations*, 43. See also Wanda Ayuso and Lonnie Henley, "Aspiring to Jointness: PLA Training, Exercises, and Doctrine, 2008–2012," in *Assessing the People's Liberation Army in the Hu Jintao Era*, ed. Roy Kamphausen, David Lai, and Travis Tanner (Carlisle Barracks, PA: Strategic Studies Institute, 2014), 171–206.

[32] Cozad, "Toward a More Joint, Combat Ready PLA?" 12.

[33] Mark Stokes and Ian Easton, "The Chinese People's Liberation Army General Staff Department: Evolving Organization and Missions," in *The PLA as Organization v2.0*, ed. Kevin Pollpeter and Kenneth W. Allen (Vienna, VA: Defense Group, Inc., 2015), 156–157.

[34] Cozad, "Toward a More Joint, Combat Ready PLA?" 18.

[35] Mei Shixiong and Zhao Guotao [梅世雄, 赵国涛], "PLA Central Theater Command Starts Its Work by Energetically Enhancing Joint Operations Command Capabilities" [中部战区起步开局大力提升联合作战指挥能力],

Xinhua [新华], April 1, 2016, available at <http://news.xinhuanet.com/mil/2016-04/01/c_128857500.htm>. The article also cites the case of Jiang Guo, a staff officer at Central Theater Command headquarters, who despite his experience within a group army, "feels that he still lacks the capability of using forces of other services while being transferred to work in the joint command framework after the founding of the theater command."

[36] Interview, June 2016.

[37] Interview, June 2016 and November 2017.

[38] See Li Chunli [李春立], "Make Efforts to Break Through the 'Two Insufficient Capabilities,'" [着力破解 "两个能力不够" 问题], *PLA Daily* [解放军报], December 30, 2014, available at <http://theory.people.com.cn/n/2014/1230/c40531-26302150.html>; Yu Qifeng [于启峰], "Start from the Source in Breaking Through the 'Five Cannots'" [破解"五个不会"难题要从源头入手], *PLA Daily* [解放军报], October 13, 2015, available at <www.81.cn/jfjbmap/content/2015-10/13/content_125880.htm>; Wang, "'The Most Difficult Battle Preparations' Cannot Be Slowed." See also Dennis J. Blasko, "Walk, Don't Run: Chinese Military Reforms in 2017," *War on the Rocks*, January 9, 2017, available at <https://warontherocks.com/2017/01/walk-dont-run-chinese-military-reforms-in-2017/>.

[39] Blasko, "Walk, Don't Run."

[40] Li Dianren [李殿仁] et al., *Study on the Development of Joint Commanding Officers* [联合作战指挥人才培养] (Beijing: National Defense University Press [国防大学出版社], 2008), 35.

[41] Interview with PLA Command Academy commandant, April 2016. For a discussion on limited "joint PME" within the PLA Navy, see Kenneth W. Allen and Morgan Clemens, *The Recruitment, Education, and Training of PLA Navy Personnel* (Newport, RI: U.S. Naval War College, 2014), 26.

[42] Kenneth W. Allen, "Chinese Air Force Officer Recruitment, Education, and Training," *China Brief* 11, no. 22 (November 30, 2011), 9–13, available at <https://jamestown.org/program/chinese-air-force-officer-recruitment-education-and-training/>. It is worth noting that this situation stands in contrast to the U.S. PME system, in which officers are able to attend war colleges outside their home Service (for example, naval officers attending the Army War College).

[43] McCauley, *PLA System of Systems Operations*, 42.

[44] Bickford, "Searing for a Twenty-First-Century Officer Corps," 321.

[45] Li et al., *Study on the Development of Joint Commanding Officers*, 38. Based on requirements contained in the Goldwater-Nichols Department of Defense

Reorganization Act of 1986, credentialing for U.S. joint officers is written into Title 10 of the *U.S. Code*. See 10 *U.S. Code* § 661—Management Policies for Joint Qualified Officers, available at <www.law.cornell.edu/uscode/text/10/661>.

⁴⁶ On the 1979 Sino-Vietnam border war, see Harlan W. Jencks, "China's 'Punitive' War on Vietnam: A Military Assessment," *Asian Survey* 19, no. 8 (August 1979), 801–815; Xiaoming Zhang, "China's 1979 War with Vietnam: A Reassessment," *The China Quarterly*, no. 184, (December 2005), 870–871.

⁴⁷ Interview with retired PLA flag officer, November 2017.

⁴⁸ Du Shanguo and Shi Liu [杜善国, 石榴], "With This Type of Training, We Will Have Confidence in Future Battles" [这样练下去，将来打起仗来心里就有底了], *China Youth Daily* [中国青年报], April 12, 2017, available at <http://news.xinhuanet.com/mil/2017-04/12/c_129529922.htm>. For a similar diagnosis of joint training weaknesses in the former Nanjing Military Region, see Cai Yingting and Zheng Weiping [蔡英挺, 郑卫平], "Deeply Absorb Historical Experience from the War of Resistance to Make Preparations for Military Struggle More Solid and Effective" [深刻汲取抗战胜利历史经验把军事斗争准备抓得更加扎实有效], *People's Daily* [人民日报], July 3, 2015, available at <http://politics.people.com.cn/n/2015/0703/c1001-27249242.html>.

⁴⁹ One U.S. author notes that "in the Navy in the mid-1980s, joint duty was considered the 'kiss of death'; it meant that one's career was over." See James R. Locher III, "Has It Worked? The Goldwater-Nichols Reorganization Act," *Naval War College Review* 54, no. 4 (Autumn 2001), 104.

⁵⁰ Fang Jiangzhe, *View on the Armed Forces Education and Training System* [军队院校培训体制] (Beijing: National Defense University Press [国防大学出版社], July 2015), 281.

⁵¹ Jeffrey Becker, David Liebenberg, and Peter Mackenxie, *Behind the Periscope: Leadership in China's Navy* (Arlington, VA: CNA, 2013), 107–22. One exception was that service as a deputy chief of the general staff became a normal avenue for appointment as PLA Navy commander.

⁵² Li et al., *Study on the Development of Joint Commanding Officers*, 14. Key moments on the U.S. path toward creating a joint force included the Defense Reorganization Act of 1958, which focused on unified command and control; the 1982 promulgation of the AirLand Battle doctrine by the U.S. Army; and the Goldwater-Nichols Act, which strengthened the authority of the regional combatant commands.

⁵³ Wang, "'The Most Difficult Battle Preparations' Cannot Be Slowed." U.S. National War College Professor Cynthia Watson has a more pessimistic assessment

of the PLA's chances to bridge this gap, arguing that the "PLA cannot hope to achieve in a few short years what has taken the United States decades, and it will need many more years of practice and experimentation to absorb the changes and derive the benefits of a more Western-style PME." Bickford, "Trends in Education and Training, 1924–2007," in *The "People" in the PLA*, 41.

[54] Li et al., *Study on the Development of Joint Commanding Officers*, 45.

[55] Ibid., 35.

[56] McCauley, *PLA System of Systems Operations*, 41.

[57] Liu Wei [刘伟], ed., *Theater Joint Operations Command* [战区联合作战指挥] (Beijing: National Defense University Press [国防大学出版社], 2016), 315.

[58] *Science of Military Strategy* [战略学] (Beijing: Academy of Military Science Press [军事科学院出版社], 2013), 203–204.

[59] Liu, *Theater Joint Operations Command*, 311–315.

[60] Xu, "Firmly Push Forward Reform of National Defense and the Armed Forces," 6.

[61] Li and Wang, "Xi Jinping: To Achieve the China Dream and the Strong Army Dream, Supply Human Talent and Knowledge Support."

[62] Chu Zhenjiang and Luo Jinmu [褚振江, 罗金沐], "Innovating Joint Operations Command Talent, Professionalizing Training Models" [创新联合作战指挥人才专业化培养模式], *PLA Daily* [解放军报], March 20, 2016, available at <www.81.cn/jfjbmap/content/2016-03/20/content_138222.htm>.

[63] "PLA National Defense University Trains Fine Commanders for Joint Operations," CCTV-7, March 21, 2016.

[64] Huang Panyue, ed., "PLA Aims to Cultivate Commanding Talents for Joint Operations," *China Military Online*, September 7, 2017, available at <http://eng.chinamil.com.cn/view/2017-09/07/content_7747234.htm>.

[65] Ibid.

[66] "PLA NDU Joint Operations College Established, Major General Zhou Licun Selected as Political Commissar" [国防大学联合作战学院已组建, 周立存少将担任学院政委], *The Paper* [澎湃新闻], August 9, 2017, available at <www.thepaper.cn/newsDetail_forward_1757313>.

[67] Guo Hongyu and Chen Zhen [果翊宇, 陈震], "Focusing on Tomorrow's Battlefields and Forging Intelligence Crack Troops" [聚焦明日战场砥砺知敌尖兵], *PLA Daily* [解放军报], April 3, 2018, available at <www.81.cn/jfjbmap/content/2018-04/03/content_203092.htm>.

68 Zhang He and Hu Xiaoqing [张贺, 胡小青], "Command College Seeks to Cultivate Teachers' Joint Operations Instruction Capabilities" [指挥学院着力培养教员联合作战教学能力], *Huojianbing Bao* [火箭兵报], June 4, 2016, 2.

69 Ibid.

70 However, it was not entirely clear if this was a new initiative. Interview with PLA service command college commandant, June 2016.

71 Yang Xiaobo and Ji Dongsheng [杨晓波, 冀东昇], "Talent Capable of Planning and Studying Operations Swiftly Rising" [谋战研战人才方阵加速崛起], *PLA Daily* [解放军报], November 30, 2016, available at <www.81.cn/jfjbmap/content/2016-11/30/content_162918.htm>.

72 Li Huamin and Jiang Boxi [李华敏, 姜博西], "Speed Up Training for Joint Operations Command Talent" [加快联合指挥人才培训], *PLA Daily* [解放军报], August 15, 2016, available at <www.81.cn/jfjbmap/content/2016-08/15/content_153536.htm>. See also Mei and Zhao, "PLA Central Theater Command Starts Its Work By Energetically Enhancing Joint Operations Command Capabilities"; Dai Feng and Cheng Yongliang [代烽, 程永亮], "Upgrading Capabilities, Strengthening Skills in Joint Operations and Joint Training" [能力升级, 练强联战联训过硬本领], *PLA Daily* [解放军报], September 1, 2016, available at <www.81.cn/jfjbmap/content/2016-09/01/content_155319.htm>.

73 Zhang Shibo and Liu Yazhou [张仕波, 刘亚洲], "Strive to Build the Highest Military Academy with the World's Advanced Standards and Chinese Characteristics" [努力建设具有世界先进水平和中国特色的最高军事学府], *PLA Daily* [解放军报], April 18, 2016, available at <www.mod.gov.cn/education/2016-04/18/content_4649689_2.htm>.

74 Dai and Cheng, "Upgrading Capabilities, Strengthening Skills in Joint Operations and Joint Training."

75 Li and Jiang, "Speed Up Training for Joint Operations Command Talent."

76 Lu Xiaolin [卢晓琳], "Military Officer System Reform, Take Off!" [军官制度改革, 走起!], *People's Daily Online* [人民网], January 8, 2017, available at <http://paper.people.com.cn/rmrb/html/2017-01/08/nw.D110000renmrb_20170108_1-06.htm>. For a discussion of ranks vs. grades, see Kenneth W. Allen, "China Announces Reform of Military Ranks," *China Brief* 17, no. 2 (January 30, 2017), 7–13, available at <https://jamestown.org/program/china-announces-reform-military-ranks/>.

77 Interviews with PLA sources, December 2016 and November 2017.

78 Wuthnow and Saunders, *Chinese Military Reform in the Age of Xi Jinping*, 18–19.

79 Ibid., 28.

[80] Interviews with PLA interlocutors, 2016–2017.

[81] Author interviews, December 2017.

[82] "Choosing People through Combat! Western Theater Command Fills 2 Brigade Commander Positions through Military Competition of 14 Officers" [以战选人! 西部战区14名军干比武竞争两个旅长岗位], *PLA Daily* [解放军报], December 11, 2017, available at <http://news.ifeng.com/a/20171211/54045910_0.shtml>.

[83] Interviews, 2016–2017. PLA interviewees indicate that civilian contract positions will not count against the PLA's post-reduction 2 million end-strength.

[84] Wuthnow and Saunders, *Chinese Military Reform in the Age of Xi Jinping*, 31.

[85] Ouyang, ed., "CMC Intensifies Supervision Over Military Training," *China Military Online*, March 21, 2017, available at <http://english.chinamil.com.cn/view/2017-03/21/content_7534230.htm>.

[86] Ibid. Punishments included "self-examinations," publicized criticisms, and "discipline punishments."

[87] Zhang Tao, "Chinese Military Academies to Cut Student Enrollment," Xinhua, October 23, 2017, available at <http://english.chinamil.com.cn/view/2017-10/23/content_7797090.htm>.

[88] Mei and Zhao, "PLA Central Theater Command Starts Its Work by Energetically Enhancing Joint Operations Command Capabilities."

[89] Zhang Kunping [张坤平], "100 Joint Campaign Staff in Martial Competition on the Same Stage" [百名联合战役参谋同台比武竞技], *PLA Daily* [解放军报], available at <www.81.cn/jfjbmap/content/2017-12/16/content_194521.htm>.

[90] Cheng Yongliang [程永亮], "Whether One May Command Joint Operations Requires 'Certification'" [能不能指挥联合作战, 需要 "考证"了], *China Youth Daily* [中国青年报], February 23, 2017, available at <http://news.sina.com.cn/o/2017-02-23/doc-ifyavwcv8556596.shtml>.

[91] Ouyang Zhimin, Ma Fei, Xiao Chiyu [欧阳治民, 马飞, 肖驰宇], "Joint Training Is a 'Chemical Reaction'" [联合训练是一场"化学反应"], *PLA Daily* [解放军报], February 3, 2017, available at <www.mod.gov.cn/power/2017-02/03/content_4771337_3.htm>.

[92] Liu Zhongtao and Zhou Pengcheng [刘中涛, 周鹏程], "Three Services Share Information on the Maritime Battlefield" [海上战场, 三军信息互联共享], *PLA Daily* [解放军报], October 13, 2016, available at <www.81.cn/jfjbmap/content/2016-10/13/content_158800.htm>.

93 "PLA Publishes New Military Training Outline, Highlights Combat," Xinhua, January 27, 2018, available at <www.xinhuanet.com/english/2018-01/27/c_136929690.htm>.

94 See Phillip C. Saunders, "Alternative Models for the Central Military Commission," *China Brief* 17, no. 13 (October 20, 2017), available at <https://jamestown.org/program/alternative-models-central-military-commission/>; Joel Wuthnow and Phillip C. Saunders, "China's Military Has a Discipline Problem. Here Is How Xi Jinping Is Trying to Fix It," *The National Interest*, November 12, 2017, available at <http://nationalinterest.org/feature/chinas-military-has-discipline-problem-here-how-xi-jinping-23163>.

95 Alternatively, if test scores and grades are given greater weight in promotion decisions, it would produce incentives for cheating and corruption of the military education system.

96 The United States implemented a joint staff structure as part of the Goldwater-Nichols reforms, though some have argued for a more comprehensive general staff model involving a permanent cadre of professional Joint Staff officers. See, for example, Jim Thomas, *Statement Before the Senate Armed Services Committee on Defense Reform*, Senate Armed Services Committee, November 10, 2015, available at <www.armed-services.senate.gov/imo/media/doc/Thomas_11-10-15.pdf>.

97 For an overview of these efforts, see Kenneth W. Allen, Phillip C. Saunders, and John Chen, *Chinese Military Diplomacy, 2003–2016: Trends and Implications*, China Strategic Perspectives 11 (Washington, DC: NDU Press, July 2017), available at <ndupress.ndu.edu/Portals/68/Documents/stratperspective/china/ChinaPerspectives-11.pdf>.

PART III

OVERHAULING SERVICES

CHAPTER 9

PLA FORCE REDUCTIONS

Impact on the Services

Daniel Gearin

In October 2013, during the Third Plenum of the 18th Party Congress, President Xi Jinping announced Beijing's intent to reform the Chinese military, with the decision document adopted at the plenum providing a brief overview of the intended reforms.[1] These remarks kicked off what would become a sweeping reform initiative, the details of which were revealed over the next few years and implemented in phases with an expected completion date of 2020. This reform program has received a fair amount of scholarly attention, which it deserves given the scale and scope of change taking place within the People's Liberation Army (PLA).[2] A subset of the overall reform initiative involves a 300,000-troop reduction, announced by Xi in September 2015 at an event honoring the anniversary of China's war with Japan. This reduction, and its impact on the PLA, has received much less attention from Western academics.[3]

The current force reduction initiative, which was "basically completed" by the end of 2017, is the eleventh of its kind in the PLA's history. An examination of past efforts in comparison to the current round of troop cuts demonstrates broad commonalities in how the PLA implements the force reductions as well as in its stated objectives. The PLA has repeatedly conducted large-scale demobilization in tandem with organizational changes, and in almost every case the goals are the same: streamline what is perceived as a bloated and inefficient military force, focus reductions primarily on noncombat troops, and utilize the force reductions and organizational changes to address longstanding cultural problems existing within the PLA.[4]

This chapter briefly examines several past force reduction efforts dating back to the 1980s to highlight Beijing's continued interest in creating a military that emphasizes quality over quantity, addressing a perceived army-centric bias within the PLA, and reducing the number of command and headquarters staff positions to enable more efficient command and control and military operations. The current round of reductions is no exception, with the bulk of demobilized forces coming from the ground forces and noncombat units. The organizational changes taking place in tandem with the force reductions are arguably the most serious example to date of Beijing's intent to overcome the PLA's historical army-centric culture and elevate the relative importance of the other military services.

The troop reduction effort and overall military reform should also be couched within Beijing's strategic goals for its military. These goals have been relatively consistent over the past several decades and were perhaps best encapsulated in remarks by Jiang Zemin in December 1997, as he laid out a "three step strategy" [*sanbuzou zhanlue*, 三步走战略] for modernizing China's military. This strategy, while vague on details, lays out three milestones for the PLA: to lay a solid foundation by 2010, to basically accomplish mechanization and make major progress in informationization by 2020, and to fully realize an informationized military by the middle of the 21st century.[5]

Xi Jinping's recent political work report at the 19th Party Congress reiterated these broad goals but added an interim milestone and modified the third goal. Xi called on the PLA to achieve modernization by 2035 and to become a world-class military by the middle of the 21st century.[6] While these goals are clearly ambitious, outside observers may be struck by the relative conservative timelines given the long-period of double-digit growth in China's military budget and the overall pace of military modernization over the past two decades. The current force reduction effort falls within this larger strategic context, as Beijing believes it is a necessary step to achieve these broader military modernization objectives.

Historical Context

The reductions announced in September 2015 were the latest in a series of personnel adjustments that have occurred within the PLA over the past several decades. The current force reduction is, again, the eleventh iteration in the PLA's history and the fourth since 1985, with the PLA having shed 1 million troops in 1985; 500,000 in 1997; and 200,000 in 2003. While the context and specific drivers for these changes differed in each case, the stated objectives that senior PLA leadership hoped to achieve are notably consistent. In general terms, force reductions were aimed at streamlining a military force that was viewed as bloated and inefficient. Furthermore, the PLA implemented organizational changes in tandem with each iteration of force reductions, in an effort to enhance the PLA's overall operational capabilities and tackle lingering cultural issues that were viewed as obstacles to further modernization.

China initiated its eighth round of military force reductions in 1985, which is a useful starting point for analysis due to the size of the reduction and because it was largely in response to changes in China's threat perceptions and domestic situation. The change in threat perception is perhaps captured best in the change made to China's military strategic guidelines at the time. The operating guidance for the military changed from "active defense, lure the enemy in deep," to simply "active defense." While a seemingly cosmetic change, this shift in jargon embodied a significant change in worldview.[7] The removal of the phrase "lure the enemy in deep" reflected not only China's embrace of economic modernization but also its growing recognition of the doctrinal shortcomings of "People's War." Reform and opening up placed economic development as the top priority for China. A military strategy of allowing the enemy to seize massive amounts of territory, particularly China's most economically valuable territory, fundamentally undermined this new development strategy.[8]

Directly related to the elevation of economic development as China's primary national objective was the recognition that the makeup of the military at the time was too large, too expensive, and wasted manpower that could be better utilized in China's private sector in order to fuel economic growth. Decreasing the size of the armed forces would also alleviate economic pressure on the government, allowing it to allocate additional resources to foster private industry and the commercial sector.

An unintended consequence of these changes was the creation of what became known as "PLA, Incorporated." As PLA budgets were slashed and as China's economy began to liberalize, the military and defense industry became increasingly involved in the commercial sector in an attempt to compensate for the lost income. This change had widespread and lasting negative influences on the PLA that Beijing is still attempting to address. Corruption within China's military grew to pervasive levels and large sections of the PLA shifted their focus away from honing operational capabilities toward economic initiatives. One purpose of the current anti-corruption campaign in China is specifically to address the challenges brought about by this cultural change.[9]

The 1985 reforms also reduced the number of military regions (MRs) from 11 to 7, disestablished 11 group armies, disbanded over 4,000 division and regimental entities, and reduced army units above the corps level by 31.[10] In addition to the desire to streamline China's military force, reductions and changes made during this time were aimed at emphasizing the importance of combined arms within the group armies. Group armies gained additional subordinate units that provided combined arms capabilities, including antiaircraft artillery, artillery, amphibious tanks, signal regiments, and engineering units. Training and exercises at the time also shifted to reflect this focus, taking on a more combined arms character.[11]

The reductions were carried out gradually over a couple years, with almost half of the goal of demobilizing 1 million soldiers achieved by December 1986 and the reduction basically completed by April 1987.[12] Overall this represented a 25 percent cut to the overall size of China's military, with the bulk of troops coming from China's ground forces.

A common target for force reductions across each iteration of reform included cuts to headquarters and staff personnel at all echelons of the PLA, decreasing the ratio of army personnel relative to the other services, adjustments to the ratio between officers and enlisted, and eliminating noncombat personnel. The 1985 iteration halved the number of personnel within the PLA's general departments, and the navy, air force, and Second Artillery all experienced growth in terms of both personnel and budget.[13]

The 1997 iteration of force reductions was intended to shed an additional 500,000 troops from the PLA. These reductions deactivated an additional three group armies and over a dozen infantry divisions, with many of these personnel transferred to the People's Armed Police.[14] Additionally, the 500,000 troops demobilized included over 200,000 officers, building on a theme established during the 1985 reductions of addressing a perceived imbalance between the number of officers and enlisted personnel within the PLA.[15]

The 1997 iteration also included significant organizational changes to the PLA to address problems inadvertently created by the previous force reduction initiative. Specifically, it was at this time that Beijing began a serious effort to divest the PLA from its involvement in private industry. By 1997, the PLA was believed to be involved in over 15,000 enterprises, totaling over $10 billion annually.[16] While some of this revenue was used to maintain and improve military installations and equipment, most of it is thought to have been siphoned off to line the pockets of individual officers, creating a culture of graft and corruption that Beijing is attempting to deal with to this day. To address this problem, Beijing provided sustained increases to the PLA's annual budget and made organizational changes meant to manage and rein in the military's reach into private industry.

In 2003, the PLA initiated its tenth troop reduction, demobilizing an additional 200,000 personnel over a 2-year period and disbanding an additional three group armies.[17] Consistent with the previous reduction initiatives, the 2003 iteration focused primarily on noncombat units within the ground force, and emphasized the removal of "lower quality" units in an effort to bolster the overall operational capability of the PLA. Once again, Beijing implemented organizational changes around the same time as the force reduction that appeared to be specifically aimed at addressing the army-centric culture within the PLA. Notably, it was in 2004 that the navy, air force, and Second Artillery commanders were added to the Central Military Commission (CMC), a symbolic step toward greater joint representation on China's highest military body.

Unlike the 1997 iteration, none of the demobilized ground troops was transferred to the People's Armed Police, thus representing a more genuine reduction to China's security forces. This round of reductions again centered on streamlining higher echelon units, which was partly accomplished by the disbandment of the headquarters and associated staff of three group armies. Furthermore, several divisions and brigades under these group armies were dissolved, while others were transferred to the reserve force.[18] A similar method of implementation is taking place currently within the PLA.

Current Iteration

Although Beijing's public commentary on the purpose of force reductions cites the effort as evidence of China's peaceful intentions and benefit to regional security, the actual objectives are likely strikingly similar to the historical examples detailed above. China's Ministry of National Defense acknowledged that the troop cuts were primarily designed to optimize the PLA's scale and structure in order to make it a more capable and efficient fighting force, and the primary target for demobilization once again involved troops with outdated equipment, headquarters staff, and noncombat personnel.[19]

Changes to the Top

Official figures on the number of personnel working within the highest echelons of China's military are difficult to come by. However, the reforms made a number of changes to the Central Military Commission and its subordinate entities. Although Beijing was probably able to trim some excess personnel from the CMC as a result of reform, outside observations of the organizational changes to these entities suggest that personnel were mainly shifted from one organization to another, rather than removed from the military entirely.

The Joint Staff Department, formerly known as the General Staff Department (GSD), probably experienced a large amount of change as a result of reform, shedding a number of second-level departments with responsibilities that fall outside the purview of operations or that fit better in some of the newly created organizations. Specifically, the GSD previously had responsibility for ground force operations that did not fall under the MR structure, to include army aviation and special forces. These departments were almost certainly transferred to the newly created army headquarters.

Similarly, the GSD's well-known third and fourth departments (the Technical Reconnaissance Bureau and Electronic Countermeasures Bureau) were absorbed by the newly created Strategic Support Force (SSF), which is responsible for all information operations in the post-reform PLA structure. These include space, cyberspace, and electromagnetic operations, in addition to the "three warfares" (psychological, media, and legal).[20] The actual reduction of personnel resulting from this change is probably negligible. Instead, the SSF is likely to see organizational growth in the coming years rather than a reduction. Placing all entities within the PLA that have a responsibility for information operations—which had previously been dispersed across several entities—under a unified command is likely to improve China's capabilities in this new warfare domain.

Other changes to the CMC involved the creation of new organizations, which may suggest a force increase rather than a decrease, but these entities all existed previously in some form within the PLA. In most cases, these organizations were subordinate entities to the previous CMC departments and were merely given new names and subordination. For instance, the Science and Technology Commission appears to be primarily comprised of former General Armaments Department organizations, and the Discipline Inspection Commission is made up of entities previously under the General Political Department.

The changes to the CMC are important and worthy of discussion, but the direct impact of the 300,000-force reduction on China's top military organization appears to be minimal. The changes instead appear to align with Xi Jinping's model for building a "strong army," with his emphasis on having a military that listens to the Communist Party's command, is capable of fighting and winning wars, and strictly maintains discipline. The fact that the leaders of the CMC Political Work Department, CMC Joint Staff Department, and CMC Discipline Inspection Commission are the only CMC department heads to have positions as CMC members reflects these priorities.

Military Regions to Combat Theaters

Below the level of the CMC, at the theater echelon, is where the PLA was probably most able to achieve some significant personnel reductions. Similar to earlier force reduction and reform efforts, the latest round of reform included the removal of some military regions. The Jinan MR was broken up and distributed to the newly created Northern Theater and Central Theater, while the Lanzhou MR was disestablished and its subordinate units absorbed within the Western Theater. Similar to the 2003 force reduction, the elimination of MR headquarters staff and their associated MR air force headquarters staff provided an opportunity for actual personnel reductions. However, it remains unclear how much of the overall staff was removed from the military vice transferred to other entities.

The theater command (TC) structure that resulted from reform has interesting operational implications. Chinese state media have noted that the newly created theater commands align to China's "strategic directions" [*zhanlüe fangxiang*, 战略方向]. While rarely enumerated in public forums, we can infer the general focus areas from the five TCs that were created, which include Taiwan and Japan, the South China Sea and South East Asia, India, the Korean Peninsula, and the defense of Beijing.[21]

The consolidation of the former Chengdu MR and Lanzhou MR into a single theater command aligned operational planning for a contingency with India under a unified staff. However, the retention of both the Xinjiang Military District and the Xizang (Tibet) Military District indicates that some degree of bifurcation remains below the theater level.[22] These two military districts each border an area of territorial dispute with India in Aksai Chin and Arunachal Pradesh, which perhaps necessitates their continued existence as military districts. The tensions between China and India in the Doklam region in the summer of 2017 provided Beijing an opportunity to test and assess the new command organization and its ability to deal with a crisis.[23] While it is difficult to determine the operational impact of the consolidation of command and control from media reporting, the change appears to be a step in the right direction for the PLA, at least conceptually.

Similarly, the Jinan MR and its subordinate entities were broken up and distributed between the Northern and Central theaters. Historically, Jinan MR has served as the PLA's strategic reserve, and would deploy its subordinate forces to other military regions to support any emerging military contingency. The newly created Central Theater absorbed the former Jinan MR 54th Group Army and probably carries forth the mission of strategic support to the surrounding military regions in the event of a conflict.

Elimination of Group Armies

As part of the force reduction, the PLA reorganized 84 corps-level entities. In April 2017, Beijing officially confirmed what had been rumored for several months—that five group armies within China's ground forces had been disbanded.[24] The 13 remaining group armies all received new unit designators (from 71st to 83rd) that aligned with the new theater structure and served as a symbolic break from the tradition and history of the PLA ground forces. The full extent of these changes is not yet clear. Similar to past instances of eliminating group armies, it appears that the headquarters offices have been disbanded but that many of the subordinate units have either been transferred to other remaining group armies or remain in a state of transition.

Of the five group armies that were eliminated, one came from each of the former seven military regions except for Guangzhou and Nanjing MRs, possibly representing the continuing operational importance of preparing for military conflict with Taiwan (a contingency for which the Guangzhou and Nanjing MRs had primary responsibility). While the elimination of five group armies represents a reduction in the number of combat troops, the total impact remains unclear. The group armies selected for elimination were arguably among the less capable and in possession of more outdated equipment.

Force Structure Adjustments

The PLA appears to have utilized this round of force reductions to implement force structure adjustments that have been under way for several years. For the ground force, this includes the wider trend of converting existing divisions and regiments into brigades. The brigade structure is meant to facilitate greater mobility and modular capabilities, a theme highlighted within the PLA for several years now (see the chapter by Blasko in this volume). Since at least 2009, the PLA has stressed the need for the ground force to be capable of rapid deployments, which it has practiced in a series of exercises including Stride [*kuayue*, 跨越] and Mission Action [*shiming xingdong*, 使命行动].[25] The purpose of these exercises is to develop the ability of ground units to rapidly deploy anywhere on China's periphery to respond to emerging contingencies; the shift to a brigade structure that is accompanying the force reduction is also meant to facilitate this change.

In addition to the continued transition to a brigade structure, the ground force is increasing its aviation and special forces units across the army. Of the remaining 13 group armies, there is increasing evidence that the ultimate goal is to have at least one army aviation brigade and one special forces brigade under every group army. This is another example of a trend that has been under way for several years, but Beijing appears to be utilizing reform and force reductions to force through changes that may have otherwise taken longer to implement. Both army aviation and special forces are viewed as key elements to the army's future concept of operations, which the PLA generally refers to as "three-dimensional" or "multidimensional" assault [*liti tuji*, 立体突击].

In contrast to the army, the other services within the PLA are likely experiencing a force increase rather than a decrease. This trend also pre-dates the current round of reform and is a component of a longstanding effort to reduce the army-centric focus of the PLA to the relative benefit of the other services. Official personnel figures for the PLA in the 2012 white paper break out to 850,000 in the army; 235,000 in the navy; and 398,000 in the air force. The figure for the Rocket Force is left unstated, but most unofficial figures put it at around 130,000 personnel. If accurate, that leaves approximately 687,000 troops within the 2.3-million-member PLA unaccounted for. That figure probably consists of civilian cadre [*wenzhi ganbu*, 文职干部] and noncombat troops, in addition to other unidentified personnel.[26]

Absent updated official figures, the post-downsizing personnel ratios within the PLA breakout are a matter of speculation. That said, the PLA Navy and to a lesser extent the PLA Air Force and Rocket Force are poised to experience potential growth in personnel end strength. This is evident from the PLA's announced prioritization of the maritime domain, as outlined in Beijing's 2015 white paper on military strategy. Furthermore, the establishment of a new marine corps headquarters and a rumored increase from two marine brigades to six hold true may produce a significant increase to the size of the navy.[27]

If the increase in the number of marine brigades proceeds as predicted, one possibility that would both accommodate the force reduction plan and allow for more rapid establishment of mission capable units would involve the transfer of existing ground force units over to the navy. The units currently within the PLA Army with amphibious capabilities would make logical sense for such a transfer. However, this would represent a significant change to the historical missions of the army and marine corps, particularly with respect to combat against Taiwan, which the army sees as one of its most important missions. Recent PLA marine exercises featuring a diverse set of climates suggest a potentially evolving role of the marine corps to one that features more expeditionary missions.[28]

Other than rumors about additional marine brigades, the PLA reforms and force reductions have had a relatively minor impact on the navy compared to the other services. The three fleets that existed prior to the creation of the geographically focused theaters still exist and retain their previous names, unlike the rebranding and flag ceremonies that have occurred elsewhere with the PLA. It is unclear at this stage whether this is an interim step with wider changes to be expected in the coming years, or if the PLA is generally satisfied with the navy's modernization pathway and will continue with established plans (see the chapter by Burns McCaslin and Erickson in this volume).

The PLA Air Force is experiencing a number of substantial changes to its force structure, primarily as a result of the reforms rather than through force reductions. As with the army, the air force has utilized the force reductions and reform initiative to implement longstanding aspirational force structure adjustments. In particular, the air force has continued its own conversion of division and regimental units into brigades, which began several years previously but appeared to have stalled. The air force brigades are designed to provide more modular capabilities at the operational level through the creation of brigades with subordinate units with dissimilar aircraft, compared to the past structure that featured entire divisions containing essentially the same operational capability.

The PLA Rocket Force is the most difficult of the services to get direct information on through open sources. However, it appears that all six operational missile bases that formerly existed within the Rocket Force's predecessor, the Second Artillery, have been retained, albeit with new numerical designations. This is noteworthy due to the mismatch between the missile bases and number of theaters, suggesting that the Rocket Force has not fully been aligned under the theater structure. This is further evident in the apparent absence of any Rocket Force leaders among the theater deputy commanders.[29] (See the discussion of the relationship between the Rocket Force and theater commands in the chapter by Logan in this volume.)

Similar to the situation with the navy, the reason for this apparent disconnect is unclear, and it may represent an interim phase with plans for a broader overhaul of the Rocket Force in the future. However, in the meantime, the changes to the Rocket Force have been largely symbolic, with the formal elevation of the organization to a service, while it had been effectively treated as such for several years previously. Unlike the ground force, there is little indication within the Rocket Force of structure changes or unit transfers. However, like the army, the Rocket Force has been issued a new set of military unit cover designators, possibly reflecting a new set of true unit designators as well.

Conclusion

The broad objectives of China's military force reduction and overall reform effort are consistent with the strategies and goals outlined in numerous official pronouncements dating back several decades. Although these objectives may not be surprising, this does not diminish their significance. Indeed, the consistency by which Beijing approaches its overall military modernization effort speaks to the level of importance and determination associated with this effort. We can conclude that China is sincere when it announces goals such as becoming a world-class military by the middle of the 21st century and that Chinese leaders are taking the necessary steps and making the required investments to achieve these objectives within their self-imposed timeline.

Overall, Chinese military force reductions have focused on streamlining the PLA, enhancing cross-service interoperability, eliminating a culture that favors the ground forces, and emphasizing qualitative improvement of the force over quantitative measures. The 2-million-person military that will exist after the completion of this round of reforms will still be among the largest in the world, indicating that reform and force reductions will likely continue beyond the current eleventh iteration. Indeed, while many of the changes taking place within the PLA today are preparing China to become a more capable and effective regional military power, a number of additional changes will likely be required as Beijing shifts from seeking to accomplish its regional ambitions to a more global orientation.

Notes

[1] "CPC Central Committee Decision on Deepening of Reforms" [中共中央关于全面深化改革若干重大问题的决定], Xinhua [新华], November 15, 2013, available at <www.gov.cn/jrzg/2013-11/15/content_2528179.htm>.

[2] Christina Garafola, "People's Liberation Army Reforms and Their Ramifications," RAND blog, September 23, 2016, available at <www.rand.org/blog/2016/09/pla-reforms-and-their-ramifications.html>; David M. Finkelstein, *Initial Thoughts on the Reorganization and Reform of the PLA*, CNA China Studies (Arlington, VA: CNA, January 15, 2016), available at <www.cna.org/cna_files/pdf/DOP-2016-U-012560-Final.pdf>; Joel Wuthnow and Phillip C. Saunders, *Chinese Military Reform in the Age of Xi Jinping: Drivers, Challenges, and Implications*, China Strategic Perspectives 10 (Washington, DC: NDU Press, March 2017), available at <http://ndupress.ndu.edu/Portals/68/Documents/stratperspective/china/ChinaPerspectives-10.pdf>; and David M. Finkelstein, *Get Ready for the Second Phase of Chinese Military Reform*, CNA China Studies (Arlington, VA: CNA, January 2017), available at <www.cna.org/cna_files/PDF/DOP-2017-U-014677-Final.pdf>.

[3] For a discussion on the resettlement process for demobilized People's Liberation Army (PLA) soldiers and its impact on society, see John Chen, "Downsizing the PLA, Part 1: Military Discharge and Resettlement Policy, Past and Present," *China Brief* 16, no. 16 (October 26, 2016); and John Chen, "Downsizing the PLA, Part 2: Military Discharge and Resettlement Policy, Past and Present," *China Brief*

16, no. 17 (November 11, 2016). Also see the chapter by Ma Chengkun and John Chen in this volume.

⁴ Dong Zhaohui, "China Releases Guideline on Military Reform," Xinhua, January 1, 2016, available at <http://english.chinamil.com.cn/news-channels/china-military-news/2016-01/01/content_6840068.htm>; and "CPC Central Committee Decision on Deepening of Reform."

⁵ *China's National Defense in 2008* (Beijing: State Council Information Office of the People's Republic of China, January 20, 2009), available at <www.china.org.cn/government/whitepaper/node_7060059.htm>; also see Huang Weimin [黄伟民], "A Scientific Guide to Advancing Military Reform with Chinese Characteristics: Experience in Studying Jiang Zemin's Collected Works" [推进中国特色军事变革的科学指南: 学习《江泽民文选》的体会], August 31, 2006, available at <http://politics.people.com.cn/GB/30178/4762395.html>.

⁶ "China to Build World-Class Armed Forces by Mid-21ˢᵗ Century," Xinhua, October 18, 2017, available at <www.chinadaily.com.cn/china/2017-10/18/content_33403375.htm>.

⁷ For an analysis of changes and adjustments in China's military strategic guidelines, see M. Taylor Fravel, "Shifts in Warfare and Party Unity: Explaining China's Changes in Military Strategy," *International Security* 42, no. 3 (Winter 2017/2018), 37–83.

⁸ Wang Junwei, "A View of Our Nation's Military Strategic Guidelines Choices and Inspiration Based on the Development of Our National Security Interests," Party Literature, May 20, 2013.

⁹ Andrew Scobell, *Going Out of Business: Divesting the Commercial Interests of Asia's Socialist Soldiers*, East-West Center Occasional Papers No. 3 (Honolulu, HI: East-West Center, January 2000); Dean Cheng, "The Business of War: The Impact of 'PLA, Inc.' on Chinese Officers," *Joint Force Quarterly* 56 (1ˢᵗ Quarter 2010), 94–96.

¹⁰ "Army to Serve China's Modernization," *China Daily* (Beijing), December 26, 1986.

¹¹ "Accelerate Our Military's Pace Toward Fewer but Better Troops," *PLA Daily* (Beijing), October 17, 2008.

¹² "PLA Progress in Streamlining, Restructuring Continues," Xinhua, December 25, 1986; "PLA Streamlining, Reintroduction of Ranks," Xinhua, April 5, 1987.

¹³ Tu Chenxi [屠晨昕], "An Exclusive Interview with Major General Xu Guangyu: Performing Arts Troupes Bear the Brunt of Force Reduction" [本端专访徐光裕少将: 裁军文工团首当其冲], *Zhejiang Xinwen* [浙江新闻], September 3,

2015; and He Youwen and Sun Weishuai [何友文, 孙伟帅], "Chen Zhou, Research Fellow of the Academy of Military Science, Interprets the PLA Downsizing of 300,000 Personnel" [军事科学院研究员陈舟解读裁军30万], *China Military Online* [中国军网], September 10, 2015.

[14] The 1985 reduction resulted in the deactivation of Shenyang Military Region's (MR's) 68th Group Army (GA), Beijing MR's 66th and 69th GAs, Lanzhou MR's 19th GA, Jinan MR's 46th GA, Wuhan MR's 43rd GA, Nanjing MR's 60th GA, Fuzhou MR's 29th GA, Guangzhou MR's 55th GA, Kunming MR's 11th GA, and Chengdu MR's 50th GA. In 1997, the PLA deactivated Shenyang MR's 64th GA, Beijing MR's 29th GA, and Jinan MR's 67th GA, providing the PLA with a total of 21 GAs.

[15] "Three Rounds of Disarmament after Reform and Opening Up," Xinhua, July 18, 2007.

[16] Andrew Tanzer, "The People's Liberation Army, Inc.," *Forbes*, March 24, 1997, available at <www.forbes.com/forbes/1997/0324/5906044a.html#66f22e0c303f>; see also Tai Ming Cheung, *China's Entrepreneurial Army* (New York: Oxford University Press, 2001).

[17] The GAs disbanded in the 2003 force reduction included the 24th GA and 63rd GA from the Beijing MR and 23rd GA from the Shenyang MR.

[18] Dennis J. Blasko, *The Chinese Army Today: Tradition and Transformation for the 21st Century*, 2nd ed. (New York: Routledge, 2012), 75.

[19] "Defense Ministry Holds Press Conference on V-Day Parade, Cut of Troops' Number," *China Military Online*, September 3, 2015.

[20] For a discussion of the Strategic Support Force, see the chapter in this volume by John Costello and Joe McReynolds; see also Benjamin Frohman and Daniel Gearin, "China's Strategic Support Force: Seeking Dominance in the 'High' and 'New Frontiers' of National Security," paper presented at the National Bureau of Asian Research, Strategic Studies Institute, U.S. Pacific Command, and Department of the Army conference on the PLA, Carlisle Barracks, PA, October 21–23, 2016, 7.

[21] Wang Hongguang, "Former Nanjing Military Region Deputy Commander: The Korean Peninsula Has Historically 'Dragged China Down,'" *People's Daily* (Beijing), October 8, 2013.

[22] "Tibet Military Region Gamba Barracks: Please Rest Assured about the Motherland!" Xinhua, September 17, 2015.

[23] Sanjeev Miglani and Ben Blanchard, "India and China Agree to End Border Standoff," Reuters, August 28, 2017, available at <www.reuters.com/article/us-india-china/india-and-china-agree-to-end-border-standoff-idUSKCN1B80II>.

24 Wang Shibin [王士彬], "Xi Jinping Receives the Newly Adjusted and Established 84 Corps-Level Officials and Issues Orders" [习近平接见全军新调整组建84个军级单位主官并发布训令], *PLA Daily* [解放军报], April 18, 2017, available at <http://jz.chinamil.com.cn/n2014/tp/content_7567108.htm>.

25 Wu Kelei, "A Certain Brigade of the 80ᵗʰ Group Held 'STRIDE-2017 Zhurihe' Mobilization Meeting" [第 80 集团军某旅举行 '跨越—2017•朱日和' 出征誓师动员大会], *PLA Daily*, August 24, 2017; Cai Pengcheng, "More Than 40,000 People from the PLA Took Part in 'Mission Action-2013' Exercise on the 10ᵗʰ" [解放军 4 万余人 10 日起参加 '使命行动-2013' 演习], *PLA Daily*, September 10, 2013.

26 *The Diversified Employment of China's Armed Forces* (Beijing: Information Office of the State Council, April 16, 2013), available at <http://en.people.cn/90786/8209362.html>.

27 Minnie Chan, "As Overseas Ambitions Expand, China Plans 400 Percent Increase to Marine Corps Numbers, Sources Say," *South China Morning Post* (Hong Kong), March 13, 2017.

28 Zhang Tao, ed., "Chinese Marines Kicks Off Exercise Jungle-2015," *China Military Online*, September 16, 2015, available at <http://english.chinamil.com.cn/news-channels/china-military-news/2015-09/17/content_6686394.htm>.

29 "China's Military Regrouped into Five PLA Theater Commands," Xinhua, February 1, 2016, available at <www.xinhuanet.com/english/2016-02/01/c_135065429.htm>.

CHAPTER 10

THE BIGGEST LOSER IN CHINESE MILITARY REFORMS

The PLA Army

Dennis J. Blasko

Since 2004, the army officially has been listed in second place for development behind the other services in China's People's Liberation Army (PLA). Accordingly, the army's progress toward its modernization objectives has been slower and perhaps less effective than the more technical services. Nonetheless, because of China's huge landmass and despite undergoing a 55 percent decrease in manpower from 1997 to 2018, the army remains the largest service in the PLA.

China's changing international environment and strategic realities resulted in the 2015 defense white paper's announcement that the "traditional mentality that land outweighs sea must be abandoned, and great importance has to be attached to managing the seas and oceans and protecting maritime rights and interests."[1] This perhaps was the final blow to the army's traditional status of being first among the services.

To contribute to maritime and joint campaigns beyond China's borders, as well as protect China's territorial integrity and sovereignty, over the past decade the army has concentrated on developing "new-type combat forces," including army aviation, light mechanized, special operations, and digitalized (cyber/information/electronic warfare) units. It has restructured its organization by mostly abandoning the former Soviet model and seeks to make the combined arms battalion the "basic combat unit" capable of independent actions on the battlefield. It has radically refined its training program to make exercises more realistic to develop both modern combined arms and joint capabilities that have never been tested in battle. Still, its forces routinely come in second in their own red-on-blue exercises.

Though it now looks like a modern army with new uniforms and equipment, PLA leadership recognizes major shortcomings in the capabilities of many units and some of its combat leaders and staff officers. With maritime threats now dominating Chinese defense planning, the army's new capabilities likely will play a supporting role in future joint maritime or aerospace campaigns. As such, for the benefit of all the PLA, second best is good enough for the army at this stage of the force's development.

Introduction

Between the technological display of the First Gulf War and the series of military exercises during the 1995–1996 Taiwan imbroglio, the senior Chinese military leadership—led by Jiang Zemin, Liu Huaqing, Zhang Zhen, Zhang Wannian, and Chi Haotian—outlined the general parameters for the continued modernization of the PLA, a process begun in the late 1970s. The force was to become smaller but more technologically advanced with a greater focus on threats from the sea. With a new maritime emphasis, naturally the PLA Navy and aerospace forces (air force and Second Artillery) would be strengthened. Nonetheless, as a continental nation, the PLA Army would still be important and continue to be modernized, albeit without the same sense of urgency as the other services.

By the late 1990s, the Chinese Communist Party leadership, Chinese government, and Central Military Commission (CMC) increased the speed and scope of PLA modernization with many years of double-digit annual percentage increases to the defense budget, even as the PLA underwent multiple manpower reductions. When President Jiang announced the 500,000 personnel reduction in 1997, the total size of the PLA was about 3 million, with an estimated 2.2 million in the army, 265,000 in the navy, 470,000 in the air force, and 90,000 in the Second Artillery, with an official defense budget of less than $10 billion U.S. dollars.[2] The army acquired its "biggest loser" status when it was cut by 18.6 percent (amounting to over 400,000 people), while the navy, air force, and Second Artillery suffered only 11.4, 12.6, and 2.9 percent cuts, respectively.[3]

The 2004 Chinese defense white paper declared that priority of development went first to "the Navy, Air Force and Second Artillery Force, and [to] strengthen [the PLA's] comprehensive deterrence and warfighting capabilities."[4] The 2013 defense white paper announced that "China is a major maritime as well as land country,"[5] but more ominously for the army, the 2015 white paper stated:

> *The traditional mentality that land outweighs sea must be abandoned*, and great importance has to be attached to managing the seas and oceans and protecting maritime rights and interests. *It is necessary for China to develop a modern maritime military force structure commensurate with its national security and development interests*, safeguard its national sovereignty and maritime rights and interests, protect the security of strategic [sea lines of communication] and overseas interests, and participate in international maritime cooperation, so as to provide strategic support for building itself into a maritime power.[6]

As part of the 300,000-man reduction and the new tranche of reforms announced in late 2015, according to its first commander General Li Zuocheng, the army now accounts for less than half of the 2 million active-duty force (which implies an army numbering less than a million personnel, though no specific figures for any service have yet been announced).[7] The army likely will see its size, influence, and status diminish further throughout the remainder of the PLA's three-step modernization strategy, scheduled for completion in 2049.[8] At the 19th Party Congress in October 2017, Xi Jinping modified the three-step strategy, calling on the PLA to achieve mechanization by 2020; the modernization of military theory, organization, personnel, and equipment by 2035; and to become a world-class military by the middle of the 21st century.[9]

The PLA's greatest overall challenge will be the shift in collective mind-set required to actually become a modern military capable of both land and maritime operations, not simply modifying its organizational structure. Changes of this magnitude are not measured in years, but in decades and generations. Yet with 14 land neighbors and the threat of transnational terrorism and extremism, a capable but smaller army is still essential to protect the Chinese mainland, deter Taiwan independence, and provide support to maritime campaigns or other joint operations beyond China's borders. To accomplish these missions, the army is developing and expanding "new types of combat forces" [*xinxing zuozhan liliang*, 新型作战力量].

This chapter examines the army's new leadership structure, its evolving order of battle, recent training and deployments, new logistics arrangements, and changes in doctrine and the education system. Throughout the chapter, evaluations of PLA capabilities and shortcomings published by its own military media are highlighted. In general, the senior PLA leadership is skeptical of the ability of its operational commanders and units to accomplish successfully the wartime missions they could be assigned and understands that much work remains to be done to improve operational readiness.

The Army's New Headquarters and Leadership

The overall level of our military power system lags behind the world's
military powers. In particular, the Army's modernization is
relatively backward. Some problems are rather prominent.
It is necessary that we downsize and optimize its structure,
innovate its form, and strengthen its functions.[10]
—PLA Army Commander Li Zuocheng

Under the PLA's old organization, the four General Departments served as the national-level army headquarters and something of a joint staff for all the PLA. The CMC, with its own small staff, exercised command of most operational army units through the four General Departments to the military regions (MRs). Within an MR, group armies (GAs) and some military districts (MDs)—specifically Tibet, Xinjiang, Hainan, and the Beijing Garrison—commanded most operational army units (a few specialized units fell under the General Staff Department). MDs also directly commanded provincial army reserve units and army border defense units through military subdistrict (MSD)/garrison headquarters. MDs further commanded militia units through People's Armed Forces Departments (PAFDs) found below MSD/garrison level. MRs directed many logistics units through joint logistics subdepartments scattered throughout the country, while the Wuhan Rear Base and Qinghai-Tibet Depot were controlled by the General Logistics Department.

With the dissolution of the four General Departments, many senior army generals saw the scope of their responsibilities and bureaucratic clout diminish considerably with the expansion of the CMC bureaucracy to 15 functional departments, commissions, and offices. For example, General Fang Fenghui, the first chief of the CMC Joint Staff Department (prior to his removal on suspicion of bribery), oversaw a much smaller organization than in his former role as Chief of the General Staff. The leaders of the three other General Departments also saw important elements of their organizations transferred to other parts of the CMC or to army headquarters. Likewise, the newly created Strategic Support Force, commanded by Gao Jin, a former Second Artillery general, assumed responsibility for national-level cyber, electronic warfare, and space operations, which previously were overseen by mostly army officers in the General Staff and General Armament Departments and contributed further to lessening the army's parochial dominance.

When the four General Departments acted as the army service headquarters, the army, by default, held a higher status than the navy and air force. After the creation of the national-level army service headquarters [*lujun lingdao jigou*, 陆军领导机构] in Beijing with a grade of theater leader, the army now has a status equal to the other three services, including the upgraded Rocket Force.[11] Unlike his service counterparts at the time, the first army commander, General Li Zuocheng, was not made a member of the CMC. At the 19th Party Congress in October 2017, the composition of the new CMC was announced, and none of the service commanders was given a seat on the CMC. Li was named chief of the CMC Joint Staff Department and became a CMC member. General Han Weiguo, previously the Central Theater commander, succeeded Li as commander of the PLA Army; Lieutenant General Liu Lei remained as the army political commissar (PC).[12]

As a service headquarters, the new army headquarters must coordinate with the CMC structure for "construction/army building" purposes as well as with the five theater leader grade joint theater commands (TCs) for operational functions. Therefore, the army headquarters staff organization must be able to interface with both the CMC and TC headquarters structures. The army headquarters staff structure, as currently known through official media reporting, is listed below (over time greater granularity is expected):

Army Discipline Inspection Commission [陆军纪委]
- Discipline and Supervision Bureau [陆军纪委纪律检查局].

Army Staff Department [陆军参谋部]
- Operations Bureau [陆军参谋部作战局]
- Training Bureau [陆军参谋部训练局]
- Arms Bureau [陆军参谋部兵种局]
- Army Aviation Corps Bureau [陆军参谋部航空兵局]
- Administration Bureau [陆军参谋部部队管理局]
- Border and Coastal Defense Bureau [陆军参谋部边海防局]
- Planning and Organization Bureau [陆军参谋部规划与编制局][13]
- Subordinate Work Bureau [陆军参谋部直属工作局].

Army Political Work Department [陆军政治工作部]
- Organization Bureau [陆军政治工作部组织局]
- Propaganda Bureau [陆军政治工作部宣传局]

- Cadre Bureau [陆军政治工作部干部局]
- Soldier and Civilian Personnel Bureau [陆军政治工作部兵员和文职人员局]
- Art Troupe [陆军政治工作部文工团].

Army Logistics Department [陆军后勤部]
- Procurement and Supply Bureau [陆军后勤部采购供应局]
- Transportation and Delivery Bureau [陆军后勤部运输投送局]
- Health Bureau [陆军后勤部卫生局]
- Finance Bureau [陆军后勤部财务局].

Army Equipment Department [陆军装备部]
- Maintenance and Repair Support Bureau [陆军装备部维修保障局]
- Aviation Equipment Bureau [陆军装备部航空装备局].

While the Army Staff Department and Political Work Department have adopted the names found in the new CMC organization, the Logistics and Equipment Departments probably will not change to current CMC nomenclature as the CMC Equipment Development Department does not appear to be responsible for overseeing equipment repair and maintenance as the General Armament Department was.[14]

The establishment of the five joint theater commands required the formation of a new level of command for the army: the TC army headquarters [*zhanqu lujun jiguan*, 战区陆军机关], each of which is a theater deputy leader grade organization. The new TC army headquarters are the same grade as the TC navy headquarters/three fleets and the TC air forces, successors to the former MR air forces.

These TC service headquarters are important links in the chain of command from operational units up to their service headquarters in Beijing (for construction) and to the regional joint TC headquarters (for joint operations). However, instead of streamlining the old command chain from MRs to group armies, the TC army headquarters actually adds a new link, no matter how necessary, in the operational chain of command. The five TC army headquarters, not the joint TC headquarters themselves, have direct command responsibility for operational army units located in the TC's area of responsibility. Operational units have a single chain of command going only to their TC army headquarters. To facilitate communications up to both TC and army headquarters and down to their subordinate units, a communications support brigade is directly subordinate to each TC army headquarters.[15] The primary relationship of operational army units to the TC army and not the TC is reflected by the fact that all TC army units wear the generic army patch, whereas previously army units assigned to an MR wore the shoulder patch of their specific MR.

TC army commanders and PCs also serve as deputy commanders and deputy PCs for the theater. As seen in table 1, the headquarters for each TC army is located some distance from the TC headquarters (therefore, we can assume the PLA has confidence in its videoconferencing capabilities and/or the TC and TC army headquarters have assigned liaison officers to each other). TC army headquarters have been assigned four main missions, serving as:

- a campaign headquarters [*zhanyi zhihui bu*, 战役指挥部] for combat operations
- a component of the theater joint command post [*zhanqu lianzhi de zucheng bufen*, 战区联指的组成部分]
- a construction headquarters [*jianshe zhihui bu*, 建设指挥部] for routine leadership and management
- an emergency response headquarters [*yingji zhihui bu*, 应急指挥部] for any of the nontraditional security tasks they must conduct.[16]

Each newly established TC army headquarters was assigned a commander and PC. As is the normal pattern, most commanders served in a single MR (their primary MR) until promotion to group army commander and potential transfer to another MR/theater. PCs were more likely to have served in more than one MR and in different types of units throughout their career. As Saunders and Wuthnow note in chapter 13, the commander and PC of each TC army headquarters came from different geographic locations and likely did not know each other well. Over the course of the following year (into 2017), 5 of the 10 new TC army commanders and PCs were transferred out of their assignments. Chinese media did not provide explanations for the reassignments. Perhaps these officers knew from the beginning that they would be placeholders in their new positions, or perhaps the early reporting of their assignments was wrong. A New York–based Web site reported that Northern TC army PC Xu Yuanlin was dismissed for disciplinary reasons, but this has not been confirmed.[17] Table 1 identifies the new leaders and indicates which leaders have been replaced.

Table 1. Theater Command Army Leaders			
TC HQ–Location	TC Army HQ Location	Commander (Primary MR/ Previous MR/TC)	PC (Primary MR/ Previous MR/TC)
Eastern TC–Nanjing	Fuzhou	Qin Weijiang [秦卫江] (Beijing/Nanjing)	Liao Keduo [廖可铎] (Beijing/Beijing)
Southern TC–Guangzhou	Nanning	Zhang Jian [张践][1] (Guangzhou/Eastern TC)	Bai Lu [白吕] (Nanjing/Chengdu)
Western TC–Chengdu	Lanzhou	He Weidong [何卫东][2] (Nanjing/Nanjing)	Xu Zhongbo [徐忠波] (Jinan/Jinan)
Northern TC–Shenyang	Jinan	Wang Yinfang [王印芳][3] (Beijing/Central TC)	Shi Xiao [石晓][4] (Chengdu/Lanzhou)
Central TC–Beijing	Shijiazhuang	Fan Chengcai [范承才][5] (Chengdu/Southern TC)	Zhou Wanzhu [周皖柱][6] (Nanjing/Nanjing)

Key: HQ: headquarters; MR: military region; PC: political commissar; TC: theater command.

[1] Original commander Liu Xiaowu [刘小午] (Guangzhou/Guangzhou).

[2] Original commander He Qingcheng [何清成] (Lanzhou/Lanzhou).

[3] Original commander Li Qiaoming [李桥铭] (Guangzhou/Guangzhou).

[4] Original political commissar Xu Yuanlin [徐远林] (Jinan/Lanzhou).

[5] Original commander Shi Luze [史鲁泽] (Beijing/Beijing); Second Commander Zhang Xudong [张旭东] (Shenyang/Northern TC).

[6] Original political commissar Wu Shezhou [吴社洲] (Guangzhou/Jinan).

Of the original commanders, only Li Qiaoming was assigned to a new theater; the other commanders all had familiarity with their subordinate group army commanders and PCs and extensive operational knowledge of the conditions in their areas of responsibility. Conversely, all of the PCs were transferred to new theaters from their last assignments. Until evidence emerges that they purchased these new posts or otherwise obtained them through corruption or connections, it seems likely that these leaders were selected for their past performance in operational leadership assignments (primarily as unit commanders, deputy commanders, chiefs of staff and political commissars, and directors of political departments) throughout their careers. None of them served primarily in the local command chain from MSD/garrison to MD (though Qin and Shi had served as MD commanders after rising through group army assignments).

As could be expected, several TC army leaders worked with each other at various points in their careers.[18] Insights into the thinking of several new commanders and PCs can be found in interviews they have given recently or articles they have written. For example, then-army Commander Li Zuocheng and PC Liu Lei wrote in February 2016, "In particular, the modernization condition of the Army remains relatively backward, with the issues of the 'Two Inabilities' and 'Two Large Gaps'[19] existing prominently. This has become a shortcoming that restricts the building of a modern military power system with Chinese characteristics."[20]

The solutions they proposed were the same as what Li had previously outlined (as seen in the epigraph that begins this section of the chapter), which, unsurprisingly, are consistent with the current reform agenda. The fact that both critiques identify concerns about the PLA's operational leadership capabilities is a criticism made frequently in the official media. Liao Keduo, Eastern TC army PC, reiterated many of the same issues in an important August 2016 article, noting that the PLA must find its own way to reform in order to narrow the gap between it and other militaries. The army must solve contradictions and problems that have existed for a long time and *gradually* [*zhubu*, 逐步, a term used frequently by PLA leaders] change from being a "following runner to a side-by-side runner [and] eventually to a lead runner."[21]

Perhaps the most important and scathing critique of "some" PLA leaders is known as the "Five Cannots" [*wuge buhui*, 五个不会], which has been prominent in the military literature since early 2015. "Some commanders" [*bufen zhihuiyuan*, 部分指挥员]:

- cannot judge the situation
- cannot understand the intention of higher authorities
- cannot make operational decisions
- cannot deploy troops
- cannot deal with unexpected situations.[22]

Changes in organization, training, and education are aimed at solving leadership problems at all levels of the PLA. Part of the solution is to decrease the responsibilities of theater commanders and their staffs (by relieving them of responsibility for day-to-day administration [construction] requirements) and to assist battalion commanders by increasing the size of their staff.

Unlike the former MR structure, the TCs and TC army headquarters do not control the local headquarters chain of command from MD to MSD/garrison to PAFD, which is responsible for conscription/demobilization as well as command of PLA reserve and militia units. Command of the military districts and below has been assigned to the CMC's National Defense Mobilization Department, with the significant exception of the Beijing Garrison and Tibet and Xinjiang MDs, which fall under the "management" of the national-level army headquarters.[23] Each of these three organizations is responsible for sensitive regions in China, command substantial combat forces, and have therefore been given the higher organizational grade of theater deputy leader compared to the other MDs that hold army leader grades. The higher grade means that these three headquarters cannot be overseen by the National Defense Mobilization Department, which also is a theater deputy leader grade organization. This arrangement probably means that operational combat units in Beijing, Tibet, and Xinjiang report to the TC army headquarters in the area where they are assigned, who then reports to army headquarters in Beijing.

Sheng Bin, director of the CMC National Defense Mobilization Department, has stated that MD headquarters serve in five capacities:

- headquarters/command department for emergencies and combat [*yingji yingzhan de zhihui bu*, 急应战的指挥部]
- military affairs department for the local Party committee [*difang dangwei de junshi bu*, 地方党委的军事部]
- construction department for reserve forces [*houbei liliang de jianshe bu*, 后备力量的建设部]
- conscription department for the government at the provincial level [*tong ji zhengfu de bingyi bu*, 同级政府的兵役部]
- coordination department for military-civilian integration [*junmin ronghe de xietiao bu*, 军民融合的协调部].[24]

Conspicuously absent from this list of responsibilities is the supervision of border and coastal defense units. It appears that command of the PLA's border and coastal defense units is being shifted to the command of TC army headquarters, with MD headquarters no longer in the chain. One report from Heilongjiang states that border defense units are being transferred to army command and a separate report indicates that coastal defense units in Shantou have been transferred to army command.[25] Throughout the country, except in Tibet, Xinjiang, and Inner Mongolia, border defense brigades have been formed from former border defense regiments.[26] Some new border defense brigades have been reinforced with new units and equipment and are responsible for areas extending over multiple provinces.[27] Consolidating multiple border defense regiments into a single brigade will allow for a reduction in the total number of staff officers required to support the same number of troops.

Both army headquarters in Beijing and TC army headquarters have a Border and Coastal Defense Bureau/Division [*bianhaifang ju/chu*, 边海防局/处] within their respective staff departments that oversee the border and coastal defense units stationed on China's borders. Furthermore, a report has stated that a Guangdong Reserve Division has been transferred to the

Figure. Old and New Group Army Structure

2017 PLA Reformed Group Army Structure

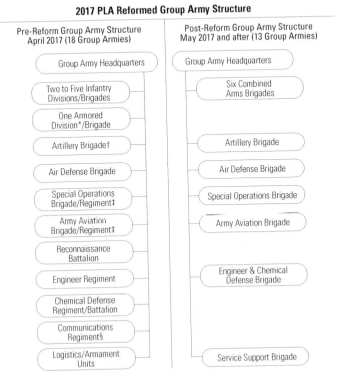

Pre-Reform Group Army Structure April 2017 (18 Group Armies)	Post-Reform Group Army Structure May 2017 and after (13 Group Armies)
Group Army Headquarters	Group Army Headquarters
Two to Five Infantry Divisions/Brigades	Six Combined Arms Brigades
One Armored Division*/Brigade	
Artillery Brigade†	Artillery Brigade
Air Defense Brigade	Air Defense Brigade
Special Operations Brigade/Regiment‡	Special Operations Brigade
Army Aviation Brigade/Regiment‡	Army Aviation Brigade
Reconnaissance Battalion	
Engineer Regiment	Engineer & Chemical Defense Brigade
Chemical Defense Regiment/Battalion	
Communications Regiment§	
Logistics/Armament Units	Service Support Brigade

*The 38th Group Army (GA) had an armored division.
†1st/42 GAs also had a long-range rocket brigade.
‡SOF/Army aviation units in some group armies.
§A few grop armies were also assigned an electronicountermeasures brigade or regiment.
Note: Prior to reform, only two GAs had similar structure.

army, which would be a change from the previous command arrangement where MDs commanded reserve units.[28] However, no mobilization staff organizations have been identified (to date) in either army headquarters in Beijing or TC army headquarters to oversee reserve unit activities.

According to unofficial reporting, provincial MD headquarters have been changing their organizational structure to include only commanders, PCs, and their deputies, while losing the former political, logistics, and armaments staff elements.[29] This is noteworthy in that several officers named for corruption have come from the MD system, and the reduction in the MD staff therefore may be an attempt to decrease the number of officers who may succumb to local temptations. Moreover, army officers are no longer the only ones who can command MD headquarters; in April 2017, in a first for the PLA, an air force major general was assigned as commander of Henan MD.[30] It is likely that many officers to be demobilized will come from this MD-MSD/garrison-PAFD chain of command.

At this time, this command structure appears to be overly complex and the details of how all these headquarters interact have yet to be explained fully to the outside world. The PLA has given itself until 2020 to work out the kinks in its new command structure.[31] Further modifications and adjustments are likely.

Army Order of Battle

Force structure remains irrational; there are too many conventional units and not enough new types of combat forces. The proportion of various arms is not balanced; officers are out of proportion to enlisted personnel. Weapons and equipment are relatively backward.[32]
—Eastern Theater Army Headquarters Political Commissar
MG Liao Keduo

The PLA Army was assessed to number about 1.6 million personnel prior to the 300,000 force reduction. That figure was more than 25 percent smaller than the estimated 2.2 million before the 1997 (500,000-man) and 2003 (200,000-man) force reductions. If, as alleged, the army now numbers less than half of a total PLA force of 2 million, the service indeed has been the biggest loser in personnel strength as a result of current reforms. To reach this bookkeeping milestone of dropping 600,000 personnel from the army's rolls, it is likely the personnel who still wear army uniforms but are assigned to the CMC staff, TC headquarters, Strategic Support Force, and new Joint Logistics Support Force are not counted against army end strength to better balance personnel among the various services and forces. This appears to be the case, as personnel assigned to each of these new organizations wear their new units' distinctive chest badges and arm patches instead of the generic army badge and patch worn by those in operational army units.

The 2013 defense white paper defined "new types of combat forces" to include "army aviation troops, light mechanized units, and special operations forces [SOF], and . . . digitalized units." It noted the army is "gradually making its units small, modular, and multifunctional in organization so as to enhance their capabilities for air-ground integrated operations, long-distance maneuvers, rapid assaults, and special operations."[33] These trends have been clearly evident in the army's changing order of battle for several years.

The 2013 white paper further revealed that 850,000 (over half) of army personnel were assigned to "mobile operational units," such as the 18 group armies and independent divisions and brigades. In early 2017, the number of operational maneuver army units assigned to group armies and independent units was estimated to include a total of approximately 21 divisions (20 infantry and 1 armored), 65 combat brigades (48 infantry and 17 armored), 12 army aviation units (7 brigades and 5 regiments), and 11 SOF units (9 brigades and 2 regiments). Additionally, some divisions and brigades were assigned smaller SOF units of battalion level or smaller.[34] Maneuver units were supported by a variety of artillery, air defense, engineer, chemical defense, and other units. Of the 18 group armies, only 2 had similar compositions of infantry and armored units. All others were uniquely configured, as were the independent combat units assigned to the Beijing Garrison Command, Xinjiang MD, and Tibet MD. The remainder of the army—some 700,000 personnel— therefore included nearly everybody in the four General Departments; MR, MD, MSD/garrison, and county-level PAFD headquarters; border and coastal defense units; and noncombatant personnel assigned to logistics/equipment support units and to the army portion of the PLA system of academies and universities.

A year after the "below-the-neck" reforms [*bozi yixia gaige*, 脖子以下 改革] began in April 2017, the number of group armies has been reduced to 13, their organization standardized and renumbered (from 71 to 83); the number of combat divisions has been cut to 6 (4 in the Xinjiang MD, 1 in the Central TC, and 1 in the Beijing Garrison), and 15 former divisions were transformed to two brigades each; and all combat brigades have been transformed into combined arms brigades [*hecheng lu*, 合成旅], and their number increased to about 82 (including three brigades in Tibet MD and 1 in Hong Kong).

Under the new standardized organization, each group army consists of six combined arms brigades and six supporting brigades, one each artillery, air defense, army aviation (or air assault [*kongzhong tuji lu*, 空中突击旅]), SOF, engineer and chemical defense [*gongbing fanghua lu*, 工兵防化旅], and service support brigade [*qinwu zhuyuan lu*, 勤务 支援旅] (see table 2). Based on Chinese media reports, combined arms brigades probably are designated either as heavy (armor or mechanized infantry) or light (light mechanized or mountain) and are assessed to command four combined arms battalions, a reconnaissance battalion, an artillery battalion, an air defense battalion, an engineer and chemical defense battalion, a communications battalion, a combat or service support battalion, and a guard and service company. Xinjiang and

Table 2. Army Transregional Exercises, 2016			
	Stride-2016 [跨越-2016] (Zhurihe)	Firepower-2016 [火力-2016] (Qingtongxia)	Firepower-2016 [火力-2016] (Shandan)
Eastern TC	Part A: 10th Armored Brigade (1st GA)	Part A: Artillery Brigade (31st GA)	Part D: Air Defense Brigade (1st GA)
Southern TC	Part D: 40th Mountain Infantry Brigade (14th GA)	Part E: Artillery Brigade (41st GA)	Part E: Air Defense Brigade (42nd GA)
Western TC	Part C: 9th Armored Brigade (47th GA)	Part B: Artillery Brigade (21st GA)	Part A: Air Defense Brigade (47th GA)
Northern TC	Part B: 77th Motorized Infantry Brigade (26th GA)	Part C: Artillery Brigade (39th GA)	Part B: Air Defense Brigade (26th GA)
Central TC	Part E: 196th Motorized Infantry Brigade (65th GA)	Part D: Artillery Brigade (54th GA)	Part C: Air Defense Brigade (65th GA)

Key: GA: group army; TC: theater command.

Tibet MDs continue to have a nonstandard structure in which both MD headquarters directly command combat units and a variety of support units, in many ways similar to a group army structure. In total, these various types of support brigades number about 87 (including those found in Xinjiang and Tibet). New combined arms battalions [*hecheng ying*, 合成营] are formed based on their primary branch (either tank or infantry) with reconnaissance, artillery (firepower), engineer, and support companies or platoons.[35]

Below-the-neck reforms have resulted in a significant increase in the number and size of new-type combat forces, such as army aviation and SOF units. Currently, each group army and the Xinjiang and Tibet MDs are assigned an army aviation brigade, for a total of 15. To form these new brigades, aircraft and personnel were transferred from the seven former brigades and five regiments and new equipment and people added. It is likely that not all army aviation brigades are at full strength, and new units will require a year or two to reach operational proficiency. Likewise, the previous 9 SOF brigades and 2 regiments have been expanded to a total of 16 SOF brigades by adding additional personnel to existing units and transforming other types of personnel and units to become SOF. Significantly, Xinjiang MD appears to have added a second SOF brigade in 2017 by combining elements of a divisional reconnaissance unit and the previously existing SOF brigade to form a new brigade stationed in Nanjiang.[36]

The army appears to have transformed one motorized infantry brigade in Shandong and multiple coastal defense units in Fujian and Shandong into four new marine brigades. As a result of the creation of these four new units, when added to the two previously existing marine brigades in the South Sea Fleet, it is likely there are now a total of six marine brigades, with two assigned to/located in each TC navy.[37]

Over time, additional details of changes to the army's order of battle probably will be discovered through continuing analysis of media reports.

Army Equipment and Battalion Staff Developments

Many military units are still upgrading equipment; the problem of new and old equipment "three generations living under one roof" is relatively prominent.[38]

The total number of personnel in operational combat and combat support units (for example, infantry, armor, artillery, SOF, army aviation, engineers, electronic/cyber warfare, and chemical defense) is probably about half that of the late 1990s. Today's smaller force is being equipped with new uniforms and personal equipment, newer tanks, armored fighting vehicles, artillery (both towed and self-propelled), helicopters, unmanned aerial vehicles (UAVs), small arms and crew-served weapons, and other support equipment and electronics. Due to the size of the force and the relatively limited production of new equipment by the Chinese defense industries, equipment modernization has been a long, drawn out process. However, reflecting the army's lower priority for modernization, all army units do not necessarily receive the best equipment the Chinese defense industries can produce.

Specifically, in 2016 *China Daily* reported that the Type-96B main battle tank—not the more advanced and expensive Type-99 series—has been selected to be the "backbone of China's tank force," replacing most older models. This appears to be supported by current inventory numbers suggesting that the second best tank has been judged to be sufficient for the most likely ground contingencies the PLA may encounter in coming decades. The *China Daily* report also stated the PLA had "more than 7,000 tanks in active service, including about 2,000 Type-96s and Type-96As, as well as about 600 Type-99s and Type-99As, so the majority of the PLA armored force is still equipped with tanks made several decades ago."[39] Those 7,000 tanks included five types of main battle tanks (Types 59, 79, 88, 96, 98/99), each with variants and three types of light tanks (Types 62 and 63A and ZTD-05). In 2018, the *Military Balance* counted a total of 6,740+ main battle tanks, with 3,390 of the Type 96/98/99 series, just slightly above half the total inventory.[40] Type 96–series tanks account for 37 percent of the force, with Type 98/99 series at 13 percent.

It is not unusual for up to 10 types and variants of a single category of equipment, such as tanks and armored personnel carriers/infantry fighting vehicles, to be found in the army and other services. The large number of variants and types of similar equipment complicates training, maintenance, and repair, especially when units go to the field. The Chinese refer to this condition as "three generations under one roof" [*sandai tongtang*, 三代同堂]. Xi's goal of achieving modernization of equipment by 2035 probably seeks, in part, to minimize this situation by eliminating weapons and equipment produced from the 1960s to 1980s and increasing the proportion of newer models throughout the entire PLA.

New weapons and technologies allow army units to move faster over more difficult terrain, including bodies of water; shoot farther and faster; and integrate their capabilities with those found in the other services more than ever before. Army commanders now have a variety of means to attack opponents out to 150 kilometers beyond their frontlines, including long-range multiple rocket launchers and artillery, attack helicopters, SOF teams, nonlethal electronic warfare and possibly cyber weapons, and supporting PLA Air Force aircraft and armed UAVs. They are supported by an ever-expanding array of ground, air, and space reconnaissance and surveillance capabilities to locate and identify potential targets. Such new capabilities, however, require new types of staff procedures and decisionmaking to select the appropriate weapons for various targets. These developments, along with massive amounts of data now available from advanced computer and communications technologies, have stressed commanders and staff in units at all levels, especially at battalion-level headquarters.

One of the most important lessons the army has learned in the past decade is that battalion commanders do not have sufficient staff to command and control combined arms operations. Recent reporting indicates that units are adding a deputy battalion commander, a battalion master sergeant [*yingshi guanzhang*, 营士官长], chief of staff [*yingcan mouzhang*,

营参谋长], and four staff officers or noncommissioned officers [*canmou*, 参谋] (NCOs) to assist the battalion commander and political instructor. Though the exact composition of the battalion staff may not yet be finalized, it appears that the following types of staff personnel have been determined as necessary:

- an operations and reconnaissance officer [*zuozhen canmou*, 作侦参谋]
- artillery/firepower and engineering officer [*paogong canmou/huoli canmou*, 炮工参谋/ 火力参谋]
- information and communications officer [*xinxi tongxin/tongxin canmou*, 信息通信/通信参谋]
- support officer [*zhanqin canmou*, 战勤参谋].[41]

No discussion has been found, however, concerning how many assistants each of these staff officers/NCOs would need in order to conduct 24-hour operations for extended periods. Standardizing these changes throughout the army will require formal modification to battalion structure and changes to the professional education and training system to prepare both officers and NCOs for these new responsibilities.

The distribution of staff responsibilities described above was seen in a recent report about a command information system [*zhihui xinxi xitong*, 指挥信息系统] set up in 2016 in the former 20th Group Army. Previously, existing information systems in its various subordinate units, such as infantry, armor, artillery, and air defense, were incompatible, and commands had to be issued separately to the units. To communicate directly with its subordinate units, the headquarters set up a command information system composed of "one network, four chains" [*yiwang silian*, 一网四链]: the command basic network, command and control chain, reconnaissance and intelligence chain, firepower chain, and logistics and equipment support chain.[42] The four staff functional responsibilities at battalion level would mesh seamlessly into such a system, which would also be found at the intervening division and brigade levels.

Fewer units and personnel mean that it will take fewer new weapons and equipment to modernize the force. Nonetheless, the army is still so large (more than twice the size of the active-duty U.S. Army) that all units cannot be equipped at the same time. Though the current reforms are geared to solve previously identified problems, new shortcomings are discovered with nearly each deployment of new equipment and in every round of field training.

Recent Training and Other Deployments

Solving the "Five Cannots" and improving command combat capabilities is an urgent task in strengthening training and preparing for war.[43]

The PLA acknowledges that there is "a large gap between the PLA's level of training and the requirements of actual combat," which is a major contradiction in its modernization process.[44] Increasing the level of realism in all PLA training by reducing formalism and cheating has been a perennial goal for decades and is frequently enunciated by the most senior PLA leaders.[45] As indicated by this typical assessment found in a 2016 *PLA Daily* staff commentator article, though the force has made some progress, the general level of advanced, integrated joint operations capabilities is lacking and more must be done to overcome the force's deficiencies: "Through development over the past more than 10 years, substantial progress has been made in our military's system-of-systems building. Yet, the overall system-of-systems operational capability remains rather weak. In some aspects, defects and weaknesses are still quite obvious."[46]

As an institution, the PLA correctly identifies the crux of the training problem to be a leadership problem at all levels, especially at battalion level and above. They often use the formula "In training soldiers, train officers [or generals] first" [*lianbing xian lianguan/lianbing xian lianjiang*, 练兵先练官/练兵先练将] to focus on the necessity of training commanders and their staffs to command and control both joint and combined arms operations.[47] That slogan underscores the problems of "some leaders" in the previously mentioned formulaic assessments known as the Two Inabilities and Five Cannots.

As Zhang Xudong, former commander of the 39th Group Army, wrote in July 2016, the PLA is a latecomer in conducting modern joint operations; its theory and practice are not yet mature.[48] For the past decade, the PLA has been seeking to push command of joint operations down to division and brigade levels [*bingtuan*, 兵团] and to enable modularized [*mokuaihua*, 模块化], combined arms battalions [*hechengying*, 合成营] to become the "basic combat unit" [*jichu zhanshu danyuan*, 基础战术单元] capable of independent actions on the battlefield.[49] (Comparatively speaking, other militaries have multiple decades of combat experience in those levels of joint and combined arms operations.)

Conducting operations at battalion level requires major change to the way the majority of army officers have been trained since the 1950s when the Soviet system of command was adopted. Under the now mostly discarded Soviet system (which is still found in the remaining PLA divisions), regiments were the lowest level at which combined arms operations were executed, and regimental headquarters did all the planning and staff work for battalions. With the "brigadization" of the force, which eliminates the regiment from the chain of command down to maneuver battalions, battalions now must be capable of planning operations and conducting them on their own. This has caused anxiety for many battalion commanders who have not been adequately trained to handle such tasks and has resulted in frequent critiques of poor coordination among units from the various arms assigned to combined arms battalions. As commander of the 41st Group Army in 2015 (before becoming commander of the Northern TC army), Li Qiaoming observed that some individual commanders had not studied adequately or were stuck in traditional modes of operations and were not able to utilize the new types of combat forces assigned to them.[50] As a result, army large unit exercises (above battalion level) emphasize leadership/staff training and evaluation as much as small unit (battalion and below) maneuver, firepower, and support operations.

A principal tool in breaking the PLA's traditional mode of operational thinking has been the roughly 74 division and brigade transregional exercises [*kuaqu yanxi*, 跨区演习] conducted from 2006 to 2016. For most of the past 70 years, army units prepared to conduct operations almost exclusively in the regions where they were located. Units concentrated on fighting potential regional enemies in familiar terrain and climatic conditions. This approach required large standing forces spread throughout the country and minimized the need for military sea and air strategic lift. As the PLA reduced its size and increased its level of weapons technology, the need to develop units that could operate outside the areas in which they were garrisoned and cooperate with forces from the other services became apparent. Most transregional exercises display some degree of joint interoperability; often headquarters or reconnaissance units are transported by air, air force aircraft provide support to ground operations, and some sea movements and amphibious operations have been included, as well as conventional support from Second Artillery/ Rocket Force units. The majority of transregional exercises were under army command, but a few have been led by navy or air force headquarters.

The first major, but unnamed, transregional exercise was held in September 2006 when the 190th Mechanized Infantry Brigade/39th GA/ Shenyang MR deployed to the Zhurihe Combined Arms Training Base in the Beijing MR. None were held in 2007, but in 2008 Jinan MR held the exercise Sharpening Troops 2008, in which the 58th Light Mechanized Brigade/20th GA traveled to Zhurihe in August, followed by exercise Joint 2008 in September, in which the 138th Motorized Infantry Brigade/26th GA undertook a sea movement from Yantai to a landing area near Dalian, Liaoning.[51]

Beginning in 2009, transregional exercises have become the marquee events in the army's annual training cycle, generating massive amounts of domestic media attention. Each exercise has been slightly different, but all involve sequential (but not simultaneous) deployments—using road, rail, military and/or civilian air, and sometimes sea transport—from home base to a distant large training base while undergoing enemy harassment or attack. After organizing for combat at the training base, several days of live-fire drills and confrontation drills between red force (friendly) and blue force (enemy) units ensued. Missions sometimes were changed to test the adaptability of commanders and staff. Observers evaluated all phases of the exercise using a 1,000-point scale. Some units underwent computer exercises in preparation for these (and other) events.

From 2006 through 2015, roughly 35 infantry and armored divisions and brigades participated in the series of Stride-2009, Mission Action–2010, Mission Action–2013, Stride-2014, and Stride-2015 exercises, which were organized by all seven MR headquarters (see appendix 1 for a chart listing each exercise and the red force unit involved). In 2014, for the first time, artillery and air defense brigades were tested in the series of 10 Firepower-2014 transregional exercises. The Firepower-2015 series sent seven artillery brigades to the Qingtongxia training area and seven air defense brigades to the Shandan training area (see appendix 2 for a chart listing each Firepower exercise and the red force unit involved). In 2015, a total of 29 brigades of all types took part in transregional training, an all-time high for such training. None of the red forces defeated the blue forces in any of the 29 exercises. To date, the only red force identified as having won a transregional brigade-level exercise is the 68th Mechanized Infantry Brigade/16th GA in Stride-2014 Zhurihe D.[52] Similar to the U.S. Army experience training at the National Training Center, red force units coming in second in most exercises is not unusual.

In 2016, army headquarters in Beijing organized the Stride and Firepower exercise series, which involved one infantry or armored brigade and one artillery and air defense brigade from each of the five new theaters' area of responsibility for a total of 15 exercises.[53] In 2017, as below-the-neck reforms were under way, army headquarters organized four of the nine Stride and Firepower exercises.[54] No sponsor was designated for the other five exercises. The Chinese media only reported on four of these exercises, Stride-2017 Zhurihe (combined arms), Firepower-2017 Qingtongxia (artillery), Firepower-2017 Shandan (air defense), and Sharp Edge–2017 Queshan (the first for SOF units). The reduction in number of transregional exercises probably was related to the disruption caused by the creation of new joint and service headquarters, which were focused on organizing and training their own newly assigned personnel to perform their duties. If, as expected, transregional joint exercises continue in future years, most probably will be organized and overseen by the various TC headquarters, following the guidance that the "CMC is in overall control, theaters are responsible for operations, and the services are responsible for construction" [*junwei guanzong, zhanqu zhuzhan, junzhong zhujian*, 军委管总, 战区主战, 军种主建].

The 15 transregional exercises held in 2016 specifically were intended to address the leadership problem of the Five Cannots.[55] These exercises were further targeted to improve SOF, electronic countermeasures, army aviation, and other new-type combat forces capabilities, while operating jointly with air force and Strategic Support Force units.[56] The units participating in 2016 transregional exercises are identified in table 2. Units from 11 of the then 18 group armies participated.

Reviewing the units involved in the totality of transregional exercises, it is apparent that units from all MRs and theaters participated in mostly equal proportions. Of the over 70 transregional exercises conducted from 2006 to 2016, only the 58th Light Mechanized Infantry Brigade/20th GA and 235th Motorized Infantry Brigade/27th GA are known to have participated in more than one exercise. This implies that no unit or region is considered more important than another and that all units must be prepared to conduct operations outside their home areas.

Another important development is the shift from both divisions and brigades participating from 2006 to 2013 to only brigades in 2014 and the expansion of the exercises to include artillery and air defense brigades. Perhaps even more significant, however, Mission Action–2013C was commanded by the air force in a major step toward jointness in the PLA. This segment of the three-part exercise primarily was an aerial exercise with support from ground-based missile and naval units.[57] Since that time, both navy and air force headquarters have commanded a handful of other joint exercises.[58]

Units not participating in transregional events conduct a variety of exercises within their home regions, some of which are joint, such as annual amphibious landing training. Many of these large exercises are named and receive Chinese media attention, but not all are publicized. They follow an annual training plan previously promulgated by MR headquarters, but in the future will probably be a joint effort involving both TC and service head-quarters passed down to TC army headquarters for execution. Training plans highlight functions to be emphasized over the year, such as night operations or air support to ground operations, and also must coordinate and deconflict other training and operational events, such as exercises with foreign coun-tries, military competitions, parades, and peacekeeping (PKO) deployments.

Because of the reorganization under way in 2016, some training events were slight aberrations from previous practice. Although the army par-ticipated in nearly 20 exercises with foreign militaries in 2016, Chinese participation was relatively small in scale. A few examples include:

- Khan Quest 2016, an international PKO exercise in Mongolia
- Exercise Tropic Twilight–2016, in which the PLA sent seven personnel to a disaster relief exercise in New Zealand
- Exercise Kowari 2016, involving small units from China, the United States, and Australia
- Panda-Kangaroo 2016, with Chinese and Australia forces
- ADMM-Plus, a humanitarian assistance, disaster relief, medical exercise in Thailand involving 18 countries with some 450 to 500 PLA personnel
- Peace Mission 2016, for which the PLA dispatched 270 personnel to an anti-terrorist exercise in Kyrgyzstan.

Perhaps the most important aspect of these exercises was that the South-ern TC oversaw the joint deployment to the ADMM-Plus exercise and the Western TC was in charge of Peace Mission 2016.[59] In 2017, while units were being reorganized, the number of army exercises with foreign militaries was cut to about six.

In previous years, most army exercises with foreign countries focused on anti-terrorist missions—sometimes with a heavy conventional combat role as seen in the Peace Mission series—and humanitarian/disaster relief operations. Many exercises were relatively small, involving a company-size or smaller element, frequently featuring SOF personnel. The number of army exercises held annually has generally increased from year to year, from 1 in 2002 when the first event was held to 10 or more since 2014, depending on what exercises are included. Although units from all MRs have participated in exercises with foreign militaries, MRs on China's western and southern borders (Lanzhou, Chengdu, and Guangzhou) provided troops most often.

Though the PLA has sent units to international military competitions in previous years, in 2016 the level of their participation was unprecedented. The 14th GA sent 10 personnel to a jungle patrol competition in Brazil, and the 26th GA sent 5 personnel from a SOF brigade to a sniper competition in Kazakhstan.[60] But the PLA's largest level of participation was at the International Army Games in Russia from July 30 to August 13, involving 1,066 personnel from all services, multiple GAs, and 11 provinces. Army units competed in 17 events including "armor, artillery, air defense, reconnaissance, engineering, chemical defense, special warfare, aviation, airborne and other professional operations, as well as repair, field kitchen, health service and other support."[61] In total, PLA teams competed in 21 events and "won the first place in one contest, the second place in eighteen contests, and the third place in two contests."[62] The PLA used its own Type-96Bs in the tank competition, while all other participants used Russian-made T-72B3s.[63] The PLA team finished second, with one tank losing a road wheel during the competition.[64] This trend of active participation in international competitions continued in the 2017 training season.

United Nations (UN) Peacekeeping Operations are another significant category of activity that has been exclusively assigned to army units. Like other high-profile events, responsibility for providing troops to UN PKO deployments has been distributed throughout most of the army, though it appears that units from the former Nanjing MR have not been so tasked. For example, units from Shenyang MR's 16th and 39th GAs provided troops to the mission to Mali; units from the Beijing MR and the 27th and 38th GAs have provided units for the missions in Liberia, Congo, and South Sudan;

Lanzhou MR's 21st GA and Xinjiang MD units have also sent units to the Congo; elements from Yunnan and the 13th and 14th GAs have been sent to Lebanon; and all GAs from the former Jinan MR have participated in deployments to Sudan, South Sudan, and Darfur.

The vast majority of units and personnel deployed to UN PKO mission have been engineers and transport and medical specialists. However, in January 2012, the PLA sent a "guard unit" from the 162nd Motorized Infantry Division/54th GA/Jinan MR to South Sudan and a "guard detachment" from the Shenyang MR to Mali in late 2013.[65] The size of these forces ranged from about a platoon to company size (170 personnel). In late 2014, the army deployed its first infantry battalion to the mission in South Sudan. The 700-strong force was composed of personnel from a motorized infantry brigade in the 26th GA and two companies from a division of the 54th GA.[66] While press reports called this an "organic infantry battalion," it was in fact a composite battalion formed from units from two different group armies. The second rotation in 2015 apparently was an organic infantry battalion, this time from the 20th GA.[67] While PLA infantry battalion commanders usually are majors, it is notable that colonels (two ranks higher than majors) were assigned as commanders of these PKO battalions. This could indicate both the PLA's attitude that these are important missions for which a higher ranking commander is appropriate and a lack of confidence that a major is ready for such responsibilities.

By assigning PKO missions to many units, the army has allowed the responsibility and experience of overseas deployments to be shared by multiple headquarters. This indicates senior leadership trust in the abilities of units from various parts of China to perform these highly visible missions and the desire for many to learn from overseas deployments. Prior to deployment, units undergo specialized preparatory training, which removes them from routine responsibilities for an even longer period than the 8 months to a year that they are deployed. Depending on circumstances, units from any part of the army may also be deployed on domestic disaster relief missions. Though emergencies may interrupt routine training, these deployments provide units with excellent opportunities for small unit leadership problem-solving and real-world helicopter, communications, and logistics support operations, often in adverse weather and terrain conditions.

New Logistics Arrangements

The traditional support model of our army is weak, with specialties not unified, backward technologies, and scattered resources making it difficult to complete system support tasks based on information systems.[68]

After the establishment of the General Armament Department in 1998, armament (or equipment) departments were added to headquarters organizations throughout the PLA. Among other duties, the Armament Department was in charge of equipment repair and maintenance as well as ammunition supply. The Logistics Department was responsible for finance, supply, fuel, food, uniforms, health care, and housing. However, these responsibilities became intertwined at the lower levels of the operational chain of command. For example, units in the field need to be resupplied with ammunition at the same time they are supplied food, water, and fuel. Transportation units need to be able to repair and perform maintenance on vehicles anywhere when in the field. As a result, small units from both the logistics and equipment systems often would locate themselves in the same general vicinity when in the field, sometimes operating together.

In 2012, PLA leadership acknowledged this reality by merging the Logistics and Armament departments at division and brigade levels into a single Support Department [*baozhang bu*, 保障部] and Support Office [*baozhang chu*, 保障处] at the regimental level. During the 2017 reforms, group armies, TC army headquarters, and the Xinjiang and Tibet MDs also have formed Support departments within their headquarters.[69] Moreover, each group army has established a service support brigade that is comprised of logistics, maintenance, communications, UAV, and electronic warfare units.[70]

The merger of logistics and armament departments into a single support department is consistent with the division of responsibilities between the CMC Logistic Support Department and Equipment Development Department. As suggested by its name, Equipment Development focuses primarily on equipment acquisition, research and development, and has transferred its repair and maintenance responsibilities to the services as a part of their "construction" responsibilities.

A major change to the former logistics structure was announced in September 2016 with the creation of the CMC Joint Logistics Support Force [*zhongyang junwei lianqin baozhang budui*, 中央军委联勤保障部队]. The "force" is comprised of the Wuhan Joint Logistics Support Base [*Wuhan lianqin baozhang jidi*, 武汉联勤保障基地] and five joint logistics support centers [*lianqin baozhang zhongxin*, 联勤保障中心] at Wuxi, Guilin, Xining, Shenyang, and Zhengzhou, with one center located in each of the new TCs.[71] It appears the Joint Logistics Support Force has incorporated many of the subordinate elements of the former 20-odd, division leader grade joint logistics sub-departments [*lianqin fenbu*, 联勤分部] into its structure, with their supply bases and depots, hospitals, and transportation units being resubordinated among the Wuhan Joint Logistics Support Base and the five joint logistics support centers, while some logistics units are being transferred to the services.[72] (See the chapter by Luce and Richter in this volume for analysis of PLA logistics and the creation of the Joint Logistics Support Force.)

The Ministry of National Defense spokesman provided a bit more information about the responsibilities of the new logistics force, noting that "special-purpose materials and equipment are supported by arms and services themselves, [g]eneral-purpose materials and equipment are supported by the joint logistic support force."[73] Such a division of labor existed previously among the former joint logistics and armament systems and the services. A graphic described the Joint Logistics Support Force's "focus of support" [*zhongdian baozhang*, 重点保障] as finance, housing, uniforms, food, transportation, and hospitals. Therefore, the army and other services must retain their own logistics systems to provide the specific functions that the new Joint Logistics Support Force does not. Exactly how that will be done has yet to be revealed and is probably the subject of experimentation and eventual further modification.

Changes in Doctrine and the Education System

[Military reform] *must address the shortage of officers who have a deep knowledge of joint combat operations and advanced equipment,* [a researcher in the Human Resources Department at the PLA Xi'an Political Academy] *said. "We have developed and deployed many cutting-edge weapons, including some that are the best in the world, but there are not enough soldiers to use many of those advanced weapons,"* he said. *"In some cases, soldiers lack knowledge and expertise to make the best use of their equipment."*[74]

The changes in PLA command and control, force structure, and logistics system will necessitate adjustments to its operating procedures and methods, what may also be called doctrine. The shift to a more joint, maritime-oriented force will also require changes to the way the PLA educates and trains its officers and NCOs. (See the chapter by Wuthnow and Saunders in this volume for more details.)

An obvious consequence of the 300,000-man reduction is that the number of officers in the PLA will be reduced. One report predicted that half of the total cuts would affect officers.[75] Accordingly, the number of cadets selected to attend the PLA and People's Armed Police system of academies was reduced in 2016 and 2017 from the 2015 intake. See appendix 3 for the numbers announced from 2005 to 2017. (The manner by which these numbers have been reported has varied over time, sometimes making year-to-year comparisons difficult.) Moreover, in 2017, *PLA Daily* announced that the National Defense Student program, which began around the year 2000, will no longer recruit (and pay) high school graduates or students already in college; instead, the military will select and recruit national defense students from graduates of civilian institutes of higher learning.[76] This change to the National Defense Student program suggests that perhaps the system was not producing the results previously expected and that by selecting graduates, rather than freshmen, the PLA can adjust the numbers based on current needs and the students' functional majors as required.

Just as important, the areas of study for the new students will be adjusted to better support the changing force structure. In 2016, the CMC Training Administration Department announced:

> Compared with last year, 24 percent fewer students will be admitted to studies related to the army, including the infantry and artillery, while logistic and support departments will see their recruits fall by 45 percent. . . . In comparison, students studying in aviation, missile, and maritime fields will increase by 14 percent. The number of recruits in sectors where there is an urgent need, such as space intelligence, radar and drones, will rise by 16 percent.[77]

These percentages show the army (and logistics forces) coming in second once more to the other services and the Strategic Support Force. Similarly, the number of PLA graduate students will be reduced in 2017, and their fields of study altered to support new requirements, most of which are not in the army:

> the number of graduate students will be reduced to 6,000 and that of doctoral students to 1,475, a decrease of 16.7 percent and 19.2 percent year-on-year, respectively. The goals of the enrolment plan in 2017 are to reduce the enrolment of students majoring in science, engineering, and medicine, and to increase the recruitment of those majoring in military-related fields, especially the fields that are closely related to construction of new-type combat forces, including strategic early warning, military aerospace, air defense and anti-missile, information-based operation, and strategic projection.[78]

As the services are rebalanced in the future, the components of the PLA education system will likely continue to be modified to provide appropriate numbers of graduates for each service and functional specialty, not only for officers but also for NCOs. For example, former academies have been merged or consolidated. Additionally, curricula in all PLA academies and universities can be expected to change to better prepare officers and NCOs for joint and combined arms operations. In particular, courses for staff officers and NCOs from battalion level up must focus on the integration of all the new types of high-technology weapons and support required to conduct maritime and aerospace operations in addition to campaigns on land. Some of this work likely will also be conducted at training bases at various points in a soldier's career after graduation from an academy or university.

In the coming years, both the PLA's education and training systems will have to work in unison to change "Big Army" [*dalujun*, 大陆军] thinking that has dominated the Chinese military for nearly a century. This shift in mindset will not occur quickly and not without pain for many still on active duty. Compared to the "old soldiers," this change will be easier for younger, more junior personnel and those just entering the service. But it is not assured that the international environment and the senior civilian Chinese leadership will be accommodating enough to allow the PLA the time it needs to make all the refinements it deems necessary to develop a modernized education structure to prepare officers and NCOs for advanced system-of-systems operations.

Conclusion

Improving the army's combat strength has become a major focus.
But the modernization level of the Chinese army is inadequate to
safeguard national security, and it lags far behind advanced global peers.
The Chinese army is not capable enough of waging modern warfare, and
officers lack command skills for modern warfare.[79]

The epigraph is one of the few instances, if not the only example, of the Two Large Gaps and Two Inabilities assessments *in English* carried by the Chinese military media (though it did not include those specific names). These and other self-assessments of the PLA's overall and functional capabilities have not made it into any of the series of defense white papers intended primarily for foreign consumption. Instead, the countless inward-looking criticisms are directed at the PLA itself in its Chinese-language media. They usually are found after a description of some type of progress the PLA has achieved. But most importantly, they underscore that everyone must work harder before the PLA can join the ranks of advanced militaries.

Despite the new uniforms and equipment and glowing reports in the Chinese media, despite the parades (there is little doubt that the PLA can outperform all foreign competition on the parade ground), despite new cyber, space, and missile capabilities, as much as it looks like a modern force, the PLA has yet to demonstrate that it can operate with the first tier of advanced militaries throughout the world. While true for the PLA as a whole, this judgment applies even more to the army.

Based only on the types of organizational reforms in motion and the open source reporting of the type and content of exercises the PLA conducts, the emphasis on improving leadership and staff abilities and conducting joint and combined arms operations is warranted. For the army, it seems likely that many individual soldiers, squads, platoons, and companies can perform their missions proficiently. (The level of tactical proficiency may vary from unit to unit and be higher in some units in other services.) But putting these units together to operate as combined arms teams at battalion level, acting independently or as part of larger units in joint operations, is an acknowledged shortcoming. The PLA's ultimate objective frequently is referred to in the Chinese literature as "turning strong fingers [small units/service arms] into a hard fist [combined arms/joint operations]."[80] The below-the-neck reforms that created combined arms brigades and battalions may help in achieving this objective, but without properly educated and trained battalion commanders and staff, it may result in small units from the non-infantry or armored branches assigned to combined arms brigades not being as fully prepared to perform their specific battlefield functions as they would be if they were part of a larger brigade of their own specialty.

Fixing these problems has been a perpetual training objective and requires additional changes in education, unit structure, and doctrine that must be formalized and implemented throughout the entire army, not just in experimental units. While the PLA has begun to address these issues over the past 10 to 15 years, many other militaries have conducted combined arms operations at the battalion level and joint operations employing larger formations in combat for multiple decades, and even they must continue to refine organization, tactics, and procedures based on changing realities.

As the army seeks to address these challenges, it also is attempting to demonstrate that it has a role in the PLA's larger maritime doctrine. Several new types of combat forces can contribute to operations conducted beyond China's landmass: helicopter units are now operating over water or from ships and may conduct attack and reconnaissance missions at sea; SOF units can be delivered to distant targets by a variety of means to conduct raids and reconnaissance; long-range multiple rocket launcher units, air defense, and electronic warfare units can be integrated into multiservice groups to defend China's exclusive economic zones; and army UAVs can be integrated into surveillance operations and perhaps eventually strike missions. Such missions, however, will be conducted as part of joint operations and all levels of army headquarters must be equipped and trained to function within that joint structure.

The tasks described above mainly involve units up to battalion size; getting larger units, especially conventional infantry and armored brigades, to distant battlefields will require strategic air and sea lift from the other services or civilian assets beyond the army's span of control. Once again, lack of strategic lift is an acknowledged PLA shortfall, but one that is beginning to be addressed by adding Y-20 large transport aircraft and a variety of amphibious ships and vessels (for example, Type-071 LPDs and Zubr air-cushioned craft) to the PLA, augmented by civilian aircraft and roll-on/roll-off ships, some of which are now designed to military specifications.

Though senior army leaders have been assigned to the vast majority of new joint command and senior staff positions, the stage has been set for non-army leaders to move into more of these slots in the future. With Vice Admiral Yuan Yubai's promotion to commander of the Southern TC and air force General Yi Xiaoguang's assignment as Central TC commander, the PLA has achieved a milestone in its modernization program and quest for jointness. Likewise, in the future, more joint exercises must be organized and led by non-army officers and staffs if the PLA is to acquire the joint capabilities necessary to conduct maritime and aerospace campaigns. As all this occurs, the army will lose the dominant role it enjoyed in past decades. The difficulty in changing the PLA's institutional mindset from an army-led land power to an advanced maritime/aerospace joint force capable of operating far beyond China's shores—and the time required to achieve these objectives—should not be underestimated. To accomplish its modernization goals, the army will have to accept its position as the PLA's biggest loser, now and far into the future, or else squander the progress made since China's last major conflict with a foreign enemy.

Appendix 1. Red Units (Inf/Arm Divs/Bdes) in Major Named Transregional Exercises, 2006–2015

MR (Total Exercises 2006–2015)	2006/2008	Stride-2009	Mission Action-2010	Mission Action-2013	Stride-2014 (Zhurihe/Sanjie)	Stride-2015 (Zhurihe)	Stride-2015 (Taonan/Sanjie/Queshan)
Shenyang (5)	2006: UI exercise, 190th Mech Inf Bde (39th GA)	115th Mech Inf Div (39th GA)			68th Mech Inf Bde (16th GA) Note: the only Red Unit judged to have "won"	119th Mtr Inf Bde (40th GA); UI Arm Bde (40th GA)	
Beijing (5)			188th Mech Inf Bde (27th GA)		235th Mech Inf Bde (27th GA)	80th Mtr Inf Bde (27th GA); 235th Mtr Inf Bde (27th GA); UI Arm Bde (65th GA)	
Lanzhou (5)		61st ("Red Army") Div (21st GA)	139th Mech Inf Bde (47th GA)		55th Mtr Inf Bde (47th GA)	UI Arm Bde (21st GA)	Mtr Inf Bde (47th GA)
Jinan (6)	Sharpening Troops 2008, 58th Lt Mech Bde (20th GA); Joint 2008, 138th Mtr Inf Bde (26th GA)	162nd Mtr Inf Div (54th GA)			58th Lt Mech Inf Bde (20th GA)	UI Mech Inf Bde (26th GA)	UI Arm Bde (54th GA)
Nanjing (5)				Part A: 86th Mtr Inf Div (31st GA)	UI Arm Bde (12th GA); 34th Mech Inf Bde (12th GA)	3rd Mtr Inf Bde (1st GA)	179th Mtr Inf Bde (12th GA)
Guangzhou (5)		121st Mtr Inf Div (41st GA)		Part B: 124th Amph Mech Inf Div (42nd GA)	122nd Mech Inf Bde (41st GA)	UI Arm Bde (41st GA)	UI Arm Bde (42nd GA)
Chengdu (4)			149th Mech Inf Div (13th GA)		UI Arm Bde (14th GA)	42nd Mtr Inf Bde (14th GA)	52nd Mnt Inf Bde (Tibet MD)
Total 35	3	4	3	2	8	10	5

Source: Chinese media reports.

Key: Amph: amphibious; Arm: armored; Bde: brigade; Div: division; GA: group army; Inf: infantry; Lt: light; Mech: mechanized; Mtn: mountain; Mtr: motorized; UI: unidentified.

Appendix 2. Units Participating in Artillery and Air Defense Transregional Exercises, 2014–2015		
Firepower-2014 (Total live exercises: 10)	Firepower-2015 (Qingtongxia) (Total live exercises: 7)	Firepower-2015 (Shandan) (Total live exercises: 7)
*Nanjing Part A: Nanjing Artillery Academy and 38th GA Artillery Brigade	*Nanjing Part A: Nanjing Artillery Academy and 20th GA Artillery Brigade	
*Zhengzhou: Air Defense Academy and 47th GA Air Defense Brigade	*Nanjing Part D: Nanjing Artillery Academy and 16th GA Artillery Brigade	
*Leting: Air Defense Academy and 40th GA Air Defense Brigade		
Korla Part A: 1st GA Long-range Rocket Brigade	Qingtongxia Part A: 20th GA Artillery Brigade	Shandan Part A: 28th GA Air Defense Brigade
Shandan: Tibet MD Air Defense Brigade	Qingtongxia Part B: 13th GA Artillery Brigade	Shandan Part B: Xinjiang MD Air Defense Brigade
Taonan Part A: 65th GA Artillery Brigade	Qingtongxia Part C: 47th GA Artillery Brigade	Shandan Part C: 13th GA Air Defense Brigade
Korla Part A: 31st GA Artillery Brigade (with long-range rockets)	Qingtongxia Part D: 16th GA Artillery Brigade	Shandan Part D: 54th GA Air Defense Brigade
Korla Part B: 42nd GA Long-range Rocket Brigade	Qingtongxia Part E: 1st GA Artillery Brigade	Shandan Part E: 41st GA Air Defense Brigade
Taonan Part B: 38th GA Artillery Brigade	Qingtongxia Part F: 42nd GA Artillery Brigade	Shandan Part F: 16th GA Air Defense Brigade
Weibei Part A: 13th GA Air Defense Brigade	Qingtongxia Part G: 27th GA Artillery Brigade	Shandan Part G: 31st GA Air Defense Brigade
Xuanhua: 40th GA Artillery Brigade		
Weibei Part B: 14th GA Air Defense Brigade		
Sanjie: 26th GA Artillery Brigade		

Source: Chinese media reports.

Key: MD: military district; GA: group army.

* Denotes preparatory computer exercise.

Appendix 3. Annual Intake of Students for PLA and PAP Academies				
Year	High School Students for PLA and PAP Academies	High School Students for National Defense Students (PLA + PAP)	PAP Academies and National Defense Students	NCOs/Conscripts into PLA and PAP Academies	Total
2017	12,000			4,800	16,800
2016	14,500	4,700		5,900	25,100
2015	15,700	6,000		5,300	27,000
2014	15,000	5,000	3,800		23,800
2013					
2012	15,000	8,000		6,000	31,000
2011	20,000	8,000		(Not specified, included among the 20,000)	28,000
2010	15,000+2,200=17,200	6,000+850=6,850		4,100	28,150
2009	15,000	7,500		7,190	29,690
2008	10,000	10,000			20,000
2007	10,000	11,000			21,000
2006	10,000	10,000		5,000	25,000
2005	20,000	12,000		5,000	37,000
2004	20,000	8,000			28,000

Source: Chinese media reports.

Notes

[1] *China's Military Strategy* (Beijing: State Council Information Office of the People's Republic of China, May 2015), available at <http://eng.mod.gov.cn/Press/2015-05/26/content_4586805.htm>.

[2] *The Military Balance 1996/97* (London: International Institute for Strategic Studies, 1996), 179–181. In 2018, China's officially announced defense budget was about 175 billion USD (based on exchange rates). For a useful discussion of the growth of the Chinese defense budget, see Richard A. Bitzinger, "China's New Defense Budget: Money and Manpower," *Asia Times* (Hong Kong), March 11, 2018, available at <www.atimes.com/chinas-new-defense-budget-money-manpower/>.

[3] *China's National Defense in 2000* (Beijing: State Council Information Office of the People's Republic of China, October 2000), available at <www.china.org.cn/english/2000/Oct/2791.htm>.

[4] *China's National Defense in 2004* (Beijing: State Council Information Office of the People's Republic of China, December 2004), available at <www.china.org.cn/e-white/20041227/index.htm>.

[5] *The Diversified Employment of China's Armed Forces* (Beijing: State Council Information Office of the People's Republic of China, April 16, 2013), available at <www.china.org.cn/government/whitepaper/node_7181425.htm>.

[6] *China's Military Strategy.* Emphasis added.

[7] "Xi Reviews Troops in Field for First Time," Ministry of National Defense, July 30, 2017, available at <http://eng.mod.gov.cn/news/2017-07/30/content_4787294.htm>. *The Military Balance 2018* (London: International Institute for Strategic Studies, 2018), 250, estimates army personnel strength to be 975,000.

[8] Both the 2006 and 2008 Chinese defense white papers described a "three-step development strategy" for defense modernization, which identified "mid-21st century" as the completion date for this process. The mid-21st century, or 2049, is also the 100th anniversary of the founding of the People's Republic of China. The three-step development strategy also provided two interim dates, or milestones: 2010 "to lay a solid foundation" and 2020 to "basically accomplish mechanization and make major progress in informationization."

[9] "China to Build World-Class Armed Forces by Mid-21st Century," Xinhua, October 18, 2017, available at <www.chinadaily.com.cn/china/2017-10/18/content_33403375.htm>; and "Xi Jinping: Build the People's Army into a World-Class Military" [习近平：把人民军队全面建成世界一流军队], *PLA Daily* [解放军报], October 18, 2017, available at <www.81.cn/jmywyl/2017-10/18/content_7791594.htm>.

[10] Feng Chunmei and Ni Guanghui [冯春梅, 倪光辉], "First Interview with Army Commander Li Zuocheng" [陆军司令员李作成首次接受媒体采访], *People's Daily* [人民日报], January 31, 2016, available at <www.81.cn/jwgz/2016-01/31/content_6882034.htm>.

[11] As of September 2016, the People's Liberation Army (PLA) apparently has begun to use the term *theater leader grade* (*zhanqu ji*, 战区级) to replace the former military region (MR) leader grade. See "Military Training Units above the Level of the Deputy War-Level Units in the Army Held in Beijing" [全军副战区级以上单位纪委书记培训班在京举办], *PLA Daily* [解放军报], September 26, 2016, available at <www.81.cn/jfjbmap/content/2016-09/26/content_157464.htm>.

[12] "China Names New Commanders for Army, Air Force in Reshuffle," Reuters, August 31, 2017, available at <www.reuters.com/article/us-china-defence/china-names-new-commanders-for-army-air-force-in-reshuffle-idUSKCN1BC3L1>.

¹³ PLA Navy headquarters has a Planning and Organization Bureau; therefore, it is logical that the army does also.

¹⁴ The names seen above continue to be reported as of March 2018. The Equipment Development Department "is mainly responsible for development and planning, [research and development], testing and authentication, procurement management, and information system construction for the whole military's equipment." See "MND Holds Press Conference on CMC Organ Reshuffle," *China Military Online*, January 12, 2016, available at <http://english.chinamil.com.cn/news-channels/china-military-news/2016-01/12/content_6854444.htm>. Note there is no mention of repair and maintenance in that statement.

¹⁵ The first of these brigades has been identified in the Northern Theater Command (TC). See "Soldiers Operate Mobile Satellite Communication System," *PLA Daily*, May 31, 2017, available at <http://english.chinamil.com.cn/view/2017-05/31/content_7623013.htm>.

¹⁶ Liu Hongjun [刘洪军], "Strengthening Theater Army's Innovation and Awareness of Warfighting and Construction" [强化战区陆军主战主建的创新意识], *China Military Online* [中国军网], May 10, 2016, available at <www.81.cn/jfjbmap/content/2016-05/10/content_144076.htm>.

¹⁷ Li Ming [黎明], "Chinese Communist Northern Theater PC Xu Yuanlin Removed from Office" [中共北部战区政委徐远林被免职 去向不明], *New Tang Dynasty* [新唐人], July 31, 2016, available at <www.ntdtv.com/xtr/gb/2016/08/01/a1278801.html>.

¹⁸ For example, Li Zuocheng worked with Bai Lu in the Chengdu MR, Liu Lei worked with He Qingcheng in the Lanzhou MR, and Liu Xiaowu served with Li Qiaoming in the 41ˢᵗ Group Army.

¹⁹ The "Two Inabilities" [*liangge nengli bugou*, 两个能力不够] are 1) our military's ability to fight a modern war is insufficient, and 2) our cadres', at all levels, abilities to command modern war is insufficient. The "Two Large Gaps" [*liangge chaju henda*, 两个差距很大] refers to gaps between the level of China's military modernization and 1) the requirements for national security, and 2) the level of the world's advanced militaries.

²⁰ Li Zuocheng and Liu Lei, "Strive to Build a Strong and Modernized New-Type Army—Study Deeply and Implement Chairman Xi Jinping's Important Discourse on Army Building" [陆军司令员政委: 建设强大的现代化新型陆军努力建设一支强大的现代化新型陆军—深入学习贯彻习近平主席关于陆军建设重要论述], *Qiushi* [求是], February 15, 2016, available at <http://army.81.cn/content/2016-02/15/content_6909160.htm>.

[21] Liao Keduo [廖可铎], "Promote Effective Army Transformation and Construction" [推进陆军转型建设落地见效], *PLA Daily* [解放军报], August 23, 2016, available at <www.81.cn/jfjbmap/content/2016-08/23/content_154414.htm>.

[22] Wang Li and Yu Wei, eds. [王李, 宇薇], "One Extraordinary Assessment" [一次不同凡响的考核], *PLA Daily* [解放军报], January 22, 2015, available at <www.81.cn/2015lzjqqh/2015-01/22/content_6318223.htm>. Xi has identified the problem as one the PLA must solve.

[23] "MND Holds Press Conference on CMC Organ Reshuffle," *China Military Online*, January 12, 2016, available at <http://english.chinamil.com.cn/news-channels/china-military-news/2016-01/12/content_6854444.htm>; Wang Jun [王俊], "Beijing Garrison Has Been Transferred from the Former Beijing Military Region Army" [北京卫成区已由原北京军区转隶陆军], *The Paper* [澎湃新闻], August 16, 2016, available at <www.thepaper.cn/newsDetail_forward_1514876>.

[24] Zhang Baoyin [张宝印] et al., "Speed Up the Construction of a New National Defense Mobilization System with Chinese Characteristics" [加快构建具有中国特色的新型国防动员体系], Xinhua, March 9, 2016, available at <www.81.cn/jwgz/2016-03/09/content_6951104.htm>.

[25] "Jixi Jun Division Border Guard Officers and Men Turned to Donate Money before the Transfer of Education" [鸡西军分区边防部队官兵转隶交前倾情捐资助学], *Bright Picture* [光明图片], available at <http://pic.gmw.cn/channelplay/12052/5300867/0/0.html>; Meng Haizhong and Chen Youguang [孟海中, 陈宥光], "The Coastal Defense Forces Belonging to the Shantou Garrison Command in Guangdong Province Transferred Their Troops to the Army in February this Year" [广东省汕头警备区所属海防部队今年2月已转隶移交陆军], *China National Defense Daily* [中国国防报], April 1, 2017, available at <www.thepaper.cn/newsDetail_forward_1653214>.

[26] "Northern and Southern TC Armies Forming Border Defense Brigades" [南部战区陆军, 北部战区陆军等均已组建边防旅], *The Paper* [澎湃新闻], May 9, 2017, available at <www.81junzhuan.com/ss/2017-05-09/11521.html>.

[27] "Brigade Party Members Carry Backpacks to Meetings" [旅党委委员背着背包来开会], *PLA Daily* [解放军报], January 10, 2018, available at <www.81.cn/jfjbmap/content/2018-01/10/content_196631.htm>.

[28] Jing Runqiang [井润强], "Official Disclosure: Guangdong Reserve Division Transferred to the Army" [官方披露: 广东某预备役师部队已转隶陆军], *China National Defense Daily* [中国国防报], April 7, 2017, available at <www.thepaper.cn/newsDetail_forward_1656910>.

²⁹ Ma Hao Liang [馬浩亮], "Four Changes to Provincial Military Districts Leadership Positions Reduced" [省軍區四變化削減領導職務], *Ta Kung Pao* [大公報], April 24, 2017, available at <http://news.takungpao.com.hk/paper/q/2017/0424/3443954.html>.

³⁰ Wang Jun [王俊], "Air Force Major General Zhou Li Transferred to Henan Provincial Military District Commander to Succeed Major General Lu Changjian" [空军少将周利调任河南省军区司令员，接替卢长健少], *The Paper* [澎湃新闻], April 12, 2017, available at <www.thepaper.cn/newsDetail_forward_1660971>.

³¹ The year 2020 is the deadline for the current phase of PLA reforms to be completed.

³² Liao Keduo [廖可铎], "Speed Up Building a Powerful Modernized New-Type Army" [加快建设强大的现代化新型陆军], *PLA Daily* [解放军报], March 29, 2016, available at <www.81.cn/jmywyl/2016-03/29/content_6980905.htm>.

³³ *The Diversified Employment of China's Armed Forces* (Beijing: State Council Information Office of the People's Republic of China, September 9, 2013), available at <www.chinadaily.com.cn/china/China-Military-Watch/2013-09/09/content_16953672.htm>.

³⁴ Order-of-battle details in this and following paragraphs are based on the author's analysis of open Chinese sources; the numbers cited are close to, but not exactly the same as, the numbers found in the *Annual Report to Congress: Military and Security Developments Involving the People's Republic of China 2016* (Washington, DC: Office of the Secretary of Defense, 2016) and *The Military Balance 2017* (London: International Institute for Strategic Studies, 2017).

³⁵ The discussion of "below-the-neck" reform is based on and updates that found in Dennis J. Blasko, "PLA Army Group Army Reorganization: An Initial Analysis," October 2017, available at <www.ashtreeanalytics.com/wp-content/uploads/2017/10/PLA-Army-Group-Army-Reorganization-An-Initial-Analysis.pdf>.

³⁶ "Who Said There Is Trust Crisis? I Say Never Leave Any Brother" [你说有信任危机? 我说绝不丢下任何一个兄弟], *PLA Daily* [解放军报], February 6, 2018, available at <www.81.cn/lj/2018-02/06/content_7934749.htm>.

³⁷ "Role Model Helps New Recruits Grow and Improve" [身边榜样助力新兵成长进步], *PLA Daily* [解放军报], September 30, 2017, available at <www.81.cn/jfjbmap/content/2017-09/30/content_189134.htm>. A new marine special operations forces (SOF) brigade with a Dragon Commando unit [*jiaolong tuji dui*, 蛟龙突击队] may also have been formed recently from existing marine assets.

See "Decrypt 'Operation Red Sea' Prototype" [解密《红海行动》原型], *Sina.com*, February 20, 2018, available at <http://mil.news.sina.com.cn/china/2018-02-20/doc-ifyrswmu3697775.shtml>.

[38] "PLA Daily Commentator: Adhere to Training to Prepare for War" [解放军报评论员文章: 坚持练兵备战], *PLA Daily* [解放军报], July 22, 2015, available at <www.81.cn/jmywyl/2015-07/22/content_6595259.htm>.

[39] Zhang Tao, ed., "Type-96B Seen as Pillar of Nation's Tank Force," *China Daily* (Beijing), August 10, 2016, available at <http://english.chinamil.com.cn/news-channels/china-military-news/2016-08/10/content_7200566.htm>. The numbers cited in this article are roughly consistent with what has been reported by *The Military Balance 2017* and U.S. Department of Defense 2016 report on the Chinese military. The 7,000 figure includes both main battle tanks and light tanks.

[40] *The Military Balance 2018*, 251.

[41] Zhang Zhaoxing [张照星], "Transformation of Combined Arms Battalion from 'Accepting Instructions Type' to 'Independent Operations Type'" [合成营由"接受指令型"向"独立作战型"转变], *PLA Daily* [解放军报], September 9, 2016, available at <www.81.cn/lj/2016-09/09/content_7249484.htm>; and Wang Renfei and Zhang Xuhang [王任飞, 张旭航], "Combined Infantry Battalion Has Command Post" [合成步兵营有了"中军帐"], *PLA Daily* [解放军报], May 27, 2015, available at <www.81.cn/jwgz/2015-05/27/content_6508696.htm>.

[42] Yang Xihe and Kang Ke [杨西河, 康克], "20th Group Army Realizes Precision Command by Breaking Information Barriers Between Arms" [第20集团军打破兵种信息壁垒实现精确指挥], *PLA Daily* [解放军报], September 25, 2016, available at <http://zb.81.cn/content/2016-09/25/content_7275473.htm>.

[43] Ma Sancheng and Sun Libo [马三成, 孙利波], "Western Theater Army Units Hold Command Ability Standards Training" [西部战区陆军部队开展指挥能力达标集训], *PLA Daily* [解放军报], March 23, 2016, available at <www.81.cn/lj/2016-03/23/content_6972534.htm>.

[44] Yin Hang and Liang Pengfei [尹航, 梁蓬飞], "All Army Symposium on Realistic Military Training Held in Beijing" [全军实战化军事训练座谈会在京召开], *China Military Online* [中国军网], June 25, 2016, available at <http://www.81.cn/jmywyl/2016-06/25/content_7119351.htm>.

[45] For a recent example of this goal stated in English, see Ouyang, ed., "Symposium Highlights Matching Military Exercises with Real Combat," Xinhua, June 26, 2016, available at <http://english.chinamil.com.cn/news-channels/china-military-news/2016-06/26/content_7120044.htm>.

⁴⁶ Jian Lin [菅琳], ed., "Lay Greater Stress on System-of-Systems Building" [更加注重体系建设], *PLA Daily* [解放军报], July 18, 2016, available at <www.81.cn/theory/2016-07/18/content_7159804.htm>.

⁴⁷ For two examples in 2016, see "For a Strong Military First Train Generals, in Training Soldiers Train Officers First" [强军先强将 练兵先练官], *PLA Daily* [解放军报], January 17, 2016, available at <www.81.cn/jfjbmap/content/2016-01/17/content_135485.htm>; and "With This Type of Locomotive in the Lead, Are the Little Partners Living It?" [有这样的"火车头"领跑，小伙伴们还坐的住吗?], *PLA Daily* [解放军报], April 12, 2016.

⁴⁸ Zhang Xudong [张旭东], "Grasp the 'Key Links' of Joint Operations" [抓住联合作战"关节点"], *PLA Daily* [解放军报], July 19, 2016, available at <www.81.cn/jfjbmap/content/2016-07/19/content_150977.htm>.

⁴⁹ Jiang Yukun [姜玉坤], "The Battalion to Become the PLA's Basic Combat Unit to Carry Out Independent Tasks" [营将作为解放军基础战术单元独立执行作战任务], Xinhua, April 25, 2008, available at <http://mil.news.sina.com.cn/2008-04-25/0632497096.html>.

⁵⁰ Liao Qiaoming [李桥铭], "Let New-Type Combat Forces Become PLA's 'Trump Cards'" [让新型作战力量成为手中"王牌"], *PLA Daily* [解放军报], July 15, 2016, available at <www.81.cn/jlwh/2015-07/15/content_6594358.htm>.

⁵¹ For a description of transregional exercises from 2006 to 2011, see Dennis J. Blasko, "Clarity of Intentions: People's Liberation Army Transregional Exercises to Defend China's Borders," in *Learning by Doing: The PLA Trains at Home and Abroad*, ed. Roy Kamphausen, David Lai, and Travis Tanner (Carlisle Barracks, PA: Strategic Studies Institute, 2012), 171–212.

⁵² Liang Pengfei and Li Yuming [梁鹏飞，李玉明], "Looking Back at Zhurihe, Seeing the Hardship" [回望朱日和，忧患之中见担当], *PLA Daily* [解放军报], August 21, 2014, available at <www.81.cn/jfjbmap/content/2014-08/21/content_85240.htm>.

⁵³ Shao Min and Sun Xingwei [邵敏，孙兴维], "Army Organizes 17 Transregional Exercises from July to September, Seven New Rules to Promote Realistic Confrontation" [陆军7至9月组织17场跨区演习 7条新规推动真打实抗], *PLA Daily* [解放军报], August 4, 2016, available at <www.81.cn/sydbt/2016-08/04/content_7189782.htm>.

⁵⁴ "2017 Army Unit Base Training Begins" [2017年陆军部队基地化训练拉开战幕], *PLA Daily* [解放军报], August 24, 2017, available at <www.81.cn/jmywyl/2017-08/24/content_7730097.htm>.

[55] Shao and Sun, "Army Organizes 17 Transregional Exercises from July to September, Seven New Rules to Promote Realistic Confrontation"; ibid.

[56] "Stride-2016 Zhurihe Series of Live Confrontation Exercises Begins" [跨越-2016•朱日和"实兵对抗系列演习拉开战幕], *PLA Daily* [解放军报], July 16, 2016, available at <www.81.cn/jfjbmap/content/2016-07/16/content_150685.htm>.

[57] Zhang Li, Wu Aili, and Zhao Lingyu, "Exercise Mission Action-2013C Led by China's Air Force," International College of Defence Studies, People's Liberation Army National Defense University, June 5, 2013, available at <www.cdsndu.org/html_en/to_articleContent_article.id=8a28e6d84adec8b-f014ae15b011900b9.html>.

[58] For joint exercises commanded by the navy and air force in 2014 and 2015, see Dennis J. Blasko, "Integrating the Services and Harnessing the Military Area Commands," *Journal of Strategic Studies* 39, no. 5–6 (August 1, 2016), 685–708.

[59] Li Mangmang [李芒茫], "ASEAN Joint Exercise Begins, Special Operations Force Participates" [东盟联合演练拉开帷幕 特战队员随队参加], *PLA Daily* [解放军报], September 6, 2016, available at <www.81.cn/tzjy/2016-09/06/content_7244105.htm>; Wang Ning and Sun Xingwei [王宁孙兴维], "'Peace Mission-2016': Listen to the Soldiers! Blood Is Flowing!" ["和平使命-2016": 众将士听令! 热血出征!], *China Military Online* [中国军网], September 12, 2016, available at <http://photo.81.cn/pla/2016-09/12/content_7253297.htm>.

[60] Zhang Tao, ed., "PLA Sends Team for International Jungle Patrol Competition in Brazil," *China Military Online*, August 11, 2016, available at <http://english.chinamil.com.cn/news-channels/china-military-news/2016-08/11/content_7202787.htm>; and Zhang Tao, ed., "China Tops International Sniper Competition," *China Military Online*, June 28, 2016, available at <http://english.chinamil.com.cn/news-channels/china-military-news/2016-06/28/content_7123197.htm>.

[61] Zhang Tao, ed., "Two Events of International Army Games 2016 Held in Kazakhstan," *China Military Online*, August 3, 2016, available at <http://english.chinamil.com.cn/view/2016-08/03/content_7199339.htm>.

[62] Zhang Tao, ed., "International Army Games 2016 Wraps Up in Russia," *China Military Online*, August 15, 2016, available at <http://english.chinamil.com.cn/view/2016-08/15/content_7207953.htm>.

[63] "Aim, Race, Win! Russia's Tank Biathlon 2016 in Most Spectacular Photos & Videos," *RT.com*, August 14, 2016, available at <www.rt.com/news/355908-russia-tank-biathlon-2016/>.

⁶⁴ "New Chinese Type-96B Tank Just Broke Down at 'Tank Biathlon' Competition," *Defence Forum India*, August 15, 2016, available at <http://defenceforumindia.com/forum/threads/new-chinese-type-96-b-tank-just-broke-down-at-tank-biathlon-competition.77216/>.

⁶⁵ Daniel Hartnett, "China's First Deployment of Combat Forces to a UN Peacekeeping Mission-South Sudan," U.S.-China Economic and Security Review Commission, March 13, 2012, available at <www.uscc.gov/Research/chinas-first-deployment-combat-forces-un-peacekeeping-mission%E2%80%-94south-sudan>; and "China to Send Peacekeeping Forces to Mali," Xinhua, July 12, 2013, available at <www.china.org.cn/world/2013-07/13/content_29412205.htm>. Some sources call the deployment to Mali the "first" deployment of a guard force.

⁶⁶ "Details of China's First Peacekeeping Infantry Battalion," *China Military Online*, December 23, 2014, available at <http://english.chinamil.com.cn/news-channels/china-military-news/2014-12/23/content_6282015.htm>.

⁶⁷ Yao Jianing, ed., "2ⁿᵈ Batch of Chinese Peacekeeping Infantry Battalion Flies to South Sudan," *China Military Online*, December 3, 2015, available at <http://english.chinamil.com.cn/news-channels/china-military-news/2015-12/03/content_6798884.htm>.

⁶⁸ Dai Feng and Wu Xu [代烽, 吴旭], "Combat and Support Integration, a 'Road' That Must Be Crossed" [战保一体，一道非迈不可的"坎"], *PLA Daily* [解放军报], July 18, 2016, available at <www.81.cn/jfjbmap/content/2016-07/18/content_150828.htm>.

⁶⁹ "83ʳᵈ Group Army Organizes Equipment Backbone Training Mobilization Activity" [第83集团军组织召开装备骨干集训开训动员活动], *PLA Daily* [解放军报], March 22, 2018, available at <http://zb.81.cn/content/2018-03/22/content_7980750.htm>; "In Order to Get Work Results Examine the Effectiveness of Learning and Implementation" [以工作成果检验学习贯彻成效], *PLA Daily* [解放军报], December 10, 2017, available at <www.81.cn/jfjbmap/content/2017-12/10/content_193914.htm>; "Fast Train and Mercedes Fusion in Tianshan North and South," *PLA Daily* [解放军报], January 19, 2018, available at <www.81.cn/jfjbmap/content/2018-01/19/content_197380.htm>.

⁷⁰ "More Than 10 Units Combine into a Brigade, Harmoniously" [10多个单位合编成一个旅,和谐相处有妙招], *PLA Daily* [解放军报], June 3, 2017, available at <www.81.cn/jwgz/2017-06/03/content_7626985.htm>.

⁷¹ "China Establishes Joint Logistic Support Force," *China Military Online*, September 13, 2016, available at <http://eng.mod.gov.cn/TopNews/2016-09/13/content_4730336.htm>.

[72] Liu Jianwei [刘建伟] et al., "From 'Department' to 'Force': The Reforms Our PLA's Joint Logistics Must Make" [从"部"到"部队":我军联勤改革要跨越啥], *PLA Daily* [解放军报], April 18, 2017, available at <www.81.cn/jmbl/2017-04/18/content_7566998_2.htm>.

[73] Zhang Tao, ed., "Defense Ministry Holds News Conference on Joint Logistic Support System Reform," *China Military Online*, September 14, 2016, available at <http://english.chinamil.com.cn/view/2016-09/14/content_7258622.htm>.

[74] Zhang Tao, ed., "PLA Restructuring Changes Focus at Military Schools," *China Daily*, April 28, 2016, available at <http://english.chinamil.com.cn/news-channels/china-military-news/2016-04/28/content_7028544.htm>.

[75] Zhao Yusha, "'Solemn' Retirement Ceremony Called for PLA Officers," *Global Times* (Beijing), June 14, 2016, available at <www.globaltimes.cn/content/988169.shtml>.

[76] Yang Hong [杨红], ed., "From 2017, No More National Defense Students Will Be Recruited from Ordinary High School Graduates" [2017年起不再从普通高中毕业生中定向招收国防生], *China Military Online* [中国军网], May 26, 2017, available at <www.81.cn/zggfs/2017-05/26/content_7619955.htm>.

[77] Zhang, ed., "PLA Restructuring Changes Focus at Military Schools."

[78] Yao Jianing, ed., "PLA Adjusts Policies on Graduate Student Enrolment," *China Military Online*, September 19, 2016, available at <http://english.chinamil.com.cn/view/2016-09/19/content_7265709.htm>.

[79] Yao Jianing, ed., "Xi Brings Strength, Integrity to Chinese Armed Forces," Xinhua, July 30, 2016, available at <http://english.chinamil.com.cn/news-channels/china-military-news/2016-07/30/content_7182049.htm>.

[80] Zhang Jiashua and Hai Yang [张佳帅, 海洋], "System of Systems Operations: Turn 'Strong Fingers' into a 'Hard Fist'" [体系作战: 变 '指头强'为 '拳头硬'], *PLA Daily* [解放军报], September 18, 2016, available at <www.81.cn/jfjbmap/content/2016-09/18/content_156883.htm>.

CHAPTER 11

MAKING SENSE OF CHINA'S MISSILE FORCES

David C. Logan

Since the start of the country's nuclear weapons programs, China's leaders have emphasized the development of missile forces. This interest in missiles was initially focused on the development of intercontinental ballistic missiles to deliver nuclear weapons but has since expanded to include a large and expanding force of conventionally armed short-, medium-, and intermediate-range ballistic and cruise missiles for regional military operations.[1] In the past two decades, the People's Liberation Army (PLA) Rocket Force (formerly the Second Artillery)—the military organization responsible for operating China's nuclear and land-based conventional missile forces—has been transformed from a small force operating liquid-fueled nuclear-armed ballistic missiles to a much larger and more modern force increasingly equipped with solid-fueled ballistic missiles. The majority of these missiles are now conventional rather than nuclear.

Changes in China's missile forces cannot be understood without referring to the broader context in which they are occurring. Jeffrey Lewis has argued that changes in China's missile forces have usually been a function of broad changes in China's political environment and bureaucratic structures, with ideological and strategic considerations of only secondary and tertiary importance.[2] The most recent military reforms have continued in this trend by demonstrating the importance of broader political and organizational changes in altering the structure and policies of China's missile forces. The reforms also raise the possibility of a more powerful and independent Rocket Force, a development that could increase the salience of strategic considerations in how China develops, sizes, and postures its missile forces. Depending on its institutional preferences, a more powerful Rocket Force might change China's missile forces in important ways, such as prioritizing conventional missions over nuclear missions or lobbying for nuclear forces to begin adopting the more assertive operational practices common to conventional elements.

This chapter attempts to answer some of the questions raised by the technological and organizational changes sweeping China's missile forces. First, it reviews the history and evolution of China's missile forces as guided by technological and bureaucratic influences. Second, it describes key features of the organizational structure and operational practices of China's missile forces on the eve of the 2016 reforms. Third, it examines the impact of the recent military reforms on the missile forces. Finally, it assesses the implications of recent changes for the future of China's missile forces, including its orientation toward either the nuclear or conventional mission sets and its relationship with other military units. The chapter employs a range of sources, including unclassified and declassified reports from the U.S. Government, Chinese state propaganda, displays of missile forces in parades and on state television, disclosures on social media, commercial satellite imagery, computer models, and open-source Chinese press reports on missile force organization, exercises, and capabilities.

Evolution of the Second Artillery Force

The Second Artillery was created in 1966, just 2 years after China's first successful nuclear test at Lop Nor.[3] Though work had begun on missile systems a decade earlier, the Second Artillery was assigned responsibility for wielding these weapons. At its founding, the Second Artillery was not an official military service [*junzhong*, 军种], but rather an "independent branch [*bingzhong*, 兵种] that is considered equal to the services."[4] For decades, the Second Artillery operated a small and relatively unsophisticated force of liquid-fueled nuclear-armed missiles. The modern incarnation of China's missile forces, the PLA Rocket Force, operates a larger force of increasingly mobile solid-fueled missiles armed with nuclear and conventional warheads.

The following section examines some of the key bureaucratic and technological drivers that have influenced the evolution of China's missile forces and the organization charged with operating them.[5]

Bureaucratic Changes

The evolution of China's missile forces has been significantly influenced by bureaucratic changes, as different organizations have guided the country's nuclear and missile policies. During the first several decades, China's decisionmaking about nuclear weapons and ballistic missiles was dominated by the bureaucracy responsible for defense research and development, the National Defense Science and Technology Commission (NDSTC) [*guofang kewei*, 国防科委] led by Nie Rongzhen from 1958 to 1975 and Zhang Aiping from 1975 to 1982. In this early period, the Second Artillery, which was not established until 1966, does not seem to have been a powerful or important player in shaping China's nuclear forces.[6]

NDSTC remained the dominant force, although its influence waned in the 1980s with the retirements of Nie and his deputy, Zhang. By the late 1990s, NDSTC, under the leadership of Nie's son-in-law, was weak enough to be replaced in 1998 with a PLA entity, the General Armaments Department (GAD) [*zong zhuangbei bu*, 总装备部]. This change was intended to make the weapons research and development process more responsive to the demands of an increasingly professional PLA and its constituent services. However, there are reasons to believe that the GAD remained a powerful and somewhat independent bureaucratic entity. Despite the significance of the creation of the GAD, it did not usher in dramatic changes in China's nuclear armed-missile force.[7]

Technological Changes

Technological advancements have been one of the key drivers of change in China's missile forces. As part of its ongoing nuclear modernization efforts, China has largely replaced its silo-based and roll-out liquid-fueled missiles with mobile solid-fueled missiles, has deployed new conventionally armed missiles, and has taken steps to improve the ability of its missile forces to penetrate adversary ballistic missile defenses.

China's first generation of ballistic missiles were liquid-fueled—the DF-2, DF-3, DF-4, and DF-5. The DF-2, with a range of approximately 1,000 kilometers, provided a rudimentary regional deterrent capability until it was phased out of the force in the 1980s. The regional deterrent was bolstered by the intermediate-range DF-3, credited with a range of roughly 3,000 kilometers, though this missile is believed to have recently been completely removed from the force. The DF-4, with a range of at least 5,500 kilometers, extended the reach of China's missile forces to Moscow and Guam. The silo-based DF-5, with an estimated range of more than 12,000 kilometers, formed the backbone of China's intercontinental force, providing the ability to strike the continental United States.

While some of these missiles were in development from the early 1960s, in March 1965 China established a plan to develop four missiles in 8 years [*banian sidan*, 八年四弹], culminating in an intercontinental ballistic missile (ICBM).[8] While some sources describe these four missiles in terms of their progressively longer ranges—the ability to strike Japan, followed by the Philippines, then Guam, and ultimately the continental United States—the real innovation embodied in the *banian sidan* plan was structuring the ICBM program around incremental technical goals. In retrospect, the DF-1 represented successful copy production, while the DF-2 was an indigenized Soviet missile. The subsequent missiles represented technical advances. The DF-3 was the first effort to cluster engines and use storable propellant (unsymmetrical dimethylhydrazine instead of liquid oxygen). The DF-4 was the first effort at staging, using a DF-3 as a first stage. Ultimately, the DF-5 integrated all these technical achievements into a full-range ICBM, making a number of technical improvements that allowed Chinese designers to create the massive missile.[9]

China completed these developmental goals in order, and largely on time. In the case of the DF-5, the successful test in 1971 was followed by a long period of disruption during the Cultural Revolution. China would conduct a full-range test in 1980 as part of the "three grasps" campaign to complete the unfinished business of the 1960s and 1970s—an operational ICBM, a submarine-launched ballistic missile, and a communications satellite.[10] An important cautionary note is that the completion of flight testing does not signal the end of development. Flight testing appears to continue as long as a missile is in service, though after deployment flight tests move from research organizations, such as the China Academy of Launch Technology [*zhongguo yunzai huojian jishu yanjiuyuan*, 中国运载火箭技术研究院], to the operational tests by either the Second Artillery's equipment department or operational brigades.[11] China often continues to make evolutionary improvements following the successful production of a missile. For example, after initial DF-3 testing and deployment, China conducted a second flight test series in the mid-1980s to produce the longer range DF-3A.

The DF-4 and DF-5 both remain in the PLA Rocket Force inventory. China undertook a program to improve the DF-5 in the mid-2000s, which the U.S. Intelligence Community calls the DF-5A. In September 2015, China paraded a missile marked DF-5B that reportedly has multiple warheads. China's nuclear-armed ballistic missiles are, in general, too small to be able to carry multiple warheads. The DF-5 was long understood to be a possible exception to this rule. It is China's largest ICBM and is massive, with a throw weight of a few thousand tons. The reentry vehicle for China's smallest nuclear warhead, developed for the road-mobile DF-31 ICBM, weighs 500 kilograms. U.S. analysts have long noted that China might be able to place three or possibly four such warheads on the DF-5. The appearance of the DF-5B during the September 2015 parade suggests that China has done it.[12]

In January 1985, the State Council and Central Military Commission reorganized China's missile programs to develop a new generation of solid-fueled missiles to replace the nuclear-armed liquid fueled missiles of the 1965 *banian sidan* plan. China's current generation of strategic missiles dates to this period: the 1,750-kilometer range DF-21/JL-1 to replace the DF-3; the 7,000-kilometer range DF-31/JL-2 to replace the DF-4; and the DF-41 ICBM to replace the DF-5. China had begun research on solid-fueled ballistic missiles in the 1960s, work that was focused on development of a submarine-launched ballistic missile. Work proceeded slowly through the 1970s, culminating in a March 1985 meeting where Nie's deputy and successor, Zhang Aiping, apparently ridiculed the notion of a sea-based deterrent by arguing that a Chinese submarine armed with the JL-1 would have to travel to the Arabian Sea for Moscow to be within range.[13] China subsequently emphasized the land-based variant, the DF-21.[14]

In the mid-1980s, Deng Xiaoping extended the timeline for the construction of the second submarine, a decision that amounted to cancelation of the program. The *Xia*-class submarine has never gone on patrol and is usually described as not operational and not deployed. It is possible that Chinese leaders might order the submarine armed with nuclear weapons in an extreme crisis, but this seems unlikely in the normal course of events. China continued development of a land-based variant of the JL-1, successfully testing the DF-21 in 1985.[15] Although China reportedly stood up the first DF-21 operational test and evaluation unit in 1985 in Jilin Province, the widespread conversion of the DF-3 to DF-21 units did not begin until the late 1990s. Establishment of operational test and evaluation units and flight testing occurs well ahead of full rate production and initial operational capability.

China first tested the DF-21 in May 1985. It then began a range extension program in August 1985, which eventually produced the DF-21A. (Development on the JL-1 appears to have stopped after an aborted program in the mid-1980s to develop underwater ignition.[16]) Testing on the DF-21 continued through the mid-1990s, with deployments beginning in the mid-1990s and continuing as the DF-21A gradually replaced older DF-3A missiles.[17] The range and deployment locations of the DF-21A suggest that it serves a regional deterrent role.[18] While research and development of the

DF-31/JL-2 began in the mid-1980s, flight testing of the DF-31 started in August 1999.[19] Flight testing was probably completed by the mid-2000s. The JL-2 sea-launched variant suffered a series of testing failures until the most recent cycle of testing in August 2012, which appears to have been successful.[20] (China has constructed at least four *Jin*-class ballistic missile submarines and appears to have deployed the JL-2 on them as of 2017.[21] Given the limited range of the JL-2, which cannot reach the continental United States from its base on Hainan Island, there is speculation that China may move on to a longer range version of the missile, usually called the JL-3). The original DF-41 program gave way to a range-extended DF-31, called the DF-31A, which has been operationally deployed with the Rocket Force.

Only in recent years has China resumed work on the DF-41. It has tested the DF-41 six times since 2012, with a noticeable increase in the pace of testing since August 2015. There are reports that China is considering rail-mobile deployment for the DF-41. China explored rail-mobile basing modes for the DF-4 during the mid-1970s but concluded that basing the DF-4 in caves under high mountains was a more feasible approach. Rail-mobile deployment would offer some advantages; as missiles become larger, road-mobility becomes a challenge, both for the transporter itself and for the supporting network of roads and bridges. The DF-41 can reportedly accommodate multiple warheads.[22] Based on the limited public information about the size of China's nuclear warheads, the DF-41 would need to resemble the U.S. Peacekeeper missile in size to accommodate about four reentry vehicles.

The Second Artillery was originally established to operate China's nuclear deterrent, but China has also developed and deployed a substantial force of conventionally armed missiles. This began in the mid-1980s, and the missiles were intended for export as the defense industry came under budgetary pressure. These missiles, initially the DF-15 and DF-25, appeared in Pakistan as the Shaheen I and Shaheen II. China has developed a large number of short-range ballistic missiles (SRBMs), although the current Rocket Force inventory appears to comprise variants of the DF-11,

DF-15, and DF-16 missiles.[23] (The DF-16 appears to be a heavily modified DF-11.) In addition to this series of conventionally armed SRBMs, China has deployed conventional variants of the DF-21 and a land-attack cruise missile called the CJ-10. China is also developing a new intermediate-range ballistic missile, the DF-26. The DF-26 is likely to be a two-stage missile that offers longer range and greater throw-weight than the DF-21 and DF-25. China also displayed a transporter-erector-launcher with a missile canister for the DF-26 in its August 2015 parade to commemorate the end of World War II. The narration provided on Chinese television pointedly noted that the missile could carry both conventional and nuclear warheads.[24]

Finally, China is taking steps to improve the ability of its nuclear forces to penetrate missile defenses. In January 2014, and again in August, China tested a hypersonic glide vehicle. Some open-source information seems to suggest that the test was a failure, while other sources argue that it succeeded.[25] The U.S. National Air and Space Intelligence Center has stated that the hypersonic glide vehicle under development "is associated with [China's] nuclear deterrent forces."[26] One possible clue is in the name of the system. The Chinese designation appears to be "DF-ZF," which probably stands for [*dongfeng zairu feixingqi*, 东风-再入飞行器] or "DF-Reentry Vehicle."[27]

This description of the evolution of China's ballistic missile force indicates that the technology push that marked the first generation of Chinese missiles is alive and well. The Chinese defense industry continues to produce incremental improvements on fielded systems, including range extensions, improvements in accuracy, and the ability to employ different types of conventional and nuclear warheads.

The Second Artillery on the Eve of the Reforms

Thanks to the bureaucratic and technological drivers described thus far, the Second Artillery that existed on the eve of the 2015 military reforms differed markedly from the Second Artillery at its founding. This section reviews key aspects of the force structure and operational features of the Second Artillery on the eve of the reforms. We discuss Second Artillery leadership and the organization of its missile bases and subordinate missile launch units. These features appear largely unchanged following the reforms, with the exception of improved integration of conventional Rocket Force missile brigades with the new theater commands (TCs). We close with a brief discussion of China's sea-based and aircraft-launched nuclear weapons.

Structure

The organizational structure of the Second Artillery (now the PLA Rocket Force) is more complicated than a simple table showing the number of missile launchers or missiles. Far more than a single truck is needed to conduct launch operations. A brigade of missile launchers requires support vehicles, as well as an infrastructure to maintain the vehicles, missiles, and warheads and to support the people who perform these tasks. As a result, it is necessary to consider the Rocket Force as an organization.[28]

The Rocket Force is commanded by a full general, who from 2004 to 2017 was also a member of the Central Military Commission. The Rocket Force political commissar is a theater leader grade officer and chairs the Rocket Force Party Committee. The commander serves as vice chairman of the Party committee.[29] The force is divided into six bases (sometimes called armies) numbered 61–66, each led by an army leader grade officer.[30] Bases 61–66 oversee subordinate launch brigades and support regiments. The Rocket Force also oversees a separate base, Base 67 (formerly Base 22), which is responsible for maintaining China's stockpile of nuclear warheads. The Rocket Force leadership also oversees three training bases and an engineering base headquartered in Luoyang. The engineering base, which was established in 2012, oversees a command in Hanzhong, Shaanxi, that is primarily responsible for tunneling; a collocated "engineering technology general group" in Luoyang, Henan, responsible for facility installation; and a specialized engineering brigade for disaster response that is garrisoned north of Beijing.[31]

Each missile base has between three and five subordinate missile brigades, with most bases operating a mix of conventional and nuclear brigades. The exception is Base 61 (formerly Base 51), which operates only conventional missiles and may have up to eight missile brigades. Within this organizational structure, command authority is exerted from the base, down through brigades, battalions, companies, and platoons.[32] Though most of China's missile bases command both nuclear and conventional brigades, these two forces appear to be subject to somewhat separate command and control arrangements. The Rocket Force's nuclear units are believed to report directly to the Central Military Commission, while there is evidence that conventional units may now be under the operational command of the theater commands.[33]

Table 1. China's Ballistic Missile Inventory

U.S. Designation	Chinese	Propellant	Mode	Range (km)	No. of Launchers	
CSS-2 Mod 2	DF-3A	Liquid	Transportable	3,000	?? (limited mobility)	
CSS-3	DF-4	Liquid	Silo and transportable	5,500+	10–15	
CSS-4 Mod 2	DF-5A	Liquid	Silo	12,000+	About 20	
CSS-5 Mod 1	DF-21	Solid	Road-mobile	1,750+	Fewer than 50	
CSS-5 Mod 2	DF-21A	Solid	Road-mobile	1,750+		
CSS-5 Conventional	DF-21C	Solid	Road-mobile	1,750+	Fewer than 30	
CSS-5 Mod 5	DF-21D			1,500+	Unknown	
CSS-6 Mod 1	DF-15/ M-9	Solid	Road-mobile	600	90–110	
CSS-6 Mod 2	DF-15A	Solid	Road-mobile	850+		
CSS-6 Mod 3	DF-15B	Solid	Road-mobile	750+		
CSS-7 Mod 1	DF-11/ M-11	Solid	Road-mobile	300	120–140	
CSS-7 Mod 2	DF-11A	Solid	Road-mobile	600		
CSS-8	B610	Solid/liquid	Road-mobile	150		
CSS-9 Mod 1	B611	Solid	Road-mobile	150		Dual launcher
CSS-9 Mod-X-2	B611M	Solid	Road-mobile	260		
CSS-10 Mod 1	DF-31	Solid	Road-mobile	7,000+	5–10	
CSS-10 Mod 2	DF-31A	Solid	Road-mobile	11,000+	More than 15	
CSS-11 Mod 1	DF-16	Solid	Road-mobile	800+		
CSS-14 Mod-X-1	P12	Solid	Road-mobile	150		Dual launcher

Table 1. China's Ballistic Missile Inventory (cont.)

U.S. Designation	Chinese	Propellant	Mode	Range (km)	No. of Launchers	
CSS-14 Mod-X-2	BP12A	Solid	Road-mobile	280		
CSS-X-15	M20	Solid	Road-mobile	280		
CSS-X-16	SY400	Solid	Road-mobile	200		8 rocket MLRS
	DF-26	Solid	Road-mobile	IRBM		Reported to be dual-ca-pable.
CSS-X-20	DF-41	Solid	Road- or rail mobile	ICBM	Not yet deployed	
CSS-NX-3	JL-1	Solid	Submarine-launched	1,700+	Not yet deployed	
CSS-NX-14	JL-2	Solid	Submarine-launched	7,000+		
	JL-3	Solid	Submarine-launched			Rumored to be under develop-ment
	YJ-63	LACM	Air-launched			
	CJ-10/ DH-10	LACM	Ground-launched			

Key: ICBM: intercontinental ballistic missile; IRBM: intermediate-range ballistic missile; LACM: land attack missile; MLRS: multiple launch missile system.

Notes: Table compiled by Jeffrey Lewis. The author gratefully acknowledges his contributions. Public U.S. Government reports suggest that all DF-3A systems may have been phased out of the force.

Each brigade has launch battalions and/or launch companies that operate a limited number of launchers. A launch platform in this context can be a silo (as in the case of the DF-5), a cave rollout to launch site (such as the DF-4), or, for mobile missiles, a transporter-erector-launcher. Table 1 chronicles China's ballistic missile inventory. The missiles and launchers also require significant communications, intelligence, and maintenance support. The structure of brigades differs for fixed-site missiles and mobile missiles, as well as for conventional and nuclear missiles. As a result, the number of missiles per brigade may vary greatly between conventional missile brigades (up to 36 launchers with as many as 6 missiles per launcher), mobile nuclear-armed missile brigades (between 6 and 12 missile launchers per brigade), and fixed-site nuclear-armed missiles (6 or fewer silos or cave rollout sites.) This reflects differences in the number of battalions, companies, and launchers assigned to each unit.

When looking at unclassified U.S. Government estimates, it usually makes sense to estimate that each nuclear-armed mobile missile brigade has approximately eight launchers—although average does not necessarily accurately reflect each unit. For example, the National Air and Space Intelligence Center assesses that China has 5 to 10 DF-31 missiles and "more than 15" DF-31A missiles.[34] Using an average of eight, China probably has one DF-31 brigade and two DF-31A brigades. Using the structure of bases, brigades, and launch units, a rough order of battle for the Rocket Force is presented in table 2.

Table 2. PLA Rocket Force Organization

Base (Previous)	Brigade (Previous)	MUCD (Previous)	Location	System
61 (52)	HQ	96601 (96151)	Huangshan, Anhui	
	611 (807)	96711 (96161)	Chizhou	DF-21
	612 (811)	96712 (96163)	Jingdezhen	DF-21A
	613 (815)	96713 (96165)	Shangrao	DF-15B
	614 (817)	96714 (96167)	Yong'an	DF-11A
	615 (818)	96715 (96169)	Meizhou	DF-11A
	616 (819)	96716 (96162)	Ganzhou	DF-15
	617 (820)	96717 (96164)	Jinhua	DF-15
62 (53)	HQ	96602 (96201)	Kunming, Yunnan	
	621 (802)	96721 (96211)	Yibin	DF-21A?
	622 (808)	96722 (96213)	Yuxi	DF-31A
	623 (821)	96723 (96215)	Liuzhou	DH-10A?
	624 (825)	96724 (96219)	Qingyuan	DF-21D
	625 (UI)	96725 (96216)	Jianshui	(UI)
	626 (825)	96726 (96319)	Qingyuan	DF-21C/D? DF-26?
	UI (UI)	96727 (UI)	Puning	(UI)
63 (55)	HQ	96603 (96301)	Huaihua, Hunan	
	631 (803)	96731 (96311)	Jingzhou	DF-5B
	632 (805)	96732 (96313)	Shaoyang	DF-31
	633 (814)	96733 (96315)	Huitong	DF-5A?
	634 (UI)	96734 (UI)	(UI)	(UI)
	635 (824)	96735 (96317)	Yichun	DH-10
	636 (826)	96736 (96318)	Shaoguan	DF-16
	637 (UI)	96737 (UI)	(UI)	(UI)
64 (56)	HQ	96604 (96351)	Lanzhou	
	641 (806)	96741 (96111)	Hancheng	DF-31
	642 (809)	96742 (96361)	Datong	DF-31A
	643 (812)	96743 (96363)	Tianshui	DF-31A
	644 (UI)	96744 (UI)	Hanzhong	(UI)
	645? (UI)	96745	(UI)	(UI)
	646 (823)	96746 (96365)	Korle	DF-21B? DF-21C?
65 (51)	HQ	96605 (96101)	Shenyang	
	651 (810)	96751 (96113)	Dalian	DF-21

Base (Previous)	Brigade (Previous)	MUCD (Previous)	Location	System
	652 (816)	96752 (96115)	Tonghua	DF-21C? DF-21D?
	653 (822)	96753 (96117)	Laiwu	DF-21C
	654 (UI)	96754 (UI)	Dalian	(UI)
66 (54)	HQ	96606 (96251)	Luoyang	
	661 (801)	96761 (96261)	Lingbao	DF-5B
	662 (804)	96762 (96263)	Luanchuan	DF-4? DF-5A?
	663 (813)	96763 (96265)	Nanyang	DF-31A?
	664 (UI)	96764 (UI)	Luoyang	(UI)
	665 (UI)	96765 (UI)	(UI)	(UI)
	666 (827)	96766 (96267)	Xinyang	DF-26?

Table 2. PLA Rocket Force Organization (cont.)

Key: HQ: headquarters; MUCD: Military Unit Cover Designator; UI: unidentified.

Source: Mark Stokes, "PLA Rocket Force Leadership and Unit Reference," Project 2049 Institute, Arlington, VA, April 9, 2018, based on open-source analysis. The author and editors thank Mr. Stokes for his generosity in sharing this information with us.

Each Rocket Force missile base and missile brigade have a headquarters, with multiple subordinate launch units. As suggested by the use of cave-based rollout sites, the Rocket Force relies extensively on underground facilities—and engineering elements responsible for digging them. Launch units are based above ground on a day-to-day basis in peacetime. Underground facilities are used for storage, as well as missile-warhead assembly, check out, and roll out. Launch units practice deploying to tunnels for short periods of time, a practice that allows the Rocket Force to ride out a nuclear attack as suggested by the country's no-first-use policy. A recent article described a "multiday survival training" exercise in which a launch battalion spent 8 days living in tunnels before conducting an exercise.[35] The article highlights the "poor living environment" of the tunnels for even short periods of time—particularly the challenge of maintaining nutrition. (Cooked meals are prohibited because the heat from a kitchen would reveal the tunnel is occupied.[36])

In addition to the land-based Rocket Force units, the Chinese navy has built at least four *Jin*-class ballistic missile submarines in the past decade. These first submarines are believed to be based in Hainan.[37] Each *Jin*-class submarine has 12 launch tubes to carry the JL-2 submarine launched ballistic missile. The slow development of the JL-2 delayed operational deployment of the system, but the missile now appears to be deployed on submarines.[38] Major operational questions, such as how China would communicate with ballistic submarines and whether China would conduct continuous at sea deterrence patrols, remain unanswered. It is not clear, for example, whether naval units will develop their own nuclear warhead storage and control system outside of the Second Artillery Base 22 structure, or whether units assigned to navy fleets would receive warheads only in a crisis.[39]

China probably does not currently maintain aircraft-delivered or tactical nuclear weapons. During the 1970s and 1980s, the United States did not identify locations at airfield for nuclear weapons storage or units responsible for nonmissile warhead handling.[40] Some estimates periodically list aircraft as possibly having "secondary" nuclear missions or speculate that China may have an interest in tactical nuclear weapons.[41] There are also reports of work on a new nuclear-capable strategic bomber currently under development.[42] However, despite recent changes to the country's nuclear forces and gradual progress toward a potential nuclear triad, China's nuclear deterrent will continue to be dominated by the Rocket Force.

Operational Features

The operational practices of the Rocket Force have been shaped largely by policy choices of civilian leadership and by the technical characteristics of the force. Civilian leadership has traditionally prioritized strict political control of its missile forces over operational flexibility. This has meant the adoption of a relatively constrained nuclear posture, including operational practices that may reduce operational readiness but maximize political control. Operational practices have also been influenced by technical considerations. For several decades following the creation of the country's missile forces, China's ballistic missile force consisted of only a few immature liquid-fueled stationary missiles. However, as part of its ongoing modernization program, China's nuclear-armed missiles have increasingly become solid-fueled and road-mobile. These technical changes have entailed potentially significant operational changes as well.

China's liquid-fueled ballistic missiles are not kept fueled during peacetime. These missiles used transporter-erectors for the DF-3As,[43] either elevate-to-launch silos or cave-rollout for the DF-4, and silo-basing for the DF-5. A typical rollout-to-launch exercise, as presented on closed-circuit television, demonstrates the operational aspects of launching liquid-fueled ballistic missiles.[44] (This launch exercise took place at a training center, as suggested by the fact that the building in which the warhead is attached is above ground.) Chinese missileers must arm the warhead inside its shelter and complete a checkout of the missile. The missile is then rolled out to the launchpad, where it is erected. The missile is fueled and guidance sets are aligned/programmed. The missile is then ready for launch. This process can take a significant amount of time, lasting hours. For silo-based ballistic missiles, there is no rollout, but the missile must be armed, fueled, and the guidance system must be aligned and programmed prior to launch.

Although the DF-3 (CSS-2) had limited mobility, the introduction of truly mobile solid-fueled missiles such as the DF-21 required new operational practices for the Rocket Force. Mobile operations can be seen in satellite images near Da Qaidam, which previously contained two cave rollout-to-launch sites but is now believed to be a training center.[45] During peacetime, the unit is located in a garrison. In the event of a crisis, the garrison would be a likely target of enemy attack. On strategic warning, the unit could deploy to hardened shelters, a holding area, or proceed directly to a launch site. There are a number of launch sites along the main road stretching from a garrison location. In satellite images, one can clearly see the pad unoccupied, then covered with vehicles in netting and tents conducting a launch exercise, then empty again.[46]

China appears to continue to store nuclear warheads separately from ballistic missiles during peacetime. A description of a mobile missile launch in the Gobi Desert—likely at the Da Qaidam training area—depicts the unit mating the reentry vehicle to the missile on the fifth day of the exercise, following maneuvers in the field, then erecting and launching the missile. However, it would seem more logical for units to mate warheads before deployment.[47]

The Rocket Force has an extensive system for handling warheads, centered on Base 67 near Baoji (formerly Base 22).[48] Each base has a warhead regiment that performs these functions. China initially stored nuclear weapons in three vaults west of the original nuclear weapons design facility near Haiyan (Koko Nor). Sometime after the late 1960s, warhead storage moved to the Second Artillery unit near Baoji. Base 67 is responsible for storing warheads, transporting them, training units in warhead handling, and communications and maintenance of warheads and special vehicles. The size and composition of these units have remained roughly the same, even as the number of Rocket Force brigades has expanded, suggesting that new Rocket Force brigades are mostly armed with conventional warheads.

Until recently, Rocket Force training has suffered from a lack of realism and a poor emphasis on conducting joint operations. However, in recent years, training has increasingly attempted to emphasize realistic conditions by undertaking more confrontation red-blue exercises and improving its ability to conduct joint operations.

The Rocket Force has taken steps to emphasize and standardize the use of red-blue confrontation exercises.[49] In 2016, the newly established Rocket Force announced the creation of its Blue Army Teaching and Research Section, led by Colonel Diao Guangming.[50] Diao has been quoted as favoring a move toward more complex scenarios in Rocket Force training, stating, "Those whose peacetime training is overly nice will suffer greatly when they take the battlefield."[51] The new section may help standardize future confrontation exercises, which had reportedly suffered in the past as blue teams were assembled ad hoc from various different units.[52] For example, past Rocket Force red-blue exercises have employed "electronic blue teams" confined to a base and presumably capable of simulating only some kinds of electronic harassment from the enemy.[53]

Impact of the 2016 Reforms

China is in the midst of sweeping military reforms that have affected the force structure, organization, and command and control mechanisms of the PLA. The reforms have the dual goals of tightening political control and improving the military's ability to conduct joint operations. The reforms elevated the Second Artillery to full service status and renamed it the PLA Rocket Force. Despite much attention paid to its new name and higher organizational status, the Rocket Force appears to be the service least affected by the reforms.[54] Here we summarize the major reforms to the PLA and assess the impact of those reforms on China's missile forces.

PLA-Wide Reforms

The Rocket Force's creation did not occur in isolation, but in the context of reforms that affected the missions and command arrangements for nearly all the Chinese military. The scope and significance of PLA reforms have been likened to those of the Goldwater-Nichols Department of Defense Reorganization Act of 1986.[55]

The PLA replaced its old system of seven military regions (MRs) with five new joint theater commands. Under the old system, the air force, navy, and Second Artillery maintained peacetime control of their units, with command and control of air force and navy assets transferring to the war zone commander in the event of actual conflict.[56] By contrast, theater commanders will use their theater joint operations command center to work through the army, navy, and air force component headquarters to command all the ground, naval, and air forces assigned to their theaters in both peacetime and wartime. The commanders of the ground, naval, and air components are dual-hatted as deputy theater commanders. The relationship between the services and theater commands appears similar to the U.S. arrangement, with the services responsible for organizing, training, and equipping units as a "force provider" and the theater commands responsible for operational planning and execution (see the chapter by Burke and Chan in this volume).[57] The reforms also established a new headquarters for the PLA Army, renamed the Second Artillery Force as the Rocket Force and elevated its status to that of a full service, and created the Strategic Support Force and Joint Logistics Support Force.

While the reforms include dramatic changes in the command and control arrangements of the other services, the Rocket Force appears largely untouched. Initial reports emphasized continuity in both China's nuclear policies and Rocket Force command and control arrangements, though more recent accounts suggest greater progress toward integrating China's missile forces with the joint operations command centers of the newly established theater commands.

Apparent Continuity of Nuclear Strategy and Policy

Media reports and official statements consistently emphasize that the creation of the Rocket Force will not entail a change in China's fundamental nuclear strategy, and especially not a change in its no-first-use policy. Reporting on the creation of the Rocket Force, a *China Daily* article stated that China's nuclear policy would remain unchanged: "Reiterating the no-first-use nuclear weapons policy and the country's defensive nuclear strategy, [Ministry of National Defense Spokesman] Yang [Yujun] said China always keeps its nuclear capability at the minimum level required for safeguarding its national security."[58] In describing the Rocket Force, Xi Jinping used language identical to that applied to the Second Artillery in the past, describing the new Rocket Force as "a fundamental force for our country's strategic deterrent, a strategic pillar for our country's great power status, and an important cornerstone in protecting our national security."[59] The same rhetorical formulation was repeated by Xi in his 2012 address to the Second Artillery, suggesting the fundamental role of the new Rocket Force will mirror that of its predecessor.[60]

Command and Control

Rocket Force command and control structures have not changed to follow the new model used by the theater commands to control army, navy, and air force units within their areas of responsibility. Mainland commentary on the Rocket Force has consistently emphasized the need for strong central control. In announcing the creation of the Rocket Force, media reports have reiterated the importance of centralized high-level command for strategic missile forces.[61] An article in *Rocket Force News* stated that the force is "a strategic military service directly controlled and used by the Central Party Committee, Central Military Commission, and Chairman Xi."[62] These comments suggest that centralized command continues to extend to not only nuclear units but also conventional ones.

Although some theater commanders claimed to control conventional missile forces within their theaters,[63] initial reports about the relationship between the services and theater commands were notable for the paucity of references to the Rocket Force. Media reports noted that the new theater commands would have dedicated forces from the army, navy, and air force but did not mention forces of the newly formed Rocket Force, suggesting that its units will remain with their home bases.[64] The theater commands were reported to have two deputy commanders from "each of the three service branches," not including the Rocket Force.[65] One report did note that 100 Rocket Force personnel have been assigned to TC headquarters as staff officers, suggesting that some mechanisms exist for integrating the Rocket Force into theater planning.[66]

Initial reports on training intended to improve the operational relationship between the Rocket Force and theater commands emphasized *coordination* between the Rocket Force and theater commands, eschewing any language suggesting direct command authority from the theater command to Rocket Force units.[67] A mock order in a training drill used the word *coordinate* [*peihe*, 配合] to describe the unit's activities in relation to TC units [*zhanqu budui*, 战区部队]. A photo essay reporting on Rocket Force joint training hosted on the Web site of the newly created Southern Theater Command stated that Rocket Force units conducted operations "according to newly revised joint operations war plans with the relevant units of each of the other services," again suggesting a role of independent support rather than command subordination.[68]

One indicator of the Second Artillery's relative independence vis-à-vis the military regions prior to the reforms was the fact that the command geography of the Second Artillery did not map directly onto the former MR borders. The Second Artillery had six missile bases commanding launch brigades and a seventh responsible for nuclear warhead storage and handling. Of the six operational bases, four were believed to command launch brigades garrisoned in different military regions. For example, Base 65 (formerly Base 51), headquartered in Shenyang, oversaw not only two nuclear-armed launch brigades garrisoned in the former Shenyang MR but also one nuclear-armed launch brigade garrisoned in the former Beijing MR and one conventionally armed launch brigade garrisoned in the former Jinan MR.[69] A similar command geography involving Rocket Force bases commanding brigades in multiple theater commands appears to be in place after the recent military reforms, though there has been significant reshuffling of missile force units between the various missile bases.[70]

Elevation to Independent Service

In some respects, the formal elevation of the Rocket Force to the level of a service merely codifies its de facto status. The Second Artillery's organizational clout had steadily grown in the last 15 years. Prior to the creation of the Rocket Force, the Second Artillery commander and other senior leaders enjoyed ranks and grades equivalent to that of their counterparts in the services. The Second Artillery had the same constellation of bureaucratic structures as the services, including a Political Department, Logistics Department, Armaments Department, and Command Academy. In 2004, Jing Zhiyuan, then-commander of the Second Artillery, and his navy and air force counterparts became ex officio members of the Central Military Committee (CMC). Wei Fenghe, the first Rocket Force commander, was a CMC member, but his successor Lieutenant General Zhou Yaning and the commanders of the other services no longer have ex officio seats on the CMC.[71]

Many reports on the Rocket Force have emphasized the significance of its higher status as a service. Previous writings about the Second Artillery's role in joint campaigns noted that while strikes conducted by Second Artillery units would be central to the importance of any operation, the Second Artillery as an institution would largely play an auxiliary or supporting role to the services.[72] However, a professor at the Rocket Force Command Academy predicted that the force would be able to "fight independently" rather than merely "support[ing]" other forces, a definition that is incompatible with the Rocket Force's capacity and actual role."[73]

Rocket Force members have stressed the independence and prestige that come with its status. The Rocket Force has reportedly already begun implementing the internal bureaucratic adjustments necessary to elevate it to the status of a full military service,[74] including a rollout of Rocket Force uniforms.[75] Internal Rocket Force reports highlight the fact that Xi personally chose the name of the Rocket Force and bestowed a new flag to the force.[76] An article published in *Rocket Force News* reflecting on the significance of the force's elevation to the level of a military service noted that the "status of the Rocket Force as a military service is getting more important than ever before."[77] The article predicted the Rocket Force would see changes in structure, status, and missions. Specifically, the "value and capability of the Rocket Force should lie in the strengthening of the credible and reliable nuclear deterrence and nuclear counterstrike capabilities referenced by Chairman Xi, along with strengthening the establishment of intermediate-range and long-range precision strike forces and enhancing counterbalancing abilities."[78]

A Rocket Force political instructor, writing about the reforms, stated that the elevation to the level of a military service would bring commensurate transformation of the force's structure and elevation of its mission, arguing that the status as a full-fledged service means that the "Rocket Force is no longer a paper tiger, placing missiles on launch platforms to scare the adversary, but rather is a strategic iron fist ready anytime to launch missiles to intimidate the enemy," perhaps suggesting a greater warfighting role for the force.[79]

Implications for the Future

Significant questions remain about the future trajectory of China's missile forces. This section addresses three key questions. First, to what extent will Rocket Force units be able to successfully participate in joint operations with the military units of other services and those assigned to the theater commands? Second, will the Rocket Force emphasize the conventional or nuclear aspect of its identity, and what implications will this have for its force structure and operational practices? Third, what does the Rocket Force's elevation mean for its relationship with other services and how could this influence control of other strategic weapons systems?

Future Joint Operations

The Rocket Force is part of a broader PLA-wide trend in emphasizing joint operations (see the chapter by Cozad in this volume). Training has appeared to focus on developing the ability to conduct joint operations, something that has long been emphasized but not fully implemented. The Rocket Force has created plans with other services, spelling out how it will coordinate in joint operations.[80] Training has reportedly tried to move away from emphasizing theories and concepts of joint operations and to focus on the actual experience and challenges of conducting such operations.[81] Recently there has been a substantial increase in joint operations training undertaken by PLA Rocket Force units, especially exercises directly involving units of other services.

As recently as 2014, though the former Second Artillery had been emphasizing the concept of joint operations, "few instances of actual joint training were reported." A review of training exercises conducted throughout the entire year of 2014 noted Second Artillery participation in only one exercise, a military-wide exercise identified as "Joint Action–2014."[82] A 2017 report, however, noted a significant increase in joint exercises, reporting that the Rocket Force "has launched hundreds of missiles in live-fire exercises over the past several years to improve its combat readiness. The missiles were fired during about 40 exercises within the force itself, as well

414

as during more than 30 joint drills between the force and other military branches and regional theater commands."[83] A *Rocket Force News* report on training improvements noted that "multi-arm, multi-service joint exercises and joint training have become the new normal."[84] The Rocket Force and Strategic Support Force have also held discussions on coordinating their respective forces in future joint campaigns.[85]

Despite the recent emphasis on joint operations, the PLA may experience difficulties in integrating Rocket Force units into joint operations. There are reports of challenges involving the force, with particular emphasis on the concepts and practices of personnel. As one brigade commander described it, "It's a problem of old wine in a new bottle."[86] A report on efforts to better coordinate between the theater commands and services noted that while members of the various services had been dispatched to help staff the theater commands and their knowledge of their own service was quite good, their understanding of joint operations exhibited "noticeable gaps."[87]

A significant development is apparent progress in integrating Rocket Force command and control structures with those of the theater commands. Initial reports following the establishment of the Rocket Force suggested that China's missile units had not yet been integrated into the theater joint command and control structures established as part of the reforms. Rocket Force command and control appeared to remain centralized and not delegated to theater commanders, which would hamper effectiveness in future joint campaigns. The greater institutional independence of the Rocket Force vis-à-vis both the theater commands and other services may have exacerbated this problem. Divided command would make it more difficult to coordinate the actions of Rocket Force missile brigades and those forces assigned directly to a theater command in a fast-moving crisis without clear command authorities and an integrated communications network.

However, more recent reports on the relationship between the Rocket Force and theater commands have emphasized efforts to improve jointness, with some language suggesting conventional Rocket Force missile units *may* be formally under the command of TC joint operations command centers. One recent report in *Rocket Force News* observes, "in the future of combat, all war will be joint, and without jointness there will be no victory."[88] The same account reports that "this base has joined the joint operations chain of command" and that "accelerating [the base's] integration into the TC joint operations command system . . . is a top priority."[89] A 2017 report on joint exercises led by the East Sea Fleet, in describing the need to enhance coordination in joint operations, mentioned the Rocket Force alongside the army and navy, suggesting a similar relationship between each of the services and the theater command.[90] A report on integrating a missile base into a TC joint operations command system noted that "when we cross the threshold into the theater command, we are like one family."[91] Several accounts from Rocket Force sources mention efforts by the missile forces to "integrate" or "build into" TC joint operations command centers and cite the presence of Rocket Force officers within TC joint operations command centers.[92] Articles as recent as early 2018 report that efforts to improve integration between Rocket Force command and control systems and those of the theater commands are ongoing and "exploratory," suggesting that the efforts are as yet incomplete.[93] It is still not entirely clear how and to what extent theater commands will directly command missile units. For example, a sample of recent reports do not explicitly describe direct command by theater commands over missile force units or the attachment of missile force units to them. However, it is clear that the Rocket Force is emphasizing efforts to enhance coordination with the theater commands and other services and is undertaking steps to deepen that coordination.

It is not yet clear how far the PLA will integrate Rocket Force units into the joint operations command and control over the theater commands or why that integration has proceeded more slowly than the integration of units from the other services. There are several possible explanations for the slow pace. PLA leadership might have decided that maintaining the current Rocket Force organization exploits economies of scale and operational synergies. Some of the missile systems operated by the force include both conventional and nuclear variants. Even missiles of different systems may share logistics, maintenance, and training requirements. Transferring control of conventional units to the theater commands would likely have required the creation of parallel and redundant structures. As one expert notes, "personnel, logistics, and training requirements for only two SRBM brigades proved unwieldy for the army when most SRBM units are assigned to the Second Artillery."[94]

There may also be operational reasons for maintaining current command and control arrangements for conventional missile units. TC leaders probably lack familiarity with missile operations and Rocket Force units. CMC leaders, including Xi Jinping, may also want to maintain tight central control over China's conventional and nuclear missile systems given their unique ability to strike targets abroad and potentially initiate a conflict due to carelessness or poor judgment. The accidental launch in July 2016 of a Taiwanese antiship missile that killed a fisherman provided a sobering reminder that such concerns are not merely academic.[95]

Alternatively, the PLA may intend to fully integrate conventional Rocket Force units into the TC command and control mechanisms, and the relatively slow pace of progress may merely reflect the challenges of integrating units that historically have been more separate from the rest of the military.

Future Force Structure and Nuclear Strategy

A more powerful Rocket Force may also be able to wield greater influence in shaping the country's nuclear strategy and policies. Some experts have suggested that as China's political leadership has become less actively focused on nuclear weapons issues, the PLA may enjoy greater autonomy in the nuclear realm. However, the Rocket Force's influence on China's nuclear strategy and policies may depend on the extent to which the Rocket Force prioritizes either the conventional or nuclear mission set.

At the moment, the Rocket Force appears to treat conventionally armed missiles differently than nuclear-armed ones. The Rocket Force has deployed conventionally armed missiles in much greater numbers than nuclear-armed missiles. The Rocket Force reportedly already controls more than 1,200 conventional short-range ballistic missiles,[96] compared to an estimated roughly 160 nuclear-capable ones, and it is estimated that more than half of personnel are assigned to conventional forces.[97] In the past decade, officers who comprise Rocket Force senior leadership were most likely to have served in Base 61 (formerly Base 52), the force's premier conventional base opposite Taiwan, and almost no officers have served in both an ICBM base and Base 61. Doctrine for conventionally armed missiles also emphasizes preemptive use, in contrast with China's no-first-use policy for nuclear weapons.

However, the Rocket Force's dual identity presents unique bureaucratic choices, and its approach to the conventional and nuclear mission sets may evolve along one of at least three lines, depending on both the Rocket Force's own institutional priorities and its relative power vis-à-vis other services and civilian leadership. The first is that a more powerful Rocket Force could advocate for the adoption of a more aggressive nuclear posture. The Rocket Force's approach to conventional missiles may represent its preferred doctrine and approach, absent the political interference that accompanies decisions about nuclear weapons. In this scenario, a more powerful Rocket Force would press to make China's nuclear doctrine and forces more closely resemble the country's conventional missile doctrine and forces.[98] This could include lobbying for a host of more assertive doctrinal and operational choices, potentially including the peacetime mating of warheads, increase in alert status, launch-on-warning posture, or abolition of China's no-first-use policy. Evidence to support this hypothesis includes statements from officers in the Rocket Force and former Second Artillery advocating the adoption of a higher alert status throughout the force and a reconsideration of no-first-use.[99]

A second possibility is that a more powerful Rocket Force may be inclined to disregard the nuclear mission and shift more of its resources and attention toward the conventional one. Like many military organizations, the Rocket Force may regard nuclear weapons as a distraction from the core mission. A review of career patterns within China's missile forces suggests that experience with conventionally armed missile units is more likely to lead to a senior leadership position within the Rocket Force. Officers who have served in units tasked with primarily conventional missions are more likely to ascend to the ranks of senior leadership than officers who have served in units tasked with primarily regional or strategic nuclear missions.[100] There is also evidence of an at least informal hierarchy among the various missile bases, with Base 61 (formerly Base 52), the Rocket Force's premier conventional missile base opposite Taiwan, sitting at the top. In addition, while China has seen only a modest growth in the size of its nuclear arsenal, its conventional forces have expanded dramatically so that, today, an estimated 80 percent of all missiles and half of Rocket Force personnel are assigned to conventional missions.[101] A more powerful Rocket Force may advocate for more emphasis and investment in conventional forces, with the nuclear deterrent persisting in its current form.

Third, civilian leaders may continue to shape operational practices and doctrines (especially in the nuclear domain), regardless of Rocket Force priorities. Despite the extent of military reforms, the impact on the Rocket Force has been notable more for continuity than change. The civilian leadership may still exert significant control over the policies and practices of China's missiles forces and continue to require a relatively restrained nuclear posture.

It is not entirely clear which of these paths the Rocket Force may take. The first two possibilities are not mutually exclusive. China could push for an expansion and prioritization of its conventional missile forces at the expense of its nuclear forces, while Rocket Force leaders simultaneously lobby for a more assertive nuclear posture. The relationship between the Rocket Force and civilian leadership is especially opaque, making it difficult to determine the extent to which the Rocket Force will be able to determine its own institutional priorities and practices. However, there are unconfirmed reports that, with the increasing professionalization of the PLA and the turning of civilian attention to other matters, the Rocket Force may be gaining increased autonomy.[102] If true, this would make it easier for the force to adopt more assertive policies and practices.

Future Interservice Politics over Other Strategic Systems

Elevation to a full-fledged service may give the Rocket Force the institutional prestige and resources necessary to compete effectively with the other services for resources and missions. As the PLA rebalances away from traditional army dominance and slower economic growth leads to slower growth in military spending, interservice rivalry, and competition to control emerging missions, will likely become more intense.

Conventional missions and forces may present such a "growth area" to the Rocket Force. With growing PLA emphasis on conducting joint conventional operations, the force might seek to expand its conventional forces and missions. While China's relatively restrained nuclear strategy may limit the growth potential of the nuclear mission, conventional operations can more easily be used to justify an expansion in force size and mission set.

Conversely, the Rocket Force maintains a comparative advantage over the other services in the nuclear realm. Chinese leadership views about the limited utility of nuclear weapons and guidance to build a "lean and effective" nuclear deterrent imply a cap on the size of nuclear forces and the missions assigned to them.[103] However, the Rocket Force could seek to capitalize on its unique nuclear role in a number of ways. First, it could push China's leadership to expand the role of nuclear forces and argue for an expanded force structure and mission set in ways that could potentially lead to more aggressive changes in overall strategy and policy.[104] The Rocket Force might also make a play for operational control of China's emergent fleet of *Jin*-class ballistic missile submarines (SSBNs). A number of Chinese and American experts have predicted that China's future SSBN force could fall under the command of the Rocket Force, though few have offered specifics about how such a command arrangement might work.[105]

The PLA Navy has little to no experience controlling nuclear weapons, as China built only one hull of the previous generation *Xia*-class SSBN, which never conducted a single operational patrol.[106] To the extent that greater operational experience with nuclear weapons increases confidence and decreases the likelihood of accidents, mistakes, and misperceptions, centralizing nuclear control under the Rocket Force might improve strategic stability by reducing the risk of accidental or unauthorized launch. Conversely, the Rocket Force has no experience running a naval fleet of any kind, let alone the kinds of complex operations required to operate and protect an SSBN force. Regardless of future command and control structures, Chinese SSBNs would undoubtedly be staffed and operated by navy crews and serviced in navy ports.

Finally, the Rocket Force could push to gain operational control of conventional strategic assets such as the DF-21D antiship ballistic missile or direct-ascent antisatellite capabilities. Both of these weapons are based on ballistic missile systems already operated by the Rocket Force, and their importance as strategic assets argues for strict centralized control.

China's sweeping military reforms have ushered in substantial changes in the relative status and relationships between different parts of the People's Liberation Army. The Rocket Force has arguably emerged as the biggest winner in the reforms. The navy and air force lost operational control of their forces to the theater commands, and the army suffered a reduction in both formal status and administrative power after the dissolution of the General Staff Department. The Rocket Force, on the other hand, has maintained direct control of its nuclear units, boosted its formal organizational status, and strengthened its ability to compete against the other services for resources and missions.

Conclusion

China's missile forces are undergoing significant changes, though it is still unclear how far those changes will go. Organizational reforms, technological developments, and operational changes all raise questions about whether the future of China's missile forces will resemble the past.

Organizationally, the Rocket Force has increased in prestige and, likely, power. For its first few decades of existence, the Second Artillery, the Rocket Force's predecessor, fielded only a few dozen unsophisticated missile systems. Today, it is estimated to command over a thousand total missile systems. The recent wave of PLA-wide military reforms saw the elevation of the Rocket Force to the level of a full-fledged service, increasing its institutional status and placing it on par with the other military services.

Technologically, China's ongoing modernization program has changed the technological makeup of its missile forces. In the nuclear domain, China's missile forces have evolved from a small and relatively unsophisticated set of liquid-fueled stationary missiles armed with single warheads into a force of increasingly advanced road-mobile solid-fueled missiles, some of which can be equipped with multiple warheads. China is also developing a sea-based leg for its nuclear deterrent, developing and deploying a new generation of SSBNs and accompanying submarine-launched ballistic missiles, and there are initial reports of a next-generation strategic nuclear-capable bomber. Just as significant for the Rocket Force, the country's land-based missiles have increasingly shifted from nuclear to conventional and, increasingly, advanced dual-capable missile systems.

Finally, the Rocket Force appears to gradually be changing its operational practices. It has placed greater emphasis on training under realistic conditions by utilizing red-blue team confrontation exercises. Perhaps most significantly, the Rocket Force has increased its integration with the theater commands and has increasingly emphasized joint operations in its training. These operational changes have, in part, been driven by both the organizational and technological changes described herein. The creation of the theater commands and the PLA-wide emphasis on joint operations have catalyzed the Rocket Force focus on jointness. Similarly, the introduction and expansion of conventional units in the Rocket Force has made the organization more relevant to the kinds of conventional conflicts for which the PLA prepares, especially a possible future conflict over Taiwan. These changes raise several important questions about the future of the Rocket Force.

First, will the Rocket Force change its fundamental policies and practices, particularly in the nuclear realm? With its recent elevation to the level of a full service, the Rocket Force may enjoy greater autonomy in deciding its future force composition and operational practices. China has historically adopted a comparatively restrained nuclear posture, but this could change.

Second, will Rocket Force units be able to effectively participate in joint operations, and what will an increased focus on jointness mean for the Rocket Force? As discussed, China's missile forces have historically remained somewhat apart from the rest of the PLA, and the Rocket Force has been comparatively slow to integrate with the newly established theater commands. Challenges persist in integrating Rocket Force units into joint operations, and it remains unclear how long it will take to overcome those challenges. The drive to jointness may end up altering the composition and identity of the Rocket Force by leading to a stronger prioritization of the conventional mission set.

Third, will the introduction and expansion of conventionally armed missiles, especially dual-capable systems, increase the escalatory risks of entanglement? Several scholars have noted that the deployment of dual-use missile systems and the possible collocation of conventional and nuclear missiles could create risks of unintentional escalation in a conflict.[107] The risks generated by this kind of technological entanglement could be mitigated or exacerbated by the operational practices under which those missiles are deployed.

Finally, what will the development of other legs of a nuclear triad mean for the future of both the Rocket Force and China's nuclear policies? The introduction of sea- and air-launched nuclear forces could push the Rocket Force to embrace its conventional identity. The introduction of new nuclear platforms could also create new opportunities or pressures for changes in China's nuclear policies. SSBN operational deployments will likely involve mated warheads and missiles, which could lead the Rocket Force to advocate peacetime mating of warheads and land-based missiles. Conversely, a more diverse and dispersed nuclear force could increase China's confidence in the survivability of its second-strike capability, causing it to forgo more assertive changes to its nuclear posture.

Notes

[1] Early Chinese interest in missiles was also driven by a desire to develop surface-to-air missiles to shoot down U.S. and Taiwanese reconnaissance aircraft that China viewed as compromising its sovereignty.

[2] Jeffrey Lewis, *The Minimum Means of Reprisal: China's Search for Security in the Nuclear Age* (Cambridge: MIT Press, 2007).

[3] Bates Gill, James C. Mulvenon, and Mark A. Stokes, "The Chinese Second Artillery Corps: Transition to Credible Deterrence," in *PLA as Organization*, ed. James C. Mulvenon and Andrew N.D. Yang (Santa Monica, CA: RAND, 2002), 517–518.

[4] Michael S. Chase, *The PLA's Second Artillery Force as a Customer of China's Defense Industry*, Study of Innovation and Technology in China Research Brief 2013-15 (San Diego: Institute on Global Conflict and Cooperation, January 2013), 2, available at <https://escholarship.org/uc/item/1tw930nf>.

[5] This section draws on arguments developed by Jeffrey Lewis and Raymond Wang of the Middlebury Institute of International Studies in Monterey. The author gratefully acknowledges their contributions.

[6] This period is described in detail by Benjamin C. Ostrov, *Conquering Resources: The Growth and Decline of the PLA's Science and Technology Commission for National Defense Science and Technology* (New York: Taylor & Francis, 1992).

[7] See especially Evan Feigenbaum, *China's Techno-Warriors: National Security and Strategic Competition from the Nuclear to the Information Age* (Stanford: Stanford University Press, 2003); and Harlan W. Jencks, "COSTIND Is Dead, Long Live COSTIND! Restructuring China's Defense Scientific, Technical, and Industrial Sector," in *The People's Liberation Army in the Information Age*, ed. James C. Mulvenon (Santa Monica, CA: RAND, 1999), 59–77.

[8] The fact that the DF-1 was an SS-2 copy accounts for a discrepancy in Chinese and U.S. designations: the DF-2 is the CSS-1, DF-3 is the CSS-2, DF-4 is the CSS-3, and DF-5 is the CSS-4. U.S. designations are based on the order in which a missile system was identified.

[9] The Chinese distinguish ranges slightly differently than Americans. Whereas the U.S. Intelligence Community categorizes the DF-4 and DF-5 as intercontinental ballistic missiles (ICBMs), Chinese sources distinguish between the two.

[10] Feigenbaum, *China's Techno-Warriors*, 79.

[11] The author is indebted to Mark A. Stokes of the Project 2049 Institute for this observation.

[12] Michael Krepon, Travis Wheeler, and Shane Mason, eds., *The Lure and Pitfalls of MRVs from the First to the Second Nuclear Age* (Washington, DC: Stimson Center, May 2016), available at <www.stimson.org/sites/default/files/file-attachments/Lure_and_Pitfalls_of_MIRVs.pdf>.

[13] John Wilson Lewis and Xue Litai, *China's Strategic Seapower: The Politics of Force Modernization in the Nuclear Age* (Stanford: Stanford University Press, 1996), 27.

[14] China continued with the submarine-launched ballistic missile (SLBM) program, listing it as one of the "three grasps" that represented an effort to conclude the unfinished business of China's first generation of strategic programs: test an SLBM, deploy an operational ICBM, and launch a communications satellite. The first JL-1 test occurred in October 1982. China's *Xia*-class ballistic missile submarine (SSBN) went to sea in 1983, but likely has never conducted an operational patrol. See Lewis and Xue, *China's Strategic Seapower*, 120.

[15] Ibid., 188.

[16] Ibid.

[17] The Office of the Secretary of Defense (OSD) indicated that the DF-21 had largely replaced the DF-3, which remained deployed by a single brigade by 2005. See *Annual Report to Congress: The Military Power of the People's Republic of China 2005* (Washington, DC: OSD, 2005), available at <www.globalsecurity.org/military/library/report/2005/d20050719china.pdf>. Analysis of commercial satellite imagery suggests that all DF-3A units have been upgraded. See Hans M. Kristensen, "Chinese Nuclear Missile Upgrade Near Dalian," Federation of American Scientists Strategic Security blog, May 21, 2014, available at <https://fas.org/blogs/security/2014/05/dengshaheupgrade/>.

[18] Gill, Mulvenon, and Stokes, "The Chinese Second Artillery Corps."

[19] Shirley A. Kan, *China: Ballistic and Cruise Missiles*, 97-391 F (Washington, DC: Congressional Research Service, August 10, 2000), 14–15.

[20] On failure, see *Annual Report to Congress: Military and Security Developments Involving the People's Republic of China 2010* (Washington, DC: OSD, 2010), 34, available at <www.defense.gov/Portals/1/Documents/pubs/2010_CMPR_Final.pdf>. On technical hurdles see *Annual Report to Congress: Military and Security Developments Involving the People's Republic of China 2011* (Washington, DC: OSD, 2011), 34, 62, available at <www.defense.gov/Portals/1/Documents/pubs/2011_CMPR_Final.pdf>. On success in 2012, see *Annual Report to Congress: Military and Security Developments Involving the People's Republic of China 2013* (Washington, DC: OSD, 2013), 31, available at <www.defense.gov/pubs/2013_china_report_final.pdf>.

[21] *Ballistic and Cruise Missile Threat 2017* (Wright Patterson AFB, OH: National Air and Space Intelligence Center [NASIC], 2017), 30, available at <www.nasic. af.mil/Portals/19/images/Fact%20Sheet%20Images/2017%20Ballistic%20and%20 Cruise%20Missile%20Threat_Final_small.pdf?ver=2017-07-21-083234-343>.

[22] Ibid.

[23] U.S. Government reports make no mention of the DF-25 having ever entered service in China.

[24] *Ballistic and Cruise Missile Threat 2017.*

[25] For a technical analysis of the apparently failed August 2014 test, see James Acton, Catherine Dill, and Jeffrey Lewis, "Crashing Glider, Hidden Hotspring: Analyzing China's August 7, 2014, Hypersonic Glider Test," Arms Control Wonk blog, September 3, 2014, available at <www.armscontrolwonk.com/archive/207443/ crashing-glider-hidden-hotspring/>.

[26] Donald L. Fuell, quoted in *China's Military Modernization and Its Implications for the United States*, Hearing Before the U.S.-China Economic and Security Review Commission, 113th Cong., 2nd sess., January 30, 2014, 36, available at <www. uscc.gov/sites/default/files/USCC%20Hearing%20Transcript%20-%20January%20 30%202014.pdf>.

[27] For more on China's hypersonic glide program, see Lora Saalman, "China's Calculus on Hypersonic Glide," Stockholm International Peace Research Institute (SIPRI), August 15, 2017, available at <www.sipri.org/commentary/topical-back-grounder/2017/chinas-calculus-hypersonic-glide>; and Lora Saalman, *Factoring Russia into the U.S.-Chinese Equation on Hypersonic Glide Vehicles*, No. 2017/1 (Stockholm: SIPRI, January 2017).

[28] For a good overview of the pre-reform Second Artillery Force, see Michael S. Chase, Daniel Yoon, and Mark A. Stokes, "The People's Liberation Army Second Artillery Force (PLASAF) as an Organization," in *The PLA as Organization v2.0*, ed. Kevin Pollpeter and Kenneth W. Allen (Vienna, VA: Defense Group, Inc., 2015).

[29] The author is indebted to Mark A. Stokes for highlighting the importance of grades in assessing where an officer stands in the protocol order.

[30] Until recently, China's missile bases were numbered 51 to 56. Sometime in 2017, the base designations were changed to number from 61 to 66. The numerical order of the previous base designations does not match that of the new designations. For an order of battle using the new base designations, see *2017 Report to Congress of the U.S.-China Economic Review Commission* (Washington, DC: Government Publishing Office, 2017), 219–220. For examples of Chinese sources

referring to missile bases by the new designations, see "Our City Holds Military Coordination Meeting to Specially Study How to Resolve Practical Troop Difficulties and Problems" [我市召开军地协调会专题研究解决部队实际困难和问题], Lanzhou Shuangyong Office, August 8, 2017, available at <www.lzsy.gov.cn/web/jsgl/sydt/486.html?402880ee5ac59a52015ac5d2da73023e,486>; "Yangshan Holds Recruit Enlistment Ceremony—125 Recruits Set Off to the Barracks" [阳山举行新兵入伍仪式—125名新兵奔赴军营], Yangshan County People's Government, September 13, 2017, available at <http://ysq.yangshan.gov.cn/info/4001435813?templateId=40546>; and "In Xianfeng County, 112 Recruits Embark on a Journey" [咸丰县112名新兵踏上征程], Chengfeng County People's Government, September 11, 2017, available at <www.xianfeng.gov.cn/xfyw/94782.jhtml>.

[31] Mark A. Stokes, *China's Nuclear Warhead Storage and Handling System* (Arlington, VA: Project 2049 Institute, March 12, 2010).

[32] The basic unit of firepower for nuclear-armed forces is the battalion, while for conventional units, it appears to be the platoon. See Kenneth W. Allen and Maryanne Kivlehan-Wise, "Implementing PLA Second Artillery Doctrinal Reforms," in *China's Revolution in Doctrinal Affairs: Emerging Trends in the Operational Art of the Chinese People's Liberation Army*, ed. James C. Mulvenon and David M. Finklestein (Alexandria, VA: CNA, 2005).

[33] Fiona S. Cunningham and M. Taylor Fravel, "Assuring Assured Retaliation: China's Nuclear Posture and U.S.-China Strategic Stability," *International Security* 40, no. 2 (Fall 2015), 44. The command and control arrangements for the Rocket Force remain opaque and difficult to evaluate. For some evidence and discussion, see David C. Logan, "PLA Reforms and China's Nuclear Forces," *Joint Force Quarterly* 83 (4th Quarter 2016), 58–60. Evidence of more recent integration of Rocket Force and theater command command and control arrangements is discussed in a later section of this chapter.

[34] *Ballistic & Cruise Missile Threat* (Wright-Patterson Air Force Base, OH: NASIC, 2013), available at <www.fas.org/programs/ssp/nukes/nuclearweapons/NASIC2013_050813.pdf>.

[35] "2nd Artillery Soldiers Hidden in Underground Caverns for 8-Day Exercise Eat Leeks and Sweet Peppers" [二炮士兵隐蔽在地下洞库8天生吃韭菜甜椒], *PLA Daily* [解放军报], May 6, 2013, available at <http://mil.news.sina.com.cn/2013-05-06/0420723740.html>.

[36] On the challenges of life underground, see Mark A. Stokes and Ian Easton, *Half Lives: A Preliminary Assessment of China's Nuclear Warhead Life Extension and Safety Program* (Arlington, VA: Project 2049 Institute, July 29, 2013).

[37] *Annual Report to Congress: Military and Security Developments Involving the People's Republic of China 2013.*

[38] *Ballistic and Cruise Missile Threat 2017* (Wright Patterson AFB, OH: NASIC, 2017), 30, available at <www.nasic.af.mil/Portals/19/images/Fact%20 Sheet%20Images/2017%20Ballistic%20and%20Cruise%20Missile%20Threat_ Final_small.pdf?ver=2017-07-21-083234-343>; "The People's Liberation Army Navy: A Modern Navy with Chinese Characteristics," Office of Naval Intelligence, U.S. Navy, August 2009, available at <www.fas.org/irp/agency/oni/pla-navy.pdf>; "China's Navy 2007," Office of Naval Intelligence, U.S. Navy, available at <www. fas.org/irp/agency/oni/chinanavy2007.pdf>; and Ronald O'Rourke, *China Naval Modernization: Implications for U.S. Navy Capabilities—Background and Issues for Congress*, RL33153 (Washington, DC: Congressional Research Service, February 8, 2012), available at <www.hsdl.org/?view&did=701351>.

[39] For more on the country's emerging SSBN fleet, see David C. Logan, *China's Future SSBN Command and Control Structure*, INSS Strategic Forum 299 (Washington, DC: NDU Press, 2016), available at <http://ndupress.ndu.edu/Media/News/ Article/1013472/chinas-future-ssbn-command-and-control-structure/>.

[40] In 1984, the U.S. Intelligence Community was "unable to identify the associated airfield storage sites" for the "small number" of nuclear capable aircraft that "probably" had nuclear bombs assigned to them. The Defense Intelligence Agency concluded that it was "improbable that China's air forces have a strategic nuclear delivery mission" because "it is unlikely that these obsolescent aircraft could successfully penetrate the sophisticated air defense networks of modern military powers." See the declassified "Defense Estimative Brief: Nuclear Weapons Systems in China," April 24, 1984, 3–4, available at <www.hsdl.org/?abstract&did=788630>. In 1993, the Intelligence Community concluded that the "Chinese air force has no units whose primary mission is to deliver China's small stockpile of nuclear bombs." See "Report to Congress on Status of China, India, and Pakistan Nuclear and Ballistic Missile Programs," U.S. National Security Council, August 4, 2000, available at <https://fas.org/irp/threat/930728-wmd.htm>.

[41] See, for example, Hans M. Kristensen and Robert S. Norris, "Chinese Nuclear Forces, 2016," *Bulletin of the Atomic Scientists* 72, no. 4 (June 13, 2016), 206.

[42] Michael S. Chase, "Nuclear Bomber Could Boost PLAAF Strategic Role, Create Credible Triad," *China Brief* 17, no. 9 (July 6, 2017), available at <https:// jamestown.org/program/nuclear-bomber-boost-plaaf-strategic-role-create- credible-triad/>.

[43] The 2017 NASIC report does not include any reference to the DF-3 system, suggesting they may have been completely phased out from China's missile systems. See *Ballistic and Cruise Missile Threat 2017*.

[44] "Guo Yafei's 'Third Eye'" [郭亚飞的 "第三只眼"], CNTV [中国网路电视台], May 4, 2011, available at <http://military.cntv.cn/program/hpnd/20110504/105020.shtml>.

[45] Hans M. Kristensen, "Extensive Nuclear Missile Deployment Area Discovered in Central China," Federation of American Scientists blog, May 15, 2008, available at: <https://fas.org/blogs/security/2008/05/extensive-nuclear-deployment-area-discovered-in-central-china/>.

[46] Ibid.

[47] Gao Hong [高航], "History: Second Artillery Missile Forces Have Become Capable of Strategic Nuclear Counterattack" [历程:二炮成为具有核反击能力的战略导弹部队], *China Military Online* [中国军网], July 31, 2005, available at <https://web.archive.org/web/20071111180904/http://news.xinhuanet.com/mil/2005-07/31/content_3282531.htm>.

[48] Stokes, *China's Nuclear Warhead Storage and Handling System*.

[49] Wei Zhigang [卫志刚], "Rocket Force Turns Eyes Toward Future War, Organizes Red-Blue Opposition Training" [火箭军着眼未来战争组织红蓝对抗训练理论集训], *Rocket Force Daily* [火箭兵报], April 29, 2016.

[50] "Diao Guangming: Change of Face Is Only to Win in War" [刁光明: "变脸"只为打胜仗], *PLA Daily* [解放军报], April 17, 2017, available at <www.81.cn/jfjbmap/content/2016-04/17/content_141844.htm>.

[51] Ibid.

[52] "Rocket Force Normalizing the Conduct of Confrontation Exercises to Enhance Actual Combat Capabilities" [火箭军常态化开展对抗演练提升实战能力], *PLA Daily* [解放军报], September 8, 2016, available at <www.81.cn/jfjbmap/content/2016-09/08/content_156037.htm>.

[53] "Exposing Our 'Electronic Blue Forces' Harassing Forces while Faking Red Team Orders" [揭秘我"电子蓝军" 干扰同时假冒红方下命令], *PLA Daily* [解放军报], April 19, 2016, available at <www.81.cn/jwgz/2016-04/19/content_7012144.htm>.

[54] Logan, "PLA Reforms and China's Nuclear Forces."

[55] Phillip C. Saunders and Joel Wuthnow, "China's Goldwater-Nichols? Assessing PLA Organizational Reforms," *Joint Force Quarterly* 82 (3rd Quarter 2016), 68–75.

[56] Ibid.

57   David M. Finkelstein, *Hearing on Developments in China's Military Force Projection and Expeditionary Capabilities*, Testimony Before the U.S.-China Economic and Security Review Commission, January 21, 2016, 114th Cong., 2nd sess., available at <www.uscc.gov/sites/default/files/USCC%20Testimony%202016_Finkelstein.pdf>.

58   Zhao Lei and Li Xiaokun, "Three New Military Branches Created in Key PLA Reform," *China Daily* (Beijing), January 2, 2016, available at <www.chinadailyasia.com/nation/2016-01/02/content_15366591.html>.

59   The author thanks Joel Wuthnow of National Defense University for this observation. See Wang Shibin and An Puzhong [王士彬, 安普忠], "Founding Ceremony for Army Leading Organization, Rocket Force and Strategic Support Force Held in Beijing" [陆军领导机构火箭军战略支援部队成立大会在京举行], *China Military Online* [中国军网], January 1, 2016, available at <http://cd.81.cn/content/2016-01/01/content_6841020.htm>.

60   Cao Zhi and Zhang Xuanjie [曹智, 张选杰], "Xi Jinping: Building a Strong Informationized Strategic Missile Force" [习近平: 建设强大的信息化战略导弹部队], Xinhua Online [新华网], available at <http://news.xinhuanet.com/politics/2012-12/05/c_113922221.htm>.

61   Zheng Wenhao [郑文浩], "China's Second Artillery Force Renamed to Rocket Force, What's the Mystery Behind Not Adding the Word Strategic?" [中国二炮部队改名火箭军 不加战略二字有何玄机], *Sina News* [新浪军事], January 1, 2016, available at <http://mil.news.sina.com.cn/china/2016-01-01/doc-ifxneept3524560.shtml>.

62   Huang Jinxin [黄金新], "My Views on the Rocket Force as a Strategic Military Service" [战略军种火箭军之我见] *Rocket Force News* [火箭兵报], January 13, 2016.

63   "Transcript of Eastern Theater Commander Liu Yuejun's Interview" [东部战区司令员刘粤军访谈录], *China Military Online* [中国军网], March 3, 2016, available at <http://jz.chinamil.com.cn/zhuanti/content/2016-03/04/content_6940918.htm>.

64   Kenneth W. Allen, Dennis J. Blasko, and John F. Corbett, "The PLA's New Organizational Structure: What Is Known, Unknown, and Speculation (Part 1)," *China Brief* 16, no. 3 (February 4, 2016), available at <https://jamestown.org/program/the-plas-new-organizational-structure-what-is-known-unknown-and-speculation-part-1/>.

65   Choi Chi-yuk, "The Rising Star in China's Military Tipped as Future Air Force Leader," *South China Morning Post* (Hong Kong), June 17, 2016, available at <www.scmp.com/news/china/diplomacy-defence/article/1976523/rising-star-chinas-military-tipped-future-air-force>. This would be consistent with the

relationship between the Second Artillery and former military regions. Unlike the services, Second Artillery officers did not serve as deputy commanders within the military region, illustrating the unique "vertical command" structure of the Second Artillery. See Roger Cliff, *Shaking the Heavens and Splitting the Earth: Chinese Air Force Employment Concepts in the 21ˢᵗ Century* (Santa Monica, CA: RAND, 2014), 23.

[66] Zhang Hui, "PLA Rocket Force Names 100 Officers to Commands," *Global Times* (Beijing), April 12, 2016, available at <www.globaltimes.cn/content/978291.shtml>.

[67] Yan Jiaqi, ed. [闫嘉琪], "Rocket Force Base Explores Standardization of Joint Operational Processes" [火箭军某基地着力探索联合作战流程规范化], *PLA Daily* [解放军报], April 1, 2016, available at <http://military.people.com.cn/n1/2016/0401/c1011-28243986.html>.

[68] Feng and Duan, "Theater Command Rocket Forces Enter Joint Training Like a Fish Taking to Water."

[69] Information on Second Artillery base and brigade locations and Military Unit Cover Designators is from Jeffrey Lewis, *Paper Tigers: China's Nuclear Posture* (New York: Routledge, 2014), 116–121; and Cunningham and Fravel, "Assuring Assured Retaliation," 7–50.

[70] Based on analysis of Rocket Force base and brigade locations and reported theater command boundaries, bases 61, 62, 63, and 64 appear to control units garrisoned in different theater commands.

[71] Zhou was promoted to succeed Wei Fenghe as Rocket Force commander in September 2017. See Mimi Lau, "China's Missile Forces Get a New Tech-Focused Commander," *South China Morning Post* (Hong Kong), September 16, 2017, available at <www.scmp.com/news/china/diplomacy-defence/article/2111497/chinas-missile-forces-get-new-tech-focused-commander>. For more on changes to the Central Military Commission, see Liu Zhen, "Xi Jinping Shakes Up China's Military Leadership," *South China Morning Post* (Hong Kong), October 26, 2017, available at <www.scmp.com/news/china/diplomacy-defence/article/2116856/what-changes-top-mean-chinas-military>.

[72] John W. Lewis and Xue Litai, "Making China's Nuclear War Plan," *Bulletin of the Atomic Scientists* 68, no. 5 (2012), 54.

[73] Zhang Zhouxiang, "Rocket Force to Protect National Interests," *China Daily* (Beijing), January 5, 2016, available at <http://usa.chinadaily.com.cn/opinion/2016-01/05/content_22933648.htm>.

[74] Du Linbo and Cai Ruijin [杜林波,蔡瑞金], "How Does the Rocket Force Build from the Basic Level Under the New Services-Equip System" [火箭军在军种主建新体制下如何抓建基层], *PLA Daily* [解放军报], April 26, 2016, available at <www.81.cn/jmywyl/2016-04/26/content_7023132.htm>.

[75] See remarks in Zhang Tao, ed., "Defense Ministry's Regular Press Conference on June 30," *China Military Online*, June 30, 2016, available at <http://english.pladaily.com.cn/news-channels/2016-06/30/content_7127994.htm>.

[76] "Deeply Implement Chairman Xi and the Central Military Commission's Decision, Work Hard to Construct a Powerful and Modern Rocket Force on a New Starting Point" [深入贯彻习主席和中央军委决策部署在新的起点上努力建设强大的现代化火箭军], *Rocket Force News* [火箭军报], March 2, 2016.

[77] Huang, "My Views on the Rocket Force as a Strategic Military Service."

[78] Ibid.

[79] Li Xuan [李璇], "From 'Force' to 'Service,' Rocket Force Must Shoulder Historic Heavy Responsibility" [由"兵" 变 "军",火箭军更要扛起历史重任], *Science and Technology Daily* [科技日报], February 23, 2016, available at <www.81.cn/depb/2016-02/23/content_6923516.htm>.

[80] Feng and Duan, "Theater Command Rocket Forces Enter Joint Training Like a Fish Taking to Water."

[81] Ibid.

[82] Kenneth W. Allen and Jana Allen, *Building a Strong Informationized Strategic Missile Force: An Overview of the Second Artillery Force with a Focus on Training in 2014* (Washington, DC: The Jamestown Foundation, 2015), available at <https://jamestown.org/wp-content/uploads/2017/10/Building-Strategic-Missile-Force_Final.pdf>.

[83] Zhao Lei, "Rocket Force More Versatile," *China Daily* (Beijing), June 21, 2017, available at <http://usa.chinadaily.com.cn/epaper/2017-06/21/content_29830330.htm>.

[84] Wang Tianlin [王天林] et al., "Revolutionary Innovation, Aiming for the Bull's-Eye of the Battlefield" [改革创新,瞄准战场靶心], *Rocket Force News* [火箭兵报], March 16, 2016.

[85] "Rocket Force and Strategic Support Force Discuss Joint Warfighting" [火箭军同战略支援部队讨论联合作战现场热烈], *PLA Daily* [解放军报], February 3, 2016, available at <http://mil.huanqiu.com/china/2016-02/8496915.html>.

[86] Feng Jinyuan and Yang Yonggang [冯金源, 杨永刚], "Certain Rocket Force Missile Brigade Organizes 'Blue Army' Supervision to Specially 'Nitpick'" [火箭

军某导弹旅组织"蓝军"督导专门"找茬"], *PLA Daily* [解放军报], June 13, 2016, available at <www.81.cn/depb/2016-06/13/content_7097562.htm>.

[87] "Central Theater Command Starts Its Campaign to Enhance Joint Operational Command Capabilities" [中部战区起步开局大力提升联合作战指挥能力], Xinhua, April 1, 2016, available at <http://military.people.com.cn/n1/2016/0401/c1011-28244657.html>.

[88] "A Certain Base for the First Time Undertakes Cluster Command 'Winning Iron Fist'" [某基地首次集群指挥锤炼 "制胜铁拳"], *Rocket Force News* [火箭军报], November 25, 2017, 1.

[89] Ibid.

[90] "Combat Readiness, Sword Pointed at New Heights" [备战, 剑指新高地], *People's Navy* [人民海军], October 21, 2017, 4.

91 "Concentrate on Sharpening the Sword, the More the Strategic Iron Fist Is Used, the Harder It Becomes" [潜心砺剑, 战略铁拳越练越硬], *PLA Daily* [解放军报], February 6, 2018, available at <www.81.cn/jfjbmap/content/2018-02/06/content_198862.htm>.

[92] "A Certain Base's Joint Training Wins 'Iron Fist'" [某基地联战联训淬炼制胜 "铁拳"], *Rocket Force News* [火箭军报], November 11, 2017, 1; "Command Academy Focuses Intently on Requirements of Winning, Reforms Military Education to Reflect Actual Combat" [指挥学院紧盯打赢需要大抓实战化教学改革], *Rocket Force News* [火箭军报], July 8, 2017, 1a; and Guo Yuandan [郭媛丹], "How China's Theater Commands Conduct Operations: By Truly Joining Systems and Fusing Command and Control Entities" [中国战区如何打仗: 中国战区如何打仗:体系深度联合、指挥一体融合, 指挥一体融合] *Huanqiu Wang* [环球网], October 8, 2017.

[93] "Concentrate on Sharpening the Sword."

[94] Dennis J. Blasko, *The Chinese Army Today: Tradition and Transformation for the 21st Century* (London: Routledge, 2006), 96.

[95] Austin Ramzy, "Taiwan Navy Accidentally Fires Antiship Missile, Killing Fisherman," *New York Times*, July 1, 2016, available at <www.nytimes.com/2016/07/02/world/asia/taiwan-china-missile.html?_r=0>.

[96] *Annual Report to Congress: Military and Security Developments Involving the People's Republic of China 2016* (Washington, DC: OSD, 2016), 25.

[97] Kristensen and Norris, "Chinese Nuclear Forces, 2016"; Jeffrey Lewis, "China's Belated Embrace of MIRVs," in *The Lure & Pitfalls of MIRVs*, 105.

[98] Eric Heginbotham et al., "Domestic Factors Could Accelerate the Evolution of China's Nuclear Posture," RAND Corporation Research Brief, 3, available at

<www.rand.org/pubs/research_briefs/RB9956.html>. For a more thorough analysis of ongoing and future changes to China's nuclear forces, see Eric Heginbotham et al., *China's Evolving Nuclear Deterrent: Major Drivers and Issues for the United States* (Santa Monica, CA: RAND, 2017), chapters 9, 10, available at <www.rand.org/pubs/research_reports/RR1628.html>.

[99] See, for example, Gregory Kulacki, "China's Military Calls for Putting Its Nuclear Forces on Alert," Union of Concerned Scientists, January 2016, available at <www.ucsusa.org/sites/default/files/attach/2016/02/China-Hair-Trigger-full-report.pdf>.

[100] David C. Logan, "Career Paths in the PLA Rocket Force: What They Tell Us," *Asian Security*, January 25, 2018.

[101] For estimates on delivery systems, see *Annual Report to Congress: Military and Security Developments Involving the People's Republic of China 2016*, 25; and Kristensen and Norris, "Chinese Nuclear Forces, 2016." For estimates on personnel distribution, see Lewis, "China's Belated Embrace of MIRVs," 105.

[102] Author communication with Chinese nuclear expert, 2017.

[103] On China's nuclear strategy and views of nuclear weapons, see M. Taylor Fravel and Evan S. Medeiros, "China's Search for Assured Retaliation: The Evolution of Chinese Nuclear Strategy and Force Structure," *International Security* 35, no. 2 (Fall 2010); and Cunningham and Fravel, "Assuring Assured Retaliation."

[104] Lewis, "China's Belated Embrace of MIRVs," 105.

[105] Liu Kun, ed. [刘昆], "Expert: Why Is the Second Artillery Being Elevated to the Rocket Force, the Fourth Military Service?" [专家:二炮为何要升格为第四大军种火箭军?], *Qianjiang Evening News* [钱江晚报], January 9, 2016, available at <http://mil.huanqiu.com/observation/2016-01/8346721.html>; Kelsey Davenport, "China Elevates Nuclear Rocket Force," Arms Control Association, March 3, 2016, available at <www.armscontrol.org/ACT/2016_03/News/China-Elevates-Nuclear-Rocket-Force>.

[106] Lewis and Xue, *China's Strategic Seapower*; and Hans M. Kristensen, "China SSBN Fleet Getting Ready—But for What?" Federation of American Scientists, April 25, 2014, available at <https://fas.org/blogs/security/2014/04/chinassbnfleet/>.

[107] See, for example, Thomas J. Christensen, "The Meaning of the Nuclear Evolution: China's Strategic Modernization and U.S.-China Security Relations," *Journal of Strategic Studies* 35, no. 4 (August 2012), 447–487; Cunningham and Fravel, "Assuring Assured Retaliation," 7–50; and Caitlin Talmadge, "Would China

Go Nuclear? Assessing the Risk of Chinese Nuclear Escalation in a Conventional War with the United States," *International Security* 41, no. 4 (Spring 2017), 50–92.

CHAPTER 12

CHINA'S STRATEGIC SUPPORT FORCE

A Force for a New Era

By John Costello and Joe McReynolds

In late 2015, the People's Liberation Army (PLA) initiated a series of ongoing reforms that have brought dramatic changes to its structure, model of warfighting, and organizational culture. Undoubtedly, among the most important changes has been the creation of a unified Strategic Support Force (SSF) [*zhanlüe zhiyuan budui*, 战略支援部队]. This force combines assorted space, cyber, and electronic warfare (EW) capabilities from across the PLA services and its former general departments.

The few statements that Xi Jinping has made about the role of the Strategic Support Force have been almost comically circumspect, affirming that it is both a "strategic" force and a "supporting" one. Even 2 years after its founding, some aspects of the SSF's organizational structure remain opaque to outside observers. However, despite this lack of transparency, a coherent picture has gradually emerged of how various SSF components fit together and the strategic roles and missions that they are intended to fulfill.

Although the Strategic Support Force is often described as having been designed to streamline the organization of China's information warfare forces and thereby improve their efficiency, such incremental advantages are not the primary reason that the SSF was created. Rather, the SSF's structure is first and foremost intended to create synergies between disparate information warfare capabilities in order to execute specific types of strategic missions that Chinese leaders believe will be decisive in future major wars. The PLA views cyber, electronic, and psychological warfare as interconnected subcomponents of information warfare writ large. Understanding the primary strategic roles of the SSF is essential to understanding how China will practice information operations in a war or crisis.

This chapter begins by examining the evolution of China's approach to the space, cyber, and electromagnetic domains over the last three decades. It then provides an analysis of military organizational reforms launched in 2015, contextualizing the SSF's creation against the backdrop of broader changes to PLA structure, command organization, and changing concepts of operations before focusing on the organizational dynamics of the SSF itself. The chapter then explores each of the SSF's operational components, those responsible for its space, cyber, EW, and psychological operations mission areas. After giving a brief overview of how peacetime-wartime command relationships have shifted in the reforms, the chapter then details the new joint force structure of the Central Military Commission (CMC) and evaluates how the responsibilities for intelligence and technical reconnaissance, network and EW, and information support missions have shifted force-wide given the preeminence of the SSF in these missions and the new CMC and regional theater command structure. Finally, the chapter outlines the key operational responsibilities of the SSF in the context of the two primary roles it plays: strategic information support and strategic information operations. The chapter then defines China's conceptualization of information warfare as applied to the SSF and notes key points where this concept aligns with and diverges from a U.S. approach.

A key observation underpinning the research for this chapter is the insight that the PLA, at least in the initial stages of its reforms, has pursued what we call a "bricks, not clay" approach to reorganization. Instead of building whole organizations from scratch, the PLA effected structural changes by renaming, resubordinating, or moving whole, existing organizations and their component parts and then redefining their command relationships within the PLA. While the names, descriptors, designators, and, in some cases, the commanders of these organizations have changed, the addresses, key personnel, phone numbers, and other unique designators have remained consistent throughout the reforms. Through analysis of hundreds of public bid and tender documents, contracts, articles, and research papers, the authors have been able to identify numerous instances where these designators remained the same, while the organizations to which they were tied underwent changes of name or affiliation. From clusters of these instances, it can be inferred which existing organizations have been renamed or shifted in the reorganization, and from that one can determine both the new structure of the SSF and changes in the PLA's larger command context.

Identifying the Military Unit Cover Designators (MUCDs) that have been assigned to the SSF, a block of numbers between 32001 and 32099, was particularly useful in this analysis. These designators are commonly used as a cover mechanism for open-source references to PLA units. Since organizations and units operating within this block are now subordinate to the SSF, one can apply the above methodology to systematically identify SSF units and their command relationships.[1]

This structural analysis informs analysis of the roles and missions of the SSF itself. Based on the assumption that the operational responsibilities of most units and organizations that were shifted to the SSF have not been fundamentally changed by the reforms, one can draw upon the existing body of Chinese military and PLA literature to gain insight into prior organizations that are now components of the SSF. With an understanding of the structure and mission of the SSF, one can then determine its broader roles and responsibilities within the PLA by evaluating this mission set against public comments, strategic literature, an understanding of the intent and impetus for reforms, as well as the broader command and organizational context under which the SFF was being formed.

The SSF in Historical Context

China's approach to the interrelated space, cyber, and electromagnetic domains—the main functional and warfighting areas for the Strategic Support Force—has undergone considerable evolution over the past three decades. In the 1990s, China identified and absorbed lessons from the 1991 Persian Gulf War, which in its view demonstrated that "the new revolution in military affairs had moved from theoretical exploration into the phase of implementation . . . drawing back the curtain on informationized warfare."[2] The lessons China took from the Gulf War fundamentally changed the way that its military planners viewed the future of warfare as well as an understanding of its own vulnerabilities, prompting a decades-long upheaval in Chinese thinking on the strategic role of information in warfare.[3]

China drew two primary lessons from the Gulf War. First, the war proved that the widespread integration of information technology in warfare could confer overwhelming military superiority. As a result, a country's progress in "informationizing" [*xinxi hua*, 信息化] itself, both in a military context and on a broader societal level, is central to its national security.[4] To this end, the PLA recognized that it would need to study and adopt operational concepts that are informed by the U.S. concept now referred to as "network-centric warfare."[5] The operational use of space-based command, control, communications, computers, intelligence, surveillance, and reconnaissance (C4ISR) attracted particular notice, with PLA writers frequently referencing it as a barometer of how informationized warfare had become.[6] Second, the PLA quickly assessed that U.S. use of these technologies created fundamental dependencies that could be exploited in wartime. This line of thinking paved the way for China's unique information warfare strategy, which seeks to "overcome the superior with the inferior" through the application of asymmetric information countermeasures against critical nodes in space, cyberspace, and the electromagnetic domains.[7] After working through a number of doctrinal iterations, by the end of the 1990s the PLA had successfully developed the foundational concepts that have guided China's strategy for and development of its information warfare forces ever since.

Chinese strategists spent the 2000s focused primarily on applying these concepts and lessons, both through force-wide concepts such as integrated network and electronic warfare (INEW) [*wangdian yiti zhan*, 网电一体战] and at the operational level. By the end of the decade, the PLA had successfully fielded a regional constellation of Beidou navigation satellites, space-based surveillance platforms, and dual-use communications and relay satellites. Taken together, they formed the foundation of a nascent Chinese C4ISR system to enable regional surveillance, reconnaissance, and precision strikes.[8] At the same time, China was rapidly developing its ability to launch offensive information operations. By 2009, PLA EW forces had fielded a basic capability to deny or disrupt U.S. space-based C4ISR and navigation.[9] China's military cyber forces attracted global attention from the mid-2000s onward due to a series of high-profile cyber intrusions that demonstrated both growing sophistication and the rapid progress that Chinese forces had made in the span of a few short years. China also demonstrated a counterspace capability with the development of a direct-ascent antisatellite system, which destroyed an obsolete satellite in a January 2007 test.[10]

The advancement of the technical capabilities of Chinese space, cyber, and EW forces stood in stark contrast with the PLA's stagnant operational structure, which remained virtually unchanged throughout the 2000s. In the years immediately leading up to the PLA's 2015 reorganization, there was a growing realization in scholarly circles that the PLA's structure and organization, not its technological capabilities, had emerged as the foremost roadblock facing modernization efforts.[11] The key organizations responsible for space, cyber, and EW missions were distributed across different parts of the PLA and remained stovepiped in their respective organizations, even as the PLA's strategic literature increasingly called for greater integration of these forces as an operational necessity.[12] It is therefore unsurprising that the PLA saw the current period of major reforms as an opportunity to finally realign its sprawling space, cyber, and EW capabilities into a unified force.

The Strategic Support Force's creation comes at an inflection point for the PLA. China has accelerated the ongoing shift of its military posture from land-based territorial defense to extended power projection, not only in the East and South China seas but also beyond them.[13] As part of this transition, China's leaders have expressed a growing desire to protect their country's interests further afield in the "strategic frontiers" of space, cyberspace, and the far seas.[14] On this point, the relatively authoritative 2013 edition of the *Science of Military Strategy* observed that "preparations and prepositioning in fighting for new strategic spaces is both an important brace-support for a country's use of these international public spaces, and also an important action in contesting new military strategic commanding heights."[15] China's 2015 Military Strategy White Paper similarly describes the three as "critical domains" and echoes their importance to China's national interests.[16] The SSF's design is a logical fit for improving China's access to the space and cyber domains in peacetime and contesting them in wartime. The SSF's "remote operations" in the far seas and beyond are aimed at achieving strategic national objectives through counterintervention and power projection.[17]

Even before the SSF's creation, the idea of forming an organization like it to meet the demands of future warfare had been germinating within the PLA's strategic theory community for years. As early as 2007, China's strategic literature called for an independent space force to unify myriad elements of Chinese organizations responsible for space operations.[18] Similarly, after the formation of U.S. Cyber Command (USCYBERCOM) in 2009, there were numerous calls for China to establish its own equivalent, with PLA scholars noting the inherent advantages of a unified command.[19] In 2012, the influential PLA information warfare specialist Ye Zheng suggested a conceptual and organizational integration of information warfare disciplines into an integrated network-electronic-psychological warfare force that partially resembles the SSF's cyber force.[20]

However, the closest conceptual forerunner for the Strategic Support Force comes from U.S. Strategic Command (USSTRATCOM). The PLA's decision to incorporate both space and cyber forces into a single service-like entity does not appear to have any clear bellwether in Chinese strategic literature. Due to USSTRATCOM's broad responsibilities for space, cyber, strategic EW, and strategic information support, it was chosen as a model for the SSF.[21] Following USSTRATCOM's example, the SSF is tasked with space and cyber missions, while also providing the theater commands with ISR support for joint operations.

The SSF and PLA Reform Efforts

The Strategic Support Force was created as part of a broader reorganization that dissolved the PLA's four former general departments, incorporating the bulk of their functions into 15 joint force "functional organs" within an expanded Central Military Commission. The General Staff Department (GSD) became the new CMC Joint Staff Department, the General Political Department (GPD) became the CMC Political Work Department, the General Armament Department (GAD) became the CMC Equipment Development Department, and the General Logistics Department became the CMC Logistics Support Department.[22] These are not exact analogues to their predecessors; some capabilities, tasking, and component parts have been transferred elsewhere within the PLA, particularly in the case of the SSF.

At the outset of the reorganization, the SSF was formed out of these departments' operational units responsible for space, cyber, and EW. This move was aimed in part to alleviate the organizational silos and other roadblocks that previously impeded the effective employment of these elements as a cohesive, coordinated strategic force under the general department system. The SSF's space mission is formed primarily from units under the former GAD and select elements of the GSD responsible for space-based C4ISR. The SSF's information warfare mission comes largely from the former Third and Fourth departments of the GSD, which had respectively held the responsibilities for technical reconnaissance and offensive cyber operations. The elements of the GPD responsible for psychological operations were also incorporated into the SSF, in keeping with the PLA's aforementioned conceptualization of cyber, electronic, and psychological warfare as interconnected subcomponents of information warfare. The psychological domain constitutes a core element of the PLA's concept of the "Three Warfares" [*sanzhong zhanfa*, 三种战法], a unique Chinese warfighting model that calls for the coordinated use of psychological operations, public opinion warfare, and legal warfare to gain an advantage over an adversary, and thus the SSF is expected to participate in Three Warfares missions. Figure 1 shows the pre-reform locations of the major components that make up the SSF. Figure 2 shows the post-reform structure of the SSF, including headquarters elements such as the Staff Department and Political

Figure 1. Pre-Reform Locations of Major SSF Components

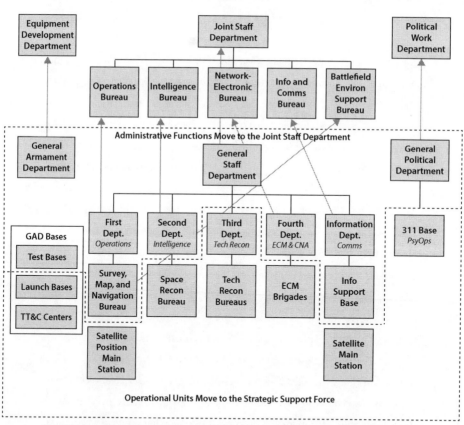

Key: ECM: electronic countermeasures; GAD: General Armament Department; PsyOps: psychological operations; TT&C: telemetry, tracking, and control; GPD: General Political Department.

Figure 2. Overall Structure of the SSF

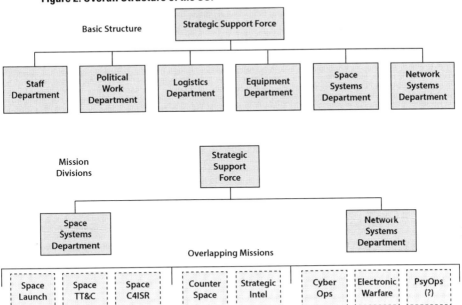

Key: PsyOps: psychological operations; TT&C: telemetry, tracking, and control.

Work Department (organized as first-level departments), the Space Systems Department (responsible for space operations), and the Network Systems Department (responsible for information operations).

When PLA leadership plotted out a multiyear course for reforms through 2020, they opted for a two-stage approach. The first stage largely consists of "above the neck" [*bozi yishang*, 脖子以上] organizational reforms that lay out the overall design of China's armed forces going forward, with "below the neck" [*bozi yixia*, 脖子以下] reforms coming later to reshape PLA institutions and operations on a more granular level. In keeping with this plan, the PLA has so far largely taken a "bricks, not clay" approach to the creation of the Strategic Support Force. That is, existing institutions have been taken in their entirety and placed within the SSF's new organizational superstructure to serve as a core around which other, smaller elements can later be arrayed. This dynamic is visible in the SSF's space and cyber warfare forces, the central components of which are formed from the

GAD's space cadre and the former GSD Third Department, respectively. These in turn act as pillars for their respective missions, with lower grade units from the GSD and services being transferred underneath them.

Prior to the PLA's reorganization, space, cyber, and EW units were organized according to their mission type—disciplines of reconnaissance, attack, or defense—rather than their warfighting domain.[23] This is most evident when looking at the PLA's cyber mission. Previously, espionage and technical reconnaissance in the cyber domain were handled by the GSD Third Department, while the targeting and attack missions were handled by the GSD Fourth Department. Separately, the former GSD Informatization Department [*xinxihua bu*, 信息化部] handled key elements of information systems defense.[24] The approach used for the SSF is intended to enable more effective full-spectrum warfighting by treating space, cyberspace, and the electromagnetic spectrum as primary warfighting domains in their own right, rather than as supporting elements of other domains.[25] In recent PLA strategic writings such as the 2015 National Defense University version of the *Science of Military Strategy*, this approach is termed "integrated reconnaissance, attack, and defense" [*zhen gongfang yiti hua*, 侦攻防一体化].[26]

PLA strategic writings reflect a recognition that employing a domain-centric force for information warfare enables levels of unified planning, force construction, and operations that would have been infeasible under the previous structure. This runs counter to the movement of the PLA's conventional armed services toward force construction and away from operations, which have been tasked to the theater commands. The difference is due to the unique requirements of the information domain, where the vulnerabilities and exploits necessary to create "cyber weapons" are discovered, refined, and deployed in a rapid, continuous loop throughout both peacetime and wartime.

Another important principle that appears to have influenced the design of the SSF is the enduring Maoist imperative of peacetime-wartime integration [*pingzhan jiehe*, 平战结合, or *pingzhan yiti*, 平战一体].[27]

Under its pre-reform organizational structure, the PLA would have been required to transition to a wartime posture just prior to the outbreak of war (or immediately following it, if China were taken by surprise). For strategic-level information operations, this operational requirement would have demanded unprecedented coordination between GSD, GAD, GPD, and military region units across multiple echelons. The creation of the SSF and the theater commands has simplified this process dramatically by organizing both China's conventional and information warfare units into permanent operational groupings that are designed to transition seamlessly into wartime command structures, though how smoothly that transition will be carried out in practice remains an open question.

Overview of the SSF as an Organization

To predict the role that the Strategic Support Force will play in wartime, it is first necessary to understand the particulars of the organization itself, as the SSF's structure will have a major impact on how its forces can be effectively employed during a conflict. Established on December 31, 2015, the Strategic Support Force is a theater command leader grade [*zheng zhanqu ji*, 正战区 级] independent military force under the direct command of the Central Military Commission.[28] General Gao Jin [高津], who previously served with the former Second Artillery Force [*di er paobing budui*, 第二炮兵部队] and then as president of the Academy of Military Science (AMS), was named as the first SSF commander.[29] General Liu Fulian [刘福连][30] served as the SSF's first political commissar until March 2017, when he was replaced by General Zheng Weiping [郑卫平].[31] General Gao's previous role as AMS president highlights the central role that AMS and its internal debates play in China's formulation of its military strategic thought—including, it appears, China's plans for the SSF. This prominence is without parallel in the military academic institutions of western countries.[32] See table 1 for a list of SSF leadership.

Table 1. Strategic Support Force Leadership, Grades, and Former Positions				
Name	Position	Grade	Rank	Former Position
Gao Jin [高津]	Commander	Military Theater Leader grade	General	Commandant, Academy of Military Science Former Second Artillery Officer
Zheng Weiping [郑卫平]	Political Commissar	Military Theater Leader grade	General	Commandant, Academy of Military Science Former Second Artillery Officer
Lu Jiancheng [吕建成]	Deputy Political Commissar and Director, Discipline Inspection Commission	Military Theater Leader grade	General	Political Commissar, Eastern Military Theater Command
Feng Jianhua [冯建华]	Director, Political Work Department	Deputy Military Theater Leader grade	Lieutenant General	Deputy Political Commissar, Jinan Military Region
Li Shangfu [李尚福]*	Deputy Commander and Chief of Staff	Deputy Military Theater Leader grade	Major General	Director, GPD Cadre Department
Sun Bo [孙波]	Deputy Chief of Staff	Deputy Military Theater Leader grade	General*	Director, GAD Xichang Satellite Launch Center
Zhang Minghua [张明华]	Deputy Chief of Staff	Corps Leader grade	Major General	Director, GSD Management Support Department
Rao Kaixun [饶开勋]	Deputy Commander	Corps Leader grade	Major General	Director, GSD Operations Department
Shang Hong [尚宏]	Deputy Commander and Commander, Space Systems Department	Deputy Military Theater Leader grade	Lieutenant General	Chief of Staff, General Armament Department
Kang Chunyuan [康春元]	Political Commissar, Space Systems Department	Deputy Military Theater Leader grade	Lieutenant General	Deputy Political Commissar, Lanzhou Military Region
Hao Weizhong [郝卫中]	Deputy Commander, Space Systems Department	Deputy Military Theater Leader grade	Lieutenant General	Director, Taiyuan Launch Center
Fei Jiabing [费加兵]	Chief of Staff, Space Systems Department	Corps Leader grade	Major General	Director, Maritime Tracking and Control Department
Zheng Junjie [郑俊杰]	Deputy Commander and Commander, Network Systems Department	Deputy Military Theater Leader grade	Lieutenant Major General	Director, GSD Third Department Director, PLA Information Engineering University

448

Table 1. Strategic Support Force Leadership, Grades, and Former Positions (cont.)				
Name	**Position**	**Grade**	**Rank**	**Former Position**
Chai Shaoliang [柴绍良]	Political Commissar, Network Systems Department	Deputy Military Theater Leader grade	Lieutenant General	Deputy Political Commissar, General Armament Department

* Li Shangfu is now director of the CMC Equipment Development Department. His replacement as SSF chief of staff has not been identified.

Key: AMS: Academy of Military Sciences; GAD: General Armament Department; GPD: General Political Department; GSD: General Staff Department; MR: military region; NSD: Network Systems Department; SSD: Space Systems Department; TC: theater command.

Administratively, the SSF operates similarly to the former PLA Second Artillery Force, which was also a force [*budui*, 部队[33]] that functioned like a service and consolidated strategic capabilities under the direct command of the CMC.[34] Of its first-level departments, the SSF has a standard four-department administrative structure that includes the SSF Staff Department [*canmou bu*, 参谋部], Equipment Department [*zhuangbei bu*, 装备部], Political Work Department [*zhengzhi gongzuo bu*, 政治工作部], and a Logistics Department [*houqin bu*, 后勤部].[35] Alongside these departments, the force also maintains headquarters for its space and information warfare forces in the Space Systems Department (SSD) [*hangtian xitong bu*, 航天系统部] and Network Systems Department (NSD) [*wangluo xitong bu*, 网络系统部], respectively.[36]

The SSF's operational responsibilities and chain of command were initially uncertain but have become clearer over time. As part of the PLA reforms, the Central Military Commission restructured the principal responsibilities of the military's main components under a new paradigm encapsulated by the official phrase "CMC leads, theaters fight, and services build" [*junwei guanzong, zhanqu zhuzhan, junzhong zhujian*, 军委管总, 战区主战, 军种主建], envisioning a division of labor that would see the new theaters focus on operations, the services on force construction, and the CMC on supervising and managing both. This approach resulted in a new dual-command structure with an administrative chain from the Central Military Commission to the services and an operational chain from the CMC to the five joint force theater commands. In theory, this would imply that subordinate SSF elements would be under the operational command of the five theater commands. In practice, however, much like the PLA Rocket Force [*jiefangjun huojian jun*, 解放军火箭军], which serves as the cornerstone of China's nuclear deterrent, the SSF's capabilities have been deemed sufficiently strategic that it reports directly to the Central Military Commission for operations.[37] The theater commands are confirmed to have subordinate command organizations for ground force, navy, and air force elements within their regions, but none have been found for the Strategic Support Force.

SSF Structure and Components

Organizationally, the Strategic Support Force's operational forces are split into two co-equal, semi-independent branches: the Space Systems Department, which heads up a force responsible for space operations, and the Network Systems Department, which heads up a force responsible for information operations. Though the force structure of these departments is largely opaque, as the reforms have progressed details have slowly emerged regarding a growing number of personnel transfers, unit consolidations, Military Unit Cover Designator conversions, and in some cases the establishment of entirely new units with no identifiable predecessor. This transitional state complicates any attempt to give a full accounting of structure and command relationships, but some basic inferences can nevertheless be drawn.

First, the SSF appears to have a bifurcated structure, whereby the SSD and NSD act as largely independent, administrative headquarters for their respective forces and the Staff Department serves as an operational headquarters. This arrangement would help explain the apparent administrative oddity of the SSD and NSD having the same grade as the Staff Department, an organization they would normally report to. Such a command structure may better enable the SSD and NSD to independently develop their own officer corps, tailor training to force needs, and prioritize their own capabilities development while allowing the Central Military Commission to integrate their operations in situations where their missions overlap, such as in certain strategic intelligence and counterspace missions.

Second, SSF units have been assigned MUCDs, the numerical codes that the PLA has long used to conceal a unit's true identity in public sources. The SSF's MUCDs fall between 32001 and 32099.[38] Analysis of these designators largely confirms that, as expected, a number of SSF units are beginning to migrate from their old designations to new MUCDs that fall within the SSF's assigned block. However, a select few appear to be newly created or do not align to known units. MUCDs are a useful tool for determining which stage of reorganization the SSF's forces are undergoing, as a new designator is generally a fair indication that their structure, grade, and command relationships have been reviewed, approved, and are likely to remain static throughout the course of the remaining reforms. On the other hand, a unit still using its pre-reform MUCD invites speculation that a new designation awaits after some administrative change or reorganization.

Finally, many SSF forces appear to be organized as "bases," a form of corps leader grade unit that is distinct to the PLA. The space force in particular had already largely been organized as bases prior to the creation of the SSF. Of the former GAD "test bases" [*shiyan jidi*, 实验基地], numbered 20 to 33, the five responsible for space operations have been confirmed to have been transferred to the Strategic Support Force, whereas the remaining bases were transferred to the Equipment Development Department and services.[39] These bases appear to have retained their previous numerical designations even under the new system. However, a newly designated unit called the "Strategic Support Force 35th Base" [*zhanlüe zhiyuan budui 35 jidi*, 战略支援部队35基地] now appears to be responsible for some of the space force's space-based survey, mapping, and navigation missions, including the management of military Beidou satellites.[40] The creation or designation of a new SSF base beyond the aforementioned five that are known to exist, with numbering that extends past what was previously the highest numbered PLA base (the 33rd), raises the possibility that there may be more space-related numerical bases in the offing. Additional bases might also be responsible for supporting the space information support and survey, mapping, and navigation missions.

The SSF has also inherited the 311 Base [*311 jidi*, 311基地], also known as China's "Three Warfares Base," from the General Political Department, though its position within the SSF's organizational structure is unclear. The 311 Base is the PLA's sole organization that is publicly known to focus on psychological warfare. Notably, one public record refers to the existence of a "Strategic Support Force Eastern Base" [*zhanlüe zhiyuan budui dongbu jidi*, 战略支援部队东部基地].[41] This invites comparisons to a similar structure used by the newly created Joint Logistics Support Force [*lianhe houqin baozhang budui*, 联合后勤保障部队], which has subordinate bases that align with the five theater commands.[42] These bases could fall directly under the SSF's staff department and serve both space and cyber force personnel or, alternatively, could be a series of bases that fall under the Network Systems Department. The former possibility would help further the SSF mission of supporting the theater commands and may explain the absence of identifiable SSF elements under them—SSF regional bases are still in the process of being created. The latter possibility would answer the question of exactly how the NSD intends to organize the loose and geographically dispersed confederation of cyber, EW, and psychological warfare forces it has inherited.

A Force in Transition

With reforms scheduled to run from 2015 until 2020, the SSF remains very much a force in transition. Its transitional state complicates efforts to fully understand how it will be permanently organized. There are several peculiarities in the current SSF structure that may either end up as permanent features of its organization (and thus consequential for understanding the SSF's operational concepts), mere transient idiosyncrasies that have been left over from larger structural reforms, or bureaucratic compromises that have yet to be ironed out.

Many of these anomalies relate to the SSF's grade [*jibie*, 级别] structure (see figure 3). The PLA's grade system is separated into 15 grades that

Figure 3. SSF Grade Structure

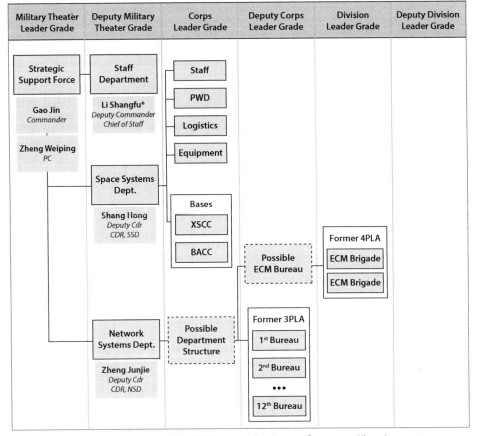

Military Theater Leader Grade	Deputy Military Theater Grade	Corps Leader Grade	Deputy Corps Leader Grade	Division Leader Grade	Deputy Division Leader Grade

* Li Shangfu is now director of the CMC Equipment Development Department. His replacement as SSF chief of staff has not been identified.

Key: BACC: Beijing Aerospace Command and Control Center; CDR: commander; ECM: electronic countermeasure; NSD: Network Systems Department; PC: political commissar; PWD: Political Work Department; SSD: Space Systems Department; XSCC: Xian Satellite Monitor and Control Center.

correspond to 10 ranks, defining both an organization's and an officer's place in the PLA hierarchy. Ranks are occasionally used for ease of coordination with foreign militaries, since most other militaries consider ranks to be paramount, but are often not referenced in the PLA's daily practice.

Traditionally in the PLA, an organization's grade, not its commander's rank, has been the determining factor for its authority, shaping which organizations it may answer to, coordinate with, or command. The grade system also defines the potential career paths for officers, providing sequential rungs upon which billets are based.[43] For many officers in the PLA, organizational mergers or streamlining reforms ultimately mean a reduction in billets, which means increased competition over fewer pathways for promotion.[44] For organizations, these changes mean a redefinition of command and coordination authorities, altering relationships within the PLA's command ecosystem. When reorganizing the PLA, planners must be conscious of both officer career paths and organizational responsibilities, balancing the need for structural change against bureaucratic and operational pressures.

Since the SSF is a massive merger between elements of the former GAD and elements of the GSD, these considerations have almost certainly played an important role in decisions about its structure. For instance, one would ordinarily expect that the SSF's Space Systems Department would mirror its Network Systems Department counterpart and have bureaus [*ju*, 局] under its headquarters. This would align with the PLA's overall organizational paradigm wherein "departments contain bureaus, which in turn contain offices" [*bu-ju-chu*, 部-局-处]. Instead the SSD has another layer of departments [*bu*, 部] where bureaus might be.[45] This nonstandard structure could either be temporary until the departments can be converted into bureaus, or it could be an indicator that the NSD will defy convention and maintain second-level departments instead of bureaus. Additionally, both the heads of the SSD and NSD are dual-hatted as deputy commanders of the SSF, giving them a "deputy theater command leader" [*fu zhanqu ji*, 副战区级] grade. The merger and demotion of former GAD elements appears to have created a bureaucratic bottleneck in promotions for much of the space mission's leadership, as many of the senior leaders there, such as the heads of the space launch bases, had already attained "corps leader" or deputy theater command leader grade. This may help explain the prevalence of former GAD officers in the SSF's leadership, as it was necessary to provide them with billets that accorded with their established grades.

The most consequential and enduring mystery in this regard is that the SSD and NSD appear to be the same grade as the SSF Staff Department, limiting the latter's ability to command and direct their operations. This arrangement may be the result of bureaucratic necessity. Since many of the former GAD launch bases were corps leader grade organizations, the Space Systems Department would need to be at least a deputy theater command leader grade to command them, requiring a grade increase that made it the equal of the Staff Department. Alternatively, it may indicate that SSF structure is in a transitional state, with further changes to come that will move the headquarters as well as the space and cyber forces into a more permanent organizational framework.

The SSD and China's Space Forces

As noted, the Strategic Support Force's space mission falls under the Space Systems Department, a deputy theater command leader grade organization that has been described as the headquarters of China's military space forces [*junshi hangtian budui*, 军事航天部队], also known informally as its "space force" [*tian jun*, 天军].[46] The initial leadership of this department consists of Major General Shang Hong [尚宏], who has led it since its inception, Political Commissar Kang Chunyuan [康春元], Deputy Commander Hao Weizhong [郝卫中], and Chief of Staff Fei Jiabing [费加兵].[47] With the exception of Kang, who formerly served as the Lanzhou Military Region deputy political commissar, all are from the former GAD and veterans of China's military space programs.[48]

This reorganization of China's myriad space capabilities into a coherent, unified space force is a response to organizational challenges that arose from space forces being dispersed throughout the military. Previously, the PLA was tasked with executing space missions using assets spread across the GAD and GSD.[49] The SSD has now subsumed nearly every aspect of PLA space operations that were formerly controlled by the GAD and GSD, including space launch and support; space telemetry, tracking, and control; space information support; space attack; and space defense (see table 2). The office overseeing China's manned space missions has stayed with the CMC

Equipment Development Department, perhaps in an attempt to avoid the appearance of militarizing China's manned space mission.[50]

Table 2. SSF Space Corps Units		
Space Launch and Support		
Name	Assessed Grade	Function and Description
Jiuquan Satellite Launch Center [中国酒泉卫星发射中心] 20th Testing and Training Base [第20试验训练基地]	Corps Leader grade	Oldest and largest launch site and the only one that conducts human space-flight launches.
Taiyuan Satellite Launch Center [中国太原卫星发射中心] 25th Testing and Training Base [第25试验训练基地]	Corps Leader grade	The center launches satellites into sun-synchronous and low-earth orbits.
Xichang Satellite Launch Center [中国西昌卫星发射中心] 27th Testing and Training Base [第27试验训练基地]	Corps Leader grade	The center launches satellites into geo-synchronous orbit. Maintains mobile tracking stations that supply data to other facilities.
Wenchang Aerospace Launch Site [文昌航天发射场]	Corps Leader grade	Completed in 2014. The center was built to use the new heavy-lift Long March 5 and to launch heavier payloads into orbit.

Table 2. SSF Space Corps Units		
Telemetry, Tracking, and Control (TT&C)		
Name	Assessed Grade	Function and Description
Beijing Aerospace Flight Control Center [北京航天飞行控制中心]	Corps Leader grade	Responsible for command and control of China's manned spaceflight program.
Xi'an Satellite Control Center [中国西安卫星测控中心] 26th Testing and Training Base [第26试验训练基地]	Corps Leader grade	Core hub for China's telemetry, tracking, and control network. Maintains a nation-wide retinue of fixed and mobile TT&C stations.

Table 2. SSF Space Corps Units (cont.)		
Telemetry, Tracking, and Control (TT&C)		
Name	**Assessed Grade**	**Function and Description**
China Satellite Maritime Tracking and Control Department [中国卫星海上测控部] 23rd Test and Training Base [第23试验训练基地]	Corps Leader grade	Provides maritime TT&C for China's space launches and intercontinental ballistic missile tests. Maintains a small fleet of Yuanwang (远望) tracking ships.

Table 2. SSF Space Corps Units		
Space-based C4ISR		
Name	**Assessed Grade**	**Function and Description**
Aerospace Reconnaissance Bureau [航天侦察局]	Deputy Corps Leader grade	Responsible for space-based intelligence, surveillance, and reconnaissance.
Satellite Communications Main Station [卫星通信总站]	Deputy Corps Leader grade	Responsible for space-based communications and data relay.
Satellite Positioning Main Station [卫星定位总站]	Deputy Corps Leader grade	Responsible for military use of the Beidou navigation system.

Although the bulk of the SSD's operational units and administrative functions are drawn from the former GAD's space cadre, some operational units and missions are also drawn from the former GSD. The components brought over from the GSD are primarily related to space-based C4ISR assets, which in the PLA are categorized as "space-based information support" [*tian ji xinxi zhiyuan*, 天基信息支援].[51] For example, although the military intelligence–focused former GSD Second Department [*zongcan er bu*, 总参二部, or *zongcan qingbao bu*, 总参情报部] remains in existence as the new Joint Intelligence Bureau [*lian can qingbao ju*, 联参情报局] under the CMC Joint Staff Department, its former Aerospace Reconnaissance Bureau [*hangtian zhencha ju*, 航天侦察局], responsible for space-based remote sensing and the Yaogan [遥感] series of optical and electronic intelligence satellites, has been separated and transferred over to the SSD.[52] The former GSD Satellite Main Station, which is responsible for satellite uplink, downlink, and managing space-based communication satellites, has also been transferred to the SSD, even as its parent organization, the former GSD Informatization Department's Information Support Base [*xinxi baozhang jidi*, 信息保障基地], has been reorganized under the CMC Joint Staff Department as the Information and Communications Bureau (JSD-ICB) [*lian can xinxi tongxin ju*, 联参信息通信局] Information Support Base.[53] Finally, the GSD Satellite Positioning Main Station [*weixing dingwei zongzhan*, 卫星定位总站], responsible for managing the PLA's use of China's Beidou navigation satellite constellation, has moved over to the SSD as well.[54] Its parent unit, the operations-focused former GSD First Department's Survey, Mapping, and Navigation Bureau [*cehui daohang ju*, 测绘导航局], has become the Joint Staff Department Battlefield Environment Support Bureau [*zhanchang huanjing baozhang ju*, 战场环境保障局].

It is currently unclear what responsibilities, if any, the SSF's space force has for antisatellite research, development, testing, and operations, nor is it known whether the SSF has a role in the related discipline of ballistic missile defense (BMD). Both missions could presumably fall under the categories of space attack and defense, respectively, which would place them under the SSF's remit. Alternatively, these missions may be assigned to the PLA Rocket Force, which already has a role in missile operations, or the PLA Air Force (PLAAF), which has already demonstrated a limited capability in both antisatellite missiles and BMD. In August 2017, the DN-3 antisatellite missile was launched from the SSF's Jiuquan Satellite Launch Center, which may indicate that the SSF has responsibility for testing or fielding these systems.[55] The current locations of many of China's offensive space capabilities, including its more experimental co-orbital attack capabilities such as the Shiyan-7 [实验-7, or SY-7] "robotic arm" satellite, remain unknown.[56]

The creation of the SSD nevertheless appears to have resolved at least some of the previous bureaucratic power struggles over space missions between the former GAD, PLAAF, and Second Artillery Force. Although the GAD had long held preeminence in space launch, support, and telemetry, tracking, and control, the capabilities necessary for contesting "space dominance" (*zhikong quan*, 制空权) by holding adversary assets at risk of denial or disruption were split among the three organizations.[57] From the mid-2000s onward, PLAAF leadership forcefully argued that its core responsibility for air defense operations should be extended into space, proposing the strategic operational concept of "integrated air and space operations" [*kongtian yiti zuozhan,* 空天一体作战] as a way toward this coupling.[58] The former PLA Second Artillery Force also promoted itself at various points as the best equipped to carry out the military's space mission set. Its arsenal of short-, medium-, and long-range ballistic missiles, as well as its inherent status as a strategic service, gave it a strong hand in arguing that its existing capabilities "could be adapted for a space intercept role by reprogramming missile guidance and fusing."[59] At least for the moment, the creation of an independent force with responsibility for PLA space missions provides a definitive conclusion to this long-running three-way dispute, perhaps reflecting a bureaucratic compromise.

There is also a broader question as to whether the SSF's primacy in space and space-based C4ISR will preclude other services from independently developing, operating, or maintaining their own space infrastructure for operations. The PLA's services have been known to defend aggressively against one another's efforts to challenge their primacy in their respective primary domains of operation.[60] It remains to be seen if the PLA's reorganization and the CMC's new functional joint model will relieve pressure on these service rivalries, or if they will intensify as a result of new competition over funding and development of "new-type" capabilities. It is possible that the SSF's space mission may represent a bureaucratic "solution" to the previous fight for space primacy between the PLAAF and Rocket Force.

The NSD and China's Cyber Forces

The Strategic Support Force's cyber mission has been given to the Network Systems Department, a deputy theater command leader grade organization that acts as the headquarters for the SSF's cyber operations force, sometimes referred to as a "cyber force" [*wang jun,* 网军] or "cyberspace operations force" [*wangluo kong jian zuozhan budui,* 网络空间作战部队].[61] Despite its name, the

NSD and its subordinate forces are responsible for information warfare more broadly, with a mission set that includes cyber warfare, EW, and potentially psychological warfare. Lieutenant General Zheng Junjie was named the NSD's first commander and Lieutenant General Chai Shaoliang as its political commissar.[62] Zheng was the director of the former GSD Third Department (3PLA) [*zongcan san bu*, 总参三部] and commandant of PLA Information Engineering University.[63] Chai previously served as deputy political commissar of the GAD and, before that, of the former Chengdu Military Region [成都军区].[64]

The NSD appears to represent a renaming, reorganization, and grade promotion of the 3PLA. Much as the institutions of the former GSD provided the partial foundation for the creation of the Space Systems Department, they also form the organizational core of the NSD. The Network Systems Department maintains the former 3PLA headquarters, location, and internal bureau-centric structure. In at least one instance, the NSD has been referred to as the "SSF Third Department" [*zhanlüe zhiyuan budui di san bu*, 战略支援部队第三部], mirroring its former appellation.[65]

The bulk of China's strategic cyber espionage forces were previously contained within the technical reconnaissance-focused GSD Third Department, which has been moved en masse into the NSD (see table 3).

Table 3. Former Third Department Units Now Likely under the SSF	
Name of Unit	Notes
Operational or Administrative Organs	
3PLA Headquarters	Now the Network Systems Department (NSD)
First Bureau (Beijing)	Assessed to be transferred to NSD
Second Bureau (Shanghai)	Assessed to be transferred to NSD
Third Bureau (Beijing)	Assessed to be transferred to NSD
Fourth Bureau (QIngdao)	Assessed to be transferred to NSD
Fifth Bureau (Beijing)	Assessed to be transferred to NSD
Sixth Bureau (Wuhan)	Assessed to be transferred to NSD
Seventh Bureau (Beijing)	Transferred to NSD
Eighth Bureau (Beijing)	Assessed to be transferred to NSD
Ninth Bureau (Beijing)	Assessed to be transferred to NSD
Tenth Bureau (Beijing)	Assessed to be transferred to NSD
Eleventh Bureau (Beijing)	Assessed to be transferred to NSD

Table 3. Former Third Department Units Now Likely under the SSF (cont.)	
Name of Unit	**Notes**
Twelfth Bureau (Shanghai)	Assessed to be transferred to NSD or Space Systems Department or Space Systems Department
Beijing North Computing Center (Beijing)	Transferred to NSD
Research Institutes	
56th Research Institute	Transferred to NSD
57th Research Institute	Transferred to NSD
58th Research Institute	Transferred to NSD
Academic Institutions	
Foreign Language Institute	Now PLA IEU Luoyang Campus
Information Engineering University (IEU)	Transferred to NSD

The Third Department's cyber missions were largely handled by its 12 technical reconnaissance bureaus [*jishu zhengcha ju*, 技术侦察局], which were responsible for both cyber espionage and signals intelligence more broadly.[66] While only three of the former bureaus can be fully confirmed to have moved into the NSD, this most likely reflects incomplete public data rather than an incomplete transition. The former GSD's 56th, 57th, and 58th Research Institutes, which previously provided research, development, and weaponization support to the technical reconnaissance mission, have also moved to the NSD.[67] Former military academic institutions, such as the PLA Information Engineering University [*xinxi gongcheng daxue*, 信息工程大学] and Luoyang Foreign Language Institute [*luoyang waiyu xueyuan*, 洛阳外语学院], have also moved over and in some cases have been consolidated.[68]

The centralization of China's strategic cyber forces is a key feature of the Network Systems Department. The NSD appears designed to address the operational coordination challenges that previously arose from the structure of the former GSD. Traditionally, computer network attack was handled by the GSD Fourth Department (4PLA), while the PLA counter-network defense mission has been handled by the GSD Informatization Department. It now appears that the former 4PLA's computer network attack forces have been transferred to the SSF to integrate with the cyber espionage elements of the former Third Department (see table 4).[69] However, it is noteworthy that the NSD does not appear to have integrated the PLA's counter-network defense mission, which remains with the Joint Staff Department's Information Support Base under its Network Security Defense Center [*wangluo anquan fangyu zhongxin*, 网络安全防御中心].[70]

The SSF and EW

Compared with the space and cyber missions, China's strategic electronic warfare mission has historically been far less divided and compartmentalized, having been concentrated almost entirely within the former GSD Fourth Department. The former 4PLA, which was also responsible for radar and computer network attack, has now been split by the reorganization along administrative and operational lines, with various elements either abolished, reorganized, or transferred to the Joint Staff Department and Strategic Support Force. At the top level, the former 4PLA headquarters has been moved to the Joint Staff Department, where it has been reconstituted as the new joint force Network-Electronic Bureau (JSD-NEB) [*wangluo dianzi ju, wang dian ju*, 网络电子局, 网电局].[71] In its new form, it likely oversees management of the cyber and EW missions across the entire Chinese military, including the SSF, theater commands, and services. The 4PLA's military academy, the PLA Electrical Engineering Institute [*dianzi gongcheng xueyuan*, 电子工程学院], has been subsumed by the National University of Defense Technology (NUDT) [*guofang keji daxue*, 国防科技大学] to become the NUDT Electronic Countermeasure Institute [*dianzi duikang xueyuan*, 电子对抗学院].[72] Meanwhile, 4PLA's GSD 54th Research Institute, responsible for research and development of operational electronic and network countermeasures, has moved over to the Strategic Support Force, likely under the Network Systems Department.[73]

At a lower, operational level, at least some of the 4PLA's EW units have been reassigned to the SSF, with Chinese media reports mentioning unidentified "electronic countermeasure brigades" under the new force and public documents revealing former 4PLA units now operating under an SSF MUCD designation.[74] Prior to the reforms, the 4PLA maintained a number of electronic countermeasure brigades, detachments, and stations nationwide, none of which has been visibly accounted for in the PLA's new structure.[75] Nevertheless, the reassignment of the GSD 54th Research Institute is a vital clue that EW now falls under the aegis of the NSD, and the former 4PLA's monopoly on strategic electronic warfare makes it a near certainty that some or all of these units have been assigned to the SSF (see table 4).

Table 4. Former Fourth Department Units Now Likely under SSF	
Name of Unit	Notes
Operational and Administrative Units	
4PLA Headquarters	Transferred to JSD as a new 'Network-Electronic Bureau'
Electronic Countermeasure Brigade (ECM) (Langfang)	Assessed to be transferred to Network Systems Department (NSD)
Langfang ECM Brigade Detachment (Yingtan)	Assessed to be transferred to NSD
ECM (Beidaihe)	Transferred to the NSD
Beidaihe ECM Brigade Detachment (Nicheng)	Transferred to the NSD
Electronic Countermeasure Center	Potentially merged with Joint Network-Electronic Countermeasure *dadui*
Satellite Main Station (Beijing)	Assessed to be transferred to NSD or Space Systems Department
Regional Satellite Station (Hainan)	Assessed to be transferred to NSD or Space Systems Department
Research Institutes	
54th Research Institute	Transferred to the NSD
Academic Institutions	
Electrical Engineering Institute	Now the National University of Defense Technology Electronic Countermeasures Institute

Integrating the cyber warfare and EW elements of the former 3PLA and 4PLA is a crucial step toward fully realizing a long-held PLA theory of how best to fight information warfare known as integrated network and electronic warfare, which envisions the close coordination of cyber and electronic warfare forces in both capabilities development and operational use. According to this school of thought, the integration of information

technology on the battlefield has created a combined "network and electromagnetic space" [*wangdian kongjian,* 网电空间] such that cyber and
EW forces "cannot be mutually exclusive, with each [force] fighting [its]
own battles."[76] On a more concrete level, integrated network and electronic
warfare was conceived by former 4PLA head Dai Qingmin in the early
2000s and represented 4PLA's side of a bureaucratic turf war between
3PLA and 4PLA as to the proper division of missions between the two
organizations.[77]

With the adoption of INEW as mainstream PLA thinking, 4PLA
took on both the GSD's offensive cyber and electronic countermeasures
missions in a partial realization of the concept, but its broader implementation remained largely incomplete.[78] Responsibilities for the cyber
and electromagnetic domains remained divided at the strategic level,
with the Fourth Department responsible for both network and electronic
countermeasures (offense) and the Third Department responsible for
cyber espionage and traditional radio-frequency signals intelligence
(reconnaissance and espionage). The Strategic Support Force's merging of
the two departments' operational responsibilities could bring the concept
full circle, creating a unified force for warfighting in the network and
electromagnetic space.

The status of this integration is unclear. For now, at least, the integration appears to be notional and largely the result of renaming and
functionally realigning rather than at a deeper level of combining of personnel, systems, and culture. That said, the reforms are still incomplete
and the next stage is intended to focus on below-the-neck reforms and
integration, under which this would presumably fall. Still, it is unclear
how foreign observers would measure or understand the progress in these
actions, as they produce fewer appearances than larger scale changes. In any
case, if successful in achieving deeper integration, this force will be fully
empowered to conduct both espionage and offense operations, a recognition
of the ways in which the two disciplines often reinforce and depend on one
another on the modern battlefield.

The JSD-NEB now seems to be pushing the INEW concept force-wide as the main successor of the 4PLA, likely overseeing force development and warfighting efforts in the Strategic Support Force, other services, and theater commands. Initially, it seemed plausible that the former 4PLA might move to the SSF to form something along the lines of a hypothetical "Electronic Systems Department" that would stand alongside the SSD and NSD.[79] The fact that 4PLA headquarters has instead been integrated in the Joint Staff Department as the Network-Electronic Bureau makes it more likely that strategic electronic warfare units have been merged with the NSD to better align with the combined network and electronic countermeasures concept that the JSD-NEB is establishing throughout the entire PLA.[80] The "network-electronic" grouping has also been spotted in other post-reform PLA organizations, such as the national joint force Network-Electronic Countermeasures *dadui* [大队] and a Theater Command Network-Electronic Countermeasure *dui* [队].[81] It is not clear if the NSD has inherited any management institutions from the former 4PLA, or if it will create new bureaus specifically for the purpose of leading the new operational EW units under its command.

The SSF and the Three Warfares

The Strategic Support Force also appears to have incorporated elements of the military's psychological and political warfare missions, a result of a subtle yet consequential reorganization of China's political warfare forces. Before the reforms, the former General Political Department had primary responsibility for carrying out military political warfare. This mission was encapsulated in a concept developed in the early 2000s known as the Three Warfares, a unique Chinese political warfare model that calls for the coordinated use of psychological warfare [*xinli zhan*, 心理战], public opinion warfare [*yulun zhan*, 舆论战], and legal warfare [*falü zhan*, 法律战] to establish "discursive power" [*huayu quan*, 话语权] over an adversary—that is, the power to control perceptions and shape narratives that advance Chinese interests and undermine those of an opponent.[82] The former General

465

Political Department separated responsibilities for these missions at strategic and operational levels, with the former Liaison Department [*lianluo bu*, 联络部] responsible for the broader mission of political warfare and the 311 Base responsible for more operational aspects of political warfare and psychological operations against Taiwan.[83] While the 311 Base was under the command of the General Political Department in peacetime, in a conflict scenario, the base, a deputy corps leader grade organization, and its six subordinate regiments, would form the core of China's psychological warfare forces in information operations campaigns.[84]

The reforms shook up this arrangement, incorporating the General Political Department into the Central Military Commission as the new CMC Political Work Department and reassigning the 311 Base to the Strategic Support Force.[85] Although the base is unaccounted for in known portions of the SSF's structure, it could potentially fall under the SSF's Political Work Department or, perhaps more likely, the Network Systems Department. The latter possibility would see the NSD in command of the full spectrum of information operations—not only cyber but also electronic and psychological warfare. The move itself appears to remove organizational impediments to coordination across the information operations disciplines, integrating them in peacetime to ease their transition into a wartime structure. PLA scholars have stressed the importance of both psychological and political operations in shaping the strategic situation ahead of conflict.[86] Integrating the 311 Base's operational forces with the SSF's space, cyber, and electronic missions empowers psychological operations forces with cross-domain intelligence and helps maximize the impact of information operations on an adversary's psychology.

What is unclear is what responsibilities the CMC Political Work Department will have for political warfare and, therefore, psychological operations. The former Liaison Department, which previously served as the PLA's political warfare command center, is unaccounted for in the PLA's structure; it has most likely remained with the CMC Political Work Department in some form. The PLA's inherent status as a Party army (not a national one) imposes on its psychological operations forces an additional imperative to ensure ideological loyalty and push Party ideals as part of its operational strategy. It is possible that the 311 Base's move signals a "decoupling" of sorts between political and psychological warfare, which have traditionally sat uncomfortably at the intersection of the General Political Department's political command and the GSD's operational command.[87] Both the PLA's revised 2010 Political Work Guidelines and the 2013 edition of the *Science of Military Strategy* indicate the need for psychological operations to more closely align with traditional, nonpolitical, military information warfare forces, and the reorganization may be a direct reflection of this imperative.[88]

Joint Command and the SSF

The reforms have also substantially altered the command context for many of the missions now under the Strategic Support Force, redefining longstanding organizational relationships and creating new responsibilities across the PLA command bureaucracy. The CMC's new Joint Staff Department may have responsibility for relaying CMC operational decisions to the SSF.[89] Understanding how each of the different components of this organization interface with the SSF is crucial to understanding PLA command and control during a wartime or crisis scenario.

The JSD was based on the former GSD, which had effectively been triple-hatted in the past—serving as a notional joint command headquarters, ground force headquarters, and as administrative headquarters for strategic missions and units. The reforms split these responsibilities apart, forming a new ground force headquarters, establishing the Strategic Support Force from pre-existing space, cyber, and EW forces, and elevating both the GSD and many, but not all, of its subordinate organs to the Central Military Commission as the Joint Staff Department. JSD bureaus oversee various aspects of military command, including operations, intelligence, cyber and electronic warfare, communications, and battlefield environment support. However, the precise manner in which the JSD commands the SSF remains unclear.

Operational Command in Peacetime and Wartime

In peacetime, the SSF appears to fall under the command of either the CMC's Joint Staff Department Operations Bureau [*liancan zuozhan ju*, 联参作战局] or its Joint Operations Command Center [*liancan zuozhan zhihui zhongxin*, 联参作战指挥中心], which are both responsible for central command and control of both the services and theater commands. Official media state that the center acts as a "strategic command" over services and theater commands.[90] In the previous Joint Staff Department Operations Bureau incarnation as the GSD First Department, it had a set of subordinate bureaus responsible for different types of operations, including both service bureaus, such as the Air Force Operations Bureau [*kongjun zuozhan ju*, 空军作战局] and Navy Operations Bureau [*haijun zuozhan ju*, 海军作战局], as well as functional bureaus such as the Special Operations Bureau [*tezhong zuozhan ju*, 特种作战局] and Information Operations Bureau [*xinxi zuozhan ju*, 信息作战局].[91] Some of these subordinate bureaus appear to have survived and been reorganized as offices [*chu*, 处], though only two have been definitively confirmed to exist: the overseas operations office [*haiwai hangdong chu*, 海外行动处][92] and air traffic control office [*kongguan chu*, 空管处].[93]

Since responsibilities for operations have shifted from the services to theater commands, it is not clear whether the former service-centric operations bureaus will ultimately survive or be replaced by geographic bureaus that directly align with theater commands. In any case, there is no clear subordinate office that would appear to be tasked with directing SSF operations. Given the SSF's mission, the chief candidate would be along the lines of a hypothetical "information operations office," a successor organization to the information operations bureau under the Operations Department before the reforms. However, an office that has clear authority over the SSF has yet to be identified.

Prior to the recent reforms, the PLA's plans for a wartime campaign entailed shifting into "operations groups" [*zuozhan jiqun*, 作战集群], temporary entities at the strategic, theater, and tactical levels that would act as joint force commands and direct operations for a particular domain, region, or type of wartime activity.[94] If this basic structure persists, the SSF will likely constitute the core component of an information operations group (IOG) [*xinxi zuozhan jiqun*, 信息作战集群], a joint force wartime construct dedicated to waging information warfare.[95] In his authoritative 2013 work *Lectures on the Science of Information Operations*, Major General Ye Zheng stated that in wartime the PLA would stand up an IOG commanding all aspects of information warfare activity.[96] Its missions would be organized as a series of subordinate elements, referred to as "groups" [*qun*, 群], for mission sets including cyber warfare, EW, psychological warfare, air defense electronic countermeasures, and information support.[97] As operations groups are further differentiated at the strategic, theater, and tactical levels of warfighting, it is plausible that any IOGs would be similarly tiered with national-level, campaign, and/ or theater-level iterations.[98]

The IOG structure used by the PLA prior to the recent reforms is in many ways the predecessor to the new joint command structure in that it similarly established joint command mechanisms overseeing individual service components at the national and theater levels. The creation of the theater commands may have obviated the need to shift the PLA into a wartime structure for regional campaigns, but the need may still be present at the national level. The Joint Operations Command Center likely facilitates command and control for national strategic missions, but it remains unclear how the organization arranges operational groupings across the services for these purposes. As of now, no joint force construct has been identified under the Joint Operations Command Center that would serve as a standing IOG. Instead, the Strategic Support Force appears to serve both operational and administrative roles. This would mean that the SSF is not a direct analogue to a wartime IOG, but rather a force that is optimized for seamless transitioning to a more operational footing. However, an IOG may still be necessary to integrate information operations capabilities from the various services at the national level.

Intelligence and Technical Reconnaissance

The reforms also substantially reorganized the intelligence responsibilities of the former GSD, creating a new Joint Staff Department Intelligence Bureau out of the former GSD Second Department as well as separating out and centralizing the strategic-level technical collection organizations under the Strategic Support Force (see figure 4).[99] At the national level, this change institutionalizes the PLA's long-standing distinction between "intelligence" [*qingbao*, 情报], which encompasses all-source analysis supporting command decisionmaking, and "technical reconnaissance" [*jishu zhencha*, 技术侦察], which refers to technical intelligence collection directly supporting military operations.[100] The structure appears to maintain the prior arrangement of intelligence flow, whereby "all military intelligence flowed upward through the GSD."[101] The new Joint Staff Department Intelligence Bureau serves the GSD's former role, incorporating intelligence from the theater commands, each which in turn has its own bureaus responsible for operational and tactical intelligence analysis.[102] Theoretically, the establishment of a separate

Figure 4. PLA's Military Intelligence System in Transition (Notional)

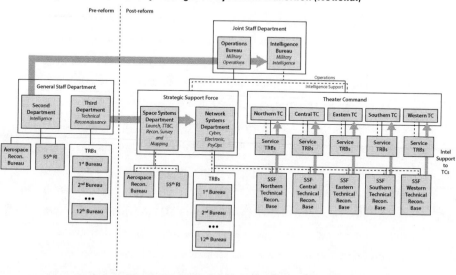

Key: PsyOps: psychological operations; RI: reconnaissance and intelligence; TC: theater command; TRB: technical reconnaissance bureau; TT&C: telemetry, tracking, and control.

ground force headquarters and the incorporation of the Intelligence Bureau into the joint staff gives it more latitude to move away from its army-dominated past and direct intelligence resources to critical missions based on operational needs.[103] However, it remains unclear what exact responsibilities the bureau will have beyond the traditional focus on all-source analysis and human intelligence and whether, in light of its elevated role, it will take on more bureaucratic responsibilities for managing intelligence demands and balancing collections requirements among different competing interests within the PLA.

Network and Electronic Warfare

The Joint Staff Department's Network-Electronic Bureau creates a new force-wide structure for the management of the cyber and electronic warfare missions in the Strategic Support Force, theater commands, and other services. The creation of the JSD-NEB suggests that the PLA is maintaining a dual-echelon structure for cyber and EW, with the SSF's cyber force assuming responsibilities for strategic national-level operations that previously rested with former GSD units, while the services and theater commands continue to be responsible for cyber and EW operations at the operational and tactical levels (see figure 5). The precise responsibilities of the JSD-NEB are unclear, but likely include oversight and integration functions such as the issuance of operational guidance, deconfliction of areas of responsibility, and establishment of rules of engagement. In one of the few public mentions of the organization tied to a specific sphere of interest, JSD-NEB Chief Major General Wang Xiaoming [王晓明] and Deputy Bureau Chief Senior Colonel Lin Shishan [林世山] held a symposium with international law experts at the Wuhan School of Law, discussing international law in cyberspace and "Tallinn 2.0," a study on applicability of international law to cyber operations performed by the NATO Cooperative Cyber Defence Centre of Excellence in Tallinn, Estonia.[104]

The reforms have also established a national Joint Network-Electronic Countermeasure *dadui*.[105] This organization appears to have corresponding

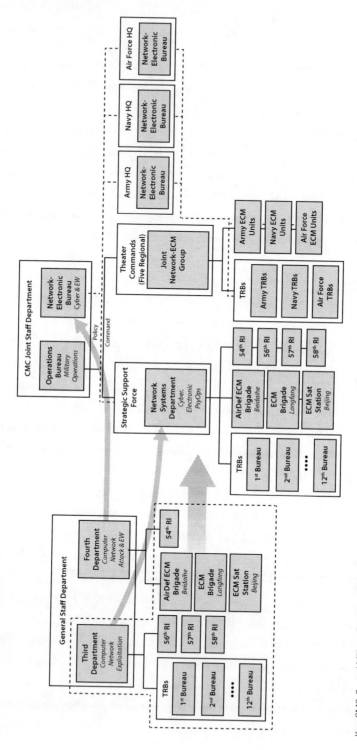

Figure 5. Network-Electronic Units in Transition

Key: CMC: Central Military Commission; ECM: electronic countermeasure; EW: electronic warfare; HQ: headquarters; PsyOps: psychological operations; RI: reconnaissance and intelligence; TC: theater command; TRB: technical reconnaissance bureau; TT&C: telemetry, tracking, and control.

472

lower echelon elements in the theater commands, called Network-Electronic Countermeasure *dui*, which are likely made up of regional service branch and theater command cyber and EW elements.[106] These organizations mirror the former force-wide network of electronic countermeasure centers (ECM centers) [*dianzi duikang zhongxin*, 电子对抗中心], which were composed of a national center collocated with the former 4PLA and lower echelon elements in the former military regions.[107] Based on the ECM center's public research, its mission appears to have focused on electronic support measures, electronic intelligence, and targeting in the electromagnetic domain.[108] The similarities suggest the former ground force ECM centers were most likely reorganized into joint force Network-Electronic Countermeasure *dadui* and *dui*, expanding the scope of their mission to include network reconnaissance and targeting. These organizations suggest that the SSF does not, as some initially thought, have a monopoly of force in cyberspace, but rather continues to share the mission with other components in the PLA.

Information and Communications

The new Joint Staff Department's Information and Communications Bureau, reorganized from the former GSD Informatization Department, has inherited responsibilities for force-wide management of information systems, communications, and support for high-level warfighting command and control. The ICB includes the PLA's Information Assurance Base [*xinxi baozhang jidi*, 信息保障基地], which has similarly moved over to the JSD.[109] However, the Strategic Support Force's control of critical ground-based satellite communication infrastructure and primacy in operating space-based data relays may indicate it is a primary organization responsible for routing and supporting information flows through outer space, which would imply an overlap with what we understand to be the JSD-ICB's responsibilities. It remains unclear if the SSF will inherit regional communications ground stations for downlink and uplink or whether those will be operated directly by the Central Military Commission, by other services, or by the theater commands. It is worth noting that the Information

473

Assurance Base appears to have maintained at least some of its subordinate communications regiments through the reforms, raising questions as to whether it might contain a joint "information support force" in the same vein as the Joint Logistics Support Force.[110]

The SSF's Strategic Missions and Roles

The Strategic Support Force demonstrates China's evolving understanding of how information serves as a strategic resource in warfare. The PLA recognizes that harnessing outer space, the cyber domain, and the electromagnetic spectrum—and denying their use to adversaries—are paramount needs if the PLA is to attain superiority in a conflict. These three domains are the primary conduits by which a military force collects, processes, transmits, and receives information. If a force is denied use of these domains, the informationized system-of-systems infrastructure that underpins modern military operations cannot properly function. For the first time in the PLA's history, the creation of the Strategic Support Force largely unifies both responsibility for fielding critical systems in these domains and conducting operations to dominate each domain's battlespaces.

These two missions, frequently summarized as "information support" and "information warfare," align in large part with the composition of the SSF's subordinate space and cyber forces. This unity of organizational design and mission set is likely to substantially improve the PLA's ability to achieve information superiority in a conflict. The reforms come at a time when the military's mandate from Xi Jinping to modernize and operate further from China's shores has placed growing demands on China's information support and information warfare forces.

Strategic Information Support

The first commander of the SSF, General Gao Jin, has emphasized the force's role in information support by stating that the SSF provides vital "support for safeguarding and raising up an 'information umbrella' [*xinxi yusan*, 信息雨伞] for the military system, which will be integrated with the actions of our land, sea, and air forces and rocket forces throughout an entire operation, [and] will be the key force for victory in war."[111] General Gao never expands on what he means by an information umbrella, but much can be inferred from a straightforward look at the types of information support the Strategic Support Force is uniquely positioned to provide.

The SSF's space force contains what the 2013 *Science of Military Strategy* refers to as the "strategic brace support" (*zhanlüe zhicheng*, 战略支撑) of space-based intelligence and communications, both of which are functions that AMS strategists envision as the primary role for space forces in the foreseeable future.[112] The terms used by authoritative sources, such as *brace support* and *information umbrella*, all carry connotations of support and extension, in this case by advancing the PLA's ability to conduct and sustain operations both within Chinese territory and in areas abroad that China understands to be vital to its national interests.

While the SSF's role in strategic information support largely derives from the plethora of intelligence and communications assets under its space force, the cyber force also maintains a deep bench of technical collection capabilities that are consequential even beyond offense and espionage operations within the cyber domain. SSF information support missions can be divided into five primary functions it offers across the military:

- centralizing technical intelligence collection and management
- providing strategic intelligence support to theater commands
- enabling PLA power projection
- supporting strategic defense in the space and nuclear domains
- enabling joint operations.

Centralizing Technical Intelligence Collection and Management. The Strategic Support Force commands a wide array of national-level technical collection assets received from the former organizations that now make up the bulk of its force. This includes space-based electro-optical imagery intelligence, synthetic aperture radar, electronic intelligence platforms from across the GSD and GAD, electronic support capabilities from the former

Fourth Department, and strategic, long-range ground-based collection systems from the former Third Department.[113] Before the reorganization, management of these systems was siloed, answerable only to their parent general department, and differentiated based on source. While the reorganization places the totality of collection assets under the same organization, the advantages inherent to centralization depend heavily on how well the technical systems, data, and organizational procedures that underpin those operations can be integrated. From a purely organizational standpoint, control over these sources of intelligence potentially allows the Strategic Support Force to gain the comprehensive perspective necessary to identify gaps in collection, assess emerging needs, and tailor operations and acquisitions to address shortfalls and new challenges. In short, the sheer breadth of what the SSF can see and hear empowers it to play a decisive role in China's comprehensive domain awareness and national defense far beyond that of any single organization that has come before.

Providing Strategic Intelligence Support to Theater Commands. While the theater command technical reconnaissance bureaus and theater-subordinate service elements maintain their own collection capabilities, they are largely focused on operational- and tactical-level intelligence, surveillance, and reconnaissance with limited coverage beyond their regional areas of responsibility. Collection is further hindered by the logistical and geographical limitations of the collections platforms themselves. Limited-range drones, surveillance planes, and shore-based radar, though each provides vital necessary reconnaissance, do not provide the type of comprehensive domain awareness necessary for actionable early warning.[114] The Strategic Support Force's space-based surveillance capacity can thus significantly extend the range of the theater command commanders' battlefield awareness, filling critical gaps in their intelligence collection.[115]

The SSF's primacy in space-based intelligence collection also places it in a unique position to develop identifiers on foreign military targets. These identifiers, which can be in the form of specific emitter signatures, signal parameters, radar signatures, infrared heat signatures, or even imagery profiles, can help detect, identify, track, and target certain operational platforms and weapons systems. The development of these indicators requires long-term technical collection on platforms and thus are a direct function of opportunities for surveillance wherein space-based technical collection systems have a clear advantage over their terrestrial counterparts. The ability to conduct space-based intelligence collection on foreign military assets thus gives the Strategic Support Force a primary role in developing these indicators, feeding them back to intelligence systems and disseminating them to operational and tactical units in the theater commands for joint force early warning, air defense, and area surveillance. In addition, the SSF may also play a similar role for nonkinetic targeting in the cyber and electromagnetic domains, where it is similarly well-positioned to identify spectrum allocation for foreign adversary sensors, communications, and radar systems for jamming and foreign adversary cyber infrastructure for targeting, intrusion, and compromise.

Enabling PLA Power Projection. The SSF enables and sustains the PLA's ability to project power in the East and South China seas and into areas beyond the first island chain. The SSF is said to field assets that cover the entirety of the "information chain," including space-based surveillance, satellite relay and communications, and telemetry, tracking, and navigation, all of which are necessary to support these types of remote operations.[116] Long-range precision strike, far seas naval deployments, long-range unmanned aerial vehicle reconnaissance, and strategic air operations all rely to varying degrees on infrastructure over which the SSF now wields exclusive control. Conventional strike, the most critical component of both the PLA's nonnuclear deterrence posture and its "counterintervention" strategy, is a prime example.[117] Despite being conducted primarily by the PLA Rocket Force, the PLA's long-range conventional strike mission depends heavily on the SSF to support operations, from initial detection, identification, and targeting, to guidance and battlefield damage assessment.

The Strategic Support Force's monopoly on space-based information infrastructure similarly places the service in a position to play an indispensable role in enabling the PLA Navy to operate in the far seas. While providing traditional intelligence support on enemy movement, early warning, and maritime surveillance, the SSF will also provide more foundational "battlefield environment support" [*zhanchang huanjing baozhang*, 战场环境保障], a term the PLA uses to describe battlespace-relevant survey, mapping, meteorological, oceanographic, and navigation information.[118] This knowledge-base is a critical factor for command decisionmaking in ship movement and operational planning. Placing China's growing fleet of maritime surveillance satellites, dual-use oceanographic and hydrological satellites, and expanding constellation of Beidou navigation satellites under the Strategic Support Force puts it in a primary position to provide this type of information. The expansion of the Beidou constellation also diminishes China's reliance on the U.S.-produced global positioning system. The constellation is expected to have global coverage by 2020, extending navigation assurance for naval deployments worldwide.[119]

Supporting Strategic Defense in the Space and Nuclear Domains. Although the SSF's responsibilities for antisatellite missile operations, ballistic missile defense, and space-based kinetic operations are unclear, its monopoly on space surveillance and early warning means it will at a minimum play a critical role in supporting these missions. Space surveillance—the ability to detect, identify, and track objects in space—is a prerequisite capability for both antisatellite and ballistic missile defense.[120] The SSF's space force has inherited three major telemetry, tracking, and control centers in Beijing and Xi'an and a fleet of *Yuan Wang*–class [远望] tracking ships. Each center provides varying degrees of space surveillance capabilities as well as telemetry functions for China's satellites, space launches, and long-range missiles. The military is also known to maintain four large phased-array radars in Huian, Korla, Longgangzhen, and Shuangyashan, possibly under the former GSD Third Department, that are capable of tracking objects in support of either counterspace or BMD operations.[121] The former 4PLA's nonkinetic counter-space mission likely means it also possessed a ground-based space tracking and surveillance apparatus, which it would have used to feed targeting data to its satellite jamming platforms.[122]

Enabling Joint Operations. The SSF's role in strategic information support directly enables joint operations by providing a connective substrate that helps to integrate disparate units and systems from the PLA's four services. The SSF's ability to provide the information umbrella of space-based C4ISR, intelligence support, and battlefield environment assessments helps forge a common intelligence picture among joint forces within each theater command, a fundamental requirement for fulfilling the PLA's mission of winning "informationized local wars."[123] According to PLA commentary, the SSF ensures the "centralized management, centralized employment, and centralized development" of support resources and acts as an "important support" for the PLA's joint operation "system of systems."[124] At the time of its establishment, Xi Jinping spoke of the need for the SSF to support system-of-systems integration, technical interoperability, information-sharing, and intelligence-fusion among the services.[125] The deputy director of the SSF's 54th Research Institute, Lü Yueguang [吕越光], goes further and states that "information-dominant system-of-systems integration" challenges will become the "fundamental requirement for future joint operations."[126]

Strategic Information Operations

In addition to its strategic information support role, the SSF is the primary force for information warfare in the Chinese military, responsible for achieving "information dominance" in any conflict. The *Science of Military Strategy* and other authoritative sources call for the coordinated employment of space, cyber, and electronic warfare as strategic weapons to achieve these ends, arguing that the PLA must "paralyze the enemy's operational system of systems" and "sabotage the enemy's war command system of systems" in the initial stages of a conflict while protecting its own.[127] These concepts are not unique to the Chinese military; many modern militaries emphasize the importance of information dominance, underscoring it as a prerequisite to victory on the battlefield.

The SSF's importance in strategic information warfare is best understood in the context of challenges posed by an "information warfare campaign," the conceptual wartime front where the SSF's forces—and an information operations group—would be employed. This campaign is likely to be a complex, multidimensional set of operations that incorporates kinetic, space, cyber, electronic, and psychological actions through all phases of conflict, and with each discipline of information operations having specific strengths at difference phases of a crisis or conflict.[128] Psychological and electronic warfare, for example, are key in the pre-crisis period to raise the political and military risks associated with aggression. EW has the potential to be a key signaling mechanism for the PLA, due to its ability to bridge the gap between cyber operations, which have a high opportunity cost in terms of blown access when used for signaling, and kinetic strikes, which mark a transition to open warfare. Electronic warfare is the workhorse in Chinese information operations and is frequently portrayed as inherently defensive (in the broadest sense of the term), pulling double duty as both a tool of coercion and information denial. China's evolving concept of "cyber-electromagnetic sovereignty" raises the possibility that the PLA will one day declare the right to deny or degrade satellite reconnaissance aimed at its territorial claims and space-based platforms, which could indirectly be understood as holding its assets at risk, complicating U.S. efforts to project power in the region.

If China's strategic objectives cannot be secured without escalating into an overt conflict, the twin disciplines of cyber operations and precision kinetic strike will likely be employed in concert by the PLA in any first strike, though PLA writings on the nature of informationized warfare suggest that such coordination is only possible once conflict is deemed inevitable and China has verifiably achieved information dominance. Both cyber operations and kinetic strike offer first-mover advantages to an attacker willing to preempt its adversary, although the intended effects may not be durable or reliable during the transition from peacetime to wartime. However, these capabilities are also prone to denial, counterattack, and uncertain effects. In the best case scenario, however, Chinese writings emphasize that the employment of cyber and kinetic strikes can create a self-reinforcing cycle that paralyzes an adversary at the outset of conflict, cementing one's own information dominance and quickly securing the adversary's compliance.[129]

The relative prominence of the information warfare disciplines shifts once again after the threshold of war is breached and protracted conflict ensues, with cyber warfare losing importance compared to electronic warfare and kinetic strike. Electronic warfare will be a key standoff weapon in any conflict that China is likely to fight, offering the potential to significantly diminish the intelligence collection and information processing capacity of an adversary even as enemy units come within range of the growing web of air, submarine, surface, and missile threats that China is extending out along its periphery. Once outright conventional warfare begins, kinetic strike once again becomes dominant, and psychological operations serve as a tool to maintain the populace's resolve, weaken the enemy's will, and shape diplomatic and political narratives in order to better enable the successful conclusion of the conflict on terms favorable to China.

The SSF evolves the PLA's ability to conduct information operations in both peacetime and wartime in a number of ways, namely, integrating these disciplines of information warfare into a unified force, integrating cyber espionage and offense, unifying information warfare campaign planning, and unifying responsibilities for information warfare command and control. This unity of command, planning, and force development enabled by the SSF potentially realizes the PLA objective to conduct the type of complex, coordinated set of operations an information warfare campaign would require.

Realizing "Integrated Information Warfare." The difficult prospect of maintaining readiness in an ever-changing information environment is a key challenge that the SSF's structural changes are intended to surmount, integrating across divisions in a way that can play to the unique realities of warfighting in the information domain. In this regard, the SSF effects a sort of "integrated information warfare," unifying China's myriad and dispersed forces across three key dimensions. First and most importantly, the force merges espionage and offense disciplines across electronic, cyber, and space warfare. Secondly, the SSF merges all the types of strategic warfighting operations that take place primarily in information domains (as opposed to physical battlespaces) under a single cohesive force. Both changes are necessary preconditions to implement the third and most important dimension: peacetime-wartime integration. By consciously mirroring the wartime IOG construct during peacetime, the PLA is better enabled to conduct intelligence preparation of the battlespace, cohesively plan cross-domain and cross-discipline information operations campaigns, and develop capabilities suited to the evolving realities of conflict.

Integrated Cyber Espionage and Offense. The creation of the Strategic Support Force optimizes China's preparation for conducting strategic information operations by reducing the degree of separation between its espionage and offense-focused disciplines, which previously only unified in war under an IOG. This prior arrangement ignored that the two disciplines are heavily intertwined, draw on common resources, and, when left uncoordinated in a conflict, can even run the risk of interfering with each other.

The SSF brings two key advantages in this context. First, integrating espionage and offense for strategic information operations allows both missions to benefit from shared reconnaissance, which is essential for identifying vulnerabilities and weaknesses around which their capabilities can be built and offensive effects can be planned. The set of conditions on which these capabilities rely do not remain static and are especially sensitive to changes in an adversary's defense posture, readiness, prevailing attitudes, and the broader shift from peacetime to wartime footing. Military readiness in such an environment means maintaining a constant operations cycle of "perpetual mobilization," wherein countermeasures and effects are constantly evaluated against a changing security landscape and the adversary's efforts.[130] The SSF's integration of espionage and offense recognizes that reconnaissance and capabilities development overlap enough between the two disciplines that both suffer if they are kept separated.

Second, grouping espionage and offense together enables commanders to balance conflicting objectives and inherent tradeoffs that can occur between the two disciplines. Espionage operations prioritize maintaining access to adversary systems and communications for the intelligence gains they may provide, whereas offensive operations may involve sacrificing those access methods in order to undermine the adversary's systems and limit his operations, even if the cost is losing a prime source of information. These tradeoffs become even more pronounced in cyber domain operations, where offense and espionage are inherently blurred; cyber accesses are notoriously "dual-use," meaning they are equally useful for intelligence or disruption. Readiness, in these cases, demands empowering commanders to continually evaluate both options against each other and against overall campaign objectives and evolving military need, a difficult proposition if espionage and offense authorities are typically separated.

Unified Operations Planning. The SSF's dual responsibilities for "force construction" and information operations empower it with both the perspective and authority to define campaign objectives and operational plans for an information warfare campaign and in turn to develop a force necessary to carry those out. Owing to the complexities of coordinating disparate elements, Chinese military scholars have stressed the importance of unified planning and command in order to "form a complete operational force and carry out integrated planning and strategy."[131] The influential 2013 work *Lectures on the Science of Information Operations* lists three primary requirements for unified planning and command in information warfare campaigns, each of which has been addressed to varying degrees by either the large structural changes in the PLA's reforms or the creation of the Strategic Support Force:[132]

- Integrated planning within larger joint and combined operations. The SSF affords information operations a status typically reserved for more traditional domains by providing a cohesive military service capable of representing constituent forces in joint force planning and operations. Its creation conceptually upgrades the status of information operations within the PLA from an auxiliary component of ground forces to a primary front of warfare alongside land, sea, and air. Fulfilling a similar role to that which other services play for their corresponding wartime operations groups, the SSF likely serves as the primary constituent service of the information operations group, shouldering responsibility for carrying out information warfare within the broader PLA framework of integrated joint operations.

- Coordinated planning across services, echelons, and theaters. The SSF's precise role in coordinating information warfare planning across other service elements and theater commands has yet to be publicly defined. Aside from the PLA Rocket Force, the SSF appears to stand alone among the services in not having any of its elements subordinate to the theater commands, either indicating that lower echelon information warfare planning may largely fall to the theater commands themselves or that these subordinate elements exist but have not yet been discovered. It is similarly unclear which organization holds planning responsibilities for China's non-PLA armed forces, including local militias and the People's Armed Police. Some military theorists indicate the SSF plays both coordinating and supporting roles in this context.[133] Given its preeminence in information warfare strategy, however, the SSF will nevertheless influence lower echelon planning at a minimum.

- Unified planning across information operations disciplines. The SSF fulfills the core requirement of unified planning and command by incorporating all information disciplines into a single cohesive force. Chinese scholars have long emphasized the inclusion of "hard-kill" measures into information warfare planning, epitomized by Ye Zheng's concept of integrated information and firepower warfare [*xin huo yiti zhan*, 信火一体战], which calls for the coordinated pairing of network and electronic warfare with conventional long-range precision strikes.[134] The SSF's concentration of technical reconnaissance capabilities provides a unique vantage point from which to identify critical nodes in an adversary's system of systems, prioritize targeting for kinetic strikes, and weigh the use of "hard" and "soft" measures against each other in campaign planning and operations.

Unified Information Warfare Command and Control. The importance of information operations in gaining unseen information and intelligence advantages in peacetime imputes upon the Strategic Support Force a unique responsibility for achieving "escalation dominance," a condition wherein China maintains the initiative in shaping adversary behavior in a crisis scenario that has not yet become a full-on conflict. This requires substantial intelligence capabilities as well as the development of a diverse set of measures for countering, influencing, or deterring an adversary, not only before the crisis occurs but also as part of a continuous process of evaluation to judge both the merits of intentional escalation and the risks of unintended escalation. This capability to engage in "calibrated escalation" reflects a highly complex mission set that requires the ability to coordinate across multiple dimensions of the military bureaucracy in order to produce a set of options that can be clearly communicated up the chain of command, where they will then be evaluated against other political, economic, and military costs. Having a singular service to produce, account for these options, and unify command and control is a marked improvement from the dispersed and siloed arrangement that existed prior to the PLA's reforms.

Comparing U.S. and Chinese Approaches to Information Warfare

While U.S. and Chinese information support and information operations concepts generally align, a key point of departure is the manner in which these two missions are understood to fit into broader whole-of-nation plans to accomplish strategic objectives.[135] The PLA, like the U.S. military, views information support and information operations as key for anticipating adversary action, setting the terms of conflict in peacetime, and achieving battlefield dominance in wartime. The PLA places a strong emphasis on dismantling the adversary's system of systems, with decapitation and paralysis rather than outright destruction being the ultimate objective. This approach is tied to the long-standing Chinese focus on *winning without fighting*, an older Maoist-era phrase that translates today to shaping an adversary's decisionmaking through actions below the threshold of outright war, accomplishing strategic objectives without escalating to open conflict. In the Chinese view, if this approach fails, the military needs to be prepared to rapidly seize the initiative in order to compel an adversary to quickly cease hostilities on Chinese terms if the threshold of open conflict is reached. Strategic information support is a key enabler, providing both the avenues and intelligence necessary for well-timed political and operational decisions and action. China's preparations for conflict and planning for these strategic campaigns are directly tied to its national emphasis on preempting and shaping enemy action.

Chinese information operations theory and force structure have historically been somewhat inconsistent on this point, recognizing that information operations defy the binary dichotomy of peacetime and wartime, while operating a force that was not up to that challenge. The Strategic Support Force comes at a time when there appears to be renewed interest in moving away from Western models of conflict, in which peace and war are distinct stages, and toward a spectrum of omnipresent "struggle," a Maoist-Marxist-Leninist paradigm that sees a broad political front in an enduring clash of political systems and ideologies, with military competition and conflict being merely one part of that whole.[136]

The strategic cultures and objectives of both the United States and China have been on opposite ends of the spectrum in many respects for decades, yet both sides have increasingly come to largely the same conclusion on the need to transcend the peace-war binary. The Chinese military has long recognized that abandoning the peace-versus-war binary better reflects the reality of modern operations but have lacked a military force structure that can properly act on that understanding. The United States has maintained a force structure that, since 1986, has merged the concept of peace and war and organized for readiness, but nevertheless maintained the strategic and political distinction between the two. The key differentiator is in how both sides view competition and conflict: as either a rising crescendo that if left unchecked results in a discrete crisis event, as the United States does, or as a long-term struggle between opposing objectives, as China does. Somewhat ironically, in the current round of reforms, the PLA is seeking to advance a traditional Maoist understanding of struggle and competition by adopting a more Western model of military structure—albeit one with Chinese characteristics. The Strategic Support Force's primary roles of information support and information warfare, on which military preparation and readiness in large part rests, are key advancements in China's ability to translate both of these paradigms into operational reality.

Although a truly authoritative insider's view of Chinese information warfare has not been made public, the 2013 *Lectures on the Science of Information Operations* by PLA scholar Major General Ye Zheng gives a comprehensive examination of the unique properties, advantages, and limitations of information operations and their use in warfare. Ye identifies four fundamental principles of Chinese thinking on information warfare that inform the SSF's approach to information operations:

- Information operations are offense-oriented. Chinese scholars believe information dominance is the core of the "three dominances" of information, air, and space that, when achieved, ensure victory. As modern warfare requires the practice of system-of-systems operations, disrupting an adversary's system of systems while preserving one's own can deprive them of strategic initiative and allow Chinese forces to rapidly achieve battlefield dominance.

- Information operations are offense-dominant. Cyber and intelligence operations in particular are fragile, sensitive to changing circumstances, and rely on techniques and access methods that lose much of their power once they have been put to use and the element of surprise is lost. Cyber accesses that enable these effects are frequently more effective in the initial stages of a conflict.

■ "Prepositioning" and "massing on the border" manifest differently in information warfare. Whereas other domains prioritize geographic prepositioning, readiness and advantage in the information domain place a priority on timing, blurring the distinction between peacetime and wartime. This in turn partially blurs the distinction between intelligence operations and military preparations.

■ Information advantage can be traded for space and time on the battlefield. A key belief in the Chinese understanding of information operations is that prepositioned effects and capabilities, achieved through either cyber implants in an adversary's systems or an intelligence advantage enabled by strategic information support, can be utilized at strategic times to anticipate, delay, and disable an adversary's ability to defend himself or project power. This means that an information domain advantage can effectively be traded for physical space and time in conflict in order to enable the achievement of China's strategic objectives.

PLA theorists believe that these characteristics of information warfare are not unique to any one nation's armed forces but instead are universal operational precepts that need to be recognized and adhered to regardless of a nation's strategic culture. It is therefore unsurprising that China's understanding of information warfare looks remarkably similar to that envisioned by the United States.

Where the Chinese view differs is in the strategic context and scenarios where they see these options being employed, stemming from a recognition of their vulnerabilities, limitations, and strategic objectives vis-à-vis those of their potential adversaries. Bureaucratic factors also play an important role. The organizational implementation of China's cyber force, for example, reflects both the similarities and differences between the Chinese and U.S. approaches. One of the key differences between USCYBERCOM and the SSF's cyber force lies in their respective scopes of responsibilities. The SSF appears to be responsible for *all* of information warfare, overseeing the employment of a broad spectrum of tools for kinetic, cyberspace, electromagnetic, and psychological domains.

The SSF reflects another point of divergence between China and the United States in the degree of organizational emphasis it places on the space domain as a core arena of information warfare. The United States certainly recognizes the intersection between the information domain and outer space; however, in both strategic writings and official publications, the PLA has continuously emphasized the link between space and cyber networks, viewing them not in isolation but as extensions of one another through their common use of the electromagnetic spectrum as a transmission medium. This may be due to the PLA's understanding that the most extreme threat scenarios it faces, such as a full-scale invasion by a foreign power, an adversary's long-range precision strike and force projection would both largely be enabled by space-based infrastructure, which would serve as both an extension of terrestrial cyber networks and a means of contesting dominance in the electromagnetic domain.

At the strategic level of war, China's plans for the defense of these three domains converge to the degree that combining them not only creates natural efficiencies but also verges on being a requirement for an effective force. The comparative lack of emphasis on operational cohesion among cyber, space, and electronic warfare in the United States can be understood as a manifestation of differing strategic priorities and threat perceptions. In the wars the United States has fought since the end of the Cold War—against armed insurgencies, terrorist groups, and relatively low-tech powers—cyber, space, and electronic warfare could be treated as separate, complementary disciplines without a demand for convergence at the strategic level as would be required when facing a technologically developed near-peer military power with a mature C4ISR system. It is possible that the U.S. 2017 National Security Strategy, which shifts focus away from combating terrorism to confronting "strategic competitors," will presage a realignment within the Department of Defense toward an organizational concept that more closely resembles the Strategic Support Force.[137]

Another key point of divergence between the SSF Cyber Force and USCYBERCOM is in the inclusion of psychological operations within the former's remit. Chinese Communist Party and PLA thinkers have long understood cyber operations to be a primary vehicle for psychological manipulation, a point not fully grasped by the U.S. Government, particularly the defense establishment, until the recent discovery and analysis of Russian interference in the U.S. Presidential election in 2016. The United States tends to view cyber warfare in terms of destruction and denial, with a particular focus on the potential for cyber attacks with kinetic effects and the destruction and manipulation of data in a conflict. Chinese leaders, on the other hand, view manipulation of information more broadly as their chief vulnerability and worry about the societal effects of an adversary undermining Chinese domestic information control. This view manifests in China's civilian cybersecurity establishment, which has taken on an expansive scope that extends beyond computer networks to physical devices, broadcast airwaves, online content, and propaganda. This understanding that failure to control information threatens the Chinese Communist Party's political power and stability in a way that it does not in democratic countries is a view shared by China's civilian and military establishments. Maintaining information control is thus viewed as a preemptive defense that obviates the need for more forceful measures, such as armed domestic actions, to be employed. For the SSF, the inclusion of content and a more information-centric approach to cyber operations is translated into the expansive remit of the cyber force, which appropriately includes psychological operations in alignment with the expansive Chinese view of cybersecurity.

Remaining Challenges

Simply reorganizing command structures and relationships is but one step in a lengthy and likely painful process the Strategic Support Force must undertake in fully integrating its myriad components into a cohesive operational force. Removing silos and integrating forces eliminate potential barriers, but without deeper changes within the space and cyber forces, the SSF will be limited in its ability to fully play its information support and information warfare roles. Similarly, in some cases there are deeper organizational tensions at play that may limit or impede overall PLA progress in the long term, such as centralizing strategic capabilities vice diffusion and balancing the cyber mission between civilian and military components. How the PLA handles these challenges is vital in realizing its goal to be a modern military able to fight and win wars.

Centralization vs. Diffusion of Control and Development of Strategic Capabilities

It is worth noting that the SSF's dual responsibilities for both "force construction" and operations are in direct tension with one of the key purposes of the reforms, namely, to transition operational responsibilities away from the services to joint force theater commands. This fundamentally defies the "CMC leads, theaters fight, and services build" paradigm implemented across the force. Although the Strategic Support Force appears to take the U.S. Strategic Command as its conceptual inspiration, the SSF diverges markedly in implementation. USSTRATCOM supports U.S. combatant commands as a joint force construct rather than as a singular service in the model of the Strategic Support Force. As a joint functional combatant command, USSTRATCOM coordinates among a number of subordinate elements from the Army, Marine Corps, Navy, and Air Force to prosecute its primary missions of nuclear operations, space operations, information warfare, strategic C4ISR support, and ballistic missile defense.

While the PLA created joint, regional theater commands analogous to U.S. combatant commands, the PLA stopped short in creating functional combatant commands, instead in the SSF's case opting to create a singular service that also serves a functional role force-wide. A similar approach was taken with the PLA Rocket Force, whose functional role of employing China's nuclear and strategic missiles has been similarly distilled into a singular service that appears incongruent with the overall intent of the reforms.

The most obvious explanation for these inconsistencies may be that the current arrangement is transitional, and the PLA intends to eventually create joint functional combatant commands—or some analog—in the future. However, there may be deeper organizational dynamics at play. In both circumstances, responsibilities for nuclear, space, and information warfare may have been deemed sufficiently strategic that the CMC elected to keep both operational and force construction functions contained within a single service, where their use and development could be more easily controlled. The lack of equivalent, mature development of these capabilities in the other services, coupled with a still-nascent joint force construct, may have convinced PLA planners that operational control and development of these capabilities were, for now, best kept contained. Chinese defense commentators have explained that the decision to construct the SSF as a separate force rather than a joint force construct was driven by lessons learned from observing foreign militaries where the distribution of strategic support across the different services resulted in redundancies in force development and a counterproductive rivalry for funding and resources.[138]

If taken at face value, this approach highlights some of the broader challenges the PLA faces in modernization and reform. The centralization of new-type force development and cutting-edge missions, such as space, cyber, and electronic warfare, seems to run counter to the objective of modernizing the PLA force-wide. The consolidation of these capabilities under the SSF, either for resource conservancy, desire to control strategic capabilities, or desire to more closely guide their development, may act as a limiting factor for other services, preventing the development of space, cyber, and information capabilities in their own missions. This raises further questions about the future of both the space and cyber missions, which in the former case may be shared with the PLA Rocket Force and PLA Air Force and in the latter case shared with the theater commands and other services. Given the above logic, it seems likely that the desire to centralize and reduce redundancy, for whatever reason, may translate to a monopoly of force, command, and development over these missions on the part of the SSF. The creation of functional services like the SSF and PLA Rocket Force appears to be a bureaucratic compromise, allowing theater commands access to these capabilities without ceding operational control, diffusing force development across other services, or risking the adoption of an unfamiliar joint force construct like USSTRATCOM by a PLA already acclimating to a new organizational model.

Mission and Force Integration

Force integration at lower organizational and administrative layers also remains a distinct challenge for both of the SSF's two main forces. The Space Systems Department is a motley mixture of higher grade bases, launch and ground stations, and experimental technology development facilities contained within a force structure that has traditionally not been optimized for combat operations. To align and coordinate its disparate component parts, the SSD will almost certainly need to stand up new administrative structures. Since the SSD's space mission brings together a disparate set of mission components from the GSD and GAD, systems integration poses an additional challenge. Each of these organizations comes to the SSD with its own operations plans, technical data sources, and infrastructure, with missions as diverse as communications, navigation, surveillance and reconnaissance, and telemetry, tracking, and control. For the SSD to fulfill the SSF's (and the PLA's) broader mandate of system-of-systems integration [*tixi ronghe*, 体系融合], it will need not only to integrate these systems together but also to seamlessly feed this information into force-wide networks such as the Integrated Command Platform [*yitihua zhihui pingtai*, 一体化指挥平台] to support both strategic missions and theater command operations.[139]

The Network System Department faces several challenges of its own. First and foremost, it will need to reform the former 3PLA's administrative structure to accommodate an expanded mission set and a newfound focus on cyber domain operations, which had previously been dispersed across multiple bureaus and treated as a subdiscipline of technical reconnaissance.[140]

Further reorganization is likely to center on consolidating myriad cyber espionage elements and integrating them with cyber and EW elements from the former 4PLA. However, these missions were deeply embedded in the force structure of their respective departments and separating these elements out to reconstitute them along either functional or organizational lines will likely require deeper reorganization.

Beyond organizational mergers, the Network Systems Department will also need to reform its personnel system. The organizational integration of all the PLA's strategic cyber and EW capabilities fulfills the long-held goal of INEW in a more comprehensive way than the previous structure, but the NSD still faces steep hurdles in integrating the two disciplines on a human level. In the past, 3PLA and 4PLA appear to have largely maintained separate personnel systems, including distinct officer corps, noncommissioned officer corps, and technical cadre career paths, all of which will need to be merged if the NSD is going to fully embrace and realize INEW. The Network Systems Department's management of professional military education and billeting will be a critical factor in any such reform. The consolidation of the Information Engineering University as the sole military academy for the cyber and electronic warfare arms of China's network-electronic forces is an important step forward that may help unify professional military education to meet the disparate needs of both forces. At this time, however, assessments of how the NSD will manage its personnel are complicated by the existence of the Network-Electronic Bureau, whose responsibilities for force-wide management of education and training in this sphere are still unclear.

It also remains an open question how the Strategic Support Force will manage conflicting or overlapping responsibilities between its space and cyber forces. For instance, a number of organizations now under the Network Systems Department once had space mission components; these presumably moved over with them to the SSF. The technical reconnaissance–focused former GSD 3rd Department's 12th Bureau [*zongcan san bu di shi'er ju*, 总参三部第十二局] or Unit 61486 [*61486 budui*, 61486 部队] has historically been responsible for space-based signals intelligence collection and the interception of satellite communications, and may also control a number of ground-based space sensing stations.[141] The transfer of units from the former 4PLA, which maintained at least two satellite ground stations and whose operational brigades possess ground-based satellite jammers, presents a similar situation.[142] If transferred to the NSD, a conflict in responsibilities with the Space Systems Department's space mission components might arise and require ironing out, either via further below-the-neck reorganization or through redesign of these units' operational responsibilities.

Challenges in Cyber Operations

While the reforms that created the SSF can be favorably compared to the reforms that occurred in U.S. military structure between 2009 and 2014 with the creation of USCYBERCOM, there are key differences between each side's baselines for reform. For the United States, a key challenge has been separating USCYBERCOM enough from the National Security Agency for independent action and planning without losing the reconnaissance capabilities required to inform military targeting. The Chinese face the opposite challenge of integration. Of China's myriad agencies with cyber portfolios, the Ministry of State Security (MSS) and PLA are the two primarily responsible for cyber operations, including both espionage and offensive action. The Mandiant report in 2014, the Xi-Obama agreement on cyber-enabled intellectual property theft in 2015, and the creation of the Strategic Support Force each in various ways forced a realignment of responsibilities between the two agencies, with the MSS focusing on foreign intelligence, political dissent, and economic espionage, and the PLA redoubling its focus on military intelligence and warfighting.

This broad division of responsibilities serves a key purpose, primarily by deconflicting their mission and targeting efforts without requiring in-depth coordination. Both the PLA and MSS have previously resisted greater integration in their intelligence efforts, with the PLA in particular heavily rebuffing oversight and coordination with civilian authorities.[143]

As their political and bureaucratic power is largely secured by controlling exclusive intelligence sources, any sharing of information could mean a diffusion of power at the expense of their influence. In China's 2017 National Intelligence Law, the provisions discussing national governance of intelligence activities exempt the military, writing that the Central Military Commission, not civilian authorities, are exclusively in control of military technical reconnaissance efforts (and thus cyber operations).[144] Despite this arrangement offering greater clarity in a bureaucratic space with clashing interests, the arrangement ultimately deprives both civilian and military missions of the resources, insight, and technical skill from each other's reconnaissance and capabilities development efforts.

The PLA's cyber operational challenges go beyond the civil-military divide. Even under the new structure, the PLA faces crucial challenges in its ability to credibly field a modern cyber force. For one, it remains unclear how the PLA will integrate the SSF's cyber operations, which appear to be overwhelmingly focused on espionage and offense, with the PLA's cyber defense mission. Currently, primary responsibility for PLA network protection remains with the Information Support Base under the Joint Staff Department's Information and Communications Bureau. The decision to separate responsibilities for cyber offense and defense between the SSF and JSD is reflected in a similar arrangement between USCYBERCOM and the Defense Information Systems Agency, which like the JSD-ICB is responsible for both network protection and network operations for high-echelon command and control. It is unclear how the SSF will work with the JSD-ICB to help secure PLA networks from cyber threat, or how its broader space information support mission will integrate with the JSD's role as a service provider to the PLA writ large.

Even less clear is what responsibility, if any, the SSF will have for cyber defense of private, civilian, and critical infrastructure networks. In an early description of the SSF, retired navy Admiral Yin Zhuo broadly suggested that the SSF plays an "important role" in "protecting the country's financial security and the security of people's daily lives."[145] It is not clear where the

SSF would have sourced the personnel or capabilities to serve in this role, as it was not a known mission area of either the 3PLA or 4PLA, the two cyber-focused organizations from which the SSF drew the bulk of its cyber forces. Given the lack of preexisting units responsible for a "national cyber protection" mission, Yin's comments, if meant literally, suggest that the SSF would need to create this capability from scratch. Even though as of this writing there has been no indication that such units have been created, they would be clear analogs to USCYBERCOM's Cyber Protection Teams under its Cyber National Mission Force.

It is also not clear how any SSF cyber defense and protection mission would conflict or be coordinated with the Ministry of Public Security [*gongan bu*, 公安部] and Cyberspace Administration of China [*guojia hulianwang xinxi bangongshi*, 国家互联网信息办公室], both of which are charged with maintaining the security and defense of China's critical information infrastructure.[146] Overlapping responsibilities for defense and security of critical infrastructure is a common issue in national cyber-security governance, one equally felt by the United States. The Chinese government would likely face challenges in clarifying roles and responsibilities and establishing necessary legal, procedural, and technical means of operational coordination and incident response in order for critical infrastructure security and protection to be meaningful. This would in turn require a level of maturity and foresight in the notoriously fraught relationship between civilian and military authorities that is not likely to be achieved in the short term.

Finally, although the structural and organizational barriers between cyber attack and espionage appear to have been decreased, PLA units responsible for operations planning have little experience in anticipating and balancing equities between the two missions. Nor does it appear that the PLA has developed a doctrine for the use of force in cyberspace under which consistent judgments can be made in a crisis. Freed from its previous organizational structure, the PLA now faces the very real challenge of defining its own ways of war in cyberspace. These peacetime decisions will shape the development of the SSF's cyber force, network warfare capabilities, espionage priorities, and operational preparation of the battlespace. Unlike in other areas of warfare, when it comes to wartime cyber operations the PLA has precious few real-world examples upon which it can draw to inform its own doctrinal development. The PLA, like many other militaries, will have to answer critical questions about peacetime and wartime targeting, escalation in situations where the divide between peacetime and wartime is not always clear, battlespace prepositioning, and the viability and wisdom of utilizing cyber operations to achieve specific strategic military objectives. Although the PLA has developed its own theories on the strategic use of cyber operations in a conflict, these ideas have not yet been tested against the hard reality of operational and organizational implementation. The restructuring of the SSF (and the PLA more broadly) will put those ideas to the test, pushing Chinese cyber operations into unfamiliar territory.

Conclusion

The creation of the Strategic Support Force heralds a new era for China's strategic posture. Its very existence is both predicated on and a reinforcement of China's growing military strength, strengthening China's preparations for "local informationized war" and shifting the PLA's horizons to projecting power farther from China's shores. The SSF demonstrates the evolution of Chinese military thought about information as a strategic resource in warfare, recognizing both the role it plays in empowering forces and the vulnerabilities that result from reliance on information systems. The inclusion of responsibilities for both information support and information dominance in the same organization is a wise decision. As China continues to develop technologically and operate beyond the first and second island chains, the asymmetric advantages it has relied upon as a land-based, technologically inferior power will narrow, and it will increasingly have to contend with adversaries on more equal terms. From this standpoint, the introduction of an organization designed to balance those equities is forward-thinking.

Success in the various roles that Chinese scholars—and Xi Jinping himself—have envisioned for the SSF will largely depend on the efficacy of the unique and unproven model of "strategic support" that the Chinese have chosen to pursue. In one sense, centralizing these components into a service rather than dispersing them in a joint manner can be seen as innovative. On the other hand, the model can be viewed as an attempt by the PLA to grapple with its deeper and more systemic issues rather than a simple desire to try something new. Since an emphasis on top-down control and distrust of bottom-up decisionmaking has been an enduring hallmark of the PRC's strategic culture, this new centralization of information power may be more a function of persistent paranoia and the need for control than a desire to explore innovative means of warfighting. China certainly has the technical and operational capability to use its strategic resources in a punctuated manner for critical operations, but its ability to do so at scale in a sustained way will require deeper cultural and organizational innovation.

Notes

[1] Sources on specific units are available to qualified researchers upon request.

[2] Ye Zheng [叶征], *Lectures on the Science of Information Operations* [信息作战科学教程] (Beijing: Military Science Press [军事科学出版社], 2013), 69.

[3] See M. Taylor Fravel, "Shifts in Warfare and Party Unity: Explaining China's Changes in Military Strategy," *International Security* 42, no. 3 (Winter 2017/2018), 37–83.

[4] Joe McReynolds and James C. Mulvenon, "The Role of Informatization in the People's Liberation Army under Hu Jintao," in *Assessing the People's Liberation Army in the Hu Jintao Era*, ed. Roy Kamphausen, David Lai, and Travis Tanner (Carlisle Barracks, PA: Strategic Studies Institute, April 2014), 207–256.

[5] Clay Wilson, *Network Centric Operations: Background and Oversight Issues for Congress*, RL32411 (Washington, DC: Congressional Research Service, March 15, 2007), available at <https://fas.org/sgp/crs/natsec/RL32411.pdf>.

[6] Both the 2013 Academy of Military Science (AMS) edition of *Science of Military Strategy* and Ye Zheng's *Lectures on the Science of Information Operations* (hereafter LSIO) remark on transfer over space-based intelligence, surveillance, and

reconnaissance (ISR) networks in support of operations in the 1991 Gulf War, 1999 strikes on Kosovo, and 2003 invasion of Iraq. Analysts observe that the U.S. military's appetite for information appears to have grown in lockstep with its relative technological sophistication. See Shou Xiaosong [寿晓松], ed., *Science of Military Strategy* [战略学] (Beijing: Military Science Press [军事科学出版社], December 2013), 95–96; and Ye, LSIO, 50–51, 69–72.

[7] James C. Mulvenon, "PLA Computer Network Operations: Scenarios, Doctrine, Organizations, and Capability," in *Beyond the Strait: PLA Missions other Than Taiwan*, ed. Roy Kamphausen, David Lai, and Andrew Scobell (Carlisle Barracks, PA: Strategic Studies Institute, 2009), 275.

[8] Andrew S. Erickson, "Chinese Air- and Space-Based ISR: Integrating Aerospace Combat Capabilities over the Near Seas," in *China's Near Seas Combat Capabilities*, ed. Peter Dutton, Andrew S. Erickson, and Ryan Martinson (Newport, RI: U.S. Naval War College Press, 2014), 88–89.

[9] *Annual Report to Congress: Military and Security Developments Involving the People's Republic of China 2011* (Washington, DC: Office of the Secretary of Defense, 2011), 37.

[10] Leonard David, "China's Anti-Satellite Test: Worrisome Debris Cloud Circles Earth," *Space.com*, February 2, 2007, available at <www.space.com/3415-china-anti-satellite-test-worrisome-debris-cloud-circles-earth.html>.

[11] Dennis J. Blasko, "The 'Two Incompatibles' and PLA Self-Assessments of Military Capability," *China Brief* 13, no. 10 (May 2013), available at <https://jamestown.org/program/the-two-incompatibles-and-pla-self-assessments-of-military-capability/>.

[12] Shou, *Science of Military Strategy*, 169.

[13] Christopher H. Sharman, *China Moves Out: Stepping Stones Toward a New Maritime Strategy*, China Strategic Perspectives 9 (Washington, DC: NDU Press, April 2015), 5.

[14] For an expansive discussion of this concept, see Zhou Bisong [周碧松], *Strategic Frontiers* [战略边疆] (Beijing: National Defense University Press [国防大学出版社], 2016); and Shou, *Science of Military Strategy*, 73.

[15] Shou, *Science of Military Strategy*, 73.

[16] "China's Military Strategy" [中国的军事战略], Xinhua [新华], May 26, 2015, available at <www.mod.gov.cn/auth/2015-05/26/content_4586723.htm>.

[17] Zhou Bisong [周碧松], "Strategic Frontiers" [战略边疆]; excerpts available online at <http://zlzy.81.cn/tb/2016-08/15/content_7231775.htm>.

[18] Kevin Pollpeter et al., *China Dream, Space Dream: China's Progress in Space Technologies and Implications for the United States* (Washington, DC: U.S.-China Economic and Security Review Commission, 2017), 94–95.

[19] *Annual Report to Congress: Military and Security Developments Involving the People's Republic of China 2017* (Washington, DC: Office of the Secretary of Defense, 2017), 35.

[20] Ye, LSIO, 81.

[21] This information is derived from Costello's conversations with a credible People's Liberation Army (PLA) source who has direct knowledge of organizational logic behind the military reforms launched in 2015.

[22] For a more in-depth discussion of PLA military reforms of the four general departments, see Joel Wuthnow and Phillip C. Saunders, *Chinese Military Reforms in the Age of Xi Jinping: Drivers, Challenges, and Implications*, China Strategic Perspectives 10 (Washington, DC: NDU Press, March 2017), 10–11.

[23] It should be noted that the PLA does not classify its forces as "cyber" forces, but rather as "network" forces, owing to a conception of the "network domain" that overlaps but does not perfectly align with the U.S. military's concept of "cyberspace." When the term *cyber* is used in this chapter in descriptions of PLA concepts and developments, it should be taken as referencing PLA network warfare units that would fall under the U.S. definition.

[24] John Costello, "The Strategic Support Force: Update and Overview," *China Brief* 16, no. 19 (December 21, 2016), available at <https://jamestown.org/program/strategic-support-force-update-overview/>.

[25] Xiao Tianliang [肖天亮], ed., *The Science of Military Strategy* [战略学] (Beijing: National Defense University Press [国防大学出版社], 2015), 388.

[26] Ibid.

[27] John Costello and Peter Mattis, "Electronic Warfare and the Renaissance of Chinese Information Operations," in *China's Evolving Military Strategy*, ed. Joe McReynolds (Washington, DC: Jamestown Foundation, 2016), 180–182.

[28] Public descriptions of the Strategic Support Force (SSF) vary considerably as to whether the SSF is a branch [兵种], meaning a subcomponent of another service, or a military service [军种] in its own right. Until clearer information is available on this point, it is best described as a "force" in English. Even if it were in some technical sense a branch, its command structure appears to connect directly to the Central Military Commission (CMC) without any intermediary from another military service. For a more involved discussion on the status of the SSF, see Kevin

L. Pollpeter, Michael S. Chase, and Eric Heginbotham, *The Creation of the PLA Strategic Support Force and Its Implications for Chinese Military Space Operations* (Santa Monica, CA: RAND, 2017), 21–22.

[29] Yue Huairang [岳怀让], "The Strategic Support Force: Gao Jin as Commander, Liu Fulian as Political Commissar, Breastplate Revealed" [战略支援部队: 高津任司令员, 刘福连任政治委员, 胸牌曝光], *The Paper* [澎湃], January 1, 2016, available at <www.thepaper.cn/newsDetail_forward_1415847>; Liu Guangbo [刘光博], "These Five 'Theater Command Leader grade' General Officers Were Just Promoted to the Rank of General" [这五位正战区级将领刚刚晋升上将], *Chang'an Street Knowledgeable* [长安街知事], July 28, 2017, available at <http://news.sina.com.cn/c/nd/2017-07-28/doc-ifyinwmp0572361.shtml>.

[30] Li Xuanliang, Zhang Xuanjie, and Li Qinghua [李宣良, 张选杰, 李清华], "Ceremony Establishing Army Leading Organ, Strategic Rocket Forces, and Strategic Support Force Held in Beijing" [陆军领导机构火箭军战略支援部队成立大会在京举行], Xinhua [新华], January 1, 2016, available at <http://news.xinhuanet.com/politics/2016-01/01/c_1117646667.htm>.

[31] "Former Eastern Theater Command Political Commissar Major General Zheng Weiping Transfers to the Strategic Support Force" [东部战区原政委郑卫平上将转岗战支部队], *United Morning Post* [联合早报], October 23, 2017, available at <www.unizw.com/mon/dapan/20171023/40725.html>.

[32] Although AMS conducts research and offers graduate degrees, its role in PLA doctrine formulation makes it more similar to parts of the U.S. Joint Staff Joint Force Development Directorate or the U.S. Army's Training and Doctrine Command than to a military academic institution.

[33] The term *dui* [队] is translated a number of ways in Chinese, though usually as 'unit' or 'team' in a military context. It is used frequently in Chinese military terminology such as in *budui* [部队], 'force' or 'corps'. When used in a unit name, the term is subject to interpretation based on context and does not give a firm indicator of unit grade or echelon on its own. For the purposes of this paper, the term is most often used in the description of joint units where the term is indicated, most often in the term itself (*dui*) and in a related term *dadui*, which connotes a high-level unit under which *dui's* fall. As there is no clear English equivalent for these terms, this paper utilizes the original Chinese while providing additional context to avoid confusion.

[34] For a more involved discussion on the status of the SSF, see Pollpeter, Chase, and Heginbotham, *The Creation of the PLA Strategic Support Force*, 21–22.

35 See "2018 Seventh Exhibition on New Technologies and Equipment for Military Logistics" [2018第七届军事后勤保障新技术与新装备展览会], *Meeting Spot* [会点], June 21–23, 2018, available at <www.hui.net/news/special/key/1sim-4hc9rsgMu>. A senior colonel, Xiao Zhiyu [肖志宇], from the SSF Equipment Department, was referenced as a speaker and attendee to the 2017 China Civil and Military Dual-Use Technology Conference [2017中国军民两用技术研讨会] held in conjunction with an opening ceremony for the newly established Changzhou Military-Civilian Fusion Industrial Park [常州军民融合产业园] on May 21, 2017. See Wang Jinghui [王晶辉], "To Help With Civil-Military Integration, Casting the Country's Treasure: Changzhou Civil-Military Integration Industrial Park Officially Opened, Entering Enterprises Enjoy Comprehensive, One-Stop Service!" [助军民融合, 铸国之重器: 常州军民融合产业园正式开园, 入园企业享受全方位, 一站式服务!], May 24, 2017, available at <http://edp.liit.edu.cn/ba/07/c7876a178695/page.htm>; Lin Yunshi [林韵诗], "Major General Feng Jianhua Promoted to Director of Strategic Support Force Political Work Department" [冯建华少将升任战略支援部队政治工作部主任], *Caixin* [财新], February 29, 2016, available at <http://china.caixin.com/2016-02-29/100913753.html>; Feng Jianhua [冯建华] is listed as a "deputy Theater Command leader grade" and was subsequently promoted to lieutenant general in October 2017. See "Breaking News—Strategic Support Force Political Work Department Director Feng Jianhua Has Been Promoted to the Rank of Lieutenant General" [战略支援部队政治工作部主任冯建华已晋升中将军衔 澎湃新闻], *Military Report* [军事报道], August 30, 2017, available at <https://xw.qq.com/cmsid/20171030A0IZEL00>. The SSF Political Work Department deputy directors have been listed as Major General Chen Jinrong [陈金荣] and Huang Qiusheng [黄秋生]. See Yue Huairang [岳怀让], *The Paper* [澎湃], February 3, 2016, available at <www.thepaper.cn/newsDetail_forward_1429068>; and Yue Huairang [岳怀让], *The Paper* [澎湃], August 1, 2017, available at <www.thepaper.cn/newsDetail_forward_1749068>.

36 "Strategic Support Force Space Systems Department Test Equipment Materials Purchasing Bureau Medical Equipment Advertisement for Public Open Bid and Tender" [战略支援部队航天系统部试验装备物资采购局医疗设备公开招标采购公告], China Government Procurement Bidding Network [中国政府采购招标网], August 25, 2016, available at <www.chinabidding.org.cn/PurchaseInfoDetails_pid_1558826.html>; "Our Board Convened the Eleventh Meeting of our Fifth Board of Directors and the 2017 Military-Industrial Enterprise Salon" [我会召开第五届第十一次理事会议暨2017军工企业沙龙], Shenzhen Promotion Association

for Small and Medium Enterprises [深圳市中小企业发展促进会], August 31, 2017, available at <www.szsme.com/cn/dtdetail/81/755.html>.

[37] Liu Wei [刘伟], ed., *Theater Command Joint Operations Command* [战区联合作战指挥] (Beijing: National Defense University Press [国防大学出版社], 2016), 340.

[38] The block falls between the one used by units assigned to the CMC (31001 to 31999) and the one used by the PLA ground forces, which starts at 32100.

[39] For the pre-reform bases, see Kevin Pollpeter and Kenneth W. Allen, eds., *PLA as Organization 2.0* (Vienna, VA: Defense Group, Inc., 2015), 145–148.

[40] The unit appears to operate under the Military Unit Cover Designator (MUCD) 32020 and is located in Wuhan. See "Historic, Proud, Responsible: CLP Jin Jiang Intends to Join Hands 35th Base to Create a Grand New Era 'Weather'" [有历史、有自豪、有担当——中电锦江拟携手35基地开创新时代宏伟 "气象"], *Zhongdian Jinjiang* [中电锦江], January 15, 2018, available at <www.jec784.com/news_detail/newsId=134.html>.

[41] Xu Nanqi [徐南启], "The Second 'Jointly Build a Strong Military Dream' Themed Party and the National Defense 2018 New Year's Party Have Ended" [我校第二届"同心共筑强军梦"主题晚会暨国防生2018年元旦晚会落幕], Nanjing University [南京大学], December 25, 2017, available at <http://news.nju.edu.cn/show_article_1_48249>.

[42] See the chapter by Luce and Richter in this volume.

[43] Kenneth Allen, "Assessing the PLA's Promotion Ladder to CMC Member Based on Grades vs. Ranks—Part 1," *China Brief* 10, no. 15 (July 22, 2010), available at <https://jamestown.org/program/assessing-the-plas-promotion-ladder-to-cmc-member-based-on-grades-vs-ranks-part-1/>.

[44] Ibid.

[45] "Most Recent News on the Military Reforms: The Central Military Commission Comprehensively Implement the Three Tiered Structure of 'Departments-Bureaus-Offices'" [军改最新消息:军委机关总体实行"部—局—处"三级体制], *Guancha* [观察], October 5, 2016, available at <www.guancha.cn/military-affairs/2016_10_05_376239.shtml>.

[46] "The Most Mysterious and Newest Force—The Strategic Support Force" [最神秘的年轻部队—战略支援部队], *China Military Network* [中国军网], September 20, 2016, available at <www.81.cn/jwsj/2016-09/20/content_7268473.htm>

[47] For Kang Chunyuan, see Wang Jun [王俊], "Officer in a Deputy Military Region Grade Position Kang Chunyuan Has Been Promoted to the Rank of Lieutenant General, Formerly Served as Deputy Political Commissar of the

Lanzhou Military Region" [副大军区职军官康春元已晋升中将军衔, 曾任原兰州军区副政委], *The Paper* [澎湃], August 29, 2016, available at <www.thepaper.cn/newsDetail_forward_1521187>. For Hao Weizhong, see Lin Yunshi [林韵诗], "The Space Systems Department of the Strategic Support Force Appears, Shang Hong as Commander" [战略支援部队航天系统部亮相 尚宏任司令员], *Caixin* [财新], April 25, 2017, available at <http://china.caixin.com/2017-04-25/101082917.html>. For Fei Jiabing, see "Leaders of the Space Systems Department Come to Our Academy to Research and Direct Work" [航天系统部领导来我院调研指导工作], China Academy of Space Technlogy [中国空间技术学院], March 31, 2017, available at <www.cast.cn/item/show.asp?m=1&d=5700>.

⁴⁸ Lin, "The Space Systems Department of the Strategic Support Force Appears."

⁴⁹ For an excellent analysis of the status of these missions prior to the reforms, see Mark A. Stokes and Dean Cheng, *China's Evolving Space Capabilities. Implications for U.S. Interests* (Washington, DC: U.S.-China Economic and Security Review Commission, April 26, 2012), 4–5.

⁵⁰ Pollpeter, Chase, and Heginbotham, *The Creation of the PLA Strategic Support Force*, 28.

⁵¹ Zhang Zhanyue and Zhu Shuguang [长占月, 祝曙光], "Trends of Space-Based Information Support Development" [天基信息支援发展趋势], *Satellite Applications* [卫星应用], vol. 9 (September 2016), 67–71.

⁵² In April 2016, it was confirmed that former Aerospace Reconnaissance Bureau Chief Zhou Zhixin [周志鑫] transferred to the SSF to head up a "certain bureau" [某局]. This is good indicator that the bureau has moved to the SSF and, given its mission, has been reassigned to the Space Systems Department. See Yue Huairang [岳怀让], "Chinese Academy of Sciences Academician Zhou Zhixin to Become the Bureau Chief of a Certain Bureau in the Strategic Support Force" [中科院院士周志鑫出任战略支援部队某局局长], *The Paper* [澎湃], April 9, 2016, available at <www.thepaper.cn/newsDetail_forward_1454253>. Zhou Zhixin is now the Commandant of the Space System Department's newly created Space Engineering University. See "Zhou Zhixin Becomes the Commandant of the Strategic Support Force's Space Engineering University" [周志鑫任战略支援部队航天工程大学校长], *Sohu* [搜狐], October 8, 2017, available at <www.sohu.com/a/196776059_495232>. For more on the Aerospace Reconnaissance Bureau's mission, see Kevin Pollpeter and Amy Chang, "The General Armament Department," in *PLA as Organization 2.0*, 145–148.

⁵³ Costello, "The Strategic Support Force."

[54] "Einstein Probe Successfully Passes Project Comprehensive Demonstration Review" [爱因斯坦探针卫星工程顺利通过立项综合论证评审], Chinese Academy of Sciences National Astronomical Observatories [中科院国家天文台], July 5, 2017, available at <www.bao.ac.cn/xwzx/zhxw/201707/t20170721_4835406.html>.

[55] Bill Gertz, "China Carries Out Flight Test of Anti-Satellite Missile," *Washington Free Beacon*, August 2, 2017, available at <http://freebeacon.com/national-security/china-carries-flight-test-anti-satellite-missile/>.

[56] The SY-7 satellite has a robotic arm that is claimed to be used to grapple onto target satellites for inspection and maintenance. Experts contend, however, that the satellite's arm could be used for co-orbital attack intended to destroy or disable an adversary satellite. For a discussion of the satellite's capabilities, see Robert Beckhusen, "China's Mystery Satellite Could Be a Dangerous New Weapon," *War Is Boring*, August 22, 2013, available at <https://warisboring.com/china-s-mystery-satellite-could-be-a-dangerous-new-weapon/>.

[57] Pollpeter et al., *China Dream, Space Dream*, 95.

[58] Stokes and Cheng, *China's Evolving Space Capabilities*, 45.

[59] Ibid. Up until the late 1990s, for instance, the PLA Air Force (PLAAF) was even limited in its ability to fly over water due to the maritime domain being considered the responsibility of the PLA Navy Air Force. In fact, it was not until the 1996 Taiwan Strait Crisis that a PLAAF plane was ordered to fly over water for the first time.

[60] Kenneth Allen and Jana Allen, "Assessing China's Response to U.S. Reconnaissance Flights," *China Brief* 11, no. 16 (September 2, 2011), available at <https://jamestown.org/program/assessing-chinas-response-to-u-s-reconnaissance-flights/>.

[61] "The Strategic Support Force Has Renamed the Former General Staff Department's Third Department as the Cyberspace Operations Force" [战略支援部队成军 原总参三部更名网络空间作战部队], *Boxun.com*, January 19, 2016, available at <www.boxun.com/news/gb/china/2016/01/201601192251.shtml>.

[62] Pollpeter, Chase, and Heginbotham, *The Creation of the PLA Strategic Support Force*, 19.

[63] "General Staff Personnel Changes; Wang Huiqing Becomes Director of the Strategic Planning Department; Zheng Junjie Becomes Director of the Third Department" [总参人事变动王辉青任战略规划部部长郑俊杰任三部部长], *Jiangwutang* [讲武堂], November 1, 2015, available at <https://web.archive.org/web/20161018223115/http://j.news.163.com/docs/99/2015110114/B7BFIC-Q405158ED3.html>.

64 Wang Jun [王俊], "Chengdu Military Region Political Department Director Chai Shaoliang Becomes Military Region Deputy Political Commissar" [成都军区政治部主任柴绍良改任军区副政委], *Ta Kung Online* [大公网], December 31, 2013, available at <http://news.takungpao.com/mainland/zgzq/2013-12/2143144.html>.

65 See Guo Rui and He Xiaoyuan [郭瑞, 贺筱媛], "Pretreatment Method for Intelligent Analysis of Battlefield Situational Data" [面向战场态势数据智能分析的预处理方法], *Electronic Technology and Software Engineering* [电子技术与软件工程], vol. 16 (2017). Guo Rui's affiliation is listed as the Fifth Bureau of the Strategic Support Force's Third Department [战略支援部队第三部第五局].

66 For a more comprehensive analysis of the former Third Department's Technical Reconnaissance Bureaus, see Mark A. Stokes, *The Chinese People's Liberation Army Signals Intelligence and Cyber Reconnaissance Infrastructure* (Arlington, VA: Project 2049 Institute, 2011).

67 For the General Staff Department (GSD) 56th Research Institute, see "Network Systems Department 56th Research Institute National Postgraduates Enrollment Exam Subject Catalog" [网络系统部第五十六研究所2017考研专业目录], Exam Training Camp [考研集训营], November 22, 2016, available at <www.kyjxy.com/yuanxiao/zhuanye/33616.html>. For the GSD 57th Research Institute, see "Shengxi Elementary School 2017 Spring Games Grand Opening Ceremonies" [胜西小学2017春季运动会隆重开幕], *Wenji8.com*, April 4, 2017, available at <www.wenji8.com/p/8cbbE3F.html>. For the GSD 58th Research Institute, see "Strategic Support Force 58th Research Institute" [战略支援部队第五十八研究所], Researcher Recruitment Network [研招网], available at <http://yz.chsi.com.cn/sch/schoolInfo--schId-367828.dhtml>.

68 "School Introduction" [学校简介], People's Liberation Army Information Engineering University Admissions Information Network [解放军信息工程大学招生信息网], available at <http://zhaosheng.plaieu.edu.cn/contents/249/508.html>.

69 See, for example, "Announcement on the Publication of the 2017 Chinese Academy of Sciences List of Preliminary Candidates Selected for Academician" [关于公布2017年中国科学院院士增选初步候选人名单的公告], Chinese Academy of Sciences Work Office of the Academic Department [中国科学院学部工作局], August 1, 2017, available at <www.cas.cn/tz/201708/t20170801_4610395.shtml>.

70 Note that this mission only appears to extend to protecting the PLA's own network, not government or nation-wide networks more generally. See Wang Weiming and Guo Biying [王伟明, 郭碧莹], "Stopping Leaks, Military Cyber Experts Teach You the Path of Solving 'Poison'" [防泄密, 军队网络专家教你解"

毒"之道], *China Military Online* [中国军网], May 23, 2017, available at <www.81.cn/jmywyl/2017-05/23/content_7613285.htm>.

71   Both Unit 31003 and the Network-Electronic Bureau have been listed at the address No. 226 North Middle Fourth Ring Road, Haidian District, Beijing [北京市海淀区北四环中路226号], the known address of the former GSD Fourth Department. For Unit 31003's address, see "Huading Decorations Successfully Signed Unit 31003" [华鼎装饰成功签约31003部队], Huading Construction [华鼎建筑], December 16, 2016, available at <www.hdzs.com.cn/index.php?m=content&c=index&a=show&catid=5&id=92>. For the Network-Electronic Bureau's address, see "XXX Network-Electronic Bureau Service Unit Single Occupant Housing Refurbish Project Open Bid Advertisement" [XXX网电局勤务队和单身干部宿舍整修改造工程施工招标公告], June 23, 2017, available at <www.bidchance.com/calggnew/2017/06/23/20745058.html>.

72   "Army Artillery Air Defense Academy and National University of Defense Technology Electronic Countermeasure Institute Debut in Hefei" [陆军炮兵防空兵学院，国防科技大学电子对抗学院亮相合肥], *The Paper* [澎湃], August 1, 2017, available at <www.thepaper.cn/newsDetail_forward_1748674>.

73   "Announcement on the Publication of the 2017 Chinese Academy of Sciences List of Preliminary Candidates Selected for Academician."

74   Zhang Qiaosu [张樵苏], "This Squad Leader Is a Little 'Zhou'—The Journal of Grade Three Sergeant Zhou Yunxiao of a Certain Strategic Support Force Brigade" [这个班长有点"轴"——战略支援部队某旅三级军士长赵云霄记事], Xinhua [新华], June 4, 2017, available at <http://news.xinhuanet.com/politics/2017-06/04/c_1121083630.htm>; Zeng Shijing, Huang Qiyuan, and Li Wen [曾世京, 黄琪渊, 李雯], "What Are the Highlights for the Military Services Symposium?" [为军服务座谈会都有啥看点?], *China Military Online* [中国军网], May 16, 2017, available at <www.81.cn/zghjy/2017-05/16/content_7603928.htm>.

75   These units include an electronic countermeasure brigade at Langfang and an air defense electronic countermeasure brigade at Beidaihe, detachments in both Shanghai Nicheng and Yingtan, and satellite stations in Beijing and Sanya. See Liu Yanqian [刘燕倩], "Visit to Give Condolences, Strong Civilian Military Relations" [慰问走访 军民情浓], Shanghai NiCheng Government [中共浦东新区泥城镇委员会], February 13, 2015, available at <https://web.archive.org/web/20160318214622/http://www.nichengdj.gov.cn/html/ArticleShow11343.aspx>; Zhu Fenni [朱芬妮], "City Investment Corporation: Carry out 'August 1ˢᵗ' PLA Day Memorial Activities" [城投公司: 开展"八一"建军节慰问活动], Shanghai NiCheng Government [中共浦

东新区泥城镇委员会], July 28, 2016, available at <http://webcache.googleusercontent.com/search?q=cache:L1wu4NnF6CIJ:www.nichengdj.gov.cn/html/articleshow14968.aspx+&cd=1&hl=en&ct=clnk&gl=us>; "On the Issue of Illegal Burning Near Unit 61906 Troops Stationed in the Area" [关于61906部队驻地附近非法焚烧排放问题], Yingtan Municipal Government [鹰潭市人民政府], December 5, 2016, available at <www.yingtan.gov.cn/gzcy/zxts_1/hbj_1/201612/t20161205_408367.htm>; Stokes, Lin, and Hsiao, *The Chinese People's Liberation Army Signals Intelligence and Cyber Reconnaissance Infrastructure*, 15.

76 Xiao, *The Science of Military Strategy*, 268. Ye, LSIO, 44.

77 Costello and Mattis, "Electronic Warfare and the Renaissance of Chinese Information Operations," 170–171.

78 Dai Qingmin [戴清民], "On Integrating Network Warfare and Electronic Warfare" [网电一体战], *China Military Science* [中国军事科学], no. 1 (February 2002), 112–117.

79 Costello, "The Strategic Support Force."

80 It is worth noting that from a purely organizational standpoint, the former GSD Fourth Department only managed a relatively small cadre of bureaus, brigades, and ground stations, which, compared with the organizational heft of the General Armament Department and GSD Third Department, may not have been enough to warrant a separate, third department in the SSF to focus exclusively on electronic warfare.

81 Li Xiaobiao and Xu Kai [李小彪, 徐凯], "Lei Feng Spirit Motivates Us to Go Forward" [雷锋精神激励我们前行], *db.81.cn*, March 28, 2016, available at <http://db.81.cn/content/2016-03/28/content_6979623.htm>.

82 Costello and Mattis, "Electronic Warfare and the Renaissance of Chinese Information Operations," 178. For an informative discussion on PLA Three Warfares strategic thought, see Elsa Kania, "The PLA's Latest Strategic Thinking on the Three Warfares," *China Brief* 16, no. 13 (August 22, 2016), available at <https://jamestown.org/program/the-plas-latest-strategic-thinking-on-the-three-warfares/>.

83 The 311 Base operates under MUCD Unit 61716 (61716部队). For a more in-depth discussion of the 311 Base and Liaison Department, see Mark Stokes and Russell Hsiao, *The People's Liberation Army General Political Department: Political Warfare with Chinese Characteristics* (Arlington, VA: Project 2049 Institute, October 14, 2013), available at <www.project2049.net/documents/PLA_General_Political_Department_Liaison_Stokes_Hsiao.pdf>.

84 On the organizational makeup of the 311 Base, see ibid., 29. On its wartime structure, see Kevin McCauley, "System of Systems Operational Capability:

Operational Units and Elements," *China Brief* 13, no. 6 (March 15, 2013), 13–17; and Ye, LSIO, 135.

[85] Major General Mei Huabo [梅华波], political commissar of the 311 Base before the reforms, was listed in that position as late as August 2016. In December, it was reported that Mei Huabo was appointed political commissar for an unnamed base under the Strategic Support Force. Other personnel transfers provide further indication the base has moved. In 2016, Mou Shan [牟珊] changed his affiliation from "China Huayi Broadcasting Company" [中国华艺广播公司], the commercial persona of the 311 Base, to a "Certain Department in the Strategic Support Force" [战略支援部队某部]. See Huang Xiaowei and Yu Shan [黄晓伟, 牟珊], "Discussion and Analysis of Taiwan Military Recruitment Promotion Advertisment and Its Effect" [台军招募文宣广告及其效果评析], *Modern Taiwan Studies* [现代台湾研究], no. 1 (2014), available at <www.cqvip.com/QK/97723X/201401/49213060.html>; Yu Shan [牟珊], "Analysis of NATO Strategic Communication Strategy" [北约战略传播策略探析], *Military Reporter* [军事记者], no. 6, (2016), available at <www.cqvip.com/qk/81377x/201606/669378161.html>.

[86] For an in-depth discussion of the Three Warfares, see Wu Jieming and Liu Zhifu [吴杰明, 刘志富], *An Introduction to Public Opinion Warfare, Psychological Warfare, Legal Warfare* [舆论战心理战法律战概论] (Beijing: National Defense University Press [国防大学出版社], 2014).

[87] An indicator of the uniqueness of the 311 Base's position is its MUCD, which fell under the GSD MUCD block even as the organization was subordinate to the former General Political Department.

[88] Costello and Peter, "Electronic Warfare and the Renaissance of Chinese Information Operations," 188.

[89] The actual grade of the Joint Staff Department may be equal to the Strategic Support Force; however, as a component of the Central Military Commission it acts under its authority in relaying operational decisions.

[90] *Annual Report to Congress: Military and Security Developments Involving the People's Republic of China 2011*, 2.

[91] "The Tenth China Air Show Flight Command Leading Small Group Meeting Was Held in Zhuhai" [第十届中国航展飞行组织指挥领导小组会议在珠海召开], Civil Aviation Administration of China [中国民用航空局], October 29, 2014, available at <www.caac.gov.cn/XWZX/MHYW/201410/t20141029_13886.html>; "The Ministry of Defense Discloses Three Operational Ways Used by Our Naval Forces to Combat Piracy" [国防部披露我国军舰打击海盗三种作战方

式], *Sina.com* [新浪], December 23, 2008, available at <http://mil.news.sina.com.cn/2008-12-23/1052536044.html>; Li Yangyang [李杨洋], ed., "Chinese-Pakistan 'Friendship-2011' Joint Anti-terrorism Training Helicopter Dadui Arrives in Pakistan" [中巴"友谊-2011"反恐联合训练直升机大队今日启程赴巴], *China Military Online* [中国军网], November 15, 2011, available at <http://military.people.com.cn/GB/42967/16251957.html>; "Writing Style of Major General Liu Xingren" [刘兴仁少将书法作品], *Chinese Army Friendship Net* [中国军谊网], October 29, 2014, available at <www.chinajunyi.org.cn/show.asp?id=1198>.

92 "Transcript of March 2016 Ministry of National Defense Routine Press Conference" [2016年3月国防部例行记者会文字实录], People's Republic of China Ministry of National Defense [中华人民共和国国防部], March 31, 2016, available at <www.mod.gov.cn/info/2016-03/31/content_4648220.htm>.

93 "Du Qiang Becomes Central Military Commission Operations Bureau Air Control Office Office Chief" [杜强任中央军委联合参谋部作战局空管处处长], *The Paper* [澎湃], January 19, 2016, available at <http://news.163.com/air/16/0119/08/BDM9D03N00014P42.html>.

94 Ye, LSIO, 108.

95 Ibid., 124–131.

96 Ibid., 134.

97 Ibid., 127.

98 Ibid., 134.

99 Peter Mattis and Elsa Kania, "Modernizing Military Intelligence: Playing Catchup (Part Two)," *China Brief* 16, no. 19 (December 21, 2016), 15–27.

100 For a deeper discussion on "intelligence" versus "technical reconnaissance," see Peter Mattis, "Chinese Military Intelligence at 90: Consistent Evolution," prepared for CAPS-RAND-NDU Conference, October 2015, 4–7.

101 Samantha Hoffman and Peter Mattis, "Chinese Legislation Points to New Intelligence Co-ordinating System," *IHS Jane's Intelligence Review*, September 5, 2017, 7.

102 Cheng Yongliang and Zhang Xiqing [程永亮, 张希庆], "Joint Iron Fist Quenches Students" [能力重塑, 联合铁拳淬火生], *China Military Online* [中国军网], October 14, 2017, available at <www.81.cn/jfjbmap/content/2017-10/14/content_189717.htm>; Peter Mattis, "China Reorients Strategic Military Intelligence," *IHS Jane's Intelligence Review*, December 2016, available at <www.janes.com/images/assets/484/68484/China_reorients_strategic_military_intelligence_edit.pdf>.

103 Mattis, "China Reorients Strategic Military Intelligence."

[104] "Professor Huang Zhixiong Holds a Seminar on International Law on Cyberspace for Relevant Military Departments" [黄志雄教授为军队有关部门讲授网络空间国际法], Wuhan Universtiy School of Law [武汉大学法学院], November 2, 2016, available at <http://fxy.whu.edu.cn/archive/detail/102263>.

[105] "Beijing Municipal People's Procuratorate Holds Symposium for Beijing Municipal People's Congress Delegate in Beijing" [北京市人民检察院召开驻京部队市人大代表座谈会], *Suibi8.com*, December 2, 2016, available at <https://webcache.googleusercontent.com/search?q=cache:ju7u3SqBfI8J:https://www.suibi8.com/essay/abf77b-11270011.html+&cd=1&hl=en&ct=clnk&gl=us>.

[106] Li and Xu, "Lei Feng Spirit Motivates Us to Go Forward."

[107] For the former Nanjing Military Region electronic countermeasure center (ECM center), also known as Unit 73677 (73677部队), see Wang Xiaowen [王晓文] et al., "Image Fusion Method Based on Visual Saliency Map" [基于视觉显著图的图像融合方法], *Journal of Jilin University (Engineering Edition)* [吉林大学学报(工学版)] (2014). For the former Guangzhou Military Region ECM center, see Xie Zhiyong [谢志勇], "PLA Representatives of the 18th Party Congress: 'Big Defense' Covers Seas and Space" [解放军十八大代表:"大国防"职责涵盖海洋太空], *Beijing News* [新京报], November 14, 2012, available at <http://military.china.com.cn/2012-11/14/content_27104914.htm>.

[108] This is based on papers published under the byline of the ECM centers, which include such topics as "A New Method of PRF Detecting Based on DTFT" [基于DTFT的一种新的PRF检测方法] and "Principles and Realization of Surface Wave Driven Plasma Antenna" [表面波激励等离子体天线的原理与实现].

[109] "After a Year of Military Reform, Review of 'New Institution Time' in the Military Newspaper's Published Articles" [军改一周年 军报刊文回眸"新体制时间"之变], *PLA Daily* [解放军报], December 2, 2016, available at <http://military.people.com.cn/n1/2016/1202/c1011-28919716.html>.

[110] Zhang Qiang, Qiao Xuewei, and Zhang Kunping [张强, 乔学伟, 张坤平], "Who Let 'Command Nerve' Be More Sensitive" [谁让"指挥神经"更灵敏?], *Science and Technology Daily* [科技日报社], July 31, 2017, available at <http://digitalpaper.stdaily.com/http_www.kjrb.com/kjrb/html/2017-07/31/content_374917.htm>.

[111] Ni Guanghui [倪光辉], "Secrets of Our First Strategic Support Force" [揭秘我军首支战略支援部队], *People's Daily* [人民日报], January 24, 2016, available at <http://military.people.com.cn/n1/2016/0124/c1011-28079245.html>.

[112] Peng Guangqian and Yao Youzhi [澎光谦, 姚有志], eds., *The Science of Military Strategy* [战略学] (Beijing: AMS Press, 2001), 179.

[113] *Annual Report to Congress: Military and Security Developments Involving the People's Republic of China 2015* (Washington, DC: Office of the Secretary of Defense, 2015), 14.

[114] "Prepared Statement of Mark A. Stokes, Executive Director Project 2049 Institute, before the U.S.-China Economic and Security Review Commission," *Hearing on Chinese Intelligence Services and Espionage Operations* (Washington, DC: U.S.-China Economic and Security Review Commission, June 9, 2016), available at <www.uscc.gov/sites/default/files/Mark%20Stokes_Written%20Testimony060916.pdf>.

[115] Liu Wei [刘伟], ed., *Theater Command Joint Operations Command* [战区联合作战指挥] (Beijing: National Defense University Press [国防大学出版社], 2016); Shou, *Science of Military Strategy*, 81.

[116] Li Dan [李丹], "What Kind of Force Is the Strategic Support Force Inspected by Xi Jinping?" [习近平视察的战略支援部队是一支怎样的力量?], *CCTV* [央视网], August 30, 2016, available at <http://news.cctv.com/2016/08/30/ARTI2Xi1zgynCfj6TYsecOcb160830.shtml>.

[117] For a detailed discussion of Chinese thinking on counter-intervention, see M. Taylor Fravel and Christopher P. Twomey, "Projecting Strategy: The Myth of Chinese Counter-Intervention," *Washington Quarterly* 37, no. 4 (Winter 2015), 171–187.

[118] A good indicator of this change of terminology is the transformation of the former GSD Survey, Mapping, and Navigation Bureau into the Joint Staff Department Battlefield Environment Support Bureau.

[119] "China to Launch 30 Beidou Navigation Satellites in Next 5 Years," Xinhua, May 19, 2016, available at <http://news.xinhuanet.com/english/2016-05/19/c_135372622.htm>.

[120] Stokes and Cheng, *China's Evolving Space Capabilities*, 23.

[121] Richard D. Fisher and Sean O'Connor, "Space Invaders—China's Space Warfare Capabilities," *IHS Jane's Intelligence Review* available at <www.janes360.com/images/assets/557/40557/Space_invaders.pdf>.

[122] *Annual Report to Congress: Military and Security Developments Involving the People's Republic of China 2015*, 38.

[123] Pollpeter, *China Dream, Space Dream*, 15.

[124] Li Xuanliang and Li Guoli [李宣良, 李国利], "Xi Jinping: Strive to Establish a Powerful, Modern Strategic Support Force" [习近平: 努力建设一支强大的现代化战略支援部队], Xinhua [新华], August 29, 2016, available at <http://news.xinhuanet.com/politics/2016-08/29/c_1119474761.htm>; Li Dan [李丹], "What Kind

of Force is the Strategic Support Force Inspected by Xi Jinping?" [习近平视察的战略支援部队是一支怎样的力量?], CCTV [央视网], August 30, 2016, available at <http://news.cctv.com/2016/08/30/ARTI2Xi1zgynCfj6TYsecOcb160830.shtml>.

125 Li Xuanliang, Zhang Xuanjie, and Li Qinghua [李宣良, 张选杰, 李清华], "Army Leading Organs, Rocket Force, and Strategic Support Force Established" [陆军领导机构火箭军战略支援部队成立], Xinhua [新华], January 1, 2016, available at <http://news.xinhuanet.com/politics/2016-01/01/c_1117646667.htm>.

126 Zou Weirong [邹维荣], "New-Quality Weapons Decide Victory on the Future Battlefield" [新质利器决胜未来战场], *PLA Daily* [解放军报], March 11, 2016, available at <http://jz.chinamil.com.cn/zhuanti/content/2016-03/11/content_6954336.htm>.

127 Shou, *Science of Military Strategy*, 129.

128 Zhang Yuliang [张玉良], ed., *Science of Campaigns* [战役学] (Beijing: National Defense University Press [国防大学出版社], 2006); Ye, LSIO, 145–150.

129 Ye, LSIO, chapter 2.

130 Ye Zheng [叶征], "Ye Zheng: The 'Seven Weapons' in the Strategic Game of Cyberspace" [叶征: 网络空间战略博弈的七种武器], *China Youth Daily* [中国青年报], August 8, 2014, available at <http://theory.people.com.cn/n/2014/0808/c40531-25427203.html>; Costello and Mattis, "Electronic Warfare and the Renaissance of Chinese Information Operations," 161–163.

131 Ye, LSIO, 146–147.

132 Ibid.

133 Wang Jinsong, Wang Nanxing, and Ha Junxian [王劲松, 王南星, 哈军贤], "Research on Cyberspace Operations Command" [网络空间作战指挥研究], *Journey of the Academy of Armored Force Engineering* [装甲兵工程学院学报] (October 2016).

134 For a more involved discussion of this concept, see Joe McReynolds, "China's Military Strategy for Network Warfare," in *China's Evolving Military Strategy*, 215–216.

135 Part of the difficulty in understanding this is in usage of Chinese terms. The United States generally differentiates between the terms *information operations* and *information warfare*, with the former being operations conducted in peace and the latter in war. The Chinese do make this distinction; however, they more generally use the term *information operations* [信息作战] interchangeably with *information warfare* [信息战争] and *information countermeasures* [信息对抗], with few consistent differences.

[136] Xiao, *The Science of Military Strategy.*

[137] *National Security Strategy of the United States of America* (Washington, DC: The White House, 2017), available at <www.whitehouse.gov/wp-content/uploads/2017/12/NSS-Final-12-18-2017-0905.pdf>.

[138] Tong Lei [童磊], "Strategic Support Force: Striding Toward the Future's New Type of People's Army" [战略支援部队: 迈向未来的新型人民军队], September 29, 2016, available at <www.qstheory.cn/laigao/2016-09/29/c_1119646359.htm>.

[139] Marcelyn L. Thompson, "PLA Observations of U.S. Contingency Planning: What Has It Learned?" in *The People's Liberation Army and Contingency Planning in China*, ed. Andrew Scobell et al. (Washington, DC: NDU Press, 2015), 44–46; Elsa Kania, "PLA Strategic Support Force: The 'Information Umbrella' for China's Military," *The Diplomat*, April 1, 2017, available at <https://thediplomat.com/2017/04/pla-strategic-support-force-the-information-umbrella for-chinas-military/>.

[140] "Prepared Statement of Mark A. Stokes."

[141] Stokes, Lin, and Hsiao, *The Chinese People's Liberation Army Signals Intelligence and Cyber Reconnaissance Infrastructure*, 7. While it is highly likely that the 12th Bureau has moved to the SSF, it has not yet been confirmed whether it has been placed under the Space Systems Department or Network Systems Department.

[142] Stokes, Lin, and Hsiao, *The Chinese People's Liberation Army Signals Intelligence and Cyber Reconnaissance Infrastructure*, 15.

[143] Hoffman and Mattis, "Chinese Legislation Points to New Intelligence Co-ordinating System."

[144] "National Intelligence Law of the People's Republic of China (Draft)," *China Copyright and Media*, May 16, 2017, available at <https://chinacopyrightandmedia.wordpress.com/2017/05/16/national-intelligence-law-of-the-peoples-republic-of-china-draft/>.

[145] "Experts: The Strategic Support Force Will Be the Key to Success Throughout the Entire Combat Operations Process" [专家:战略支援部队将贯穿作战全过程是致胜关键], *People's Daily* [人民日报], January 5, 2016, available at <http://military.people.com.cn/n1/2016/0105/c1011-28011251.html>.

[146] Lu Xiaomeng, "Scoping Critical Information Infrastructure in China," *The Diplomat*, May 22, 2018, available at <https://thediplomat.com/2018/05/scoping-critical-information-infrastructure-in-china/>.

PART IV

CENTRALIZING AUTHORITY

CHAPTER 13

LARGE AND IN CHARGE

Civil-Military Relations under Xi Jinping

By Phillip C. Saunders and Joel Wuthnow

Chinese military modernization has made impressive strides in the past decade.[1] The People's Liberation Army (PLA) has achieved progress in key technological areas, ranging from precision-guided missiles to advanced surface ships and fighter aircraft; PLA personnel are more highly trained and skilled, capable of carrying out increasingly complex operations near to and farther away from China's shores; and Chinese military doctrine has been updated to emphasize modern, joint maneuver warfare on a high-tech battlefield.[2] This progress has been undergirded by significant increases in Chinese defense spending every year since 1990.[3] Taken together, these changes better enable the PLA to fight what the U.S. Department of Defense describes as "short-duration, high-intensity regional conflicts."[4]

As the title of a 2015 RAND report suggests, however, PLA modernization has been "incomplete."[5] Among the major weaknesses outlined in that report is the PLA's antiquated organizational structure, which had experienced few major changes since the 1950s. Key problems include the lack of a permanent joint command and control (C2) structure, inadequate central supervision—which bred corruption, lowered morale, and inhibited the development of a professional force—and institutional barriers in the defense research and development (R&D) process.[6] Prior military reforms made only limited and incremental adjustments to the PLA's structure; more comprehensive reform efforts stalled in the face of bureaucratic resistance.

Since the early 1990s, PLA reformers had argued for comprehensive changes to the military's structure. There were two basic reasons. First was the trend of modern warfare toward joint operations, most notably in the maritime and aerospace domains. This required the PLA to rebalance from the army to the navy and air force, and to institute a joint C2 structure that could integrate the capabilities of all the services as well as command, control, communications, computers, intelligence, surveillance, and reconnaissance assets. The need to conduct effective joint operations in multiple domains only increased as China's national economic and political interests expanded outward to the maritime periphery and, later, to a global scale.[7] Second, the general departments and military regions had amassed too much power and were too poorly supervised, leading to growing financial waste and corruption throughout the force. This, in turn, raised serious concerns about PLA combat readiness and proficiency.[8]

To address these problems, the PLA embarked on a series of institutional reforms during the Central Military Commission (CMC) chairmanships of Jiang Zemin (1989–2004) and Hu Jintao (2004–2012). Important changes included reducing the PLA's size by 500,000 in 1997 and 200,000 in 2003; establishing a professional noncommissioned corps (NCO) in 1998; increasing resources to the navy, air force, and Second Artillery Force in 2004; and restructuring the research, development, and acquisition process in 1998.[9] However, more fundamental changes to the PLA's C2 and administrative structure eluded reformers. Resistance to change was likely strongest among the potential losers of reform, including the ground forces and general departments. Moreover, the relative weakness of Jiang and Hu within the military made bureaucratic opposition much harder to overcome.[10]

Conversely, Xi Jinping has been willing to invest significant amounts of time and political capital in pushing forward an ambitious PLA reform agenda. Prior to the initiation of the reforms, Xi's signature military initiative was the directive that the PLA must focus on "fighting and winning an informationized war."[11] Xi appears to place a high personal priority on sovereignty and territorial disputes; a more effective military would be an important tool in strengthening China's ability to resolve these disputes on favorable terms.

Revelations about widespread corruption within the PLA and the limited authority that former CMC Chairman Hu wielded over senior PLA officers also raised important questions about Chinese Communist Party (CCP) control over the military.[12] The corollary to Mao Zedong's dictum that "political power grows from the barrel of a gun" is that "the Party must always control the gun." The extent of corruption within the PLA—and the fact that neither political ideology nor existing supervisory mechanisms could control it—was evidence that Party control over the PLA had eroded, perhaps to dangerous levels. More broadly, Xi appears to believe that emphasizing ideological conformity and obedience to Party central leadership are necessary conditions for continued CCP rule.

A final point involves the extent to which Xi seeks to overturn the norms of CCP collective leadership that Deng Xiaoping painstakingly constructed.[13] Given Xi's apparent desire to build his personal power at the expense of collective leadership norms, the military is an area where he (as the sole member of the Politburo Standing Committee with direct responsibility for military issues) has important advantages over potential political rivals. If Xi's efforts to reassert CCP control over the PLA also build his personal authority over the military and create a senior officer corps that is personally loyal to him, this would be an important political asset.

This chapter is organized in four parts. The first section examines problems in civil-military relations in China from a historical, theoretical, and empirical perspective. It focuses on identifying the problems that PLA reforms are intended to solve: ineffective information-sharing between military and civilian authorities, corruption and cronyism, and a perceived waning of ideological commitment to Party ideals and values within the PLA. The second section examines how specific organizational and political aspects of the reforms are intended to address these problems. Given that the reforms will adversely affect the organizational and personal interests of some parts of the PLA and some PLA senior leaders, reformers anticipated resistance. The third section examines some of the political tools and tactics that Xi has used to push reforms through. The conclusion assesses whether this political strategy is likely to succeed in building a PLA that is more capable of executing joint operations to "fight and win wars" and in reasserting CCP control—and perhaps Xi's personal authority—over the Chinese military.

Problems in Chinese Civil-Military Relations

A key dilemma for civil-military relations is how to build an army strong enough to fight and win the nation's wars that does not pose a threat to a civilian regime or social order.[14] In mature democracies, the problem is often alleviated by military professionalism and broad acceptance of the principle of civilian control, aided by institutions such as legislative oversight, the rule of law, and a free press.[15] In these circumstances, militaries can serve as a professional warfighting force but are constrained in the extent to which they can (or desire to) interfere in domestic politics. In transitional democracies and some civilian-led authoritarian states, the problem is more acute because of weak social norms and weak institutions limiting military encroachment into internal affairs. Indeed, in many cases the military played a pivotal role not only in the founding of the regime but also in post-revolutionary governance.[16] Getting the military out of politics in such cases is no easy feat.

Chinese reformers have learned firsthand how difficult it can be to extricate the military from political affairs. During the Mao era, the PLA played a key role in elite politics as well as in domestic governance. Uniformed officers held high Party posts and on occasion became so powerful (and had ideas so divergent from Mao's) that they had to be purged, as in the cases of Peng Dehuai and Lin Biao. The military also played a role in social and economic affairs at the grassroots level, most notably during the Cultural Revolution.[17] During this period, shared belief in Marxism-Leninism by civilian and military elites helped CCP leaders exercise what Samuel Huntington called "subjective control" over the PLA.[18] Common ideology and objectives were reinforced by "objective control" measures such as the political commissar system and the CMC, which gave the top CCP civilian leader formal authority over military decisions. Following Mao's death, Deng Xiaoping and his co-reformers sought to reduce the military's role in political affairs, including encouraging the PLA to focus on its professional military responsibilities. However, this required an uneasy bargain in which the PLA was granted significant autonomy over its own affairs and given compensation for limited defense budgets in the 1980s by being granted permission to engage in a range of commercial activities.[19] Reduced oversight and encouragement to participate in China's booming civilian economy proved to be a potent recipe for wide-scale corruption.

Deng's successors, Jiang Zemin and Hu Jintao, had to wrestle with the consequences of this bargain. Both Jiang and Hu sought to make the PLA into a more competent warfighting force, as well as to revise China's national security architecture to cope with a more diverse set of security challenges, but neither was able to fully implement their plans. For instance, Jiang's 1998 decision to remove the PLA from business ventures was only partially successful, as many of these enterprises were simply transferred to close relatives of senior officers.[20] The creation of a National Security Council (NSC)-like entity, which Jiang and Hu both supported in order to produce more effective responses to regional crises, was stunted in part due to the PLA's unwillingness to share information with civilian officials or coordinate with civilian ministries.[21] The problem was exacerbated by Jiang and Hu's lack of knowledge of military affairs and limited influence within the military; neither had served in the PLA nor had significant ties to it.

Thus, Xi Jinping inherited a military that was making incremental progress toward jointness and where Party control over the PLA had eroded significantly in some areas. Xi recognized that the lack of effective civilian (and especially Party) oversight limited the military's ability to become a truly professional force focused on fighting and winning wars. At worst, the military might not follow the Party's orders in the event of a national crisis. This was especially worrisome given the perception that China was facing increasing national security challenges both at home and abroad, such as separatism, maritime disputes, and strategic challenges from the United States.[22]

Xi wrestled with several distinct but interrelated civil-military challenges. These included the military's reluctance to share information and intelligence with civilian authorities, corruption and cronyism, and a perceived waning of ideological commitment to Party ideals and values within the PLA. These challenges are discussed in turn.

Information-Sharing

As part of the Deng Xiaoping–era bargain that reduced the PLA's political role, the military was granted extensive autonomy to manage its own affairs. From the "principal-agent" perspective, this autonomy created a number of information asymmetries between the Party (the "principal") and PLA (as its "agent").[23] Civilian Party elites had limited insight and control over the PLA's internal finances, R&D activities, and perhaps even some operational decisions. The fact that a significant share of PLA revenue was coming from "off-budget" commercial activities before the 1998 divestiture reduced the effectiveness of budgets as an instrument of civilian control. The PLA also kept tight control over military intelligence and information about Chinese military capabilities and operations as a bureaucratic advantage, and it was often reluctant to share this information with either senior leaders or civilian ministries (such as the Ministry of Foreign Affairs, which occupied a lower bureaucratic grade). At the heart of the problem was an extremely thin institutional nexus between the civilian Party elite and PLA—only the CMC Chairman himself bridged this divide.[24]

Limited information-sharing contributed to a number of secondary civil-military problems. The first was prolific corruption and financial mismanagement within the PLA (discussed below). Second was the inability of senior leaders to anticipate and manage key decisions and announcements from the PLA. Two prominent examples were the negative international response to the January 2007 test of an antisatellite weapon, which appeared to catch Hu and other civilian officials off guard, and the January 2011 test of a J-20 stealth fighter, which led to a diplomatic kerfuffle as it coincided with the visit of U.S. Secretary of Defense Robert Gates to Beijing. Although there are several possible explanations for these incidents, the most convincing is simply that Hu and his advisors were not kept abreast of the specific operational details and timing of the tests.[25] This does not mean that the PLA had gone rogue, but, as PLA expert Andrew Scobell argues, does suggest that it was able to act roguishly—or in a way that caused embarrassment to top Party officials.[26]

A third problem was China's limited ability to coordinate effective civil-military responses to domestic and foreign crises. One of the key drivers for proposals to institute a Chinese NSC was the perception of weak and ineffective whole-of-government responses to incidents such as the May 1999 accidental North Atlantic Treaty Organization bombing of the Chinese embassy in Belgrade and the April 2001 collision of U.S. and Chinese military aircraft in the South China Sea.[27] Part of the problem, as already noted, was the PLA's bureaucratic disincentive to share military information and cooperate with civilian ministries. To be sure, the military was represented on the National Security Leading Small Group, which was intended to facilitate stronger coordination, but this was only an ad hoc arrangement with little institutional support and no ability to compel the PLA to share information or respond to requests from civilian agencies.

Corruption and Cronyism

Another legacy of Deng's bargain with the PLA was ineffective external (as well as internal) supervision of the military, often resulting in corruption and mismanagement. The most well-known examples of graft within the PLA are those that came to light following the anti-corruption campaign initiated by Xi and his colleagues at the end of 2012 (which was not limited to the PLA but covered the entire Party apparatus and state organizations as well). Those cases involve investigation and purges from the Party of high-ranking cadres such as former CMC vice chairmen Xu Caihou and Guo Boxiong, and former General Logistics Department deputy director Gu Junshan, who was suspected of selling military ranks. However, corruption was found at many levels of the PLA, and in many areas. More quotidian examples of malfeasance include the unlawful privatizing of military housing, disobeying traffic regulations, travelling extravagantly, and abusing retirement benefits.[28] PLA-run businesses, such as military hospitals, were also frequent targets of corruption allegations.[29]

System-wide corruption had several major negative consequences for civil-military relations. First was that Party leaders may not have been able to rely on the PLA as an effective warfighting instrument. No military, of course, is optimized for combat when some (if not many) of its senior officers earned their positions through bribes rather than professional qualifications. Second was the military's resistance to reform. As early as 1998, then PLA Chief of the General Staff Fu Quanyou warned that substantial reforms to the PLA's size and structure would be difficult because they would "inevitably involve the immediate interests of numerous units and individual officers."[30] It is likely that graft-prone parts of the PLA, such as the political work and logistics systems, were particularly averse to restructuring. Third were the negative effects that corruption likely had on morale among those personnel who were genuinely interested in serving the Party's, rather than their own, interests.

A key factor contributing to corruption in the PLA was the lack of effective self-policing. At a theoretical level, authoritarian regimes often try to overcome principal-agent problems and concomitant information asymmetry through two means: creating quasi-independent supervisory mechanisms, such as secret police, and by instituting rules and norms intended to shape behavior toward that preferred by the regime.[31] The PLA attempted both techniques, but with limited results. First, beginning in its formative period in the 1920s, the PLA developed an "interlocking and reinforcing" system of political commissars, Party committees, and discipline inspection commissions. These helped to ensure Party control by, respectively, ensuring that Party decisions were followed at each level, managing appointments, and investigating violations of rules governing Party members in the PLA.[32] Because these "objective" mechanisms to control the military were all implemented by PLA officers, their effectiveness depended on political commissars acting as loyal members of the Party (that is, having the correct "subjective" political values and interests) rather than pursuing their individual or PLA institutional interests. Instead of objective and subjective control mechanisms being mutually reinforcing, failure of the subjective mechanisms eroded the effectiveness of the objective mechanisms. The widespread incidence of corruption in the PLA demonstrated that these control mechanisms were not effective and that in some cases, such as graft in the promotion system, the supposed monitors were complicit in the problem.[33]

A second effort to strengthen objective control mechanisms, beginning in the 1980s, involved efforts to regularize [*zhenggui hua*, 正规化] the PLA by instituting laws and regulations governing military activities. This was part of a larger transformation of governance in China from a system based on fiat [*renzhi*, 人制] to one based on laws [*fazhi*, 法制] that was designed to prevent abuses of power and promote better management of Party and state affairs. Hence, the Party restored military ranks (which had been eliminated during the Cultural Revolution) in the late 1980s, and issued regulations on issues such as recruitment, promotions, retirement, procurement, and auditing.[34] Figure 1 depicts the increase in laws and regulations from 1998 to 2012. However, cultivating a rule of law within

Figure 1. Increase of PLA Laws and Regulations, 1998–2012

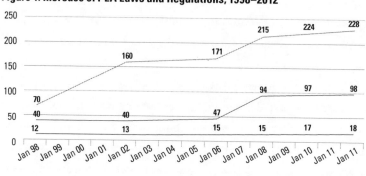

—Military Laws ——Military Regulations ——Military Administrative Rules

Source: Adapted from Shinji Yamaguchi, "Xi Jinping's Military Reform and Party-Military Relations in China," paper presented at the Japanese Association of International Relations, October 14, 2016.

the PLA was bedeviled by various obstacles. As Chinese law expert Susan Finder notes, those problems include the lack of professionalization of military courts and prosecutors, gaps in military legislation, isolation of the military judicial system from its civilian counterpart, and perhaps most seriously, commanders who think that "their word is law."[35]

Ideological Laxity

The most nebulous, but also perhaps the most nefarious, problem in China's civil-military relations involved concerns about the Party's waning ideological appeal within the PLA. In Huntingtonian terms, this suggested a decline in the Party's subjective control of the army. Speaking at the November 2014 Gutian political work conference—held at the site of a 1929 gathering that cemented the PLA's status as subordinate to the Party—Xi stated that the most fundamental political problems were ideological, including those related to "ideals and beliefs," "Party spirit," and "revolutionary spirit."[36] A *PLA Daily* commentary published shortly thereafter stated that the root of the ideological malaise was the clash of competing value systems, in which the ideas of PLA members are becoming "more independent, more selective, more changeable, and more diversified."[37] Although not explicit, this certainly refers to concerns about foreign, and especially Western, ideological influence both in the PLA and in the larger society (from which the military draws its personnel).

Of greatest concern for Party leaders were signs of a renewed discourse of nationalization [*guojia hua*, 国家化] and depoliticization [*fei zhengzhi hua*, 非政治化] in the PLA. A 2014 essay in the Party's flagship journal *Qiushi* explained that the idea of rebranding the PLA as a national (and not a Party) army has blurred the understanding of "some officers and men" in the PLA about the principle of the Party's "absolute leadership" over the military. The author stated that "some" have also "blindly admired" Western models of civil-military relations, in which armies serve national goals, and not those of individual political parties. If those ideas gained prominence, the PLA would "lose its soul" and thus its ability to defend the Party.[38]

These arguments are not new, but rather rooted in the Party's anxieties about the impact of Western influence—an inevitable consequence of China's economic opening—on the Party's grip on power. The case of the Soviet Union, in which a similar opening contributed to the end of one-party rule, is never far out of mind. Regarding the PLA, concerns peaked during the 1989 Tiananmen crisis, when some PLA units refused to obey orders to disperse the student protesters. This was blamed on unnamed Western conspirators as well as on ousted Party General Secretary Zhao Ziyang, whose alleged support for "nationalization" of the army was believed to have weakened Party control.[39] The crisis led to an increased emphasis on political work in the PLA, including a major emphasis on the Party's "absolute leadership" of the military. In the ensuing years, the same themes were stressed at regular intervals. In 2007, for instance, CMC Vice Chairman Cao Gangchuan argued that "some hostile forces" had made it their goal to "separate the military from the Party leadership," while in 2011 CMC member Li Jinai blamed "domestic and foreign hostile forces" for spreading similar ideas.[40] Xi's comments at the Gutian conference and elsewhere are fully consistent with this pattern.

Whether the problem of ideological laxity has become more serious since Xi took office is difficult to assess. Senior PLA officers continue to ritualistically proclaim their loyalty to Xi and the Party in speeches and meetings. It is not clear who, if anyone, in the PLA actually supports delinking the PLA from the Party.[41] Nevertheless, there are two reasons to think that Xi's exhortations are more than a simple reminder. First is the declining relevance of Marxism as a guiding concept within the Party-state (witness, for instance, senior PLA officers who spend as much time purchasing luxury goods as they do attending meetings on their visits to the United States). Second is the increasing role of nationalism as a growing ideological force within China. CCP leaders have tried to compensate for the declining relevance of Marxist ideology by positioning the Party as the only vehicle for fulfilling nationalist goals such as building China into a powerful and respected state and resolving outstanding territorial disputes, including the status of Taiwan. However, this approach means that support for the Party based on nationalism is conditional on its performance in achieving nationalist goals. It is not hard to imagine deep resentment within the PLA toward leaders viewed as unduly soft toward China's perceived enemies and perhaps even talk about ineffectual Party leaders as national traitors [*maiguozei*, 卖国贼]. That does not mean that a nationalist coup is likely as in the Soviet Union in 1991, but it does mean that the Party has to continually reassert its influence in the army.

Structural and Procedural Changes

An initial sign of Xi's intent to strengthen Party control over the PLA came at the Third Plenum of the 18th Party Congress in November 2013. At the plenum, the Party decided in general terms to upgrade management of the PLA, noting the need for more effective leadership, bureaucratic processes (such as those related to the PLA's personnel, budgetary, and procurement systems), and laws and regulations. In addition, the plenum sought to better integrate the military into the broader national security system by creating a national security council (NSC).[42] These changes were designed to increase objective control in the PLA by reducing the problems of limited information-sharing and corruption. At the same time, there was an added emphasis on political work in the PLA, as evidenced by Xi's speech at the Gutian conference. This sought to strengthen subjective control, especially by reiterating Party loyalty within the army. Party control was also strengthened by changes to the personnel assignment system featuring more frequent rotation of senior officers. This section discusses these changes.

Improving Information Flows

Two sets of structural changes were designed to increase the Party's ability to understand and control PLA activities. First was disbanding the 4 general departments and replacing them with a new system of 15 offices, departments, and commissions reporting directly to the CMC. This is depicted in figure 2. This change was intended to reduce the influence of the general departments, which had become powerful enough to limit the CMC's ability to exercise "unified command" over the military.[43] Specific functions previously ensconced within the general departments, such as training, mobilization, and strategic planning, were placed under direct CMC control. Moreover, as discussed below, supervisory organs including the Audit Office, Political and Legal Affairs Commission, and Discipline Inspection Commission also became direct CMC reports. This meant that information on PLA affairs that once would have gone through the general departments (and thus was subject to manipulation) would now be able to

Figure 2.

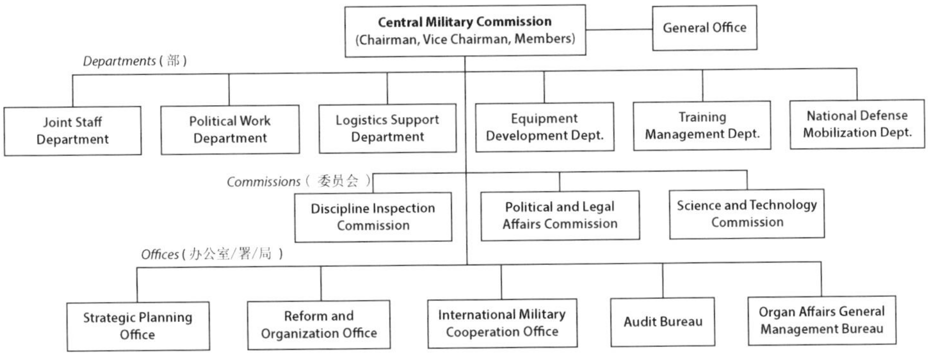

reach CMC members directly.

A second change was the establishment of the NSC. Although the Third Plenum was vague about the nature of this organization, the Politburo soon clarified that it is a Party organ under the Central Committee and that it would be led by Xi. The two vice chairmen are the second- and third-ranking Party members (currently Li Keqiang and Li Zhanshu). Although perhaps focused more on internal than external challenges, the NSC is designed to improve information-sharing and coordination between the PLA and civilian agencies, which if successful could increase the chances for effective crisis response. The organization will do this by maintaining a permanent structure, unlike the ad hoc National Security Leading Small Group, and by including PLA representation at a senior level and as staff liaisons.[44] Anecdotally, the NSC has already begun to improve information flows by forwarding situation reports from the PLA's East China Sea joint operations command center to senior Party officials.[45]

However, these changes are at best only a partial solution to the information asymmetries inherent in Party-army relations. One problem is that the PLA still retains control of military intelligence and information about military capabilities and operations, and it can decide what information to share with civilian Party elites. Another problem is that the institutional nexus between Party and PLA remains thin, located mainly in Xi's hands. The reforms did not increase the involvement of civilians in military affairs (though it might be expected that Xi's successor, when named, could become a CMC vice chairman).[46] A third challenge is that significant power over diverse issues remains in the hands of the general departments' successor organizations, namely the CMC Joint Staff, Political Work, Logistics Support, and Equipment Development departments. Those departments have considerable bureaucratic clout and opportunities to shape the decisionmaking agenda.

Reducing Corruption

The PLA also enacted a series of structural reforms to reduce corruption and promote more effective internal governance. A first change came in October 2014, when the PLA Audit Office was returned to the CMC from the General Logistics Department, where it had resided since 1992. The office's director explained that the transfer was meant to enhance "independence, authority, and effectiveness" of auditors within the military, allowing for greater supervision of "high-level leading organs and cadres."[47] A *PLA Daily* report noted that, between 2013 and 2015, the office had audited 4,024 cadres at or above the Regiment Leader level, resulting in 21 dismissals, hundreds of demotions and other penalties, and recovery of 12.1 billion RMB (approximately $1.9 billion in 2018 U.S. dollars) in losses due to waste and mismanagement.[48]

Further changes were made as part of a CMC reorganization announced in January 2016. The Discipline Inspection Commission, which had been part of the General Political Department (GPD) since 1990, was returned to the CMC. The PLA also announced that teams of discipline inspectors had been created and would be conducting investigations of Party members across the PLA, just as the Central Discipline Inspection Commission has conducted investigations of Party members in the civilian bureaucracy and in state-owned enterprises as part of Xi's anti-corruption campaign. CMC Vice Chairman Xu Qiliang encouraged the inspectors to "take advantage of their new standing" within the PLA to verify "officers' political loyalty, power, and responsibility."[49] In addition, hotlines were established so that military members could anonymously report Party violations to the Discipline Inspection Commission.[50] On January 15, 2018, the PLA formally issued a new CMC Inspection Work Regulation governing the discipline inspection process and specifying the responsibilities of the CMC Inspection Work Leading Small Group, its subsidiary inspection groups, and similar bodies established in the services and the People's Armed Police.[51] Another organizational change was the transfer of the Political and Legal Affairs Commission, responsible for military courts and prosecutors, from the GPD to the CMC.

These reforms were potentially useful because they extricated supervisory functions from the corruption-prone general departments and gave investigators, judges, and auditors greater bureaucratic independence from those they were supposed to be supervising. Status as part of the CMC also gave these units more authority and allowed CMC leaders (including Xi) to exercise tighter control. This was not so much an innovation as a return to the earlier system of "interlocking" directorates in which the Party maintained several distinct channels of control.[52] In this respect, the Audit Office, Discipline Inspection Commission, and Political and Legal Affairs Commission will reinforce the political commissar and Party committee systems (which reside in the Political Work Department, successor to the GPD). Taken together, this could result in a greater ability to identify, investigate, prevent, and punish corruption at higher levels of the PLA, especially in the former general departments. However, a key limitation is the continued lack of significant external checks on PLA activities (such as a free press or independent legislative oversight). To the extent that there is corruption within the auditing, discipline inspection, and military judicial systems themselves, structural changes will have little impact.

A related area of change was the announcement of new regulations designed to strengthen the rule of law within the PLA and encourage a stronger professional ethos among servicemembers. One important development was new restrictions on the PLA's ability to engage in commercial activities, such as accepting civilian patients in PLA hospitals, leasing warehouses, and contracting out military construction units.[53] This helped to close loopholes that allowed the PLA to stay in business despite the 1998 divestiture. In addition, rules were promulgated to prevent garish displays of power by PLA officers, such as use of military license plates to avoid traffic laws, use of luxury cars, opulent banquets, and excessive foreign travel.[54] Still other regulations targeted the personnel system by mandating dismissal of officers on the basis of incompetence and clarifying retirement ages.[55] This was meant to pave the way for a younger, more capable and professional officer corps. Nevertheless, concerns remained about the efficacy of such laws. CMC Vice Chairman Xu Qiliang noted that "We need to correct the phenomenon of having law but not enforcing it, not enforcing the law strictly, and not pursuing those who break the law."[56]

Improving Ideological Commitment

A third area of efforts to increase Party control is in the ideological arena. A key feature of the PLA's political work in recent years has been a renewed emphasis on the principle that the "Party commands the gun." As early as the 18th Party Congress in November 2012, the CMC reiterated that the PLA must "unswervingly uphold the absolute leadership of the Party over the army," guarantee "absolute loyalty and reliability," and support the new generation of Party officials under Xi.[57] Xi himself stressed the same themes at the November 2014 Gutian political work conference and elsewhere.[58] At the same time, the CMC highlighted the need for "reliable" Party cadres in the army, defined in one document as those who have "resolute" political views, carry out military and political orders "without hesitation," and are able to resist "incorrect ideological trends."[59] Senior PLA officers were also required to *biaotai*, or publicly pledge their dedication to the Party and its leadership.[60]

There is nothing inherently unique about the recent emphasis on Party loyalty in the PLA. The fact that this theme reappeared after the 18th Party Congress does not imply specific concerns about disloyalty to the Party or to Xi personally within the army (although it is impossible to rule out such concerns). Rather, it is consistent with a pattern established in the immediate post-Tiananmen era of periodic political campaigns deemed necessary to ensure that Party control does not waver—or what David Finkelstein calls the "re-redding" of the PLA.[61] Indeed, a CMC instruction on political work released in January 2015 reaffirmed the need to "forge the soul" of the army to follow Party commands, requiring continued ideological education at all levels, but "especially in the upper echelons."[62] Hence, even as officer training and promotion criteria increasingly stress operational capabilities, the need for Party education and bona fides will remain central to the PLA's personnel system. Indeed, one PLA officer suggested in a 2017 conversation that political loyalty has become the most important factor in promotions.

A secondary emphasis of PLA political work has been on reinvigorating support for Marxist principles. Overall, the CMC requires that the army be educated with the "important theories of communism and socialism with Chinese characteristics," in addition to the specific principles exhorted by Xi.[63] This has led to an emphasis on socialist norms such as austerity, intra-Party democracy, service to the people, criticism and self-criticism, and upright actions.[64] The goal is to instill values that counteract more self-interested impulses that give rise to materialism and ultimately to corruption and lack of discipline. However, as already noted, the appeal of Marxism in Chinese society has waned considerably since the 1980s. This is no less true in the PLA, as illustrated in the extreme in cases of self-aggrandizement such as those of Xu Caihou and Gu Junshan. PLA members might thus vocalize support for Marxism, but it is unclear that those values are being re-internalized to any significant degree.

Personnel Assignment Changes

A fourth aspect of efforts to tighten Party control over the PLA involves rotating senior officers to reduce the risk of collusion between commanders and political commissars and to break up existing patronage networks that might facilitate corruption. Rotation is a traditional means of preventing senior officers from developing their own local political networks that might challenge civilian control. In the case of the PLA reforms, the assignment pattern of commanders and political commissars varied at different levels of the ground forces. At the theater command (TC) level, four of the five inaugural commanders were previously assigned to other military regions, while all five of the political commissars were local. At the (newly established) TC army level, four of the five commanders were local, while all of the political commissars rotated from other military regions. At the group army level, almost all of the commanders of the group armies were transferred from other military regions, while most of the political commissars were from the local area.[65]

This pattern of personnel assignments balanced the benefits of familiarity with the operating area and subordinate officers with the enhanced political control provided by transferring officers to new locations and breaking up existing patronage networks. These rotations meant that in most cases the commander and political commissar did not have an existing personal relationship and were therefore less likely to trust each other and engage in corrupt behavior. They also meant that if a theater commander contemplated ordering subordinate ground units to engage in unauthorized activity, the operational chain of command included a TC army commander and group army commanders that he did not know well. Taken as a whole, this pattern of senior officer assignments enhanced Party control and the supervision provided by the political commissar system, but likely at some cost to operational effectiveness because the theater commander, political commissar, and subordinate commanders were all unfamiliar with each other.

Xi's Political Strategy for Implementing Reforms

PLA reformers have advocated structural reforms since the early 1990s, but previous reform efforts (including some backed by Jiang Zemin and Hu Jintao) were stymied by bureaucratic opposition within the PLA. How has Xi Jinping succeeded where his predecessors failed? Xi has employed a number of tools and tactics to pursue the reform goals of building a PLA that can fight and win informationized wars by improving its joint operations capability and strengthening CCP control over the PLA. This section describes the elements of Xi's political strategy and the political tools available to pursue his military reform agenda.

Embed Military Reforms in a Broader Reform Agenda

Key elements of the military reforms were unveiled in the Third Plenum decision document approved by the Central Committee in November 2013.[66] The plenum not only identified key areas of military reform, but also sent a powerful message that fundamental organizational changes to the PLA were an important part of China's overall national reforms and were widely supported by the top CCP leadership. By embedding the PLA reforms in a broader reform agenda, and elevating the decision mechanism to the Central Committee level (where the power of PLA senior leaders was diffused), Xi made it harder for potential opponents to resist the reforms. As one PLA officer noted, incorporating military reforms into the national reform agenda elevated military reform "to the will of the Party and act of state."[67] The plenum decision document outlined key aspects of the reforms, sometimes in vague terms that indicated the desired direction of change without providing specific details. This is an effective device for building consensus on the reform agenda while deferring divisive internal debates (for example, over which services would gain or lose personnel in the PLA restructuring).

Emphasize Xi's Personal Involvement

Xi has used his personal involvement in the reform process to demonstrate his commitment to making the reforms succeed. Widely considered the most powerful Chinese leader since Deng Xiaoping, Xi has invested his time and attention to military matters in ways that his predecessors Jiang Zemin and Hu Jintao did not.[68] For example, in his first 3 years as CMC chairman (November 2012–December 2015), Xi made 53 publicized appearances at military events. During the equivalent period of time from 2004–2007, Hu made only 36 appearances.[69] One nonauthoritative Chinese media report claims that Xi spends a half-day every week at his CMC office, in contrast to Hu, who rarely used his office.[70] Moreover, as Nan Li argues, Xi's more assertive leadership style has allowed him to exert greater influence within the PLA than either Jiang or Hu.[71] Xi has also highlighted the "CMC chairmanship responsibility system," which emphasizes that he bears ultimate responsibility over all military matters.

Xi has used his positions as chairman of the CMC and chairman of the CMC Leading Small Group on military reform established in January 2014 to lead efforts to flesh out the details of military restructuring, including chairing meetings to study the feasibility of various options.[72] More than 20 working groups were established under the CMC to research and consider various aspects of the reforms, with extensive consultations with military and civilian units at various levels and more than 150 revisions of the reform plan.[73] Xi personally announced the first details on the reforms at a military parade in Beijing in September 2015, stating that the PLA's size would be reduced by 300,000 by the end of 2017, bringing total personnel down from 2.3 to 2 million.[74] In November 2015, he chaired the CMC meeting that adopted the detailed reform plan.[75]

Since the reforms were announced, Xi has been personally involved in pushing them forward. One means involved making formal speeches to military audiences to launch key elements of the reforms, including a December 27, 2015, speech at the PLA newspaper *Jiefangjun Bao* and a major address on the reforms to CMC and senior PLA leaders at a December 31, 2015, ceremony to establish the army as a separate service, rename the Second Artillery as the Rocket Force and elevate it to full service status, and stand up the Strategic Support Force.[76] Xi met with the leaders of the new services and personally awarded them banners to serve as symbols of their services.[77] He made a similar appearance and speech at a January 11, 2016, ceremony to establish the reorganized CMC with its new departments, commissions, and offices.[78] Xi used these appearances and a photo opportunity at the CMC joint operations command center to highlight the missions and importance of the new services and the reorganized CMC and to reinforce his authority as CMC chairman and his personal commitment to the reforms. He also led a 2-day conference on military reform in December 2016 that reaffirmed the need for a smaller, more agile military.[79]

Since Xi himself cannot be personally involved at all times and in all aspects of the reforms, he has installed trusted agents within the PLA who can ensure that his instructions are being followed. One such individual is Lieutenant General Qin Shengxiang, director of the CMC General Office from December 2012 until September 2017, who was also dual-hatted as director of the new CMC Reform and Organization Office, which has a leading role in formulating reform plans and ensuring implementation.[80] Another key figure is Major General Zhong Shaojun, who has been a senior civilian aide to Xi since Xi's time as Zhejiang Party secretary. When Xi became CMC chairman, Zhong was given a military rank of senior colonel and designated as CMC General Office deputy director and director of Xi's personal office within the CMC. His close association to Xi and responsibilities in the General Office likely gave him significant influence despite his relatively low formal rank and grade.[81] Major General Zhong was subsequently promoted to replace Lieutenant General Qin as director of the CMC General Office.

Protect Senior Officers

The PLA organizational restructuring is a major transformation that saw the end of the general departments, the transition from seven military regions to five theater commands, and the establishment or change in status of three services. Some senior PLA officers stayed in essentially the same jobs under a new organization structure; others changed to new positions, sometimes in different geographic areas. One tacit principle is clear, however: all senior (MR-grade and above) PLA officers were given jobs at their current grades and kept their current ranks. This proved to be a transitional arrangement that only lasted through the personnel shifts prior to the 19th Party Congress in October 2017, which also named a new Central Military Commission and removed the service chiefs and directors of the CMC Equipment Development and Logistics Support departments from their ex officio seats on the CMC. Protecting the personal career interests of senior PLA officers (as opposed to forcing officers whose organizations were disestablished to retire early) is an important means of defusing opposition to the reforms from leaders whose organizations would lose personnel, authority, or budget in the reorganization.

Compensate Reform Losers

Despite its traditional dominance in numbers and the PLA leadership ranks, the army has lost status, budget share, and end strength relative to the other services in recent years. Since 2004, Chinese defense white papers have emphasized the need for increased funding for the navy, air force, and Second Artillery. "Optimizing the composition of the services and arms of the PLA" has meant reductions in "technologically backward" army units and personnel increases for the other services.[82] Most of the 300,000 troops that will be cut from the PLA will come from army ranks, and the army is widely perceived as the likely loser in current PLA organizational reforms.[83] Elimination of the general departments and establishment of a new army commander and headquarters reduced the army to bureaucratic equality with the other services. The army also lost direct control of space and cyber units, which were transferred to the new Strategic Support Force.

Nevertheless, the reforms provided compensation that may actually have increased the army's power, at least in the short term.[84] The new joint C2 structure gives theater commanders both wartime and peacetime operational control over all army, navy, air force, and conventional rocket force units within their areas of responsibility. This significantly expands the authority of theater commanders relative to commanders of the former military regions. All five of the initial theater commanders and four of the five initial theater political commissars were ground force officers (and the other political commissar has spent most of his career in the army). Giving all the theater commander positions to army officers provided a degree of assurance to the army, although subsequent personnel reshuffles named navy Admiral Yuan Yubai as commander of the Southern TC and air force General Yi Xiaoguang as commander of the Central TC.[85]

Another effort to defuse potential opposition involves ensuring that those officers and NCOs who will lose their positions as part of the 300,000-person downsizing of the PLA will receive pensions, civilian jobs, and compensation to which they are entitled. Two PLA National Defense University researchers published an article in the *PLA Daily* warning that salary and pension issues needed to be addressed properly to ensure that military downsizing did not destabilize the military and society.[86] The PLA has learned important lessons from previous force reductions and has codified the benefits that conscripts, NCOs, and officers should receive, which vary based on status, years of service, and how they separate from the PLA.[87] Challenges include allocating sufficient resources to pay earned benefits, ensuring that local officials fulfill their responsibilities to provide benefits to PLA veterans, and pressuring state-owned enterprises and local government offices to fulfill their responsibility to provide civilian jobs to PLA veterans who are entitled to them.

One aspect of the reforms gives responsibility for veterans affairs to the new CMC Organ Affairs General Management Bureau.[88] Senior leaders, including Xi, have repeatedly stressed the importance of local officials fulfilling their obligations to veterans.[89] These measures, and the establishment of a new Ministry for Veterans Affairs in March 2018, are efforts to demonstrate the Party's commitment to take better care of downsized soldiers than in the past.[90] The October 11, 2017, protest by disgruntled PLA veterans in front of the Ba Yi building serves as a vivid reminder of the potential for veterans to engage in embarrassing and politically sensitive protests.[91] (See the chapter by Ma and Chen in this volume for more details on the force reduction process.)

Enlist Support from Reform Winners

Generally speaking, the navy, air force, and rocket force are likely to be the organizational winners from PLA reforms. They have already benefited from an increased share of the PLA budget since 2004 and are likely to be protected from significant force cuts in the 300,000-person downsizing and may even increase their size. Although the army dominated the initial theater command senior leadership and the senior CMC staff, the emphasis on jointness in the reforms created opportunities for the other services to increase their policy influence and their share of senior officer positions. One early indicator was the number of air force and navy officers in theater deputy commander positions. In the pre-reform system, air force and navy officers held only 10 of the 32 MR deputy commander positions, the minimum possible given air force and navy responsibility for commanding seven MR air forces and three fleets.[92] After the reforms, officers from those services occupied 16 of 31 deputy commander positions in the five theaters.[93]

As noted above, a navy officer subsequently became commander of the Southern TC and an air force officer was named as Central TC commander.

Use Threat of Corruption Investigations to Intimidate and Punish Opponents

Investigations into former CMC vice chairmen Guo Boxiong and Xu Caihou not only revealed their complicity in corruption on a massive scale but also confirmed the widespread practice of PLA officers paying large bribes for promotion to senior positions. This suggests that most senior PLA officers are vulnerable to corruption investigations that would reveal their complicity in the pay-to-play promotion system. However, in the initial phases of the reform, anti-corruption investigations focused primarily on the logistics and political systems (which, along with military district commands, offer the most opportunities for corruption). Senior PLA operational commanders were largely spared (with the potential exception of some officers with close ties to Guo, Xu, and the network run by Bo Xilai and Zhou Yongkang). Nevertheless, the threat of investigation is a potent tool to intimidate or remove any officers who might obstruct reform efforts or show insufficient loyalty to Xi Jinping.[94] Once the organizational reforms were implemented, Xi demonstrated his willingness to use this tool by launching corruption investigations into then CMC Joint Staff director Fang Fenghui and then CMC Political Work director Zhang Yang.[95]

Use Control over Promotions to Reward Allies and Supporters of Reforms

Guo and Xu were evidently able to extract such large bribes for positions because Hu Jintao was not actively involved in the promotion and selection process, essentially rubber-stamping decisions made by the CMC vice chairmen. Conversely, Xi Jinping appears to be significantly more engaged in the promotion and assignment process, and reportedly conducts interviews with candidates for senior military positions.[96] Xi's personal engagement in the selection process provides opportunities to place supporters of reforms in key positions and to reward officers with whom he has close ties or who display personal loyalty to his leadership.[97] This approach would be consistent with his broader approach to civilian personnel appointments within the Party and government. The reshuffle of senior PLA officers in the runup to the 19th Party Congress in 2017 provides additional evidence of Xi's involvement in PLA personnel decisions (see the chapter by McFadden, Fassler, and Godby in this volume for an analysis).

Conclusion

The previous section indicates that Xi has an extensive range of tools to influence the PLA and suggests that he employed a reasonably coherent and phased political strategy to push the reforms through. How effective will he be in pursuing the long-term goals of building a PLA with a stronger joint operations capability that can fight and win informationized wars and strengthening CCP control over the PLA?

One starting point is to ask whether Xi's objectives are compatible with the interests and goals of senior PLA leaders.[98] Despite the potential negative impact on some organizational and individual interests, there is likely considerable support within the PLA leadership for reforms that will improve PLA combat capability. The organizational reforms draw upon insights from the PLA's study of foreign military operations and on theoretical study of the nature of modern war.[99] Moreover, senior PLA leaders were involved in drawing up the details of the military reforms, which appear to incorporate some compromises to protect the interests of individual leaders, major organizations, and those soldiers who will be let go as part of the military restructuring.

Conversely, Xi's efforts to strengthen Party control will reduce the autonomy of the PLA as an institution and potentially have some negative effects on both operational effectiveness and on the organizational and personal interests of PLA leaders. Will the increased emphasis on political work interfere with efforts to build a more operationally effective PLA? Every hour spent on political education is 1 hour less spent on training, so some tradeoffs are inevitable. Will the emphasis on regularization and stronger supervisory mechanisms lead to paralysis or disruption in major parts of the PLA, especially if the anti-corruption campaign continues indefinitely as an instrument of Xi's personal control?

At a more fundamental level, can efforts to use political work to rekindle the ideological flame of belief in Marxism-Leninism succeed? Senior PLA officers have been willing to say the correct slogans and swear their loyalty to the Party and to Xi as the core leader of the Party. But formal compliance is not the same as genuine belief, and may not produce better behavior over the long term or loyalty to the Party in a political crisis. Moreover, the hypocrisy of CCP leaders pursuing an anti-corruption campaign when their own family members have amassed fortunes by trading on their political connections will likely undermine efforts to produce cleaner governance.[100]

The CCP's insistence on reiterating the principle of absolute loyalty to the Party suggests that CCP leaders themselves are not fully confident about PLA loyalty. If the means of ensuring objective control over the PLA require a high degree of subjective control (in the form of ideological belief by those officers doing the supervision) to be effective, then Xi's efforts to improve supervisory mechanisms may not succeed.[101] Even if these measures are effective in the short term, they will require continued high-level attention from Xi himself. This could become a problem in the future if Xi's attention gets drawn away to deal with other pressing challenges. A permanent anti-corruption campaign, like the permanent revolution Mao called for during the Cultural Revolution, is likely to be highly disruptive.

The PLA reforms are still a work in progress, and the PLA is engaged in figuring out how to make its new joint C2 system work. Knowledgeable observers differ in their assessments of whether the reforms are likely to make a significant difference in operational effectiveness.[102] Observing the PLA's progress in building an effective joint operations capability that can, as Xi Jinping says, "fight and win wars," will be challenging, especially in the absence of actual combat, but at least there will be some exercises and operations to observe and some tangible indicators of progress.[103]

Assessing Xi's efforts to reassert Party control over the PLA will be much more difficult. Senior PLA officers are likely to say the right things; any officers who refuse to profess loyalty to the Party and to Xi will not last long. But the real test would only come in a major political crisis or if the CCP's efforts to maintain economic growth and to achieve nationalist goals falter. Until then, our assessment that the reforms are more likely to succeed in improving PLA operational performance than in reasserting CCP control over the military must remain a tentative judgment.

Notes

[1] For an overview, see *Annual Report to Congress: Military and Security Developments Involving the People's Republic of China 2015* (Washington, DC: Office of the Secretary of Defense, 2015), available at <www.defense.gov/Portals/1/Documents/pubs/2015_China_Military_Power_Report.pdf>.

[2] See James C. Mulvenon and David M. Finkelstein, eds., *China's Revolution in Doctrinal Affairs: Emerging Trends in the Operational Art of the Chinese People's Liberation Army* (Arlington, VA: CNA, 2005).

[3] For an excellent analysis, see Adam P. Liff and Andrew S. Erickson, "Demystifying China's Defence Spending: Less Mysterious in the Aggregate," *China Quarterly*, no. 216 (December 2013), 805–830.

[4] *Annual Report to Congress*, i.

[5] Michael S. Chase et al., *China's Incomplete Military Transformation* (Santa Monica, CA: RAND, 2015).

[6] Brian Lafferty, Aaron Shraberg, and Morgan Clemens, *China's Civil-Military Integration*, SITC Research Brief 2013-10 (San Diego, CA: Study of Innovation and Technology in China, January 2013).

[7] For a discussion of China's global interests, see Phillip C. Saunders, *China's Global Activism: Strategy, Drivers, and Tools* (Washington, DC: NDU Press, 2006); and David Shambaugh, *China Goes Global: The Partial Power* (New York: Oxford University Press, 2013).

[8] Chase et al., *China's Incomplete Military Transformation*, 48–49.

[9] For an excellent overview, see Kenneth W. Allen et al., *Institutional Changes of the Chinese People's Liberation Army: Overview and Challenges* (Arlington, VA: CNA, 2002).

[10] See, for instance, Minnie Chan, "Hu Jintao's Weak Grip on China's Army

Inspired Xi Jinping's Military Shake-Up: Sources," *South China Morning Post* (Hong Kong), March 11, 2015, available at <www.scmp.com/news/china/article/1734663/ hu-jintaos-weak-grip-chinas-army-inspired-president-xi-jinpings-military>.

[11] "Xi Stresses Joint Battle Command for Military Reform," Xinhua, April 21, 2016, available at <www.chinadaily.com.cn/china/2016-04/21/content_24709910.htm>.

[12] See Phillip C. Saunders and Joel Wuthnow, *China's Goldwater-Nichols? Assessing PLA Organizational Reforms*, INSS Strategic Forum 294 (Washington, DC: NDU Press, April 2016), available at <http://ndupress.ndu.edu/Portals/68/ Documents/stratforum/SF-294.pdf>.

[13] See Alice Miller, "The PLA in the Party Leadership Decisionmaking System," in *PLA Influence on China's National Security Policymaking*, ed. Phillip C. Saunders and Andrew Scobell (Stanford: Stanford University Press, 2015), 58–83.

[14] Peter D. Feaver, *Armed Servants: Agency, Oversight, and Civil-Military Relations* (Cambridge: Harvard University Press, 2003), 5–7.

[15] Richard H. Kohn, "How Democracies Control the Military," *Journal of Democracy* 8, no. 4 (1997), 140–153.

[16] Samuel P. Huntington, "Reforming Civil-Military Relations," *Journal of Democracy* 6, no. 4 (1995), 9–17.

[17] Jaehwan Lim, *The Emergence and Demise of Military Governance in China: From Cultural Revolution to Deng Xiaoping* (Nagoya, Japan: Nagoya University Press, 2014).

[18] On the concept of "subjective" and "objective" control, see Samuel P. Huntington, *The Soldier and the State: The Theory and Politics of Civil-Military Relations* (Cambridge: Harvard University Press, 1957). For a review of the literature on civil-military relations in China, see Michael Kiselycznyk and Phillip C. Saunders, *Civil-Military Relations in China: Assessing the PLA's Role in Elite Politics*, China Strategic Perspectives 2 (Washington, DC: NDU Press, 2010), available at <http://ndupress. ndu.edu/Portals/68/Documents/stratperspective/china/ChinaPerspectives-2.pdf>.

[19] For an overview, see James C. Mulvenon, *Soldiers of Fortune: The Rise and Fall of the Chinese Military-Business Complex, 1978–1998* (New York: Routledge, 2000).

[20] James C. Mulvenon, "PLA Divestiture 2.0: We Mean It This Time," *China Leadership Monitor*, vol. 50 (Summer 2016).

[21] Phillip C. Saunders and Andrew Scobell, "Introduction," in *PLA Influence on China's National Security Policymaking*, 8.

[22] For a summary of the Chinese government's view of the security environment, see *China's Military Strategy* (Beijing: State Council of the People's Republic

of China, 2015).

[23] For two recent analyses employing a "principal-agent" framework to assess civil-military relations in China, see Jaehwan Lim, "Drawing a Fine Line Between Society and Military: A Political Logic of Military Reform in China," paper prepared for the Japan Association of International Relations Conference, Tokyo, October 14, 2016; and Shinji Yamaguchi, "Xi Jinping's Military Reform and Party-Military Relations in China," paper prepared for the Japan Association of International Relations Conference, Tokyo, October 14, 2016.

[24] It is worth noting that the Central Military Commission (CMC) vice chairmen hold ex officio seats on the Politburo and several senior PLA officers are represented on the Party Central Committee, though there is little evidence that these Party organs have played a significant role in military affairs.

[25] On the antisatellite test, see James C. Mulvenon, "Rogue Warriors? A Puzzled Look at the Chinese ASAT Test," *China Leadership Monitor*, vol. 20 (Winter 2007). On the J-20 test, see Andrew Scobell, "The J-20 Episode and Civil-Military Relations in China," Testimony Before the U.S.-China Economic and Security Review Commission, Washington, DC, March 10, 2011.

[26] Andrew Scobell, "Is There a Civil-Military Gap in China's Peaceful Rise?" *Parameters* 39, no. 2 (Summer 2009), 4–22.

[27] Joel Wuthnow, "China's New 'Black Box': Origins, Prospects and Obstacles for the Chinese Central National Security Commission," *China Quarterly*, no. 232 (December 2017), 886–903.

[28] Chase et al., *China's Incomplete Military Transformation*, 48–49.

[29] Mulvenon, "PLA Divestiture 2.0."

[30] Kenneth W. Allen et al., *Institutional Reforms of the Chinese People's Liberation Army: Overview and Challenges* (Arlington, VA: CNA, 2002), 67–68.

[31] Tom Ginsburg, "Administrative Law and the Judicial Control of Agents in Authoritarian Regimes" in *Rule by Law: The Politics of Courts in Authoritarian Regimes*, ed. Tom Ginsburg and Tamir Moustafa (Cambridge: Cambridge University Press, 2008), 58–72.

[32] David Shambaugh, "The Soldier and the State in China: The Political Work System in the People's Liberation Army," *China Quarterly*, no. 127 (September 1991), 536–550.

[33] One claim made in Chinese media was that former CMC Vice Chairman Xu Caihou had netted $3.25 million for the sale of a military region command position. Cited in Cheng Li, "Promoting 'Young Guards': The Recent High Turnover in the PLA

Leadership (Part 1: Purges and Reshuffles)," *China Leadership Monitor*, vol. 48 (Fall 2015).

[34] Thomas A. Bickford, "Regularization and the Chinese People's Liberation Army: An Assessment of Change," *Asian Survey* 40, no. 3 (June 2000), 456–474.

[35] Susan Finder, "Ruling the PLA According to Law: An Oxymoron?" *China Brief* 15, no 21 (November 2, 2015), available at <https://jamestown.org/program/ruling-the-pla-according-to-law-an-oxymoron/>.

[36] "All Army Political Work Conference Opens in Gutian, Xi Jinping Delivers an Important Speech" [全军政治工作会议在古田召开习近平出席会议并发表重要讲话], Xinhua, November 1, 2014, available at <http://news.xinhuanet.com/politics/2014-11/01/c_1113074055.htm>.

[37] Zhang Yu and Chang Xuemei [张玉, 常雪梅], eds., "It Is Urgently Required to Settle Apparent Problems in Political Work" [政治工作存在的突出问题亟须解决], *PLA Daily* [解放军报], November 5, 2014, available at <http://cpc.people.com.cn/pinglun/n/2014/1105/c78779-25978483.html>.

[38] Yu Guang [禹光], "Looking at Casting the Army's Soul from the Modern Values of the Gutian Conference" [从古田会议的当代价值看铸牢军魂], *Qiushi* [求是], July 31, 2014, available at <www.qstheory.cn/dukan/qs/2014-07/31/c_1111827487.htm>. The author is director of the PLA Press, part of the former General Political Department.

[39] Shambaugh, "The Soldier and the State in China," 555–557.

[40] "PLA Reiterates Loyalty to CPC Leadership," Xinhua, July 17, 2007, available at <www.chinadaily.com.cn/china/2007-07/17/content_5438017.htm>; "No Nationalization of Military in China," *China Daily*, June 20, 2011, available at <www.chinadaily.com.cn/china/2011-06/20/content_12739234.htm>.

[41] It was also unclear who supported nationalization of the PLA during the Jiang and Hu years. See Michael D. Swaine, "Civil-Military Relations and Domestic Power and Policies," Carnegie Endowment for International Peace, November 2, 2005.

[42] The full text of the Third Plenum decision (in English) is available at <www.china.org.cn/china/third_plenary_session/>.

[43] Wu Ming [吴铭], "Remolding Our Military's Leadership and Command Structure Is a Necessary Step in the PLA's Rejuvenation" [重塑我军领导指挥体制是强军兴军的必然选择], *PLA Daily* [解放军报], November 30, 2015, available at <http://jz.chinamil.com.cn/n2014/tp/content_6791140.htm>.

[44] Wuthnow, "China's New 'Black Box.'"

[45] Michael D. Swaine, "The PLA Role in China's Foreign Policy and Crisis Behavior," in *PLA Influence on China's National Security Policymaking*, 146.

[46] Xi served as CMC vice chairman from 2010 to 2013, as did Hu Jintao from

1999 to 2005.

47 Wang Xiaoyi [王晓易], ed., "Effectively Use the 'Sharp Sword' of Auditing to Build a Defense Line of Supervision" [用好审计"利剑" 筑牢监督防线], *PLA Daily* [解放军报], March 7, 2015, available at <http://news.163.com/15/0307/06/AK363OKJ00014AED.html>.

48 Jiang Pingping and Cheng Hongyi [姜萍萍, 程宏毅], eds., "Push Forward the Innovative Development of Army Audit Work from a New Starting Point" [在新起点上推动军队审计工作创新发展], *PLA Daily* [解放军报], January 29, 2015, available at <http://cpc.people.com.cn/n/2015/0129/c83083-26471805-2.html>.

49 Nectar Gan, "PLA's New Top-Level Anti-Corruption Units Swing into Action," *South China Morning Post* (Hong Kong), May 5, 2016, available at <www.scmp.com/news/china/policies-politics/article/1941520/plas-new-top-level-anti-corruption-units-swing-action>.

50 Yao Jianing, ed., "Chinese Military Opens Channels for Reporting Disciplinary Violations," *China Military Online*, February 16, 2016, available at <http://english.chinamil.com.cn/news-channels/china-military-news/2016-02/16/content_6912001.htm>.

51 "Central Military Commission Regulations on Roving Inspection Work" [中央军委巡视工作条例], PRC Ministry of National Defense, January 17, 2018, available at <www.mod.gov.cn/shouye/2018-01/17/content_4802593.htm>.

52 Shambaugh, "The Soldier and the State in China," 527–568.

53 Mulvenon, "PLA Divestiture 2.0," 1.

54 Carlos Tejada, "China's New Leaders Ban Lavish Military Banquets," *Wall Street Journal*, December 22, 2012, available at <www.wsj.com/articles/SB10001424127887324461604578194641136585674>; William Wan, "China Curbs Use of Coveted Military License Plates in Latest Anti-Corruption Move," *Washington Post*, April 1, 2013, available at <www.washingtonpost.com/world/asia_pacific/china-curbs-militarys-luxury-cars/2013/04/01/264d2eba-9ac0-11e2-9a79-eb5280c81c63_story.html>.

55 Li, "Promoting 'Young Guards.'"

56 Finder, "Ruling the PLA According to Law"; Susan Finder, "Shoring Up the 'Rule of Law' in China's Military," *The Diplomat*, February 4, 2015, available at <http://thediplomat.com/2015/02/ruling-the-pla-according-to-the-law/>.

57 Wan Peng and Zhao Jing [万鹏, 赵晶], eds., "Matter of Key Importance at Present, Most Important Political Task" [当前头等大事 首要政治任务], *PLA Daily* [解放军报], November 20, 2012, available at <http://theory.people.com.cn/n/2012/1120/c49151-19633004.html>.

[58] See, for example, "Xi Stresses Military Headquarters' Loyalty to Party," Xinhua, September 22, 2014, available at <http://news.xinhuanet.com/english/china/2014-09/22/c_133663216.htm>; "Xi Brings Strength, Integrity to Chinese Armed Forces," Xinhua, July 30, 2016, available at <http://english.chinamil.com.cn/news-channels/china-military-news/2016-07/30/content_7182049.htm>.

[59] Yu, "Looking at Casting the Army's Soul from the Modern Values of the Gutian Conference."

[60] Zhang Hong, "PLA Generals Take Rare Step of Swearing Loyalty to President Xi Jinping," *South China Morning Post* (Hong Kong), April 3, 2014, available at <www.scmp.com/news/china/article/1463386/pla-generals-take-rare-step-swearing-loyalty-president-xi-jinping>.

[61] David M. Finkelstein, *Initial Thoughts on the Reorganization and Reform of the PLA* (Arlington, VA: CNA, 2016), 19.

[62] "PLA Pledges Allegiance to Party's 'Absolute Leadership,'" Xinhua, January 30, 2015, available at <www.china.org.cn/china/2015-01/30/content_34702143.htm>.

[63] Ibid.

[64] "Commentary: Improved Party Life Vital to Advanced CPC," Xinhua, October 31, 2016, available at <http://news.xinhuanet.com/english/2016-10/31/c_135794711.htm>; "The CMC General Office Issues a Notice Requiring All PLA and PAP Units to Diligently Study, Propagate, and Implement the Spirit of the Sixth Plenum of the 18th Party Congress" [中央军委办公厅发出通知要求全军和武警部队认真学习宣传贯彻党的十八届六中全会精神], Xinhua, October 30, 2016, available at <http://news.xinhuanet.com/politics/2016-10/30/c_1119815230.htm>.

[65] See Joel Wuthnow and Phillip C. Saunders, *Chinese Military Reforms in the Age of Xi Jinping: Drivers, Challengers, and Implications*, China Strategic Perspectives 10 (Washington, DC: NDU Press, 2017), 14–21.

[66] "CPC Central Committee Decision on Deepening of Reforms for Major Issues" [中共中央关于全面深化改革若干重大问题的决定], Xinhua, November 15, 2013, available at <http://news.xinhuanet.com/politics/2013-11/15/c_118164235.htm>.

[67] Bai Zonglin, "Perspective on China's Military Reform," *International Strategic Studies*, no. 2 (2016), 22.

[68] Nan Li, "The Top Leaders and the PLA: The Different Styles of Jiang, Hu, and Xi," in *PLA Influence on China's National Security Policymaking*, 120–140.

[69] These figures are based on a search for each leader's name in the military issues section of the *China Vitae* database for the relevant periods.

[70] Ji Beiqun [季北群], "To Reshuffle Military Generals as Fast as Mao: Xi

Jinping's 'Foresight'" [军队换将直追毛泽东习近平 "深谋远虑"], Duowei Newsnet [多维新闻], January 10, 2015, available at <http://china.dwnews.com/news/2015-01-10/59629032.html>.

[71] Li, "The Top Leaders and the PLA."

[72] "China's Reform Leading Group Holds First Meeting," Xinhua, January 22, 2014, available at <http://news.xinhuanet.com/english/china/2014-01/22/c_133066240.htm>.

[73] Bai, "Perspective on China's Military Reform," 22–23.

[74] "China to Cut Troops by 300,000: Xi," Xinhua, September 3, 2015, available at <http://news.xinhuanet.com/english/2015-09/03/c_134583730.htm>. For an analysis, see John Chen, "Downsizing the PLA, Part 1: Military Discharge and Resettlement Policy, Past and Present," *China Brief* 16, no. 16 (October 26, 2016), 20–26; and John Chen, "Downsizing the PLA, Part 2," *China Brief* 16, no. 17 (November 11, 2016), 6–11.

[75] "At CMC Reform Work Meeting, Xi Jinping Stresses: Comprehensively Implement Reform and Military Strengthening Strategy, Resolutely Take Path to Strong Military with Chinese Characteristics" [习近平在中央军委改革工作会议上强调全面实施改革强军战略坚定不移走中国特色强军之路], Xinhua, November 26, 2015, available at <http://news.xinhuanet.com/politics/2015-11/26/c_1117274869.htm>; and Liu Xiaopeng [刘晓朋], ed., "CMC Opinions on Deepening National Defense and Military Reforms" [中央军委关于深化国防和军队改革的意见], Xinhua, January 1, 2016, available at <http://news.xinhuanet.com/mil/2016-01/01/c_1117646695.htm>.

[76] "Faithfully Perform the Sacred Missions Assigned by the Party and the People" [忠实履行党和人民赋予的神圣使命], *PLA Daily* [解放军报], January 2, 2016; also see Li Jing, "President Xi Jinping Lays Down the Law to the Chinese Army in First 'Precept' Speech Since Mao Zedong," *South China Morning Post* (Hong Kong), January 4, 2016. Li stresses the imperative nature of Xi's precept speech, known as a *xun ci* ["admonishing words"].

[77] Li Xuanliang, Zhang Xuanjie, and Li Qinghua, "Meeting on Establishment of Army Leading Organ, Rocket Force, Strategic Support Force Held in Beijing"; and "Xi Jinping Confers Military Banners to Army, Rocket Force, Strategic Support Force Units of the People's Liberation Army and Delivers Speech," Xinhua, January 1, 2016.

[78] Li Xuanliang [李宣良], "Xi Jinping Meets with Responsible Comrades at Various Departments of the CMC Organ, Emphasizing the Requirements of Stressing Politics, Striving for Winning, Rendering Services, Playing an Exemplary Role, Endeavoring to Build the CMC Organ With 'Four Iron Qualities'" [习近平在接见军委机关各部门负责同志时强调讲政治谋打赢搞服务作表率努力建设 "四铁" 军

委机关], Xinhua, January 11, 2016.

[79] "Xi Calls for Smaller but More Capable Army," Xinhua, December 3, 2016, available at <http://news.xinhuanet.com/english/2016-12/03/c_135878424.htm>.

[80] "CMC General Office Director Qin Shengxiang Will Concurrently Serve as Director of the CMC Reform and Organization Office" [军委办公厅主任秦生祥兼任军委改革和编制办公室主任], *The Paper* [澎湃新闻], August 28, 2016, available at <http://news.qq.com/a/20160828/009988.htm>.

[81] Edward Wong, "The 'Gatekeeper' in Xi Jinping's Inner Circle," *New York Times*, September 30, 2015, available at <http://sinosphere.blogs.nytimes.com/2015/09/30/the-gatekeeper-in-xi-jinpings-inner-circle/>.

[82] "China's National Defense in 2004," State Council Information Office of the People's Republic of China.

[83] Saunders and Wuthnow, *China's Goldwater-Nichols?*; Kenneth W. Allen, Dennis J. Blasko, and John F. Corbett, Jr., "The PLA's New Organizational Structure: What Is Known, Unknown, and Speculation (Part 1)," *China Brief* 16, no. 3 (February 4, 2016); *China Security Report 2016: The Expanding Scope of PLA Activities and PLA Strategy* (Tokyo: National Institute for Defense Studies, 2016), 62.

[84] Phillip C. Saunders and John Chen, "Is the Chinese Army the Real Winner in PLA Reforms?" *Joint Force Quarterly* 83 (4th Quarter 2016), available at <http://ndupress.ndu.edu/Media/News/Article/969659/is-the-chinese-army-the-real-winner-in-pla-reforms/>.

[85] Choi Chi-yuk, "Admiral Named to Head PLA's New Southern Theatre Command," *South China Morning Post* (Hong Kong), January 19, 2017, available at <www.scmp.com/news/china/policies-politics/article/2063649/admiral-named-head-plas-southern-theatre-command>; and Teddy Ng, "China's Air Force Gets a Lift with Pilot's Promotion to Top Military Job," *South China Morning Post* (Hong Kong), February 14, 2018, available at <www.scmp.com/news/china/diplomacy-defence/article/2133405/chinas-air-force-gets-lift-pilots-promotion-top>.

[86] Sun Kejia [孙科佳] and Han Xiao[韓笑], "Stepping Up Preparations to Integrate Military Reform into Country's Strategic Planning" [加強統籌, 把軍隊改革納入國家戰略規劃], *PLA Daily* [解放軍報], November 19, 2015. See also Jun Mai, "PLA Pay Deal Could 'Destabilise' Chinese Society," *South China Morning Post* (Hong Kong), November 19, 2015.

[87] For details, see Chen, "Downsizing the PLA, Part 1."

[88] Liu Zhiming [刘志明], "Follow the Requirements of the 'Four Railways'

to Create First-Class Service Security Agencies" [按照"四铁"要求打造一流服务保障机构], *PLA Daily* [解放军报], April 20, 2016, available at <www.mod.gov.cn/topnews/2016-04/20/content_4650021_4.htm>.

[89] Yin Shen and Tong Zongli [尹深, 仝宗莉], "Two Ministries: No State-Owned Company May Refuse to Accept Retired Soldiers" [两部委: 任何国有企业不得拒绝接收退役士兵], *People's Daily* [人民日报], December 28, 2015, available at <http://politics.people.com.cn/n1/2015/1228/c1001-27986615.html>.

[90] See Kevin J. O'Brien and Neil J. Diamant, "Contentious Veterans: China's Retired Officers Speak out," *Armed Forces & Society* 41, no. 3 (2015), 563–581.

[91] For an assessment of the likely effectiveness of these efforts, see Chen, "Downsizing the PLA, Part 2."

[92] *Directory of PRC Military Personalities March 2014* (Washington, DC: Department of Defense, 2014).

[93] *Directory of PRC Military Personalities March 2016* (Washington, DC: Department of Defense, 2016).

[94] See Derek Grossman and Michael S. Chase, "Why Xi Is Purging the Chinese Military," *The National Interest*, April 15, 2016, available at <http://nationalinterest.org/feature/why-xi-purging-the-chinese-military-15795?page=show>.

[95] Zhang Yang committed suicide in November 2017, and it was announced in January 2018 that Fang Fenghui was under investigation for "giving and taking bribes." Chris Buckley, "Chinese General under Investigation, Joining a Line of Fallen Commanders," *New York Times*, January 9, 2018, available at <www.nytimes.com/2018/01/09/world/asia/china-general-corruption.html>.

[96] Author interviews with two PLA officers, 2017.

[97] See Cheng Li, *Chinese Politics in the Xi Jinping Era: Reassessing Collective Leadership* (Washington, DC: Brookings Institution, 2016).

[98] See Isaac B. Kardon and Phillip C. Saunders, "Reconsidering the PLA as an Interest Group," in *PLA Influence on China's National Security Policymaking*, 33–57.

[99] Andrew Scobell, David Lai, and Roy Kamphausen, eds., *Chinese Lessons from Other Peoples' Wars* (Carlisle Barracks, PA: Strategic Studies Institute, 2011).

[100] At the Sixth Plenum in October 2016, the Central Committee apparently voted down a proposal for an "assets-disclosure sunshine regulation" that would have required Central Committee members, their spouses, and their children to disclose their assets. See Willy Wo-Lap Lam, "Xi Jinping Uses New 'Leadership Core' Status to Boost His Faction," *China Brief* 16, no. 17 (November 11, 2016), 5–6.

[101] For a more positive assessment, see Chien-wen Kou, "Xi Jinping in Command: Solving the Principal-Agent Problem in CCP-PLA Relations?" *China Quarterly*, vol. 232 (December 2017), 866–885.

[102] Michael S. Chase and Jeff Engstrom, "PLA Reforms: An Optimistic Take," *Joint Force Quarterly* 83 (4th Quarter 2015), 49–52; and Roger Cliff, "PLA Reforms: A Pessimistic Take," *Joint Force Quarterly* 83 (4th Quarter 2015), 53–56.

[103] "'Be Ready to Win Wars,' Xi Orders Reshaped PLA," Xinhua, August 2, 2017, available at <www.china.org.cn/china/2017-08/02/content_41332028.htm>. For one list of potential indicators, see Saunders and Wuthnow, *China's Goldwater-Nichols?*

CHAPTER 14

THE NEW PLA LEADERSHIP

Xi Molds China's Military to His Vision

By Joel McFadden, Kim Fassler, and Justin Godby

In October 2017, the 19th Party Congress resulted in dramatic changes to the Central Military Commission (CMC), China's highest military decisionmaking body. Outsiders looking in can only speculate that the deliberations surrounding the selection of these top generals involved a high-stakes negotiation involving sensitive and critical questions of competence, loyalty, and the future direction of the People's Liberation Army (PLA). Although we may never know the content of these debates, the outcome of those negotiations—the new CMC structure and leadership lineup—is a window into the whims of the country's top leaders on political loyalties, Party-military relations, and China's military modernization.

Overall, the changes to China's high command reflect leaders giving priority to joint operations and emphasis on having capable, well-rounded commanders from across the services take charge of a rapidly modernizing force. They also reveal a concerted effort by the Chinese Communist Party (CCP), especially since 2012, to accelerate the careers of a new generation of senior military officers who are in lockstep with President Xi Jinping's agenda and who apparently avoided the worst of the endemic corruption that reached to the highest echelons of the PLA. Over the next 5 years and beyond, these new leaders will oversee the PLA's continued expansion into a capable, global military that is attempting training and overseas missions that are unprecedented in recent Chinese history. They will also be expected to meet key goals, including a 2020 deadline for implementing the most comprehensive changes to the PLA's command structure in recent decades.

Background: PLA Priorities and Party-Military Relations under Xi

To understand the mindset of Xi Jinping and other Chinese leaders involved in making these selections ahead of the 19th Party Congress, it is worth examining the changes that have taken place in the PLA during the past 5 years. The incoming Party leadership that rose to power at the 18th Party Congress in 2012 did not delay in announcing its priorities for the PLA. On November 16, 4 days after the congress concluded in Beijing, newly appointed CMC Chairman Xi Jinping and his outgoing predecessor, Hu Jintao, addressed an enlarged session of the CMC. After thanking Hu for his stewardship of the PLA, Xi first reminded military leaders that the PLA must "unswervingly adhere to the Party's absolute leadership over the armed forces." Second, Xi instructed the PLA to "resolutely complete various tasks of military struggle," including safeguarding national security and sovereignty and raising combat capabilities. Finally, Xi exhorted the PLA to uphold the military's "glorious tradition and fine style." Xi included in this sentiment a warning to top generals to "take a firm stand against corruption," foreshadowing a sweeping anti-corruption campaign across the Party and military.[1]

Xi and the new leaders' sense of urgency about reforming the PLA in part probably stemmed from issues in civil-military relations during Hu's tenure, many of which were only brought to light after the 18th Party Congress. Headlining these were poor discipline and widespread corruption that apparently reached all the way into the top ranks. The rampant problems must have caused deep anxiety among Party leaders not only about the PLA's loyalty, but also about the corrosive effect of shady procurement deals and buying positions on military readiness. The extent of corruption in the PLA was revealed in dramatic fashion in 2014 and 2015 when the two highest ranking generals and top military advisors to Hu were arrested in retirement for corruption.[2]

As a result of these fears, in 2012 Party leaders led by Xi intensified efforts around these three priorities: Party control of the armed forces, combat capability, and discipline. First, the Party firmly reasserted its symbolic control over the PLA and bolstered propaganda around Xi's authority as commander in chief. On November 1, 2014, Xi convened a critical all-army political work conference in Gutian, Fujian Province. This historic location was the site of an important 1929 meeting where Mao Zedong cemented Party authority over the Red Army and which thus serves as a potent political symbol of the Party's control over the armed forces. Political propaganda before and after the meeting has stressed the principle of the Party leading the army, stridently rejected Western-style nationalization of the armed forces, and strongly reiterated the concept of the "CMC Chairman Responsibility System," which emphasizes the singular authorities of the CMC chairman (Xi) in running the military.[3]

Similarly, Xi formally was named commander in chief of the CMC Joint Operations Command Center, an honorific title signaling the chairman's place at the top of the operational command chain. From the start as head of the CMC, Xi also took an early and active interest in military affairs, frequently visiting military units and meeting with officers and soldiers. In July 2017, wearing military fatigues and riding in a jeep, he presided over a massive military demonstration to celebrate the 90th anniversary of the PLA's founding, during which he again exhorted the PLA to obey the Party's command and transform itself into an elite fighting force.[4]

Xi's second exhortation to the military to "resolutely complete various tasks of military struggle" has been most vividly illustrated in the intensified training, exercises, missions beyond China's borders, and reforms to the PLA's command structure intended to equip the PLA to be able to defend evolving Chinese interests. In 2004, then-CMC Chairman Hu Jintao ordered the PLA to be prepared to perform new missions, including defending China's overseas interests. Xi's guidance to the PLA, issued early and often during his tenure, to be able to "fight and win"[5] compounds this guidance. It is both a reflection of the PLA's rapidly developing and externally facing capabilities and the leadership's need for a force that can defend China's growing domestic and overseas interests from threats. Chinese ships and aircraft now operate more frequently and farther from China's immediate borders than at any time in recent history—as China's growing presence in the East and South China Seas illustrates. Meanwhile, China's first overseas logistics hub in Djibouti and the 24th Counterpiracy Task Group to the Gulf of Aden, both completed in 2017, underscore China's growing global interests and the PLA's increasing global presence. Lastly, the whole-scale restructuring of the PLA that began in late 2015 finally abolished the military's outdated organizational structure and brought the high command in line with longstanding operational goals, such as refining joint operations.[6]

Finally, Xi and the leadership have taken a firm stand against corruption at all levels of the military. These measures have included inspections of military units across China, updated guidelines for proper behavior, more frequent political indoctrination sessions, and corruption investigations into top military leaders. In December 2012, the CMC announced 10 regulations to rein in bad behavior in the PLA, including banning alcohol at banquets. Since then, the campaign has netted dozens of officers whose names and crimes have been publicly announced in the Chinese press. In August 2017, corruption rumors emerged around two CMC members, Chief of the Joint Staff Fang Fenghui and Political Work Department Director Zhang Yang, when their names were not included on a list of representatives to the 19th Party Congress.[7] The list instead contained a surprising percentage of first-time delegates from the PLA, by some accounts up to 90 percent. These developments suggest that leadership does not intend to slow down military anti-corruption efforts anytime soon; instead, anti-corruption measures are likely to have an enduring impact on all aspects of military life, including promotions.[8]

The Central Military Commission

The new CMC reflects the themes of Xi's tenure thus far. It was slimmed down from 11 to 7 members and retained a civilian chairman (Xi), two military vice chairmen, the defense minister, and the directors of the Joint Staff and Political Work Departments. The new structure added the secretary of the PLA's Discipline Inspection Commission, while the leaders of the Logistics Support Department, Equipment Development Department, navy, air force, and Rocket Force were removed. This structure and the backgrounds of the new elites provide some insight into the Party's considerations for military leadership selection and its goals for the PLA during the next 5 years and beyond.

Analyzing the New Leadership

Much can be said about the structure and membership of China's new CMC, but it is evident that it aligns closely with Xi's three-pronged agenda for the military: "follow the command of the Party, build capability to win battles, and maintain a fine work style."[9] Although many will argue that cutting the CMC from 11 to 7 seats and displacing the service chiefs and half of the former general departments from the body reflect yet another example of Xi's personal drive to consolidate all authority under himself, a stronger case can be made that it enhances efficiency, decisionmaking, and clarifies roles in a much more effective way in the wake of ongoing structural reforms.

Atop a body of 15 CMC entities is now a smaller leadership core that can serve as an advisory body and focus more succinctly on oversight and issuing guidance to an overhauled PLA. The CMC leadership reflects the priorities that Xi views as most essential and is better positioned to ensure the success of the ongoing structural reforms. This is technically the smallest CMC since the 1930s, but it looks very similar to the 1982 body that Deng Xiaoping brought out of the bloated Cultural Revolution era and streamlined to the needs of the coming era.[10] The CMC leadership structure was the last piece of the PLA not touched by reforms, and its new membership finally reflects the PLA's shift into a new command structure. Analysts assessed the CMC would either become a larger Politburo-like body bringing on all the service chiefs, five theater commanders, and heads of new CMC departments, or become smaller and push some of its former responsibilities down. With their missions shifting to focus on administration, the services were bumped off the CMC, and it is now clear that logistics and equipment development are viewed as important yet secondary enablers compared to operations, Party affairs, and ensuring accountability and loyalty in the force.[11]

The new high command with Xi sitting unchallenged at its apex is well-balanced between an old guard of three CMC veterans and an inbound group of three newcomers who have seen their careers fast-tracked during Xi's tenure. For the first time, the top PLA officer did not rise up through the ground forces, but has been at the forefront of a modernizing military that has taken on an increasingly joint appearance. A decade ago it would have been unthinkable for a Rocket Force commander to become China's primary face for external engagement, but Wei Fenghe was named China's defense minister during the National People's Congress in March 2018. Finally, the easily dismissed resonance of the CMC having two "war heroes" with rare combat experience and the elevation of the Discipline Inspection Commission (led by a Rocket Force star) could not more clearly signal Xi's priorities for a military he wants to be "world class" by 2050.[12]

The Old Guard: Precursor to a New Era

Vice Chairman Xu Qiliang (born 1950/CMC member since 2007). The PLA Air Force (PLAAF) fighter pilot could have been pressed to retire after serving two-full CMC terms. On the cusp of hitting the informal "seven up, eight down" retirement norm, Xu is the first officer to serve this length on the high command since former Vice Chairman Chi Haotian. Xu is the PLAAF golden boy who always was the youngest, fastest rising officer in his cohort. Younger than his successor, Ma Xiaotian, he has made a career of hitting "firsts" within China's modernizing force. It was in 2004 when the service chiefs were first elevated to the CMC that Xu and former navy commander Wu Shengli were the first non–ground force officers named as deputy chiefs to the then–General Staff Department. This gave them the requisite grade level for promotion to the CMC and clarified their designation as the heirs-apparent to lead their services. During the course of his five-decade military career, Xu has been in the vanguard of a rapidly evolving PLA, reflecting reform and modernization priorities put forward by Jiang Zemin, Hu, and now Xi. It is only apropos that this military prodigy who joined the PLA at age 16 and achieved milestones in so many areas of joint representation should become the PLA's top officer today.

According to his official biography, Xu was born March 1950 in Linqu, Shandong. He trained at three of the PLAAF's aviation schools to become a pilot in the late 1960s. During the early 1980s, he served in the PLAAF's 4th Army Air Corps and was chief of staff (COS) of its Shanghai base. After attending the basic course at China's National Defense University (NDU) from 1986 until 1988, Xu was transferred to the 8th Army Air Corps in Fuzhou where he ultimately became its commander from 1990 to 1993. Xu took his first staff job in 1993 when named as a deputy COS of PLAAF headquarters, a corps-level assignment, and then as COS from 1994 to 1999. Xu was transferred to the Shenyang Military Region (MR) in 1999, where he was dual-hatted as a deputy MR commander and as the PLAAF MR air force commander until 2004. In June 2004, he was promoted to become a deputy chief of the General Staff Department (GSD) for 3 years before being named commander of the PLAAF and CMC member in 2007.[13]

Xu, like all in the new CMC lineup, received some higher education. He consistently pursued educational opportunities throughout his career including coursework at the Air Force Command College and four separate study stints at China's NDU.[14] Although not a combat veteran, one source suggests his air force unit may have mobilized in 1979 in Guangxi in support of the war against Vietnam.[15]

Although much has been made of (and speculated about) Xu's ties to Xi Jinping, his air force career really started to take off during Jiang's tenure and, according to some reports, with the direct help of Deng ally and PLA stalwart, Zhang Zhen. Zhang, who was charged by Deng to oversee the establishment of NDU in 1985, apparently took a liking to Xu when Xu was in the first class of the basic course at the school with other rising cadre like future PLAAF Commander Ma Xiaotian and Deputy Chief of the PLA General Staff Zhang Qinsheng. It was during Zhang's tenure as CMC vice chairman (1992–1997) that Xu was transferred out of the Nanjing MR to PLAAF headquarters to help lead air force operations, first as a deputy COS and then as COS. During Hu Jintao's 8 years atop the military, Xu became the first air force officer to join the GSD leadership, after which Hu selected him over more senior competitors to helm the PLAAF and to join the CMC.[16]

Xu probably developed some ties to Xi Jinping in Fuzhou between 1990 and 1993 when Xi was the Party chief of the city and Xu was COS and later commander of the 8th Army Air Corps. At the time, Xi served concurrently as the Fuzhou military district's first Party secretary. It is not clear to what extent they remained in touch afterward, and Xi probably would not have been well positioned to support Xu until decades later. More likely, Xu's rise came from his stellar reputation as a first-rate fighter pilot, serving for decades in units across from Taiwan, who embodied the skills and leadership traits that Chinese leaders were looking for in building a modern air force.

He reached the rank of major general by age 41 and was voted as an alternate member of the CCP Central Committee at age 44, the same year he was named PLAAF headquarters COS. On his watch, the PLAAF undertook some it most critical modernization efforts and emerged as a force aligned to support China's evolving national security interests. Viewed as a young innovator by several top civilian and military leaders, Xu even caused ripples in 2009 for his reported advocacy for the air force to develop both defensive and offensive space warfare capabilities and his belief that the eventual militarization of space was inevitable.[17]

Xu, in his role as CMC vice chairman during the past 5 years, has overseen at least two of Xi's top priorities for the PLA: cleaning up the force and implementing the largest structural reorganization since the 1980s. Since

2012, Xu has headed the CMC Leading Group for Inspection Work, giving him responsibility for monitoring discipline inspection, judicial, auditing, and supervision.[18] Xu also was tasked as the point person for implementing the reform plan as the executive secretary of the CMC Leading Group for Military Reform.[19] Regardless of any previous ties to Xi, he clearly has earned Xi's trust as his top military aide.

Vice Chairman Zhang Youxia (born 1950/CMC member since 2012). Zhang, the princeling perhaps best known for his family connections to Xi, has taken a relatively modest profile since his elevation to the high command 5 years ago. First as the head of the General Armament Department and then as head of its post-reform version, the Equipment Development Department, Zhang appears to have quietly but successfully pressed ahead in meeting objectives for China's weapons modernization program. The rare PLA officer who can tout combat experience, even in the less than complex battle environment along the Sino-Vietnamese border, he is arguably the PLA's most experienced operator after nearly 50 years split between command postings in the Chengdu MR in China's rugged southwest and since the mid-2000s in the Beijing and Shenyang MRs.[20]

Appointed to the CMC in 2012, the low key Zhang has shown little to corroborate the claims in some media sources that he is Xi's "sworn brother" and staunchest ally on China's top military body.[21] Notwithstanding the credibility of reports about his enduring family connections to Xi, Zhang, like Xu, probably benefited just as much from the support of Hu Jintao and military patrons from previous generations, including the disgraced former CMC Vice Chairmen Guo Boxiong and Xu Caihou. In fact, the launching point for Zhang's rise was his transfer to be a deputy commander in the Beijing MR in 2005, years before Xi had a toehold in either the Party or military leadership. It was also during Hu's tenure that Zhang was elected to the Party's Central Committee in 2007 and that same year given the trusted post of commander of the Shenyang MR bordering the Korean Peninsula.[22] Xi probably would only have been positioned to indirectly help Zhang until 2010, when he was named to the CMC as the first civilian vice chairman under Hu. Notably, other princelings with rumored ties to Xi such as Liu Yuan, Zhang Haiyang, and Liu Yazhou all retired when they reached the requisite age.

Zhang was born in Weinan, Shaanxi Providence, according to his official biography.[23] Like Xu, he attended the basic course at the PLA Military Academy (the precursor to NDU) and attained a junior college education early in his career. Zhang served nearly three decades in command posts in the 14th Group Army (GA) near Kunming in the Chengdu MR. After taking additional training in combined arms operations at NDU in the mid-1990s, Zhang moved to the 13th GA near Chongqing, where from 1994 to 2005 he served as deputy commander and then commander. Picked by leaders in Beijing for greater things, he was sent to the Beijing MR as a deputy commander in 2005 before serving a full 5-year term as Shenyang MR commander in advance of joining the CMC in 2012.[24]

We do not know what part Zhang's family connections may have played in advancing his career, but he has longstanding ties to Xi's family and many others associated with the revolution. Zhang's father, Zhang Zongxun, led the PLA General Logistics Department in the 1970s and commanded the Northeast Army Corps (or First Field Army) in 1947 when Xi's father was its political commissar. Both Zhang and Xi are Shaanxi natives and second-generation revolutionaries with family who were later purged in the Cultural Revolution. At the same time, Zhang made a name for himself early, when at the age of 26, as a company commander, he led his unit into combat during the border war with Vietnam in the late 1970s and in later skirmishes in the 1980s.[25] His service in three different MRs gave him a wide-ranging background in critical security issues such as Tibet, China's sometimes lawless southwest border, capital defense, and North Korea. Since 2012, in leading the PLA's weapons development and acquisition programs he has emphasized civil-military integration and emerging issues such as space and lunar exploration.[26] Relatedly, Chinese press claims he attended the first class focused on high-tech training at the National University of Defense Technology in 1998.[27]

Minister of National Defense Wei Fenghe (born 1954/CMC Member since 2012). As with all officers rising through the secretive Second Artillery Force (now the PLA Rocket Force), we have only modest details on Wei Fenghe's background and career.[28] The nuclear officer rose to prominence in late 2010 when he was named as the first Second Artillery Force officer to fill one of several prestigious posts as a deputy chief of the General Staff Department. The promotion to the GSD—giving him the requisite grade increase needed for promotion to the CMC—all but guaranteed his later promotion to commander of his service in 2012.

According to several official and unofficial biographical sources, Wei was born in Liaocheng, Shandong Province. He reportedly has served in a variety of command posts associated with China's nuclear forces. For example, he may have risen through the 54th Base located near Luoyang, serving as COS from 2001 to 2002. Prior to that, he served in an unidentified brigade as COS then as its commander between 1990 and 1994. He then led the 53rd base near Kunming until 2004.[29] In 2004, he was named to the leadership of the Second Artillery headquarters as a deputy COS before taking the COS post in 2006. Wei was promoted to the rank of major general in 2004, lieutenant general in 2008, and general after joining the CMC in 2012.[30] During several periods of his career, he took time to pursue educational and training opportunities. For example, he attended the Second Artillery Command Academy from 1982 to 1984 and NDU in 2006 and in 1997–1999 for full-time study.[31]

Like Xu Qiliang and the air force, Wei has served at the forefront of the Rocket Force's growing representation across the PLA, taking on responsibilities never previously available to officers from his service. As the youngest deputy among the GSD leadership, Wei spent substantial time supporting China's military-to-military relations with other nations. From late 2010 until the fall of 2012, he was involved in extensive foreign engagement both at home and abroad including supporting CMC Vice Chairmen Guo Boxiong and Xu Caihou, as well as then-defense minister Liang Guanglie. In fall 2011, Wei joined Guo on a trip to Cuba, Colombia, and Peru and traveled with Xu to Mongolia in May 2012.[32] In June 2011, Wei joined Liang as a "key member" of the PLA delegation to the Shangri-la Dialogue in Singapore.[33]

It is unclear how well Xi Jinping knew Wei before 2012, though Xi's first promotion as CMC chairman was promoting Wei to general. Under Xi, Wei and fellow Rocket Force officers Zhang Shengmin and Gao Jin have risen to unprecedented seniority in the PLA hierarchy. Heading two services and holding two of the six seats on the new CMC, the once backwater missile men have arrived.

The New Guard: Bridging the Past and Future

Joint Staff Department Chief Li Zuocheng (born in 1953/CMC member since 2017). Perhaps more a late riser than a newcomer, Li was promoted to chief of the Joint Staff Department in late August 2017, replacing Fang Fenghui. He rose to prominence in 1979 as the company commander who successfully led an offensive again Vietnamese forces during a month-long battle along the border. Li sustained multiple injuries and was later awarded the honorific title of "Combat Hero" by the CMC for his bravery.[34] The distinction apparently also earned him a seat on the dais as part of the 12th Party Congress presidium at age 29 in 1982.[35]

Li made major general in 1997 but saw little movement with his career until 2008, when he was transferred out of the Guangzhou MR after four decades to become a deputy commander of the Chengdu MR. In 2009, he was promoted to lieutenant general, appearing to benefit from the support of then-CMC Chairman Hu Jintao and top military leaders, even though he did not make the cut for selection to the Central Committee. However, Li has seen his career take off during Xi's tenure.[36]

Born in Meicheng, Hunan Province, Li received an undergraduate degree in Marxist theory and graduate degree from NDU later in his career. During the fight that made him famous in 1979, he reportedly captured four enemy personnel along with enemy supplies. Li rose through the 41st GA in Guangxi in the Guangzhou MR and was named the unit's commander in 1998. From 2002 to 2008, he served as a deputy COS of the Guangzhou MR before his transfer to the Chengdu MR. After his combat exploits, he developed a reputation as a skilled administrator who successfully oversaw several disaster relief efforts, such as responding to massive flooding in Guangxi in 1994 and along the Yangtze River in 1998.[37]

After 5 years as a deputy commander, Li was promoted to Chengdu MR commander in July 2013 in the first notable shuffle of senior military personnel under Xi. Along with Li, 31st GA veteran Wang Ning was named a GSD deputy chief and Song Puxuan was appointed NDU commandant. None of these officers were members of the Central Committee, suggesting Xi was already seeking to advance the careers of officers outside established PLA leadership circles.[38] Li's career also appears to have risen in parallel with Eastern Theater Commander Liu Yuejun. Both officers come from Guangxi and fought in the Sino-Vietnamese war, then served together in the 41st GA.[39]

Until his promotion to the high command, Li's biggest achievement—and a signal that Xi viewed him as having potential for greater things—was his appointment as the inaugural commander of the new PLA Army headquarters, established after top-level organizational reforms were announced in December 2015. This followed his promotion to general earlier that summer.[40]

It is clear that Xi and Chinese leaders value the symbolism of Li's war hero status and his reputation as an experienced veteran who has seen the reality of combat. At the same time, Li brings to his new role a plethora of more practical experiences from his decades commanding units in China's rural southern and western regions. His tenure in Chengdu from 2008 to 2015 gave him a leading role in disaster relief campaigns and managing ethnic unrest. He almost certainly played a key part in the response to the uprisings in Tibet in 2009 and the Sichuan earthquake in 2010.[41] According to Xinhua and local news reports, Li also helped facilitate the Chengdu MR's involvement in the 2010 Mission Action mobility exercise where units crossed through multiple MRs on a deployment that extended 2,000 kilometers.[42] Li has also authored works on civil-military integration, an important element in Xi's military strategy.[43]

Li probably also would have had some association with former CMC member and Political Work Department head Zhang Yang (who committed suicide in November 2017 while under investigation for corruption), as they both spent decades in the Guangzhou MR. This speaks to the difficulty of understanding why some officers have been targeted even as their peers have risen.

Political Work Department Director Miao Hua (born 1955/CMC member since 2017). A clear Xi favorite among the next generation of military leaders, Miao is one of only two members of the new CMC who is eligible to serve another term on the military's top body starting in 2022, if retirement norms hold. Miao is the first among an elite group of officers who earned their spurs toiling in the 31st GA in the Nanjing MR near Xiamen. Under Xi, with his close association to that area, Miao and others, like Wang Ning and new PLA Army Commander Han Weiguo, have seen their careers fast-tracked. Miao, born in Fuzhou, is a career political officer who spent almost his entire tenure in the Nanjing MR, including stints as the political department director of the 31st GA (1999–2005) and political commissar (PC) of the 12th GA.[44]

In late 2010, Miao was transferred to the Lanzhou MR to serve as the director of the political department. The timing notably coincided with Xi's appointment that fall to the CMC. In mid-2012, Miao was promoted to a deputy PC of the Lanzhou MR and secretary of its discipline inspection commission. In July 2012, he was made the MR's PC. Considering that the Lanzhou MR was long seen as Guo Boxiong's powerbase, Miao may have had a role in supporting the investigation against Guo and removing remnants of his influence in the region. Miao was made major general in 2001 and then lieutenant general in 2012. He was a member of the larger Central Discipline Inspection Commission body overseen by Wang Qishan from 2012 to 2017. He has a bachelor's degree in project management from the National University of Defense Technology.[45]

Miao was among the dozens of senior PLA leaders who in April 2014 published articles in the same paper pledging loyalty to Xi.[46] A political track officer from the ground forces, Miao was transferred in late 2014 to the PLA Navy to serve as its PC.[47] The move appears similar to others like Wang Ning's crossover to become the People's Armed Police (PAP) commander, which may reflect Xi's placement of trusted outsiders in service headquarters to monitor and clean up malfeasance and fix lingering issues with graft. Reflecting his candidacy for CMC elevation, Miao was promoted to the rank of admiral in mid-2015 alongside others who have benefited from Xi's trust, including Li Zuocheng, Wang Ning, and Song Puxuan.[48]

Discipline Inspection Commission Secretary Zhang Shengmin (born 1958/CMC member since 2017). Arguably the most surprising and impactful move in the unveiling of the new CMC and its membership was the elevation of the newly appointed head of the PLA's Discipline Inspection Commission, Zhang Shengmin. Zhang is the youngest member of the high command and, alongside Miao, he is well-positioned to serve two terms through at least 2027. Hailing from Shaanxi Province like Xi and Zhang Youxia, his 42 years in the PLA represent the shortest tenure among his CMC peers.

As with his Rocket Force counterpart Wei Fenghe, Zhang's career details are shrouded in mystery. According to an unofficial biography from Phoenix News and other reports, Zhang got his start in the Lanzhou MR before taking a staff officer post in the then–General Political Department's General Office. Starting in 2004, in just a decade, he served in senior political posts at four separate missile bases (Bases 55, 53, 56, and 54) across China. During one of those years, Zhang served as the PC of the Rocket Force Command College. By late 2014, Zhang was leading the political department of the then–Second Artillery Force headquarters.[49]

Despite his diverse career spanning multiple bases and MRs, in recent years no other officer has benefited more from the top-level changes necessitated by the reform effort than Zhang. His positioning as a rising star probably helped beforehand from major shuffles in a number of top positions in the Second Artillery in 2014 and 2015, possibly spurred by corruption concerns and moves to remove the lingering influence of Xu Caihou and Guo Boxiong.[50] The late 2014 shuffle appeared to be focused on the navy, Second Artillery, PAP, senior PLA academies, and the Beijing MR. The personnel overhaul represented the first time that all senior officers at the MR-leader level were born after 1950.[51] The changes also included a number of transfers and swaps of posts that probably were conducted in place with an eye on 2017 and the revamped military leadership structure. For example, among those moving alongside Zhang were Gao Jin, Miao Hua, and Wang Ning—some of whom were on their second posting within a year. This was the first tangible sign that Xi and his top military deputies were intent on resetting the promotion lineup in the coming years.[52]

Zhang has served in several newly created posts since the PLA was reorganized in late 2015. In just 2 years, his status has soared as he was first named the inaugural PC of the new CMC Training and Administration Department in early 2016, then only a few months later in October was reassigned to replace Xi ally and anti-corruption champion Liu Yuan as the new CMC Logistic Support Department PC.[53] The move coincided with a number of other top-level changes in the navy and among the political officer corps. In March 2017, not even a year later, Zhang was elevated again to become the PLA's top graft-buster as the secretary of the Discipline Inspection Commission. This was part of another sweeping personnel overhaul that saw dozens of senior officers step down from their posts.[54]

The elevation of the PLA's Discipline Inspection Commission to the CMC aligns its prestige to that of its parent organization, the Central Discipline Inspection Commission, whose leaders serve on the Politburo Standing Committee. It also tracks with the bolstering of the PLA's inspection, judicial, and audits mechanisms since 2012, including giving them the authority and imprimatur of Xi and other CMC leaders. Zhang, with his CMC seat and sitting atop a department with responsibilities now viewed on par with operations and Party matters, should have a freer hand to institutionalize the military's anti-corruption processes and use his 10 roving inspection teams to ensure that PLA officers are following Xi's exhortation to "conduct themselves well."[55] In January 2018, Xinhua announced that full-time inspection teams will start supervising Party members at and above the corps level, including organizations under the CMC, underscoring a continued emphasis on discipline through Xi's second term.[56]

Outlook and Implications

Xi's work report at the opening of the 19th Party Congress called for the PLA to perfect its new post-reform joint command system in the face of "profound changes" in China's security environment. This may have caused leaders to opt for modest continuity in the midst of historic organizational change for the military. Despite rumors to the contrary before the congress, the leadership stuck with its decade-long practice of maintaining two uniformed vice chairman posts and did not appoint a potential successor to Xi as a civilian vice chairman.[57] Similar to the civilian transition, the final results of the CMC turnover appear to reflect a balanced lineup of relatively clean, competent, and loyal officers with diverse career experiences. The age 67 norm was also upheld on the military side, with older generals such as Fan Changlong stepping down and Vice Chairmen Xu Qiliang and Zhang Youxia, both 67, selected to serve on the Politburo through 2022.

Retaining a mix of seasoned veterans while injecting new blood into the CMC is not unusual, yet it suggests Xi wants to maintain momentum on military reforms as he cultivates a diverse generation of talented leaders. Xi's friendship and decades-long familiarity with the two vice chairmen also affords him trusted, capable officers he can rely on during a pivotal time for China's rise—a major contrast to the adverse circumstances Hu Jintao faced when dealing with Jiang Zemin's appointees in the Guo Boxiong and Xu Caihou era.[58] In addition to spending years together in China's coastal provinces and overlapping with Xi on the CMC since 2010, Xu Qiliang was an early, vocal proponent of the military's reform efforts even before serving as Xi's top deputy on the PLA reform leading group. Zhang Youxia in his former role embraced calls for improved civil-military integration and technological development, two of Xi's top priorities for the coming years outlined in his marathon speech during the congress. Furthermore, the combat experiences of Zhang and Li Zuocheng, albeit dated, will prove valuable in setting an example if hot spots flare up on China's periphery during their tenures.

Wei Fenghe, who was named defense minister in March 2018, is no stranger to foreign engagement and is well-postured to serve as the face of China's military diplomacy abroad. In addition, Li Zuocheng's selection represents a refreshing change compared to the old-school officers formerly responsible for PLA operations. His relative youth and combat experience, combined with his recent tenure as the first army service chief, prepare him to address readiness issues precipitated by reform implementation. In the next few years, he should be able to apply these lessons learned by translating Xi's guidance to the PLA and prepare to "fight and win."

Finally, Miao Hua's transfer from navy headquarters to run political affairs and Zhang Shengmin's elevation to oversee PLA discipline strongly imply the anti-corruption campaign has become further institutionalized at the highest levels of the military and is likely to become ingrained for years to come. The success of Miao and Zhang in their respective posts will be vital if Xi hopes to complete a once-in-a-generation cultural shift in the PLA.

The new lineup, however, still leaves observers with some important questions. For example, it remains to be seen how the absence of service chiefs on the CMC will affect operational decisionmaking, particularly during a crisis. It is also unclear how and from whom Xi intends to receive service-specific advice during CMC gatherings or through which venues the service chiefs will advocate for service priorities in acquisitions. However, the new leaders previously occupied top positions in the services, which probably made this change more palatable. Relatedly, it is unclear how a CMC that appears to be more joint, at least symbolically, will practically improve the military's ability to conduct joint operations in the timeline Beijing has unveiled. In reality, this transition probably will take several years, if not decades.

We also do not know what, if any, political concessions or compromises were hammered out in the deliberations about the CMC. From a management perspective, the choice to have a smaller CMC membership overseeing an expanded CMC organization with 15 disparate organs seems counterintuitive. The leaders probably will have to rely on the CMC General Office more than ever if they hope to coordinate across a sprawling bureaucracy, arbitrate disputes over missions and resources, and implement troop cuts in the coming years. To this end, Xi has named Zhong Shaojun, a civilian and trusted advisor who has worked closely with Xi for more than a decade, to lead the General Office. In 2012, when Xi became CMC chairman, he picked Zhong to lead his personal office and gave him the rank of senior colonel.[59] Previous Chinese leaders Jiang Zemin and Hu Jintao also kept an eye on the PLA by appointing confidantes to the General Office, but the large-scale changes afoot in the military arguably make Zhong's job more complicated than it was for his predecessors.

The removal of Fang Fenghui and Zhang Yang unveiled the first investigations during Xi's tenure into members of the CMC and sends a strong message to younger leaders about a new level of scrutiny in promotions and new expectations for officers at all echelons. The generals' downfall affected the final outcome, as both were eligible to remain on the CMC.[60] In addition, the dramatic revelations about Zhang's suicide and Fang's investigation punctuated an overhaul of military representatives in the Central Committee to include new and younger officers. In fact, according to Cheng Li of the Brookings Institution, the congress may have been the "largest-ever turnover of military elite in the history of the PRC."[61] This generational change probably affected associates of Zhang, Fang, and the old guard, and signals that the anti-corruption campaign in the PLA is far from over.

If Xi's exhortations to the PLA during the 19th Party Congress are any indication, the new military leadership has a challenging agenda to accomplish. With a new leadership team in place, Beijing is well-poised to address its goals for modernizing and reforming the PLA to address future security challenges. The congress produced one of the smallest leadership lineups in the PLA's history and enshrined the CMC Chairman Responsibility System into the Party's constitution, reflecting the culmination of Xi's efforts to centralize the CMC's authority—and his own—over the entirety of the armed forces. This should make Xi even better poised to push his priorities for the PLA than at the start of his tenure. What remains to be seen is what Xi will do with that added authority over an increasingly capable and global military. However, there is little doubt Xi and his generals emerged in a stronger position to steer the PLA toward fulfilling its part in the "great rejuvenation" of the Chinese nation.

Notes

[1] "Hu Jintao, Xi Jinping Attend Enlarged Meeting of Central Military Commission, Deliver Important Speeches" [胡锦涛习近平出席中央军委扩大会议并发表重要讲话], Xinhua [新华], November 17, 2012, available at <http://politics.people.com.cn/n/2012/1117/c1024-19611030-1.html>.

[2] Lim Yan Liang, "Xi's Reforms Have Reshaped, Modernized Military," *Straits Times* (Singapore), October 12, 2017, available at <www.straitstimes.com/asia/xis-reforms-have-reshaped-modernised-military>.

[3] Zhang Hui, "Party Commands the Gun: Xi," *Global Times* (Beijing), November 3, 2014, available at <www.globaltimes.cn/content/889686.shtml>; "The Work System Must Be Made Stricter and More Realistic—Discussion Three on Putting Great Efforts into Strengthening the Building of the Various Levels of Party Committee Leading Groups" [工作制度要进一步严起来实起来——三谈大力加强各级党委班子建设], *PLA Daily* [解放军报], January 28, 2015, available at <www.81.cn/jmywyl/2015-01/28/content_6325633.htm>.

[4] Xiang Bo, ed., "Chinese Military Takes Solid Steps Toward Strong Army over 5 Years: Xi," Xinhua, July 31, 2017, available at <www.xinhuanet.com/english/2017-08/01/c_136490561.htm>.

[5] A concept first introduced under Jiang Zemin.

[6] Minnie Chan, "China Has the World's Biggest Military Force, Now Xi Jinping Wants It to Be the Best," *South China Morning Post* (Hong Kong), October 19, 2017, available at <www.scmp.com/news/china/diplomacy-defence/article/2115968/xi-orders-massive-military-shake-meet-threats-worlds>.

[7] Zhang committed suicide in November 2017, and it was announced in January 2018 that Fang is under investigation for "giving and taking bribes." Chris

Buckley, "Chinese General under Investigation, Joining a Line of Fallen Commanders," *New York Times*, January 9, 2018, available at <www.nytimes.com/2018/01/09/world/asia/china-general-corruption.html>.

8   Rowan Callick, "PLA Purged in Roll Call for Party Congress," *The Australian*, September 29, 2017, available at <www.theaustralian.com.au/news/world/pla-purged-in-roll-call-for-chinese-communist-party-congress/news-story/7232f77e3fc39a3fde4f4990ce16963d>.

9   "Xi Calls for Building a Strong Army," Xinhua, October 26, 2017, available at <www.xinhuanet.com/english/2017-10/26/c_136708142.htm>.

10   David Shambaugh, "The Pinnacle of the Pyramid: The Central Military Commission," in *The People's Liberation Army as Organization: Reference v. 1.0*, ed. James C. Mulvenon and Andrew N.D. Yang (Arlington, VA: RAND, 2002), 95–121.

11   Phillip C. Saunders, "Alternative Models for the Central Military Commission," *China Brief* 17, no. 3 (October 20, 2017), 18–22.

12   "Full Text of Xi Jinping's Report at the 19th CPC National Congress," Xinhua, November 3, 2017, available at <www.xinhuanet.com/english/special/2017-11/03/c_136725942.htm>; Liu Zhen, "Xi Jinping Shakes Up China's Military Leadership . . . What Changes at the Top Mean for World's Biggest Armed Forces," *South China Morning Post* (Hong Kong), October 26, 2017, available at <www.scmp.com/news/china/diplomacy-defence/article/2116856/what-changes-top-mean-chinas-military>; "Xi Calls for Building a Strong Army."

13   "Xu Qiliang—Member of the Political Bureau of CPC Central Committee," Xinhua, October 25, 2017, available at <www.xinhuanet.com/english/2017-10/25/c_136705645.htm>.

14   Ibid.

15   Chin Chien-Li [今千里], "One of the Key People in Chinese Communist Combat Operations against Taiwan: Biography of Xu Qiliang" [中共副总参谋长许其亮中将评传], *Frontline* [前哨], vol. 172 (June 1, 2005), 71–75.

16   Minnie Chan, "General Xu Qiliang: How a Chinese Air Force Top Gun Shot to the Top of the Military," *South China Morning Post* (Hong Kong), October 25, 2017, available at <www.scmp.com/news/china/diplomacy-defence/article/2116939/general-xu-qiliang-how-chinese-air-force-top-gun-shot>.

17   Ibid.; Peter Foster, "Space Arms Race Inevitable Says Chinese Commander," *The Telegraph*, November 2, 2009, available at <http://www.telegraph.co.uk/news/worldnews/asia/china/6486030/Space-arms-race-inevitable-says-Chinese-commander.html>.

[18] "The CMC's 10 Inspection Groups to Strengthen Oversight Duties," *Ta Kung Pao* [大公报], July 28, 2017; Tan Xiaolin and Yin Hang [谭晓林, 尹航], "Xu Qiliang Addresses PLA Meeting on Army Inspection Organs" [许其亮在军队巡视机构成立暨巡视干部培训会议上强调], *PLA Daily* [解放军报], November 19, 2013.

[19] "Report: Xi Jinping Presides over the First Meeting of the CMC Leading Group for Deepening Defense and Military Reforms" [习近平主持召开中央军委深化国防和军队改革领导小组第一次全体会议强调], Xinhua [新华], March 18, 2014; Cao Zhi and Li Xuanliang [曹智, 李宣良], "Military Affairs Column: At a Meeting on the Work to Reform the Size, Structure, and Organization of the Armed Forces Held by the Central Military Commission" [中央军委军队规模结构和力量编成改革工作会议], Xinhua [新华], December 3, 2016.

[20] "Zhang Youxia—Member of the Political Bureau of CPC Central Committee," Xinhua, October 24, 2017, available at <www.xinhuanet.com/english/2017-10/25/c_136705654.htm>.

[21] Minnie Chan, "General Zhang Youxia: Xi Jinping's 'Sworn Brother' Now His Deputy on China's Top Military Body," *South China Morning Post* (Hong Kong), October 25, 2017, available at <www.scmp.com/news/china/diplomacy-defence/article/2116936/general-zhang-youxia-xi-jinpings-sworn-brother-now-his>.

[22] "Zhang Youxia."

[23] Ibid.

[24] Ibid.

[25] Chan, "General Zhang Youxia."

[26] Ibid.

[27] Jia Xiping, Xi Qixin, and Qiu Wenwei, "Generals Learn about High Technology—Sidelines on First All-Army High-Tech Knowledge Training Class for High-Ranking Cadres," Xinhua [新华], June 14, 1998.

[28] Based on precedent, Wei almost certainly will replace Chang Wanquan as minister of national defense and state councilor at the National People's Congress's next session in spring 2018.

[29] "Wei Fenghe" [魏凤和], *Baidu* [百度], available at <https://baike.baidu.com/link?url=CxbqTHamQvrlVYp4hyOLN8iDcR8YFlOdHoFRFMOOV-8CaQC4p5-E8oi3adY6FMKN6FHSYBhTGvNyhPqmEniJA0sAgSxffr3sbwssEL-NVSZj2hjH5NN2cfPCIwgrXtZag7>.

[30] "Second Artillery Chief of Staff Wei Fenghe Promoted to PLA Deputy Chief of General Staff" [二炮原参谋长魏凤和升任解放军副总参谋长], *Sina.com*, January 15, 2011, available at <http://dailynews.sina.com/gb/chn/chnpolitics/

sinacn/20110115/16192163540.html>; "Wei Fenghe," *China Vitae*, available at <http://chinavitae.com/biography/weifenghe>.

³¹ Wei Fenghe biography [魏凤和简历], March 19, 2018, available at <http://www.xinhuanet.com/politics/2018lh/2018-03/19/c_1122560874.htm>; "Wei Fenghe"; Minnie Chan, "'Reticent' General Wei Fenghe Could Be China's New Defense Minister, Sources Say," *South China Morning Post* (Hong Kong), February 24, 2018, available at <www.scmp.com/news/china/diplomacy-defence/article/2134555/reticent-general-rockets-ranks-central-military>; Mark Stokes and Russel Hsiao, "China's Second Artillery Leadership," *The Diplomat*, October 1, 2011, available at <https://thediplomat.com/2011/10/chinas-second-artillery-leadership/>.

³² "Chinese Central Military Commission Vice Chairman Guo Boxiong Leaves Beijing on Official Goodwill Visit to Cuba, Colombia, Peru," *PLA Daily* [解放军报], October 25, 2011; "Chinese Central Military Commission Vice Chairman Xu Caihou Leaves Beijing on Official Goodwill Visit to Mongolia," *PLA Daily* [解放军报], May 10, 2012.

³³ "Chinese DM to Attend Shangri-La Dialogue to Boost Regional Security Cooperation," Xinhua, June 3, 2011, available at <www.china-embassy.org/eng/gdxw/t828180.htm>.

³⁴ Zhao Lei, "PLA Promotes Three Officers to Top Posts," *China Daily* (Beijing), September 8, 2017, available at <www.chinadaily.com.cn/cndy/2017-09/08/content_31716930.htm>.

³⁵ Chen Baocheng [陈宝成], "Li Zuocheng Promoted to Chengdu Military Region Commander" [李作成升任成都军区司令员], *Caixin* [财新], August 6, 2013, available at <http://china.caixin.com/2013-08-06/100565903.html>.

³⁶ "Xi Jinping Molds Military Brass to His Image," *Nikkei Asian Review*, September 2, 2017, available at <https://asia.nikkei.com/Politics-Economy/Policy-Politics/Xi-Jinping-molds-military-brass-to-his-advantage>.

³⁷ Yu Dong, Pan Mengqi, and Zhao Liangmei [于冬, 潘梦琪, 赵良美], "Officers Born in the 1950s Take Over the Leadership of All Military Regions" [大军区正职 "50后" 接棒], *Southern Weekend* [南方周末], August 9, 2013, available at <http://www.360doc.com/content/13/0809/10/1427567_305791174.shtml>; "Hong Kong Report: Li Zuocheng in Charge of Chengdu Military Region" [港报: 李作成掌成都军区 七大军区高层调整完成] China News Service [中国新闻网], July 10, 2013, available at <http://www.chinanews.com/mil/2013/07-10/5023939.shtml>; "Li Zuocheng Named Central Military Commission Joint Staff Department Chief" [李作成任军委联合参谋部参谋长], *Southern Metropolis Daily (Shenzhen)* [南方都

市报(深圳)], August 27, 2018, available at <http://news.163.com/17/0827/00/CSQA-JVSR000187VE.html>; Chen, "Li Zuocheng Promoted to Chengdu Military Region Commander"; "Li Zuocheng," Phoenix News Media, August 27, 2013, available at <http://renwuku.news.ifeng.com/index/detail/231/lizuocheng>; "Li Zuocheng," *China Vitae*, available at <http://chinavitae.com/biography/Li_Zuocheng/full>.

[38] Ma Haoliang [馬浩亮], "Intensive Reshuffle of 20 High-Ranking Military Officers" [20位高級將領密集履新], *Ta Kung Pao* [大公报], August 2, 2013; Choi Chi-Yuk, "War Hero Li Zuocheng Appointed to Top PLA Post," *South China Morning Post* (Hong Kong), July 11, 2013, available at <www.scmp.com/news/china/article/1279850/war-hero-li-zuocheng-appointed-top-pla-post>.

[39] Choi, "War Hero Li Zuocheng."

[40] Zhao, "PLA Promotes Three Officers to Top Posts."

[41] Minnie Chan, "Leaner Lineup Unveiled at Top of Military Machine," *South China Morning Post* (Hong Kong), October 25, 2017, available at <www.scmp.com/news/china/diplomacy-defence/article/2117004/xi-jinping-rolls-out-leaner-top-line-chinas-military>.

[42] Liu Yonghua and Zhu Yingtao [刘永华, 朱映涛], "Military Units and Supplementary Units of the Chengdu Military Region Participating in the 'Mission Action 2010' Conduct Three-Dimensional Long-Distance Delivery" [使命行动 2010 成都军区参演部队及配属分队向演习地域展开远程立体投送], Xinhua [新华], October 15, 2010; Zao Meihua [遭美华] et al., "Whole Division Successfully Completed Forced Crossing of the Yellow River with All Operation Elements" [某师整建制全要素成功强度黄河], *Zhanqi Bao* [战旗报], October 20, 2010.

[43] Li Zuocheng [李作成], "Several Important Thoughts on Pushing Forward the Integration of People's Air Defense Building and Socioeconomic Development Systems" [推进人民防空建设融入经济社会发展体系的几点思考], *National Defense Journal* [国防杂志], July 2012, 4–7.

[44] Ma Haoliang [馬浩亮], "Five Admirals Assume New Offices at the PLA Navy Headquarters" [海軍總部五將軍履新], *Ta Kung Pao* [大公报], December 28, 2014; "Miao Hua," Phoenix News Media, December 25, 2014, available at <https://web.archive.org/web/20150907010024/http://renwuku.news.ifeng.com/index/detail/972/miaohua>; "Miao Hua," *China Vitae*, available at <www.chinavitae/biography/miaohua>; "Who Is Miao Hua, China's Youngest General?" China News Service [中国新闻社], August 4, 2015, available at <http://news.china.com/jiedu/20150804/>.

[45] "Miao Hua"; "After Reform, the Positions of the Four Members of the Central Military Commission Were Adjusted One by One; Miao Hua Succeeded

Zhang Yang as Director of the Political Work Department" [军改后中央军委四名委员职务先后调整，苗华接替张阳出任政治工作部主任], *Shanghai Observer* [上观新闻], September 7, 2017, available at <www.jfdaily.com/news/detail?id=64325>; "Who Is Miao Hua, China's Youngest General?"

46 "PLA Senior Generals Reaffirm Support for Xi," *PLA Daily* [解放军报], April 18, 2014, available at <www.chinadaily.com.cn/china/2014-04/18/content_17446318.htm>.

47 "Miao Hua."

48 "China Promotes 10 Officers to General," Xinhua, July 31, 2015, available at <www.xinhuanet.com/english/2015-07/31/c_134469023.htm>.

49 "Detailed Personnel Information," Phoenix Network [凤凰网], March 1, 2016, available at <http://renwuku.news.ifeng.com/index/detail/1077/zhangshengmin>; "Comrade Zhang Shengmin's Biography" [张升民同志简历], China Central Commission for Discipline Inspection [中国中央纪律检查委员会], November 29, 2017, available at <www.ccdi.gov.cn/xxgk/ldjg/zsm/201711/t20171129_113916.html>; Choi Chi-yuk, "China Names New Political Commissar of PLA Logistics Department," *South China Morning Post* (Hong Kong), October 19, 2016, available at <www.scmp.com/news/china/policies-politics/article/2028999/china-names-new-political-commissar-pla-logistic>.

50 "Trusted Followers of Xu Caihou, Guo Boxiong Are Removed from Leading Posts in the Capital Region and in the Second Artillery in the Reshuffles on an Unprecedented Scale" [京畿二炮将领空前大洗牌徐才厚郭伯雄亲信遭踢走], *Ming Pao* [明报], January 3, 2015; Mao Haoliang [马浩亮], "Six Generals of Second Artillery Corps Assume New Posts, Political Work Posts Reshuffled" [而炮六将履新政工岗位易人], *Ta Kung Pao* [大公报], January 4, 2015, available at <http://news.takungpao.com/paper/q/2015/0104/2876888_print.html>.

51 Ge Chong [葛冲], "Overseas Returnee Bai Jianjun Appointed Beijing MR Deputy Commander: Major Reshuffle of PLA Generals Involves General Staff Organs, Navy, and Academy of Military Science" ["海归" 白建军任北京军区副司令解放军将领大调整涉总部机关海军军科院等], *Wen Wei Po* [文汇报], January 7, 2015, available at <http://paper.wenweipo.com/2015/01/07/CH1501070006.htm>.

52 Ao Lei [敖雷], "Changes Come to Nearly 50 Military Region Deputy Commander Grade Positions" [近50副大军区岗位易将], *Hong Kong Commercial Daily* [香港商报], January 16, 2015, available at <www.hkcd.com/content/2015-01/16/content_903117.html>; Suburo Tanaka, "Large-Scale Reshuffling of High-Ranking PLA Officers, Promotions of Young Officers All Stemming from Rooting Out of

Corrupt Officers, as Central Military Commission Chairman Xi Jinping Strives to Build a 'Fighting Army,'" *Gunji Kenkyu*, June 2015, 182–195.

[53] Suburo Tanaka, "Establishment of PLAA Headquarters, Transformation from Military Regions to Theater Commands, Second Artillery Upgraded to a 'Service,' Formation of 'Strategic Support Force,'" *Gunji Kenkyu*, May 2016, 66–77; Choi, "China Names New Political Commissar of PLA Logistics Department."

[54] Minnie Chan, "Xi Jinping Appoints New Man to Tackle PLA Corruption," *South China Morning Post* (Hong Kong), March 2, 2017, available at <www.scmp.com/news/china/diplomacy-defence/article/2075243/china-replaces-top-general-charge-tackling-military>.

[55] "Stronger Discipline Inspection System of the PLA" [軍紀委十大紀檢組加強監督], *Ta Kung Pao* [大公报], July 29, 2017; Cao Siqi, "Xi Stresses Combat Capabilities, Party Building in Military," *Global Times* (Beijing), October 18, 2017, available at <www.globaltimes.cn/content/1070900.shtml>.

[56] "China's Armed Forces to Set Up Full-Time Inspection Teams," Xinhua, January 17, 2018, available at <http://en.people.cn/n3/2018/0117/c90000-9316193.html>.

[57] Minnie Chan, "Xi Jinping Clears Decks for Top-Level Changes to China's Military," *South China Morning Post* (Hong Kong), October 3, 2017, available at <http://www.scmp.com/news/china/diplomacy-defence/article/2113054/xi-jinping-clears-decks-top-level-changes-chinas>.

[58] Chan, "General Zhang Youxia."

[59] Choi Chi-yuk, "Young Guns Including Xi Jinping's Top Military Aide Expected to Move Up the Ranks," *South China Morning Post* (Hong Kong), September 13, 2017, available at <www.scmp.com/news/china/diplomacy-defence/article/2110742/young-guns-including-xi-jinpings-top-military-aide>.

[60] Minnie Chan, "Xi Jinping Rolls Out Leaner Top Line-Up for China's Military Machine," *South China Morning Post* (Hong Kong), October 26, 2017, available at <www.scmp.com/news/china/diplomacy-defence/article/2117004/xi-jinping-rolls-out-leaner-top-line-chinas-military>.

[61] Cheng Li, "Why China's Military Facelift Ahead of the Party Congress Could Be a Sign of Bigger Changes," Brookings Institution blog, October 10, 2017, available at <www.brookings.edu/blog/order-from-chaos/2017/10/10/why-chinas-military-facelift-ahead-of-the-party-congress-could-be-a-sign-of-bigger-changes/>.

PART V

INTEGRATING WITH SOCIETY

CHAPTER 15

KEEPING UP WITH THE *JUNDUI*

Reforming the Chinese Defense Acquisition, Technology, and Industrial System

By Tai Ming Cheung

X i Jinping has established strong control over the People's Liberation Army (PLA) since becoming its commander in chief and the
country's paramount leader in 2012. He has used this authority
to press ahead with an ambitious and bone-crunching reform agenda to
make the defense establishment more politically loyal, less corrupt, and
better able to fight and win future wars.

One area of particular attention for Xi is the defense acquisition, technology, and industrial (DATI) system, which covers the defense technology
and industrial apparatus and PLA agencies overseeing acquisition matters.
The central goal of these reforms is to transform the DATI system from a
predominantly absorptive development model toward a system better able
to engage in original higher end innovation. Among the key requirements
necessary for this upgrading are building a more advanced R&D base,
developing an operating culture that is more risk-tolerant, greater market
competition, and closer integration between the civilian and military segments of the national economy. This chapter examines the reforms that are
currently taking place within the Chinese DATI system and what can be
expected in the near-, medium-, and long-term future.

The State of the Chinese Defense Industry in the Mid-2010s

The Chinese defense industry in the mid-2010s is enjoying a golden age of record revenues and profits. Driven by leadership concerns of mounting challenges to the country's external security environment and rapid advances in the global technological order, investment into research, development, and acquisition has soared, greater efforts are being made to acquire and absorb foreign technologies, and the existing defense innovation system is being remade.

This has resulted in significant improvements in technological, economic, and industrial performance. The country's 10 major state-owned defense corporate groups, which together control the defense industry's six sectors, have enjoyed nearly double-digit annual growth in revenues and profits over the past decade. Between 2004 and 2015, total profits of the big 10 increased from Rmb 15 billion to Rmb 120 billion (see figure 1). The ordnance, space, electronics, and aviation industries were the most profitable sectors, while the shipbuilding industry has struggled because of a severe global downturn. While the robust expansion of the defense industry is a bright spot amid slowing growth in the rest of the Chinese economy, its future prospects depend on continuing defense budget increases that now appear to be slowing. The rate of increase for the 2016 defense budget was only 7.6 percent, which may mark the end of the double-digit budget increases that began in the early 1990s.[1]

However, the official defense budget represents only one source of funding for the defense industry, which has access to funding and resources from a diversified array of sources. Funding for defense-related research and development, for example, comes primarily from other areas of the central government budget, most notably those allocated to the State Administration for Science, Technology, and Industry for National Defense (SASTIND), which is not included in the official defense budget. Moreover, around half of the defense industry's revenue and profits comes from civilian business, and in some sectors like ordnance and nuclear this could be as high as 80 to 90 percent.[2] In addition, since 2013, the defense industry has

Figure 1. Financial Performance of the Chinese Defense Industry, 2004–2015

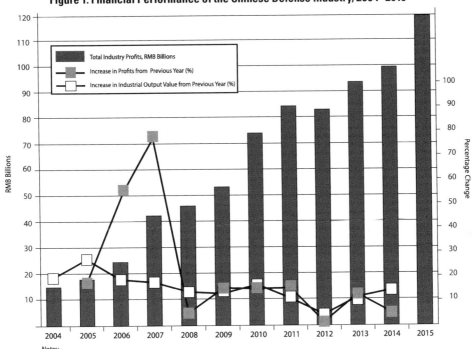

Notes:
Total profit data is incomplete for 2014. No 2014 figure was available for CNEC as of March 1, 2016.
Total profit data is incomplete for 2015. No 2015 figures were available for CNEC and CSIC as of March 1, 2016.

Sources: Information obtained from annual reporting of the 10 defense corporations. See also *China Civil-Military Integration Development Report 2015* [中国军民融合发展报告2015] (Beijing: National Defense University Press [国防大学出版社], 2015), 61.

been allowed to seek investment funding from capital markets that provide access to large pools of financial resources, including shareholder funds, bank loans, and bonds, which will be discussed later in this chapter. These different sources will allow the defense industry to mitigate the impact of slowing official defense budget increases.

The aviation sector, for example, is simultaneously engaged in the development or production of more than half a dozen combat and transport aircraft. The shipbuilding industry has at least four active nuclear and conventional submarine programs along with research, development, and construction of aircraft carriers, destroyers, and numerous other surface warships. The PLA Navy is estimated to have laid down, launched, or commissioned more than 60 naval ships and smaller craft in 2014 alone, with the same number expected in 2015.[3]

An important new trend is also becoming apparent in the performance of the shipbuilding industry. Until the mid-2000s, Chinese naval shipyards relied heavily on the importation of foreign, primarily Russian, technology transfers for their industrial development. As Chinese shipbuilders absorbed these transfers, they have been able to substantially reduce their foreign reliance in the past decade. The U.S. Office of Naval Intelligence (ONI) notes that since the beginning of the 2010s, the PLA Navy's "surface production shifted to platforms using wholly Chinese designs and that were primarily equipped with Chinese weapons and sensors (though some engineering components and subsystems remain imported or license produced in country)."[4] These include the *Jiangkai*-class (Type 054A) frigate series, *Luyang*-class (Type 052B/C/D) destroyer series, and the upcoming new cruiser (Type 055) class, which ONI considers to be "comparable in many respects to the most modern Western warships."[5]

The space and missile industry has also been among the leaders in promoting technological self-reliance in the defense industry. Chinese authorities were especially keen to signal the industry's potency in offensive missile capabilities at a military parade in September 2015 to celebrate the 70th anniversary of the end of World War II, with more than half a dozen short-, medium-, and long-range ballistic missiles and cruise missiles on display. These included the DF-15B short-range ballistic missile, DF-21D and improved DF-26 medium-range antiship ballistic missiles, and DF-5B and DF-31A intercontinental ballistic missiles.

The accelerating pace of output of the Chinese defense economy is taking place at the same time as it is confronted with deep-seated structural problems. The principal constraints and weaknesses that the Chinese defense economy faces stem from its historical foundations and the uncertain efforts to overcome the corrosive legacy of its difficult past. The institutional and normative foundations and workings of the Chinese defense industry were copied from the former Soviet Union's command defense economy and continue to exert a powerful influence.

The PLA and defense industrial regulatory authorities are seeking to replace this outdated top-down administrative management model with a more competitive and indirect regulatory regime, but there are strong vested interests that do not want to see any major changes.

High-Level Leadership Support

High-level and sustained support and guidance from Chinese Communist Party, state, and military leadership elites have been essential in the defense industry's transformation efforts. Leadership backing and intervention have been vital in addressing entrenched bureaucratic fragmentation, ensuring adequate resource allocations, and tackling chronic project management problems. Without high-level leadership engagement, much of the recent progress of the defense industry probably would not have happened.

Leadership involvement in the defense industry often occurs through small groups and special committees. The committed involvement of the country's top leaders is especially critical, and the DATI system has been fortunate that Xi Jinping has taken a keen and active interest in defense science, technology, and innovation issues. Between November 2012 and October 2016, Xi took part in more than 30 publicly reported events related to PLA and DATI issues, which is considerably higher than his predecessors such as Hu Jintao or Jiang Zemin (see figure 2). Activities that signal his interest on defense S&T issues include:

■ Inspection of the Liaoning aircraft carrier and J-15 carrier fighter plant in Liaoning Province in September 2013: within his first year as Central Military Commission (CMC) chairman, Xi made a high-profile visit to tour the Liaoning aircraft carrier in Dalian and look at the progress in the development of the J-15 fighter aircraft at Shenyang Aircraft Corporation. This was a clear demonstration of Xi's keen interest in China's naval airpower capabilities.

Figure 2. Publicly Reported Visits to Military and Defense Science and Technology–Related Facilities by Xi Jinping, November 2012–October 2016

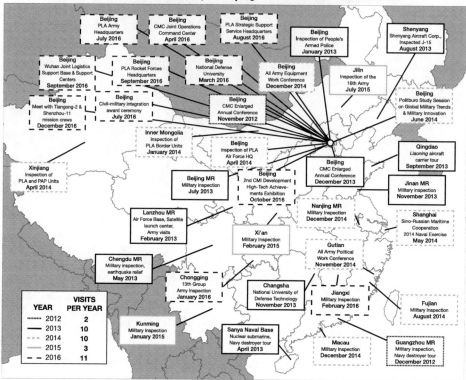

- Tour of National University of Defense Technology in Changsha, Hunan, in November 2013: Xi has emphasized on his military visits that the defense science and technology (S&T) establishment's duty is to serve the needs of warfighters. He noted during an inspection at the National University of Defense Technology, the military's leading high-tech R&D establishment, that the work of defense scientists and engineers should be "closely linked with real combat and army service."[6] This fits with Xi's calls to the PLA to strengthen its preparations for "military struggle," which means enhancing combat readiness.

- Convening a Politburo study session on military innovation: Xi chaired a study session of the full Politburo in August 2014 devoted to the examination of global trends in military innovation. Xi pointed out that a global revolution in military S&T affairs is currently taking place "at a speed so fast, in a scope so wide, at a level so deep, and with an impact so great that it has been rarely seen since the end of World War II."[7] Xi stated this represented both a challenge and opportunity that required China's defense establishment "to vigorously promote military innovation."

■ Keynote speech at the All-Army Armament Conference in Beijing in December 2014: With the leaderships of the PLA's armament apparatus and defense industry in attendance, Xi affirmed the "historical achievement" in the PLA's weapons development, and urged accelerating the pace of construction. He emphasized the importance of "unifying thinking" and "gathering consensus," which may have been hints of policy differences over the Third Plenum reform issues.

Preparing for the Next Stage of Defense Industrial Advancement

The Xi administration signaled its intention to carry out a major overhaul of the defense industry as part of an ambitious national program of economic and military reforms at the Third Plenum of the 18th Party Congress in 2013. A flurry of activity since then by defense industrial decisionmakers has produced new medium- and long-term defense industrial development strategies, plans, and institutional arrangements that collectively represent a potentially key turning point in the defense industry's evolution from an innovation follower to becoming an original innovation leader.

The reform planning effort began in earnest in March 2014 when the CMC established a leading group on national defense and military reform. This group was headed by Xi Jinping and acted as the command headquarters for designing reform plans, coordinating work among different departments, and implementing policy.[8] The leading group conducted more than 800 forums and seminars involving 690 military units. After almost 2 years of investigation, a reform plan titled the Proposal on Deepening Defense and Military General Reform Plan was approved at the leading group's third meeting in July 2015. The plan was subsequently released at the CMC Working Conference on Reform in November 2015, which marked the formal start of the implementation of the most far-reaching structural reform of the PLA in its history.[9]

While the reforms focused on the PLA's central management, military regions, and services, they also had important implications for the armament management system, which plays a highly influential role in defense science, technology, and industrial matters. At the end of 2015, the PLA's armament system underwent a far-reaching reorganization:[10]

- The PLA General Armament Department (GAD) was reorganized into the CMC Equipment Development Department (EDD) [*zhuang-bei fazhan bu*, 装备发展部] and given responsibility for "centralized unified management" [*jizhong tongguan*, 集中统管] of the military armament system.[11] One of the now-defunct GAD's chief roles was to oversee the armament development of the ground forces. GAD units responsible for this function have been transferred to the newly created PLA Army headquarters.
- The GAD Science and Technology Committee was elevated to a commission-level rank reporting directly to the CMC and renamed as the CMC Science and Technology Committee (CSTC) [*kexue jishu weiyuanhui*, 科学技术委员会].

Although it will take some time before these reforms are fully implemented and can be adequately assessed, some initial speculative thoughts can be offered. First, the promotion of the CSTC from the GAD to the CMC demonstrates that Chinese military authorities, especially Xi, are serious about engaging in higher end science, technology, and integration (STI) activities and establishing a high-level coordinating mechanism through the CSTC to provide operational leadership and guidance. Lieutenant General Liu Guozhi, who was the GAD S&T Committee director, will lead the CSTC. He has spent much of his career engaged in high-tech R&D. Liu has a doctorate in physics from Tsinghua University, is a member of the Chinese Academy of Sciences, and has technical expertise in accelerator physics and high-power microwave technology.[12]

Second, the ability of the EDD to carry out its mandate of providing centralized management of the armament system looks to have a greater chance of success than the GAD, which was hamstrung by its institutional bias toward the ground forces. The nature of the relationship between the EDD and the armament departments belonging to the service arms will be critical in determining how much jointness versus compartmentalization will be present in PLA armaments development. The authority and influence of the EDD initially benefited from the appointment of GAD Director General Zhang Youxia as its head. Zhang reportedly has close ties with Xi through princeling-related links and was subsequently promoted to be a CMC vice chairman in October 2017.[13] The new EDD director is Lieutenant General Li Shangfu, who spent much of his career working in the space launch system before serving as a deputy director of the GAD and then as a deputy director of the Strategic Support Force.[14]

In parallel, the state defense industrial bureaucracy formulated new strategies and plans for a less ambitious but still significant adjustment to the defense industry as well as to chart its medium- and long-term transformation. One of these key plans is the 13th Defense Science, Technology, and Industry Five Year Plan (13th Defense S&T FYP). This plan was issued at the beginning of 2016 and sets out six key tasks through 2020:

- facilitating leapfrog development of weapons and military equipment
- enhancing innovation capabilities in turnkey areas
- improving overall quality and efficiency
- optimizing the structure of the defense industry and vigorously promoting civil-military integration (CMI)
- accelerating the export of armaments and military equipment supporting national economic and social construction
- supporting national economic and social construction.[15]

Compared to its predecessor, the 13th Defense S&T FYP has a stronger focus on the development of high-tech weaponry and civil-military integration. It also signals a significant shift in the direction of defense industry development from absorption and reinnovation to greater emphasis on original innovation. The 13th FYP also shows that China is seeking to build on the inroads it has been steadily making in the international arms market.

Chinese arms sales have almost doubled over the past 5 years, according to the Stockholm International Peace Research Institute.[16] China now supplies arms to 37 countries, with three-quarters of the exports to customers within the Asia-Pacific region, led by Pakistan, Bangladesh, and Myanmar.[17]

A longstanding Achilles' heel of the Chinese defense industry being addressed by defense planners is a lack of higher end manufacturing capability. In 2015–2016, SASTIND put together the Defense S&T Industry Strong Basic Engineering Project 2025 that is aligned closely with the national-level Made in China 2025 Advanced Manufacturing Plan aimed at lifting the overall level of the country's industrial equipment manufacturing base and curtailing excessive dependence on foreign core technology and products. The defense industry features prominently in the Made in China 2025 plan, especially in the space and aviation sectors.[18]

In a further signal of Chinese leaders' efforts to chart a long-term course for the country's defense S&T development, SASTIND announced in June 2015 that it was establishing a defense S&T Development Strategy Committee to conduct research and provide policy input that would help the country's leadership in its decisionmaking on long-term defense R&D over the next 20 to 30 years. The key goals of this committee are to implement the Communist Party leadership's strategic decisions and plans; focus on strategic, comprehensive, and forward-looking studies; and provide policy recommendations and consultation on defense S&T development and innovation.

This Development Strategy Committee is headed by the SASTIND director and its membership features many prominent figures in the Chinese national and defense scientific community, including 10 academicians from the Chinese Academy of Sciences and Chinese Academy of Engineering.[19] In addition, there are officials from a range of other governmental agencies such as the National Development and Reform Commission, Ministry of Education, Ministry of Science and Technology, Ministry of Finance, and PLA armament units.

Targeting Breakthroughs in Core Technological Capabilities

Another trend in the Chinese national and defense S&T system in the Xi era is a stronger emphasis on making breakthroughs in core technological capabilities, also referred to as turnkey technological capabilities. A key reason behind the focus on promoting breakthrough science and technology is Xi Jinping's belief in the critical role of advanced technology in enhancing China's competitiveness and acquiring international political power. Xi has commented that the previous IDAR (introduction, digestion, assimilation, and reinnovation) development strategy pursued by Hu Jintao's administration is no longer as effective today, since it has become much more difficult and often impossible for China to purchase core technologies from foreign countries. Those technologies can only be developed through original innovation.[20]

Hand in glove with this shift, in 2016 the Chinese leadership formally promulgated an "innovation-driven development" strategy, which aims to strengthen the country's original innovation capacity and enable China to move up the innovation ladder.[21] Identifying and making breakthroughs in turnkey technology areas is a key component of this new development strategy.

At the 5th Plenum in November 2015 that discussed the 13th FYP, Xi Jinping stressed that there must be more "serious prioritization" of "technological innovation in key sectors and implementation of important technological projects that affect the national big picture and long-term future"—a point he has made previously in multiple other venues. Xi also called for China to pursue an asymmetric strategy to catch up with developed countries, stating that "China should develop its own strengths and explore 'asymmetric' measures in core technologies that would otherwise be unlikely for China to catch up by 2050. More efforts should be put into these critical, bottleneck fields."[22]

A number of technological fields have been designated as turnkey for short-, medium-, and long- term development, and this is reflected in the selection of major projects. In his speech at the National Science and Technology Conference in June 2016, Xi confirmed that China has decided to speed up implementation of 16 megaprojects, such as high-end all-purpose chips, integrated circuit equipment, broadband mobile communication, high-grade numerical machinery, nuclear power plants, and new drugs.[23] Many of these projects were included as high-priority developments in the 2006–2020 Medium- and Long-Term Science and Technology Development Plan.

Additionally, China is adding a new round of megaprojects that "embody national strategic intentions" with a timeframe of achieving breakthroughs in the industries by 2030. This new initiative is part of a new program called Science, Technology, and Innovation 2030 that was announced in the national 13th FYP. Projects selected for this program include aero-engine and gas turbines, quantum communication, information network and cyber security, smart manufacturing and robotics, deep-space and deep-sea exploration, key materials, neuroscience, and health care. To support this initiative, the Ministry of Science and Technology (MOST) requested proposals for its new National Key Research and Development Program in early 2016 in fields that are aligned with the 2030 Program.

Chinese authorities also announced plans in 2015 to establish large-scale national laboratories modeled on U.S. and foreign entities such as Los Alamos and Lawrence Berkeley national laboratories to support the pursuit of breakthroughs in big science endeavors. Xi Jinping has pointed out that "national laboratories are important vehicles in which developed countries seize the high ground in technological innovation."[24] For China, these national laboratories are viewed as critical platforms to accelerate fundamental and applied research that will enable it to reach the global frontier.[25]

The idea to establish national laboratories dates back to 2000, when MOST started an experiment to build seven national laboratories over 3 years.[26] Progress was very slow, however, and only two laboratories in Shenyang and Qingdao were established. Despite measured initial progress made by those pilot national laboratories in improving China's innovation capability, their future prospects are unclear because of unstable financial support and divided opinions about the contributions of the laboratories to basic research.

However, as the new national laboratories initiative is labeled a key priority in the 13th FYP and has Xi's strong endorsement, this situation is expected to change. Xi stated that China

> urgently needs to establish comprehensive integrated national laboratories of greater dimensions and greater cooperation among disciplines, driven by national objectives and strategy and aimed at international technological frontiers to optimize the distribution and arrangement of talent and material resources and form a new structure of coordinated innovation.[27]

A series of national laboratories will be established in new sectors that create "important strategic innovation power that can take the international technological high ground."

As such, the old development model for pilot national laboratories will be abandoned. According to MOST officials, a new development plan is being drafted where MOST, the Ministry of Education, Chinese Academy of Sciences, and Chinese Academy of Engineering jointly study the national laboratory construction plan and the Ministry of Finance and the National Development and Reform Commission work on institutional mechanisms.[28] Though it is still too early to tell where this initiative will lead, the building of national laboratories will "represent major transformation of China's R&D system," according to Chinese Academy of Sciences president Bai Chunli.[29]

The new national laboratories will be significantly different from the existing pilot laboratories, both in scope of focused areas and development model. Instead of targeting single subjects, the new national laboratories will be multidisciplinary and will work in both civilian- and defense-related fields. It is not yet clear which technological sectors these national laboratories will be focused on, but if they are modeled on the U.S. system, then high-tech weapons R&D may be an important consideration. In addition to these national laboratories, SASTIND has called for building defense laboratories and defense science, technology, and industry innovation centers to further support China's national defense S&T innovation system.[30]

Vigorously Promoting Civil-Military Integration

CMI has been promoted in China since the early 2000s but with little tangible success because of limited leadership engagement, unclear strategy, ineffective implementation, and weak civil-military coordination. Despite the weak progress, Chinese civilian and military authorities see CMI as essential in the drive for original innovation and defense modernization.

Efforts to promote CMI have focused primarily on reforms of state-owned defense conglomerates and on the implementation of policies, platforms, and other mechanisms by which private-sector technology can flow smoothly into defense projects.[31] Each of the half a dozen sectors that make up the Chinese defense industry is controlled by one or two defense corporations. Efforts to promote competition in the late 1990s by dividing these monopolistic behemoths into competing entities were largely a failure because of poor institutional design. Consequently, Chinese authorities began to remerge these firms, especially so they could compete with much larger foreign firms on the global arms market. This began in the late 2000s with the consolidation of the aviation sector, but there was a long hiatus before the next merger took place at the beginning of 2018 between the two principal firms in the nuclear sector, China National Nuclear Corporation and China National Engineering Corporation. The shipbuilding industry appears next in line for restructuring as one of its two dominant conglomerates, China State Shipbuilding Corporation, has been adversely affected by a sharp downturn in the global civilian shipbuilding market.

The transfer of state-owned defense technology to the private sector also receives strong emphasis in the plan and is important to support China's "innovation-driven development" and the financing of China's defense industry. China's efforts to increase its high-tech industrialization through programs such as the Made in China 2025 plan also feed directly into CMI, and efforts have been made to coordinate these programs to emphasize areas that will directly benefit China's defense industry.

In 2007, Hu Jintao attempted to broaden CMI's scope and push for deeper implementation, although with only limited success. Ultimately, Hu's aim to implement "overall coordination" [*tongchou guihua*, 统筹规划] stalled due to persistent obstacles such as poor coordination among top-level decisionmaking bodies, insufficient regulatory structures to allow transfer of technology between civilian and military entities, poor intellectual property rights (IPR) protection, especially for defense industry–originated IPR, and lack of universal industry and technology standards across civilian and military sectors. While Hu's attempt at top-down leadership support should have been enough to catalyze CMI implementation, it proved insufficient to mobilize all the needed actors and agencies.

Two modest successes of Hu's push include broadening the thinking on CMI away from its former limited understanding of "combining the civilian and military sectors" [*junmin jiehe*, 军民结合] to an understanding more reflective of the deep implementation required through "integration of civilian and defense sectors"; and broadening the scope of CMI to include all available economic resources in the promotion of the defense industry, including capital, technology, human capital, facilities, and information.[32]

The Xi administration has made a renewed push to make CMI a viable policy tool. CMI has been relabeled as military-civil fusion (MCF) [*junmin ronghe*, 军民融合] to distinguish the new approach. To address deficiencies in the previous CMI strategy that was ad hoc, structurally misaligned, and of low policy importance, Xi designated MCF as a national priority in 2015 and defined it as a development strategy. According to Xi, a central goal of the MCF strategy is to build an "integrated national strategic system and strategic capabilities." The development of such a strategic system and capabilities will allow China to "implement key science and technology projects and race to occupy the strategic high ground for science and technology innovation."[33]

Key elements of this national strategic system are detailed in some of the MCF implementation plans that have been formulated since the adoption of the MCF strategy. This includes the 13th 5-Year Special Plan for Science and Technology MCF Development issued in 2017 by the CSTC and MOST. This plan detailed the establishment of an integrated system to conduct basic cutting-edge R&D in artificial intelligence, biotechnology, advanced electronics, quantum, advanced energy, advanced manufacturing, future networks, and new materials "to capture commanding heights of international competition."[34] This plan also noted the pursuit of MCF special projects in areas such as remote-sensing, marine-related technology, advanced manufacturing, biology, and transportation.

The political significance of MCF gained even more prominence with the formation of the "Commission for Integrated Civilian-Military Development" (CICMD) [*zhongyang junmin ronghe fazhan weiyuanhui*, 中央军民融合发展委员会] in January 2017. The importance of this organization in leading MCF policymaking and implementation was made clear with the appointment of Xi as its chair and Premier Li Keqiang as a vice chair. At the CICMD's first meeting in June 2017, Xi stated that there was a "short period of strategic opportunity" to implement MCF, pointing out the most fruitful areas that included infrastructure, equipment procurement, training, military logistics, and defense mobilization.[35] In its September 2017 meeting, the CICMD issued a series of plans and guidelines tied to the 13th Five Year Plan on MCF that covered defense industrial development and military logistics.[36]

Supporting High-Tech Defense Industrialization

The Chinese authorities are currently engaged in a comprehensive effort to boost advanced manufacturing capabilities in high-tech industries, of which defense and dual-use capabilities are a central priority. Led primarily by civilian agencies, this effort aims to support China's innovation-driven development strategy that focuses on broader economic growth. For the defense industry, directing China's overall plans to develop its high-tech industries with particular emphasis on CMI-related industries is a key factor that will enable it to produce innovation at higher levels.

Chief among China's actions to develop its manufacturing base is the Made in China 2025 plan issued in May 2015. The plan outlines a three-step strategy for China to comprehensively upgrade its industrial economy and achieve its goal of becoming a world-leading manufacturer by 2049.[37] The plan outlines policies to deepen institutional reforms, strengthen financial and tax support, complete a talent training system, and also introduces five sub-plans intended to facilitate government involvement when market mechanisms alone are insufficient.[38] The plan also prioritizes 10 industrial sectors for policy and funding support:

- new-generation information technology
- automated machine tools and robotics
- space and aviation equipment
- maritime equipment and high-tech shipping
- modern rail transportation equipment
- new energy vehicles and equipment
- power generation equipment
- agricultural equipment
- new materials
- bio-pharmaceutical and advanced medical products.

Close coordination took place between civilian and defense agencies in drafting the Made in China 2025 plan to emphasize CMI priorities, including space and aviation equipment, high-tech shipping, and new materials. SASTIND continues to be closely involved in the implementation of the plan. In June 2015, the State Council established a "State Strong Manufacturing Power Building Leading Small Group" [*guojia zhizao qiangguo jianshe lingdao xiaozu*, 国家制造强国建设领导小组] led by Vice Premier Ma Kai and administered by Ministry of Industry and Information Technology (MIIT) to oversee Made in China 2025. SASTIND Director Xu Dazhe sits as 1 of 20 representatives on the leading small group, as do many other leaders of major agencies with a vested interest in CMI development.[39] The body also directs the work of other subgroups, such as the " Manufacturing Power

Building Strategy Advisory Group" [*zhizao qiangguo jianshe zhanlüe zixun weiyuanhui*, 制造强国建设战略咨询委员会], which also includes SASTIND representatives, and is tasked with issuing a technical "green paper" every 2 years to act as an update to the 10 original sectors in the Made in China 2025 plan.[40] All indicators are that CMI-related industries will continue to receive priority attention in these plans. SASTIND is also preparing a Defense S&T Industry 2025 plan that will set additional goals toward development of CMI-related industries. Information on this plan has been scarce, but there is a large expectation that turbo-fan engines will receive significant focus.[41]

Outside of Made in China 2025, many additional efforts are being made to strengthen China's high-tech industrialization. One such industry receiving attention from many fronts is the integrated circuit (IC) industry, which has been the focus of a new State Council plan titled Guidelines on Developing and Promoting the National Integrated Circuit Indus-try,[42] a new leading small group named the "Leading Small Group for IC Industry Development" [*jicheng dianlu chanye fazhan lingdao xiaozu*, 集成电路产业发展领导小组],[43] and an approximately $25 billion National Integrated Circuit Industry Investment Fund.[44] MIIT's Special Action Implementation Program calls for creating military IC products and the promotion of civil-military IC production lines, and the 2016 SAP states that a Civil-Military Dual-Use Integrated Circuit Development Special Action Plan will be drafted along with a document outlining "high-level plans and programs" for the IC industry development in CMI areas.[45] These efforts—and continued movements as China deepens CMI imple-mentation—are intended to produce a defense R&D base more capable of sourcing prime technology domestically.

Restructuring the Defense Research Institute System

Although the Chinese defense industry has made significant progress tran-sitioning from centralized planning to a market-oriented modern enterprise system, one overlooked area has been the status of research institutes (RIs) that belong to or are affiliated with the big 10 defense corporations. While these RIs are a core component of the R&D capabilities of the defense firms, they are designated as "government-affiliated institutions" [*shiye danwei*, 事业单位], which means they are subject to state ownership restrictions and cannot be restructured into listed entities.

Many defense RIs have developed advanced technologies that are potentially lucrative and are viewed as cash cows by their parent defense corporations. For example, 30 percent of the profits of the China Shipbuilding Industry Corporation in 2014 reportedly came from its 28 RIs.[46] The barriers in listing defense RIs have become a major bottleneck for the defense industry's ongoing efforts to securitize their assets on the capital markets. Besides the ownership problem, the corporate restructuring of defense RIs has also run into difficulties in other areas. The issues include asset management, personnel placement, income distribution, social welfare, taxation, and secrecy considerations.

However, the restructuring of defense RIs is viewed as critical to overall efforts to reform the defense industry and to improve innovation capacity.[47] Consequently, in 2016, Chinese authorities began tackling defense RI reform and drafted a number of reform policies. These include the Scheme on Classification of Defense Research Institutes, Defense Research Institutes Classified Reform Implementation Plan, and Supporting Policies on the Restructuring of Defense Research Institutes under Public Institution Reform. In the latter document, SASTIND drafted a total of 31 policies on party-building, personnel placement, income distribution, social welfare, and security and secrecy issues.[48] In addition, defense RIs will be divided into three categories that will determine the nature of their ownership structures.[49] These proposals were then sent to the major defense corporations for comments, and it now appears that the long-awaited RI restructuring process may begin.[50] Defense corporations with the largest number of RIs, such as the two space and missile conglomerates China Aerospace Science and Technology Corporation and China Aerospace Science and Industry Corporation, will be allowed to take the lead in reform implementation.[51]

Chinese authorities hope that a successful restructuring of the defense RIs will be a colossal boost for the defense industry. Analysts argue that this will significantly promote innovation, optimize resource allocations, increase the efficiency in state investment, facilitate civil-military integration, and bring in more investment for defense R&D from the capital markets.[52]

In addition to the reform of the defense RI system, the country's civilian R&D apparatus is being overhauled to make it more capable and effective in producing higher end innovation. One major initiative is the consolidation of S&T plans operated by numerous state agencies into just five plans. This streamlining is intended to address structural problems such as duplication, nontransparency, and corruption that have caused widespread waste and inefficiency. Key plans that have or will be merged include the 863 Plan, the 973 Plan, and the National Science and Technology Infrastructure Plan that is managed by MOST. Research plans administered by the National Development and Reform Commission and MIIT will also be affected. The five new comprehensive S&T plans will be:

- National Natural Science Fund
- National Major Science and Technology Plan
- National Key R&D Project (NKRDP)
- Special Fund for Technology Innovation and the R&D Base
- Professional Special Plan.[53]

The NKRDP is by far the largest and most important of these five new plans and was officially established in February 2016. It is designed to be as wide-ranging and inclusive, supporting research and development in areas such as agriculture, health care, energy, environment, industrial competitiveness, innovation, and national security.[54] Unlike the legacy programs that the NKRDP replaces, which were divided according to their position on the R&D spectrum from basic research to engineering development, the new plan covers all phases from research to development and production with the goal of improving commercialization rates.[55] The other four remaining plans were expected to be launched at the end of 2016, although full-scale implementation was not scheduled until 2019.[56]

Leveraging Capital Markets for Defense Investment

The defense industry is being opened up to the capital markets, and the big 10 state-owned defense corporations are seeking to take advantage of the lucrative financial opportunities that this may offer for them to better manage and leverage their assets. With enough recent orders to keep production lines churning, a pipeline full of new generations of equipment under development, and plenty of high-level leadership support, the defense industry is attracting plenty of interest from a growing proliferation of domestic investment vehicles that has appeared in the past couple of decades, and especially in the past few years.

While defense companies have been allowed to list subsidiaries on stock markets in China and Hong Kong since the early 1990s, this was limited to their civilian operations. Chinese authorities—led by the Commission for Science, Technology, and Industry for National Defense—began to prepare defense firms to tap into the capital markets from the mid to late 2000s by establishing a regulatory framework to ensure a secure and orderly process (see table for details). Detailed procedures were promulgated in 2007 that emphasized three principles: allow nonpublic capital to enter the defense industry, encourage the defense industry to make increased use of capital markets, and encourage the defense industry to diversify investments and ownership.[57] An initial round of deals were allowed to take place in 2007 in the shipbuilding and aviation sectors.[58] Additional guidelines followed that encouraged further opening up to capital markets by the defense industry.

Table. State Guidelines Promoting Diversification of Investments and Use of Capital Markets by Defense Industry			
February 2007	Guiding Opinions from COSTIND Regarding Non-Public Ownership Economic Participation in Construction of Defense S&T Industry[1]	COSTIND	Encourage and guide non-public capital to enter defense S&T industries; encourage non-publicly owned enterprises through purchasing shares, shareholding, and mergers and acquisitions to participate in developing civil-military dual-use products that emphasize nonmilitary uses.
March 2007	Guiding Opinions Regarding the Development of Defense S&T Industry for Civilian Industry[2]	COSTIND	Fully utilize capital markets to promote industrial development; encourage introduction of capital into military and civilian enterprises through acquisitions, asset swaps, and joint ventures; encourage companies that sell military products approved for nonmilitary production to list.
March 2007	Certain Opinions Regarding Deepening Reform of Investment System for Defense S&T Industry[3]	COSTIND	Promote diversification of investment and ownership in defense S&T enterprises; expand investment from the social sphere in defense S&T industry to implement management of different classes divided into open, restricted, and prohibited classes.
May 2007	Guiding Opinions Regarding Promoting Shareholding System Reform for Defense S&T Industry[4]	COSTIND	Complete shareholding reform for qualified military industrial enterprises; diversify investments; promote the establishment of modern enterprise structures and modern ownership structures by military industrial enterprises.
November 2007	Interim Measures for Implementation of Shareholding Reform for Defense Enterprises[5]	COSTIND	Allow domestically listed companies to reacquire military industrial enterprises.
October 2010	Certain Opinions Regarding Establishment and Improvement of Civil-Military Integration of Weapons and Equipment Research and Production Systems[6]	COSTIND	Promote shareholding reform through asset restructuring, listing, mutual shareholding, mergers and acquisitions; actively and steadfastly promote the reform of military research institutes and actively promote the applied research institutes to restructure along the commercial basis; establish modern enterprise systems or convert into large corporate R&D centers.
March 2011	"Guiding Opinions Regarding Categorically Promoting Reform of Public Institutions"[7]	COSTIND	Promote the reform of public institution, and particularly for scientific institutions, promote the reform of production activities.
June 2012	"Implementation Opinions for Encouraging and Guiding Private Capital in Entering Defense Industries"	COSTIND	Encourage and guide private capital in entering defense industries; allow private companies to undertake R&D and production tasks for weapons and equipment; guide and support the involvement of private capital in restructuring of military enterprises; encourage private capital to undertake R&D for technologies fit for both military and civil uses.
August 2013	Rules for Defense S&T and Industry Fixed Assets Investment Program Management	COSTIND	Allow defense corporations to undertake large-scale share placements using military assets as securitization.
April 2014	Guidelines on Promoting Civil-Military Integration	COSTIND	Make new progress in giving private capital access to the defense industry.
January 2016	Related Issues for Non–State Owned Enterprises Applying for Military Industrial Fixed Assets Investment Programs	COSTIND	Outlines methods by which non–state owned actors can invest in fixed assets of defense industry.

Key: COSTIND: Commission for Science, Technology, and Industry for National Defense; CMC: Central Military Commission; R&D: research and development; S&T: science and technology; SASTIND: State Administration for Science, Technology, and Industry for National Defense.

Notes

[1] "Guiding Opinions from COSTIND Regarding Non-Public Ownership Economic Participation in Construction of Defense S&T Industry" [关于印发《非公有制经济参与国防科技工业建设 指南》的通知], Commission for Science, Technology and Industry for National Defense, People's Republic of China, August 8, 2007, available at <www.gov.cn/zwgk/2007-08/07/content_708284.htm>.

[2] "Guiding Opinions Regarding the Development of Defense S&T Industry for Civilian Industry" [《大力发展国防科技工业民用产业的指导意见》发布], Commission for Science, Technology and Industry for National Defense, People's Republic of China, March 2, 2007, available at <www.gov.cn/gzdt/200703/02/content_539623.htm>.

[3] "Certain Opinions Regarding Deepening Reform of Investment System for Defense S&T Industry" [《深化国防科技工业投资体制改革的若干意见》], Commission for Science, Technology and Industry for National Defense, People's Republic of China, March 5, 2007, available at <www.china.com.cn/policy/txt/200703/05/content_7905219.htm>.

[4] "Guiding Opinions Regarding Promoting Shareholding System Reform for Defense S&T Industry" [国防科工委 发展改革委 国资委关于推进军工企业股份制改造的指导意见], Commission for Science, Technology and Industry for National Defense, People's Republic of China, June 23, 2007, available at <www.gov.cn/gzdt/2007-06/23/content_658955.htm>.

[5] "Interim Measures for Implementation of Shareholding Reform for Defense Enterprises" [《军工企业股份制改造实施暂行办法》], Commission for Science, Technology and Industry for National Defense, People's Republic of China, November 21, 2007, available at <http://gov.finance.sina.com.cn/chanquan/2007-11-21/50173.html>.

[6] "Certain Opinions Regarding Establishment and Improvement of Civil-Military Integration of Weapons and Equipment Research and Production Systems" [国务院中央军委关于建立和完善军民结合寓军于民武器装备科研生产体系的若干意见], State Council and Central Military Commission, People's Republic of China, October 24, 2010, available at <www.jxgb.gov.cn/2011-1/20111111433114.htm>.

[7] "Guiding Opinions Regarding Categorically Promoting Reform of Public Institutions" [中共中央国务院关于分类推进事业单位改革指导意见], State Council, People's Republic of China, March 23, 2011, available at <www.gov.cn/jrzg/2012-04/16/content_2114526.htm>.

The initiative to allow firms to tap the domestic equity markets was curtailed by the 2008–2009 global financial crisis, and this hiatus continued into the early 2010s. As a consequence, many defense companies delayed undertaking management, financial, and other reforms, such as becoming shareholding entities that would allow them to issue shares to outside investors.

The situation changed in 2013 when SASTIND began to permit firms to issue share placements using military assets as securitization.[59] This opening up of the defense industry to investment from capital markets is part of a broader initiative by Chinese authorities to forge closer integration between the science and technology system and financial markets. Premier Li Keqiang stated in 2014 that:

it is necessary to increase the efficiency of science and technology innovations with institutional innovation . . . and let the market decide allocation of innovative resources. We should intensify financial support, guide more enterprises and social capital to increase input in research and development. We should pay particular attention to activating stock assets and enhance capital usage efficiency.[60]

China Shipbuilding Industry Corporation (CSIC) became the first defense firm to undertake a private share placement in September 2013 and raised Rmb 8.5 billion ($1.4 billion) from 10 Chinese parties to acquire production facilities to manufacture warships. More than one-third of the funds (Rmb 3.275 billion) was earmarked for the acquisition of medium- and large-sized surface warships, conventional submarines, and large landing ships, while Rmb 2.66 billion was designated for arms trade–related undertakings and civil-military industrialization projects, and the remaining Rmb 2.54 billion was allocated as working capital.[61] CSIC explained that the funds would "satisfy the development and manufacture of a new generation of weapons and equipment," adding that "we need urgent large-scale technological improvements and need to expand our financing channels."[62] Dalian Shipyard is one of the CSIC facilities that are slated to receive proceeds from the share placement, and it is reportedly China's first domestically designed aircraft carrier.[63]

All 10 big defense conglomerates have begun actively issuing public and private equity offerings and bond issuances, although to varying degrees. Total funds raised in public and private equity offerings between 2010 and June 2016 totaled nearly Rmb 207.6 billion ($31.14 billion), with most of these funds going specifically to military development projects. Funds raised decreased from 2010 to 2012, but have significantly increased annually thereafter. Funds raised in 2016 were expected to register a significant jump from 2015, as total funds raised in the first half of the year had already exceeded total funds raised in 2015 by Rmb 4.3 billion ($645 million).[64]

The shipbuilding and aviation industries raised by far the largest amount of funds, significantly dwarfing the other defense industrial sectors. Between 2010 and June 2016, the shipbuilding industry raised Rmb 63 billon ($9.45 billion) while the aviation sector brought in Rmb 65 billion ($9.75 billion). The space industry raised Rmb 31.9 billion ($4.79 billion), ordnance industry Rmb 27.1 billion ($4.07 billion), electronics industry Rmb 17.3 billion ($2.6 billion), and nuclear industry came last with Rmb 3.4 billion ($510 million). See figure 3.

Bond issues by defense firms were also substantial and totaled Rmb 211.5 billion ($31.73 billion) between 2010 and June 2016. Shipbuilding came first in total bonds raised during this period with Rmb 101.8 billion ($15.27 billion). Surprisingly, the nuclear industry came second with Rmb 40.8 billion ($6.12 billion). Space came in third at Rmb 20 billion ($3 billion),

Figure 3. Chinese Defense Corporate Equity Deals, 2010–June 2016

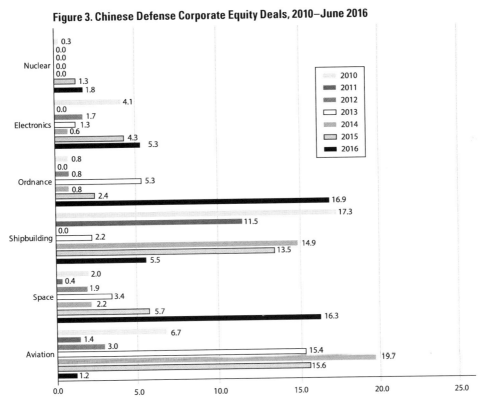

Figure 4. Chinese Defense Corporate Debt Issuances, 2010–June 2016

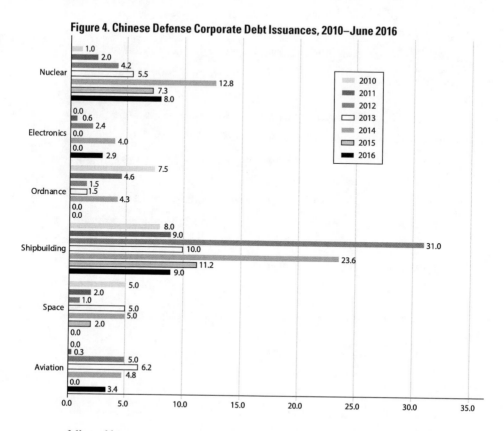

followed by aviation at Rmb 19.6 billion ($2.94 billion) and ordnance with Rmb 19.4 billion ($2.19 billion). Electronics came last with Rmb 9.9 billion ($1.49 billion). See figure 4.

Total equity and bond offerings between 2010 and June 2016 reached Rmb 419.16 billion ($62.87 billion), which is equivalent to 8.9 percent of the official Chinese defense budget total of Rmb 4.7 trillion ($704.39 billion) for the same period. See figure 5.

Defense corporations will be able to continue to raise large amounts from asset securitization deals and bond issues as well as from bank loans in the coming years. As of March 2016, the big 10 defense companies had 80 subsidiaries listed on China's stock exchanges, which accounted for around 25 percent of their total assets.[65]

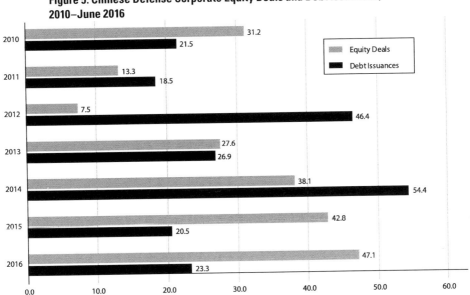

Figure 5. Chinese Defense Corporate Equity Deals and Debt Issuances, 2010–June 2016

Analysts estimate that if China follows the United States, which has around 70 percent of defense industrial assets listed, this could allow Chinese firms to raise upward of another Rmb 1 trillion of funds. Aviation Industry Corporation of China's Deputy General Manager Wu Xiandong stated, "Not all military industrial enterprises are suitable to marketize and undergo shareholder reform, but the vast majority are suitable."[66] As an example of the magnitude and speed of growth at which the Chinese firms may grow, the China Aerospace Science and Technology Corporation plans to triple its asset securitization rate from its current 15 percent to 45 percent by the end of the 13th Five-Year Plan.[67] Other defense conglomerates can be expected to strive toward similar growth.

Weaknesses in the Chinese Defense Industry

The principal constraints and weaknesses that the Chinese defense industry faces at present stem from its historical foundations and uncertain efforts to overcome the corrosive legacy of its difficult past.[68] The institutional and normative foundations and workings of the Chinese defense industry were copied from the former Soviet Union's command economy and continue to exert a powerful influence. The PLA and defense industrial regulatory authorities are seeking to replace this outdated top-down administrative management model with a more competitive and indirect regulatory regime, but there are strong vested interests opposed to any major changes.

Monopolies

One of the biggest hurdles that PLA and civilian defense acquisition specialists point out is the defense industry's monopoly structure. Little competition exists to win major weapons systems and defense equipment because each of China's six defense industrial sectors is closed to outside competition and is dominated by a select handful of state-owned defense corporations. Contracts are typically awarded through single-sourcing mechanisms to these corporations. Competitive bidding and tendering only takes place for noncombat support equipment, such as logistics supplies.

An effort in 1999 to inject more competition by splitting corporations that monopolized their sectors into two separate entities did little to curb monopolistic practices because these firms focused on different areas of business in their domains and there was little direct rivalry. These powerful defense firms have subsequently sought to reverse this effort at demonopolization by finding ways to remerge or collaborate. In 2008, the aviation industry made the first and so far only successful challenge by consolidating its two post-1999 entities back into a single monopoly structure. There have been occasional reports that the space and shipbuilding sectors might also seek to reestablish a single holding company arrangement.

Bureaucratic Fragmentation

A second serious weakness that has seriously handicapped the effectiveness of Chinese defense economy is bureaucratic fragmentation. This is a common characteristic of the Chinese organizational system,[69] but is especially virulent within the large and unwieldy defense sector. A key feature of the Soviet approach to defense industrialization that China imported was a highly divided, segmented, and stratified structure and process. There was strict separation between the defense and civilian sectors as well as between defense contractors and military end-users, compartmentalization between the conventional defense and strategic weapons sectors as well as among the different conventional defense industrial subsectors, and division between R&D entities and production units. Key reasons for this excessive compartmentalization include an obsessive desire for secrecy and the powerful influence of the deeply ingrained Chinese model of "vertical functional systems" [*tiao tiao*, 条条] that encouraged large-scale industries like those in the defense and supporting heavy industrial sectors, such as iron, steel, and chemicals, to become independent fiefdoms.

This severe structural compartmentalization is a major obstacle to the development of innovative and advanced weapons capabilities because it requires consensus-based decisionmaking that is carried out through extensive negotiations, bargaining, and exchanges. This management by committee is cumbersome, risk-adverse, and results in a lack of strong ownership that is critical to ensure that projects are able to succeed the thicket of bureaucratic red tape and cut-throat competition for funding.

The research, development, and acquisition (RDA) system also suffers from compartmentalization along many segments of the RDA process. Responsibilities for research and development, testing, procurement, production, and maintenance are in the hands of different units, and under-institutionalization has meant that linkages among these entities tend to be ad hoc in nature with major gaps in oversight, reporting, and information-sharing.[70] The fragmented nature of the RDA process may help to explain why Hu Jintao was apparently caught by surprise by the first publicized test flight of the J-20 fighter aircraft that occurred during the visit of U.S. Defense Secretary Robert Gates in January 2011.[71]

Weak Management Mechanisms

A third major weakness is that the PLA continues to rely on outdated administrative tools to manage projects with defense contractors in the absence of the establishment of an effective system. The PLA did implement the use of contracts on a trial basis in the late 1980s with the introduction of a contract responsibility system.[72] These contracts are administrative in nature, though, and have little legal rights because of a lack of a developed legal framework within the defense industry. Consequently, contracts are vague and do not define obligations or critical performance issues, such as quality, pricing, or schedules. Contracts for complex weapons projects can be as short as 1 to 2 pages, according to analysts.[73]

Moreover, the PLA acquisition apparatus is woefully backward in many other management approaches and tools that it uses compared to its counterparts in the United States and other advanced military powers. It has yet to adopt total life-cycle management methods, for example, and many internal management information systems are on standalone networks that prevent effective communications and coordination. One analyst stated that this often meant that the only way for project teams to exchange information was through paper transactions.[74]

Outdated Pricing Regime

A fourth serious weakness is the lack of a transparent pricing system for weapons and other military equipment, representing a lack of trust between the PLA and defense industry. The existing armament pricing framework is based on a cost-plus model that dates back to the planned economy, in which contractors are allowed 5 percent profit margins on top of actual costs.[75] There are a number of drawbacks to this model that hold back efficiency and innovation. One is that contractors are incentivized to push up costs as this would also drive up profits. Another problem is that contractors are not rewarded with finding ways to lower costs such as through more streamlined management or more cost-effective designs or manufacturing techniques. Contracts rarely have performance incentives, which discourage risk-taking and any willingness to adopt innovative approaches. Yet another issue is that contractors are dissuaded from making major investments in new technological capabilities or processes because of the low 5 percent profit margin that is available.

To address this longstanding problem, the PLA, Ministry of Finance, and National Development and Reform Commission held a high-level meeting on armament pricing reform in 2009 that concluded the outdated pricing system had seriously restricted weapons development and innovation.[76] A number of reform proposals were put forward that provide incentives to contain costs, switch from accounting procedures that focus on ex post pricing to ex ante controls, and expand from a single-pricing methodology to multiple pricing methods. Some of these ideas were incorporated in a document issued after the meeting titled "Opinions on Further Pushing Forward the Reform of Work Concerning the Prices of Military Products."

At the beginning of 2014, the GAD announced that it would conduct and expand on pilot projects on equipment pricing. These reforms include the strengthening of the pricing verification of purchased goods, improving cost controls, and shifting from singular to plural pricing models, from "after-purchase pricing" to "whole-process pricing," and from "individual-cost pricing" to "social average–cost pricing."[77] These represent modest steps in the pricing reform process, but the PLA will continue to face fierce opposition from the defense industry on this issue.

Corruption

A fifth impediment is corruption, which appears to have thrived with the defense industry's uncertain transition from centralized state planning to a more competitive and indirect management model.[78] PLA leaders have highlighted the RDA system as one of a number of high-risk areas in which corruption can flourish along with the selection and promotion of officials, enrollment of students in PLA-affiliated schools, funds management, and construction work.[79]

At the PLA's annual conference on military discipline inspection work in January 2014, CMC Vice Chairman General Xu Qiliang, who heads the PLA's anti-corruption efforts, pointed out that armament research, production, and procurement was one of two areas that required "better oversight."[80] The other area that Xu highlighted was construction projects, which have been plagued by a number of high-profile corruption scandals in recent years including the case of the General Logistics Department Deputy Director Lieutenant General Gu Junshan, who amassed a huge fortune from lucrative real estate kick-backs.[81]

The almost complete absence of public reporting on corruption in the defense industry and RDA system means that the extent of the problem is not known. Military authorities justify this lack of transparency, as many of the cases involve classified programs. In the latest anti-corruption crackdown that began with Xi Jinping's ascent to power at the 18th Party Congress in November 2012, there have only been a handful of cases of defense industry executives being arrested on corruption charges.[82] A rare instance of official reporting into defense industrial–related corruption was when the Central Discipline Inspection Commission sent a team to investigate SASTIND for 2 months in the spring of 2016. SASTIND was required to set up a "comprehensive rectification program" [*fankui zhuanxiang*, 反馈专项] covering 100 measures and the investigation led to 2 officials being subject to "party discipline" [*dangji zhengji chufen*, 党纪政纪处分], 14 officials were "verbally admonished" [*jiemian tanhua*, 诚勉谈话], 3 officials were moved from their positions, and 10 officials were given letters of criticism.[83]

Implications for U.S.-China Military Technological Competition

Chinese defense industry efforts to successfully transition from an innovation follower to an original innovator able to engage in higher end technological development appear likely to succeed because of the confluence of powerful factors discussed in this chapter. What are the implications for the intensifying military technological competition with the United States from a more capable and innovative Chinese defense industry?

First, as the Chinese defense industry becomes more self-reliant and less dependent on foreign sources, this will allow it greater ability to forge a more independent development path. This is an important policy consideration because Chinese analysts have pointed out that a key goal in the U.S. Third Offset Strategy is to lure potential adversaries to compete in areas that the United States chooses and in which it enjoys a decisive advantage. According to one analysis in the *PLA Daily*, China should avoid this temptation and "persevere in taking our own development road, continue to stress and strengthen the domains where we enjoy superiority, and not be influenced by the United States."[84]

Second, as the pace and intensity of the Chinese defense industry's restructuring efforts quicken, the United States will find it has a narrowing window of opportunity to pursue the Third Offset and other related initiatives and restore its strategic superiority before China is able to catch up in critical areas. The next 5 to 10 years could be a decisive period in shaping the nature of U.S.-China military technological competition. This is a viewpoint that is shared by Chinese decisionmakers, including Xi Jinping, who see China engaged in a zero-sum global race for technological leadership in both the civilian and defense S&T domains.[85]

Notes

[1] "China Announces 7.6 Percent Defense Budget Rise, Lowest in Six Years," Xinhua, March 5, 2016, available at <www.xinhuanet.com/english/2016-03/05/c_135158243.htm>.

[2] "China Civil-Military Integration Development Report 2015" [中国军民融合发展报告2015] (Beijing: National Defense University Press [国防大学出版社], 2016), 59.

[3] *The PLA Navy: New Missions and Capabilities for the 21ˢᵗ Century* (Suitland, MD: U.S. Office of Naval Intelligence, April 13, 2015), available at <https://fas.org/nuke/guide/china/plan-2015.pdf>. See also Tai Ming Cheung, "Innovation in China's Defense Technology Base: Foreign Technology and Military Capabilities," *Journal of Strategic Studies* 39, nos. 5–6 (2016), 728–761.

[4] *The PLA Navy*, 15.

[5] Ibid., 13.

[6] "Xi Stresses Military Talent," Xinhua, November 6, 2013, available at <www.china.org.cn/china/third_plenary_session/2013-11/06/content_30544430.htm>.

[7] "Xi Jinping Addresses CCP Central Committee Political Bureau 17th Collective Study Session, Emphasizes Need to Acurately Grasp New Trend in the World's Military Development, Advance with the Times to Vigorously Promote Military Innovation" [习近平在中共中央政治局第十七次集体学习时强调准确把握世界军事发展新趋势 与时俱进大力推进军事创新], Xinhua [新华], August 30, 2014, available at <www.xinhuanet.com/politics/2014-08/30/c_1112294869.htm>.

[8] "Xi Jinping Chaired the First Meeting of the CMC National Defense and Military Small Leading Group" [习近平主持中央军委深化国防和军队改革领导小组第一次全体会], State Council, People's Republic of China, March 15, 2014, available at <www.gov.cn/xinwen/2014-03/15/content_2639427.htm>.

[9] "Documentary of the Design Process of Deepening Defense and Military Reform by Xi Jinping and the CMC" [习主席和中央军委运筹设计深化国防和军队改革纪实], Sina News Center [Sina 新闻中心], December 30, 2015, available at <http://news.sina.com.cn/o/2015-12-30/doc-ifxncyar6047368.shtml>.

[10] "Central Military Commission Issues 'Opinions Concerning Deepening the Reform of National Defense and the Armed Forces'" [中央军委印发"关于深化国防和军队改革的意见"], Xinhua [新华], January 1, 2016, available at <www.xinhuanet.com/mil/2016-01/01/c_1117646692.htm>.

[11] "Ministry of National Defense Holds News Conference on CMC Administrative Reform and Reorganization," *China Military Online*, January 11, 2016.

[12] "Former GAD S&T Committee Director Liu Guozhi Appointed Director of New CMC S&T Committee," *The Paper* [澎湃新闻], January 11, 2016.

[13] "Former GAD Director Zhang Youxia Becomes New Director of CMC Armament Development Department," *The Paper* [澎湃新闻], January 14, 2016.

[14] Zhao Lei, "PLA Says Chief of Its Arms Wing Replaced," *China Daily* (Beijing), September 19, 2017, available at <www.chinadaily.com.cn/china/2017-09/19/content_32187194.htm>.

[15] "2016 National Defense Science, Technology and Industry Working Conference Was Held in Beijing" [2016 年国防科技工业工作会议在京召开], State Council, People's Republic of China, January 9, 2016, available at <www.gov.cn/xinwen/2016-01/09/content_5031770.htm>.

[16] Laura Zhou, "China Almost Doubles Weapons Exports over Past Five Years, with Pakistan Biggest Buyer: Think Tank," *South China Morning Post* (Hong Kong),

February 22, 2016, available at <www.scmp.com/news/china/diplomacy-defence/article/1915140/china-almost-doubles-weapons-exports-over-past-five>.

¹⁷ Ibid.

¹⁸ Liu Zhongcai [刘重才], "'Defense 2025' Is Coming Soon: Aero-Engines May Become the Breakthrough" ["军工版2025"呼之欲出航空发动机将成突破], Xinhua [新华], June 19, 2015, available at <http://news.xinhuanet.com/fortune/2015-06/19/c_127931606.htm>.

¹⁹ "Defense Science, Technology and Industry Development Strategy Committee Was Established" [国防科技工业发展战略委员会成立], Ministry of National Defense, People's Republic of China, June 6, 2015, available at <http://news.mod.gov.cn/headlines/2015-06/05/content_4588445.htm>. Xu Dazhe was the initial head of the committee when he was State Administration for Science, Technology, and Industry for National Defense (SASTIND) director, but he was transferred to become governor of Hunan Province in September 2016.

²⁰ *Selection of Xi Jinping's Comments on Science, Technology, and Innovation* [习近平关于科技创新论述摘编] (Beijing: Central Party Literature Press, 2016), 42–43. China continues, though, to undertake a comprehensive and sophisticated effort to acquire foreign technology and know-how through diverse means. See Tai Ming Cheung, "Innovation in China's Defense Technology Base."

²¹ "Outline of the National Strategy of Innovation-Driven Development" [国家创新驱动发展战略纲要], Chinese Ministry of Science and Technology, May 23, 2016, available at <www.china.com.cn/zhibo/zhuanti/ch-xinwen/2016-05/23/content_38515829.htm>.

²² *Selection of Xi Jinping's Comments on Science, Technology, and Innovation*, 41.

²³ Cao Kun [曹昆], ed., "Xi Jinping Pointed Out Three Directions for Technological Innovation" [习近平指出科技创新的三大方向], *People's Daily* [人民日报], June 2, 2016, available at <http://politics.people.com.cn/n1/2016/0602/c1001-28406379.html>.

²⁴ *Selection of Xi Jinping's Comments on Science, Technology, and Innovation*, 50–51.

²⁵ "The 13ᵗʰ Five-Year Plan" [十三五规划纲要(全文)], Xinhua [新华], March 18, 2016, available at <http://sh.xinhuanet.com/2016-03/18/c_135200400_2.htm>.

²⁶ "What Dragged National Laboratory: Still under Development after Ten Years" [谁拖了国家实验室的后腿：十多年仍难去"筹"], Sohu News [搜狐新闻], March 3, 2016, available at <http://news.sohu.com/20160303/n439195452.shtml>. These laboratories included Shenyang National Laboratory for Material Sciences,

Beijing National Laboratory for Condensed Matter Physics, Hefei National Laboratory for Physical Sciences at the Microscale, Tsinghua National Laboratory for Information Science and Technology, Wuhan National Laboratory for Optoelectronics, Beijing National Laboratory for Molecular Sciences, and Qingdao National Laboratory for Marine Science and Technology.

27 "13th Five-Year Plan."

28 "We Could Have Comprehensive National Laboratories" [综合性国家实验室: 这个可以有], *Science and Technology Daily* [科技日报], March 12, 2016, available at <http://news.sciencenet.cn/htmlnews/2016/3/340373.shtm>.

29 "CAS President: A Number of National Laboratories Will Be Established Targeting Major Science and Technology Issues" [中科院长: 将建一批国家实验室解决重大科技问题], Sina News Center [Sina 新闻中心], February 4, 2016, available at <http://mil.news.sina.com.cn/china/2016-02-04/doc-ifxpfhzk8866244.shtml>.

30 "SASTIND Takes Measures to Accelerate National Defense Science, Technology, and Industry Coordinated Innovation" [国防科工局多措并举加快推进国防科技工业协同创新], State Administration for Science, Technology, and Industry for National Defense, People's Republic of China, June 29, 2016, available at <www.sastind.gov.cn/n112/n117/c6603042/content.html>.

31 There were nine state-owned defense industrial corporations as of mid-2018: China National Nuclear Corporation, China State Shipbuilding Corporation, China Shipbuilding Industry Corporation, North Industries Group Corporation, China South Industries Group Corporation, China Electronics Technology Group Corporation, China Aerospace Science and Industry Corporation, China Aerospace Science and Technology Corporation, and Aviation Industry Corporation of China.

32 Daniel Alderman et al., "The Rise of Chinese Civil-Military Integration," in *Forging China's Military Might: A New Framework for Assessing Innovation*, ed. Tai Ming Cheung (Baltimore: Johns Hopkins University Press, 2014), 112.

33 "Xi Calls for Deepened Military-Civilian Integration," Xinhua, March 12, 2018.

34 *13th Five-Year Special Plan for the Development of Military Civil Fusion* [十三五科技军民融合发展专项规划] (Beijing: CMC Science and Technology Commission and Ministry of Science and Technology, September 26, 2017), available at <www.aisixiang.com/data/106161.html>.

35 "Xi Jinping Chairs First Plenary Session of the Central Commission for Integrated Military and Civilian Development" [习近平主持召开中央军民融合发展委员会第一次全体会议强调], Xinhua [新华], June 20, 2017.

[36] "Xi Jinping Chairs Second Plenum of Central Commission for Integrated Military and Civilian Development" [习近平主持召开中央军民融合发展委员会第二次全体会议强调], Xinhua [新华], September 22, 2017.

[37] "Interpret 'Made in China 2025': 'Three-Step' Strategy to Become a Manufacturing Power" ["中国制造2025"解读之六: 制造强国"三步走"战略], Ministry of Industry and Information Technology, People's Republic of China, May 19, 2015, available at <www.miit.gov.cn/n1146295/n1146562/n1146655/c3780688/content.html>. See also Tai Ming Cheung et al., *Planning for Innovation: Understanding China's Plans for Technological, Energy, Industrial, and Defense Development* (Washington, DC: U.S.-China Economic and Security Review Commission, September 2016).

[38] "Made in China 2025 Plan Unveiled to Boost Manufacturing," Xinhua, May 19, 2015, available at <www.xinhuanet.com/english/2015-05/19/c_134252230.htm>.

[39] "Office of State Council on Notice on Establishment of State Strong Manufacturing Power Building Leading Small Group" [国务院办公厅关于成立国家制造强国建设领导小组的通知], State Council, People's Republic of China, June 24, 2015, available at <www.gov.cn/zhengce/content/2015-06/24/content_9972.htm>.

[40] "State Manufacturing Power Building Leading Small Group Established with Ma Kai as Chair" [国家制造强国建设领导小组成立 马凯任组长], *Observer* [观察者], June 24, 2015, available at <www.guancha.cn/politics/2015_06_24_324516.shtml>.

[41] "SASTIND Statement Confirms for the First Time 'Defense S&T Industry 2025'" [国防科工局表态首次确认'国防科技工业 2025'], Shanghai Securities News [上海证券报], June 19, 2015, available at <http://military.china.com/important/11132797/20150619/19871906_all.html>.

[42] Author interview with semiconductor industry representative, January 14, 2016.

[43] "Guidelines on Developing and Promoting the National IC Industry" [国家集成电路产业发展推进纲要], Ministry of Industry and Information Technology, People's Republic of China, June 24, 2014, available at <www.miit.gov.cn/n1146295/n1652858/n1652930/n3757021/c3758335/content.html>.

[44] *A Decade of Unprecedented Growth: China's Impact on the Semiconductor Industry—2014 Update* (London: PricewaterhouseCoopers, January 2015), available at <www.pwc.com/gx/en/technology/chinas-impact-on-semiconductor-industry/assets/china-semicon-2014.pdf>.

[45] "SASTIND Issues 2016 SASTIND Civil-Military Integration Special Action Plan" [国防科工局发布2016年军民融合专项行动计划], State Council, People's Republic of China, March 17, 2016, available at <www.gov.cn/xinwen/2016-03/17/content_5054670.htm>.

⁴⁶ "Defense Research Institute Reform May Be Implemented Soon" [军工科研院所分类改革文件或近期落地], Xinhua [新华], January 15, 2016, available at <http://news.xinhuanet.com/finance/2016-01/15/c_128631763.htm>.

⁴⁷ "Defense Research Institutes Reform Need to Deal with Six Issues" [机构:军工科研院所改制需直面六大问题], Xinhua [新华], July 23, 2014, available at <http://finance.ifeng.com/a/20140723/12778652_0.shtml>.

⁴⁸ "Defense Research Institute Reform May Be Implemented Soon."

⁴⁹ "Defense Conglomerates Will Start Classification Reform, 87 Enterprises Are Listed" [军工集团将启动分类改革 已有 87 家企业上市], *cnstock.com*, September 6, 2015, available at <http://news.cnstock.com/industry/sid_zxk/201509/3553950.htm>.

⁵⁰ "Research Institutes Restructuring Starts, Greatest Potential in Electronics and Space" [军工行业:院所改制发令枪响,电科航天弹性最大], *Tencent Finance*, May 12, 2016, available at <http://finance.qq.com/a/20160512/026066.htm>.

⁵¹ "Reform of Defense Research Institutes Made Breakthroughs, Space Sector May Take the Lead" [军工院所分类改革迎突破 航天系望成"领头羊"], Shanghai Securities News [上海证券报], February 4, 2016, available at <www.cnstock.com/v_industry/sid_rdjj/201602/3703256.htm>.

⁵² "Defense Research Institutes Reform Need to Deal with Six Issues."

⁵³ "Plan on Deepening Reform of the Central Government S&T Plan (Projects, Funds, etc.) Management" [关于深化中央财政科技计划（专项、基金等）管理改革的方案], State Council, People's Republic of China, December 3, 2014, available at <www.gov.cn/zhengce/content/2015-01/12/content_9383.htm>.

⁵⁴ "Policy Explanation on Deepening the Management Reform Central Funding of S&T Plans (Items and Funds)" [《关于深化中央财政科技计划（专项、基金等）管理改革的方案》政 策解读], Ministry of Science and Technology, People's Republic of China, January 1, 2015, available at <www.most.cn/kjzc/zdkjzcjd/201501/t20150106_117286.htm>.

⁵⁵ Ibid.

⁵⁶ Ministry of Science and Technology Vice Minister Hou Jianguo stated that the set of S&T reforms outlined in Doc. No. 64 would be completed in 3 years. See *Science and Technology Daily* [科技日报], February 17, 2016.

⁵⁷ Five separate policy documents issued in 2007 established these principles. See included State Guidelines table for additional details.

⁵⁸ For example, in January 2007, China State Shipbuilding Corporation subsidiary Hudong Heavy Machinery issued a private placement of Rmb 12 billion

($1.5 billion). The funds were used to buy shipyards and invest in new technology. See Charlotte So, "Hudong Heavy Eyes 12b Yuan in Placement," *South China Morning Post* (Hong Kong), January 30, 2007, available at <www.scmp.com/article/580095/hudong-heavy-eyes-12b-yuan-placement>.

[59] "SASTIND Issues Notice on Rules for Defense S&T and Industry Fixed Assets Investment Program Management" [国防科工局关于印发国防科技工业固定资产投资项目管理规定的通知], State Administration for Science, Technology, and Industry for National Defense, People's Republic of China, August 27, 2013, available at <www.opt.ac.cn/jg/glbm/kjyglb/xagjsjgglwj/201309/W020140328373812704712.pdf>.

[60] "Li Keqiang Stresses Innovative Macroeconomic Measures at CAS, CES Meeting," Xinhua, June 10, 2014.

[61] "CSIC Releases Plan for 8.48 Billion Set, Creates Precedent for Defense Asset Injection" [中国重工 84.8 亿定增预案出炉 开创重大军工资产注入先河], *Shanghai Securities News* [上海证券报], September 11, 2013, available at <http://finance.sina.com.cn/stock/s/20130911/023716724295.shtml>.

[62] "China Navy Plots Course to Stock Market," *Financial Times*, September 11, 2013, available at <https://next.ft.com/content/4f27d80a-1abb-11e3-a605-00144feab7de>.

[63] Ibid.

[64] Calculations for public and private equity offerings and bonds were aggregated from an IGCC database collecting capital market transactions of China's defense companies. Data for these transactions are compiled from numerous online sources for each of China's 10 big defense conglomerates from 2010 to June 2016. Official announcements were referenced where possible. Data primarily reflect only capital market transactions of the parent companies. Also, data for Chinese domestic capital transactions are believed to be complete, but Hong Kong and overseas transactions may have missing data. Bonds do not distinguish between public bonds and interagency bonds, and for private placement deals still being finalized, details such as investor and deal size are subjected to change.

[65] "Military Industrial Asset Securitization Rate Decreases; Industry Calls for Policy Support" [军工资产证券化率偏低业界呼吁政策支持], Xinhua [新华], March 25, 2016, available at <http://news.xinhuanet.com/fortune/2016-03/25/c_1118447808.htm>.

[66] Ibid.

[67] "CMI Is Trending, Do You Know How to Sort Out Core Stocks?" [军民融合这么火 你知道怎么梳理核心概念股吗?], *Securities Times* [证券时报], April 5, 2016, available at <http://finance.sina.com.cn/stock/t/2016-04-05/doc-ifxqx-qmf4052133.shtml>.

[68] This section is based on the chapter titled "Weaknesses in PLA Defense Industries," in *China's Incomplete Military Transformation*, ed. Michael Chase et al. (Washington, DC: RAND, October 2014).

[69] Kenneth Lieberthal and Michel Oksenberg, *Policy Making in China: Leaders, Structures, and Processes* (Princeton: Princeton University Press, 1988), 35–42. See also Kenneth Lieberthal and David Lampton, eds., *Bureaucracy, Politics, and Decision Making in Post-Mao China* (Berkeley: University of California Press, 1992); and David Lampton, ed., *Policy Implementation in Post-Mao China* (Berkeley: University of California Press, 1987).

[70] See Liu Hanrong and Wang Baoshun, eds., *National Defense Scientific Research Test Project Management* [国防科研试验项目管理] (Beijing: National Defense Industry Press [国防工业出版社], 2009).

[71] John Pomfret, "Chinese Army Tests Jet During Gates Visit," *Washington Post*, January 12, 2011; and Elizabeth Bumiller and Michael Wines, "Test of Stealth Fighter Clouds Gates Visit to China," *New York Times*, January 12, 2011.

[72] Tai Ming Cheung, *Fortifying China: The Struggle to Build a Modern Defense Economy* (Ithaca, NY: Cornell University Press, 2009), 83–85.

[73] Author interview with PLA acquisition specialist, Beijing, November 2011.

[74] Ibid.

[75] Mao Guohui, ed., *Introduction to the Military Armament Legal System* [军事装备法律制度概论] (Beijing: National Defense Industry Press [国防工业出版社], 2012), 158–159.

[76] Zong Zhaodun and Zhao Bo [宗兆盾, 赵波], "Major Reform Considered in Work on the Prices of Our Army's Armaments" [我军装备价格工作酝酿重大改革], *PLA Daily* [解放军报], November 13, 2009.

[77] Zhang Xiaoqi [张晓祺], "Armament Work: It Is the Right Time for Reform and Innovation" [装备工作:改革创新正当其时], *PLA Daily* [解放军报], February 13, 2014.

[78] *Corruption* is defined broadly in China as covering the improper behavior of state, party, or military officials, but the more common Western definition is the abuse of public office for personal gain in violation of rules.

[79] "PLA Gets Tough on Duty Crimes," Xinhua, December 1, 2014, available at <www.chinadaily.com.cn/china/2014-12/01/content_19005244.htm>.

[80] Zhang Qian and Yao Chun, eds., "CMC Vice Chairman Stresses Effective Anti-Corruption," Xinhua, January 17, 2014, available at <http://en.people.cn/90786/8515367.html>.

[81] "How a PLA General Built a Web of Corruption to Amass a Fortune," *Caixin Wang*, January 16, 2014, available at <www.chinafile.com/reporting-opinion/caixin-media/how-pla-general-built-web-corruption-amass-fortune>.

[82] See, for example, "Wu Hao, Deputy General Manager of AVIC Heavy Machinery Under Investigation for Corruption," *Xinjing Bao*, June 4, 2014.

[83] "Second Central Inspection Team Sent to SASTIND Party Committee to Inspect the Situation" [中央第二巡视组向国防科工局党组反馈专项巡视情况], Central Commission for Discipline Inspection Supervision Web site [中央纪委监察部网站], June 8, 2016, available at <www.ccdi.gov.cn/special/zyxszt/djlxs_zyxs/fkqk_18jzydjl_zyxs/201606/t20160613_80395.html>.

[84] Zhao Yang and Liu Na [赵阳, 刘娜], "The Best Way of Predicting the Future Is to Create the Future: An Analysis of the Technical Background of the U.S. High-Profile Presentation of the Third 'Offset Strategy'" [预测未来的最佳途径是创造未来—美国高调提出第三次"抵消战略"的技术背景分析], *PLA Daily* [解放军报], May 6, 2016, available at <www.81.cn/jfjbmap/content/2016-05/05/content_143605.htm>.

[85] See Tai Ming Cheung and Thomas Manhken, eds., *The Gathering Pacific Storm: Emerging U.S.-China Strategic Competition in Defense Technological and Industrial Development* (Amherst, NY: Cambria Press, 2018).

CHAPTER 16

CIVIL-MILITARY INTEGRATION AND PLA REFORMS

By Brian Lafferty

In December 2015, the People's Liberation Army (PLA) formally launched reforms that have been described as the "most wide-ranging and ambitious restructuring since 1949."[1] Central Military Commission (CMC) Chairman Xi Jinping announced his intention to pursue these changes by calling them the "only way to develop a strong military and the key to deciding the future of the PLA."[2] The PLA's new plan set several goals for 2020: achieving "breakthrough development" in joint operations command system reforms and leadership management system reforms, as well as "significant results" in military force reductions, reforms to improve defense policies, and civil-military integration (CMI) development.[3] CMI's inclusion as a key pillar in a transformative reform agenda confirmed its importance to the PLA's overall modernization, and China's unwavering embrace of it as a national strategic imperative.

CMI began slowly taking root in China as a military modernization strategy in the 1990s, and has since become steadily more institutionalized within the PLA and China's national security sector.[4] Chinese reliance on CMI in military and economic development has increased significantly under Xi Jinping, who has called for CMI to extend into more technology areas, cover more military and economic activities, and generate more tangible achievements.[5] He has provided a theoretical justification for change by arguing that China's CMI has entered a new phase, transitioning from its initial institutionalization toward a deep integration of the civil and military sectors. To spur a greater focus on CMI's importance, in March 2015 Xi announced that it would be raised to a "national strategy" [*ba junmin ronghe fazhan shangsheng wei guojia zhanlüe*, 把军民融合发展上升为国家战略], and this decision was ratified by the Politburo a year later.[6]

Chinese commentators have voiced their support for this policy direction by emphasizing the critical importance of CMI, arguing that it is a "strategic requirement" [*zhanlüe xuqiu*, 战略需求] and the only way to build a military capable of winning informationized wars.[7] As a recent article in *Qiushi* argued, "CMI has become the one and only choice for strengthening national comprehensive strength and defense competitiveness. . . . If a state does not pursue CMI then it is difficult to preserve technological dominance."[8] The same article also asserted that CMI development had become a new area of fierce competition between states, and any major country that did not quickly adopt CMI would inevitably fall behind its rivals.[9]

While Chinese CMI reforms have received saturation coverage in China, they remain underexplored elsewhere, hindering efforts to understand their potential impact on the PLA's current round of reforms. In particular, CMI has emerged as an integral part of Chinese efforts to promote defense science and technology development and bring additional resources more efficiently into defense modernization. Its success or failure will in turn have a corresponding influence on a broad range of PLA activities, and as such, it is helpful to better understand China's efforts to implement CMI, as well as its problems and prospects.

This chapter provides an overview of four aspects of China's push for civil-military integration. First, it surveys the broad impetus and objectives for CMI, highlighting why Chinese leaders consider it so vital to the overall PLA reform program. Second, it describes the operationalization of CMI, noting where and how China has tried to pursue CMI reforms. Third, it focuses on some of the key problems that have hindered the effectiveness of CMI reforms. Finally, the chapter discusses the creation of the Central Commission for Integrated Military and Civilian Development [*junmin ronghe fazhan weiyuanhui*, 军民融合发展委员会], and how it offers a credible new path for resolving some of the most entrenched CMI obstacles.

Broad Impetus for Civil-Military Integration

China's impetus for pursuing CMI as a core component of its PLA reforms is in large part a result of its reckoning with modern technology-driven warfare. After the first Gulf War, Chinese military strategists reached a consensus on the decisive role played by technology in military conflicts, and the reforms that have followed were geared toward creating a PLA that was better equipped and better prepared to fight on the battlefield. The many U.S. military engagements since 1991 have only reinforced for Chinese strategists that modern warfare has transitioned from the mechanized warfare of the industrial age to the informationized warfare of the network age.[10] This change has dramatically affected Chinese thinking on military modernization and the role of civil-military integration in their national security strategy. In particular, it has focused Chinese strategic attention on the issues of technology development and resource allocation.

Technology Development

The 2013 edition of the Academy of Military Science's *Science of Military Strategy* addressed the importance of science and technology (S&T) for military development at length: "Science and technology is the key foundation for combat strength," and "the ferociously fast development of new and high technology . . . has profoundly changed the content and mode of combat strength."[11] CMI theorist Hou Guangming also analyzed the changing impact of technology on the PLA, noting in a 2014 book on innovation in the Chinese defense industries, from the "state's perspective, the global revolution in military affairs continually promotes upgrades in high-tech weaponry, and the core of military competition is changing toward science and technology."[12] Thus, the race to upgrade defense technology has become an overarching strategic imperative, and PLA strategists have stressed that China's weapons development pace will be inadequate if the country fails to catch up in technology innovation.[13] This imperative has already been enshrined in policy documents, as the 18th Party Congress in 2012 concluded, "[s]cience and technology innovation is a strategic support for raising social productivity and comprehensive national strength, and we must place it in a core position within our national security posture."[14] Xi Jinping amplified this mandate in 2016 when he stated that the "state needs the strategic support of science and technology more urgently than any other time in the past" and warned that China was in a precarious position in terms of its ability to innovate. He stated, the "situation that our country is under others' control in core technologies of key fields has not changed fundamentally, and the country's S&T foundation remains weak."[15] Most recently, China included similar sentiments in the 19th Party Congress final report, which stated, "We must keep it firm in our minds that technology is the core combat capability, encourage innovations in major technologies, and conduct innovations independently."[16]

China's efforts to overcome its deficiencies in defense science and technology are hampered by the fact that the resource commitment needed to reach and maintain technological parity with other major military powers (let alone preeminence) is enormous. Chinese analysts have made numerous references to the increasing costs of next-generation weapons platforms, citing, for example, that the research and development (R&D) expenditures for global first-generation fighters were under Rmb 500,000, while the cost to develop fourth-generation fighters was between Rmb 10 and 40 billion.[17] The financial requirements for R&D alone, exacerbated by how long the R&D cycle now stretches, pose a significant resource challenge. Chinese analysts have also drawn attention to the rapidly rising cost of military operations, both in terms of finances as well as materiel consumption.[18] Compounding these issues, the government is also confronting the enormous cost of transforming its economy in an effort to build China into an S&T power.

Resource Allocation

Given these demands on its finite resources, China's official policy statements have repeatedly warned that the country's much-publicized defense budget increases would be insufficient to meet the PLA's development needs.[19] The head of National Defense University's China Institute of National Defense Finance Studies [*zhongguo guofang jinrong yanjiu hui*, 中国国防金融研究会] highlighted the PLA's budgetary constraints in a May 2016 speech, stating, "[r]ight now . . . we face the reality that there is an intensified contradiction between the rigid demand for increases in defense investment and the state's fiscal situation. In relying solely on state finances for defense investment, we are already unable to support major advances in the development of our defense."[20] This dynamic has arguably worsened over the last 2 years, as China's official defense budget increase was well below media expectations in 2016, and rose by an even smaller margin in 2017, thanks in part to slower economic growth.[21] While China's official defense budget does not capture all of its defense-related spending, it does capture most defense expenditures.[22] Moreover, to the extent that China's economic growth has slowed to a "new normal," declining defense budget increases are most likely not overly disproportionate with trends in its total defense-related spending.[23]

As a result, there are no expectations that China can achieve its defense modernization goals solely by increases in the defense budget. Chinese leaders have been clear that the solution to this problem will not be guns-versus-butter budgetary tradeoffs that prioritize short-term military needs at the expense of economic imperatives. Their reluctance to raise defense spending more dramatically stems in part from the belief that it would harm economic growth (and thus the foundation for long-term military strength), as well as from the common perception that one of the major causes for the fall of the Soviet Union was its ruinous attempts to match U.S. military spending.

CMI Reforms as Strategic Response

China's current CMI reforms have evolved directly from concerns about resource constraints versus the need to promote defense modernization.[24]

Xi Jinping has stated that they are the product of research into how best to coordinate building the country's economy and defense capabilities, and indeed, they reflect what has been a slow evolution in policy toward broader, deeper civil-military resource-sharing.[25] As currently conceived, CMI reforms offer a way to ease PLA competition for resources by broadening and strengthening the resource base that China can use for building up defense. Phrased another way, they involve the "leveraging of dual-use technologies, policies, and organizations for military benefit."[26] Their basic prescription is the abandonment of governing norms that closed off [*fengbi*, 封闭] military and defense institutions from the rest of the country, and granted them their own dedicated resources, management systems, and policy and standards environments. Instead, Chinese CMI seeks to dramatically increase cross-fertilization and sharing between military and civilian institutions in a growing spectrum of activities like technology development, logistics, finance, and training. It seeks to merge civilian and military development resources into a combined system that pursues substantially more cost-effective "coordinated development" [*xietiao fazhan*, 协调发展] and resource-sharing [*ziyuan gongxiang*, 资源共享] to satisfy the requirements for China's national security and economic strategies.[27] CMI's idealized application is a situation in which "military" and "civilian" development is organically blended into a single whole, the distribution of civil and military resources are optimized, and the overall efficiency of resource utilization is improved to the point where "one kind of resource investment produces multiple kinds of benefits" [*yizhong ziyuan touru chansheng duozhong xiaoyi*, 一种资源投入产生多种效益].[28]

While CMI touches on a wide range of activities, it is primarily concerned with an efficient allocation and use of resources [*ziyuan peizhi he shiyong*, 资源配置和使用].[29] Chinese analysts have often taken inspiration from the example set by U.S. moves toward CMI, which they feel considerably lightened the U.S. military's burden on overall spending.[30] To that end, China seeks to create coordinating institutions and mechanisms between military, political, economic, and social organizations that reduce allocative redundancies, achieve multiplier effects, and eliminate working at cross-purposes. As one analyst argued:

> Under the premise of preserving core national defense building abilities [baochi hexin guofang jianshe nengli, 保持核心国防建设能力], [CMI] should fully bring about the market's determinative utility in resource allocation, and promote dual directional flow of resources between the military and local areas in things like technology, industrial arts, equipment, facilities, labor, capital, and information. It should make national defense construction even more fully utilize the fruits of economic and social development, and actively bring into play the important "pull effect" [ladong zuoyong, 拉动作用] that defense and military modernization have on economic and social development. We want a maximized "military benefit" for economic construction, and a maximized "economic benefit" for defense construction.[31]

In this fashion, China's leaders feel they can create savings and make government spending more effective by doing things like minimizing redundant development efforts, such as when defense and civilian institutions are separately receiving grants to conduct similar research on the same technologies; finding cheaper civilian sources for generic goods and services that do not need to use specialized military providers; and ensuring consideration for defense needs in economic planning, so that spending and investments are mutually beneficial to the military and local economies.

Chinese strategists argue that CMI reforms can achieve the unification of the "strong army" and "rich country" ideals [*fuguo he qiangjun xiang tongyi*, 富国和强军相统一], providing a blueprint for overcoming structural impediments to military and economic development. Their support for the reforms is enhanced by the fact that CMI serves as a compelling strategic response to four major characteristics of modern informationized warfare. First, Chinese leadership has reached an analytical conclusion that military development and economic development are mutually dependent to a greater extent than ever before. They believe it is impossible to be a global military power without also being a global economic power. This viewpoint took root decades ago, when Deng Xiaoping's military reforms were conditioned by his belief that a country's military strength was dependent on its economic base. However, the resource requirements for modern warfare are so extensive now that Chinese analysts are especially conscious of how vital an advanced economy is to PLA modernization. As Yu Chuanxin, one of the Academy of Military Science's more prolific CMI experts explained, China's pursuit of a strong military requires a leading economic and S&T foundation, which is only possible if China's economy develops further, productivity levels increase, and its strength in S&T advances to the global forefront.[32] At the same time, Yu argues that given the complex and increasing security threats facing China from foreign and domestic enemies, its economy and society need a strong military that can ensure security, stability, and peace.[33] The defense sector can also contribute to economic development through multiple channels, such as the transfer of defense technologies for civilian use, integrating defense conglomerates into the broader economy, and contracting out for goods and services needed by the military. Therefore, national security and economic development should be thought of as a "single piece of steel" [*yikuai zheng gang*, 一块整钢] that serves China's fundamental national interest.[34]

The second characteristic of modern warfare that favors a move toward CMI reforms is that technology is increasingly dual-use, blurring [*mohuhua*, 模糊化] the lines between military and civilian.[35] CMI analysts regularly claim that over 80 percent of technologies in the equipment used by leading military powers are dual-use, highlighting an imperative to more effectively promote civil-military technology sharing in China.[36] In addition, the narrow but deep specialization needed to develop next-generation technologies has ensured that an ever-increasing number of industries are involved in defense technology development and production. Chinese researchers have cited statistics claiming that products from more than 1,000 industrial technology categories were involved in the equipment used to conduct combat operations during the first Gulf War, up from the roughly 160 used for World War II.[37] These trends have only accelerated. As such, the limitations of relying primarily on military and defense industry resources to pursue defense-related S&T have been brought into stark relief. The technology demands of modern combat are so great that they far exceed [*yuan yuan chaochule,* 远远超出了] the research and production capacity of military academic, research, and defense industry institutions.[38] CMI analysts have been critical of how slow China has been to adapt to these dual-use trends, citing widespread wasteful duplication in R&D efforts—stemming from bifurcated military and civilian research streams—as well as serious difficulties in converting R&D discoveries into the production of new defense technologies.[39]

China's slow response to dual-use dynamics has clear consequences in an era in which the civilian sector has increasingly become a source of major technological innovation.[40] As one analysis in *Qiushi* observed, in the "20th century, defense science and technology was the locomotive for technological revolutions, and the main direction for the spread of new technology was from military to civilian sectors. However, disruptive technological change in the 21st century now usually starts in the civilian sector."[41] As this implies, in an increasing number of technology fields, civilian R&D has surpassed the capabilities of military and defense industry research institutions.[42] Therefore, China has national security interests in helping its civilian technology sector develop as quickly as possible, as well as in ensuring that the PLA is able to rapidly absorb and apply whatever advanced technologies it produces. Given how fast technology is changing, an inability to develop or apply advanced S&T capabilities can have progressively dire effects on a country's security.[43] This logic was clearly evident in China's New Generation Artificial Intelligence Development Plan [*xin yidai rengong zhineng fazhan guihua,* 新一代人工智能发展规划], released in July 2017, which established a goal of making China the world's premiere global artificial intelligence innovation center by 2030, and also explicitly promoted a CMI strategy to ensure that corporate and civilian advances in artificial intelligence could be leveraged for national defense.[44]

The third characteristic of modern warfare relevant to CMI reforms is its unprecedented resource demands, which has created incentives to more fully eliminate the distinction between peacetime development and preparation for war. "Combining peacetime and wartime preparations" [*pingzhan jiehe*, 平战结合] has long conditioned party leaders' approach to domestic development strategies, but Chinese analysts have begun to advocate for a more extreme version due to their assessment that victory in a conflict between major powers is no longer determined by simple measures, such as numbers of ships and planes or industrial capacity. Instead, winning is determined by comprehensive national security systems, encompassing the whole of a country's national security resources. Everything is brought to bear in a major conflict, and the state that is able to fuse its disparate resources together to exert the most strength is likely to emerge victorious. As a result, they argue that China must approach its military reforms from a systems engineering perspective, in which multiple disparate elements work together toward an overall goal. The factors involved in winning informationized conflicts—the investments to promote S&T development, reforms to promote innovation, infrastructure to support rapid deployments, training to ensure that troops can handle the complexities of informationized operations, and so forth—must be defined to include a very broad range of activities so that areas not normally viewed through the prism of defense are included in military reform and development strategies. Moreover, given the importance of these factors, they must be addressed continuously, not simply when security concerns are more urgent.

In recognition of these conditions, Chinese CMI analysts now describe war between states as a contest between entire systems [*tixi duikang*, 体系对抗], encompassing (to a much more consequential degree than in previous eras) political, economic, scientific, technological, and cultural strength.[45] As such, failing to recognize the interdependence of defense reforms with the country's overall policy environment is untenable: "In the information era the lines are increasingly blurred between concepts like security and development, economic and military development, civil and military,

636

peacetime and wartime, frontlines and rear areas, and military-use versus civilian-use. These concepts are being increasingly fused together."[46]

The last characteristic of modern warfare that makes CMI a compelling strategic response to military reform requirements is that informationized war has increased the value of quality over quantity. China has enshrined this as official policy under Xi Jinping, who has stated that streamlining the PLA's "scale, structure, and power composition" is an important part of the PLA's ongoing reforms.[47] As he noted in a July 2017 Politburo study session, "Quantity should be reduced and quality improved to build capable and efficient military forces, which should be science and technology–oriented rather than relying on labor intensity."[48] To this end, Xi has continued the PLA's longstanding efforts to shed excess manpower. In January 2016, the CMC announced a plan to cut the PLA's size by 300,000, focused in part on noncombat organizations and personnel [*fei zhandou jigou he renyuan*, 非战斗机构和人员].[49] Chinese commentators have noted that the troop cuts are a sign that the PLA will change "from big to strong" [*you da dao qiang*, 由大到强], but the consequence of moving toward a leaner, meaner fighting force is that the PLA will be increasingly reliant on civilians, reserves, and militias to fulfill certain noncombat roles and responsibilities.[50] CMI's focus on promoting civil-military resource-sharing and using civilian capabilities to support the military is therefore well aligned with the needs arising from a smaller PLA.

Operationalizing Civil-Military Integration

Having established why China wants to pursue a CMI development strategy, this section examines how and in what areas it has tried to apply CMI. It is important to recognize that even though China has been promoting CMI reforms in earnest for over 10 years, in most areas the reforms are still at early stages of development. At the start of this process the basic infrastructure for CMI—organizations to administer, regulations to govern, and institutional mechanisms to facilitate—needed to be established either from scratch or from rudimentary foundations.[51] Defense conversion [*jun zhuan min*, 军转民] was the only component of CMI reforms that could be considered solidly institutionalized, but this was due to policies that began at the start of the post-Mao era.[52] China was unprepared to implement the other main components of what it wanted to accomplish with CMI—namely, promoting the flow of civilian technology, talent, capital, and information into the defense sector and encouraging a freer cross-exchange of civil and military resources. As a result, initial CMI reforms focused on identifying organizations with managing responsibilities for particular activities, crafting first-step regulations that removed barriers to civil-military coordination and/or facilitated better cooperation, creating better information flows between relevant civil-military actors, and pushing relevant actors to engage in CMI reform tasks.[53] It was about laying groundwork rather than producing immediate results.

The process of breaking down civil-military barriers and establishing cross-cutting civil-military resource-sharing has moved slowly precisely because it upended entrenched norms and interests. CMI reforms required disruptive change, but Chinese leaders' own unfamiliarity with CMI and their uncertainty about its impact helped pushed them toward a cautious policy approach. As one 2008 analysis observed, "CMI is a big issue and new topic, and our understanding and research is still in its initial stage."[54] Therefore, much of what China's leadership promoted for CMI prior to Xi Jinping's administration amounted to relatively basic reforms that took piecemeal steps to realign institutional behavior, such as changes that allowed private companies to begin to contract goods and services to the PLA, or the effort to encourage joint research, technology transfer, and personnel training agreements between civil and military companies, universities, and research institutions.[55] The focus was in reorienting political, corporate, and military leaders toward collaborative development processes in which they had little to no experience.

China's effort to create a basic infrastructure for CMI has been complicated by the fact that the operationalization of CMI reforms are unavoidably complex, involving interaction between an array of political, military, and corporate organizations in different administrative levels and geographic areas, and across multiple areas of responsibility. It is at least "cross disciplinary" [*kua lingyu*, 跨领域] and "cross-departmental" [*kua bumen*, 跨部门], but is more accurately understood as a "system of systems for coordinated military and economic development."[56] Xi Jinping has described it in similar terms, stating that "CMI development is a systems engineering issue, requiring systemic thinking, systemic methods, and systemic science in making relevant policy prescriptions."[57] As such, the activities that are potentially affected by CMI reforms, and the institutions involved, are vast, and the interaction between all of them conditions how effective the reforms will be.

Due in part to this complexity, China focused its initial CMI reform efforts in only four high-priority areas: weapons and equipment development, social support for the PLA [*jundui shehuihua baozhang*, 军队社会化保障], defense personnel training, and defense mobilization.[58] In each of these areas, China identified CMI reform goals, authorized or created managing organizations to oversee activity, modified or created rules and regulations to support activity, and reviewed implementation to identify ways to improve outcomes. It also developed multiple channels for information-sharing so that relevant actors could be more aware of CMI resources and opportunities.[59]

In practice, thanks in part to relentless advocacy for CMI reforms from political and military leaders, and political expectations for results, a broad swath of Chinese actors at both central and local levels has engaged in CMI activities. With so much room to improve, and so many actors involved, this participation has generated some notable positive outcomes. These include steadily broader and more substantive participation in PLA contracting work from civilian-owned companies, fueled in part by the PLA General Armament Department's launch of the online All-Army Weapons and Equipment Procurement Information Network [*quan jun wuqi zhuangbei caigou xinxi wang*, 全军武器装备采购信息网] in January 2015. The Web site, now operated post-reorganization by the CMC Equipment

Development Department, became the PLA's first authorized clearinghouse for defense procurement notices. More than 1,000 projects were put up for competitive bid in both 2016 and 2017—in theory, promoting cheaper, more efficient supply services—and the PLA hopes to double that number by 2020.[60] CMI's positive results also include the PLA's increased reliance on contractors for basic supplies and simple military services such as barracks maintenance, heating supply, power supply, and cleaning, which is already common in more urban areas and is increasingly getting adopted in lower level and more remote areas.[61]

Positive developments aside, the operationalization of CMI reforms has thus far not fully met the government's aspirations. Anecdotal evidence and the complaints of Chinese leaders (see below) suggest that implementing CMI reforms has not unleashed pent-up energies for CMI. The government has so far been willing to let CMI participants use a certain amount of initiative in implementing CMI measures, in the hopes that self-interested behavior would help discover best practices, but civil and military leaders have not aggressively embraced new opportunities for collaboration and resource-sharing. This could be interpreted as a signal that there is opposition to the reforms, but Chinese leaders and strategists have instead blamed the slow pace of meaningful compliance on the government's inability to effectively respond to the difficulties involved in implementing the reforms.

Operationalizing CMI Reforms under Xi

Xi Jinping did not immediately seek to leave his mark on China's CMI policies when he first took office, but in early 2015 he initiated major new theoretical guidelines for CMI work that have shaped reforms since. At a meeting with PLA representatives in advance of the 2015 National People's Congress, he announced a new phase in CMI reforms, stating, "China's CMI development has just entered a transitional phase, from initial integration [*chubu ronghe*, 初步融合] to deep integration [*shendu ronghe*, 深度融合]."[62] It was at this same meeting that Xi elevated CMI to a national strategy, setting CMI reforms on their current path of serving as a core component of the PLA reform program. Both of these ideas reflected Xi's belief that a CMI develop-ment strategy could "break new ground in the PLA's capability building."[63]

In promoting this new phase of CMI development, it is notable that Xi—despite the mixed record of success in China's CMI reforms to this point—decided to dramatically expand the scale and scope of implementa-tion. He has called for using CMI in a broader range of activities and raising the level and degree of integration wherever it is applied. While retaining CMI's focus on weapons development, social support for the PLA, training, and mobilization, Xi has called for expanding CMI processes into new areas, specifically citing sea, space, and cyberspace [*haiyang, taikong, wan-gluo kongjian,* 海洋、太空、网络空间] as priorities.[64] He has also ordered China's academic, corporate, and research institutions to take the initiative in discovering, cultivating, and applying cutting-edge technologies that can help build up China's military and national defense capabilities.[65]

In addition to new technology areas, Xi wants CMI reforms to focus more on organizational innovation, specifically in "three systems" [*san ge tixi,* 三个体系]:

- a *management system* that features unified leadership and coordination between the PLA and local governments
- an *operational system* in which work is led by the state, driven by demand, and unified by market operations
- a *policy system* that features a well-conceived set of policies (which cov-ers all necessary areas), a complete set of policy linkages, and effectively encourages desired outcomes.[66]

Essentially, Xi is calling for CMI processes to begin working the way poli-cymakers have hoped they would.

Indeed, Xi has been critical of the pace of progress made so far in CMI reforms, specifically flagging the country's inability to quickly generate new ideas and concepts to guide CMI activity; the government's inability to keep up with the demand for CMI-related policies, legislation, and operating mechanisms; and a lack of top-level, unified management systems. Notably, he has also complained that CMI reform work was not being pursued with enough intensity [*gongzuo zhixing lidu bugou,* 工作执行力度不够].[67] As he has stated, "We can do some things even better and some things even faster with respect to using CMI in S&T areas . . . and we will more quickly transform our military toward models based on quality and efficiency and concentrated science and technology."[68]

Problems in Implementing CMI

Xi Jinping is not the only critic of CMI's operationalization, as scholars and political and military experts have been cataloging its unresolved problems for years. The critiques are motivated by the sense—clearly shared by Xi—that given how important CMI reforms are for PLA modernization, they have advanced far too slowly. For all the legitimate progress that has been made, it is still true that China has only succeeded in establishing a basic framework for CMI. Moreover, critical reforms such as the restructuring of defense industry scientific research institutions into corporations have taken much longer than originally expected, and are only now getting started.[69]

Thanks to the lack of transparency regarding China's defense spending, it is hard to gauge how effective CMI has been at promoting a more efficient use of defense resources. However, it is telling that experts still discuss CMI's ability to usher in a more productive use of resources in aspirational rather than empirical terms, and this style of argumentation suggests that there is not yet a wealth of relevant data to cite. In terms of CMI's impact on defense science and technology, despite some encouraging signs of technological progress in advanced critical technologies like quantum communications, Chinese leaders have stated that China still lacks sufficient international core competitiveness in technological innovation.[70] This is, of course, a matter of national security concern given how strength in science and technology is considered vital to China's security and its ability to develop into a more advanced military power.

Problems with Execution

Despite the government's clear prioritization of CMI reforms, Chinese analysts have observed a lingering (and at this point, increasingly problematic) lack of buy-in from actors impacted by the reforms. Some military and civilian operations still remain closed off [*fengbi yunxing*, 封闭运行] because administrators are not actively seeking out opportunities to work across the civil-military divide. Other officials act as if national defense was not an economic concern and vice versa.[71] Analysts have also cited a widespread persistence of "no action, no initiative, no self-reliance" [*deng, kao, yao*, 等, 靠, 要] behavior among lower level officials, arguing that they too often wait for higher level administrators to deal with CMI implementation problems instead of taking them on themselves. In addition, analysts accuse some local officials of not treating CMI reforms with a sufficient level of importance, noting that they promote local interests at the expense of consideration for CMI development, as if CMI were only a priority for the national government or the military.[72]

These critiques point to issues of misaligned incentives between national and local officials, but Chinese officials and analysts have avoided describing the problem in those terms. Instead, they have blamed these issues on a persistent superficial understanding of CMI, relating to what it entails, why it is important, and how it should guide behavior. The annual report on CMI development overseen by the Ministry of Industry and Information Technology and National Development and Reform Commission has found that some Chinese believe that any contact between civilian and military actors is evidence of successful CMI, and therefore limit their ambitions to simple activities that promote army-government and army-civilian unity rather than working on more substantive aspects of CMI. Some organizations have also overemphasized one component of CMI, as if it was simply about civilian support for the PLA or military interaction with civilian political and economic sectors, without understanding that CMI now prioritizes mutually beneficial bidirectional interaction.[73] This latter problem is especially prevalent in the defense industries, where companies with long experience and comfort in developing products for the civilian market focus on that aspect of CMI without expending much effort to utilize civilian resources in their operations. These assessments of the problems affecting CMI implementation are directly reflected in how Chinese leadership has responded, with calls for better education and guidance from the top.

The flip side of concerns about apathy is that with so many units participating in reforms—across industrial sectors; across military, political, academic, and business activities; and across central and lower level administrative units—CMI operationalization has been overly fragmented. The participants in a 2012–2013 year-long consultative investigation into the defense industry's CMI development strategy, sponsored by the Chinese Academy of Engineering, found that individual industries and departments were pursuing idiosyncratic CMI strategies that had them scattering off in different directions.[74] China's military, economic, and political institutions at different administrative levels (for example, national, provincial, municipal, and so forth) established organizations to manage CMI work within their specific jurisdictions, but there was little regular coordination between them, and coordination work was slow, cumbersome, and consultative, not collaborative. In general, these institutions were working individually, but not collectively, to advance CMI policies. They were not used to the level (and extent) of coordination being asked of them, and in the absence of clear guidance and authoritative pressure, it has been easier to remain in their comfort zone.[75] This is problematic for a policy that requires cross-sectoral, cross-industry, and cross-administrative cooperation to work optimally. Indeed, CMI work—in the words of one recent commentary—has thus far only been implemented to a "narrow, shallow, and superficial" degree.[76]

Problems with Top-Level Coordination

Chinese analysts have blamed the above problems on ineffective top-level design [*dingceng sheji*, 顶层设计], a suboptimal outcome that stems from the inescapable fact that Chinese CMI is a massive management challenge. It requires coordination and cooperation among the leading institutions in charge of the military, national economy, administrative institutions, and industrial sectors, and affects a broad, cross-sector range of activities, including science and technology, education, and the economy. Traditionally, this level of coordination has not been ingrained within Chinese institutions, and in the absence of strong national guidance with clear incentives, Chinese actors have found it much easier to avoid the effort and sacrifice required to make dramatic behavioral changes. This resistance has made the generic benefits of CMI—integrating economic and military development into unified strategic planning and allocating resources more efficiently—much more difficult to achieve.[77]

These problems reflect China's inability to effectively coordinate the more complex aspects of CMI policymaking among CMI's leading stakeholders. Functional departments under the State Council and CMC have had oversight over individual aspects of CMI, like defense industries, defense S&T development, civil air defense, national defense transportation, and defense education, but none has had clear lines of authority over the others to lead and coordinate action. As a result, although there is a consensus among both military and civilian leaders concerning the importance and urgency [*jinpoxing*, 紧迫性] of CMI, there are still significant differences between military and local civilian actors [*jun di zhijian de renshi piancha bijiao da*, 军地之间的认识偏差比较大] regarding the concrete steps to accomplish these goals. Areas of contention include determining civil-military functions, division of responsibilities, and operational processes.[78] China has also failed to settle on ways to routinize stable operational processes for interagency coordination, as well as for other CMI management activities such as linking available resources to requirements and implementing civil-military resource-sharing.[79]

Experts have consistently argued for years that many of the problems in CMI implementation are due to the central government's disjointed management of the issue, which affected its ability to educate and guide behavior. Until January 2017, when the government launched the new Central Commission for Integrated Military and Civilian Development (discussed below), China had avoided giving any single institution leadership over the CMI portfolio. Most likely, this was due to the fact that CMI straddled both military and economic activities but was only designed to affect some aspects of military and economic development. Thus, a supra agency with managing authority over only a limited range of its subordinates' activities was not practical or feasible. Instead, China relied for years on the Department of CMI Promotion [*junmin jiehe tuijin si*, 军民结合推进司]—a subordinate unit in the Ministry of Industry and Information Technology—to serve as the government's highest administrative body devoted solely to CMI work.[80] In practice, the department only had limited value in advancing reforms, as it had no discernible ability to set or enforce CMI policy and lacked the authority to play much of a managing role. It was ostensibly charged with promoting greater integration between civil-military S&T institutions, but since the actual management of these institutions fell to a host of other higher ranking agencies (among them the Ministry of Science and Technology, Ministry of Commerce, National Development and Reform Commission, and State Administration for Science and Technology for National Defense), it could do little to affect actual behavior. As a result, its activities were restricted to serving as a CMI facilitator, in which it acted as an information resource for CMI opportunities and brought various stakeholders together to find opportunities to deepen CMI development.[81]

The problem of diffused national leadership over reforms was exemplified by the 2010 Opinions on Establishing and Improving a "Civil-Military Integration" and "Locating Military Potential in Civilian Capabilities" Weapons Research and Production System [*guanyu jianli he wanshan junmin ronghe yu jun yu min wuqi zhuangbei keyan shengchan tixi de ruogan yijian*, 关于建立和完善军民融合寓军于民武器装备科研生产体系的若干意见] issued by the Central Military Commission and State Council. This document was the most authoritative guideline for the CMI reform agenda through the 12th Five-Year Plan (2011–2015), and in that context it is worth noting how many institutions were given responsibility for CMI implementation. The Opinions were addressed to the People's governments in each province, autonomous region, and provincial-level city, the ministries and directly managed organizations under the State Council, the People's Armed Police, each of the PLA's services and branches, the four PLA general departments, each military region, each military district, the Academy of Military Science, the National Defense University, and the National University of Defense Technology. They called on "relevant departments" in the PLA and State Council to formulate concrete methods and policies to address CMI requirements, to focus their planning on developing links between units involved in CMI, and to implement CMI policies in close coordination with each other, based on their (unspecified) division of responsibilities. They also called on local governments and military equipment management departments at each level to actively work in concert and implement a full set of measures to ensure the smooth advancement of development for the CMI weapons research and production system. As one analysis highlighted, this guidance—in a top-level document that shaped CMI development in weapons research and production for years—placed overall managerial responsibilities in the hands of at least 20 different institutions under the CMC and State Council.[82]

China sought to mitigate these problems by creating top-level coordination groups, such as the Inter-Ministerial Coordinating Small Group for the Development of the (CMI) Weapons Research and Production System, which debuted in 2012. Led by the Ministry of Industry and Information Technology, the small group featured senior officials from 23 military and civilian departments.[83] It has met every year since its launch, and according to reports the meetings typically focus on discussing each member's respective efforts to support the current CMI priorities.[84] While this information-sharing is presumably helpful, the body is not equipped to resolve conflicts or disagreements, given that all members are on the same levels of the administrative hierarchy.

A diffused management of CMI was less consequential when China's key tasks were focused on developing a basic institutional framework for CMI. However, as CMI has progressed along its development path, the problems of disorganized management of CMI have become more obvious and acute. They are not only confined to the issues of coordination and superficial implementation, described above. As Chinese analysts have argued, inadequate management has also affected the pace of technology innovation, created widespread unnecessary duplication in investment and policies, failed to sufficiently encourage competition, and ultimately led to a huge amount of waste [*juda langfei*, 巨大浪费].[85]

Improving Top-Level Design

Given the difficulty in resolving the management issues described above, Chinese CMI experts have promoted the creation of a national-level managing organization with the authority to oversee top-level design of CMI reforms.[86] These calls have now been answered. China launched a Central Commission for Integrated Military and Civilian Development [*jun-min ronghe fazhan weiyuanhui*, 军民融合发展委员会]. This commission, announced on January 22, 2017, is chaired by Xi Jinping, and its original members included three other Politburo Standing Committee (PBSC) members (Li Keqiang, Liu Yunshan, and Zhang Gaoli) as vice chairmen, as well as CMC Vice Chairmen Xu Qiliang and Fan Changlong.[87] According to news reports, the commission was specifically created to provide unified leadership of CMI decisionmaking, acting as a top-level coordinating organization overseeing the most significant issues affecting CMI development. It reports directly to the Politburo and PBSC, and its importance is reflected in the fact that Zhang Gaoli was chosen to lead the commission's General Affairs Office [*bangongshi*, 办公室].[88] As the *South China Morning Post* article on his appointment observed, the head of the General Affairs Office is more typically a lower grade leader, so it is unusual that a PBSC member was chosen to lead the commission's day-to-day operations.[89]

In a sign of how important its work is considered, the commission has already met three times—in June and September 2017 and in March 2018. At the September 2017 meeting, Xi called on members to strengthen top-level design of CMI development and urged them to insist on making key breakthroughs, while focusing both on present and long-term strategies for CMI development.[90] The members also reviewed accomplishments since the first meeting and discussed work items relating to the passage of recent CMI guidelines, including the Guidelines for Defense Science and Technology Industry Development During the 13th Five-Year Plan (2016–2020), Opinions on Promoting Deep Development of Civil-Military Integration in the Defense Science and Technology Industries, and Opinions on Implementing Deep Development of Civil-Military Integration in Military Logistics During the 13th Five-Year Plan.[91] The commission's third meeting called for strengthening the leading role of strategy and ideology, for the CMI development strategy to take root in each region and department, and for reforms to achieve effective results in key domains, regions, and industries. It also highlighted the need for key reform breakthroughs, such as quickly eliminating barriers to defense conversion [*jun zhuan min*, 军转民] and civilian participation in the defense industries [*min can jun*, 民参军] and hastening key reforms in areas like defense S&T industries, PLA equipment acquisition, pricing of military supplies, and unbalanced civil-military taxation policies.[92]

While the launch of the commission is an important step for the management of CMI reforms, none of the management challenges that existed before its creation has melted away. It must still deal with a sprawling network of institutions (with a diverse set of functions) that implement CMI directives. It also still faces the problem of misaligned incentives between national- and local-level actors, as party leadership appears to expect lower level compliance with CMI directives without acknowledging that they may be at odds with corporate and organizational interests. However, CMI operationalization is now led by a higher authority that can issue concrete guidance, push authoritatively for greater interagency cooperation, and more credibly demand a focus on overarching goals. In addition, the commission allows the government's CMI management system to move toward a more rational division of labor—where top-level management organs make policy decisions, interministerial coordinating organs allow leaders from relevant departments to consult with their counterparts, CMI departments lead, and relevant departments carry out centralized management.[93]

Conclusion

Xi Jinping's assessment that China has only just emerged from its initial phase of CMI development serves as a useful reminder that CMI is still a work in progress, with fundamental questions about how to operationalize and manage it still unsettled. In particular, despite full agreement on the abstract need for CMI, China's aspirations for it involve an extremely complex level of system of systems (interministerial, cross-sectoral, center-local, and civil-military) cooperation, and substantive buy-in for this degree of integration is not yet widespread. As described in this chapter, Chinese actors throughout the CMI universe have shown varying levels of commitment to CMI reforms, and while the sustained drumbeat of pressure from top-level leadership makes it unlikely that disinterested actors can fully resist efforts to deepen CMI, they can surely limit how far CMI behavior is institutionalized. As such, China's prospects for fully integrating CMI processes into day-to-day PLA functions remain in doubt, and the track record suggests that even positive returns will involve a longer and more difficult process than the party currently acknowledges.

However, China is clearly improving its understanding of CMI-related policy challenges and has shown a commitment to working through them despite their obvious complexity. Even before the creation of the Central Commission for Integrated Military and Civilian Development, one of China's leading voices on CMI strategy argued that China had started the process of taking on the deep-rooted obstructions that had hampered CMI development.[94] This effort is reflected in the designation of CMI as a national strategy in 2015, and Xi's engagement on the issue, which has created a new urgency to generate substantive CMI returns. According to the reform timeline that the CMC described when it announced its PLA reform plan in January 2016, CMI reforms would be a focus from 2017 to 2020. As such, the effort to adjust, optimize, and improve its workings is just getting started, and still has 3 years to go.[95] It is too early to assess how well it has gone.

The government has set a goal of "breakthrough" development in CMI by 2020, and while this is a vaguely defined objective, there is reason for Chinese leaders to think it is reachable. An institutional framework for CMI operations is already in place, a better management structure has been devised, and invested leaders have accrued several years' worth of watching CMI in practice and working through policy solutions to emergent problems. As a result, although CMI reforms have thus far not delivered on their promise, and still face significant hurdles, there is more of a chance for CMI to take hold. If it does, it will mark a turning point in the PLA's reforms, with tangible and significant multiplier effects in areas such as defense science and technology, logistics, military education, and mobilization. By the same token, it would be equally important if China continued to struggle with CMI implementation. A failure to deepen CMI reforms would serve as a drag on the PLA's reform process and impair China's ability to fully meet the challenges—as it currently sees them—of modern informationized warfare.

Notes

[1] Joel Wuthnow and Phillip C. Saunders, *Chinese Military Reforms in the Age of Xi Jinping: Drivers, Challenges, and Implications*, China Strategic Perspectives 10 (Washington, DC: NDU Press, 2017), 1.

[2] Cao Zhi, Li Xuanliang, and Wang Shibin, "Xi Jinping: Unswervingly Implement Comprehensive Reforms for the Strong Army Strategy and Take the Path of a Strong Army with Chinese Characteristics" [习近平: 全面实施改革强军战略坚定不移 走中国特色强军之路], Xinhua [新华], November 26, 2015, available at <http://news.xinhuanet.com/politics/2015-11/26/c_1117274869.htm>.

[3] Ibid.

[4] As Chinese analysts have noted, China has a long tradition of integrating military and civilian resources and functions, including the "PLA, Inc." that thrived under Deng Xiaoping. However, the People's Republic of China had not previously used civil-military integration (CMI) as a modernization strategy.

[5] Jiang Luming, "The Overall Strategy for National Security and Development" [统筹国家安全和发展的总方略], *China Defense Daily* [中国国防报], June 2, 2016, 3, available at <www.81.cn/gfbmap/content/2016-06/02/content_146372.htm>.

[6] Ibid., 3.

[7] Jiang Luming, "Why Civil-Military Integration Has Been Raised to a National Strategy" [军民融合发展缘何上升为国家战略], *PLA Daily* [解放军报], February 3, 2017, 7; Wang Weihai, "Uphold Taking the Strong Army Road of Civil-Military Integration with Chinese Characteristics" [坚持走中国特色军民融合强军之路], *Qiushi* [求是], August 2, 2017, available at <www.qstheory.cn/wp/2017-08/02/c_1121421061.htm>.

[8] Wang Lu, "Achieve a Unification of 'Rich Country, Strong Army' in the Great Rejuvenation of the Chinese People" [在民族伟大复兴进程中实现富国和强军相统一], *Qiushi* [求是], April, 26, 2017, available at <www.qstheory.cn/dukan/qs/2017-04/26/c_1120876410.htm>.

[9] Ibid.

[10] Jiang Luming, *A Selection of Lectures by Jiang Luming* [姜鲁鸣讲稿自选集] (Beijing: National Defense University Press [国防大学出版社], 2014), 71.

[11] Shou Xiaosong, ed., *The Science of Military Strategy* [战略学] (Beijing: Military Science Press [军事科学出版社], 2013), 267–268.

[12] Hou Guangming and Li Cunjin, *Applied Research in Methods to Promote Defense Industry Innovation* [军工企业创新方法推广应用研究] (Beijing: Science Press [科学出版社], 2014), 1.

[13] "Suggestions on Implementing Innovation-Driven Development in Defense Areas, and Promoting Civil-Military Integration-Style Development" [关于在国防领域实施创新驱动发展战略, 推进军民融合式发展的建议], in *Civil-Military Integration Development Strategy* [军民融合发展战略], ed. Chinese Academy of Engineering [中国工程院] (Beijing: Higher Education Press [高等教育出版社], 2014), 440.

[14] Hou and Li, *Applied Research in Methods to Promote Defense Industry Innovation*, 1.

[15] "President Xi Says China Faces Major Science, Technology 'Bottleneck,'" Xinhua, June 1, 2016, available at <http://news.xinhuanet.com/english/2016-06/01/c_135402671.htm>.

[16] Xi Jinping, "Secure a Decisive Victory in Building a Moderately Prosperous Society in All Respects and Strive for the Great Success of Socialism with Chinese Characteristics for a New Era," Xinhua, October 18, 2017, available at <www.xinhuanet.com/english/download/Xi_Jinping's_report_at_19th_CPC_National_Congress.pdf>.

17 Li Jia, He Siyuan, and Lu Pei, *The Civilian Contracting Big Screen Has Opened,* [We Discuss] *Preferred Platform Companies* [民参军大幕开启, 优选平台型公司] (Guiyang, China: Hua Chuang Securities [华怆机械军工], June 24, 2015), 9. To be clear, in this instance the authors are speaking of worldwide generations of fighters, rather than Chinese fighter generations specifically.

18 Yu Chuanxin, *Actual Combat Series on National Defense and Armed Forces in the New Situation* [实战化的军民融合] (Beijing: PLA Publishing House [解放军出版社], 2015), 005–006.

19 Eric Hagt, "Emerging Grand Strategy for China's Defense Industry Reform," in *The PLA at Home and Abroad: Assessing the Operational Capabilities of China's Military,* ed. Roy Kamphausen, David Lai, and Andrew Scobell (Carlisle Barracks, PA: Strategic Studies Institute, 2010), 481–546.

20 "Liu Yasu's Speech at the Opening Ceremony for the China Institute of National Defense Finance Studies" [刘亚苏在中国国防金融研究会成立大会上的讲话], China National Defense Finance Association [中国国防金融研究会], May 12, 2016, available at <www.chinaelections.org/article/1974/243072.html>.

21 Hu Zhengyang and Zhen Yi, *Looking at the Next 15 Years in Military Power and Defense Industries from the Perspective of Defense Budgets* [从军费看军力, 军工未来十五年] (Guangzhou, China: GF Securities [广发军工], March 23, 2016), 4; Michael Martina and Ben Blanchard, "China Confirms 7 Percent Increase in 2017 Defense Budget," Reuters, March 6, 2017, available at <www.reuters.com/article/us-china-parliament-defence/china-confirms-7-percent-increase-in-2017-defense-budget-idUSKBN16D0FF>.

22 Adam P. Liff and Andrew S. Erickson, "Demystifying China's Defense Spending: Less Mysterious in the Aggregate," *China Quarterly,* vol. 216 (December 2013), 805–830.

23 In other words, China seems unlikely to be hiding dramatically higher increases in other budgetary areas that affect defense modernization, while allowing the rate of increase in its defense budget to fall.

24 Liu Shuoyang, "Grand Strategy to Promote the Defense Economy Development" [推进国防经济发展的宏伟方略], *Military Economic Research* [军事经济研究], no. 11 (2015), 14.

25 Luan Dalong, "Promote Mixed Ownership Reform with the Help of Defense Industry Asset Securitization" [借助军工资产证券化促进混合所有制改革], *Defense Science and Technology Industry* [国防科技工业], no. 9 (2016), 38.

26 *Annual Report to Congress: Military and Security Developments Involving the People's Republic of China 2017* (Washington, DC: Office of the Secretary of Defense, 2017), 67.

[27] Wang Shunian, "Coordinate Economic and National Defense Construction—Take the Road of Civil-Military Integration-Style Development with Chinese Characteristics" [统筹经济建设和国防建设 走中国特色军民融合式发展路子], *China Reform Daily* [中国改革报], December 26, 2012, available at <www.crd.net.cn/2012-12/26/content_6143909.htm>; Zhang Fengpo, "Civil-Military Integration Inserts Soaring Wings for a Strong, High-Tech Military" [军民融合为科技强军插上腾飞的翅膀], *PLA Daily* [解放军报], June 21, 2017, available at <www.stdaily.com/index/toutiao/2017-06/21/content_554673.shtml>.

[28] Jiang Ying, "Military Reforms and Deep Civil-Military Integration" [军队改革与军民深度融合], *National Defense* [国防], no. 5 (2017), 14; Zhong Tao and Li Yaping, "The Role of National Guidance in Deepening Civil-Military Integration" [论军民融合深度发展的国家主导作用], *China Military Science* [中国军事科学], no. 5 (2016), 75.

[29] Zhu Qinglin et al., *The Theory of Military and Civilian Integration* [军民融合论] (Beijing: Haichao Press [海潮出版社], 2014), 4; Jiang Luming, *A Selection of Lectures by Jiang Luming* [姜鲁鸣讲稿自选集] (Beijing: National Defense University Press [国防大学出版社], 2014), 1.

[30] Li Xin and Wang Maosen, *Defense Industry Mid-Year Strategy Report* [军工行业年中策略报告] (Nanchang, China: AVIC Securities, June 30, 2016), 14.

[31] Gu Tongfei, *Optimizing the Structure of the Civil-Military Integration Equipment Market* [军民融合装备市场结构优化] (Beijing: National Defense Industry Press [国防工业出版社], 2017), 9.

[32] Yu, *Actual Combat Series on National Defense and Armed Forces in the New Situation*, 004.

[33] Ibid.

[34] Jiang, *A Selection of Lectures by Jiang Luming*, 72.

[35] Yang Shaoxian, "2017 Development Trends in Civil-Military Integration" [2017年军民融合的发展趋势], *Defense Science and Technology Industry* [国防科技工业], no. 4 (2017), 31.

[36] Wang, "Achieve a Unification of 'Rich Country, Strong Army' in the Great Rejuvenation of the Chinese People."

[37] Jiang, *A Selection of Lectures by Jiang Luming*, 71.

[38] Ibid., 72.

[39] Ma Xianzhang, "A Study on the Deep Development of Civil and Military Integration" [军民融合深度发展问题研究], *Proceedings of the 5th Conference on Chinese Command and Control* [第五届中国指挥控制大会论文集] (Beijing:

Publishing House of Electronics Industry [电子工业出版社], 2017), 9; Daniel Alderman et al., "The Rise of Chinese Civil-Military Integration," in *Forging China's Military Might*, ed. Tai Ming Cheung (Baltimore, MD: Johns Hopkins University Press, 2014), 109–135.

[40] Wang Weihai, "The New State of Global Civil-Military Integration Development" [世界军民融合发展新态势], *PLA Daily* [解放军报], February 17, 2017, 7.

[41] Wang, "Achieve a Unification of 'Rich Country, Strong Army' in the Great Rejuvenation of the Chinese People"; He Xinwen and Hou Guangming, "Constructing National Defense Science and Technology Innovation Organizational Systems on the Basis of Civil-Military Integration" [基于军民结合的国防科技创新组织系统的构建], *China Soft Sciences Supplement* [中国软科学增刊 (上)], no. 1 (2009), 333.

[42] Lin Luning, "Some Thoughts on Promoting CMI Development in Our Defense S&T Industries" [关于推进我国国防科技工业军民融合发展的若十思考], *Defense Science and Technology Industry* [国防科技工业], no. 8 (2010), 33.

[43] Shou, *The Science of Military Strategy*, 269; Jacques S. Gansler, *Defense Conversion* (Cambridge, MA: MIT Press, 1998), 9–13.

[44] Elsa Kania, "The Dual-Use Dilemma in China's New AI Plan: Leveraging Foreign Innovation Resources and Military-Civil Fusion," Lawfareblog.com, July 28, 2017, available at <https://lawfareblog.com/dual-use-dilemma-chinas-new-ai-plan-leveraging-foreign-innovation-resources-and-military-civil>.

45 Jeffrey Engstrom, *Systems Confrontation and Systems Destruction Warfare: How the Chinese People's Liberation Army Seeks to Wage Modern Warfare* (Santa Monica, CA: RAND, 2018); Wang, "Uphold Taking the Strong Army Road of Civil-Military Integration with Chinese Characteristics"; Yu Chuanxin and Zhou Jianping, eds., *Theory and Practice of Civil-Military Integration Development* [军民融合式发展 - 理论与实践] (Beijing: Military Science Publishing House [军事科学出版社], 2010), 32.

[46] Jiang, "Why Civil-Military Integration Has Been Raised to a National Strategy," 7.

[47] An Baijie, "Xi: Reform of PLA Calls for 'All-Out Efforts,'" *China Daily* (Beijing), July 26, 2017, available at <www.chinadaily.com.cn/china/2017-07/26/content_30246927.htm>.

[48] "China Targets Smaller but Better Structured Armed Forces," *China Military Online*, July 26, 2017, available at <http://eng.chinamil.com.cn/view/2017-07/26/content_7690835.htm>.

[49] "The Central Military Commission's Opinion on Deepening Military and National Defense Reforms" [中央军委关于深化国防和军队改革的意见],

Xinhua [新华], January 1, 2016, available at <http://news.xinhuanet.com/mil/2016-01/01/c_1117646695.htm>.

50   Jiang Luming, "Winning the Tough Battle That Is Military Reform" [打赢军队改革这场攻坚战], *Guangming Daily* [光明日报], July 25, 2017, 2, available at <http://epaper.gmw.cn/gmrb/html/2017-07/25/nw.D110000gmrb_20170725_1-02.htm>.

51   The current Chinese term for CMI [*junmin ronghe*, 军民融合], which conveys the kind of thorough integration of civilian and military resources that the government now promotes, became canon after it appeared in the 17th Party Congress's final report in 2007.

52   Tai Ming Cheung, *Fortifying China: The Struggle to Build a Modern Defense Economy* (Ithaca, NY: Cornell University Press, 2009); Chen Xianfan, Zhou Ershuang, and Zhu Yueru, *Civil-Military Integration: National Strategy, Strong Country and Invigorated Military* [军民融合: 国家战略, 强国兴军] (Suzhou, China: Soochow Securities, Feburary 22, 2016), 25.

53   The best example of these types of reform measures was the "Opinions on Establishing and Improving a 'Civil-Military Integration' and 'Locating Military Potential in Civilian Capabilities' Weapons Research and Production System" [*guanyu jianli he wanshan junmin ronghe yu jin yu min wuqi zhuangbei keyan shengchan tixi de ruogan yijian*, 关于建立和完善军民融合寓军于民武器装备科研生产体系的若干意见] that the Central Military Commission and State Council released in 2010, which set the CMI reform agenda in defense science and technology through the 12th Five-Year Plan (2011–2015).

54   Zhu et al., *The Theory of Military and Civilian Integration*, 2.

55   Alderman et al., "The Rise of Chinese Civil-Military Integration."

56   Di Bian, "Group Together Policy and Strength to Collectively Advance Defense Contracting" [群策群力共推民参军], *Defense Science and Technology Industry* [国防科技工业], no. 6 (2014), 14; Gu Tongfei [顾桐菲], *Optimizing the Structure of the Civil-Military Integration Equipment Market* [军民融合装备市场结构优化] (Beijing: National Defense Industry Press [国防工业出版社], 2017), 9–10.

57   "Focus Hard on Key Areas in Civil-Military Integration Development" [向军民融合发展重点领域聚焦用力], *Changjiang Daily* [长江日报], September 23, 2017, 8.

58   Zhu et al., *The Theory of Military and Civilian Integration*, 5.

59   These include a series of annual catalogs of dual-use and defense conversion technologies seeking investment support and declassified defense patent catalogs published by the Central Military Commission Equipment Development Department's National Defense Intellectual Property Rights Bureau, which are designed

to help lower defense research and development costs for academic institutions, research institutes, and civilian contractors.

⁶⁰ Jiang, "Military Reforms and Deep Civil-Military Integration," 16; *2018 Investment Strategies for the Defense Industries* [军工行业2018年度投资策略] (Beijing: Northeast Securities Co., Ltd., November 10, 2017), 9.

⁶¹ Jiang, "Military Reforms and Deep Civil-Military Integration," 17; Yan Guiwang [严贵旺], "Tibet Advances the Building of an Army-Local Civil-Military Integration Guarantee System" [西藏军地推进军民融合保障体系建设], *China Defense Daily* [中国国防报], January 12, 2017, available at <http://news.xinhuanet.com/mil/2017-01/12/c_129442916.htm>; "PLA Invites Civil Logistics Firms to Help Distribute Materials," *China Military Online*, May 3, 2017, available at <http://eng.chinamil.com.cn/view/2017-05/03/content_7586584.htm>.

⁶² Sun Yanhong, Yuan Wei, and Chen Li, "A Study of Xi Jinping's Strategic Thought on Civil-Military Integration" [习近平军民融合发展战略思想研究], *China Military Science* [中国军事科学], no. 2 (2017), 12.

⁶³ "China's Xi Calls for Closer Civil-Military Integration to Boost Army Combativeness," Xinhua, March 12, 2015, available at <http://news.xinhuanet.com/english/2015-03/12/c_134062544.htm>.

⁶⁴ Gu Tongfei [顾桐菲], *Optimizing the Structure of the CMI Equipment Market* [军民融合装备市场结构优化] (Beijing: National Defense Industry Press [国防工业出版社], 2017), 10.

⁶⁵ Sun, Yuan, and Chen, "A Study of Xi Jinping's Strategic Thought on Civil-Military Integration," 13.

⁶⁶ Bi Jingjing and Xiao Dongsong, eds., *China Civil-Military Integration Development Report 2016* [中国军民融合发展报告2016] (Beijing: National Defense University Press [国防大学出版社], 2016), 27–61; Wang, "Achieve a Unification of 'Rich Country, Strong Army' in the Great Rejuvenation of the Chinese People."

⁶⁷ Jiang, "The Overall Strategy for National Security and Development," 3.

⁶⁸ Li Xuanliang, Wang Jingguo, and Wang Yushan, "Xi Jinping: Accelerate the Setting Up of a Civil-Military Integration Innovation System in Order to Provide a Powerful Support for Our Army Building" [习近平: 加快建立军民融合创新体系为我军建设提供强大科技支撑], Xinhua [新华], March 12, 2017, available at <http://news.xinhuanet.com/politics/2017lh/2017-03/12/c_1120613988.htm>.

⁶⁹ Yu Xiangming, "The First Batch of Military Research Institutes Have Begun Restructuring—Accelerating the Implementation of Civil-Military Integration" [首批家军工科研院所转制启动—军民融合加速实施], Shanghai Securities News [上

海证券报], July 10, 2017, available at <http://stock.qq.com/a/20170710/003913.htm>; Bank of China, "Mechanized Defense Industry 2015 Fall [Investment] Strategy" [机械军工2015年秋季策略], August 14, 2015, 26.

70 Elsa Kania and Stephen Armitage, "Disruption under the Radar: Chinese Advances in Quantum Sensing," *China Brief* 17, no. 11 (August 17, 2017), 15–21; Elsa Kania and John Costello, "Quantum Leap (Part 1): China's Advances in Quantum Information Science," *China Brief* 16, no. 18 (December 5, 2016), 11–16; Elsa Kania and John Costello, "Quantum Leap (Part 2): The Strategic Implications of Quantum Technologies," *China Brief* 16, no. 19 (December 21, 2016), 21–27; Lian Weiliang, "Use Reform and Innovation to Advance Civil-Military Integration Development" [以改革创新促进军民融合发展], *Qiushi* [求是], October 31, 2016, available at <www.qstheory.cn/dukan/qs/2016-10/31/c_1119817228.htm>.

71 Wen Xiaoge, "In-Depth Civil-Military Integration of Science, Technology and Industry for National Defense" [论国防科技工业军民融合深度发展], *China Military Science* [中国军事科学], no. 1 (2016), 48.

72 Zhong and Li, "The Role of National Guidance in Deepening Civil-Military Integration," 77.

73 Bi Jingjing and Xiao Dongsong, eds., *China Civil-Military Integration Development Report 2015* [中国军民融合发展报告2015] (Beijing: Defense University Press [国防大学出版社], 2015), 12–13.

74 "Recommendations for Reforming the Top-Level Management System and Mechanisms for Civil-Military Integration Development" [关于改革完善军民融合发展顶层管理体制机制的建议], in *Civil-Military Integration Development Strategy*, 439.

75 Zhong and Li, "The Role of National Guidance in Deepening Civil-Military Integration," 75–79.

76 Xie Wuzhong, "Five Development Concepts to Guide the Deeper Development of Civil-Military Integration" [以五大发展理念引导推动军民融合深度发展], *PLA Daily* [解放军报], January 25, 2016, 6, available at <www.81.cn/jfjbmap/content/2016-01/25/content_136357.htm>.

77 Zhong and Li, "The Role of National Guidance in Deepening Civil-Military Integration," 75–76.

78 Ma, "A Study on the Deep Development of Civil and Military Integration," 9–10.

79 Zhong and Li, "The Role of National Guidance in Deepening Civil-Military Integration," 75–76.

80 Task Group for "Research on Chinese Defense Science and Technology Industries' Civil-Military Integration Development Strategy Project" ["中

国国防科技工业军民融合式发展战略研究"项目课题组], "Research Report on Chinese Defense Science and Technology Industries' Civil-Military Integration Development Strategy" [中国国防科技工业军民融合式发展战略研究报告], in *Civil-Military Integration Development Strategy*, 448.

[81] Dong Xiaohui, Zeng Li, and Huang Chaofeng, "The Present Condition of Military and Civilian Integration Development of National Defense Industry Base and the Countermeasure" [国家工业基础军民融合发展现状与对策], *Military Economics Research* [军事经济研究], no. 4 (2012), 19.

[82] Ibid.

[83] Task Group for "Research on Chinese Defense Science and Technology Industries' Civil-Military Integration Development Strategy" Project, 448.

[84] "The Sixth Meeting of the Inter-Ministerial Coordinating Small Group for the Development of 'Civil-Military Integration' and 'Locating Military Potential in Civilian Capabilities' Weapons Research and Production System" [军民结合寓军于民武器装备科研生产体系建设部际协调小组第六次会议召开], Changzhou Jianeng Management Consulting [常州嘉能管理咨询], April 6, 2017, available at <www.jmrhw.org/gczx/20170406/1695.html>.

[85] "Recommendations for Hastening Civil-Military Integration-Style Development in China's National Defense Science and Technology Industries" [关于加快我国国防科技工业军民融合式发展的建议], in *Civil-Military Integration Development Strategy* [军民融合发展战略], ed. Chinese Academy of Engineering [中国工程院] (Beijing: Higher Education Press [高等教育出版社], 2014), 437.

[86] Yu Chuanxin, "Some Thoughts on the Top-Level Design of Civil-Military Integration Development" [军民融合式发展顶层设计的几点思考], in *Civil-Military Integration Development Strategy* [军民融合发展战略], ed. Chinese Academy of Engineering [中国工程院] (Beijing: Higher Education Press [高等教育出版社], 2014), 94–97.

[87] Choi Chi-yuk, "In Unusual Move, Xi Appoints Top Party Leader to Lead Daily Affairs of Key Committee," *South China Morning Post* (Hong Kong), June 21, 2017, available at <www.scmp.com/news/china/policies-politics/article/2099248/xi-jinping-further-consolidates-power-commission>. It is unclear what the senior leadership of the commission will look like in the wake of Liu and Zhang's retirement at the 19th Party Congress. News items about the third meeting of the commission, held on March 2, 2018, did not describe personnel changes but noted that Li Keqiang, Zhang Gaoli, and Wang Huning were in attendance. Zhang was presumably in attendance because his term on the Politburo did not

officially expire until later in March 2018. See "Xi Jinping: Truly Grasp and Work to Firmly Implement the Civil-Military Integration Development Strategy, Open up a New Aspect of the New Era of Deeper Civil-Military Integration Development" [习近平: 真抓实干坚定实施军民融合发展战略 开创新时代军民融合深度发展新局面], Xinhua, March 2, 2018, available at <www.xinhuanet.com/politics/2018-03/02/c_1122478435.htm>.

[88] Li Junhai and Wang Nianchun, *Central Commission for Integrated Military and Civilian Development Is Created, and This Is Good for the Long-Term Development of the Defense Industries* [军民融合发展委员会成立, 利好军工长期发展] (Shenzhen, China: Guosen Securities [国信证券], January 23, 2017), 1.

[89] Choi, "In Unusual Move, Xi Appoints Top Party Leader to Lead Daily Affairs of Key Committee."

[90] "Focus Hard on Key Areas in Civil-Military Integration Development," 8.

[91] Ibid.

[92] Xi Jinping: Truly Grasp and Work to Firmly Implement the Civil-Military Integration Development Strategy."

[93] You Guangrong and Zhao Linbang, *Development of Civil-Military Science and Technology Integration—Theory and Practice* [军民科技融合发展 — 理论与实践] (Beijing: National Defense Industry Press [国防工业出版社], 2017), 13.

[94] Yu Chuanxin, "On the Four Principal Points in the Strategy of Civil-Military Integrated Development" [论军民融合发展战略的四个关节点], *China Military Science* [中国军事科学], no. 6 (2016), 109.

[95] "Central Military Commission Opinion on Deepening Military and National Defense Reforms."

CHAPTER 17

SYSTEM OVERLOAD?

The 2015 PLA Force Reduction, Military-Locality
Relations, and the Potential for Social Instability

By Ma Chengkun and John Chen

On September 3, 2015, Chinese Communist Party (CCP) General Secretary and Central Military Commission (CMC) Chairman Xi Jinping announced a reduction in the overall size of the People's Liberation Army (PLA) from 2.3 million personnel to 2 million, a reduction of about 11 percent of the military's end strength.[1] The announcement was followed by a Work Conference on Central Military Commission Reform [*zhongyang junwei gaige gongzuo huiyi*, 中央军委改革工作会议] in which Xi initiated his military reform plan.[2] A flurry of organizational and structural reforms to the PLA soon followed, and continues apace today.

The reforms were to be implemented in three main stages. First, top leadership and management organs of the PLA were to be reorganized and the joint operations command structure reformed before the end of 2015. Next, changes in force structure and size, along with reforms to the military education system and the People's Armed Police, were to be implemented before the end of 2017. Finally, the above reforms, along with changes to the policy system and civil-military integration, were to be adjusted, advanced, optimized, and completed from 2017 to 2020.[3]

To those ends, the Ministry of National Defense announced that the reduction of 300,000 personnel from the PLA would be completed by the end of 2017.[4] Broadly speaking, Xi's reform directives explicitly included rationalizing the structure and organization of the military force, reducing numbers of administrative and noncombat personnel, and adjusting and improving the ratio of different services.[5] The troop reduction was widely interpreted as a means of implementing these overarching directives. Noncombat billets are likely to be targeted for elimination, and PLA interlocutors have suggested that the ratios of navy and air force personnel will increase relative to their army counterparts.[6]

Downsizing 300,000 PLA personnel while simultaneously upending and reorganizing the operational and administrative components of the military would inevitably bring considerable turmoil and dislocation. Xi's downsizing policy also forced Chinese society to absorb and reintegrate a substantial portion of these 300,000 personnel in the span of approximately 2 years. At a minimum, any failure or inefficiency in accommodating these personnel and their families could jeopardize the pace and effectiveness of the military reforms; at worst, neglect or poor execution of the downsizing could lead to potentially regime-threatening social instability.

The risks of a botched troop reduction were not lost on the Xi regime. Xi himself has consistently reiterated the importance of properly reintegrating downsized military personnel back into Chinese society, and he has emphasized the work of veteran administration and support at the central government level to forestall dissatisfaction from downsized personnel.[7]

This chapter argues that although force reductions are especially fraught for the local governments responsible for accommodating veterans, the effort will ultimately be successful due to a number of countervailing forces in play during this latest reduction effort. These offsetting forces range from the benevolent encouragement of veteran entrepreneurship to the more ominous specter of Xi's ongoing anti-corruption campaign, and most importantly, the supremacy of party rule over any potential legal, economic, and political contradictions. The announcement in March 2018 that the troop reduction was "basically complete" supports this judgement, while the establishment of a new Ministry of Veterans Affairs [*tuiyi junren shiwu bu*,退役军人事务部] speaks to the military-locality tensions and conflicts of interest that had to be managed and overcome in the process.[8]

The chapter proceeds in four parts. The first section gives a brief historical overview of military-locality relations and documents changes in relations that have increasingly pushed the burdens of troop reductions and personnel resettlement onto local governments. The second section describes key parts of the military-locality administrative system and the legal regulations overseeing the 2015–2017 troop reduction. The third section explores political, economic, and legal issues that complicate force reduction efforts, and describes the intermittent protests by dissatisfied veterans that have resulted from past complications. The chapter concludes with an examination of several countervailing considerations and various factors unique to the Xi era that are likely to offset the difficulties of the reduction, albeit at the expense of strains in military-locality relations.

Evolving Military-Locality Relations

The PLA's modern-day efforts to reduce its end strength are dependent on good relations with the localities that must absorb the burden of troop reductions. Military-locality relations in the years before Deng Xiaoping's late 1970s reforms focused primarily on providing moral and material support to the PLA and its predecessors. After Deng's reforms began to take hold, however, the realities of China's emerging market economy began to substantially increase pressure on localities charged with handling troop reductions. These difficulties have extended to the present day.

Early Military-Locality Relations

The PLA has a long history of drawing support from the people, dating back to the 1927 founding of its predecessor military organization, the Chinese Workers' and Peasants' Red Army [*zhongguo gongnong hongjun*, 中国工农红军]. In the years leading up to 1949, interactions between the military and the people, referred to as "military-locality relations" or "double support work" [*shuangyong gongzuo*, 双拥工作] by the Communist Party, initially emphasized preferential treatment for Red Army soldiers and their dependents in order to increase recruitment and political and logistical support for the Communist cause, and later expanded to demobilization and mobilization efforts.[9]

The resolution of the First Red Army Representative Assembly [*minxi di yi ci gongnong bing daibiao dahui xuanyan ji jueyian*, 闽西第一次工农兵代表大会宣言及决议案], held in Fujian in March 1930, provided a monthly stipend to Red Army soldiers and called for CCP members to shape the societal atmosphere to improve the social position of the Red Army.[10] This treatment was later extended to Red Army dependents in 1934: the CCP 2nd National Soviet Assembly adopted the Resolution on Preferential Treatment of Red Army Dependents [*zhongguo gongchangdang zhongyang weiyuanhui, zhonghua suweiai gongheguo renmin weiyuanhui guanyu youdai hongjun jiashu de jueding*,中国共产党中央委员会、中华苏维埃共和国人民委员会关于优待红军家属的决定], emphasizing the necessity of extending this resolution into a social movement for the purpose of strengthening the combat determination of the Red Army and encouraging more people to join the forces.[11]

The founding of the People's Republic of China (PRC) in 1949 introduced demobilization of military personnel as a major new task for military-locality relations. Military victory over the Kuomintang on the mainland precipitated a pressing need to reduce the size of the PLA, which led to an initial force reduction in March 1950.[12] Newly anointed PRC officials set up governing and administrative infrastructure according to socialist ideology for national development. Early centrally planned mechanisms for resettling and reintegrating demobilized soldiers in their hometowns provoked relatively little controversy between the military and various localities because the interests of central and local governments often overlapped—for instance, the PLA needed to shed personnel, and local governments needed labor.

Mao Zedong's decision to send PLA troops to the Korean War abruptly upended the initial process of demobilization and sent defense mobilization to the top of the priority list of military-locality issues. On December 2, 1950, the Central Government Interior Affairs Ministry and General Political Department of the People's Revolutionary Military Commission issued "Instructions for Supporting Policy and Loving the People and Initiating Movement of Supporting Military Personnel and Their Dependents" [*guanyu xinjiu nianguan kaizhan yongzheng aimin he yongjunyoushu yundong de zhishi*, 关于新旧年关开展拥政爱民和拥军优属运动的指示], formally establishing a mechanism of interaction for local governments to mobilize logistics and recruitment support for the army.[13] This was the first official directive by the Chinese government codifying a mechanism for mobilization efforts from the Chinese population.

Defense mobilization, preferential treatment for military personnel and their dependents, and resettlement of demobilized military personnel remained the core issues of military-locality relations until 1979, along with a strong emphasis on maintaining popular support for the military. The provision of preferential benefits to soldiers and codification of mobilization efforts were supplemented by patriotic parades and ceremonies organized by local governments on significant days for the PLA. The main responsibility for military-locality interaction fell largely on the people, who were charged with showing their respect and support for military personnel.

Popular moral support for the military belied the comparatively underdeveloped nature of demobilization mechanisms. After the PRC was founded in 1949, the government kept the military permanently mobilized as it continually perceived serious hostility from the international community. Under these circumstances, the PLA had little chance to transform itself from a revolutionary force organized mainly by rural citizens into a regular army with regular conscription and a demobilization mechanism. Time in service was not well defined. Personnel could remain in the military until they decided to leave or the military believed they were too old to continue service. While mobilization mechanisms relied heavily on popular local support, demobilization mechanisms remained comparatively underdeveloped.

Reform and Opening Up, Military Modernization, and Military-Locality Relations, 1979–Present

China's leaders initially sought to maintain existing military-locality relations even as Deng Xiaoping's 1979 reform and opening up [*gaige kaifang*, 改革开放] shifted the direction of the national zeitgeist from revolution to peaceful development. The December 14, 1979, "Notice to Enhance the Glorious Tradition of Supporting Military Personnel and Dependents, Supporting Policy and Loving the People, and Further Strengthening Military-People Unity" [*guanyu fayang yongjunyoushu, yongzheng aimin de guangrong chuantong, jinyibu jiaqiang junmin tuanjie de tongzhi*, 关于发扬拥军优属, 拥政爱民的光荣传统, 进一步加强军民团结的通知] exemplified this extension of the status quo and confirmed existing mechanisms of military-locality interaction.[14]

In the early 1980s, however, China's program of defense modernization presented a new major challenge to military-locality relations. Deng announced a force reduction plan in June 1985 that would trim 1 million military personnel from the PLA as part of a broader defense modernization and cost reduction effort.[15] The announcement of the massive troop reduction was followed soon by a notice placing the responsibility of resettling demobilized personnel at the top of the priority list for localities. The July 27, 1985, "Notice on Respecting the Military and Actively Supporting Military Reform and Construction" [*guanyu zunzhong, aihu jundui jiji zhichi jundui gaige he jianshe de tongzhi*, 关于尊重, 爱护军队积极支持军队改革和建设的通知] elevated resettlement [*anzhi*, 安置] for demobilized PLA personnel as the most important task that localities could undertake to support the reforms.[16]

At first, local governments were usually able to resettle demobilized PLA personnel into corresponding high- or low-level positions. Local governments had more billets available than the central government and proved able to accommodate demobilized personnel one way or another. Officers were offered local government positions roughly equal to their former military grade and became civilian officials; enlisted personnel, for whom the local government had no resettlement responsibility, were nonetheless often pointed toward lower level grassroots labor units to forestall potential unemployment.

As Deng's economic reforms accelerated, however, China's transition to a market economy made military resettlement much more difficult. Market pressures for organizational and financial reform in government sectors to reduce personnel spending and improve government efficiency made it increasingly difficult to accommodate demobilized PLA personnel. Local governments, given wide latitude to implement their own reforms, began privatizing state-owned enterprises, reducing redundant billets, laying off underperforming employees, or at least slowing the hiring of new personnel. The remaining collectively run government enterprises were hit especially hard, facing stiff competition from foreign and foreign-invested competitors.

This rush to privatize state-owned enterprises disenfranchised demobilized PLA personnel. Newly privatized enterprises began to shirk their responsibilities to resettle and retrain veterans in their drive to compete in the marketplace. The 1993 "Notice Concerning Problems of Enterprises Canceling Worker Identification Boundaries and Fully Implementing the Labor Contract System" [*guanyu qiye quxiao gongren shenfen jiexian shixing quan yuan laodong hetong zhi ruogan wenti de yijian de tongzhi*, 关于企业取消工人身份界限实行全员劳动合同制若干问题的意见的通知] was one such example; the notice allowed enterprises to cancel the national cadre identity of former military cadres in order to establish more normal, efficient personnel systems within the enterprise.[17] It also freed enterprises from the burden of subsidies, as well as medical and social insurance for these military cadres, all of which had been promised by the government when they left the military.

In an attempt to respond to reports of shirking, the central government promulgated a series of legal and organizational measures intended to ensure better military-locality relations. A National Double Support Work Leading Group [*quanguo shuangyong gongzuo lingdao xiaozu*, 全国双用工作领导小组] was established in 1991 by the State Council and CMC to coordinate and unify the work of provincial, county, city, and municipal Double Support Offices [*shuangyong bangongshi*, 双用办公室].[18] To further clarify regulations regarding the treatment of separated officers, the State Council and CMC issued the *Provisional Measures for Resettling Transferred Officers* [*jundui zuanye ganbu anzhi zanxing banfa*, 军队转业干部安置暂行办法] in 2001. These measures remain in force today as the primary reference document governing the treatment of demobilized, retired, or downsized PLA personnel; the measures have been supplemented by additional laws codifying the treatment of enlisted personnel. The administrative organs and the legal regulations guiding the resettlement of PLA personnel are covered in detail in the following section.

Administrative and Legal Mechanisms for Force Reduction

As the 2015 PLA personnel reduction has proceeded, several details about troop reduction have surfaced. Half of the downsized personnel are reportedly officers,[19] and generally speaking, administrative and command billets have been reduced.[20] For the most part, these discharged personnel will have a number of separation options available according to a collection of laws passed and overseen by two main organizations of the State Council. This section examines key components of the separation process, giving an overview of the legal mechanisms and organizations responsible for accommodating discharged PLA personnel.

Resettlement and Separation Options

Soldiers leaving the PLA have a number of separation options available to them according to their grade and time in service.[21] Resettlement and separation options for conscripts, noncommissioned officers (NCOs), and officers are governed by a variety of relevant laws discussed in the text and figures below.[22]

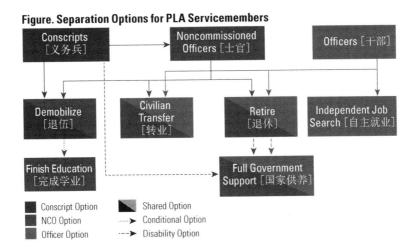

Figure. Separation Options for PLA Servicemembers

Conscripts (义务兵). As late as 2007, conscripts appeared to have only one main option for separation from the PLA. They could choose to simply be released from service [*tuiwu*, 退伍] after their 2-year service commitment with no government obligation to provide job placement, or they could decide to extend their term of service and become NCOs, after which they would enjoy the separation benefits and options described in the next section. Those who chose to leave have traditionally returned home and continued their old way of life.[23]

Conscripts that left after fulfilling their service obligation were entitled to certain benefits, including a small resettlement allowance and assistance in job-hunting. However, these entitlements had often been ignored or doled out unevenly across China, sparking complaints and aggravating civil-military tensions.[24] Dissatisfaction with inconsistent disbursement of benefits led the central government to codify the benefits available for discharged conscripts. The most obvious changes are manifested in 2011 revisions to the Military Service Law [*zhonghua renmin gongheguo bingyifa*, 中华人民共和国兵役法] and Enlisted Personnel Resettlement Regulations [*tuiyi shibing anzhi tiaoli*, 退役士兵安置条例], which declared conscripts eligible for a one-time independent subsidy [*zizhu jiuye yicixing tuiyijin*, 自主就业一次性退役金], in which they would look for a job themselves and collect a one-time subsidy from the military.[25] As of September 2015, demobilized conscripts also receive a one-time demobilization subsidy [*tuiwu buzhufei*, 退伍补助费], a one-time healthcare subsidy [*tuiwu yiliao buzhufei*, 退伍医疗补助费], a subsidy consisting of next month's allowance [*lidui xiayue jintie*, 离队下月津贴], prorated living expenses for the month they leave [*lidui dangyue shengyu tian huoshi fei*, 离队当月剩余天伙食费], and living expenses for the month after demobilization [*lidui xiayue huoshifei*, 离队下月伙食费], among additional healthcare and retirement subsidies.[26]

Noncommissioned Officers (士官). NCOs enjoy more separation options and benefits than conscripts. As of 2007, enlisted personnel who had served up to 6 years beyond their initial 2-year conscription period were considered junior NCOs [*chuji shiguan*, 初级士官] and were eligible only for demobilization [*tuiwu*, 退伍]. NCOs who had served between 8 and 16 years beyond their initial 2-year conscription period were referred to as mid-level NCOs [*zhongji shiguan*, 中级士官] and were eligible for transfer to civilian state positions [*zhuanye*, 转业] after 10 years of total service. Senior-level NCOs [*gaoji shiguan*, 高级士官], or NCOs who had served at least 14 years beyond their conscription period, were eligible to retire [*tuixiu*, 退休] after 30 years of total service.[27]

Major changes to discharge and resettlement policy enacted in 2011 expanded resettlement options and simplified separation benefits. Revisions to the Military Service Law outlined five major separation and resettlement options: independent job-searching [*zizhu jiuye*, 自主就业]; government job placement [*anpai gongzuo*, 安排工作], also known as civilian transfer [*zhuanye*, 转业]; full retirement [*tuixiu*, 退休]; government support [*gongyang*, 供养]; and completion of education [*jixu wancheng xueye*, 继续完成学业].[28] The 2011 revision to the Enlisted Personnel Resettlement Regulations simplified eligibility rules for separation benefits: NCOs who had served less than 12 years would receive essentially the same benefits as conscripts, including the same one-time independent job-searching subsidy per year of service from the military, along with possible further financial subsidies from local provincial and municipal governments.[29] NCOs who had served more than 12 years were eligible for government job placement (also known as resettlement),[30] while those who had served at least 30 years, were disabled in war or public service, were 55 years or older, or had to retire for health reasons were eligible for full retirement or government support.[31]

Officers (干部). Officers have the most options available for separation from the PLA and enjoy greater benefits than either enlisted soldiers or conscripts.[32] Officers are required to apply for separation from the PLA. Of those whose applications are accepted, officers who have served for 30 years are eligible for full retirement. Division leader grade officers with less than 30 years of service and officers at the battalion leader grade or lower with less than 20 years of service are to be transferred to civilian state employment. Battalion and regiment leader grade officers who have served between 20 and 30 years are allowed either to accept a transfer to a civilian job or to accept a partial pension while they independently seek employment in the private sector [*zizhu zeye*, 自主择业].[33]

Officers transferred to civilian positions are entitled to the same levels of pay and benefits they would have earned at their duty grade level in the PLA,[34] and their years in military service count toward retirement at their civilian positions.[35] Civilian transfers also collect subsidies for living expenses [*shenghuo buzhufei*, 生活补助费] and home settlement [*anjia buzhufei*, 安家补助费].[36] Officers who choose to independently seek employment accept an 80 percent pension that persists unless they accept a job in the government sector.[37] They are also eligible for a job-search subsidy [*zizhu zeye buzhufei*, 自主择业补助费] on top of the living expenses and home settlement subsidies offered to civilian transfers.[38] Officers that retire collect full pensions and are eligible for a number of allowances, including one-time payments for living expenses and home settlement,[39] along with housing, healthcare, and other benefits.[40]

Most officers leaving the PLA must return to the location of their original household registration [*hukou*, 户口]. Some consideration is made for the locations of spouses or parents,[41] although the policy does not elaborate on who makes the decision. Those leaving under the auspices of independent job-searching, as well as aviation and naval officers who have served 10 or more years, are also allowed a degree of flexibility in resettlement.[42] Discharged officers can also be placed in other regions as needed.[43] Some officers may simply be transferred to locations as needed rather than transferred home, especially to government regions in central and western China "eagerly hunting for talented people."[44]

Full Government Support (国家供养). A special discharge option is full government support [*guojia gongyang*, 国家供养] for all military personnel who are disabled in public service and includes considerable disability compensation payments based on the level and type of disability. Disabilities are classified on a scale of severity from Levels 1 to 10 (1 is the most severe) and sorted by combat, work, or illness disabilities. Personnel with disability ratings from Level 1 to Level 4 are eligible for full government support and receive substantial compensation payments in addition to health care and housing allowances.[45]

Key Trends. Changes in the PLA's separation and resettlement processes since the last major troop reduction in 2003 can be characterized in three main ways.

First, conscripts have increasingly enjoyed greater benefits for their service, and as the PLA continues to seek more college-educated personnel, it will feel compelled to better enforce existing demobilization policy and improve the conscript demobilization package by providing more generous benefits. The 2011 revisions to discharge policy afforded much greater financial assistance to conscripts by opening up independent job selection to a group that was simply demobilized and returned home in the past. Some demobilized conscripts ostensibly leave the force with marketable job skills and useful certifications such as a driver's license,[46] although their employment prospects are in doubt in an economy that increasingly values higher skilled workers. The PLA faces no shortage of available conscripts,[47] but in recent years it has been forced to relax physical standards to attract better educated personnel.[48] As it continues to compete with the private sector for college-educated personnel, the PLA will have little choice but to continue increasing expenditures on demobilized conscripts as one way to attract desired talent.

Second, the PLA has placed increasing emphasis on higher education as a separation pathway, especially for its enlisted and noncommissioned personnel. This is evident in the various incremental revisions to NCO discharge and resettlement policies. Starting in 2011, NCOs who have been discharged for longer than a year, have tested into a full-time higher education program, and are participating in independent job-searching are also entitled to a yearly tuition subsidy of up to 6,000 RMB (roughly $942 USD in 2018)[49]—a figure that was adjusted upward in 2014 to 8,000 RMB ($1,257) a year for undergraduate programs and 12,000 RMB ($1,885) a year for graduate programs.[50] Discharged enlisted personnel who choose independent job selection are also entitled to attend local government vocational education for up to 2 years at no cost.[51]

Third, the civilian transfer process for officers has become increasingly competitive. Though the burden of resettling transferred officers is the legal responsibility of local governments[52] and rejecting officers is not allowed,[53] there appears to be a priority order for the best positions. Division and regiment leader grade officers eligible for civilian transfer must undergo an evaluation process [*kaohe*, 考核] that assigns civilian positions based on moral virtue, grade, military rank, time in service, specialty skills, hardship duty, and military commendations. Eligible officers at the battalion leader grade or lower would undergo the above evaluation process and an additional testing process [*kaoshi*, 考试] administered by the receiving province, consisting of a written test and an in-person interview.[54] The competitive nature of civilian transfers has generated considerable anxiety over transfer prospects.[55]

Separation and resettlement mechanisms have changed over time according to various needs and pressures. The PLA's desire for college-educated personnel precipitated an increase in benefits for demobilized conscripts, while the looming expense and difficulty of finding jobs for NCOs led officials to highlight education as an increasingly important pathway for discharged troops. The opacity of the officer civilian transfer process prompted officials to clarify the process in an attempt to defuse criticism from the affected group. In each case, the PLA and the relevant civilian agencies have taken deliberate steps to address a need or a potential problem.

Resettlement Organizations

The task of reintegrating PLA personnel into Chinese civil society falls to a pair of State Council small groups [*xiaozu*, 小组] comprised of various agency officials with relevant roles. These national-level small groups nominally oversee a larger nationwide ecosystem of corresponding provincial, county, and municipal groups responsible for disbursing a variety of benefits to discharged PLA personnel, ranging from placement in civilian government-arranged jobs to lump sum pension and buyout payments. Although the exact bifurcation of responsibilities remains unclear, generally speaking the State Council Military Cadre Transfer and Resettlement Work Small Group is responsible for transferring military officers to civilian government jobs, while the National Double Support Work Leading Small Group handles the resettlement of retiring military personnel and civilian cadres [*wenzhi ganbu*, 文职干部].

Resettlement and Transfer Work. The organization primarily responsible for transferring military personnel to civilian government jobs is the State Council Military Cadre Transfer and Resettlement Work Small Group [*guowuyuan jundui zhuanye ganbu anzhi gongzuo xiaozu*, 国务院军队转业干部安置工作小组]. This group is headed by the director of the Ministry of Human Resources and Social Security [*renli ziyuan shehui baozhang bu*, 人力资源社会保障部][56] and has typically been comprised of members from the former General Political Department, Ministry of Public Security, Ministry of Civil Affairs, and several other government, party, and military organizations.[57]

Table. Separation Options and Major Associated Benefits for PLA Servicemembers		
Separation Mechanism	Eligibility	Major Associated Benefits
Demobilize [退伍]	Conscripts; NCOs with less than 12 years of service	One-time demobilization subsidy (4,500 RMB per year of service); one-time independent job-searching subsidy (2,000 RMB); one-time healthcare subsidy; pro-rated last month's living expenses; following month's living expenses (750 RMB)
Finish Education [完成学业]	NCOs demobilized more than a year ago who have tested into a full-time higher education program and are independently job searching	Tuition subsidy: 8,000 RMB per year for undergraduate programs; 12,000 RMB per year for graduate programs; up to 2 years of free access to local government vocational education
Civilian Transfer [转业]	NCOs with more than 12 years of service; division-leader grade officers with less than 30 years of service; battalion-leader grade officers or lower with less than 20 years of service	Salary equivalent to pay level at time of discharge; years in military service count toward civilian retirement; living expenses subsidy: none for less than 8 years of service; 3 months salary for 8 to 9 years of service; additional 1 month salary for each year of service beyond 9, up to 16 years; home settlement subsidy: 4 months salary for 14 years of service or less; additional half-month salary for each year of service beyond 15 years
Independent Job Search [自主择业]	Battalion and regiment leader grade officers with more than 20 but less than 30 years of service	Monthly pension payment worth 80 percent of monthly salary; job search subsidy: 1 month salary for every year of service under 15 years; additional 1.5 month salary for each year of service beyond 16 years; same living expenses and home settlement subsidies as civilian transfers
Retire [退休]	NCOs and officers at the age of 55 or with 30 or more years of service	Full monthly pension; one-time living expenses subsidy: 4 months salary; home settlement subsidy: 8 months salary for troops returning to rural areas; 6 months salary for troops retuning to cities
Full Government Support [国家供养]	Conscripts, NCOs, and officers disabled in public service	Health care, caretaking, and housing allowances; annual compensation payments corresponding to disability level and type, ranging from 5,000 to 52,000 RMB

Key: NCO: noncommissioned officer; RMB: renminbi.

The General Office of the Transfer and Resettlement Small Group [*guowuyuan jundui zhuanye ganbu anzhi gongzuo xiaozu bangongshi*, 国务院军队转业干部安置工作小组办公室], also known as the Military Officer Transfer Resettlement Department [*junguan zhuanye anzhisi*, 军官转业安置司], carries out most of the actual work of resettling transferred officers to civilian government roles at the national level. Specifically, the General Office plans military cadre transfer resettlement, trains and educates on policy and resettlement plans, makes adjustments to the resettlement system, and handles Beijing-area transfer resettlements. The organization is also partly responsible for resolving problems that arise with transfers to industries, and manages independent job-searching services [*zizhu zeye*, 自主择业].[58] The national level small group oversees the work of local provincial, county, and municipal leading small groups that undertake the same transfer resettlement tasks as the General Office.[59]

Double Support Work System. The administrative system officially responsible for coordinating overall military-locality relations is headed by the National Double Support Work Leading Small Group (NDSWLSG) [*quanguo shuangyong gongzuo lingdao xiaozu*, 全国双用工作领导小组], operating under the authority of the CCP Central Committee, State Council, and CMC.[60] Led by a vice premier, the NDSWLSG is made up of 7 deputy directors and 31 members representing a wide variety of government, party, and military organizations, including the political work departments of the four former PLA general departments and the People's Armed Police.[61]

The General Office of the NDSWLSG [*quanguo shuangyong gongzuo lingdao xiaozu bangongshi*, 全国双用工作领导小组办公室] is charged with disseminating information to and liaising with provincial, county, and municipal Double Support Offices [*shuangyongban*, 双拥办],[62] which are typically situated under the authority of local civil affairs departments.[63] The General Office has two subordinate groups: the Secretariat [*mishuzu*, 秘书组], charged with organizing and coordinating meetings and communication between national and local Double Support Offices, and the Policy

Research Group [*zhengce yanjiu zu*, 政策研究组], responsible for drafting reports and publications of the NDSWLSG.[64]

The NDSWLSG is responsible for resettling certain types of discharged military personnel. The director of the Special Care Resettlement Bureau [*youfu anzhi ju*, 优抚安置局] of the Ministry of Civil Affairs (MCA) [*minzhengbu*, 民政部] is a member of the NDSWLSG,[65] and the bureau is responsible for the resettlement of discharged enlisted personnel [*tuiyi shibing*, 退役士兵] demobilized cadre [*fuyuan ganbu*, 复员干部], retired military cadre [*jundui li tuixiu ganbu*, 军队离退休干部], and retired non-military staff [*wu junji tuixiu tuizhi zhigong*, 无军籍退休退职职工].[66] The bureau's subordinate units include a Comprehensive Office [*zonghe chu*, 综合处] and a Policy and Law Office [*zhengce fagui chu*, 政策法规处]. Both are affiliated with the Secretariat and Policy Research Group of the General Office of the NDSWLSG, respectively.[67]

Overall, the Ministry of Civil Affairs and the PLA's CMC Political Work Department are the primary loci of responsibility for double support work, with a heavy emphasis on resettlement of military personnel. The director and deputy director of the MCA occupied two of the seven NDSWLSG deputy director positions in 2013, and the MCA deputy director was dual-hatted as the head of the General Office of the NDSWLSG. Two of the three deputy directors of the General Office hailed from the CMC Political Work Department Mass Work Office [*zong zhengzhi bu qunzhong gongzuo bangongshi*, 总政治部群众工作办公室]; the third was the deputy director of the Special Care Resettlement Bureau of the MCA.[68]

Broader Characteristics. At the national level, the composition of these small groups suggests that a variety of agencies have important equities in managing resettlement and separation of PLA personnel. Several agencies have representatives present as members of both small groups, specifically the Ministry of Human Resources and Social Security, CCP Central Organization Department, political departments of the various former PLA general departments, and ministries and administrations for national development and reform, finance, education, housing, taxation, and industry and commerce.[69]

Many of the participating organizations in both the Double Support and Resettlement LSGs have other primary functions, and the rotational nature of LSG membership extends to both national- and local-level LSGs. The overwhelming majority of members in both groups are deputy directors of their respective "home" organizations, serving on the groups as part of a rotational assignment; a few are assistants to directors.[70] New rosters with different members are announced every 4 to 5 years.

While the responsibilities at the national level seem clear, the lines of responsibility are not always so at the local level. Both double support work and resettlement work are the responsibilities of local civil affairs departments, but it is not clear if double support work includes resettlement, or if double support work and resettlement are considered separate tasks under separate units. The NDSWLSG considers resettlement to be within its purview, describing resettlement work as a critical part of double support work.[71] Some provinces include resettlement and transfer work under the auspices of double support work.[72] Several cities, however, direct "double support work" at active military personnel and their dependents, and consider double support work to be distinct from resettlement work.[73]

Problems with Resettlement

While the codification of preferential treatment and job placement for discharged PLA personnel represented a concerted attempt to formalize a discharge and separation process, the effort has suffered from complications. A lack of standardization in converting military grades to civilian equivalents has led to complaints about resettlement, and restrictive legal measures limit the options of local governments. At a macro level, the localities charged with resettling PLA personnel into civilian jobs face political and economic pressures that profoundly undercut their ability to complete this task quickly and efficiently.

Complications

The lack of a standardized conversion between military and civilian grades has spawned widespread complaints that personnel resettlement differs across provinces. While the *Provisional Measures for Resettling Transferred Officers* stipulates that military officers should be emplaced into positions of equal grade,[74] the measures do not specify what the corresponding civilian grades are. According to one PLA officer, the military uses a system based on 15 grades and equivalent civilian systems have 11 or 12 grades.[75] Although there is discussion about unifying the two systems, as of 2017, the conversion from military to civilian grades varied from province to province.[76] Problems with resettling regiment and division grade officers are particularly acute.[77] In the past, many regiment and division grade officers would have readily found arranged employment in local government billets as dictated by the State Council, typically as county mayors [*xianzhang*, 县长], office heads [*chuzhang*, 处长], administration heads [*juzhang*, 局长], or department heads [*tingzhang*, 厅长].[78] As more regiment and division grade officers left the PLA across multiple troop reductions, however, local governments struggled to accommodate all of these personnel at the dictated civilian grade level. Instead, local governments began backsliding on these assignments, sometimes failing to assign discharged personnel to civilian positions or assigning them to lesser sinecures as a way to fulfill their obligation. Discharged regiment and deputy regiment grade officers continue to face this problem: many are currently being forced to accept lower grade positions while working their way up the civilian promotion ladder to positions to which they should have already been legally entitled.[79]

Local governments, however, do not have full authority to assign discharged PLA personnel to whichever positions they wish; their autonomy is restricted by laws passed to reform China's civil service. The 2005 Civil Servant Law [*gongwu yuanfa*, 公务员法] states that all non-leadership positions lower than senior section member [*zhuren keyuan*, 主任科员] must be filled using open examination, strict testing, and equal competition to select the most qualified candidates.[80] Article 25 of the same law states that civil service positions will be "filled within the limits of the authorized size" and when there are "vacancies of corresponding posts to be filled up."[81] Structurally, this means that local government positions at the township [*xiang*, 乡] level and below are subject to open examination and fair competition practices and cannot be simply assigned to discharged military personnel;[82] all billets must be filled according to set, existing vacancies, severely restricting the ability of local governments to create positions for discharged PLA personnel.

Broader efforts to streamline and reform the administrative elements of local and national governments, along with corresponding efforts to reduce military administrative billets, have also greatly complicated the resettlement and accommodation of discharged PLA personnel. Accelerated reform efforts in both the PLA and in local governments have upset patronage networks and "iron rice bowls" that previously provided for military cadres and government officials.

Breaking Military and Government Iron Rice Bowls

The recent PLA reorganization has focused on slimming down noncombat and administrative organs, upending the PLA's iron rice bowl and resulting in a surplus of discharged PLA personnel who must be offered civilian positions commensurate to their military grade.[83] In the past, unit commanders often extended the military careers of officers who did not win promotion to increasingly competitive command track positions in combat units by transferring them to administrative or noncombat billets. This process was especially common for division and regiment grade officers and helped commanders avoid embarrassing personnel downsizings that would weaken their fiefdoms. These billets are now being reduced en masse, resulting in a large number of less-qualified discharged division and regiment grade officers who must be accommodated by local governments.

In the past, local governments responded to the ballooning number of discharged military personnel by creating civilian billets with little substantial responsibility to accommodate additional troop reductions. Today, however, local governments face a mandate to slim down their administrative organs—the same ones that would ordinarily provide civil service billets for demobilized or discharged PLA personnel.[84] Local governments often have little recourse left but to offer lower grade positions, register these veterans and ask them to wait, or hope veterans accept buyouts to participate in independent job-searching.

The pressure to slim down both civilian and military administrative positions has created significant difficulties in finding appropriate positions for field grade officers at the division- and regiment grade levels. The resettlement of these officers is one of the most difficult problems in personnel resettlement and has been amplified by the lack of a standardized conversion between military and civilian grades, leading to widespread complaints that personnel resettlement differs across provinces.[85] Regiment and deputy regiment grade officers, among others, have often been forced to accept lower grade positions while working their way up the civilian promotion ladder to positions they may have already been legally entitled to.[86]

The Effects of Market Reforms and Economic Adjustment

China's shift toward a market economy has also profoundly reduced the ability and willingness of localities to accommodate discharged PLA personnel. In the past, state-owned enterprises (SOEs) were to accommodate discharged personnel into positions in industry and commerce, but increasing privatization and market liberalization have incentivized these companies to shirk their responsibilities to veterans. Some economic reforms, like the 1993 Notice Concerning Problems of Enterprises Canceling Worker Identification Boundaries and Fully Implementing the Labor Contract System [*guanyu qiye quxiao gongren shenfen jiexian shixing quan yuan laodong hetong zhi ruogan wenti de yijian de tongzhi*, 关于企业取消工人身份界限实行全员劳动合同制若干问题的意见的通知] not only were meant to create more efficient and competitive personnel systems in state-owned industries,[87] but also allowed enterprises to cancel the national cadre identity of these former military cadres, freeing the companies from the burden of medical and social insurance.

The ultimate result of this privatization for enterprises was organizational reform, large-scale layoffs, and veteran dissatisfaction. Newly unemployed military veterans were told that the enterprise had already become a private business, so SOEs had no responsibility for their subsidies and medical care promised by the government. Local governments claimed they had fulfilled their obligation to veterans by finding them jobs, and the military viewed these veterans as civilians and ultimately refused to intercede on their behalf.

Economic readjustment and rebalancing are slated to accelerate under Xi Jinping, leaving localities with an even more daunting task ahead of them. The government is embarking on "structural reforms" to reduce over-capacity in the steel and coal sectors, potentially shedding millions of jobs, many in the economically depressed Northeastern rust belt.[88] The sweeping pace and scope of the anticipated economic reforms have prompted officials to promise that China can handle the economic adjustments;[89] the government quickly announced that it would earmark some 100 billion RMB (roughly $15.7 billion USD in 2018) to offset pending unemployment.[90] Nonetheless, local governments will likely be hard pressed to find appropriate jobs for discharged military personnel amid the upheaval caused by the latest tranche of economic reforms.

Overall, local governments are under increasing pressure to accommodate PLA personnel leaving the military, but their viable options for doing so are dwindling. Problems with resettlement policy and restrictive legal measures limit the ability of local governments to handle the most recent troop reduction quickly and without incident. When combined with the effects of accelerating reform in military, civil, and economic sectors, the processes of resettlement and dispensing preferential treatment for PLA veterans look set to significantly increase military-locality tensions and potentially create problems for the regime.

Protests

Many of the problems described above have resulted in increasingly visible protests by disenfranchised PLA veterans in the last 15 years. In April 2005, more than 1,600 discharged military personnel came from 20 provinces to hold a peaceful sit-in demonstration in Tiananmen Square, where they protested their unemployment even though they were supposed to receive corresponding jobs after they left the military.[91] Protests continued as market reforms deepened after Hu Jintao's inauguration. In 2007, more than 1,000 discharged military members clashed with the police in Heilongjiang, with several injured and arrested.[92] In Hunan, more than 300 discharged personnel protested in front of a provincial government building, prompting the local government to use special police forces to suppress the demonstration.[93]

The Central Military Commission responded to these protests by increasing subsidies for these former cadres, but the situation did not improve because protestors had already been stripped of their national cadre identities by local SOEs. In March 2008, roughly 6,000 discharged military cadres signed a petition to show their disapproval of the situation. This petition appealed to the central government to recover their cadre identity and associated subsidies, medical, and social insurances.[94] Protests continued into 2009, as hundreds of former cadres demonstrated and petitioned members of the local Shandong government assembly and asked the government to recover their cadre identity and to implement the resettlement policy of the central government.[95] Although the local government suppressed this demonstration, a larger protest occurred only 6 months later.[96]

The potential for troop reduction to create social instability is probably the single weightiest concern for the party.[97] Authorities appear to have ample reason for wariness: veterans complain that state-owned companies often renege on promised benefits and local officials embezzle funds meant for veterans,[98] and reports of protests have increased in the last year. As many as 4,000 veterans assembled at the offices of the CMC in July 2016 to call for the full payment of benefits.[99] Another protest in October 2016 brought hundreds of veterans to the CMC headquarters building in Beijing,[100] followed by another in early January 2017.[101]

Troop reduction will inevitably increase tensions between local governments and the central government and the PLA. Official media writings acknowledge these difficulties, noting that local governments will bear the heaviest burden of finding jobs for transferred officers and emphasizing the importance of alleviating this pressure.[102] The requirement that downsized personnel return to their home provinces virtually ensures that the troop reduction will impact Chinese provinces unevenly, as local governments in economically depressed regions of China will be charged with finding jobs for discharged personnel who likely joined the military in greater numbers to escape poor economic prospects. This could be harder if the PLA decides to cut large numbers of higher-ranking officers, who are entitled to scarce high-paying jobs.

Troop Reduction in the Xi Jinping Era

In spite of the organizations and regulations put in place to manage the separation of 300,000 military personnel from the PLA, the 2015 troop reduction has almost certainly encountered political, economic, and legal headwinds. The local governments that would otherwise accept discharged PLA personnel as civil servants face a political mandate to slim down their administrative ranks that has intensified as Xi Jinping's anti-corruption campaign continues apace. Large SOEs, previously major employers of discharged PLA personnel, face a similar political zeitgeist compounded on two sides by statist pressures for strong economic performance and market pressures wrought by privatization and free market competition. To make matters worse, the organizations responsible for resettlement are typically low on the pecking order, and legal mechanisms ensuring preferential treatment for discharged military personnel conflict with legislation designed to reform government civil service. At first glance, the 2015 troop reduction is likely to seriously disrupt military-locality relations thanks to these political, economic, and legal obstacles—recent suggestions that the deadline for force reductions will be extended until 2020 likely prove as much.[103]

Nevertheless, the party's worst fears about a troop reduction gone wrong are unlikely to come to pass in the era of Xi. Though the potential implications for social instability are serious, a number of considerations are likely to mitigate the problems of the ongoing troop reduction. Expertise gained from past troop reductions, general demographic characteristics of the downsizing, and the government's active efforts to strengthen supervision of veterans' affairs may help attenuate the difficulties of the current reduction effort. A number of countervailing forces unique to Xi Jinping's rule may temper objections and force cooperation, including recent initiatives for entrepreneurship, Xi's ongoing anti-corruption campaign, and the ultimate supremacy of party rule over the rule of law. On balance, the party will likely successfully reduce the size of the PLA without threats to its rule, even at the cost of greater tension in military-locality relations.

Countervailing Considerations

The PLA and Chinese government have extensive experience managing troop downsizing, implementing at least 11 large force reductions since 1949. Past reductions have been much larger and were accomplished in part by transferring personnel to the People's Armed Police.[104] Recent reduction efforts were similar in size, scale, and method to the current downsizing: the 1997 troop reduction cut 500,000 troops in 3 years, and the most recent troop reduction in 2003 downsized 200,000 troops in 2 years.[105] Though historical experience is no guarantee that Chinese authorities will successfully navigate the ongoing downsizing, both the PLA and relevant civil authorities have gained substantial insight into the possible problems associated with large troop reductions.

The demographics of the latest reduction may be less problematic than it initially appears. Though dissatisfied veterans might pose a political risk for China's leaders, they may constitute a relatively small percentage of discharged soldiers. Officers transferred to civilian jobs should be mollified by a position with equivalent pay and benefits, while retired officers can expect extensive benefits and a full pension. The biggest losers of the downsizing will be those officers who choose independent job-searching but subsequently have difficulty finding work on their own. Statistics from 2014, however, indicate that only 22.5 percent of the discharged officers choose independent job-searching,[106] amounting to an estimated 11,600 to 13,000 officers per year during the downsizing. This is no small figure, but authorities have already stepped up efforts to help these officers find employment by organizing conferences, giving classes, and teaching entrepreneurship skills.[107]

The transfer of PLA personnel to state-owned enterprises may also prove less painful than speculated. Statistics from past years suggest that only 1.5 to 2 percent of eligible officers are placed into SOEs,[108] roughly equivalent to 1,160 officers per year for the current troop reduction. Past economic reforms split SOEs into public and commercial categories, with several "strategic" industries kept under strict government control that will face a strong mandate to find jobs for eligible discharged PLA personnel.[109] Though the percentage of enlisted personnel transferred to SOEs is unknown, the government has reportedly made accommodation for enlisted personnel, announcing that 5 percent of jobs at SOEs would be reserved for discharged soldiers.[110]

While recent protests by PLA veterans have made for splashy headlines, these protestors are likely less of a threat to regime stability than reports indicate. Many of the demonstrators in these protests were older veterans from past conflicts like the 1979 Sino-Vietnamese War, for whom the primary concern is pension and benefits, not employment and resettlement.[111] These protesters are more likely to be placated by appropriate disbursement of subsidies and pose a less difficult logistical problem for local governments.

At a higher administrative level, the central government and PLA have undertaken several steps meant to strengthen supervision of veterans' affairs and eliminate corruption in the system. An October 2015 report indicated the PLA is considering establishing an independent body responsible for veterans' affairs.[112] The PLA's recent organizational reforms dismantled the four general departments that previously handled veterans' affairs for themselves[113] and placed the newly formed Organ Affairs General Management Bureau [*zhongyang junwei jiguan shiwu guanli zongju*, 中央军委机关事务管理总

局] in charge of veterans' affairs under direct CMC supervision.[114] Changes in resettlement and separation policy have expanded and codified benefits for discharged soldiers, and current policy allows the central government to simply assign officers to jobs outside their home province if necessary.[115] Pronouncements from the highest levels of China's leadership warn against contravention of demobilization and resettlement policy.[116]

The Chinese government has also demonstrated a tacit willingness to extend deadlines in order to forestall any potential future disruptions brought on by the troop reduction. PLA officers have suggested that the original deadline for reductions will be extended from the end of 2017 until 2020, giving more time for the relevant parties to arrange for the downsizing and subsequent treatment of discharged personnel.[117] While the deadline extension is an indicator of the difficulties inherent in trimming the PLA's end strength, it is also undoubtedly intended to relieve pressure on both PLA commanders charged with making reductions and the local governments tasked with providing benefits to discharged personnel.

Countervailing Factors in the Xi Era
Although the convergence of political, economic, and legal obstacles depicts bleak prospects for a smooth PLA personnel reduction, a variety of counter-vailing factors suggests that the reduction will nonetheless be successfully implemented. For instance, the various party and government organs charged with accommodating discharged PLA personnel will encour-age less burdensome alternative separation paths for them. Xi Jinping's anti-corruption campaign will punish some military personnel and leave them ineligible for preferential treatment, while cowing others into forego-ing aggressive efforts to secure their full benefits. Xi's recent consolidation of power at the 19th Party Congress is likely to steer governance away from institutionalization and rule of law and further toward party supremacy and personalized rule by Xi himself, making it less likely that legal barriers and local concerns will truly stand in the way of swiftly executing troop reduction and resettlement efforts that have Xi's backing.

Alternative Separation Options. Higher education, independent job-searching, and entrepreneurship initiatives benefiting discharged soldiers are increasingly attractive for the local governments and SOEs already hard pressed to accommodate former military personnel. Higher education bonuses and reduced pensions for independent job-searchers are ultimately much less expensive and easier to arrange than retirement with full pensions or transfer to civilian billets.[118] Chinese authorities are placing a stronger emphasis on these separation options. Military authorities have already stepped up efforts to help officers find employment by organizing conferences, giving classes, and teaching entrepreneurship skills;[119] provincial human resources offices have added more classes to improve entrepreneurship ability for discharged soldiers.[120] Provincial civilian and military organizations responsible for the troop reduction have begun holding ceremonies for soldiers who leave the PLA to obtain higher education.[121]

These separation options benefit multiple stakeholders in the discharge and resettlement processes and may alleviate the burden on localities charged with accommodating discharged soldiers. The military is able to jettison the personnel it no longer wants, and discharged PLA personnel are able to secure some benefits while pursuing futures in the private sector. Hard-pressed local authorities are absolved of resettlement obligations beyond a buyout payment for veterans who chose independent job-searching; they are similarly absolved of further obligations for personnel who choose to pursue higher education. Neither of these options are as expensive as retirement or civilian transfer, and nominally, neither option explicitly excludes PLA personnel that may have been charged with corruption. At scale, these alternative separation options could have benefits for the central government's effort to rebalance the economy; each veteran who starts a business is one less veteran on the payroll of a local government or state-owned enterprise.

The Anti-Corruption Campaign. Should education bonuses and entrepreneurship classes fail to satisfy the demands of PLA veterans, Xi's anti-corruption campaign adds a powerful coercive tool to the central government's toolkit for implementing the troop reduction on Xi's terms. The anti-corruption campaign has accelerated at an extraordinary pace since 2013, with 4,024 officers above lieutenant colonel punished since 2013[122] and 4,885 officers punished in 2016 alone.[123] At least 13,000 military officers have been punished since the campaign began in 2012.[124] According to article 13, section 2, of the *Provisional Measures for Resettling Transferred Officers*, regiment grade officers and below who have committed a crime are not eligible for resettlement benefits; anyone convicted of a crime is likewise ineligible for civil service jobs of any kind.[125] While some of these officers may remain in PLA service and are not part of the latest troop reduction, those who leave the PLA will not enjoy preferential treatment from the party.

The anti-corruption campaign also has a strong coercive and deterrent effect on military personnel and local government officials who have not officially been convicted of corruption. Many of the administrative and noncombat military organizations facing personnel reductions were hotbeds of corruption given their frequent interaction with commercial industry and civilian business. The specter of guilt and criminal charges withheld is likely to be compelling enough to force corrupt military personnel to leave the PLA without claiming the veterans' resettlement and benefits owed by the government. Even the hint of prosecution for corruption may have cowed Xi's political opposition into compliance before the 19th Party Congress; a similar dynamic will likely hold true for both the military personnel leaving the PLA and the local governments and SOEs charged with accommodating the discharged personnel. PLA veterans may be more willing to accept less than they are due rather than make complaints that risk triggering a corruption investigation.

Coercion and silencing effects aside, the national scope of the anti-corruption campaign may also free up civilian billets for discharged PLA personnel who do not have the black mark of corruption charges on their records. Local government officials and SOE leaders are not immune from the anti-corruption campaign; indeed, the campaign has thus far ensnared nearly 100,000 higher officials since it began in 2012, and the "tigers and flies" nature of the effort has targeted local officials as well.[126] Some of these recently vacated positions may be open for discharged PLA personnel.

Xi Ascendant: A More Compliant Governing Apparatus? Xi's consolidation of power at the top of the CCP will lead to a party that is more compliant and more likely to override legal mechanisms of resettlement should the need arise. Most agree that China is a country under "ruled by law" rather than "rule of law," despite attempts to portray China as the latter.[127] In other words, China's highest governing authorities, namely Xi and the CCP, may be more inclined than ever to adjust, override, contravene, or outright ignore existing law if the troop reduction threatens their rule.

Xi's anti-corruption campaign and subsequent coronation as core leader of the CCP hint at an increasing unity of command throughout the party that controls all aspects of the Chinese state and government. Given the party's longstanding emphasis on its control of the military and the military's continued allegiance to protecting the party,[128] central party leaders will not look kindly upon laws or local officials that restrict their ability to extend preferential treatment to PLA veterans. Military-locality relations will undoubtedly be strained by the troop reduction, but the well-worn maxim that the party comes before all else in China is likely even more true under Xi's consolidated rule than in years past. This centralization of power and emphasis on party rule will likely override local difficulties in accommodating PLA veterans.

Conclusion

The People's Liberation Army and relevant civilian agencies were well aware of the potential negative impact the force reduction could have on morale and social stability and have worked hard to anticipate and ameliorate problems from past force reductions. Expanding and increasing benefits to demobilized conscripts, providing more exit opportunities to NCOs in the form of education stipends, and clarifying the civilian transfer process for officers all represent calculated efforts by the Chinese government to soften the negative impact of force reductions on discharged soldiers. The government announced in March 2018 that the force reduction was "basically complete," although some PLA officers have privately suggested that the force reduction process could extend beyond the originally announced 2017 deadline until 2020.[129]

Nonetheless, the troop reduction significantly strained military-locality relations. Tensions were likely most aggravated in the localities hit hardest by the economic downturn that face underfunded mandates to find jobs for discharged PLA personnel. Still, the success of the force reduction indicates that challenges such as increased costs are serious but solvable: the government would likely find the monetary resources needed to make separation and pension payments if serious threats to social stability emerged. Furthermore, recent veteran protests appear to be aimed at eliciting central government pressure to rectify local injustices and protect veterans' rights, rather than directing dissatisfaction at the CCP and central government.[130] If social instability rises to a level that requires suppression, the Chinese internal security apparatus has amply demonstrated its ability to stifle any substantial disruption of social stability, applying its expertise most recently against veteran protesters in 2015.[131] The party's ability to control, co-opt, coerce, or otherwise suppress dissent is well documented by past incidents and verified by the party's continued rule.

The biggest challenge in any force reduction lies in finding civilian positions for discharged soldiers in poorer parts of China. Failure on this front could exacerbate tensions between the PLA and local governments, and more importantly, between the PLA and a party obliged to care for its military. However, this challenge does not seem to have posed a severe threat to party rule since the PLA and Chinese government were well positioned to mitigate the difficulties that arose from the force reduction. The claim that the force reduction is basically complete suggests that the challenges were manageable.

In March 2018, the Chinese government responded to the issues that emerged in the force reduction by establishing a new Ministry of Veterans

Affairs to "to maintain the legitimate rights and interests of the military personnel and their families, strengthen the building of the service and support system for veterans, build and optimize a concentrated, integrated, and well-defined service and support system for veterans, so as to make the military a better respected career in China."[132] The ministry is intended partly to serve as an advocate for veterans and to press local governments to meet their responsibilities. However, it is unclear whether this new organization will be successful in overcoming the inherent conflicts in interest between the military and local governments.

This chapter is based on a conference paper prepared for the 2016 CAPS-RAND-National Defense University People's Liberation Army Conference and a two-part article published by the Jamestown Foundation's *China Brief*. See Ma Chengkun, "Xi Jinping's Military Reform and Military Locality Relations," November 18–19, 2016; John Chen, "Downsizing the PLA, Part 1: Military Discharge and Resettlement Policy, Past and Present," *China Brief* 16, no. 16, October 26, 2016, available at <https://jamestown. org/program/downsizing-pla-part-1-military-discharge-resettlement-policy-past-present/>; and John Chen, "Downsizing the PLA, Part 2: The Potential for Social Instability," *China Brief* 16, no. 17, November 11, 2016, available at <https://jamestown.org/program/downsizing-pla-part-2-military-discharge-resettlement-policy-past-present/>.

Notes

[1] Shen Mengzhe and Liu Shaohua [申孟哲, 刘少华], "Chinese Military Reduction of 300,000 Personnel Draws Worldwide Praise" [中国裁军30万迎来世界点赞], *People's Daily Overseas Edition*, September 11, 2015, available at <www.mod.gov. cn/intl/2015-09/11/content_4619049.htm>.

[2] People's Liberation Army (PLA) General Political Department, "Resolutely Win the Tough Battle of Deepening Reform of National Defense and the Armed Forces—Thoroughly Study and Implement Xi Jinping's Important Expositions on Deepening the Reform of National Defense and Armed Forces" [坚决打赢深化国防和军队改革这场攻坚战——深入学习贯彻习主席关于深化国防和军队改革重要论述], *China Military Science*, no. 6 (2015), 1–6.

³ Liu Xiaopeng [刘晓朋], ed., "CMC Opinions on Deepening National Defense and Military Reforms" [中央军委关于深化国防和军队改革的意见], Xinhua, January 1, 2016, available at <http://news.xinhuanet.com/mil/2016-01/01/c_1117646695.htm>.

⁴ Sun Yanxin, Wang Jingguo, and Li Xuanliang [孙彦新, 王经国, 李宣良], "Ministry of National Defense Holds News Conference to Explain Military Parade and Troop Reduction Questions" [国防部举行新闻发布会详解阅兵和 裁军等问题], Xinhua, September 3, 2015, available at <http://news.xinhuanet.com/2015-09/03/c_1116457865.htm>.

⁵ Liu, "CMC Opinions."

⁶ Huang Zijuan [黄子娟], "Major General: Troop Reduction Will Focus on 'Joint Warfare'; Navy and Air Force Troop Ratios Could Increase" [少将: 裁军将围绕"联合作战"的核心; 海空军比例或增加], *People's Daily* (Beijing), September 7, 2015, available at <http://military.people.com.cn/n/2015/0907/c1011-27550619.html>.

⁷ Wang Jingguo [王经国], "Xi Jinping: Care and Show Concern for Resettling Military Cadre—Innovate Resettlement Work System" [习近平: 关心关爱军转干部 创新安置工作机制], Xinhua, June 7, 2016, available at <http://news.xinhuanet.com/politics/2016-06/07/c_1119007068.htm>.

⁸ "Defense Ministry's Regular Press Conference on March 29," *China Military Online*, March 30, 2018, available at <http://english.chinamil.com.cn/view/2018-03/30/content_7987841.htm>.

⁹ "Double support work" is a contraction of a Chinese phrase that roughly means "Locals support the troops and their dependents, troops support governments and love the people" [地方拥军优属, 军队拥政爱民]. See Hao Sijia [郝思嘉], ed., "How Much Do You Understand about Double Support Common Knowledge?" [这些双拥常识, 你了解多少?], Nantong Double Support Network [南通双拥网], July 5, 2017, available at <www.81.cn/zjsymfc/2017-07/05/content_6609115.htm>.

¹⁰ For one examination of early preferential treatment reserved for Red Army troops, see Dong Guangcun [董广存], "Early Era Military Personnel Stipends of the People's Liberation Army" [中国人民解放军建军早期的军人津贴], China Files [中国档案], January 26, 2009, available at <http://dangshi.people.com.cn/GB/8722624.html>.

¹¹ "Central Committee of the Communist Party of China, Chinese Soviet Republic People's Committee Decision Regarding Preferential Treatment for Red Army Dependents" [中国共产党中央委员会、中华苏维埃共和国人民委员会关于优待红军家属的决定], *Selected Documents of the Chinese Communist Party*

Central Committee, vol. 10 (1934–1935), available at <http://cpc.people.com.cn/GB/64184/64186/66640/4489969.html>.

[12] Li Tao [李涛], "Ten Historical Troop Reductions of the People's Liberation Army" [人民解放军历史上的10次大裁军], *PLA Daily* [解放军报], November 18, 2015, available at <www.81.cn/20151126jg/2015-11/18/content_6885147.htm>.

[13] For a discussion of this decision in historical context, see Bai Li [白黎], "People and Military United as One, Try and See Who Could Resist! Recollections of the Development of China's Double Support Work" [军民团结如一人，试看天下谁能敌: 忆我国双拥工作的发展], Qiushi Network [求是网], July 30, 2016, available at <www.qstheory.cn/wp/2016-07/30/c_1119309252.htm>.

[14] "A Brief History of the Development of Double Support Work" [双拥工作发展简史], *China Double Support Magazine* [《中国双拥》杂志], available at <http://syzz.mca.gov.cn/article/syjg/201405/20140500638856.shtml>.

[15] Li, "Ten Historical Troop Reductions of the People's Liberation Army."

[16] "Central Committee of the Communist Party of China, State Council Notice on Respecting the Military and Actively Supporting Military Reform and Construction" [关于尊重, 爱护军队积极支持军队改革和建设的通知], *Selected Important Documents of the 12th National Party Congress*, available at <http://cpc.people.com.cn/GB/64184/64186/66679/4493919.html>. The actual Chinese text is *jieshou anzhi hao zhuanye ganbu, shi dangqian difang dui jundui gaige he jianshe de zuida zhichi*, 接收安置好转业干部, 是当前地方对军队改革和建设的最大支持.

[17] For the text of the notice circulated to Shenzhen, see "Labor Department General Office Transmits to Shenzhen City Notice on Opinions Concerning Problems of Enterprises Canceling Worker Identification Boundaries and Fully Implementing the Labor Contract System" [劳动部办公厅转发深圳市《关于企业取消干部工人身份界限实行全员劳动合同制若干问题的意见》的通知], Shenzhen City Labor Bureau, July 5, 1993, available at <http://law.lawtime.cn/d521214526308.html>.

[18] Ministry of Civil Affairs [民政部], "A Brief Description of Double Support Work" [双拥工作简介], China Double Support Network [中国双拥网], available at <http://sy.mca.gov.cn/article/zzjg/sygk/200707/20070700000959.shtml>.

[19] Fang Yongzhi [房永智], "Media: Demobilization Ceremonies Should Be Held for the Nearly Half of the 300,000-Personnel Troop Cut That Will Be Officers" [媒体: 裁军30万近半是军官应举行退役仪式], *China Youth Daily* [中国青年报], June 13, 2016, available at <www.81.cn/jwgz/2016-06/13/content_7098812.htm>.

[20] Zhang Xiangyi, ed., "PLA Daily Editors' Department Essay: Military Reforms Have Entered the Era of 'New Organization'" [军报编制部文章: 改革强军

进入新体制时间'], *PLA Daily* [解放军报], April 8, 2016, available at <http://news.eastday.com/c/20160408/u1a9288279_K26843.html>; and Li Dongxing, Li Liang, and Wang Pei [李东星, 李亮, 王沛], "Organizational Reconstruction: How to Lead 'Large Armed Forces' with 'Small Organizations'" [体制重塑, '小机关' 如何指导 '大部队']," *PLA Daily* [解放军报], July 29, 2016, available at <http://military.people.com.cn/n1/2016/0729/c1011-28594372.html>.

²¹ Chinese laws do not appear to specify transfer to the People's Armed Police (PAP) as a regularly available option for soldiers leaving the PLA, although some past reductions have transferred entire PLA units to the PAP. Considering the amount of state media attention surrounding other demobilization methods and goals, such wholesale transfers are unlikely to represent a significant portion of the ongoing force reduction.

²² For a seminal treatment of Chinese demobilization policies in the open literature, see Maryanne Kivlehan-Wise, "Demobilization and Resettlement: The Challenge of Downsizing the People's Liberation Army," in *Civil-Military Relations in Today's China*, ed. David M. Finkelstein and Kristen Gunness (Armonk, NY: M.E. Sharpe, 2007).

²³ Ibid., 260–261.

²⁴ Ibid.

²⁵ "What Is Living Expenses Policy Like for Demobilized Conscripts? A Group of Questions and Answers in Reply" [退伍义务兵生活待遇政策怎么样? 一组问答告诉你], Financial Affairs Section of the Nanjing Military Region Joint Logistics Department, People's Frontline News Weixin [人民前线报微信], August 8, 2015, available at <www.mod.gov.cn/intl/2015-08/08/content_4613364.htm>.

²⁶ Huang Yanghai [黄杨海], ed., "Demobilized Soldiers, Don't Miss Out on These Benefits If You Want to Start Your Own Business" [退伍了, 如果你想创业, 这些优惠不要错过], *PLA Daily Reporter's Weixin* [军报记者微信], September 7, 2015, available at <www.81.cn/jwgz/2015-09/07/content_6669758_4.htm>.

²⁷ Kivlehan-Wise, "Demobilization and Resettlement," 262.

²⁸ "People's Republic of China Military Service Law" [中华人民共和国兵役法], National People's Congress, revised October 29, 2011, available at <www.npc.gov.cn/npc/xinwen/lfgz/zxfl/2011-10/31/content_1678464.htm>.

²⁹ See articles 18 and 19, "Enlisted Personnel Resettlement Regulations" [退役士兵安置条例], State Council of the People's Republic of China and Central Military Commission of the People's Republic of China, November 1, 2011, available at <www.gov.cn/zwgk/2011-10/30/content_1981589.htm>.

[30] See article 29, "Enlisted Personnel Resettlement Regulations."

[31] Ibid., article 41.

[32] The term *ganbu*, 干部, is actually best translated as *cadre*, and includes both military officers and PLA civilians [*wenzhi ganbu*, 文职干部]. The more specific Chinese term for *officer* is *junguan*, 军官, but PLA demobilization regulations tend to use *ganbu* in reference to officers. This chapter uses *officers* to refer to both uniformed military officers and PLA civilians.

[33] *Provisional Measures for Resettling Transferred Officers* [军队转业干部安置暂行办法] (Beijing: State Council of the People's Republic of China and Central Military Commission of the People's Republic of China, January 19, 2001), chapter 4, article 22, available at <www.mohrss.gov.cn/SYrlzyhshbzb/zcfg/flfg/xzfg/201605/t20160506_239559.html>. See also Kivlehan-Wise, "Demobilization and Resettlement," 263–266.

[34] *Provisional Measures*, chapter 5, article 34.

[35] Ibid., chapter 5, article 37.

[36] See table for details, which summarizes information from "Two Hundred Questions on Living Expenses Policy for Officers and Men" [官兵生活待遇政策200问], Ministry of National Defense of the People's Republic of China, March 11, 2015, available at <www.mod.gov.cn/policy/2015-03/11/content_4574146.htm>.

[37] "Opinions Regarding Problems Managing the Resettlement of Officers Selecting Independent Job-Search" [关于自主择业的军队转业干部安置管理若干问题的意见], State Council of the People's Republic of China, August 24, 2001, available at <www.gov.cn/gongbao/content/2002/content_61487.htm>.

[38] See table for details.

[39] "Two Hundred Questions on Living Expenses Policy for Officers and Men" [官兵生活待遇政策200问].

[40] Kivlehan-Wise, "Demobilization and Resettlement," 260.

[41] *Provisional Measures*, chapter 3, article 16.

[42] Ibid., chapter 3, article 19.

[43] Ibid., chapter 3, article 21.

[44] Zhang Tao, ed., "Troop Cuts to Boost PLA Capability and Efficiency," *China Military Online*, September 9, 2015, available at <http://english.chinamil.com.cn/news-channels/china-military-news/2015-09/09/content_6673474.htm>.

[45] "Ministry of Civil Affairs and General Staff Department Explains 2014 Demobilized Enlisted Personnel Resettlement Policy" [民政部总参谋部解答2014年度退役士兵安置政], Ministry of Civil Affairs of the People's Republic of

China, March 10, 2015, available at <www.mod.gov.cn/regulatory/2015-03/10/content_4643949.htm>.

[46] Kivlehan-Wise cites anecdotal evidence documenting this trend, which likely applies to rural conscripts more than those from the cities. See Kivlehan-Wise, "Demobilization and Resettlement," 268.

[47] Dennis J. Blasko writes that new recruits are "drawn mostly from a pool of over 10 million males that reach conscription age annually," suggesting that conscript supply still outnumbers demand. See Dennis J. Blasko, *The Chinese Army Today* (New York: Routledge, 2012), 59.

[48] Zhao Lei and Cang Wei, "PLA Eases Standards for Recruitment," *China Daily* (Beijing), June 17, 2014, available at <http://usa.chinadaily.com.cn/china/2014-06/17/content_17592194.htm>.

[49] "Opinions Regarding Implementation of Financial Subsidization Policy for the Education of Demobilized Enlisted Personnel" [关于实施退役士兵教育资助政策的意见], Ministry of Finance and Ministry of Education, October 25, 2011, available at <www.mof.gov.cn/preview/jiaokewensi/zhengwuxinxi/zhengcefabu/201110/t20111031_603544.html>.

[50] "Notification Regarding the Adjustment and Perfection of National Educational Debt Subsidization Policy Measures" [关于调整完善国家助学贷款相关政策措施的通知], Ministry of Finance, Ministry of Education, People's Bank of China, and China Banking Regulatory Commission of the People's Republic of China, July 18, 2014, available at <www.mof.gov.cn/zhengwuxinxi/caizhengwengao/wg2014/wg201409/201503/t20150331_1210835.html>.

[51] Niu Chenfei [牛晨斐], "Ministry of Civil Affairs General Staff Department Interprets 2014 Enlisted Personnel Demobilization and Resettlement Policy" [民政部总参谋部解答2014年度退役士兵安置政策], *China Military Online* [中国军网], November 6, 2014, available at <www.81.cn/sydbt/2014-11/06/content_6216297.htm>.

[52] *Provisional Measures*, chapter 1, article 8.

[53] Yuan Jing, "Beijing Officer Resettlement Work Conference Requests That No Unit Refuse Transferring Officers" [本市转业干部安置工作会要求任何单位不得拒收军转干部], *Beijing Daily* [北京日报], July 15, 2016, available at <www.beijing.gov.cn/sjbsy/jrbj/t1441308.htm>. See also Liu Jianjun [刘建军], "An Advisor Replies to A Young Officer's Concerns about Civilian Transfer" [年轻军官的转业烦恼, 谢顾问为你解答], *PLA Daily* [解放军报], July 5, 2016, available at <www.81.cn/jwgz/2016-07/05/content_7134792.htm>.

54 "Opinions Regarding the Problems and Improvement of Measures for Civilian Transfer for Demobilized Officers" [关于改进计划分配军转业干部安置办法若干问题的意见], Communist Party of China Organization Department et al., Inner Mongolia Ministry of Human Resources and Social Stability, January 21, 2012, available at <www.nmg.gov.cn/xxgkpt/rst/xxgkml/201708/t20170821_635361.html>.

55 Liu, "An Advisor Replies."

56 Jun Zhuanxuan, "State Council Military Cadre Transfer and Resettlement Work Small Group Meets in Beijing" [国务院军队转业干部安置工作小组会议在京召开], *China Organization and Human Resources Report* [中国组织人事报], May 8, 2017, available at <www.alldem-center.com/html/htmlganbugong-zuo201705082446.html>.

57 The last complete roster of the Transfer and Resettlement Small Group was released in 2008; the 2013 and 2017 press releases do not mention the actual composition of the groups. See "Personnel Adjustment for State Council Military Cadre Transfer and Resettlement Work Small Group" [国务院军队转业干部安置工作小组组成人员调整], State Council of the People's Republic of China, *Liaoning Provincial People's Government Report*, 2008, available at <www.ln.gov.cn/zfxx/lnsrmzfgb/2008/d9q/gwybgtwj/200806/t20080602_219353.html>.

58 "Military Officer Transfer Resettlement Department" [军官转业安置司], Ministry of Human Resources and Social Security, People's Republic of China, January 31, 2013, available at <www.mohrss.gov.cn/jgzyzzs/ltxgbjzz/201301/t20130131_78467.html >.

59 For an example, see "Military Cadre Transfer Resettlement Department" [军官转业安置处], Fujian Provincial Department of Human Resources and Social Security, available at <www.fjrs.gov.cn/zw/jgszyzn/tjgcs/jzb/>.

60 Hao Sijia [郝思嘉], ed., "A Description of the National Double Support Work Leading Group" [全国双拥工作领导小组介绍], China Double Support Network [中国双拥网], July 31, 2015, available at <www.81.cn/zjsymfc/2015-07/31/content_6609076.htm>.

61 For a full list of organizations with high-level equities in double support work, see the roster of the national leading small group at Cui Xiaosu and Yao Yi [崔小粟, 姚奕], eds., "Adjustment of the National Double Support Work Leading Small Group Roster" [全国双拥工作领导小组组成人员名单调整], News of the Chinese Communist Party, November 11, 2013, available at <http://renshi.people.com.cn/n/2013/1111/c139617-23496497.html>.

[62] Hao, "A Description of the National Double Support Work Leading Group."

[63] General Office of Hebei Province Double Support Work Leading Small Group, "Double Support Work Responsibilities and Work System" [职责和工作制度], Hebei Province Department of Civil Affairs, available at <www.hebmz.gov.cn/mzyw/sygz/>

[64] Hao, "A Description of the National Double Support Work Leading Group."

[65] Cui and Yao, "Adjustment of the National Double Support Work Leading Small Group Roster."

[66] "Special Care Resettlement Bureau" [优抚安置局], Ministry of Civil Affairs, People's Republic of China, July 2015, available at <www.mca.gov.cn/article/jg/jgsj/201507/20150700847756.shtml>.

[67] Ibid.

[68] Cui and Yao, "Adjustment of the National Double Support Work Leading Small Group Roster."

[69] See appendix for a comparison of the 2008 rosters for both working groups.

[70] Cui and Yao, "Adjustment of the National Double Support Work Leading Small Group Roster."

[71] "Demonstrate Superiority in Double Support Work, Strongly Support the Deepening of National Defense and Military Reform" [全国双拥工作领导小组: 发挥双拥工作优势, 大力支持深化国防和军队改革], National Double Support Work Leading Small Group, Ministry of Civil Affairs, People's Republic of China, May 23, 2016, available at <www.mca.gov.cn/article/zwgk/mzyw/201605/20160500000635.shtml>.

[72] "Double Support Work Responsibilities and Work System" [职责和工作制度], General Office of Hebei Province Double Support Work Leading Small Group, Department of Civil Affairs, available at <www.hebmz.gov.cn/mzyw/sygz/>.

[73] "Guidance on Executing Double Support Work" [双拥工作办事指南], Tai'an City Department of Civil Affairs, available at <www.tamz.gov.cn/html/bszn/syyfaz/shuangyong/69.html>.

[74] *Provisional Measures.*

[75] Interview of PLA officer by authors, November 2017.

[76] Xu Jingjing, "How to Understand 'Arranging Corresponding Duty Grades' in Military Transfer and Resettlement" [军转安置中"安排相应职务"咋理解], *National Defense News* [国防报], February 14, 2017, available at <http://military.people.com.cn/n1/2017/0214/c1011-29078672.html>.

[77] Ibid.

[78] One document from 1985 detailed civilian grade equivalents for military personnel transferring out of the PLA. Division grade leaders [*zheng shi zhi*, 正师

职] were to be assigned as local administration or department heads [*ju, ting zhang,* 局, 厅长], deputy division grade leaders [*fu shi zhi,* 副师职] to vice administration or department heads [*fu ju, ting zhang,* 副局, 厅长], regiment leaders [*zheng tuan zhi,* 正团职] to office heads [*chu zhang,* 处长] or county mayors [*xian zhang,* 县长], and deputy regiment leaders [*fu tuan zhi,* 副团职] to vice county mayors [*fu xian zhang,* 副县长] or deputy office heads [*fu chu zhang,* 副处长]. See State Council and Central Military Commission, "Notice on the Problem of Salaries and Treatment of Transferred Military Cadre" [军队转业干部工资待遇问题的通知], November 19, 1985, available at <www.bjrbj.gov.cn/LDJAPP/search/zxfgdetail.jsp?no=201208211103400341>.

[79] Meng Leilei [孟磊磊], "What Did This Transferred Military Cadre Rely upon to Become a Deputy County Mayor in Sixteen Months?" [一年零四个月, 这名军转干部靠什么成为副县长?], *China Military Online* [中国军网], May 10, 2017, available at <www.81.cn/jwgz/2017-05/10/content_7596327.htm>.

[80] See article 21 of "Civil Servant Law of the People's Republic of China" [中华人民共和国公务员法], Central Organization Department of the Chinese Communist Party, available at <www.gov.cn/flfg/2005-06/21/content_8249.htm>.

[81] Ibid., article 25.

[82] For a conversion between the number of civil service grades and administrative (county, township, and so forth) grades, see "Regulations on Managing Civil Servant Grades and Levels" [公务员职务与级别管理规定], Ministry of Human Resources and Social Security, People's Republic of China, April 9, 2006, available at <www.mohrss.gov.cn/SYrlzyhshbzb/zcfg/flfg/xzfg/201605/t20160506_239550.html>.

[83] Zhang, "PLA Daily Editors' Department Essay"; Li, Li, and Wang, "Organizational Reconstruction."

[84] Many of these downsizing mandates are motivated by concerns about mounting local government debt. For a discussion of past downsizing efforts, see John P. Burns, "'Downsizing' the Chinese State: Government Retrenchment in the 1990s," *China Quarterly,* vol. 175 (September 2003), 775–802. See also Frank Tang, "China's Spiraling Local Government Debt Still Out of Control, Says Outspoken Lawmaker," *South China Morning Post* (Hong Kong), March 9, 2017, available at <www.scmp.com/news/china/economy/article/2077367/chinas-spiralling-local-govt-debt-still-out-control-says>.

[85] Xu, "How to Understand 'Arranging Corresponding Duty Grades' in Military Transfer and Resettlement."

[86] Meng, "What Did This Transferred Military Cadre Rely upon to Become a Deputy County Mayor in Sixteen Months?"

87 For the text of the notice circulated to Shenzhen, see "Labor Department General Office Transmits to Shenzhen City Notice on Opinions Concerning Problems of Enterprises Canceling Worker Identification Boundaries and Fully Implementing the Labor Contract System" [劳动部办公厅转发深圳市《关于企业取消干部工人身份界限实行全员劳动合同制若干问题的意见》的通知], Shenzhen City Labor Bureau, July 5, 1993, available at <www.govyi.com/zhengcefagui/quan-guofagui/200707/52528.shtml>.

88 Jane Perlez and Yufan Huang, "Mass Layoffs in China's Coal Country Threaten Unrest," *New York Times*, December 16, 2015, available at <www.nytimes.com/2015/12/17/world/asia/china-coal-mining-economy.html>.

89 See Tian Shaohui, ed., "China Can Deal with Economic Challenges: Official," Xinhua, February 3, 2016.

90 Zhao Xiaohui [赵晓辉], "China Initiates Fight Against Production Overcapacity; Government Allocates 100 Billion Yuan for Worker Resettlement" [中国打响去产能攻坚战 政府斥资千亿元用于职工安置], Xinhua, February 25, 2016, available at <http://news.xinhuanet.com/fortune/2016-02/25/c_1118157288.htm>.

91 See Benjamin Lim, "China Veterans Stage 2,000-Strong Protest," Reuters, April 16, 2005; and Edward Cody, "China Grows More Wary Over Rash of Protests," *Washington Post*, August 10, 2005, available at <www.washingtonpost.com/wp-dyn/content/article/2005/08/09/AR2005080901323.html>.

92 Lu Jianwei, "A Thousand Demobilized Military Personnel Clash Bloodily with Hundreds of Special Police in Heilongjiang" [黑龍江千名退伍軍人 與數百特警流血衝突], Central News Agency, September 9, 2007.

93 Zhang Qian [張謙], "China's Demobilized Military Personnel Hit the Streets for Their Rights; Hunan Government Deploys Special Police as a Precaution" [中國退伍軍人上街爭權 湖南派特警戒備], Central News Agency, April 20, 2007, available at <www.epochtimes.com/b5/7/4/20/n1684680.htm>.

94 "Nearly 6,000 Demobilized Chinese Military Cadres Publicize Petition Appealing for Equal Treatment" [中国近6千军转干部发表要求同等待遇请示书], *Radio Free Asia* [自由亞洲電台], March 26, 2008, available at <www.epochtimes.com/b5/8/3/26/n2059023.htm>.

95 Guo Meilan [郭玫兰], "Large-Scale Demonstration by Demobilized Military Cadres Explodes in Yantai" [煙台爆發軍轉幹部大規模抗議行動], Central News Agency, December 16, 2009, available at <www.epochtimes.com/gb/9/12/16/n2756491.htm>.

96 Guo Meilan [郭玫兰], "Over 400 Demobilized Military Personnel Petition the Yantai Government" [400多名退伍軍人到煙台市政府請願], Central News Agency, May 20, 2010, available at <www.secretchina.com/news/gb/2010/05/20/350544.html>.

97 Kivlehan-Wise, "Demobilization and Resettlement," 257.

98 Jeremy Page, "As China's Economy Slows, Unrest Among Veterans Rises," *Wall Street Journal*, April 26, 2016, available at <https://blogs.wsj.com/chinarealtime/2016/04/26/as-chinas-economy-slows-unrest-among-veterans-rises/>.

99 These protests are, unsurprisingly, not covered by official state media. See Qu Ming, ed., "More Than 4,000 Demobilized Soldiers Gather at the Central Military Commission Holding Banners to Protect Their Rights" [4000余退役军人聚中军委拉横幅维权], *New Tang News*, July 18, 2016, available at <www.ntdtv.com/xtr/gb/2016/07/19/a1276834.html>.

100 "China Blockades Streets Around Military Building as Hundreds Protest in Capital," Reuters, October 11, 2016, available at <www.reuters.com/article/us-china-military-protests/china-blockades-streets-around-military-building-as-hundreds-protest-in-capital-idUSKCN12B12V>.

101 Chi-yuk Choi, "PLA Veterans Stage Another Protest in Beijing over Unpaid Benefits," *South China Morning Post* (Hong Kong), January 4, 2017, available at <www.scmp.com/news/china/policies-politics/article/2059225/pla-veterans-stage-another-protest-beijing-over-unpaid>.

102 Fang Yan, "Demobilization Bugle Call Sounds: The Pressures of Civilian Transfer and Resettlement Will Not Be Small" [裁军号角吹响: 转业安置压力不会小], *China Youth Daily* [中国青年报], March 3, 2016, available at <www.81.cn/rd/2016-03/03/content_6939115.htm>.

103 Information from PLA officers, November and December 2017.

104 Li Tao [李涛], "The 10 Large Troop Reductions in People's Liberation Army History" [人民解放军历史上10次大裁军], *PLA Daily*, November 18, 2015, available at <http://military.people.com.cn/n/2015/1118/c1011-27827138.html>.

105 Ibid.

106 Huang Fuyou, ed., "Media: Where Can Downsized Officers Go?" [媒体: 被裁的军官们都能去哪儿?], *Beijing Daily* [北京日报], September 4, 2015, available at <http://news.ifeng.com/a/20150904/44584202_0.shtml>.

107 Chen Guoquan and Li Youtao [陈国全, 黎友陶], "Navy and Ministry of Human Resources Hold Joint Training Class on Independent Job Selection, Job Searching, and Entrepreneurship" [海军与人社部联合举办自主择业军转干部就

业创业培训班], *PLA Daily* [解放军报], August 9, 2016, available at <www.81.cn/jwgz/2016-08/09/content_7196968.htm>.

[108] Huang, "Media: Where Can Downsized Officers Go?"

[109] "Opinions Regarding the Guidance of Delineation and Categorization of State-Owned Enterprise Capabilities" [关于国有企业功能界定与分类的指导意见], Ministry of Finance, People's Republic of China, December 30, 2015, available at <www.mof.gov.cn/zhengwuxinxi/zhengcefabu/201512/t20151230_1638704.htm>.

[110] Song Yu, ed., "British Media: China Requests State-Owned Enterprises Reserve 5% of Jobs for Demobilized Enlisted Soldiers" [英媒: 中国要求国企按招新5% 比例聘用退役士兵], *Reference News*, December 30, 2015.

[111] See Minnie Chan, "Why Former Chinese Soldiers Are Skeptical about Xi Jinping's Promise of Better Treatment," *South China Morning Post* (Hong Kong), November 5, 2017, available at <www.scmp.com/news/china/policies-politics/article/2117765/why-former-chinese-soldiers-are-sceptical-about >; and Christopher Bodeen, "China Veterans' Protests for Pensions Pose Test for Leaders," Associated Press, October 17, 2016.

[112] Zhao Lei, "Veterans to Receive Better Income, Pensions Package," *China Daily*, October 9, 2015.

[113] Mark A. Stokes and Ian Easton, "The Chinese People's Liberation Army General Staff Department: Evolving Organizations and Missions," in *The PLA as Organization v2.0*, ed. Kevin Pollpeter and Kenneth W. Allen (Vienna, VA: DGI, Inc., 2015), 160–161.

[114] Liu Zhiming [刘志明], "Adhere to the 'Four Iron' Demands to Build a First-Rate Support Organization" [按照 '四铁' 要求打造一流服务保障机构], *PLA Daily* [解放军报], April 20, 2016, available at <www.mod.gov.cn/topnews/2016-04/20/content_4650021.htm>.

[115] See *Provisional Measures*, chapter 3, article 21.

[116] See Yin Shen and Tong Zongli [尹深, 仝宗莉], eds., "Two Departments: No State-Owned Enterprises Are Allowed to Reject Demobilized Enlisted Personnel" [两部委: 任何国有企业不得拒绝接收退役士兵], *People's Daily* [人民网], December 28, 2015, available at <http://politics.people.com.cn/n1/2015/1228/c1001-27986615.html>; and Yuan Jing [袁京], "Beijing Officer Resettlement Work Conference Requests That No Unit Refuse Transferring Officers" [本市转业干部安置工作会要求任何单位不得拒收军转干部], *Beijing Daily* [北京日报], July 15, 2016, available at <www.beijing.gov.cn/sjbsy/jrbj/t1441308.htm>.

[117] Information from PLA officers, November and December 2017.

[118] See table for details.

[119] For examples, see Chen and Li, "Navy and Ministry of Human Resources Hold Joint Training Class on Independent Job Selection, Job Searching, and Entrepreneurship"; and Leng Xinggao and Li Bingfeng [冷兴高, 李兵峰], "Rocket Force Organization Job Search and Entrepreneurship Classes Help Independent Job Search and Civilian Transfer Military Cadre Enter the 'Sea of Commerce'" [火箭军组织就业创业培训为自主择业军转干部融入"商海"搭桥], Xinhua, August 31, 2017, available at <http://news.xinhuanet.com/mil/2017-08/31/c_1121579275.htm>.

[120] See Yunnan Provincial Office of Human Resources and Social Security, "Notice Regarding Holding Entrepreneurship Training Courses for Independent Job-Searching Military Cadre" [关于举办自主择业军转干部创新创业能力提高培训班的通知], Yunnan Human Resources and Social Security Network, December 14, 2016, available at <www.ynhrss.gov.cn/NewsView.aspx?NewsID=20437&ClassID=558>.

[121] Guangdong Provincial Office of Human Resources and Social Security, "Guangdong Province Holds First Ceremony for Transferring Military Cadre Entering Higher Education and Special Training Schools" [广东省举办首批军转干部进高校专项培训开学典礼], September 20, 2017, available at <www.gdhrss.gov.cn/gzdt/20170920/10520.html>.

[122] Zhao Lei, "Scores of PLA Officers Punished," *China Daily* (Beijing), January 30, 3015, available at <http://usa.chinadaily.com.cn/china/2015-01/30/content_19444889.htm>.

[123] Liu Mengjiao, ed., "PLA Daily Vows Strict Discipline for Chinese Army," Xinhua, March 27, 2017, available at <http://news.xinhuanet.com/english/2017-03/27/c_136161188.htm>.

[124] Minnie Chan, "Xi Jinping Clears Decks for Top-Level Changes to China's Military," *South China Morning Post* (Hong Kong), October 3, 2017, available at <www.scmp.com/news/china/diplomacy-defence/article/2113054/xi-jinping-clears-decks-top-level-changes-chinas>.

[125] For the relevant prohibition in the *Provisional Measures*, see chap. 2, art. 13, sec. 2. For the corresponding prohibitions in civil servant law, see art. 24 of "Civil Servant Law of the People's Republic of China."

[126] "Robber Barons, Beware: A Crackdown on Corruption Has Spread Anxiety among China's Business Elite," *The Economist*, October 22, 2015, available at <www.economist.com/news/china/21676814-crackdown-corruption-has-spread-anxiety-among-chinas-business-elite-robber-barons-beware>.

[127] Josh Chin, "'Rule of Law' or 'Rule by Law'? In China, a Preposition Makes All the Difference," *Wall Street Journal*, October 20, 2014, available at <https://blogs.wsj.com/chinarealtime/2014/10/20/rule-of-law-or-rule-by-law-in-china-a-preposition-makes-all-the-difference/>.

[128] For a discussion of the relationship between the party and PLA, see James C. Mulvenon, "China: Conditional Compliance" in *Coercion and Governance: The Declining Political Role of the Military in Asia*, ed. Muthiah Alagappa (Stanford: Stanford University Press, 2001).

[129] "Defense Ministry's Regular Press Conference on March 29," *China Military Online*, March 30, 2018, available at <http://english.chinamil.com.cn/view/2018-03/30/content_7987841.htm>.

[130] Qu, "More Than 4,000 Demobilized Soldiers Gather at the Central Military Commission Holding Banners to Protect Their Rights."

[131] More recent reports have indicated that some veteran activists have been taken away by security services. See Chan, "Why Former Chinese Soldiers Are Skeptical about Xi Jinping's Promise of Better Treatment."

[132] "Defense Ministry's Regular Press Conference on March 29."

Appendix

Comparison of National-Level Working Groups Responsible for Military-Locality and Demobilization, 2008			
Military Cadre Transfer and Resettlement Work Small Group		**National Double Support Work Leading Small Group**	
State Council	Director, Ministry of Human Resources and Social Security [人力资源社会保障部部长]*	Vice Premier, State Council [国务院副总理]*	State Council
State Council	Deputy Director, Ministry of Human Resources and Social Security [人力资源社会保障部副部长]**	Director, Ministry of Civil Affairs [民政部部长]**	State Council
PLA	Assistant to Director of General Political Department [总政治部主任助理]**	Deputy Director, CCP General Office [中央办公厅副主任]**	CCP
CCP	Deputy Director, Central Organization Department [中央组织部副部长]	Deputy Director, Central Organization Department [中央组织部副部长]**	CCP
CCP	Deputy Director, Propaganda Department [中央宣传部副部长]	Assistant Secretary General, State Council [国务院副秘书长]**	State Council
CCP	Deputy Director, State Commission Office for Public Sector Reform [中央编办副主任]	Deputy Director, Propaganda Department [中央宣传部副部长]**	CCP
State Council	Assistant Secretary General, State Council [国务院副秘书长]	Deputy Director, Ministry of Civil Affairs [民政部副部长]**	State Council
State Council	Deputy Director, National Development and Reform Commission [发展改革委副主任]	Deputy Director, National Development and Reform Commission [发展改革委副主任]	State Council
State Council	Deputy Director, Ministry of Education [教育部副部长]	Deputy Director, Ministry of Education [教育部副部长]	State Council
State Council	Deputy Director, Ministry of Public Security [公安部副部长]	Deputy Director, Ministry of Science and Technology [科技部副部长]	State Council
State Council	Deputy Director, Ministry of Civil Affairs [民政部副部长]	Deputy Director, Ministry of Industry and Information Technology [工业和信息化部副部长]	State Council
State Council	Deputy Director, Ministry of Finance [财政部副部长]	Deputy Director, Ethnic Affairs Commission [国家民委副主任]	State Council
State Council	Deputy Director, Ministry of Housing and Urban-Rural Development [住房城乡建设部副部长]	Director, Political Department, Ministry of Public Security [公安部政治部主任]	State Council

Comparison of National-Level Working Groups Responsible for Military-Locality and Demobilization, 2008			
Military Cadre Transfer and Resettlement Work Small Group		**National Double Support Work Leading Small Group**	
State Council	Assistant to Director, People's Bank of China [人民银行行长助理]	Deputy Director, Ministry of Justice [司法部副部长]	State Council
State Council	Deputy Director, Administration of Taxation [税务总局副局长]	Deputy Director, Ministry of Finance [财政部副部长]	State Council
State Council	Deputy Director, Administration for Industry and Commerce [工商总局副局长]	Deputy Director, Ministry of Human Resources and Social Security [人力资源社会保障部副部长]	State Council
State Council	Deputy Director, Administration of Press, Publication, Radio, Film, and Television [广电总局副局长]	Member, Party Committee, Ministry of Land and Resources [国土资源部党组成员]	State Council
PLA	Political Commissar, General Logistics Department [总后勤部政治委员]	Deputy Director, Ministry of Housing and Urban-Rural Development [住房城乡建设部副部长]	State Council
PAP	Director, Political Department [武警部队政治部主任]	Deputy Director, Ministry of Transport [交通运输部副部长]	State Council
PLA	Deputy Director, General Political Department Cadre Department [总政治部干部部副部长]	Deputy Director, Ministry of Railways [铁道部副部长]	State Council
State Council	Deputy Director-General, Ministry of Human Resources and Social Security [人力资源社会保障部副司长]	Deputy Director, Ministry of Water Resources [水利部副部长]	State Council
		Deputy Director, Ministry of Agriculture [农业部副部长]	State Council
		Deputy Director, Ministry of Commerce [商务部部长助理]	State Council
		Deputy Director, Ministry of Culture [文化部副部长]	State Council
		Deputy Director, Ministry of Health [卫生部副部长]	State Council
		Deputy Director, State-Owned Assets Supervision and Administration Commission [国资委副主任]	State Council
		Deputy Director, Administration of Taxation [税务总局副局长]	State Council

Comparison of National-Level Working Groups Responsible for Military-Locality and Demobilization, 2008		
Military Cadre Transfer and Resettlement Work Small Group	**National Double Support Work Leading Small Group**	
	Deputy Director, Administration for Industry and Commerce [工商总局副局长]	State Council
	Deputy Director, Administration of Press, Publication, Radio, Film, and Television [广电总局副局长]	State Council
	Director, General Staff Department Political Department [总参谋部政治部主任]	PLA
	Director, General Political Department Mass Work Office [总政治部群众工作办公室主任]	PLA
	Director, General Logistics Department Political Department [总后勤部政治部主任]	PLA
	Director, General Armaments Department Political Department [总装备部政治部主任]	PLA
	Deputy Political Commissar, People's Armed Police [武警部队副政治委员]	PAP
	Vice Chairman, All-China Federation of Trade Unions [全国总工会副主席、书记处书记]	NGO
	Secretary, Central Secretariat, Communist Youth League [共青团中央书记处书记]	CCP
	Vice Chairman, All-China Women's Federation [全国妇联副主席、书记处书记]	NGO
	Vice Chairman, All-China Federation of Industry and Commerce [全国工商联副主席]	CCP
	Director, Ministry of Civil Affairs Special Care and Resettlement Bureau [民政部优抚安置局局长]	State Council

Notes: Heads [*zu zhang*, 组长] of these two groups are denoted with one asterisk; deputy heads [*fu zu zhang*, 副组长] have two asterisks. Positions in red are common to both groups, but few of the actual personnel are dual-hatted with positions in both groups. All information is sourced from the 2008 rosters, which is the last year both rosters could be found. See State Council of the People's Republic of China, "Personnel Adjustment for State Council Military Cadre Transfer and Resettlement Work Small Group" [国务院军队转业干部安置工作小组组成人员调整], Liaoning

Provincial People's Government Report, available at <www.ln.gov.cn/zfxx/lnsrmzfgb/2008/d9q/gwybgtwj/200806/t20080602_219353.html>; and Duan Hongjie, ed., "State Council General Office and CMC General Office Notice on Adjustment of Personnel in National Double Support Work Leading Small Group" [国务院办公厅中央军委办公厅关于调整全国拥军优属拥政爱民工作领导小组组成人员的通知], Jilin Provincial People's Government, available at <www.jl.gov.cn/zw/xxgk/jlgb/2008/200809/200809GBF/200812/t20081228_2275705.html>.

CHAPTER 18

CONCLUSION

Assessing Chinese Military Reforms

Phillip C. Saunders and Joel Wuthnow

China's military reforms are driven by Xi Jinping's ambition to reshape the People's Liberation Army (PLA) to improve its ability to win informationized [*xinxihua*, 信息化] wars and to ensure that it remains loyal to the Chinese Communist Party (CCP). There is broad political support within the party for Xi's goal of building a stronger military. The outline of the current military reform agenda was endorsed at the third plenum of the 18th Party Congress in November 2013, and Xi played a central role in working with PLA leaders to develop detailed reorganization plans and implement the reform agenda.[1] At the first meeting of the new leading group on military reform in early 2014, Xi declared that the overriding goal was to produce a military that can "fight and win battles."[2] The 19th Party Congress work report in October 2017 advanced the timeline for Chinese military modernization, calling for achieving mechanization and making strides on informationization and building strategic capabilities by 2020 and building "world-class forces" [*shijie yiliu jun*, 世界一流军] by mid-century.[3]

The reforms are unprecedented in their ambition and in the scale and scope of the organizational changes. Virtually every part of the PLA now reports to different leaders, has had its mission and responsibilities changed, has lost or gained subordinate units, or has undergone a major internal reorganization. The relationships between and among the Central Military Commission (CMC) departments, offices, and commissions, the services, and the theater commands have all changed. The military education system has been reformed to reduce duplication and place greater emphasis on jointness, and changes to the military assignment, promotion, and grade/rank systems are still to come. The reforms will have important implications for the PLA's responsiveness to political direction and ability to achieve the modernization goals that the CCP has set for it.

The chapters in this book explore various dimensions of Xi's PLA reform agenda in detail. This conclusion draws the analytical threads together to assess what difference the reforms are likely to make for the PLA's ability to conduct joint operations, for the CCP's control of the army, and for civil-military integration. The analytic judgments draw on some of the arguments, evidence, and assessments presented in the individual chapters, but those authors do not necessarily share all our conclusions.

Assessing the Reforms

While the reforms are not complete, the chapters in this book show how much has been accomplished in a relatively short period. One important judgment is that Xi and fellow PLA reformers have succeeded in forcing the military to adopt needed reforms that previous CMC Chairmen Jiang Zemin and Hu Jintao were unable to push through and that the PLA could not adopt on its own. Xi's political strategy for pushing his reform agenda through bureaucratic opposition appears to have succeeded, with the reforms breaking up the four general departments (previously described as "independent kingdoms"), reducing the institutional power of the previously dominant ground forces and purging the senior PLA officer corps of many potentially disloyal and corrupt elements.[4]

The structural reorganization of the PLA is basically complete, with the responsibilities and constituent parts of the four general departments redistributed to CMC departments, commissions, and offices or sent to the new army headquarters, Strategic Support Force, or the Joint Logistic Support Force. The seven military regions have been converted into five joint theater commands, which now exercise operational control over the ground, naval, air, and conventional Rocket Force units within their areas of responsibility. The army has stood up its new headquarters, the Rocket Force is now a full-fledged service, and the Strategic Support Force and Joint Logistics Support Force are both operational. Ground force group armies and air force fighter and fighter-bomber units have been reorganized into a standardized "group army/corps-brigade-battalion" structure. The PLA claims to have completed its downsizing of 300,000 officers and troops, cutting over 1,000 units and 30 percent of commissioned officers by the end of 2017.[5] The military education system has been reorganized and downsized to achieve efficiencies and increase emphasis on joint operations and technology. Changes have also been made to the People's Armed Police, which handles domestic security as part of China's armed forces. Planned changes to the military assignment, promotion, and grade/rank systems—which will have a major impact on the ultimate success of the reforms—are yet to be implemented.

Improving Joint Operations Capability

The reforms revised the division of labor within the PLA, with the CMC providing "general management" [*junwei guan zong*, 军委管总], the theater commands focusing on operations [*zhanqu zhu zhan*, 战区主战], and the services managing force-building [*junzhong zhu jian*, 军种主建].[6] The resulting theater joint command and control structure, with the theater commands exercising control of ground, naval, and air forces through service-specific theater component headquarters, rectifies a major problem with the pre-reform command and control structure, where the military region headquarters did not have peacetime command of naval, air, and missile units within its area of responsibility. The new construct should be much better suited to joint planning, training, and operations. PLA joint exercises at the theater level appear to be focused on developing the ability of commanders and their staffs to employ joint forces effectively. There have been significant growing pains as the theater commands and their components adjust to new command relationships and learn how to work together, but the basic joint command structure appears to be workable. The disruption caused by the organizational reshuffling and personnel downsizing has probably reduced the PLA's near-term combat readiness, but the reforms are likely to produce significant improvements in the PLA's ability to plan and execute larger and more complex joint operations within 2 to 3 years.

Important questions remain about the relationships between the CMC's Joint Staff Department (JSD) and theater commands and about how theater commanders will tap nuclear and nonnuclear strategic capabilities that remain under CMC command. The reforms established joint command and control structures at the national level (under the CMC's JSD, which also has nominal control of operations beyond China's periphery) and at the theater level (the theater commands). But the precise division of labor and willingness of the CMC to delegate decision authority to the theater commander remains unclear. Will the JSD (acting on behalf of the CMC) view its role primarily as providing supporting strategic capabilities (such as antiship ballistic missiles, intelligence derived from space and cyber systems, counterspace and offensive cyber capabilities, and long-range precision strike) to help a theater commander execute his war plan, or will the JSD (run by a CMC-member grade officer senior to the theater commanders) attempt to micromanage the theater's operations? The prevailing PLA organizational culture emphasizes caution and deference to authority, not taking responsibility for actions not fully vetted with more senior leaders.[7] The notion of empowering military officers to exercise initiative to carry out the intent of their commanders (known as mission command), which is integral to some Western militaries, is not culturally accepted in the PLA at present.[8] Integrated communications systems and a common operational picture provide both opportunities for timely support and temptations to intervene in the decisions of subordinate commanders.

A second question is the role of the services in supporting joint operations and building a joint force. In principle the reforms remove the service headquarters from operations, but in practice all of them have held onto some operational command responsibilities. Army headquarters retains responsibility for border and coastal defense; navy headquarters supervises the counterpiracy patrols in the Gulf of Aden; air force headquarters retains centralized control of bomber, transport, and airborne assets; and the Rocket Force has operational control over strategic forces. Moreover, all the services are using service-specific training requirements (including multi-theater exercises) as a means of asserting a continued operational role. The theater command service component commanders report to both the theater command headquarters for operations and to their service headquarters for service training and administration. How they will reconcile competing (and potentially incompatible) demands remains to be seen.

While the services are responsible for building forces to support joint operations, there is ample evidence of interservice rivalry and competition for missions and resources. Ian Burns McCaslin and Andrew Erickson show in their chapter how the higher priority accorded to the maritime domain by Xi Jinping has prompted efforts by the air force, Rocket Force, and even the army to develop and showcase capabilities relevant to maritime operations.[9] Similar trends are evident in long-range precision strike, where the navy, air force, and Rocket Force all have systems that perform similar missions. Especially in an environment where military budgets are growing more slowly, interservice competition over missions and resources may impede operational cooperation. This may also be the case in the nuclear domain as the PLA Navy's submarine-launched ballistic missile–equipped nuclear submarines become operational and if the PLA Air Force develops nuclear capabilities. The tension between the services desire to maximize their budgets and capabilities and the needs of theater commanders for trained forces that can work jointly to achieve operational synergies is real. One question going forward is whether the removal of the service commanders from membership on the CMC will allow that organization to override parochial service considerations and make procurement decisions that maximize PLA joint capabilities.

Achieving the potential synergies of a joint force will ultimately depend on the PLA's ability to successfully recruit, educate, and train operational commanders and staff officers who can lead and work effectively in a joint environment.[10] The PLA recognizes this as a current weakness, and some planned military reforms are aimed at fixing these problems. PLA Army officers currently spend the bulk of their careers in a single group army, in a single theater, with limited opportunities to work with units from other locations or services. This system produces officers and commanders who may be proficient in their service tasks and assigned responsibilities in specific contingencies, but who have a very limited perspective. Building effective joint commanders will require changes not only to the military education system to teach soldiers about the other services and how to conduct joint operations but also to the military assignment, promotion, and grade/rank systems. Without cross-fertilization and broader operational experiences, PLA effectiveness could be stunted.

However, these changes are interdependent and would constitute a major disruption of longstanding PLA practices. For example, a rotational assignment system would allow officers to gain experience with other services, localities, and job responsibilities and help them develop into well-rounded commanders capable of leading joint operations. But rotational assignments would require developing new military housing and schools for dependent children to entice officers to accept assignments in remote regions.[11] They would also likely require a shift to a centralized promotion system that evaluates officers fairly and rewards them for their experience and qualifications rather than their relationship with their local commander.[12] Such changes to the assignment and promotion systems are being contemplated and experimented with, but conversations with PLA officers suggest that military leaders remain cautious about implementing reforms that will reshape career incentives and affect every member of the PLA.

Ensuring CCP Control over the Military

A second major driver for the reforms was Xi Jinping's desire to strengthen party control over the military, which had eroded during Hu Jintao's tenure as CMC chairman. Rampant corruption within the PLA was one major problem, but the potential for the military not to follow orders from the CCP (and from Xi himself) was an even bigger issue. Xi asserted his authority over the PLA by emphasizing the "CMC Chairman Responsibility System" [*zhongyang junwei zeren zhi*, 中央军委责任制], which gives the chairman the ultimate authority over military affairs, and by using anti-corruption investigations to root out senior officers who might be disloyal, including retired CMC Vice Chairmen Xu Caihou and Guo Boxiong (both appointed by Jiang Zemin). The example set by these cases—and the vulnerability of other corrupt officers to investigation—proved to be a potent weapon in defusing potential opposition to military reforms.

Xi has implemented a series of structural and personnel changes designed to combat graft and ensure political orthodoxy among the officer corps. These include reducing the susceptibility of PLA supervisory mechanisms to the influence of commanding officers by elevating the Discipline Inspection Commission to independent status, raising its secretary to CMC member status and placing the audit bureau and the military court system under direct CMC oversight. It also includes efforts to reemphasize the importance of party organs and political work at all levels of the PLA, including the requirement to incorporate Xi's writings on military issues into the military education system. Finally, Xi has used corruption investigations, rotations of senior officers, forced retirements, and promotion of younger officers to reshape the ranks of the senior PLA officer corps, eliminating or sidelining officers deemed to be potentially disloyal and promoting those viewed as politically reliable and relatively free from corruption.

These measures have marginalized potential opposition to Xi's PLA reform agenda and have likely been effective at uprooting officers who might have been part of patronage networks tied to Xu and Guo. The structural changes to the CMC's organization should improve the effectiveness of monitoring mechanisms, while the appointment of Zhong Shaojun as head of the CMC General Office gives Xi's long-time personal aide the ability to monitor communications and activity within the CMC. Xi's personal involvement in the promotions of senior officers and ability to initiate (or withhold) investigations are powerful carrots and sticks to help ensure an obedient officer corps. However, the continued effectiveness of these measures requires Xi to continue to dedicate significant time to military personnel issues and is likely to create a climate of toadying and fear that may stimulate resentment and inhibit diverse or contrary military advice.

More generally, efforts to use political work to rekindle the ideological flame of belief in Marxism-Leninism will be difficult. Senior PLA officers are willing to mouth the correct slogans and swear their loyalty to the party and to Xi as its core leader. But formal compliance is not the same as genuine belief and may not produce better behavior over the long term or loyalty to the CCP and to Xi personally in a political crisis. Moreover, the hypocrisy of CCP leaders pursuing an aggressive anti-corruption campaign when their own family members have amassed fortunes by trading on their political connections is likely to breed cynicism and undermine efforts to produce a cleaner PLA.

Strengthening Civil-Military Integration

A third major driver of PLA reforms is the desire to strengthen civil-military cooperation, known as civil-military integration [*junmin ronghe*, 军民融合] (CMI) or civil-military fusion. The PLA has long relied on defense mobilization to reduce military expenditures by tapping civilian transportation, personnel, and supply resources in a crisis or conflict. However, a major focus of CMI is finding ways for the military to leverage breakthroughs in the civilian science and technology (S&T) sector and to ensure that military science and technology needs are met. CMI also involves other types of military and civilian cooperation, including expanding reliance on civilian contractors in the military supply chain and incorporating military specifications into the design of civilian transport ships, which could be mobilized during wartime (especially during an amphibious invasion of Taiwan). As Brian Lafferty discusses in this volume, strengthening CMI has been part of the PLA's reform agenda since the 1990s, but its implementation has been hindered by ineffectual top-level management, bureaucratic stove-piping, and other obstacles.

The PLA reforms include several initiatives to enhance CMI. One involves upgrading the PLA's Science and Technology Commission, previously subordinate to the General Armaments Department, to a higher level CMC organization that reports to Xi Jinping. This commission is responsible for the military's coordination with civilian experts in critical technological areas. Another change involves reforms to the military educational and research systems. For instance, several technical research institutes were merged into the PLA's Academy of Military Science, helping to more closely integrate technology advances with innovations in China's military doctrine.[13] To improve management and supervision of the process, the government declared civil-military integration to be an official development strategy in 2015 and created a new Central Commission for Integrated Military and Civilian Development in January 2017, with Xi as chairman.[14]

In their chapters in this volume, Brian Lafferty and Tai Ming Cheung analyze the prospect for intensified CMI efforts to build on the existing foundation and produce important breakthroughs in military technology. Cheung sees the adoption of civil-military fusion as an official development strategy, the establishment of the new commission, integrated civilian and military S&T planning, efforts to develop China's advance manufacturing base as part of the "Made in China 2025" plan, and reforms of defense research institutes as creating the conditions for major innovations. He concludes with a positive assessment of "prospects for the Chinese defense industry to successfully transition from an innovation follower to an original innovator that is able to engage in higher end technological development."[15] Lafferty has a more measured assessment, noting that the Chinese government has laid an initial foundation for CMI, improved its understanding of challenges in implementing CMI, and shown a commitment to tackling them, but that success is not guaranteed.[16]

Although there are clearly potential civil-military synergies in some areas, the large-scale cooperation envisioned by CMI advocates requires Chinese companies and government agencies to reduce their organizational autonomy by opening up their decision processes to incorporate the views and interests of other actors. The contradiction between the CCP's desire to incorporate all civilian and military interests into economic and S&T decisionmaking and the reluctance of companies and agencies to cede control to others may make it difficult for China to move beyond formal compliance (for example, establishing mechanisms to participate in CMI) to actual accomplishments. The CCP's ability to appoint the leaders of Chinese state-owned enterprises is a powerful tool, but it has not prevented these leaders from pursuing the financial and institutional interests of the companies they run and resisting implementation of mandates that would interfere with profits.

Signposts for the Future

How can we gauge the extent to which PLA reforms are succeeding? In the absence of a regional conflict that would put the PLA's new joint command structure to the ultimate test, joint training and exercises will provide the best window into improvements in PLA joint operations capability. Large exercises that involve multiple PLA services working together against an adaptive enemy would be the best evidence that new joint command and control structures can not only plan joint operations but also execute them and respond to changing battlefield conditions. Effective use of Strategic Support Force and Joint Logistics Support Force units to support theater exercises—and the ability to integrate other strategic capabilities controlled by the CMC or the services—would be additional evidence of improvements in higher level joint operational capabilities.

Another metric will be the extent to which joint operations and forces take priority over their service counterparts. A crude metric for assessing reductions in ground force dominance is the army's share of overall personnel, theater command positions, important jobs in the CMC, and slots in the joint military education courses that will train future PLA leaders. A more sophisticated metric will be observing whether officers with joint experience enjoy a promotion advantage over peers who stick to traditional service-centric career paths. The U.S. military ultimately required congressional intervention to make joint experience a requirement for promotion to general officer; a similar PLA regulation would be an important milestone for jointness. Of course, major changes to the PLA assignment and promotion system would be necessary to support such an action. The U.S. experience suggests that building an effective joint force can takes decades, since it requires a new generation of senior leaders that has experience working with other services and that develops a mindset that prioritizes joint operations over service interests.[17]

Another question is whether the CMC eventually develops the ability to contain interservice rivalry and discipline service desires for new weapons systems that advance service equities rather than joint objectives. The removal of the service chiefs from CMC membership in October 2017 may mark an important evolution in jointness within the PLA. The addition of the navy, air force, and Second Artillery commanders to the CMC in 2004 marked what might be called "representational jointness," with those services gaining a voice in high-level PLA decisions. The removal of the service commanders from CMC membership as part of Xi's reforms could mark a transition to "directed jointness," where the CMC imposes its decisions about how to build a joint force on the services. Given the service-centric nature of the PLA, the CMC is unlikely to play this role anytime soon, but this would be an important development if it occurs.

Assessing the degree to which Xi's efforts to reassert CCP control over the PLA have succeeded will be a much more difficult analytic challenge. All senior PLA officers are likely to say the right things in public; any officers who refuse to profess loyalty to the party and Xi will not last long. But the real test would only come in a major political crisis or if the CCP's efforts to maintain economic growth and to achieve nationalist goals falter and call Xi's leadership (and the party's legitimacy) into question. Until then, our assessment that the reforms are likely to strengthen CCP control over the military in the short term, but will not guarantee military support in a crisis, must remain a tentative judgment.

Identifying markers of progress in civil-military integration is also difficult because the priority that CCP leaders place on the program requires Chinese companies and agencies to pay lip service to CMI and emphasizes procedural improvements rather than substantive outputs. The clearest evidence of success would be a leap forward in innovation in Chinese weapons systems that incorporate dual-use technologies and production processes. Another indicator would be a major expansion of PLA use of civilian contractors and Chinese defense industries subcontracting important parts of weapons system development to civilian companies or state-owned enterprises outside the defense sector.

Implications

If PLA reforms succeed, they will have significant implications for China's neighbors, competitors, and opponents. A better trained, organized, and equipped PLA will be in a stronger position to accomplish its primary functions: winning modern wars, especially what the U.S. Department of Defense terms "short-duration, high-intensity regional conflicts"; deterring both large and small competitors; performing a variety of military operations other than war (also known as nontraditional security missions); and protecting Chinese interests in Asia.[18] A more effective joint command structure will enable the PLA to more quickly and seamlessly transition from peacetime to combat operations, as well as to more capably oversee complex peacetime missions that may require participation from multiple services, such as large-scale disaster relief or noncombatant evacuations. That system will be further improved as the PLA educates and trains commanders and staff to employ joint forces, and as more advanced capabilities in the various domains of warfare come online.

Rival territorial claimants, such as Vietnam, the Philippines, Japan, and India, will face a more confident and capable adversary in the South and East China seas and across the Sino-Indian border. Reforms to the broader Chinese armed forces, including placing the People's Armed Police under firm CMC control, could permit closer coordination between PLA, coast guard, and maritime militia forces, thus giving Beijing a strong hand in gray zone operations against other claimants. Taiwan will have to contend with a PLA that can more credibly plan and execute joint operations, such as amphibious landings, blockades, and joint missile strikes.[19] This will further strengthen the need for the Taiwan military to develop and implement asymmetric and innovative approaches to respond to the threat posed by a more capable PLA. U.S. forces operating throughout the Indo-Pacific region will face a PLA that can respond more quickly to regional crises and conduct counter-intervention operations more effectively. Moreover, a Chinese military and defense industry that can effectively harness civilian S&T breakthroughs to create advanced and innovative weapons would be an even more formidable strategic competitor over the long term. This latter point is important to counter the U.S. defense strategy that seeks to regain its technological edge over time to sustain a favorable regional balance of power.

A Future Expeditionary PLA?

One future requirement that the current PLA reforms do not fully address is the potential need to command and support a broader range of military operations beyond China's borders. In the last several decades, PLA overseas operations have been limited to participation in United Nations peacekeeping operations, counterpiracy patrols in the Gulf of Aden (since 2008), short-term deployments to participate in military exercises and conduct military diplomacy, and a few noncombatant emergency evacuations.

The theater commands are better equipped to respond to a range of regional contingencies than was possible under the pre-reform military regions. However, their ability to plan and execute operations has geographic limits depending on their areas of responsibility and the specific contingencies they are assigned.[20] For example, the Southern Theater Command already routinely conducts operations that extend into the far reaches of the South China Sea, while the other theater commands have more limited areas of operations. However, in the event of a Taiwan contingency, the PLA Navy may be tasked to operate even farther from Chinese territory into the Western Pacific, and it is not clear whether the Eastern Theater Command, navy headquarters, or the CMC's Joint Staff Department would have operational control over forward-deployed naval forces. Command and control arrangements are even less clear in the event of a conflict with India that involves both ground operations along the Sino-Indian border and naval operations in the Indian Ocean, since the Western Theater Command does not have a naval component to conduct contingency planning or take charge of naval operations in a war.

The PLA is devoting considerable effort to developing power projection capabilities, doctrine, and political justifications that would support expeditionary operations well beyond China's land borders and outside the second island chain.[21] The new PLA logistics base in Djibouti provides the ability to sustain peacetime naval operations in a permissive environment and a nascent capability to support other types of operations that may involve a combat role. These operations are justified domestically by the need to protect China's overseas interests and internationally by the claim that the Chinese military can provide public goods and contribute to international stability.[22]

PLA operations beyond the theater command areas of responsibility are currently handled differently depending on the type of operations. For example, navy headquarters appears to retain responsibility for the counter-piracy operations in the Gulf of Aden, with each escort task force composed of ships drawn from a different fleet. Conversely, the Joint Staff Department's Overseas Operations Office is in charge of PLA deployments to support United Nations peacekeeping operations. Unlike the U.S. military, which assigns every part of the world to a geographic combatant command responsible for contingency planning and operations within its area of responsibility, the PLA has gaps where potential operations fall outside the areas of responsibility of the theater commands. Moreover, it does not appear to have established a standing or ad hoc joint task force mechanism to command such operations.

To date, most PLA independent overseas operations (such as the evacuation of Chinese citizens from Libya in 2011) have been small, of short-duration, and in relatively permissive environments.[23] These types of operations could be assigned to either the Joint Staff Department or one of the service headquarters depending on the nature of the operation. However, these mechanisms are likely to prove inadequate if PLA overseas operations become larger, require joint forces, last for extended periods of time, or occur in nonpermissive environments where deployed forces face threats from hostile state or nonstate actors. Conducting multiple simultaneous overseas operations would further stress the PLA's ability to command overseas operations. If the PLA begins to regularly conduct such operations, new joint command and control mechanisms will likely be necessary.

Conclusion

This volume has traced the drivers of the PLA's ambitious reform agenda, examined how the reforms affect the component parts of the PLA and their relationships to each other, and assessed the opportunities and challenges that will affect the success of the reform agenda. The reforms that have been implemented have already had a major impact on how the PLA is organized and how it expects to plan, train, and execute combat operations. The reforms that are still to come—which will affect the military recruitment, education, assignment, promotion, and rank/grade systems—are likely to play a decisive role in determining whether a reformed PLA can realize Xi Jinping's goal of building a joint force capable of fighting and winning informationized wars. As the PLA begins conducting larger and more sophisticated joint operations and potentially expands the range and scope of its overseas operations, experience is likely to reveal the need for additional adjustments to joint command and control mechanisms to fully support China's growing military ambitions.

Notes

[1] "CCP Central Committee Decision on Deepening of Reforms for Major Issues" [中共中央关于全面深化改革若干重大问题的决定], Xinhua, November 15, 2013, available at <http://news.xinhuanet.com/politics/2013-11/15/c_118164235.htm>.

[2] "Xi Leads China's Military Reform, Stresses Strong Army," Xinhua, March 15, 2014, available at <http://english.cntv.cn/20140315/102892.shtml>.

[3] "Full Text of Xi Jinping's Report at the 19th CPC National Congress," Xinhua, November 3, 2017, available at <www.xinhuanet.com/english/special/2017-11/03/c_136725942.htm>.

[4] See Minnie Chan, "Chinese General's New Job Suggests Army Revamp Finished," *South China Morning Post* (Hong Kong), June 25, 2016.

[5] "Facts and Figures on China's Military Reform," Xinhua, December 19, 2017, available at <www.xinhuanet.com/english/2017-12/19/c_136837189.htm>.

[6] "Central Military Commission Opinion on Deepening National Defense and Armed Force Reforms" [中央军委关于深化国防和军队改革的意见], Xinhua, January 1, 2016, available at <http://news.xinhuanet.com/mil/2016-01/01/c_1117646695.htm>.

[7] Roger Cliff, "Chinese Military Reforms: A Pessimistic Take," *Joint Force Quarterly* 83 (4th Quarter 2016), 53–56.

[8] Eitan Shamir, *Transforming Command: The Pursuit of Mission Command in the U.S., British, and Israeli Armies* (Stanford: Stanford University Press, 2011).

[9] See Ian Burns McCaslin and Andrew S. Erickson, "The PLA and Maritime Security Challenges," in this volume.

[10] See Joel Wuthnow and Phillip C. Saunders, "A Modern Major General: Building Joint Commanders in the PLA," in this volume.

[11] See Shanshan Mei, *People of the PLA* (Maxwell Air Force Base, AL: China Aerospace Studies Institute, 2018).

[12] See Peng Wang and Jingyi Wang, "How China Promotes Its Officers: Interactions Between Formal and Informal Institutions," *China Quarterly*, no. 234 (June 2018), 399–419.

[13] Interviews with People's Liberation Army (PLA) Academy of Military Science personnel, 2017.

[14] "Xi to Head Central Commission for Integrated Military, Civilian Development," Xinhua, January 22, 2017, available at <www.xinhuanet.com/english/2017-01/22/c_136004750.htm>.

[15] See Tai Ming Cheung, "Keeping Up with the *Jundui*: Reforming the Chinese Defense Acquisition, Technology, and Industrial System to Engage in Advanced Innovation," in this volume.

[16] See Brian Lafferty, "Civil-Military Integration and PLA Reforms," in this volume.

[17] PLA officers have asked U.S. counterparts how the U.S. joint professional military education system works to develop a "joint mentality" among the U.S. officer corps.

[18] *Annual Report to Congress: Military and Security Developments Involving the People's Republic of China 2016* (Washington, DC: Office of the Secretary of Defense, 2016), i; "China's Military Strategy (Full Text)," Xinhua, May 27, 2015, available at <http://english.gov.cn/archive/white_paper/2015/05/27/content_281475115610833.htm>.

[19] Phillip C. Saunders and Joel Wuthnow, "What Do China's Military Reforms Mean for Taiwan?" *NBR Commentary*, May 19, 2016, available at <http://nbr.org/research/activity.aspx?id=692>.

[20] See Andrew Scobell et al., eds., *The People's Liberation Army and Contingency Planning in China* (Washington, DC: NDU Press, 2015).

[21] Kristen Gunness and Oriana Skylar Mastro, "A Global People's Liberation Army: Possibilities, Challenges, and Opportunities," *Asia Policy*, vol. 22 (July 2016), 131–155.

[22] This theme is prominent in China's 2012 defense white paper. See *The Diversified Employment of China's Armed Forces* (Beijing: State Council Information Office of the People's Republic of China, April 16, 2013).

[23] See Michael S. Chase, "The PLA and Far Seas Contingencies: Chinese Capabilities for Noncombatant Evacuation Operations," in Scobell et al., *The People's Liberation Army and Contingency Planning in China*, 301–319.

Nathan Beauchamp-Mustafaga is a Policy Analyst at the RAND Corporation, where he focuses on Asian security issues. Prior to joining RAND, Beauchamp-Mustafaga was the Editor of the Jamestown Foundation's *China Brief*. He has also spent time with the International Institute for Strategic Studies (IISS), the Stockholm International Peace Research Institute (SIPRI), the Center for International and Strategic Studies at Peking University (CISS) under Wang Jisi and Zhu Feng, and the U.S.-China Economic and Security Review Commission (USCC). Beauchamp-Mustafaga graduated from the dual-degree MSc in International Affairs program at the London School of Economics and Peking University, and earned a bachelor's degree in International Affairs and Chinese Language and Literature from the Elliott School of International Affairs at The George Washington University.

Dennis J. Blasko is an Asian Analyst in the China Security Affairs Group at CNA Corporation. He is a retired Lieutenant Colonel in the U.S. Army. He served as an army attaché in Beijing and in Hong Kong from 1992 to 1996. Blasko is the author of *The Chinese Army Today: Tradition and Transformation for the 21st Century*, 2nd edition (Routledge 2012).

Edmund J. Burke is a senior intelligence and defense researcher at the RAND Corporation. Mr. Burke has served in and out of government as a China specialist since 1988. Immediately prior to joining RAND, he was a Senior Executive and the senior China officer at NGA. Mr. Burke was in the private sector from 2001-2009; in 2003 he founded a consulting firm, which was eventually acquired by a large defense contractor. From 1997-2001 Mr. Burke was an all source analyst, manager and PDB briefer at CIA. He spent his first nine years of government service as a China analyst at the

National Photographic Interpretation Center. is a senior intelligence and defense researcher at the RAND Corporation.

Arthur Chan was previously a policy analyst at the RAND Corporation. Prior to joining RAND, he worked at the National Bureau of Asian Research, the American Enterprise Institute, the NYU Department of Politics and the U.S. Embassy in Paris, France. Arthur holds a Masters in European Affairs from Sciences Po Paris and a BA in political science and French from New York University. He is a native speaker of Cantonese and has professional proficiency in Mandarin and French.

John Chen is a Research Associate at the Special Programs Division of SOS International, where he conducts China-related research and analysis on foreign policy, national security, and science and technology issues using Chinese-language sources. He received an AB from Dartmouth College and an MA from Georgetown University.

Tai Ming Cheung is Director of the Institute on Global Conflict and Cooperation (IGCC) located at the University of California, San Diego in La Jolla. He leads the institute's Study of Innovation and Technology in China project that examines China's efforts to become a world-class science and technology power. Dr. Cheung is also a professor at the School of Global Policy and Strategy at UC San Diego, where he teaches courses on Chinese foreign and defense policy and Chinese security and technology policy. Dr. Cheung is a long-time analyst of Chinese and East Asian defense and national security affairs, especially defense economic, industrial and science and technological issues. He is the author of *Fortifying China: The Struggle to Build a Modern Defense Economy* (Cornell University Press, 2009), editor of *Forging China's Military Might: A New Framework for Assessing Innovation* (Johns Hopkins University Press, 2014), and co-editor of *The Gathering Pacific Storm: Emerging US-China Strategic Competition in Defense Technological and Industrial Development* (Cambria Press, 2018). He was based in Northeast Asia (Hong Kong, China, and Japan) from the mid-1980s to 2002 covering political, economic, and strategic developments in Greater China and East Asia as a journalist for the *Far Eastern Economic*

Review from 1988-1993 and subsequently as a political and business risk consultant for a number of companies, including PricewaterhouseCoopers. Dr. Cheung has a PhD in War Studies from King's College, London.

John Costello is Director of the Office of Strategy, Policy, and Plans in the National Protection and Programs Directorate at the Department of Homeland Security. He coauthored this chapter before taking his current position. Previously, he served as a Cybersecurity Policy Fellow in New America's Cybersecurity Initiative and a Senior Analyst for Cyber and East Asia at Flashpoint. He is also a former Congressional Innovation Fellow for majority staff in the U.S. House of Representatives Committee on Oversight and Government Reform. During his time on the Hill, Costello helped investigate the 2015 breach into the Office of Personnel Management and helped oversee federal IT management. Previously, Costello was a research analyst at Defense Group, Inc., where he concentrated on Chinese cyber espionage, information warfare, and intellectual property theft. He is a U.S. Navy veteran, former NSA analyst, and is fluent in Mandarin Chinese, having graduated with honors from the Defense Language Institute. His insights have appeared in *Wired*, the *Wall Street Journal*, the *New York Times*, Reuters, and the Jamestown *China Brief*. Costello's research focuses on Chinese cyber forces, evolving technology and innovation environment, and quantum technologies.

Mark R. Cozad is a senior international defense research analyst at RAND. Previously, he served in both the military and intelligence community in a variety of areas including intelligence analysis, targeting, operational planning, and strategy development. Cozad's work at RAND focuses on strategic warning, intelligence analysis, and security issues in Europe and East Asia. In his final assignment in the intelligence community he served as the deputy to the Assistant Deputy Director of National Intelligence for the President's Daily Brief (PDB). Immediately preceding his assignment to the ODNI, he was the Defense Intelligence Officer for East Asia, the senior intelligence officer on that issue within the Department of Defense.

Andrew S. Erickson is a Professor of Strategy in the U.S. Naval War College (NWC)'s China Maritime Studies Institute (CMSI). As a core founding member, he helped to establish CMSI and to stand it up officially in 2006, and has subsequently played an integral role in its development. CMSI has inspired the creation of other research centers, to which he has provided advice and support. Since 2008 Erickson has been an Associate in Research at Harvard University's John King Fairbank Center for Chinese Studies. He is a term member of the Council on Foreign Relations.

Kim Fassler is a political-military analyst at the U.S. Department of Defense where her focus includes U.S.-China relations and East Asia political and security issues. She holds an M.A. in international relations from the Johns Hopkins University School of Advanced International Studies (SAIS) and a B.A. in political science and Chinese from Williams College. Ms. Fassler also studied at the Hopkins-Nanjing Center on a National Security Education Program Boren Fellowship. Originally from Honolulu, she worked in journalism, public relations, and energy consulting before starting her career with the U.S. Government.

David M. Finkelstein is a Vice President of CNA and Director for China and Indo-Pacific Security Studies. A retired U.S. Army Officer, Dr. Finkelstein held command and staff positions in various field units and China-related positions at the Pentagon. He also served on the faculty at West Point, where he taught Chinese and Japanese history and the history of warfare in Asia. Finkelstein holds a Ph.D. in Chinese and Japanese history from Princeton University, is a graduate of the United States Military Academy, the U.S. Army Command & General Staff College, and the Army War College. He also studied Mandarin Chinese in Tianjin, China at Nankai University. A long-time student of Chinese security affairs, his edited volumes include *Chinese Warfighting: The PLA Experience Since 1949* (ME Sharpe), *China's Revolution in Doctrinal Affairs: Developments in the Operational Art of the People's Liberation Army* (CNA), *Civil-Military Relations in Today's China: Swimming in a New Sea* (ME Sharpe), and *China's Leadership in the 21ˢᵗ Century: The Rise of the Fourth Generation* (ME Sharpe).

His historical monograph, *From Abandonment to Salvation: Washington's Taiwan Dilemma, 1949-50* (George Mason University and Naval Institute Press), was hailed in *Presidential Studies Quarterly* as "blazing a new trail" and as certain to "take an important place in the literature of U.S.-China relations in the mid-20th Century."

Daniel Gearin is a liaison officer with the Department of Defense, currently serving in Taipei, Taiwan. Daniel previously served as an analyst with the Department of Defense, focusing on China's military capabilities. Before joining the Department of Defense, Daniel held research positions with the Center for a New American Security (CNAS), the U.S.-China Economic and Security Review Commission, the National Defense University, and the Brookings Institution. He obtained a B.A. in International Affairs from Northeastern University, and an M.A. in International Affairs from the George Washington University. Daniel also spent two years living in Beijing, China studying Mandarin Chinese.

Justin Godby is a Department of Defense political-military analyst specializing in East Asia security issues. He previously served as a liaison officer to the Office of the Secretary of Defense for Asia-Pacific Security Affairs and as a researcher for James Madison University's Institute for National Security Analysis. Mr. Godby will graduate in 2018 with a M.S. in Strategic Intelligence from the National Intelligence University created by the Office of the Director of National Intelligence. Mr. Godby attended James Madison University and graduated with a B.S. in Information Analysis and a minor in Asian Studies.

Brian Lafferty is a Chinese language researcher at the Special Programs Division of SOS International, specializing in research on China's defense science and technology development. He has written a number of articles, briefs, and conference papers concerning China's civil-military integration. Dr. Lafferty holds a B.A. from Cornell University and received his Ph.D. from Columbia University.

David C. Logan is a Ph.D. Student in Security Studies at Princeton University's Woodrow Wilson School of Public and International Affairs, where his research focuses on U.S.-China security relations and nuclear strategy and arms control. His writing has been published by *Asian Security, Nonproliferation Review, Foreign Affairs, Joint Force Quarterly,* and the *Bulletin of the Atomic Scientists.* Mr. Logan attended Grinnell College and received his MPA in International Relations from the Woodrow Wilson School at Princeton University.

LeighAnn Luce is an independent analyst specializing in Chinese civil-military integration and science and technology development with a particular focus on defense electronics and information technology. She has previously worked as a senior engineer at SOS International's Special Programs Division as well as an Associate Deputy Director of Technical Analysis at Defense Group Incorporated's Center for Intelligence Research and Analysis. Ms. Luce attended the George Washington University's Elliott School of International Affairs and received a dual B.A. in International Relations and Chinese Language and Literature, with concentrations in Asian Studies and International Economics.

Ma Chengkun is Professor and Dean of the College of PLA Studies at Taiwan's National Defense University. Professor Ma received his Ph.D. in China's war behavior study from National Taiwan University and specializes in People's Liberation Army affairs. His articles include "China's security strategy and military development" and "China's three warfares against Taiwan." Professor Ma is currently researching China's military strategic thinking and military transformation and participates in international academic exchanges about China's military modernization with various countries.

Joel McFadden is a specialist in East Asian politics and security issues with the U.S. Department of Defense. Prior to joining the federal government in 2008, he worked for U.S. Senator Dianne Feinstein (D-Calif.) as a senior aide on defense and greater China policy. Mr. McFadden holds a master's degree from Johns Hopkins University School of Advanced International Studies (SAIS) and has also studied Chinese history and language at Fudan University in Shanghai. He spent most of his youth living in the Asia-Pacific region including Taiwan.

Joe McReynolds is a Principal Cyber Analyst at SOS International. His research interests primarily center on China's approach to computer network warfare and defense science & technology development. Mr. McReynolds has previously worked with the Council on Foreign Relations and the Pacific Council for International Policy, and is a graduate of Georgetown University's School of Foreign Service and Graduate Security Studies programs. He speaks and reads Chinese and Japanese, and has lived and studied in Nagoya, Guilin, and Beijing.

Ian Burns McCaslin is a contract researcher at the U.S. National Defense University's Center for the Study of Chinese Military Affairs and a China Aerospace Studies Institute (CASI) Associate. Previously, he worked as an intern at the Project 2049 Institute. He received his B.A. in International Studies with a minor in Mandarin Chinese from Ohio Wesleyan University and his M.A. in International Relations from the National University of Singapore (NUS). At NUS his thesis focused on the role of the People's Liberation Army (PLA) in China's foreign policy and behavior abroad using the Korean War, 1995-1996 Taiwan Strait Crisis, and the South China Sea as case studies. He has also studied at National Taiwan University and Fudan University.

Erin Richter is a Senior Intelligence Officer for the Defense Intelligence Agency where she has specialized in Chinese military capabilities and civil-military interdependencies for the last 14 years. Erin has served for the last 20 years in the United States Marine Corps as a logistics officer, intelligence officer, and reserve attaché, completing reserve and active duty assignments throughout the Indo-Pacific, in the Middle East, Balkans, and within the continental United States. She is a graduate of the Marine Corps Command and Staff College and Joint Forces Staff College, and holds a M.A. in International Affairs from American University and a B.A. in Anthropology from the University of Maryland.

Phillip C. Saunders is Director of the Center for the Study of Chinese Military Affairs and a Distinguished Research Fellow at National Defense University's Institute for National Strategic Studies. Dr. Saunders previously worked at the Monterey Institute of International Studies, where he was Director of the East Asia Nonproliferation Program from 1999-2003, and served as an officer in the U.S. Air Force from 1989-1994. Dr. Saunders is co-author with David Gompert of *The Paradox of Power: Sino-American Strategic Restraint in an Era of Vulnerability* (NDU Press, 2011) and co-editor of five books on Chinese military and security issues. Dr. Saunders attended Harvard College and received his MPA and Ph.D. in International Relations from the Woodrow Wilson School at Princeton University.

Andrew Scobell is a Senior Political Scientist at the RAND Corporation. He was previously an Associate Professor of international affairs at the George H.W. Bush School of Government and Public Service at Texas A&M University. He is the author of *China's Use of Military Force: Beyond the Great Wall and the Long March* (Cambridge University Press, 2003) and co-authored *China's Search for Security* (Columbia University Press, 2012). In addition to editing or co-editing 12 books, Dr. Scobell has written dozens of reports, monographs, journal articles, and book chapters. He holds a Ph.D. in political science from Columbia University.

Joel Wuthnow is a Research Fellow in the Center for the Study of Chinese Military Affairs at National Defense University's Institute for National for Strategic Studies. He also serves as an adjunct professor in both the Eisenhower School at NDU and the Edmund A. Walsh School of Foreign Service at Georgetown University. Dr. Wuthnow has worked as a China analyst at CNA, a postdoctoral fellow in the China and the World Program at Princeton University, and a pre-doctoral fellow at The Brookings Institution. He is the author of *Chinese Diplomacy and the UN Security Council* (Routledge). Dr. Wuthnow holds degrees from Princeton University (A.B., summa cum laude, in Public and International Affairs), Oxford University (M.Phil. in Modern Chinese Studies), and Columbia University (Ph.D. in Political Science).

Made in the USA
Middletown, DE
07 September 2024

60523785R00433